For Randall and our poet friends
Adrienne, Allen, Berryman, Cal, Dee,
Eleanor, Elizabeth, Fitzgerald, Heather, Karl,
Marianne, Mr. Ransom, Red, Bob Watson;
and to the memory of
"All we said, and did, and thought —
The world we were."

Randall Jarrell's Letters

Randall Jarrell's
LETTERS

AN
AUTOBIOGRAPHICAL
AND LITERARY
SELECTION

EDITED BY
MARY JARRELL

Assisted by Stuart Wright

faber and faber

Copyright © 1985 by Mary Jarrell

Printed in the United States of America

First published in Great Britain in 1986
by Faber and Faber Limited
3 Queen Square London WC1N 3AU

British Library Cataloguing in Publication Data
Jarrell, Randall
 Randall Jarrell's letters : an autobiographical
 and literary selection.
 1. Jarrell, Randall — Biography   2. Poets,
 American — 20th century — Biography
 I. Title   II. Jarrell, Mary
 811'.54   PS3519.A86 $\mathcal{CC}$
 ISBN 0-571-13829-2

The author is grateful for permission to quote the following material:
 Letters from Randall Jarrell to *The New Republic*, March 1941 and Oc-
tober 1941. Reprinted by permission of *The New Republic*, © 1941, The
New Republic, Inc.
 Letters from Randall Jarrell and Conrad Aiken to *The Nation*, June
12, 1948. Reprinted by permission of *The Nation*.
 Excerpts from *Alumni News*, Spring 1966 (volume 54, number 3),
issue devoted to Randall Jarrell. Reprinted by permission of the Alumni
Association, University of North Carolina at Greensboro.

CONTENTS

ILLUSTRATIONS

ACKNOWLEDGMENTS

I wish to express my gratitude to a number of libraries, institutions, and friends who have helped me since I began this book in 1967. For the use of Randall Jarrell's letters in their possession I am grateful to the University of Chicago, Harvard University, the University of Indiana, the Library of Congress, the Berg Collection of the New York Public Library, the Rosenbach Foundation, Princeton University, the Humanities Center at the University of Texas, and the Beinecke Library at Yale University. My thanks also for letters from the files of Atheneum Publishers, the *Atlantic Monthly,* the *Kenyon Review, The Nation,* the *Partisan Review,* and *Poetry.* And special thanks to the estates of Hannah Arendt and Elisabeth Eisler and to Alleyne Boyette, Sister Bernetta, Michael di Capua, Marjorie Dickinson, Harry Ford, Bernard Haggin, Beatrice Hofer, Adrienne Rich, and Sara Starr Wolff, for the use of letters belonging to them.

I have been continuously aided by the staff of the Jackson Library at the University of North Carolina at Greensboro, particularly by Emily Mills of the Special Collections and Nancy Fogarty and Mark Schumacher of the Reference Department. I am indebted to Charles M. Adams for valuable information from his *Bibliography of Randall Jarrell 1935-1958* (University of North Carolina Press) and to Stuart Wright for his *Bibliography of Randall Jarrell 1936-1983* (University Press of Virginia, 1984). Keith Monroe suggested the geographical divisions of the book and supplied some missing names of authors, titles, and other data, as did Fred Chappell, Arthur Dixon, Suzanne Ferguson, and Robert Watson. The poems of Randall Jarrell that appear in this book are reprinted from *The Complete Poems,* by permission of Farrar, Straus and Giroux.

I am most appreciative to Mary Louise Gordon and Shirlee Rothrock for their cheerful company during the many months they transcribed Randall Jarrell's handwriting into typescript. I wish to thank Randall's friend — and my editor — Robie Macauley for his expertise in determining the last one hundred letters to cut, which I had found such reluctance in giving up but *knew* should come out. I deeply appreciate Clay Morgan, the manuscript editor, for his caring concern and high standards that enabled us to remedy flaws and errors of omission in the textual parts. And I am exceedingly grateful to Stuart Wright, assistant indefatigable, for his wise counsel, his ready encouragement, and his inspired research that decoded most of the literary allusions on these pages that might otherwise have frustrated, if not baffled, their readers.

Finally, I want to express thanks more than words can say to my daughters, Alleyne Boyette and Beatrice Hofer, for their interest and for the enlivening details they recalled for me about their stepfather; and to Emily Huntley of Garden Studio for *café au lait* after my daily six-hour stint with the letters, for her cut flowers, and for her convivial dialogues on Max Beckmann self-portraits, May Sarton novels, Venice, Rhode Island history, the artistic temperament, and pets, which have sustained my spirit across fifteen years.

M.J.

INTRODUCTION

The young writer we meet in Jarrell's letters in 1935 was twenty-one, short of funds, and fiercely determined to write. He was a Marxist intellectual in his senior year at Vanderbilt and was pelting Robert Penn Warren with poems for the *Southern Review*. As the letters continue into the later 1930s, one is impressed with how the older writers Warren, Allen Tate, and John Crowe Ransom appreciated and advised Jarrell and how Edmund Wilson, too, took him under his wing, giving him books to review for the *New Republic* and recommending his poetry to the *Atlantic Monthly*.

In the letters of the 1940s we meet Private Randall Jarrell of the Air Force, on his way up to sergeant and with two published books of poetry: *Blood for a Stranger* and *Little Friend, Little Friend*. In the last months before his discharge, Jarrell wrote his own appreciative and advisory letters to Robert Lowell, concerning the poems in *Lord Weary's Castle* — letters of such empathy and generosity that the youthful friendship, begun between Jarrell and Lowell at Kenyon, became a permanent part of both their lives.

In the year after the war, when Jarrell was literary editor of *The Nation*, he gained — through Lowell — his other long-time close friend, Peter Taylor, the fiction writer. Drawn to Taylor's Southern stories as he had been to Lowell's Yankee poems, Jarrell involved himself in Taylor's writing to the extent that Taylor said, "I doubt if I could have started writing again [after the war] if I had not had Randall to talk to."

In 1963, Michael di Capua, a young editor in children's literature at Macmillan, became Jarrell's third most valued male friend and correspondent. For years Jarrell had switched from one editor to another, because all his editors had made him "feel as if publishing the poems was a cultural duty they performed without the slightest enthusiasm." He had always dreamed of an editor who would give him, as he wrote James Laughlin, "a Happy Smile — that look of joy, or mild pleasure, or *something* . . . and not the feeling that a window-dummy made out of ectoplasm" was publishing him. Di Capua was this dream come true. He devoted himself to Jarrell as a friend, and he invented Jarrell as a writer for children. In return, Jarrell gave him his three forthcoming adult works for publication at Macmillan, ranked him with his favored few, and dedicated his final book of poetry, *The Lost World,* to him.

These were the major friendships, and Jarrell fostered several minor ones, but he was not a gregarious person. Eager to receive letters, he was slow to answer them, and a high percentage of his replies begin, "I should have written long ago . . ." When he stopped writing to Tate, he substituted Hannah Arendt and Elizabeth Bishop. Ten years later, Arendt's letters dwindled to nothing and were replaced by Adrienne Rich's. Compared to the number of writers Lowell and Taylor kept up with, Jarrell's group was small. He was often bored by his own kind, and he backed away at any sign of pretentiousness or self-importance. On the other hand, it should be noted that when occasion permitted, he was overjoyed to see Eudora Welty, for instance, or J. F. Powers, Brendan Gill, Meyer Schapiro, Wallace Stevens, W. D. Snodgrass, Robert Graves, Robert Frost; and the list could go on: he simply did not write to them. One would have expected more leters to William Carlos Williams or Philip Booth or Marianne Moore: but no. In the last two years of his life, "write Berryman" touchingly made Jarrell's lists underneath "bank, stamps, haircut" and was repeatedly carried over but never crossed off.

Fortunately, Jarrell had no trouble writing his wives, and his first wife preserved ninety Army letters whose contents furnished poems such as "The Lines," "Mail Call," "Gunner," "Soldier [T.P.]," and "The Sick Nought." His second wife preserved ninety letters from Princeton whose contents read like a section of his academic satire *Pictures from an Institution,* but one that reveals actual names.

To speak about the selection itself, the following 350 or so letters were chosen from 2500 that were recovered, and they represent, I believe, those letters of general interest that are the most literary and biographical. Except for the responses to attacks Jarrell sent to the *New Republic* and *The Nation,* none of his letters were written with an eye to publication, as Edmund Wilson's were, nor as part of a literary estate, as Rilke's were. Rarely dated and rarely typed, Jarrell's were written more often from hammocks or trains or on his lap than from a desk, and sometimes by a hand still shaking from three sets of tennis. They are the letters, as Jarrell wrote a friend in Vienna, of a person "whose principal work-and-amusement is reading, writing and thinking about things." They are bookish and full of references to books without their titles, titles without their authors, and essays without either one, such as "I saw a piece in *Kenyon* ..." But they are rich with Jarrell's thoughts on Alexandra Danilova, Lotte Lehmann, Oskar Kokoschka, or the new design for the Jaguar's headlights, as well as merry quips about Richard Eberhart, Paul Goodman, Harry Levin, and Dudley Fitts.

There are some regrettable blanks in this collection as there are in every series of letters from St. Paul's to Flannery O'Connor's: blanks left by letters lost, destroyed, or withheld. Lost or destroyed were all Jarrell's adult letters to his mother except the few included here; and Peter Taylor chose to withhold those written to him. Since Jarrell and Taylor were frequently together or in easy telephone range, the number of those letters is not large; but the loss of any single one to this unique friend is grievous. Therefore, whenever Taylor is part of the narrative, I have had to make use of italicized commentary to materialize him from his letters to us and from my memory, and for this I ask the reader's indulgence.

In seeking to preserve the letters as an endangered species — which letters surely have become — I felt a responsibility to use them to fill Randall Jarrell's biographical space in the "American Bloomsbury Circle" of the fifties. I also valued them to memorialize the poignant, enduring affection that existed between Jarrell and Taylor and Lowell. Finally, I saw his letters as an autobiographical source in which he tells us what it was like for him to read and teach and write for thirty years, allowing those acquainted with him only through his writing to know some of the thoughts behind it on his art, his cat, his intellectual hobbies, his closest friendships, and the women he loved and who loved him.

Just as Freud's and Mozart's letters speak for Freud and Mozart, Jarrell's letters *are* Jarrell; and in lieu of actually meeting the writer, they are a way of meeting the writer. Readers will find him less guarded in his letters than Wallace Stevens, for instance, and not as long-winded as Archibald MacLeish. He is as honest in them as Conrad Aiken in his, but not so abject; as reportorial as Evelyn Waugh, but kinder; as entertaining as Louise Bogan, but more profound; and as witty as W. H. Auden, but not so naughty. I cannot tell how Jarrell, the person, will come through in his letters. Will they discredit him somewhat, as Frost's did? Or ennoble him, as Sandburg's did? I only know that if the judgment is harsh I can find comfort in Harry Moore's words to Rilke's detractors: "Those doing the judging could not have written the poems."

Finally, to return to Jarrell himself: In a letter he wrote to Robert Penn Warren in September of 1965, Jarrell was still telling him about poems. He commented on being "very glad to be [his] usual self again" after recovering from a midlife crisis, and said he had been "thinking about the passage of time and what it's like to have lived a certain number of years in the world." He thought it was "sure to turn into some poems in the long run." In less than a month Jarrell was struck by a car and killed, and we were robbed of the poems and letters that would have come from the "hard, green, serene old age" predicted for him in a letter from Robert Lowell.

In the end, the poet-critic we say goodbye to at Jarrell's grave is a mellowed intellectual who had traded Marx for Kennedy; who had a credit card; and who had achieved in his fifty-one years seven books of poetry, four books of criticism, a novel, translations of Chekhov's *The Three Sisters* and Goethe's *Faust: Part I,* anthologies of Kipling and Russian short novels and stories, and four books for children.

Mary Jarrell
Greensboro, North Carolina

EDITOR'S NOTE

The principles guiding my work on these letters have been (1) to clarify their content and background for the reader's widest comprehension and (2) to preserve — after transcribing them from Randall Jarrell's handwriting to type — their original flow, tone, and mood.

As Jarrell dated fewer than a dozen letters, approximate dates usually appear in brackets at the upper right-hand corners of the letters. For the purpose of identification, omitted first or last names, book titles, and brief miscellaneous information are given in brackets in the letters. Explanatory details are provided in italicized passages between letters, as are descriptions of Jarrell by his contemporaries, as quoted from *Randall Jarrell, 1914-1965,* edited by Robert Lowell, Peter Taylor, and Robert Penn Warren (New York: Farrar, Straus and Giroux, 1967) and the *Alumni News* of the University of North Carolina at Greensboro (Spring 1966, volume 54). These sources are acknowledged in the text by the initials RJ and AN, given in parentheses after the quotations. Repetitions, travel schedules, and minor irrelevancies have been trimmed without indication; however, most of the letters may be read in their entirety at the institutions that own them.

As for the love letters to Elisabeth Eisler and Mary von Schrader (Jarrell), the salutations and farewells have been deleted and the literary and biographical excerpts that appear have been extricated, whenever possible, from their romantic surroundings.

In seeking to avoid footnotes, ellipsis points, and other editorial invasions foreign to the prose and poetry of Randall Jarrell, I hope that his individual style of responding to the persons and situations in his letters will shine through.

M.J.

Randall Jarrell's Letters

Nashville, Tennessee,
1935–1937

*R*andall Jackson Jarrell was born on May 6, 1914, in Nashville, Tennessee, to Owen and Anna Campbell Jarrell. Some time after he was a year old, the family went west to California. By the time Jarrell was six, the family had settled in Long Beach, where Jarrell's father was a partner in Kramer-Jarrell Portrait Pictorialists. By the time he was ten, his parents were divorced, and he, his younger brother Charles, and their mother returned to Nashville. Except for his never-to-be-forgotten year-long visit to his paternal grandparents in Hollywood, Jarrell lived in Nashville with his mother and brother — even during his college years — until 1938.

When he was seventeen, Jarrell discovered, or was discovered by, the Fugitive writers Robert Penn Warren, Allen Tate, and John Crowe Ransom, who occasionally included their precocious young friend at literary evenings with their Vanderbilt University colleagues Donald Davidson and Charles Sanborn.

On first meeting him, Tate described Jarrell as "arrogant," but later softened toward him and published his poems "The cow wandering in the bare field" and "Fear" in the short-lived American Review Tate edited in 1934.

Warren, who had allowed the freshman Jarrell into his Sophomore Survey of Literature course "because he had read everything," wrote, "He was a very gentle and polite young man, though sometimes overwhelmed by the spectacle of human dumbness. At such times he might cover his face and moan aloud. But pity and despair would quickly pass as some flash of intelligence and perception appeared before him. Then his face would light up with generous appreciation and deep impersonal joy." (AN)

As a protégé of Warren's, Jarrell was eventually invited with him to what Warren called "jolly Jewish dinners" at the home of the Breyers. The Breyers were *representative of a type of cultivated, well-to-do Southern Jewish family who enjoyed being hospitable to intellectuals. They were the first of several such friendships Jarrell had during his life, including the Milton Starrs, the Marc Friedlaenders, Mrs. Laura Cone and her son Edward.*

At the time these letters begin, Jarrell was in love with the Breyers' eldest daughter, Amy. Amy was a statuesque medical student at Vanderbilt, and a few years older than Jarrell. She read Baudelaire in French, played a strong game of tennis, and vaguely wanted to write. Warren said she was "brilliant, good-looking and charming," and Jarrell wrote many poems to her while they were together and several more after they parted.

At the time of the opening letter to Warren, Jarrell was in his senior year at Vanderbilt, majoring in psychology; he was twenty-one. Robert Penn Warren, thirty, was a Vanderbilt graduate and a Rhodes scholar, and he had moved to Baton Rouge, Louisiana, to teach and to help edit the Southern Review *with his friend Cleanth Brooks. Warren's* Thirty-Six Poems *was about to come out; he had already published* John Brown: The Making of a Martyr *and, along with Brooks, was writing* An Approach to Literature. *Warren was the youngest of the Fugitives and was intelligent, earthy, comical, and, above all, kind. He was good company and an understanding mentor, and when he left Nashville, Jarrell keenly felt the loss. This letter is typical of those he wrote to Warren (a number of which do not appear in this book because they are repetitive). His letters to Warren were basically about his own writing, or Warren's, and contained inquiries as to when Warren would be coming to Nashville or hopeful plans for visiting Warren at LSU.*

TO ROBERT PENN WARREN

[May 1935]

Dear Red:

Here are the poems. I'd have sent them before except they weren't fixed before. I should have written before and said what a nice time I had and all that, but I was sure you'd appreciate the letter more if the poems came along with it. They haven't any titles — just call any "A Poem" like that. The more you use the better — I'll have plenty for the group.

If you use [John Peale] Bishop's group of poems in the second issue, I would like it a lot if you would put mine in the third. By that time I'll have all the ones I'm writing finished, and some new ones written. I'll be able to give you thirteen or fourteen, I imagine, some of them fairly long.

If you want the [Edna St. Vincent] Millay or the [W. H.] Auden article for the second issue I can have it all ready; I have been working since I got home on the Auden one. I think it's probably the more interesting. I really know Auden's poetry pretty well. Outside of your introductory essay, he hasn't been remotely well treated in this country.

Will you write me a note as soon as you get this and tell me what poems you're going to use, and which article you want and so forth?

Pardon the very Writer-to-Editor tone of this letter so far — I just put all that material in a lump.

I'm having to write all my psychology experiments and make up the school I missed and get up the last *Masquerader* and play a tennis match every other afternoon and I'm getting to have a mild version of the harried expression you had gotten. I've won all the matches I've had in games with other schools.

I hope you'll have time to rest and write as well this summer. Everybody was worried about your having so much work you scarcely had time to sleep.

I've had to interrupt this letter for an hour to play with a three year old boy that visited us. He was very interesting telling about the dark man, and the rain man, and the thunder man. They live above the clouds, in the sky, with God; God makes them do what they do. The dark man is all covered with dark, the thunder man with thunder. The dark man doesn't live in the sun, but along with the rest of them. He got me to draw him a picture of the dark man. The dark man looks exactly the same as he does, except he is grown up. At night after he goes to sleep he thinks about the dark man; he doesn't play in his dreams or do anything except think about the dark man.

I had a fine time at LSU and I was glad to get to stay with you as long as I did. I hope you'll get to come up here before you go west for the summer.

Mr. Ransom told me all about his Harvard lecture; it's a long metaphor comparing poetry and a masquerade.

Yours,
Randall

Give my love to Cenina and thank her for caring for me while I was there.

Two of the poems mentioned in the letter above were printed in the first issue of the Southern Review: *"And did she dwell in innocence and joy" and "Looking back in my mind I can see." Neither was called "A Poem"; they were simply identified as "I" and "II," and "II" was later retitled "The Elementary Scene."*

The mention of Warren's essay refers to his review of W. H. Auden's Poems *and* The Orators *in the May 1934 issue of the* American Review.

Jarrell planned to write his master's thesis on Auden and wanted to do an article about him first. Warren, however, did not assign him either piece, and while this was the first and last time Jarrell would volunteer to write about Millay, he worked at, laid aside, and referred to this "Auden article" over the next six years. He finally submitted it to the Southern Review, *and it was published in autumn of 1941 under the title "Changes of Attitude and Rhetoric in Auden's Poetry."*

The Masquerader *was the university humor magazine, and Jarrell was its editor.*

Jarrell had recently visited LSU to attend the Writers' Conference there. After making up his lost laboratory time, Jarrell graduated Phi Beta Kappa and magna cum laude with a B.A. in psychology.

TO ROBERT PENN WARREN

[October 1935]

Dear Red:

To get the business part of this letter over:

1. When do you want an Auden article? Brooks said in a letter, for the next number; you said there was no hurry. Tell me which — I don't care a bit either way.

2. Shall I review [D. H.] Lawrence's book [*Selected Poems*]? If so, send it to me and tell me when the review has to be in.

Really do write me about these — I hope I'll never again have to write so much in so short a time as I did with all those charming novels. I'll remember to give you back *A Preface to Maturity:* you'll be sorry, though.

I've seen Mr. Ransom a good deal — he is engrossed in aesthetics. We rather argue; he wants me to do a thesis on that, but I'm afraid I could hardly make it experimental. I reread [Benedetto] Croce and said the original part in Croce (the intuition as expression) was purely psychological, or to use a word he loves, behaviouristic; he gave me a thoughtful look, with doubt, concern, and regret mixed in, and said he had never seen it looked at from that point of view before. I have more fun talking with him than I used to; I like to talk shop, and aesthetics more or less is, politics and freeing the slaves not much. Did you know the *Saturday Review* cut out the nasty last paragraph of his Wm. Rose Benét review? Giving him the *Southern Review* poetry review ["Autumn of Poetry"] was a good and witty idea.

I've been at the [Charles] Sanborns' a good many times; the last time he showed me his college magazine in which he and William Ellery Leonard were accustomed to write verse. It was amusing in a pathetic naive way:

halfway between Pope and Tennyson, on Salamis, Alexander, War, Nature. I felt the same way when he told me, with a sort of innocent pride, that [Louis] Untermeyer said Leonard was one of the five greatest American poets of all time.

I am slowly accumulating poetry, like a stalagmite — painlessly too, I don't know how good; it's more objective, (I mean this, not using it re-viewer fashion), and needs less sympathy on the reader's part. I got four or five stanzas done over the last part of the summer; that sounds ridiculous but I never can do anything in the summer. Still, I must have 150 to 200 lines you haven't seen. Considering that I haven't shown you any *new* poetry for a year and a half, that's hardly surprising.

My brother [Charles] mentioned with awe, meeting you.

I hope you can come up before Christmas; anyway, I'd like very much to come down then. Christmas in such a semi-tropical climate should inspire one of us to write a poem like Kipling's "Christmas in India," or "Far brighter than this gaudy melon-flower"; and we can live on the anthology royalties.

Was the review all right? If I'd had a few decent books I could have been more constructive, but less entertaining. You know, I'm really very old-fashioned when it comes to reviews, the majority of my tendencies are not at all Eliot-ish and didactic. (Can you recite a review from memory when you finish it? I was astonished to find I could.)

Give my love to Cenina and everybody. Amy [Breyer] is getting along well, except she says the hospital telephones her at 12 or 1 in the morning to come to autopsies. I guess the corpses are due at a funeral the next day, and they have to hurry with them. She says she likes most of it well enough, but that there's one who always pulls out the intestines as if he were coiling a garden hose.

Yours,
Randall

Nothing came of the review of D. H. Lawrence's poems.

Ransom said that the Jarrell of this period was "the star of my advanced writing class" but was "an insistent and over-bearing talker ... belligerent in argument" and "always put his adversary down by virtue of his quicker intelligence and a wit that scathed." (AN) He went on to say, "Randall was like those brow-beating Sophists of The Dialogues *who went about inflict-ing their wisdom on any victim within reach." Cal (Robert) Lowell de-scribed Ransom and Jarrell in argument as "each expounding to the other's deaf ears his own inspired and irreconcilable interpretation." (RJ) The two*

*were often at odds, and they vexed each other with their dialectics; but in his
heart, Ransom was proud of his brash, brilliant student, and Jarrell, in his
heart, knew all that he owed his learned, unyielding teacher.*

*The "review" Jarrell refers to was entitled "Ten Books" and was pub-
lished in the* Southern Review *of autumn 1935. In his letter accompanying
it, Jarrell wrote, "I have tried to temper justice with mercy." The authors of
the books reviewed were Ellen Glasgow, Erskine Caldwell, Stark Young,
James Hanley, Jule Brousseau, Gale Wilhelm, Tess Slesinger, Willa Cather,
Rachel Field, and Raymond Holden.*

*Amy Breyer's hospital duties and study hours cut deeply into her time
with Jarrell, and in a poem he wrote for her called "In Those Days" he ends
with:*

> How poor and miserable we were,
> How seldom together!
> And yet after so long one thinks:
> In those days everything was better.

TO ROBERT PENN WARREN

July 27, 1936

Dear Red, Cleanth, or whoever's in charge:

Here are the poems I'm entering for your poetry prize; they are accompanied by a self-addressed stamped envelope, and this is the signed statement
entering them in the contest. There are about four hundred and eighty-five
lines in all.

I hope all of you are feeling better than I am — finishing the long poem
has tired me out completely. How soon are you coming up here?

Yours,
Randall
or Randall Jarrell for purposes
of the signed statement.

The Southern Review *contest was judged by Allen Tate and Mark Van
Doren. Seven of Jarrell's poems were selected for publication from 478 un-
signed manuscripts. The long poem (over 300 lines) he submitted was
"Orestes," and it won the poetry prize but was not printed.*

*In a subsequent letter to Albert Erskine, Jarrell wrote, "If you know
why Tate and Van Doren excluded 'Orestes' I wish you'd write back and
tell me; I'm curious. And tell Red and Cleanth they can publish it later if*

*they want, and if they don't they're missing the chance of a lifetime! (I'm
entirely unprejudiced, of course.)" The* Southern Review *had excluded the
poem because of a lack of space, and it finally appeared in the Winter 1943
issue of the* Kenyon Review *as "Orestes at Tauris."*

TO ROBERT PENN WARREN

[February 1937]

Dear Red:

I was under the impression that I was certain to get a fellowship here,
but [Professor Walter] Curry tells me I have a "very good chance" —
which is something so beautifully ambiguous I think I'll send it to William
Empson. So do you think you might get me one there [at LSU]? If you do,
write me back about what information, recommendations, and assorted
junk I should send, and I'll be real grateful.

This is my second year of graduate work and I'll have an English M.A. I
think I was about eighth or tenth in my class; I can get you some admiring
letters from Curry, Ransom, Davidson, Sanborn, etc., etc. Also, all this year
I've been grading the papers of two of Ransom's classes, one freshman and
one advanced. Also, as a merit that will strike home more directly, I could
read stuff and proof for you and Cleanth.

Curry says that everybody is delighted with my work, but there are five
or six people for three places so he can't tell me anything definite. The possibility (or probability, as it naturally seems to me) of not getting a fellowship here annoys me; I have been going to Vanderbilt for five years and have
never managed to get a fellowship, scholarship, or anything else; after I
made a letter in tennis I was allowed to go to football games free, except for
the government tax; but they stopped that a year ago, so I can be grateful to
Vanderbilt proper only for having been allowed to get into five football
games by paying the government tax. The person I am grateful to is Mr.
Ransom, who got me a little NYA [National Youth Administration] job
grading his papers; fortunately Vanderbilt had nothing to do with that.

I leave off the imitation of Isaiah; I've written twenty or thirty poems
since summer, some of which I send. (For you to read and comment on,
saying that they make you cry or the top of your head come off or something similar.) Send me your long one.

I see a lot of Mr. Ransom, who is well and wise but not writing poetry; I
guess from posterity's point of view it would be better to have him sick and
silly, but writing. At the moment I'm sick and I feel silly enough, but I do
write poetry constantly — so posterity should appreciate me.

I am working some on my thesis about Auden; I play football a lot and

broke my finger. I hope you and Cenina and Cleanth and Tinkum are well
and happy; write soon about the fellowship, won't you?

Yours,
Randall

*There was no fellowship at LSU, and no offer came from Vanderbilt.
Tinkum was Brooks's wife.*

*   *   *

*At this time, President Gordon Chalmers of Kenyon, a small Episcopal col-
lege in Gambier, Ohio, offered Ransom a Carnegie Professorship there. Ransom submitted the proposal to his English department, supposing that (after
some twenty years of teaching, several published books, and many editorships,
prizes, and distinctions) Vanderbilt would match little Kenyon's offer and
all would continue as before. To the astonishment of many and the outrage
of Jarrell, mighty Vanderbilt decided to pass. In a fury, Jarrell circulated a
petition to keep Ransom, and got hundreds of signatures from faculty members and students. But the English department and the chancellor of the university were unmoved, and Ransom went. Jarrell knew who in the
department had held back, and he held it against them for the rest of his
life. Twenty-five years after the event, an aged emeritus professor from the
Ransom days called on Jarrell, who was at his mother's home on a visit to
Nashville, and pathetically tried to clear himself and "explain the other
side." Jarrell listened coldly, showed him out, and then burst forth, "Tell
me. He didn't lift a finger because he wanted Ransom to go. They all did.
They were jealous, and he was, too." Still scowling, he added, "Wasn't that
abject!"*

TO CLEANTH BROOKS AND ALBERT ERSKINE

July 14, 1937

Dear Cleanth and Albert:

Red wrote me and told me when he was here that I'd get paid for my
Fall poems on July 1; since I haven't heard from you, I'm writing. I suppose
Red sent you the new poems he got from me; counting those and the
poems you had already decided to use, there are 250 lines. Will you send me
the money if the University comes through with it, or a gentle note to
soothe my grief, if it didn't?

I enjoyed re-reading the *Waste Land* piece. It certainly had some amusing comments on the Trotsky piece, it was clever to think of getting them.

I'm going up to Kenyon this fall with Mr. Ransom as a sort of part-time instructor. I hope to get to come down there and see everybody next year. I understand I have Christmas and Easter vacations both, so I imagine I will. Give my love to Tinkum and tell her I owe her a letter. And do send the money, if possible, by the wings of the morning, for I am wasting away with no ice cream cones and tennis balls.

Yours,
Randall

Cleanth Brooks's "The Waste Land: An Analysis," which Jarrell refers to above, appeared in the Summer 1937 issue of the Southern Review.

Gambier, Ohio,
1937–1939

❧

*T*he job at Kenyon that Ransom had arranged for Jarrell involved teaching the Freshman Survey and coaching the tennis team. Ransom later wrote, "Jarrell read more books from the library than any student we had, and of wider range than any professor would have chosen." (AN)

Grateful as he was to have this job, Jarrell found that the income barely paid his keep, and he gladly accepted the Ransoms' offer of free room in their attic along with a twenty-year-old student from Boston, Robert "Cal" Lowell. In a letter to Richard Eberhart, Lowell described Jarrell at this period as "upsettingly brilliant" and "knowing everything — Marx, Empson, Auden, Kafka and the ideologies and current events of the day . . . everything, except Ransom's provincial world of Greek, Latin, Aristotle and England" [Ian Hamilton, Robert Lowell: A Biography (New York: Random House, 1982)].

Lowell further described Jarrell as crying out, after skiing the mild slopes at Gambier, "I felt just like an angel," and wrote, "Randall did somehow give off an angelic impression, despite his love for tennis, singular mufflers knitted by a girl friend, and disturbing improvements of his own on the latest dance steps. His mind, unearthly in its quickness, was a little boyish, disembodied and brittle. His body was a little ghostly in its immunity to soil, entanglements and rebellion. As one sat with him in obvious absorption at the campus bar, sucking a fifteen-cent chocolate milk shake and talking eternal things, one felt, beside him, too corrupt and companionable."

Throughout that winter the English instructor and the classics major fought and froze in their attic and forged a friendship that withstood marriages, divorces, honors, and breakdowns. Still at Kenyon in 1938, the two of them moved to Doug-

lass House and were joined by a third Tate protégé and Ransom follower, Peter Taylor of Memphis, Tennessee.

The letters from Gambier are preoccupied with poetry and publishing, though at the same time Jarrell was writing his master's thesis, whose topic he had shifted, at Professor Davidson's insistence, from Auden to A. E. Housman. Typical of Jarrell, where others would have gossiped about people in their letters, he gossiped about books.

TO ROBERT PENN WARREN

[September 1937]

Dear Red:

Gambier is rather like Siberia with nothing to do but otherwise rewarding. It's wonderful to get paid, though. You asked me in June if I would give you all my poems for the [LSU] University press to publish in a book, did that go through or not? If it didn't, I wish you'd tell me, so that I can start getting them ready to send to a publisher.

When I was reading your winter issue I saw my name in the contributors to the Spring and Summer issues; does that mean you want me to send you some poems? I have eight or nine, some new and some old that you haven't seen, besides the finished and unfinished ones you have (the "Nursery Rhyme" and the one I couldn't finish for the Fall issue ["Love, in its separate being"]). I'll send them to you if you need poems; if you have more than enough say so.

Amy and I stayed all one day at the Tates [in Clarksville, Tennessee]; they talked for hours about the Fords' visit, until I was sick from laughing so much.

Untermeyer visited us yesterday. I hope he chokes.

Tell me when you're coming to Nashville or here, so I can be there when you do. Give my love to Cenina and Cleanth and Tinkum and Albert.

Yours,

Randall

Before visiting the Tates, Ford Madox Ford, the English novelist and critic, had attended the Rocky Mountain Writers' Conference in Boulder, Colorado, with Ransom and Lowell. The best student there was an aspiring novelist named Jean Stafford, who impressed the older writers and attracted Lowell.

At this time Louis Untermeyer's anthologies were held in low esteem by the Southern poets, who thought he chose not widely nor too well from among them. As time passed, they came to find "Louie" likable, helped him to better his taste, and became quite friendly with him.

*   *   *   **

Just before Christmas in 1938, Amy broke with Jarrell, and he poured his misery into poems. In a letter to him, Amy cited how badly they had been getting along, especially during the past summer when they had visited some Nashville friends, Milton and Zaro Starr, at Folly Beach, South Carolina. She had planned to make the break when he left for Kenyon that fall and put her on the train for New Haven, but she had delayed until after their Thanksgiving holidays together. There were many reasons she couldn't keep on with him, she thought: the way they had grown up, for instance — she in a large, gregarious, warm family, which made Jarrell's asocial and family-rejecting behavior a strain for her. And while she, too, was intelligent and used to being "top of the stack," she resented Jarrell's need to be right, to be "omniscient" and to dominate her mind with his. Furthermore, his brilliance unnerved her and made her fear he would "see through" her pretensions. A letter Jarrell was finally able to write her about this in 1942 somewhat clarifies the situation between them (see page 64); and the following poem, written in 1940, indicates the clinical terminology Jarrell had picked up from Amy, as well as his painful feeling of abandonment.

THE CHRISTMAS ROSES

The nurse is at the tree, and if I'm thirsty no one minds.
Why don't they finish? . . . If it's metastasizing
I wish that it would hurry. Yesterday it snowed.
The man they took before me died today.
When I woke up I thought I saw you on the bed,
You smiled at me and said, "It's all all right,"
And I believed you and went back to sleep.
But I was lucky: the mortality's so high
They put it in a foot-note or don't mention it.

Why don't you write to me? . . . The day nurse sits and holds
The glass for me, but yesterday I cried
I looked so white. I looked like paper.
Whiter. I dreamt about the pole, and bears,
And I see snow and sheets and my two nurses and the chart
I make all by myself with my thermometer
In red that's like the roses that are like the blood

That's gone, that's gone for good — and what's left's spoiled,
The silly culture I keep warming for my death.

How could I believe you, how could I believe them?
You were lying, and I am dying; and you knew. . . .
I dreamed it, I woke and laughed at it; and then I saw
That there was nothing else that could be so,
I knew, I knew. And now I know you never meant
The least letter of the poorest kiss
You thought about and gave me; you and life were tired of me,
You both thought — quickly, quietly, in a dream —
To kill me, to be rid at last, for good, for good,

Of that blind face that still looked up to you
For love, and then pity, and then anything.
And now I'm dying and you have your wish.
Dying, dying; and I have the only wish
That I had strength or hope enough to keep,
To die: to lie here ruined and dumb and done,
And lose at last what I have left to lose, the shame
And need and pain, the unendurable desire:
What I was given for a world. . . . Now when I see myself

Even in my own thoughts or dreams or — or desire,
It's only as a nuisance, Want out of a play
There begging in your bed; but it's I who am in bed
Really, O isn't it? — and it's not right, not right
Even to die so badly, once you loved me, too,
And I'm not angry now, I'm dying now, I —
Come to me! come to me! . . . How can I die without you?
Touch me and I won't die, I'll look at you
And I won't die, I'll look at you, I'll look at you.

*   *   *

Allen Tate, thirty-eight, Kentucky-born, was another illustrious Vanderbilt graduate. He had published biographies, poetry, fiction, and essays; had lived in Greenwich Village and Paris; and was continually serving as a fellow or chancellor or adviser in the literary establishment. A fountain of gossip about literary politics, awards, and reputations, he had access to persons of influence in academe, Madison Avenue, and Washington, and he used it unstintingly to advance younger writers such as Hart Crane, Lowell, Taylor, and Jarrell. At the time the following letter was written, Tate was

teaching at the Woman's College in Greensboro, North Carolina (now Uni-
versity of North Carolina — Greensboro), and his novel The Fathers *had*
just been published.

TO ALLEN TATE

[February 1939]

Dear Allan: (I'm crazy, like the first edition of *White Buildings*)

Thanks very much for writing about my poems; I'm very grateful to you
for wanting to bother with getting them printed, and I'd like it if you could
get Scribner's to print them. (I'd prefer Scribner's to New Directions, I
think.) I've been getting them typed and finished and one or two changed a
little; I'll send them in a week or two.

I've been working hard at a review of [Yvor Winters's] *Maule's Curse*
and as hard as I know how to (which isn't very) at trying to get a job for
next year; they're economizing here, giving most of the English courses
every other year, and so have no need for me.

I liked your Dickinson review very much — when I read the book [*This
Was a Poet: A Critical Biography of Emily Dickinson,* by George Whicher] in
the fall I was appalled by much the same things. Tell me how you like my
Winters piece when you see it, will you? I had to cut it a lot.

I hope I can see you this summer; I enjoyed seeing you a lot at
Christmas — I don't get to talk or, better, hear about poetry much.

Seeing Red at Christmas was a great disappointment (shock) to me.
He's changed so much that he hardly seems his former self at all. I'd seen
him just about once, for a couple of hours, in three or three and a half years,
and I hadn't realized it.

When I send the poems will you tell me whether you want any letters to
go along with them? I'm calling them *Blood for a Stranger:* a happily or un-
happily characteristic title, I'm afraid.

Have you seen *New Verse* or any of the others? The English are really
quarreling — like a pie-fight in a comedy.

Give my love to Nancy and Caroline, and tell Nancy I apologize for eating half her grapefruit at Christmas.

Yours,
Randall

In the salutation, Jarrell's misspelling of "Allen" referred jokingly to the
misspelling that appeared in a few copies of Tate's introduction to Hart
Crane's White Buildings.

New Verse *was an English literary anthology.*
Tate's wife was the Catholic writer Caroline Gordon, and Nancy was
their daughter.

TO ROBERT PENN WARREN

[March 1939]

Dear Red:

I want to ask a favor of you. I'm trying to get a job at Texas (they're economizing here, hence giving most English classes alternate years, hence no longer needing me), and am getting various letters of recommendation; would you write me one? The person to address is Professor J. B. Wharey, Chairman of the Committee of Professors of English; if you'll send me the letter I'll send it to him with the others.

I enclose the formal letter to you we spoke about at Christmas, the one asking about my book; particularly now that I haven't any job, and want to get one, I'd like to have the poems published in the next three or four months — I'd rather have you [LSU Press] publish them then for sentimental reasons, that is, because I'm grateful to you for printing so many in the [*Southern*] *Review* and wanting to have a book of them.

I liked your review on [Matthew] Arnold; Mr. Ransom was crazy about it, and spoke of it one day as "about the best review ever written." Tell me if you like (or don't like) mine of *Maule's Curse,* will you?

What are you doing this summer? I hope I can see you some time; I was disappointed missing you so almost completely at Christmas. I saw Allen [Tate] a good bit. Did you know that Amy had pneumonia, and had to go home and then to Florida to convalesce?

Yours,
Randall

TO ALLEN TATE

March 13, 1939

Dear Allen:

Thanks for your nice note. I've had a letter to [Delmore] Schwartz written for three weeks, but *Poetry* has had the five or six best poems I have (with characteristic perspicuity they wanted only the worst), the ones I wanted to send to Schwartz, and I just got them back. I sent them to him yesterday.

I haven't answered yours because I'm so mixed up about that damn book. Red and the LSU people wrote back that they wanted it badly, would print it immediately, etc. I haven't known what to do. Anyway, I'm sending you the manuscript. If Scribner's or Random House want it now, O.K., if not, I can send it on to Red, as I guess I ought to anyway. As for the North Carolina University Press, you're of course welcome to use my name in any way, and I'll give you, if you want it, next spring, a book the size of this one: I've saved about ⅔, as many as there are in this book, good ones I mean — I've lots of bad. I have good unfinished ones, and I'll certainly be writing eight or ten before then: I'll have more than enough. Is that all right? Anyway, don't go to any trouble with Scribner's or Random House, Allen; if they want it right away, O.K., if not, Red does.

I've been finishing my thesis and magazine article, and, what with classes and coaching tennis every afternoon and writing and typing at night, I've been nuts.

I was delighted to hear about Princeton.

The *Review* here has been in great and comic difficulties; no one sent in stuff, and they've been frantic, and are waiting in agony for an article, much overdue, by John Peale Bishop on the World's Fair.

I'm sorry not to have written; it's poor thanks for your having been so kind; I just didn't know what to do and so did nothing.

                                                        Yours,
                                                        Randall

Delmore Schwartz was poetry editor at Partisan Review *and a friend of Tate's.*

The book for the University of North Carolina Press was to be part of a series of books by American poets that Tate had advised them to publish, but nothing came of this.

Princeton University had invited Tate to teach there.

John Crowe Ransom had founded the Kenyon Review *in 1938, but it was winter 1939 before the first issue came out. Included in the first issue were Bishop's "World's Fair Notes" and Jarrell's poem "The Winter's Tale."*

TO DONALD DAVIDSON
                                                    April 26, 1939
Dear Mr. Davidson:

I am sending you my thesis in a separate envelope; I hope it will be all right in its present form. I have made all the corrections that you and Mr.

[Richmond] Beatty suggested, cut out the parts you didn't like, and written between thirty-five and forty new pages — in this new work I tried to go by the suggestions in your letter. I hope the tone is formal enough now; I'll be glad to make any changes you think desirable for the sake of more formality. I have cut out the chapter about my own poem, and have substituted for it the analysis of Shelley's "To the Moon"; I examine fifteen or twenty poems of Housman's other than those I had treated. I have tried to indicate the scope and nature of the work, to contrast perfect with simpler or partial examples of the type, etc., as you asked me to.

Do you think that "Implicit Generalization in Housman" would be a proper name for the thesis? If you do, I should like to use it.

I'm sorry not to have gotten the thesis in sooner; the new work took more time than I thought it would, and for some time, also, I was unable to work on it.

I don't know how much postage on sending it back to me will come to — some fabulous amount; I will send you the stamps when I find out.

Spring is just beginning up here; living in the north is making a good patriotic southerner of me.

Yours faithfully,
Randall

Donald Davidson, one of the Fugitive poets and critics, was a professor at Vanderbilt and Jarrell's thesis adviser. "Implicit Generalization in Housman" was accepted by Davidson, and Jarrell was able to add an M.A. in English to his teaching qualifications.

TO ALLEN TATE

[April 1939]

Dear Allen:

Random House would be just as good as Scribner's; you might try it first, if you think that better. I'll send you the stuff in a little.

I've been reading [Allen Tate's] *The Fathers* — I had read about half when I was at your place Christmas before last. What I liked awfully about it was the feel of another world it gives you — I haven't read any other book about the south of those times that makes it such a different, odd, and real place. (The historical imagination of the Faustian mind, I guess.) I thought most of the reviews of it were rather as if they were reviewing a book of historical essays, and as if the *I* of the book were you.

Imagine my astonishment to suddenly come on the parts of your poem

["Records"] there toward the end of the book. Did many people notice them?

Poor [Philip] Rice had to give a lecture on modern poetry to the Faculty Wives' Club, about a month after Mrs. Chalmers had told them to be sure that all this modern stuff was just trash — stick to the classics like Robert Frost and Edna Millay.

Have you read [T. S. Eliot's] *Family Reunion*? I thought it one of the very worst and silliest plays I ever read.

I'm trying to get a job at Texas, and this letter is partly to ask you to write me a letter of recommendation there, if you'd be kind enough to. Prof. J. B. Wharey, Chairman of the Committee of Professors of English, Texas University, Austin, Texas. Gee, it's almost like writing to God, isn't it? Well, I know I wish that God were going to decide about the job, and not any English professors — though I suppose one has as much reason to distrust him as his creatures.

You should have sent your Meredith poem ["The Trout Map"] to the World's Fair Poetry Award Committee, to become rich and famous. I haven't written any poems for three or four months — about all I want to do here is go to sleep. I hope you have better luck with some more.

I'm homesick for the south, and I'll be glad to be home Easter.

Yours,
Randall

Mrs. Chalmers was the wife of the president of Kenyon College.

Tate sent Blood for a Stranger *to his own publisher, Scribner's. At the same time he suggested that James Laughlin use a few of Jarrell's poems in a New Directions anthology of young poets.*

TO ALLEN TATE

[April 1939]

Dear Allen:

The name *is* W H A R E Y — I can think of one misspelling which might easily anger him.

I wrote back to [Joe] Horrell [at the University of North Carolina, Chapel Hill] to do anything he could — to tell me whether I should send letters, a transcript, "and all the baggage of the tomb"; to quote the modern poet. As soon as I hear from him I'll write you about it; I hope you can do something there — in fact, if anybody does anything anywhere I'll be just charmed. I feel like Smith's economic man turned inside out.

I'm very glad you liked the review [of *Maule's Curse*]; no news from the Western front, as yet.

I wrote Red a long time ago, asking him for permission to give the poems to somebody else. I've had no answer at all, and if I don't get one in three or four days I'm just writing him that I consider the absence of any reply a consent. I have the poems about half-typed; if, when you get them, you feel strongly that any should be left out, please tell me.

I, too, don't see how science can treat poetry, since, as I understand it, the whole development of science has come about by rigidly excluding any aesthetic considerations or considerations of value from it. Before I quit, the psychology I was much the most interested in was Gestalt psychology, which is all mixed up with philosophy and very non-positivistic in attitude. Most psychologists are like English professors: they make a great fetish of scientific method and are very much charmed by tables and formulas and figures, precisely because they know their subjects aren't "really" scientific, and they hate to feel inferior to, and be ridiculed by, the real scientists. I can conceive of a psychology that would be some help with the criticism of po-etry — but not at all as a yardstick, a superior and objective substitute for taste or whatever you want to call it; only to describe and very imperfectly what does happen. (I've always been told that science is just description.) Anyway, it's an academic question: such a psychology isn't even remotely near existing. I feel very frivolous and unconcerned about it anyway; I think all in all I've got a poetic and semifeminine mind, I don't put any real faith in abstractions or systems; I never had any certainties, religious or metaphys-ical, to lose, so I don't feel their lack — I don't mean that I don't *show* their lack, I may very well. I think my mind is *really* unsystematic; along with that or perhaps because of it, I can't help thinking the world (as such little animals see it anyway because I can't help thinking that) is too. When you carry any analysis past a certain point things get contradictory and incom-prehensible, if you look at anything long enough you stop moving and fall through the ice into the abyss you (Allen Tate here) talk about. And of course I feel contradictorily and as strongly as I can that when I'm good I *am* good. And when poetry's good it *is* good — that the values are really values, and thoroughly important. And I'm not at all bothered by the con-tradictions, and like very much science as such — it seems inevitable to me, and I raised myself on Russell and Hume — and am, I guess, all in all, an absurd phenomenon. Anyway, pray don't get vexed at all this free con-fession, which is facetious and partial and pretty silly, but just the same pretty much *so*. For me, I mean. Logically, perhaps, I should hate science for destroying poetry; but I don't think it can, and besides, I don't want to be

Randall Jarrell at twenty-four

logical, just sensible. (You have a right here to say incredulously *"Sensible!"* and burst out laughing.) [Philip] Rice was talking the other day about women — and Southerners, as I remember — taking people just as people, and putting too much importance on that, instead of considering mostly their ideas (this was in relation to ordinary life, not philosophy and controversy); and I laughed to myself and thought, "I should hope." When I hear people talking gravely and importantly and at great length about these same "ideas"; I can't help thinking childishly, "How ridiculous for these two grown-up men to take all this so seriously and finally" — and so forth; and most intelligent people certainly are like that. When I know something I *know* it: I mean, as if I were the thing (or at least I hope so) and not as if I were — O, Mattheiessen (or however you spell his absurd name — this is a Freudian block, I'll bet a dollar) or a sociologist.

I must stop this river and take this to the postoffice in time for the train. Would it do any good for me to come over to N.C. myself? I *could* — I'll be in Nashville from the 5th to the 15th, at 2524 Westwood.

Yours,
Randall

The Maule's Curse *review appeared in the Spring 1939 issue of the* Kenyon Review, *under the title "The Morality of Mr. Winters." Yvor Winters, who lived on the West Coast, remained quiet.*

Nothing came of Jarrell's job application to the University of North Carolina at Chapel Hill.

TO JAMES LAUGHLIN

[June 1939]

Dear Mr. Laughlin:

I've just received the New Directions [catalogue] you were kind enough to send me, and I see that I quite misunderstood the nature of the plan you mentioned in your letter: I had thought that you were talking about publishing several books of poetry, mine among them. That I should have been interested in; unfortunately, I am not at all interested in having fifteen or twenty poems published along with equal amounts from five or six others, since I can't, in the circumstances in which I find myself, see that this would do my poems, or me, or anybody else, any good whatsoever. You see, I've been writing poems for almost ten years, and I have quite a big bunch, more nearly enough for two books than for one; and they're fairly homogeneous, that is, if there's any point in printing any there's the same point in printing the rest. I didn't know that it was so difficult to get first books published; the LSU press had asked me to give them a book, and I hadn't settled things with them just because Allen had asked me for mine when he believed that he was bringing out that series of books at North Carolina. However, if all these circumstances were different, the proposal you make would be a good thing; since they are as they are, I want to thank you for asking me, and to say that I'm sorry that I can't.

I think your plan is a good idea, and the book ought to sell well and create interest in the poets it uses. I don't know anyone good to suggest for it whom you wouldn't know already; I thought of George O'Donnell and Harry Brown, and I'm sure they occurred to you.

Anyway, thanks very much for both the invitation and the New Directions.

Yours,
Randall Jarrell

James Laughlin founded New Directions Publishers in 1936 and dedicated the company to publishing selected avant-garde authors, such as Henry Miller and William Carlos Williams, whom other publishers would not touch. Laughlin knew and said that first books of poetry were financially suicidal, but he found attractive the suggestion of Selden Rodman that he publish an anthology of five promising young poets who were relatively unknown.

George O'Donnell was a Vanderbilt graduate who had studied under Tate and Ransom. Although he had been a classmate of Jarrell's at Vanderbilt, they were not friends. They had vied for honors, for followers, and for Tate's and Ransom's approval. Total opposites in lifestyle and politics, they were, in fact, enemies whom Peter Taylor said had loud arguments in public, addressing each other as Mr. O'Donnell and Mr. Jarrell. Ransom believed that Jarrell "brow-beat" O'Donnell unmercifully; yet it was typical of Jarrell to recognize some merit in O'Donnell's poetry and recommend it to Laughlin.

Harry Brown had left Harvard without graduating and had turned to writing poetry.

Austin, Texas,
September 1939–February 1943

🎜

*P*rofessor *Wharey approved the recommendations of Tate, Ransom, and Warren, and Jarrell went to the University of Texas with an instructorship waiting, with* Blood for a Stranger *awaiting a reading at Scribner's, and with a free heart. Austin is where he met his first wife, Mackie Langham, where he first saw his cat Kitten, and where he wrote the biting reviews of Conrad Aiken, Frederic Prokosch, Marya Zaturenska, and Horace Gregory that won him a little following of lifelong friends and enemies. Jarrell left Austin with his teaching job turned over to Mackie, his book* Blood for a Stranger *published by Harcourt, Brace, and his future in the hands of the United States Army.*

TO ALLEN TATE

[September 1939]

Dear Allen:

Texas is lovely: the students meek, the professors amiable or indifferent; I am taking piano lessons, and have written about 150 lines since I've been here. I've got an office on the twenty-third floor, a really enormous one: the book shelves would hold several hundred books, and look comic with my six or eight. So far I've met nobody who knows anything about poetry, but I should worry. Nobody knows anything about me, either — except I've become famous, since I'm the best badminton player, at the university, and am getting a permanent modest look (*very* unbecoming) from responding to compliments. My classes are nice and not too much work: all in all, it's a lot nicer for me than Kenyon.

My new poems are very plain, suited for the advanced kindergarten student; you know, objective, like your fishing poem ["The Trout Map"]. I liked it — I'd read it before at your house, of course it certainly is a queer feeling when your old style comes through like an explosion or a mermaid, at the very end.

I never did write to say how much I enjoyed staying with you in August; I guess I thought I'd wait for something exciting to write about, but it didn't arrive.

How is Princeton, and how are your exceptional students, really exceptional? I've got one who, at eighteen, has read Rilke, Kafka, Proust, Spengler, everybody, but she's European and doesn't count. The rest make up for her.

I know some people who knew Kafka, and used to have him to dinner.

I felt quite funny when Freud died, it was like having a continent disappear.

I met a student who, for a year, made up, for two of the respectable English professors here, a Concordance to the Poems of Sidney Lanier. There's something wonderfully representative and *true* about this story.

I hope Princeton's nicer than you thought it would be; give Caroline and Nancy my love, and tell Nancy I'd write her a letter if I thought she'd write back.

(A girl here wanted to write a thesis about the Fugitives' poetry; she read yours and Ransom's and said she couldn't understand yours and didn't like his. You come off best, don't you?)

Yours,
Randall

TO JAMES LAUGHLIN

[October 1939]

Dear Mr. Laughlin:

I want to thank you for the last two letters I've gotten from you, the one written before and the one written after I wrote my last letter. All the details about the anthology make it look quite different; to tell you the truth, what you said about it in *New Directions* did it no justice. Also, I'm very grateful for the arguments that, naturally, come from a sort of knowledge and experience I am naked of: what I know about publishing and selling books could be put in a vacuum tube without materially impairing it. I'll write in a week or two and tell you definitely about the anthology — when Allen wrote me a few weeks ago he said he was giving the manuscript to Scribner's, and I'd better hear about that before saying anything.

I guess your main duty to your poems is to get them read by as many people as possible. (What you told me about the sale of books by a university press I knew; I guess my attitude was completely pessimistic. I thought every first book of poetry — unless, of course, you're a *good* writer, like Paul Engle or Edna Millay — sold so.) So I will think about having two or three times as many readers.

Anyway, it's certainly awfully nice of you to take so much trouble, especially in the middle of a trip that must be a pain in the neck.

I left my pen at home, and borrowed one, and look what I got; isn't it impressive?

Yours,
Randall Jarrell

Laughlin entitled his anthology Five Young American Poets, *and Jarrell frequently referred to it in writing as 5YAP. Laughlin's plan was for each poet to submit a photograph, a poem in handwriting, a "preface to his poetry," and a brief biography of himself. Jarrell wrote back that he would substitute a poem for the preface, saying, "I think I'll wait until I can have a few hundred pages before I tell the world what I think about poetry." Laughlin insisted on the preface and made some comments on the forbearance it took to work details out with poets, and Jarrell answered, "I was amused at your letter, and sympathetic, too (I shouldn't like to have to get on with poets; they — always excepting me and thee — are more things for Mother to love than the great big world outside)."*

TO ALLEN TATE

[November 1939]

Dear Allen:

I was amused and rather pleased with Laughlin's letter. I had written him several days before saying that I was interested in the anthology now that he'd sent me the details, and that when I heard from you about Scribner's I'd be able to tell him definitely. I'd gotten a quite bad impression of it from the account in *New Directions* (that's all I knew of it, and Laughlin's preface style in N.D. is, as you know, not too prepossessing: rather like God giving a rough account of what he would have done during the six days if he'd had a free hand); from what you say, and from the new letters he's written me, I think I'd better do it. Thanks very much for the advice about it, which I value a great deal.

Laughlin's notion of what we thought the world would do when it saw our poems (bray and yell with joy) is so exactly and perfectly wrong, so far as I'm concerned, that it's funny. *I* had the notion that any first and about any last poems, except Engle's or Millay's, sold next to nothing. Publishing poetry has always seemed to me like throwing it down a well: mostly nothing, a few echoes if you're lucky.

You understand, I still don't *like* the anthology, but my personal preferences seem to me irrelevant: so far as I have any duty to poems, it's to get them read by as many people as possible, I suppose; and this seems to be the best thing for that. Anyway, the whole question of how my poems get published seems to me so beautifully unimportant.

I was awfully glad you liked the "Emigrant" ["For an Emigrant"]. I'll send in this letter several you haven't read, for a Christmas present. I've written about a million.

Tell Nancy I am writing: that, in fact, I sit for hours wondering about the tone of my letter. I've about decided to use Marcus Aurelius as a model; or else Addison.

I got a nice long letter from Cal.

Princeton sounded funny and nice in spots.

The "Christmas Roses" poem [see page 12] is supposed to be *said* (like a speech from a play) with expression, emotion, and long pauses. It of course needs a girl to do it. I can do it pretty well for myself, to anybody I get embarrassed. I'd like to hear it done really nicely by somebody like Bette Davis.

I've almost finished a sequel to the "Emigrant": exactly the same length, stanzas, everything. It's less even, but the best parts are better; though of course it isn't as *lucky.*

I said [your] "Last Days of Alice" to somebody with judgment; she said it was wonderful. I hope you like secondhand compliments — I like any sort.

Yours,
Randall

"Cal" Lowell was engaged at this time to Jean Stafford, the aspiring novelist he had met at the Writers' Conference in Boulder two years before. He was also converting to her faith, Roman Catholicism.

"For an Emigrant" appeared in Blood for a Stranger but was revised for Jarrell's Selected Poems and retitled "To the New World." The sequel to "For an Emigrant" was probably "A Winter's Tale," which describes an emigrant's dreams but has fewer lines.

The person with judgment was a colleague of Jarrell's in the English

department, Mackie Langham, a member of Phi Beta Kappa with B.A.
and M.A. degrees in English from the University of Texas.

TO JAMES LAUGHLIN

[February 1940]

Dear Laughlin:

I thought Lola Pergament an unmitigated pain in the neck; I think you
are right, though, about getting a girl for the anthology.

Yes, I'd be very glad to have Allen advise me on dividing material for
the two books or on anything else. I'm pretty clear on how to do it, I think;
I'll write him and see what he thinks of the way.

I think it would be better not to run the poems together but to give a
page for each.

Your letters were especially pleasant, since I'd heard nothing about
Scribner's.

I just reviewed two of your books, among a million others, for *Partisan
Review* ["Poetry in a Dry Season": March–April, 1940]. I said no one could
afford not to get the Dylan Thomas [*The World I Breathe*], or to get the
Kenneth Patchen [*First Will and Testament*]. More or less. Alas, I don't
know any lady for the anthology.

Yours,
Randall Jarrell

*Jarrell's concern about dividing his poetry between two books refers to the
poems that would be left over from the anthology for inclusion in* Blood for
a Stranger.

*Mary Barnard was the "girl" Laughlin chose to include with Jarrell,
John Berryman, W. R. Moses, and George Marion O'Donnell in the anthology.*

*The manuscript at Scribner's may have fallen behind some editor's desk,
for nothing was heard from them until after Jarrell's death, when it sur-
faced without explanation and was sent to Mary Jarrell.*

TO JAMES LAUGHLIN

[Nashville]
[June 1940]

Dear Laughlin:

Here are the poems. I never found exactly how many you wanted,
whether they were to be printed solid or not; so I've sent what will, I sup-

pose, be a lot too many, with a list here that gives their approximate order of removal — what to take away first, second, and so on, when you have to take away:

1. ~~Fat, aging, the child clinging to her hand~~
2. The Loves of the Magician
3. Up in the sky . . .
4. Beheading
5. London
6. Fear
7. To Play Hard-to-Get . . .
8. The Hanged Man on the Gallows . . .
9. February, 1938.
10. 1789–1939
11. The Bad Music
12. Because of me, because of you . . .
13. The refugees
14. Love, in its separate being . . .
15. Eine Kleine Nachtmusik

But the more you use the better, as far as I'm concerned.

You can arrange them as you please, except for the first and last; I'd like "On the Railway Platform" to be the first poem, and I'd like "A Little Poem," "For the Madrid Road," "Che Farò Senza Euridice," and "For an Emigrant" in that order, to be the last four poems. Or that as nearly as possible.

I put in a title-page; I didn't want to use the name I have for a book, so I borrowed "The Rage for the Lost Penny."

I'll be up at Cape Cod about the tenth or twelfth or so; I'll write you when and where — so I can correct proof or do such things up there.

I hand wrote "For the Madrid Road"; leaving the title off was deliberate, I thought it spoiled the looks.

The photograph is enclosed; I don't like it much but it's literally the only one I have in the last four or five years. Outside of one making a smash.

I enclose as little biographical data as possible. You *will* keep a strictly statistical tone, won't you? At least, please do for mine; or else use it as it's written. This is just a sweet request, I don't mean to sound demanding.

I hope I've put in everything. I'm quite sorry to have been late with it; my circumstances were such that it was difficult for me to write my article.

After the biographical data, picture, and handwriting I started to go on to a fingerprint and a lock of hair.

If you want anything else, or any revisions or such (I don't mean in the poems) do write me immediately, and I will.

Yours,
Randall Jarrell

RANDALL JARRELL   BIOGRAPHICAL DATA

I was born in 1914 and grew up in Tennessee and California, and went to school at Vanderbilt. There I studied psychology; but after I had to learn radiophysics I went over into English where I belonged. (~~I remember getting to the point of thinking it would be better for everybody if I lay down on the table, and let the cat set up the cathode ray oscillograph.~~) I taught English for two years at Kenyon College, and teach it now at the University of Texas. ~~This exhausts me.~~

Jarrell's title for his section in Five Young American Poets, *"The Rage for the Lost Penny," refers to the inscription on Beethoven's posthumously published "Rondo a capriccio in G" and expresses his underlying vexation at having to comply with Laughlin's request for a preface to the poems and a biographical sketch.*

The circumstances that made it difficult for Jarrell to finish his preface, "A Note on Poetry," included the end of the semester, the task of grading examinations, and also the wedding festivities surrounding his marriage to Mackie Langham in Nashville on June 1. Like Amy, Mackie was "brilliant, good-looking and charming." Unlike Amy, she was trim of figure, with dark eyes and hair — and she did not play tennis.

The Jarrells were planning to visit the Milton Starr family on Cape Cod.

TO ALLEN TATE

[December 1940]

Dear Allen:

If I'd a safe-deposit box, I'd put your last letter in it. As the next best thing, I put it in the blank pages of Audubon's *Birds of America* I write in: so I can answer it point for point.

Don't worry. I'm peculiarly interested in pleasing you with the reviews.

I know what you mean about the Kilmer: I meant to dispose of it in a couple of sentences, but it was so really nasty — so *Catholic* in the absolutely insupportable sense of the word — that it could have goaded me into about anything. I too thought the Pound review ever so much better: I was disappointed with the other after it was too late to do anything about it.

To talk about 5YAP: I'm sure you're right about some of my lines being limp (though I do think that in the future when people are thoroughly used to reading accentual verse some of them will seem a lot stiffer); and I hope I can improve; but it's an occupational risk, a defect of a quality. In other words, I'd rather seem limp and prosaic than false or rhetorical, I want to be rather like speech — rather I did want all that; I've gone so far in that direction I'm interested in the opposite now. But you know what I mean; suppose somebody had said to you in 1925, "Mr. Tate, you tend to overwrite." I suppose you'd have answered, "I'll take the risk." But I'll think it over — I assure you I've thought it over plenty. (I've been moaning to myself all this fall about being too prosy, and when, lately, I did some that weren't at all, I felt wonderful.)

I agree with you *exactly* about [W. R.] Moses: it's just a complete Bore. (The capital *b* is a nice example of a Freudian error — it was quite unconscious.) I don't think anything in the world would help Mrs. Barnard sufficiently. As for O'Donnell, prompted by love of Beethoven, not dislike of O'Donnell, my nasty remark about the Op. 111 piece gave you the wrong impression: I *don't* think all of him's that bad. He has real talents; for instance, he has a better feel for phrase, often, than Berryman; but there's so much pure fake, so much posing and pretentiousness and imitation and romantic forcing, that the good qualities are pretty well vitiated. I think if we went over his poems line for line we'd agree almost always. I say this much on an unimportant subject because I don't want you to think my critical judgment weak enough to be overturned by my personal feelings. Doesn't that sound vain? But we have our little vanities, and that's a nice big one of mine.

I thought Berryman much better than O'Donnell so far as the negative virtues are concerned; as for positive ones, there the difference is smaller. I think Berryman has a pretty inferior feel for language for one thing; and to talk about your old favorite, the poetic subject, he's obviously not really found his.

The book was quite pretty and mild, wasn't it? I was afraid of some typical Laughlin blurbs. I hope it sells well. You may say, Why? So I'll get twenty-five dollars more.

I told them [the English department at the University of Texas] about your third year at Princeton, stressing the unprecedented honor angle; they were very much impressed. So they will talk all about it, and if they get the money this summer, they may very well invite you to come after next year; but you know how administrations are, Allen, I don't know how much they mean by what they say. I don't know what the other full professors think, and have no way of finding out. They'll probably ask Brooks all about you when he's here this summer; and *surely* he'll talk about you as if you were — O, God, or T. S. Eliot.

You know, you said my "Description of Some Confederate Soldiers" is quite as good as "A Little Poem." Boy, I think so too: better, in lots of ways. But it (C. S.) was absolutely the best poem I could write then (1936) and I wasn't recommending "A Little Poem" (1940) for the Anthology, as anything more than a very nice odd poem, one that I thought would appeal to you particularly. I left out "The cow wandering" because for a long time I've been trying to change part that I think bad. I don't mean to give the impression that I think I can write lots better poetry now: I can't write as exciting language, even, but I can construct lots better and say what I mean more clearly; and say more.

Do write me with the book [*Five Young American Poets*] by you [i.e., beside you for reference], as you say you will in your letter.

Whether Laughlin will do *Blood for a Stranger* I have no idea. I hope all my *New Republic* stuff (they're printing three poems and another review — [Edmund] Wilson's really an angel) will impress him; but I'm afraid he'll be so badly annoyed at the nasty things I say about his idol Pound, that all the *New Republic* in the world wouldn't help. Maybe if I get some good reviews it'll help.

[Philip] Rahv wrote me a complimentary letter about the Pound review and asked me to do a long article about the general state of modern poetry for *Partisan Review*.

I certainly wish you could come here. I'll be here till the cows come home, I guess.

I've been finishing poems all fall; one of the poems in the *New Republic* ["London"] has the first eight lines of accentual verse I ever wrote.

Is your Putnam's book a collection of essays, or is it the book on Flaubert? I wish it were going to be a book of poems.

Thanks ever so much for what you say about Putnam's and my book.

Don't worry about the dishes keeping me humble: here no one even reads the *New Republic,* or anything else I'm in. Seriously, not a single soul here has mentioned reading my Pound review, 11,000 students, 700 or 800 faculty, and not a soul!

We had a good Christmas at home with our cat; otherwise it was pretty dreary. The couple of people I like were away. I miss Nashville.

Randall Jarrell, Kitten, and Mackie Jarrell, 1949

Thanks a lot for what you said about the reviews, especially the unfavorable things.

I forgot to congratulate you on the third year; they certainly must have been bowled over.

Yours, affectionately,
Randall

Excuse the writing; Mackie lost my pen, I'd had it two years, and it had gotten so I could write with it fine, and nobody else would write with it at all.

Jarrell's defense for ridiculing Joyce Kilmer's brand of Catholicism in his review entitled "A Job Lot of Poetry: Joyce Kilmer, Sidney Salt, J. Calder Joseph, Elder Olson" (New Republic, *December* 1940) *was to reply to Tate's defense of it. Despite his affection for Tate, Jarrell could not help thinking that, in this case, Tate the near-Catholic was prevailing over Tate the critic. (Tate's wife and daughter were Catholic, but he did not convert until 1950.) Jarrell's Pound review, "Poets: Old, New and Aging," appeared in the* New Republic *and treated books by Leonard Bacon, Witter Bynner, Frederic Prokosch, and Ezra Pound.*

Jarrell's reference to "the Op. 111 piece" was to O'Donnell's poem "Prayer Against the Furies" in Five Young American Poets. *He found particularly distasteful O'Donnell's lines*

> Under the pressure of your urgent hands
> The sounds old deaf Beethoven pre-arranged
> Are patterned into time, into this deranged
> Time ...

The long article about modern poetry that Jarrell refers to was entitled "End of the Line" and appeared in The Nation *rather than the* Partisan Review.

Tate's book for Putnam's was his collection of critical essays entitled Reason in Madness.

TO EDMUND WILSON

[January 1941]

Dear Mr. Wilson:

I sent the [Conrad] Aiken–[Raymond] Holden review ["The Rhetoricians"] to the *New Republic* yesterday and I'm sending this letter there because I blush to say it, I couldn't read the address you wrote in at the end of your letter.

As for these two new ones [Aiken's *And in the Human Heart* and Holden's *Arrow at the Heel*] — they aren't really below the level of what I've been reviewing, the big one [by Conrad Aiken] has a sort of gaseous merit.

I'm glad you're printing the poems ["90 North," "Variations," and "London"]. I don't think Allen had read "90 North" very carefully when he suggested leaving out the fifth stanza. To do so would make the first line of the 6th stanza nonsense (it would say the precise opposite of what it does); and the stanza is an essential part of the argument, which compares the imaginary conclusive death at the Pole, in the child's warm bed, to the life, the inconclusive going-away, at the real Pole. (This is all just on a meta-phorical level, of course.) I suppose anyone who writes such a pessimistic poem ought just to nod with gloomy satisfaction at seeing it spoiled; but I have no heroic consistency at all and would be sorry to see it ruined. Read it with the stanza left out and see if it doesn't do what I say. [See poem fol-lowing this letter.]

I was naturally very pleased and complimented at having you say that you were interested in what I write, and that I ought to take prose more seriously. I like writing it, and am learning to, more or less; I never wrote any until recently because nobody asked me to. A poem doesn't exist till it's written, but prose criticism is what you think or say anyway (mostly) so you don't have much tendency to write it all out, if you have no idea whether it will be used or not. At most I would make notes — I have them for dozens of articles. I've made them for a book on modern poetry — I read all last spring trying to get a better understanding than the usual of how neo-classicism turned into romanticism; Rahv asked me for an article on modern poetry for *Partisan Review,* and they ought to be useful for it. Any-way, I'm enjoying it a lot. If you have any suggestions about it, do give them to me.

In the past I've reviewed more criticism than poetry, and I quite like doing it. If you haven't somebody better, I wish you'd give me some such book as Delmore Schwartz's essays to review. I'd like awfully to have a good book to review, and be able to make some favorable judgments; the books I've reviewed have been so bad I'm afraid the readers will start thinking, "O, *him.* He doesn't like anything."

Would you mind my making an objection to a recent review ["If We Had Some Eggs," by Harry Levin, *New Republic,* December 30, 1940]? I thought Levin's treatment of [*The Expense of Greatness* by] Blackmur was pretty regrettable, for a number of reasons. There are some things wrong with Blackmur (Louise Bogan was good on them, in what I thought a swell review ["Sensibility and Luggage," *The Nation,* December 7, 1940]); but just about every good critic I know is really interested in him, and thinks he's really hot. It wasn't just that Levin's judgments were wrong: I couldn't help feeling that they were determinedly and maliciously so, that he'd have torn to pieces in the same way *any* book of criticism, just to show how superior he is, how contemptuously he can look down on his inferior's efforts. And I've had the same feeling about other reviews of his. I remember that of an anthology of modern criticism where he said that there is no good modern criticism and then he named the four best critical books of that year as examples of the unspeakable depths to which criticism has fallen.

(The last paragraph is just to you in your strictly private position, *not* to you as collector of sentences for the poetry Mailbag. I just wrote it because Blackmur is a good critic hardly read by the public, and it's a shame to see them run away from him so.)

I'm glad my review ["Poets: Old, New and Aging"] was a success in New York; it was neither a success nor a failure here, nobody read it. Out of 11,000 students and 750 professors, not one even mentioned it. So, to make up for that, I read it several times, and laughed and applauded.

Yours, faithfully,
Randall Jarrell

90 NORTH

At home, in my flannel gown, like a bear to its floe,
I clambered to bed; up the globe's impossible sides
I sailed all night — till at last, with my black beard,
My furs and my dogs, I stood at the northern pole.

There in the childish night my companions lay frozen,
The stiff furs knocked at my starveling throat,
And I gave my great sigh: the flakes came huddling,
Were they really my end? In the darkness I turned to my rest.

— Here, the flag snaps in the glare and silence
Of the unbroken ice. I stand here,
The dogs bark, my beard is black, and I stare
At the North Pole . . .
                              And now what? Why, go back.

Turn as I please, my step is to the south.
The world — my world spins on this final point

Of cold and wretchedness: all lines, all winds
End in this whirlpool I at last discover.

And it is meaningless. In the child's bed
After the night's voyage, in that warm world
Where people work and suffer for the end
That crowns the pain — in that Cloud-Cuckoo-Land

I reached my North and it had meaning.
Here at the actual pole of my existence,
Where all that I have done is meaningless,
Where I die or live by accident alone —

Where, living or dying, I am still alone;
Here where North, the night, the berg of death
Crowd me out of the ignorant darkness,
I see at last that all the knowledge

I wrung from the darkness — that the darkness flung me —
Is worthless as ignorance: nothing comes from nothing,
The darkness from the darkness. Pain comes from the darkness
And we call it wisdom. It is pain.

*   *   *

Edmund Wilson, forty-five, was the complete man of letters. His literary works included criticism, history, fiction, social comment, poetry, and drama. An "intellectual circle" formed wherever Wilson went — Princeton, the Partisan Review, *the* New Republic, *wherever. At this time he had written* Axel's Castle, The Triple Thinkers, The Wound and the Bow, *a novel, a book of poetry, and studies of Freud and Marx; and this was just a fraction of his enormous literary and editorial accomplishments still to come. Jarrell's writing had caught his eye, and, as an editor at the* New Republic, *he sought to favor his readers with it.*

Harry Levin wrote on Joyce and Shakespeare, had all the academic credentials, and taught at Harvard.

R. P. Blackmur wrote poetry and literary essays, had only a high school diploma, and taught at Princeton.

Louise Bogan wrote brief (but powerfully influential) paragraphs, which she called "blurbs," about books of poetry and related subjects for The New Yorker. *She was on "Wystan" and "Bunny" terms with Auden and Wilson, and was an ardent fan of Theodore Roethke's. She did not care in the least for Jarrell's poetry — nor he for hers.*

TO ALLEN TATE

[January 1941]

Dear Allen:

I was charmed to hear about your poem ["Jubilo"]. Now that you've started again we ought to write alternate lines of a poem by postcard to keep you in the habit. And I was awfully glad you liked the *New Republic* poems of mine so much.

What did you think of Levin's review of [*The Expense of Greatness* by] Blackmur? (I hoped you would write to Wilson complaining about it.) I wrote saying what a shame I thought it was; Wilson answered only — I quote from memory but accurately I believe: "I was interested in what you said about Blackmur. Personally I am well-disposed toward him, but I find his work boring." Gee!

He was very kind about my poems; said that they are "haunting, and linger in my memory." I'll certainly miss him from the *New Republic;* God knows whether [Malcolm] Cowley will ever give me anything to do. As the chess champion who lost to [Wilhelm] Steinitz said, "I can do without the fame, but not the money."

I met another quotation that pleased me, from a Russian named [Lou] Novikoff, the west coast hitter who was reproached for always hitting at bad balls. He answered, "When you can get to them with a bat they ain't bad balls no more."

Did you see Babette Deutsch's review of 5YAP in the *Herald Tribune?* It pleased me very much, since I'd bet Mackie somebody would say Miss Barnard was the best of us, and Mackie had said that no one could be so foolish. But I knew. Also, I had a malicious satisfaction in being the only male who got even one kind word: imagine the feelings of the others. But that's my lower self.

Yeats's letters [*Letters on Poetry from W. B. Yeats to Dorothy Wellesley,* 1940] certainly were appealing; Wellesley's are one of the most embarrassing exhibitions I've ever seen. Poor Yeats! you go in for the aristocracy and that's what you wind up with. Her letters were as middle-class as (the present) Queen Elizabeth. Her sentence about believing love is constructive and hate destructive really got me.

Tell me how you like my Aiken-Holden review. I think and hope it will please you.

I appreciated your advice about "90 North" and feel bad about not being able to show my gratitude by taking it. But if the stanza is removed the first line of the next becomes nonsense (says the opposite of what it now does) and an essential part of the argument is lost. The poem may very well be too long and the stanza may be bad; but it's impossible just to remove it. When you see the poem again see if you don't think so.

My "Variations" is a result of all the late Beethoven I've got; the variations form is too good not to steal.

If you'll send back my manuscript [*Blood for a Stranger*], I'll add one or two poems to it that I can't bear leaving out (the *Poetry* one you liked ["The Ways and the Peoples"] and a couple of better ones, I hope) and change a few words in one; also, some more have been printed, so I have to change the acknowledgments a little. And do let me send you the stamps for it — as I remember, sending it before cost some fabulous sum, forty or sixty cents, I forget — I just remember my pained indignation.

Have you got any suggestions about leaving out ones, or are there parts that cry out to be changed, or anything like that? I wish you'd tell me about anything of the sort; probably, if you did, I'd just think, horrified, "How can he say that about *that?* that gem!" — people are fools, me too — but I might not.

I have forty-five sophomores and *one* of them had heard that faith and works were religious terms. All the rest went to church, 5 or 6 were Catholics, too. I said, "What do your preachers talk to you about?" One girl said (I thought), "About election."

I thought of you, the Ode, I mean ["Ode to the Confederate Dead"] and was going to answer, "Well, that's a good thing to talk about," when I realized that she had used the plural.

Yours,
Randall

The Queen Elizabeth referred to was Elizabeth the wife of George VI.

TO ALLEN TATE:

[March 1941]

Dear Allen:

You said I'd get rich and famous writing for the *New Republic,* but said nothing of my becoming poor and infamous being written about for it. To tell the truth, I was so enchanted by the silly over-favorable things Cowley said [in "Poets as Reviewers," *New Republic,* February 24, 1941] about my being witty that I couldn't work up any indignation about all the silly other things. Anyway, looking at it not *sub specie aeternitatis* but sensibly, it serves me right for being so tough: what I said was true but I hardly said it discreetly. Looking at it *sub specie aeternitatis* it shows lots of things, mostly that people sure love some bad poetry. Anyway, I've had some fun and some money out of it — and wasn't Cowley's article wonderfully funny? I wrote a good-humored letter back to the *New Republic* — I thought I'd send it to you and see how you like it, especially the motto for critics. I hope it's as successful as your answer to [David] Daiches, that marvelous creature, which I thought wonderfully pleasant and telling.

I've been writing *lots* of poems, some of which I'll send you.

We've just moved for the spring into a cottage in the country: a big river thirty yards from the door, cows to the left, horses to the right — like Red's old place except rattier. Kitten loves it: he was born in the nearest house.

I saw a picture of [James] Joyce that looked like you. Have you ever noticed that Wordsworth's eye sockets, in all the pictures, are exactly like Red's? (End of Better Resemblances Week.)

Give my love to your family and write me yourself if the logic's done [*Reason in Madness*].

Mackie's latest game is calling me all the names she can get from letters on reviews complaining of me. I rarely get called anything but *arrogant and pretentious creature* or such. I just answer scornfully, Brilliant! brilliant! Wittier than *anybody!*

Affectionately yours,
Randall

Tate had written a letter to the New Republic *in answer to a letter from David Daiches, the British critic and writer, in which Daiches complained that Tate's review of his book* Poetry and the Modern World *implied that he (Daiches) judged literature "politically" and did not really like literature. Tate later apologized for this publicly.*

Warren's old place outside of Nashville was a roomy, run-down frame house Jarrell and Amy had often visited.

*   *   *

Jarrell's Aiken–Holden review ("The Rhetoricians," New Republic, *February 17, 1941) had pleased Tate but highly displeased Aiken's loyal friend Malcolm Cowley. In the review Jarrell had said that the sonnets in Aiken's* And in the Human Heart *were "written with impressive fluency and command" and that "their materials and mechanisms are ones Mr. Aiken has used so many times before, under so much more difficult circumstances, that he seems as much at ease as Merlin pulling a quarter from a schoolboy's nose." He went on to say: "The ostensible subject of the sonnets was a generalized love-affair; but their real subject was a particular rhetoric Aiken had been developing for a long time. He is in love with a few dozen words . . . the traditional magic-making words of English romantic poetry. . . . In the forty-three sonnets, the sun, moon and stars are mentioned more than fifty times; love 50; flower and flower names, 58; time, 33 . . . etc."*

Jarrell concluded: *"The content of Mr. Aiken's best poems has almost disappeared; these are only their emptied and enormously inflated rhetorical shells. To him, now, the world exists as a thesaurus from which to derive the glittering and immaculate counters that arrange themselves, almost automatically, into a poem."*

In a brief but pointed aside early in the review, Jarrell took Aiken to task for being an enemy of modern poetry, writing, *"A few months ago, writing from England to the* Atlantic Monthly *he began a crusade against contemporary poetry. It was hard not to be impressed with it: anyone would be impressed with a crusader who says Auden, Tate, Ransom, Warren, MacNeice, and Muriel Rukeyser all write just alike."*

Cowley chose to defend Aiken in the New Republic *in a piece entitled "Poets as Reviewers" (February 24, 1941). His attack was directed at Jarrell, except for one sentence condemning Louise Bogan's Aiken review in* The New Yorker. Cowley *began by exalting Aiken as "one of the few . . . poets by profession" who had never "played the literary game" of reading for the radio, lecturing to women's clubs, attending autographing parties, and "scratching backs, rolling logs, or mending fences." Cowley wrote that in* And in the Human Heart *Aiken's poetry had taken a new direction, one "more emotional and straightforward," which he had thought the literary world would discuss with interest and review widely. But he then had to admit that in all Aiken had gotten only seventeen reviews, none of them in "the bookselling mediums like the* New York Times, *the* New York Herald Tribune, *the* Saturday Review, The Nation *and the* Atlantic Monthly." Cowley *went on to say that the review in the* New Republic *"was used by Randall Jarrell as the occasion for a diatribe against rhetoric — a brilliantly written diatribe, but one which had only a formal connection with Mr. Aiken's book." He continued, "Mr. Jarrell is a talented poet . . . [and] as a book reviewer he is about the wittiest we have. . . . And this is a clue to the nature of Mr. Jarrell's book reviews: they are a form of art in which the technical skill and the attitude — the* dandysme *— of the reviewer are more important than the subject matter. The poet who gets a going-over by Mr. Jarrell is like the scared Negro at a county fair who sticks his head through a sheet while people throw baseballs at it, three balls for a* *dime. He is doing something like that in his review of* And in the Human Heart."

Cowley then faulted Jarrell for understating the subject of the sonnets as *"a generalized love affair" when they really dealt with "two lovers parted during an illness that threatens to be fatal" and complained that "besides missing the subject, Mr. Jarrell does not say anything about the music of Mr. Aiken's verse." In his last paragraph, Cowley condemned all poet-reviewers as "psychologically unable to like anything whatever, for fear of helping a rival or hurting their own reputations," and stated that "Often they convey the impression that all the other poets are cretins or zanies, hog-callers, copyists, or rhetoricians."*

Aiken was so pleased by "Poets as Reviewers" that he wrote Cowley, *"Thanks thanks thanks thanks — your letter was balm, manna, panacea and goulash, all in one — and it came in the nick of time, too, as I was still staggering under the first-round pounding of mr. jarrell"* (Selected Letters of Conrad Aiken, *ed. Joseph Killorin [*New Haven: Yale University Press, *1978]). He went on to say that he had a lot of respect for Jarrell and thought him "damned intelligent," and that he was one of the few new people he would go out of his way to read; but that he couldn't understand this "monstrous hate" Jarrell had for him. Then he added, "I think the Tate-to-Blackmur-to-Warren-to-Brooks-to-Ransom roundelay is becoming a menace . . . and ought to be dealt with, but they're tough babies. And that 0-so-private language of theirs! Jesus." (Aiken's "roundelay" consisted of the pillars of the school of criticism known as the "New Criticism," which would never include Malcolm Cowley or Harry Levin among its members.)*

Jarrell's response to Cowley's "Poets as Reviewers" ("Mr. Jarrell Replies") *appeared in the letters section of the March 17, 1941, issue of the* New Republic.

TO THE NEW REPUBLIC

[March 1941]

Mr. Jarrell Replies

Sir:

I am so flattered at Mr. Cowley's overestimation of my wit [the *New Republic,* February 24] that I hardly like to object to his underestimation of my judgment. Besides, there is something agreeably odd about reviewing a book for a magazine and having the review reviewed, as a typical crime, by one of the magazine's editors; I feel as if my decision had been overruled by the Supreme Court.

Mr. Cowley says that Louise Bogan's review treated Mr. Aiken's book only as "one of the texts for a sermon against the grand poetic manner," and that mine treated it only as "the occasion for a diatribe against rhetoric" which was simply irrelevant. Isn't it a coincidence that both Miss Bogan and I should decide to waste our reviews of Mr. Aiken on irrelevant attacks on rhetoric and the grand style? Really both of us made pretty much the same objections to the book; perhaps we were wrong about it; but then perhaps Mr. Cowley was. I wasn't attacking *rhetoric* (an old friend), but the ornamental and empty romanticism of the particular rhetoric in *And in the Human Heart;* and there was more wrong with the book than rhetoric. Though Mr. Cowley thinks not, I noticed and admired the skill and "music" of the poems: I compared them to Liszt finger-exercises, and found them "beautifully able" verse, written with "impressive fluency and command." Mr. Cowley finds them good poetry as well; but this amiable failing I cannot share.

I doubt that my own reviews furnish a very good text for a sermon against poetry-reviewing; most reviewers would say hastily, "The damn things aren't like *mine*." According to Mr. Cowley, I review poets by making the cleverest and nastiest attacks on them that I can manage: I am like Pope's parrot (the one who yelled names at passers-by), if the parrot had been a little smarter. The report of my method seems to me a good deal exaggerated. A good many of the books I get to review do seem bad to me, and I say so — a string of sober *no's* would bore any reader, so I try to phrase my *no's* as well as I can. But so far as I know I've never been dishonest enough to say unfavorable things for a chance to be witty. And I do like (and say that I like) some of the books I happen to review; so I can hardly be Mr. Cowley's typical poetry reviewer, who does neither. That my reviews seem to Mr. Cowley disproportionately severe indicates a divergence of our tastes which can hardly fail to be a source of gratification to us both.

I had thought a good motto for critics might be what the Persians taught their children: *to shoot the bow and speak the truth;* but perhaps a better one would be Cordelia's *love and be silent.*

Randall Jarrell

TO EDMUND WILSON

[March 1941]

Dear Mr. Wilson:

It's really extraordinarily kind of you to have gone to so much trouble over my letter ["Mr. Jarrell Replies," *New Republic,* March 17, 1941] — I hardly know how to thank you. The *New Republic* had told me nothing

about any such letter from [J. V.] Healy; Nigel Dennis thanked me for my
letter (he said they "liked it very much") and said that the next few correspondence columns would be fun for me to read, there'd be some letters For
me and some Against me. If I'd known about all the denunciation I'd have
written differently — the books were bad, I said so, and I'm glad, is the way
I feel. My last paragraph was pure irony, of course, and rather nasty under
the surface; but coming after a letter like Healy's it would have looked
awful, as if I were more or less apologizing, something I shouldn't even
dream of, of course.

Isn't this whole business a joke? Or it would be a joke if it didn't show
what most poetry-reviewing's like. I have to laugh unbelievingly when I
think of three little unfavorable reviews by a quite unknown reviewer making such a mess — it's completely absurd.

I'm glad you liked the poems so much (glad you liked the Aiken review,
too, but of course I care about the poems a million times more). What you
said in your last letter about repeating points in my reviews I had no difficulty in recognizing as the truth: I wrote the reviews pretty much as collections of fragments, and I'd make a joke which meant what another one had
at the beginning of the review (two weeks before).

I was glad to see what you said about Kipling's later stories: I've always
been particularly interested in them, their entire neglect is wonderfully stupid. When people talk about Kipling's stories it almost always turns out
they mean the Indian ones or such — I remember Mr. Ransom saying
"They're awfully crude little things, aren't they?" and he was talking about
(as typical) *Plain Tales from the Hills!* Kipling was a great waste; what he
could have done grieves you to think of. (But I can read even *Puck of Pook's
Hill* and *Rewards and Fairies* with pleasure; I remember when I first read that
I didn't even know who the *Browning* and *Ruskin* referred to were. And I
remember when I first read *Kim* I tried to go bare foot and got a nail in my
foot. So I'm hardly an impartial judge of Kipling.)

What caused Cowley's article ["Of Clocks and Calendars"], anyway? So-
licitude for Aiken?

I'll stop this pretty dopey letter — I just wanted to write immediately to
thank you. I was typing poems when you called and welcomed the inter-
ruption; I thought I'd enclose one of the poems I was typing ["The Skat-
ers"], to see if you like it; it's got the "90 North" *milieu* pretty much.

Yours,
Randall Jarrell

I find to my great shame I've lost your address, so I'll just have to send this
c/o *N. Republic.*

Nigel Dennis was an associate editor at the New Republic.

Among other letters criticizing Jarrell in the New Republic *was one from J. V. Healy, a poet from Maine who denounced Jarrell in an attack entitled "The Poet's Bloody Corner." He was furious at the treatment given Aiken, Pound, and Prokosch, the latter of whom he considered "one of the best poets of my generation." In "Poets: Old, New and Aging," Jarrell had described Prokosch as "a sort of decerebrate Auden, an Auden popularized for mass consumption," and had gone on to write: "Mr. Prokosch's success in the romantic and superficial exploitation of Auden's materials and methods is really incomparable ... (A person who knows Auden's poetry well will notice his influence in* Death at Sea *many hundreds of times in tone, form, images, rhetoric and content) ... [and] the poems pour out like sausages, automatic, voluptuous and essentially indistinguishable."*

Healy requested that the New Republic *justify Mr. Jarrell's review or else apologize to Mr. Aiken, Mr. Pound, and Mr. Prokosch. "Failing that," he added, "please cancel my subscription." Cowley obliged with a short piece entitled "Of Clocks and Calendars" that concluded that poetry reviewing was indeed in a "disheartening state."*

In a subsequent letter to the New Republic, *Prokosch himself wrote, "No one should be seriously disturbed by a critic if he is clever and entertaining (like Mr. Jarrell) even though his deficiencies in reading power and critical education might lie apparent in every line." What Prokosch found "intolerable" was that "these lacks should be garnished by such high pretentiousness and arrogance." He added that "I shall publish no further verses in America where they have met with [such] vituperation." And he implored the* New Republic *editors, "Never, never, entrust your reviews to poets old, new or aging; good, bad or mediocre."*

TO LOUISE BOGAN

March 25, 1941

Dear Miss Bogan:

I'm so grateful for your letter that I certainly can't thank you properly. I've always read and liked your reviews, so naturally I'm awfully glad you like mine: and it's so good to have someone know *why* a reviewer has to write mostly unkind reviews; Mr. Cowley's answer is *Vanity, vanity.*

I felt rather shy about pulling your name into my letter; but your review [of *And in the Human Heart* by Conrad Aiken, *The New Yorker*, Dec. 28, 1940] was implicated in the point I wanted to make, and your review had

been condemned even as mine, though hardly so spectacularly. I was pleased
enough at the agreement of the reviews to want to defend yours too.

I've particularly liked your reviews lately, partly (naturally) because we
made about the same judgements on several poets, and that gave me a comfortable sense of community, a feeling there was a Mrs. Judge Jeffries to
share my guilt. But I think the one I liked best was your *Nation* review of
[*The Expense of Greatness* by] Blackmur; I wrote to Edmund Wilson complaining about Levin's review, and cited yours as just the way it should have
been done. I was awfully sorry to see yours lumped with Levin's [in *Partisan
Review*] in the heat of battle; but righteous indignation carries everybody
into excess.

What I've always felt grateful to you for is the way you've treated
Auden; to accept him with unjudging admiration is exactly what nobody
(no good critic, that is — you'll know all the ones I'm talking about, Empson, even Blackmur, Tate, Eliot, Winters, etc.) of the generation before him
has done. And I was simply charmed by something you said (in *Partisan
Review*, I think) about the feel of early romanticism at its best; I feel so, too.
It's such a shame to see all the good — really good — middle-aged critics as
stupid about the romantics as Arnold was about Dryden and Pope. I understand why they are, of course; it's what they liked when they were very
young, and revolted against, and it's what they are — in the last extraordinary extension — in their poetry; and so protest too much about, like Gertrude in the play [*Hamlet*]. But it's too bad they can't get over it, one or
two at least, so late, so very late as this.

I was interrupted in writing this letter by the extraordinary arrival of a
poor wonderfully scrubby half-starved four-months-old dark brown Persian;
the extraordinary comes from the fact that very obviously — from his looks
and some more data — he's the half-brother of our own Kitten, who at the
age of seven and a half months weighs twelve pounds. We fed him; he was
wonderfully good, and our cat was too; they're both fast alseep on the floor,
looking like the lion and the lamb (I don't think the new one weighs two
pounds). My wife's also asleep on the floor, everything's perfectly dark and
quiet except for a cow that moos occasionally outside; I feel as if I'd wandered into the Sleeping Beauty's castle.

It was awfully kind of you to tell me not to mind the unkind remarks;
and to tell the truth I couldn't; in real life I know I'm normally sensitive to
disapproval, but in the disreputable Limbo of magazines I simply manage to
take the things said as anything more than queer and wonderfully funny.
(Of course I do take them seriously as signs of the usual bad state taste, poetry, criticism — and why should I leave out Life? — are in.) Somebody

ought to write about the way most poetry *is* reviewed: the formulas, the amount of comprehension, etc.

I liked your rhymed review of [Donald Parson's] *The Glass Flowers;* the Deepening Sense of Awe keeps recurring to me. I read an odd book, the memoirs of an 18th century Jewess, not much as literature but somehow very enlightening; and I wrote a poem about it (considerably looser than yours) which I send as a grateful gift, not a Greek gift, I hope.

I certainly enjoy reviewing, and hope I'll be permitted to continue; in fact, I hope we both get to, until finally we die all wrinkled and gray from reading so much bad poetry. And I hope the True Critics of poetry all meet Proper Fates. I thought up a Proper Fate for Otis Ferguson the other day: that he'll become so popular he'll get a daily newspaper column.

This long letter is supposed to show how grateful I was for yours, which I will treasure.

Yours faithfully,
Randall Jarrell

"Mrs. Judge Jeffries" refers to Judge George Jeffreys (1645–1689), who was known for his harsh denunciation of, and penalties for, insurrectionists during the reign of James II. In "Poets as Reviewers," Malcolm Cowley had written, "A revolutionist coming before Judge Jeffreys . . . at the Bloody Assize of 1685 had a better chance for his life than a poet who faced Mr. Jarrell."

Otis Ferguson is best known as a film critic. He also wrote book reviews for the New Republic.

TO ALLEN TATE

[April 16, 1941]

Dear Allen:

Thank you so much for *Reason in Madness.* I was sick when I got it and reading it made me feel a lot better. Having read the individual essays didn't prepare me for how well they'd fit together — all of them make a much bigger impression. The latest one is swell.

The *New Republic* and *Nation* asked me to send them titles I wanted to review — I put it first on both lists; and *The Nation* sent it to me today — so I'll get to review it.

Cleanth was here, I saw him for about twelve hours. I had a wonderful time talking to him and was crazy about him. He was much liked here.

I've been working hard. I wrote a lot this winter, poems I mean. I've been sick or dopey for the last couple of weeks.

I don't know whether you'll like my Auden review [of *The Double Man, The Nation,* April 12, 1941] or not (I hope you do); I fancy I liked the poem better than you. Wilson liked it much better than I did; Cleanth said that [Delmore] Schwartz was denouncing the poem to everybody when he met him.

I'm going to Mexico this summer where there'll be no school, duties, or anything, and work all summer, I hope.

I admired your prose style very much. I hope your aura or something will affect Blackmur's style.

Did you see the review [of *The Expense of Greatness*] he got in *Poetry?* It was incredible. About all his reviews have been a crime; I could have seen you be even nastier to [Harry] Levin without minding.

The New Yorker tried to print a very short poem of mine with nine changes in the — punctuation!

Hasn't Harry Brown's poetry disintegrated?

I'm reviewing MacNeice's [*The Poetry of W. B.*] *Yeats* — a bad vexing book.

This is silly chatter and I don't feel up to more — I just wanted to thank you for the book. I only hope it gets the reviews it deserves; though that's a temporal mercenary wish, really I guess it doesn't matter.

Doesn't Daiches do *anything* but write letters about you?

Yours affectionately,

Randall

Two of Harry Brown's books of poetry — The End of a Decade *and* The Poem of Bunker Hill — *appeared in 1941. Brown was on the poetry staff at* The New Yorker, *and Jarrell assumed it was he who had sought to make the punctuation changes in Jarrell's poem "The Blind Sheep."*

TO ALLEN TATE

[May 1941]

Dear Allen:

[The first page of this letter has been lost.]

You know, *your* public style certainly is different from your private. When I tell posterity about my dear kind friend Mr. Tate, how charming he was, smiled on rich and poor alike and was loved by all, it will look blankly and unbelievingly at me and say "What about all these essays? And letters? And controversies? Etc.?" You don't even make the same sort of jokes in your letters and your public writings: your public facade is stern and absolute, compared. This isn't reproach, just description. I'm sure your readers, when they hear you on the radio [on "Invitation to Learning"], are astonished at how mild and gentle, how unexpectedly so, you are.

I was reading your *Sonnets at Christmas* the other day and admiring them — it, rather. They certainly are beauties — just conversational enough and just exciting-language enough, just hard enough, very complicated under an easy surface. I like that sort of treatment of "What's become of religion? Where are we going to go?" so much better than Eliot's, for instance; its form fits the situation so much better. If you disagree with what I say it will be cheapening your own wares, so you'd better not.

I've been writing stuff that flows glibly off, without emotion but wittily, I hope, anyway — why it comes out I've no notion, it's certainly not anything I've ever done or meant to do. I am looking at it askance as 1740 and waiting for a Romantic Revival about next fall. To quote the modern poet [Jarrell, in "Esthetic Theories: Art as Expression"]: "Poems, like lives, are doing what we can/ And very different from what we know./ They start surprisingly, like blood in bones;/ The unlucky wake up bleeding at the nose . . ." But here I stop.

Red asked me for a Yeats article, as I assume he did you (an honor for me). I'm doing the periods, language change, the re-written poems, and some value judgements. Yeats' letters made me remember my old attachment very vividly. He's certainly a writer I'm grateful to.

If I had something I meant to say in this letter I've hopelessly lost it under the mass of what I have said; I'll quit with best wishes to everybody, give my love to Nancy.

Affectionately yours,
Randall

"Invitation to Learning" was an intellectual radio-conversation series. The public sent in questions about literature, classical music, nature, and art, and these were spontaneously answered by Tate, Mark Van Doren, John Kieran, Oscar Levant, Huntington Cairns, and others. They participated not for refrigerators or $64,000 but to address the public's interest, and they received a sensible fee and a certain amount of prestige.

Jarrell's essay on Yeats was entitled "The Development of Yeats' Sense of Reality." Warren wanted it for the Yeats issue of the Southern Review, *Winter 1941.*

TO EDMUND WILSON

[Mexico City]
[August 5, 1941]

Dear Mr. Wilson:

I just got a letter from [the editor] Edward Weeks saying the *Atlantic Monthly* was using two of my poems, so I thought I'd write and thank you for it.

I haven't had such a hot summer; my wife had pneumonia in June, and I was pretty sick and had to write that *New Republic* article at the same time. Just now I'm half way through an interminable Auden article and very tired of it. The most amusing thing I've done in Mexico is to help coach a boys' football team — I don't know any Spanish, so the operation of coaching is pretty funny.

I was asked to contribute to an English book about writing and the war, and was told that you were being asked. Are you going to write anything? Do you think it's worth doing?

My wife and I were charmed with your wife's story ["The Man in the Brooks Brothers Shirt" by Mary McCarthy] in *Partisan Review;* we were in Baton Rouge when we read it, and we got into long arguments with the *Southern Review* staff, saying that they should have printed it instead of their stories.

I've just finished a review ["Town Mouse, Country Mouse"] of [Marya] Zaturenska and [Horace] Gregory for *The Nation* that ought to be printed in a few days — tell me how you like it, will you?

Speaking of reviews, Otis Ferguson certainly did a ghastly one of you. Will you, as one on the inside, tell me why the *New Republic* adores him in large quantities? From the outside it's inexplicable; or, anyway, disquieting.

What do you think of the war stand *The Nation* and *New Republic* have taken? They should have slogans like: We hate War; we love wars. Or: The latest war is never economic. They should list (like the ways to tell a Snark from a Boojum) the ways to tell an Imperialist from a Crusader. How did you like the arguments for and against declaring war in the letter to contributors?

The newspapers here, about the Roosevelt–Churchill marriage of minds, are lovely. The war aim — Great Britain and the United States as the armed police force of the world — is surely beyond any parodist's talents or dreams.

Here in Mexico City they have rival telephone companies, both foreign: there is no communication between the systems. All the "nice people" are delighted with the government, which has gone beyond their fondest dreams. Food prices have increased enormously — meat is twice as high, since so much of it is being shipped to the United States. I have never seen so many policemen and soldiers. The policemen's uniforms are incredibly varied, running even into gold braid — the motorcycle policemen wear a beige and brown Hollywood creation, and look pretty and barbered enough to be one of the real attractions of the city. The soldiers wear drab olive-green cotton uniforms, French helmets, and bristle with equipment; they are almost all young Indians. A regiment looks astonishingly French-Colonial — Annamese, say.

Mexico is absolutely covered with very big contented dogs, of no definite breed, often resembling nothing you've ever seen, who lie confidently asleep on the pavements or in the market-aisles. If a Mexican dog barks at anyone he is taken to a psychoanalyst. The pet cats are tied on little strings.

The upper classes have an unconscious tight hard look, as if they had got on top and were going to stay there. That's very impressive. The nicest things in Mexico, probably, are all Indian: to judge by a vague impression.

I know it's conventional to say how bad American tourists are, but here the exclamation is simply wrenched from you. There are three classes: the well-to-do, the cultured, and the plain Americans — the last are much the best. The nicest remark I've heard was a fat woman's dismayed "This plate ain't got no boids on it." I think eventually there will be a system where the people with money enough will stay at an American hotel, eat all their meals at Sanborn's — as a matter of fact, they already do this — and see the country only from a portable American diving sphere all of whose windows will be equipped with the latest assortment of camera-filters. Much of the tourist profit is already made by Americans.

The thing is, of course, that the tourists are mostly unrepresentative, people you'd like no better in the United States. I'm quite homesick for the United States and — not coffee, or baths, or screens, or any of the usual — a *library:* any Carnegie.

I hope you've had a good summer; what are you writing?

Sincerely,
Randall Jarrell

Otis Ferguson's review of Wilson's The Boys in the Back Room, *entitled "Pencil, Pad and Purpose," appeared in the July 7, 1940, issue of the* New Republic.

TO ALLEN TATE

[October 1941]

Dear Allen:

I was awfully amused at your last letter — you really are the best letter-writer I know. I'm afraid you're right about (my) patronizing style, although I do think you exaggerate it a lot — I think *that* because other people don't, or say they don't, notice it (about the style). Anyway, I'll try to improve; and I believe I am getting better — when you've read the Auden piece I have in the *Southern Review* and a piece about modern poetry in *The Nation* ["End of the Line"], tell me if you don't think them better in that respect.

How right you were about the disgrace of being in the *Atlantic Monthly*! They put my poem ["The Head of Wisdom"] in the middle of pieces most freshmen would be ashamed to write; and in the contributors' column they said that R. J. "writes criticism and poetry when the spirit moves him." Also, they didn't mention that I'd ever had anything else published, in order to give the impression that I was a find of the *Atlantic Monthly*. But I felt lucky when I saw that the poet above me had "elemental love of the soil."

If you see the poem will you tell me how you like it? — the first and last, that is — I know the middle is too abstract.

I forgot to mention the saving fact that I got paid a dollar a line. Another saving fact is that it will make more impression on the poor ole professors here than having forty-six years work in the regular magazines. But it was a ghastly experience.

Boy, I hope the [Mesure] lecture goes through; it would really have more effect on the department than having a couple of books published. The people here are the usual lunatics: I've been told that several disapprove of my having things in "that radical magazine, *The Nation*"; others said that they disapproved of my having so much published, since it must mean that I was neglecting my classes. (I'm on only ¾ time, you know.) If I had equal amounts of stuff published in the PMLA they'd make me a full professor.

But why should I go on talking about things that are obvious to you *à priori*?

I hope you are well by now or getting better — we've been sick enough in the last six months to make me very sympathetic.

You're certainly right about Ransom's letter; when I saw it my heart sank. I'd been afraid (he'd told me he was writing) that it was going to be one of those horrible times when he loses his temper and everything else.

It's a shame — the review was so rotten, too. If he ever gets an equally bad one let's write letters in ourselves to keep him from having to.

Besides my regular classes (which are swell) I have a student from New York — educated, literate, with literary acquaintances — who is doing with me a course 567K is its pretty name, that involves only picking a professor and writing things for him. It's fun; I was surprised to be picked by anybody, I think generally they pick [J. Frank] Dobie (and learn to ride) or the full professors.

Mackie's well and sends her love. We've got a nice house close by.

This is a silly chatty letter and I don't feel like anything better.

If you want to see wicked me being patronized at four or five pages length look at Mary Colum in the *American Mercury;* I'm told I've suffered out in the provinces from never having known any real literary people to correct my views, and that I should read Saintsbury.

Well, I must go to the library.

Yours affectionately,

Randall

The lecture Jarrell refers to was part of a Princeton lecture series called the Mesure Lectures in American Criticism, and Tate had recommended Jarrell as one of the speakers.

Ransom's letter was in response to Louise Bogan's review of his book The New Criticism *in the July 12, 1941, issue of* The Nation. *What elicited Ransom's incensed reply was, among other censures, an accusation that he displayed a new kind of snobbery that held that it was vulgar "to think and to express oneself in images."*

TO ALLEN TATE

[October 1941]

Dear Allen:

This is a thank-you letter pure and simple: you don't know how grateful I am. I'll like giving the lecture, seeing you, and — most of all, since this is a business culture — getting in good with the department here. I'm particularly grateful because it seems to me that other people, in your place, wouldn't have done the same thing, whether or not they liked my criticism — or me.

I wish you could see the football team here. It's even better than people say. The Princeton–Vanderbilt game ought to delight you; I'm assuming Princeton hasn't won you over so far as football's concerned. I confess that if Texas played Vanderbilt I'd be yelling myself hoarse for Texas. They have an extremely just and reasonble system here — Crain and Layden do the same work and get the same money that the worst men on the third team do. You'd be astonished at the good humor and good feeling — I know some of the players and have played touch football with them, and it's surprising.

I've got an all-state freshman back in my class; he runs the hundred in 9.7, is a first-rate broken-field runner, a good punter and passer, and he's cold as a corpse — possibly owing to the fact that he's an undertaker's assistant in the summers. He wrote a Defoe theme on his job. The contrast between his tone and his subject-matter was so extreme that some of the girls half fainted when I read it — to the class. His name is Lawler and I'll bet he'll be famous in two years.

How's your Yeats coming along? I'm tired of writing and can barely force myself to work on mine.

If you'd give me some advice about the lecture I'd be grateful: what the others were like, what the audience is like, how hard or general to be, etc., if the lectures were read or said? Who's doing it this year besides [Kenneth] Burke and Blackmur?

Daiches wrote a letter to the *New Republic* about me — rather angrier than his letter about you — I answered mildly; see if you like the tone. He called me a good many things, *ignorant* was the mildest.

I've written a little poetry — it's not prosey, either, thank goodness.

I hope you're quite well now. Does school take up much of your time?

Yours affectionately,

Randall

TO THE NEW REPUBLIC

[October 6, 1941]

Critical Scholars

Sir:

Mr. Daiches has written [the *New Republic*, August 18] that it is "quite untrue" that modern critics have been instrumental in effecting any change in taste about Donne, Herbert, Marvell, Webster, Fulke Greville, Hopkins and so forth. It was an "academic job": the scholars did it all, and the "brilliant young critics" simply "followed meekly behind." Mr. Daiches' tone of polite, sober and factual good sense is almost enough to recommend the theory; certainly there is not much else to recommend it. It is a theory that has a superficial plausibility if applied to any critical change whatsoever. If modern critics had resurrected Cowper, Surrey, Christopher Smart and Cowley, Mr. Daiches could have said — would have said — using the same arguments and with just as much truth: "Why, these young critics have simply followed the scholars. Didn't Professor So-and-So, in 1916, bring out a new edition of Cowper? Hasn't Professor A, in his edition, pleaded for a resurrection of Surrey? and Professor B for a resurrection of Christopher Smart? and Professor C for a resurrection of Cowley? It is the *scholars* who have engineered this change in taste!"

There is no poet, no period that scholars have not tried valiantly to resurrect, to overrate; scholars — who have a vested interest in their own particular specialties — notoriously exaggerate the importance of them as much as they can. To select a very small part of this indiscriminate incoherent mass of advocacy, and then to call *that* a critical change, is fantastic. Scholarship is like the man who jumped on his horse and rode off in all directions: no matter which way criticism goes, Mr. Daiches can say that it is merely following scholarship.

Mr. Daiches' only attempt at proving his theory is the citation of — four *editions.* According to his astonishing logic, all that is necessary to effect a critical change, a "rehabilitation" of a poet, is a new edition of his poems. Or, worse still, of his letters. Mr. Daiches cites as one of his proofs Abbott's edition of Hopkins, without mentioning that it is an edition of his *letters,* published long after his poetry had become famous. His citation of the very recent edition of Fulke Greville is just as bad: the interest in Fulke Greville came long before any modern edition of his poems existed — it was the interest which was responsible for the edition. Why did Mr. Daiches resort to examples like these?

Mr. Daiches' picture of scholarship in the English universities made my mouth water; but I could not, try as I would, manage any identification between his ideal scholars and everyday reality. Of course, I have not had the good fortune of hearing what they say, but I have had the bad fortune of reading what they write. It is hard for me to reconcile Mr. Daiches' knowledge of the men with my own knowledge of the books; but perhaps such a scholar is just the opposite of Goldsmith — talks like an angel, and writes like poor Poll.

Mr. Daiches finishes with the unkind remark that the preferences expressed in Cleanth Brooks's *Modern Poetry and the Tradition* were a "critical commonplace" in English universities from 1920–40. Some of Mr. Brooks's preferences are entirely too acute, and some are entirely too personal, to be "commonplace" anywhere at any time. If the book was a critical commonplace in England, why did it get such good reviews there? Why did Empson — an English critic quite as likely as Mr. Daiches to recognize an English critical commonplace — waste so much praise on it?

Mr. Daiches' letter is simply the old game of keeping the *status quo* as nearly as possible intact, by insisting that the radicals' advances are only what the old guard wanted all the time and finally managed to get; Mr. Daiches is exactly in the position of the conservative legislators who, forced by radical pressure to consent to social legislation, give the credit for the whole thing to the Conservative Party.

Randall Jarrell

TO EDMUND WILSON

[October 1941]

Dear Mr. Wilson:

I got your note about the review ["Town Mouse, Country Mouse"]. I'm afraid the criticism is just; when I start talking about the virtues of so-so people my style collapses, I hardly know how to say the things I feel obliged to say — certainly saying them well or wittily is beyond me. I guess I'll have to practice — seriously, I've thought of doing that; being able to is practically a necessity for the Perfect Reviewer. The *deserves one's gratitude or awe* was a little ambiguous stylistic grace that evidently doesn't get over. I agree with you, entirely, about the Gregory Family [Horace Gregory and Marya (Zaturenska) Gregory]. It amused me to think of their reading the review.

I've just had a very hard week's work (not enough time, and I hadn't enough space) doing an article on modern poetry ["End of the Line"] for *The Nation*. I wish I'd done up my theory better (I'm going to, later, at very great length); this was supposed to be a sort of *patent applied for* affair but it may have the effect of dampening any widespread interest in infringing the copyright. I thought I'd send you a carbon and see how you like it. I was so pressed for space that I had to cut out long, already-written paragraphs and replace them with sentences: the ones I regret most are ones on Imagism, another movement, and the singular development of modern music, which I cut entirely. Anyway, make allowances for that, won't you, and see how you like the theory. I've been working on it for years and have waste baskets full of notes.

I've been amused by the fact that, try whom he will, Cowley can't get favorable reviews of poetry; his pet lamb, Aiken, is unkindest of all, and dismissed MacNeice, Cummings, and John Peale Bishop in one issue [in a review entitled "Poetry as Entertainment"].

I have a vague memory that I'd like you to corroborate, if you can: did Yeats ever say anything about Pound's having helped change his style? I'm almost sure I remember reading it (perhaps in that little publisher's pamphlet that came out eight or nine years ago with different writers' praise of Pound — you may have been in it, and might remember). If you know where (or that) such a statement exists, I'd be grateful.

I remember seeing reviews of yours, four or five years ago, grieving about how bad poetry was getting — which might recommend my theory to you. When I went through Baton Rouge I told it at length to Cleanth Brooks; I was surprised to find he thought it mostly true. He said his own experience, as editor, certainly confirmed it; that the young poets almost invariably got worse, or certainly didn't develop; that the old poets sent in bad poems; that it was excessively difficult to get good poetry.

The theory (though it came from the detailed judgments, not the other way around) is, implicitly, so heavily Marxist that I tried to make the surface neutral; I don't know whether I succeeded.

Yours,
Randall Jarrell

Jarrell's "theory" in "End of the Line" was that the change from romantic poetry to modernist poetry was evolutionary and not revolutionary. While other critics contended that the poetry of Pound, Eliot, Crane, Tate, Stevens, Cummings, and MacLeish established "a violent break with romanticism," Jarrell believed that it was "an extension of romanticism, an end product in which most of the tendencies of romanticism have been carried to their limits."

TO ALLEN TATE

[November 1941]

Dear Allen:

I wrote this letter almost two weeks ago — I've been waiting to hear whether they'd let me make the lecture; I expected and didn't get the information every day — it had to go through the Chairman and Budget Council on up to the President. Permission was given with cries of joy — you wouldn't believe how much effect the whole thing has had on the department; all the old professors look lovingly at me, the honor was announced in department meeting, everybody has congratulated me (everyone seems to think it does the department even more good than it does me), and I'm a new man. You're really an angel, Allen; if I get an extra class next year, and get to write poetry in my spare time instead of articles, it will be your doing.

I've been having a funny time: I had a couple of teeth more or less dislocated, playing football; the dentist shoved them back in place, and for two weeks I've ached and put on hot salt water and — worst of all — lisped. I can at last talk perfectly normally and I think they're not going to die. You should have heard my first lecture while my mouth was still quite swollen: I was so funny I'd break down and laugh at myself every two or three minutes.

We've had another financial miracle besides the lecture: a rich Hungarian wants his daughter coached in English eight or ten hours a week, and Mackie will make quite a lot of money out of it in the next few months — *quite a lot* on a small scale, that is.

Tell me how you like my Auden article in the *Southern Review,* will you?

I hope you're well and happy — it'll certainly be fun to see you in the spring.

Yours affectionately,
Randall

P.S. An unknown donor, me, really, would give R. P. Blackmur $5.00 if he'd never again use the word *nub.*

> *The title of Jarrell's Mesure lecture was "Levels and Opposites," and in a note to Tate about his travel plans to Princeton, he wrote, "Dear Allen, thanks partly, largely, for this lecture you've wangled for me, the Department has given me another class and I'm full-time. I can't express my gratitude sufficiently, since money talks so much louder than anything else in this world."*

*   *   *

> *In another letter to Tate, Jarrell wrote, "Thanks a lot for helping select the poems [for* Blood for a Stranger]. *Select well, O Allen, or — but I can't think of any threat horrid enough; besides, how'll I know whether you select well or not?" He went on to joke, "Red Warren said ... that the Navy hadn't accepted you because of a wretched shoulder; is that right? Whether I get drafted or not depends on how they reclassify; if they assume Mackie can get a job they might take me."*

TO LAMBERT DAVIS

[December 1941]

Dear Mr. Davis:

I'd like very much for you to publish the poems. I have no obligations anywhere else. We might write back and forth about when and what, and settle it finally when you come down.

I've had about seventy poems published, and we could get most of the book from those; but there are plenty more to choose from. As for size, you know much more about that than I do. I remember Allen Tate's saying that more than forty or so poems bewilders everybody, especially reviewers. The sooner the better, so far as the time's concerned.

Suppose you write me about the size and the selection, and I'll fix up a sort of trial manuscript from what you say (just now I've plenty of time, since it's Christmas vacation); then you can tell me which poems you dislike, I can send substitutes for those, and we can have it in proper shape for going-over when you come yourself. Incidentally, when you come do have dinner with us; I'd say come and stay with us, but you'd have to sleep on the sofa with the cat, and the cat weighs fourteen pounds and is very playful.

I remember talking to you at Kenyon, and I'll enjoy seeing you again; and I'll enjoy talking about the poetry, too, since I see about one person a year who reads my poems. I was pleased that you liked them and wanted to print them because of that — in letters from another publisher I noticed that liking the poems didn't, at least practically, have anything to do with printing them.

Anyway, I was delighted to get such a Christmas letter, and I'm looking forward to having Harcourt, Brace publish the poems.

Sincerely,
Randall Jarrell

Lambert Davis of Harcourt, Brace was a Southerner with a solid career in New York publishing. As a long-time friend of Allen Tate's, he gave a special reading to Tate's protégés, and, in addition to Jarrell, he subsequently published Robert Lowell and Peter Taylor.

During his final review of the Blood for a Stranger *manuscript, Jarrell disregarded Tate's selections and made his own. He also changed the order of the poems in the book, which surprised and angered Tate when he was told about it some months later.*

TO EDMUND WILSON

[April 1942]

Dear Mr. Wilson:

I feel rude and guilty for not having written for so long. I wanted to write a long answer to your letter, and so put it off — I was writing three articles and in a pathetic state; then I got sick, more than miserably sick, for between two and three months; by the time I was well I felt about as Hamlet did over neglecting to murder his uncle. So far as I'm concerned, Hamlet acts in a thoroughly understandable and naturalistic manner; but I'm sounding like Coleridge and will stop.

I meant to start this letter by saying I agreed with almost everything you said in yours; but at this date you'll probably answer, "What did I say?" First of all, I agree about modern critics of poetry: what I said about them in that *New Republic* article ["Contemporary Poetry Criticism," July 21, 1941] was just for a certain audience and a certain purpose, and if I'd talked at length about all their faults it would have helped make them more unread than they are, while I wanted to do what I could to get them read now. I think that extensively they're misguided or crazy (particularly so about anything scientific, economic, social, and so on) but that intensively they're (2 or 3 of them) the best who have existed. But I guess you can tell pretty well what I think about politics, economics, and so on — and it's just the opposite of what they think.

I was grateful for what you said about [James] Joyce, whom I'd stupidly forgotten — I put in a few words, with credit, when I was rewriting the article. What you said about the article being much too limited is true: partly that's because it was short and doing just one thing, but partly it's because I started writing intensive limited criticism and haven't got out of it yet. I hope my Auden article ["Changes of Attitude and Rhetoric in Auden's Poetry," *Southern Review,* Autumn 1941] was better that way.

What you said about Modern Poetic Drama (that it's a joke) charmed me. I certainly agree. I did the best I could to devastate one section of it (I guess you've been told about the *New Republic* fuss over that *Fall of the City* article) but I'm afraid I did about as much good as Munchausen's Huntsman who blew the calls that froze in his horn.

I wish you'd tell your wife [Mary McCarthy] how much I enjoy her short stories. Writing intelligent instead of sensitive stories is a new idea in our time. I read hers ["Ghostly Father, I Confess"] in *Harper's Bazaar* and felt good all afternoon.

I'm going to be up North the end of this month, and I'd like awfully much to see you, if I could. I'm supposed to make one of the Mesure lectures at Princeton on April 30; I'll get there the 28th or 29th and leave the 31st — I have to rush back and forth because of school. Well, I wonder if you're going to be in New York any of those days (I don't know how often you go down or how far away you live or anything); if you are I'd like to see you and talk some. I would simply come up and see you, but I have to be in Princeton two of those days, and do some business at Harcourt Brace's on the other; so if you *are* going to be in New York it would be better for me. If you're not though, I'll try to come up anyway.

I've got a lot of ideas for the lecture — it's about *Structure in Poetry,* a

stiff knowing title — but I've put off the actual writing and won't have anything very elegant. I have about a pound of notes. I'm calling the lecture
"Levels and Opposites," and part of it is to the effect that the "logical"
structure of poetry is, very often, roughly dialectical, this with many examples; but don't tell this to my friends, for they would disown me, or to my
superiors, for they would discharge me — or would if they knew or cared
what *dialectical* meant. I think I'll introduce it as a word Heraclitus and
Plato were fond of, and not carry it down to date; perhaps Kant will be safe,
and I have a charming quotation from Blake: "In poetry Unity and Morality
are secondary considerations." I'm kidding — halfway.

Four economists from the university went to that Dallas anti-labor
meeting and tried to speak; they were given no chance to (the rally was, of
course, about as spontaneous as a mink coat — many of which were worn),
and went home and said so — the papers mentioned them. Immediately a
judge wrote to the Board of Regents saying that the Economics department
was teaching Communism — he ended by demanding that the four men be
fired.

The war hasn't had an unusual effect here, to put it mildly; but in a
couple of months there'll be a camp with 75,000 soldiers 15 miles out, and a
big magnesium factory, and things will be different then. I'm full of facts
about it — supposed to write an article — but I won't inflict them on you. I
wouldn't mind reporting if somebody else would write up the facts. The
only thing I thoroughly hate to do — so much so that I'm haunted by it,
that it blackens my innocent days — is writing articles. Doesn't this sound
silly? I wish it weren't so.

I'm afraid this is beginning to sound like "My Day" at best, so I'll quit.
I hope you're getting along well with your long book.

Do you ever listen to "Invitation to Learning"? What do you think of
Mark Van Doren? I'd tell you what I think except it would sound absurdly
exaggerated. I think that in the hereafter philosophers are punished by having Van Doren tell them about philosophy; and historians by having . . .
and so on. When Allen was on all the time I'd listen, pretty much just for
the sound of his voice; it's certainly something now. [Jacques] Barzun peculiarly affects me, too: when he said that [William H.] Prescott's *Conquest
of Mexico* was better than Herodotus, because it told a more improbable
story, and improbability was the essence of history (or words to that effect),
I felt helplessly that nothing that could ever happen to him could possibly
be enough.

Once upon a time I heard Herbert Agar talking to Allen about History;
he had gotten to Marx; he made a sweeping gesture and said in a rich voice,

"What did *Marx* know about history?" I was there with a girl, and we stared at him as if he were in a zoo; but the other people there — there were six or eight — made an approving murmur.

I went to a dinner party and the lady sitting by me said, "I just *love* the British Empire." I said, "Why?" She said, "Because I feel so *English*." Her brother, who is a banker, says that Roosevelt should be impeached.

But she's in quite a minority here: people here blame the defeats not on the British government but on the British people, and feel vaguely that there's just something wrong with the British.

I don't know how I got off on these anecdotes.

Thanks to your getting me in the *Atlantic Monthly* [the poem "Head of Wisdom"], I've received several wonderful letters; the best was from a girl who signed herself *Olive Lightfoot, Sophomore in Home Economics;* she said that I was a defeatist. I told her that when she woke up some morning transfixed with a meat skewer she'd see whether or not I was a defeatist.

As a matter of fact, being in the *Atlantic Monthly* got me something better than that. A full professor, a large white-haired man who lisps badly, congratulated me on an elevator; he said, "I always say there are only two sorts of poets: Those who have been published in the *Atlantic Monthly* and those who aren't good enough to be."

I'm afraid my anecdotes have become almost unbelievable, so I'll really quit this time.

Yours,
Randall Jarrell

Jarrell's denunciatory review of Archibald MacLeish's Fall of the City *appeared a year later in the* Sewanee Review, *but it may have been submitted to the* New Republic *earlier, and rejected.*

Jarrell stayed with Robert Lowell and his wife, Jean Stafford, in New York before the Princeton lecture, and he spent an afternoon with Wilson in Wellfleet, Massachusetts, before leaving for Austin.

The anecdote about the four pro-labor economists from the University of Texas reflected Jarrell's own strong Marxist sympathies. Knowing Wilson's, he thought this story would amuse him.

"My Day" was a somewhat anecdotal syndicated newspaper column written by Eleanor Roosevelt while her husband was president.

Wilson's "long book" was an untitled novel.

Herbert Agar, poet, critic, and Pulitzer Prize–winning historian, was at one time associated with the Southern Agrarians, and, as a friend of Allen Tate's, Agar met Jarrell at Vanderbilt.

TO ALLEN TATE

[August 1942]

Dear Allen:

I've had a kind of horror of writing letters the last two months, and haven't written anybody; which is very rude, because I meant to write you at once and tell you what a good time I'd had staying with you, and so forth. I've done absolutely nothing worth writing about; when I got home there was so much school work piled up I'd no time for anything, and when I got to Mexico (June 1) I promptly got sick, and was sick or dopey half the time — not to mention that we were so increasingly bored and horrified by Mexico that we left in the middle of the summer. I suppose you're at Clarksville [Tennessee], and glad to be there after three years of the northeast, that wretched direction. Are you going to LSU next year?

I've taken great pleasure in reading Red's late poems, which are wonderful [*Eleven Poems on the Same Theme*]. How was he when you saw him?

I read many improving books in Mexico, the most improving being the *Greater Logic,* rather like the abyss in *Paradise Lost.* Have you read [F. O.] Matthiessen's *Little Giant?* It's a dumb dull book. The worst book I read — almost the worst I've ever read was [Thackeray's] *Henry Esmond.*

In Mexico most of the people think the U.S. sank their tankers to get them in the war.

My nose has been bleeding every day for the last week, why I don't know; and I've noticed that the blood is the freshest gayest most innocent red imaginable, without a thought in its pretty head. It's like seeing the Statue of Liberty for the first time and finding it light green.

I read your "Poetry 1941" review [of *New Poems: 1942,* ed. Oscar Williams, in the *Nation,* June 13, 1942] in Guadalajara, surrounded by Indians wearing sandals made of worn-out tires. I enjoyed it.

Gee, the United States is a wonderful place. This first week I've done nothing but feel it and sigh with joy. If you read these sentences unsympathetically, just try living in Mexico four months in two summers and you'll appreciate them.

I'll enclose half a poem (unidentified) and see how you like it. I've written so little poetry lately I'd welcome your assurance that I still can.

Tell me how things are in middle Tennessee. Nashville always seems so empty (for my purposes) when I go back that I'm horrified; and this is horrifying, because it still feels like home to me.

Six four-motored bombers have flown by my window in the last five minutes.

How does Nancy like being back in the South?

This is a sorry letter; travel is very coarsening, not to mention dulling — no man is a hero to his Cook's tour, believe me.

I thought Wilson very like what you'd told me.

I am writing around to magazines trying to get Red's poems to review, if it's not too late; I should love to say what I think of them.

Have you ever read Maurice Dobb's *Political Economy and Capitalism*? It's an awfully good book on economics, one of the best I've ever read; I think you'd enjoy it.

Give my love to everybody; I hope you're all well and happy and I wish I could see you.

Yours,
Randall

This letter, though ostensibly friendly, was by any standard a belated reply to Jarrell's host and benefactor; and Jarrell closed with "Yours" instead of the usual "Affectionately." Perhaps more significant, Jarrell did not write Tate again for two and a half years. Tate wrote, later, that during the Princeton visit Jarrell, the guest of honor, "would leave the company and play with my young daughter and her friends, whom he enjoyed more than he did us." (AN) Though it was well known that Jarrell enjoyed children, it was equally well known that he despised small talk, general conversation, and gossip: too much of that may have driven him to the children. Tate, still smoldering over Jarrell's rejection of his advice for Blood for a Stranger, *may have expected an apology and not gotten it from Jarrell. At any rate, this letter seems to mark the beginning of the rift between them that was evidenced by the slighting or mocking tone Jarrell occasionally took with Tate in print, and by Tate's own comment, years later, that "For some inscrutable reason — I never understood Randall — he liked me very much for some years but not much later on." (RJ)*

Tate was not hired by LSU but spent the year in Monteagle, Tennessee, with his family and the Robert Lowells. He had writer's block and was unable to finish his sequel to The Fathers, *but this seemed to remove his poetry-writing block and he was able to write "Jubilo" and other poems and complete his new book,* The Winter Sea.

*   *   *

On reading an advance copy of Blood for a Stranger *in September, Jarrell wrote Lambert Davis congratulating him on the book, "which has no typographical errors at all and which (especially the dust-jacket) is pretty as a*

*picture." He then requested "one more copy of the book at once — I especially
need it." Having learned that Amy was back in Nashville, Jarrell wanted
to send her a copy.*

TO AMY BREYER DE BLASIO

[October 1942]

Dear Amy:

I never got a letter from you I liked better, or felt more. It's all true, I
think — or almost all. A lot of it I'd known myself, but some of it I never
had.

Amy, do you remember the letter I wrote you after I saw you last year?
When you wrote me last summer you said you'd been sick, and said you'd
forgotten it. I told you how much it meant to me to see you again, and how
fond of you I was, and how wonderful I thought you were — *wonderful*
sounds silly but you know what I mean by it. I don't think, as people do in
books, "How could I have suffered so much for this stranger?" I thought,
"Yes, I was right to, it was worth it all."

It's all true about the growing up — you'd lived at home, in one place,
in the middle of the Biggest Family in the World, and never been alone at
all. I've lived all over, and always been separated from at least half of a very
small family, and been as alone as children ever are. As long as I can remember I'd been so different from everybody else that even trying to be like
them couldn't occur to me. I never realized at all that you felt I'd eventually
"see through you" and leave you: how could I, when you were the only
thing I had in the world, the only thing I cared about at all? Everything I
did — I mean *everything,* really believe me — was just a way of wasting time
while I was waiting to see you — the weeks were just things to get through
until Saturday, the days something to get through until I saw you in the
late afternoon when we went home together.

I see what you mean about the way you were about the poetry — and I
knew then you couldn't see why I thought your opinion worth anything;
but I thought this was just part of your extraordinary attitude towards
yourself — the trying so hard mixed with completely distrusting yourself,
blindly minimizing everything you did or were.

I knew you felt the way you did about trying to be like other people — I
was very conscious of that and used to argue with you; and about wanting
to be liked by other people — I always had too much fierceness and con-
trariness to go in for that, *though really* I'm in a queer way like you about it;
and "being at the top of the stack" — this had been my vice, too, for so
long that it had ceased to be a trial, since I just automatically thought my-

self there, and disliked even being compared with other people. I never thought, ever thought, of your worrying about "living up to me," for a lot of reasons. In the first place I knew you were extremely intelligent and generally wonderful (I've certainly never met any woman more intelligent than you) and like a fool I suppose I felt you must, underneath, feel *that* yourself, and certainly know that I knew it. Besides, you were part of me, and who thinks of part of himself worrying about "living up to himself"?

I'm sure you're right about your writing. I used to think that Chemistry, Biology and Medicine were as bad a mistake for you as they'd have been for me (so far as withering a real enormous part of one is concerned). I wish so much you'd write now. For to write what you can about the world makes it almost bearable —

I didn't know that you'd decided what you had before I left for Kenyon [1938]. I know things were bad then, and I remember one quarrel we had when I was omniscient in my worst way. We'd driven somewhere in East Nashville for Mr. Ransom, I think, and I was very nasty and superior about your choosing the wrong road, when really it turned out to be right. But your resolution must have broken down when I came home that Thanksgiving, because I don't remember ever being happier with you, and you seemed as happy.

When you say you're "just now getting over all our years together" I believe you — and yet, all these years I didn't realize it. Somehow it always seemed that you'd just stopped loving me, that it was all over, cut off easily for you. Except for guilt — because I *did* know, always, how sorry you were for me. I guess everybody's pretty naive at bottom, and since everybody knows that people who leave others forget them and get along well, and that the left ones are the miserable ones who remember — what could I think except that *you* were all right, and that I was the one who remembered everything? When I first learned that you'd been getting along badly and had been ill for months I didn't know what to think, or to feel either.

It took years, and great changes in me, for me to be able to understand about us, what we were to blame for, and what we weren't. We were worst about one thing: seeing each other. I mean the worst thing you did was seeing me less than you should, and the worst thing I did was my constant attacks on you for that, ones so severe and miserable and prolonged that they would have made anyone in the world feel guilty and in need of all the justification in the world. So far as that's concerned I can't bear to think of the way we treated each other.

But we had almost everything against us, and still managed to be as happy as we were — and surely nobody ever was happier than we were, some part of those years. And to change each other as we did; because if you like the poems, or me, you like what you made. It's really just that the poems should make you understand what you didn't, because you're responsible for them in every way you could possibly be.

Nobody will ever write anything about the poems that will give me such a thrill as what you've written. What you say about "On the Railway Platform" and about what it meant about us and Kenyon, is all so; and though I guess nobody else but you would know, "A Story" is autobiography. I wrote it with "I" meaning "me" for a couple of stanzas before I thought out the story, and then the emotion was certainly mine.

No, Amy dear, none of what you wrote made me think you were fancying yourself in love with me again (though once I couldn't have read it and borne not to think so); I know exactly how you feel about me and I feel just that way about you — I *do* understand. I used to think to myself about us, "It's all come to nothing! All of it! All of it!" When I saw you last year and when I read this letter I knew it didn't come to nothing, that we weren't cut off from everything we had once.

Yes, "The Bad Music" is certainly your private poem. So is "Che Farò"; so are so many others. But whether you're right, and it really tells the truth about things, I don't know. I know I've so often exaggerated or said things I only half meant, in poems, that I don't trust them as truth — except as the way things felt. When I saw you in New York and you said to me about the poems, that I'd written them about how miserable and guilty we'd been but nothing about all the rest, I told you I'd write some poems about the rest, and I've thought of it many times, but I never did, never knew how. After I saw you in Nashville last year, I wrote down lots of things to say, but I wasn't writing poems then and couldn't — I still carry them around with me, but I've never managed to. The future won't know what you were like any better than the present —

You don't know how happy your letter made me, A, or how glad I am that you've got so much out of the last unlucky years. You are at last really grown up. You do know, don't you, that you are as completely "justified" as anyone could ever be? And that, except for Mackie, you are the one person I care about most in the world?

I want to send you this as soon as possible and I'll send you some poems later. You should see me sitting in a Trainer with the hood down anxiously trying to get the airspeed, altitude, and direction all right at the same time. It's a pathetic sight.

I wish so much I could see you and talk to you.

Love,
Randall

TO EDMUND WILSON
                                                    [November 1942]
Dear Mr. Wilson:

I have — this is my usual condition — been meaning to write you for
many months; so I feel rude, ashamed, and generally dopey. I started to
write a long letter, full of political information, from Mexico; but I knew it
would get censored there, and didn't write it, and now I hardly remember
and certainly don't care. But it might amuse you to know that two-thirds of
the Mexicans think *we* torpedoed the Mexican tankers to get Mexico in the
war. We got so sick of Mexico — which is like a pageant or *Everyman,* full
of highly visible Evil — that we came back in the middle of the summer.

Forgive me for not sending you *Blood for a Stranger* any sooner — the
letter's delay delayed it. I started to write a touching inscription to you *qua*
editor — you know, to the One who drew me from the sea of anonymity
and exposed me, all dripping, to the world — or at least to the readers of the
New Republic; but I couldn't bear to desert the Christmas-present formula
(to — from —) I love.

I'm in the Air Corps, and start getting flight training in a couple of days;
if I can get through ten months training I'll be a ferry pilot, flight instructor, or co-pilot on an airline. We go to classes six hours a day (7–11 a.m.,
8–10 p.m.) and fly one or two hours besides, and get paid nothing for the
ten months, just room and board; but it's fun, more use than being a private
in the army, and there's next to no military discipline — for the first four
months I live in a dormitory here at school and eat at the school cafeteria,
and so on.

In a review someone said I was influenced by Wordsworth; this is the
most unexpected thing that's happened to me.

I've enjoyed the poems of yours that have come out relatively recently; I
thought the couplets were really handled beautifully — they didn't have any
period feel at all. The nearest thing to couplets I've ever managed to do
(except in comic verse, where I can do them till the cows come home) is
stuff like "For the Madrid Road" or "The Blind Sheep." Did you ever hear
what [George L.] Kittredge said about [Robert] Hillyer's couplets? "Just
like Pope, only better!" That's the last word on the Scholar as Critic.

I had an awfully good time visiting you [in Wellfleet]; I thought Nabokov just wonderful, an extremely charming person.

Are you still working on your novel?

This is later. I didn't finish the letter before I got in the army, and have
hardly had a chance to since. Flying is pretty dull and I'm bad at it; ground
school is easy. It takes more time than I thought, though; you spend about

two hours a day riding in a school bus to and from the airport; besides all the rest.

Have you read Robert Warren's poems, the ones in a New Directions book named *Eleven Poems on the Same Theme*? Several of them are awfully good, I think.

I haven't had time or heart to write anything, but I had something printed — a long poem in the *Kenyon Review* ["Orestes at Tauris"]. If you read it tell me how you like it. I spent more time than you'd believe writing it.

I meant to write you a long and interesting or at least, readable, letter but I hardly seem up to it — I'll try again. I hope your book is getting along well. Has your wife written any more stories? I tried hard to get her book [*The Company She Keeps*] to review, but nobody would give it to me.

Yours,

Randall Jarrell

Wilson's novel was never finished, and no further correspondence from Jarrell was found among his papers.

TO LAMBERT DAVIS

[January 1943]

Dear Lambert:

I've been meaning to write. Thanks for the Simenon [*Maigret and M. L'Abbé*]. The prospects of my dying in any financially rewarding way, I'll have to tell you, are pretty bad; disregard this, I've just been ordered to Sheppard Field [Texas]. I was washed out (I got into a spin on a check ride and the chief pilot, as he said, decided I wasn't a safe flyer). Since I was the best in ground school (I had just won a dollar bill for making a 100 in C.A.R. [Civil Air Regulations], and a large ugly computer for making a 100 in navigation) they asked Washington to make me a ground instructor; until we hear from Washington I'm just continuing the ground school. However, don't despair; they may train me to be a navigator, which is dangerous both for you and everybody else in the plane.

I never expected to see my poetry recommended in *Vogue:* didn't the Hon. Daisy Fellowes come by the office next day for a copy, a free one? I was quite surprised to have so many good or pretty good reviews; the old Hatfield-McCoy spirit isn't what it used to be. Speaking *qua* Golden Mean, how did you like my "Orestes" poem?

If you've got extra copies of reviews you might send them to me or lend them to me; for a couple of months I was busy all day and probably missed some. I know that, like [Arthur Wing] Pinero, I ought to pretend I read nothing but the *Engineering Journal* and see no reviews as a result.

Tell [Robert] Giroux he's certainly got it all over me as a flyer, but that I've got it all over him as Old Unimpressionable. *I* thought flying about as thrilling, or romantic, as juggling three oranges. Joking aside, I was awfully disappointed; if I wrote a flying book it would be just like a Mexico book: entirely discouraging. I've certainly got a prosaic nature. I can't seem to write serious improving articles, but the prospect of telling *View* readers what I think, first of them, and second of magazines, was more than I could resist. So I'm happily making up nasty remarks. I'm going to call Reinhold Niebuhr The-Homage-Which-Nominal-Infidelity-Pays-to-Faith.

I hope you're well and happy; write me a long gossipy letter, after all it's just a matter of sitting and talking to your secretary, *she* does the work. Incidentally, if she is still *The* secretary — by that I mean the one who likes my poetry — ask her wouldn't she like me to write her out a poem or do some of the customary absurd things writers are always panting to do for readers. Perhaps I could cast her horoscope for her. O no, that's Yeats.

At present I'm surrounded by thirty flying cadets from Massachusetts — [Arthur] Kober's Massachusetts, to judge from their accents; their instructor's general remark is "What?" They are dressed in spruce-green eight-year-old C.C.C. uniforms, which makes me look like Helena among the robots.

I must quit; I'm about to go along (with several friends) to watch discouragingly as the Texas legislature passes a bill to outlaw labor unions — at least, that's the general effect. Did you ever figure out how we (we means Congress and such, here) got into the war on the side we're on?

I hope you're well and that all your little children are well.

Yours,
Randall

Daisy Fellowes was an English society woman often quoted in Vogue *magazine.*

   Robert Giroux was a rising junior editor at Harcourt, Brace who had been educated at Columbia University during the time of Mark Van Doren and who liked modern poetry. Amiable and considerate, Giroux had a gift for being an author's friend. In Jarrell's case he had taken time off to don his navy blue suit and travel from New York to Princeton to hear Jarrell's Mesure *lecture. Later he would become T. S. Eliot's editor, and after join-*

ing Farrar, Straus and Giroux would publish John Berryman, Elizabeth
Bishop, Jarrell, Robert Lowell, Marianne Moore, and many others.

View *was a pocket magazine edited by Charles Henri Ford. In a letter*
*to Ford that appeared in the October 1942 issue, Jarrell wrote, "*View *is,*
really, the weirdest magazine I've ever seen — a triumph that ought to touch
its contributors."

Reinhold Niebuhr was professor of applied Christianity at Union Theo-
logical Seminary and a prolific writer and activist for moral social reform.
In Jarrell's opinion, Niebuhr's recent two-volume work The Nature and
Destiny of Man *was too Christian and too popularized — in other words,*
the kind of homage nominal liberals such as Niebuhr paid to Marxism.

Arthur Kober wrote humorous pieces for The New Yorker.

Sheppard Field, Wichita Falls, Texas, February–April 1943

*W*hen Jarrell was sent away from his wife and his cat to a Replacement Center with 50,000 soldiers, he wrote Mackie, "Being in the army is like being involved in the digestive processes of an immense worm." A day or so later he wrote, "I don't think I'll be able to do any writing much — your whole tendency is to leave after dinner and read or listen to music; since you get up so early you have to go to bed early, too."

In the months they were apart, Jarrell wrote Mackie nearly one hundred letters from Sheppard Field, Chanute Field, and Davis-Monthan Field that almost make a book on their own. About one-third of the letters were selected for this volume, and a number of excerpts from those omitted are included to maintain continuity as well as give more clarity and balance.

In Jarrell's first numbed communication to Mackie, he wrote, "I am sitting on my bed in the barracks writing this; I've been here about 24 hours. Most of the people are quite nice to you; it's not nearly as rough and tough as people say but the soldiers are, in general, strictly from Steinbeck . . . In my barracks there are a good many from Louisiana who'd rather speak French than English; one is named Rousseau."

Jarrell described Sheppard Field as "rather like the country around Browning Airport — dry, dusty and nothing but mesquite. You can't even see that from the camp. There are so many low, frame identical buildings that you can't see beyond them in any direction and you get the impression you're living by some seaside resort for the indigent pauper . . . The barracks is queer at night; you're in the middle of a just-moving sea of sleeping people who cough, or make little snoring sounds, or give little moans — at any time you wake there is someone making some sound. At 4:30

you are wakened by a very queer sound: somebody running down the street as fast as he can blowing a whistle — the whistle gets louder and louder (accompanied by footsteps) and then vanishes away." In Jarrell's poem "Soldier [T.P.]," the open-ing lines are "When the runner's whistle lights the last miles of darkness / And the soldier stumbles into the hard green clothes . . ."

In another letter to Mackie, Jarrell deplored the mediocre selection of books in the soldiers' library, although he did admit that it had the first volume of Proust. After looking to see how many readers had checked it out, Jarrell reported, "It was never kept longer than two or three days, or just until they finished reading the fun in bed parts." In a letter after this, he asked Mackie to send him the daily comic strips of Terry and the Pirates.

Another letter commented on the food: "Our dinner consisted of two wienies, beans and potatoes, and some canned peaches. If I were a salad I'd eat myself." On a cheerier note he wrote Mackie, "I keep forgetting to tell the charming piece of news: I didn't have to shave off my moustache. I didn't have to have my hair cut short. Imagine!" Once, after a restful weekend, he wrote, "Gee, Sundays are wonderful! About the middle of the day you can see the soldiers return to their normal selves and to act a little like civilians. Charming word! I'm going to start a political party the members of which are going to call each other Civilian!"

Since the possibilities for reading and writing were so limited, Jarrell's main concern was to be classified and assigned to "some place where brains count." Weather observation, meteorology, Officer Candidate School, and Link Trainer School were some of the opportunities available, and Jarrell took numerous tests for general intelligence and aptitude. Meanwhile, he worked in the mail room, and later he was assigned to "Classification," where he interviewed soldiers like himself for assignment. In one letter he reported passing his Army Specialist Test with a high grade — 138 — but added that "In all probability nothing whatever will come of it. The lieutenant in charge explained that the training for psychologists was completely up in the air, that nobody knew when or, really, if anything would be done."

After two months, when Jarrell was more used to the army and used to his place in it, he wrote Mackie, "Perhaps if I ever have the time, I can write some good, dreary poems about the army; but they won't be printable while I'm in the army, and they won't be liked by anybody until the '20's [A.D. 2020] — when they re-turn."

Shortly after this, Jarrell began revising two old poems that were in what he called his "political economy" style and started a new poem, "Soldier [T.P.]." He said the latter was in his "army" style, and it led to "Mail Call," "A Lullaby," "Gunner," "The Lines," and "The Sick Nought," all of which have details and phrases lifted directly from these letters he wrote Mackie.

TO MACKIE JARRELL

Saturday, 6 o'clock
[February 27, 1943]

Darling:

Alas, I should have written you an hour or so ago — I was in a good humor then; but now everybody's in a bad humor — we've just been told that we get no more Sundays off, but have to work every day. Fortunately I'm not tired: I've had an easy day of walking, listening to gas lectures, and practising putting on the gas mask. All my stakes are straightened out, and I count as having done the first ten; there are only fifteen more I have to do. Also, I think I'll at last, at last, be given the classification test Monday or so; and *then* I can start applying for O.C.S. [Officer Candidate School].

I'm just delighted with all the pictures — I look at them over and over. I want some more of Kitten and some more of you; the duck, the black and white cat, and the Orange Cat are done up brown. Gee, the house and trees and car and you and Kitten look just too good to be true. And I was so pleased with Kitten's lock of hair — to use the very inaccurate term.

I'm not very critical here at camp and rather enjoyed the *Poetry* review [Jessica Nelson North's review of *Blood for a Stranger*] — it was so unlike anything I'd expected. But what was really good for my morale was the [March 1, 1943] copy of *Time* I bought last night. Imagine *me* reviewed as better than [Karl] Shapiro in *Time*! I'm sure even the English department reads *Time,* and will be much impressed. It was certainly nice of *Time* to quote that much from one of my two or three best poems, and to talk seriously about my "spiritual significance" instead of whatever the other reviews did talk about.

Wasn't Laughlin's letter funny?

Imagine, I have to go to a lecture at 7 tonight. Wicked old Sheppard Field. I hope a flood comes and improves it.

I just heard, late this afternoon, that Micky Mayne, Fambrough [University of Texas students], and a number of Texas boys have been sent here; I'll look them up.

The cowpasture in the afternoons is a wonderful sight. Imagine a perfectly flat, perfectly barren and desolate plain; the soil is a kind of loess — it's one tremendous dust-pile; on this plain, for as far as you can see, there are men running, doing calisthenics, and playing rough children's games — tens of thousands of men. Tremendous clouds of dust hang over the field all afternoon; when the wind rises there is a dust storm so extreme that you can't see men fifty or a hundred yards away. The only structures on this field

are meaningless surrealist or geometrical figures made out of two-by-fours
(the obstacle courses) and raised platforms for the calisthenics instructors;
seen from a distance the men on the platforms look *exactly* as if they were
crucified there over the heads of the troops — you know those distant View
of Calvary paintings. The dust storms are extraordinary: in one today I
could barely see people a few yards away, and the wind knocked over a garbage can and rolled it a block away. When you grit your teeth, there at the
cowpasture, you sound like a child shoveling sand.

Resuming our conversation: tell Guy [Steffens] and Herschel [Baker]
that I implore them to stay out of the army, *as enlisted men,* by hook or by
crook, as long as they can; they should try to get commissions as teachers in
the Navy, or something of that sort. They are helping the war far more
right now than they would as privates: the army is managed so that it gets
the same amount of good out of an intelligent and cultivated person that it
does from a low-grade moron. The army is everyone's lowest common denominator. I am getting along well for many reasons; but tell them they'd
dislike it *extremely.* Quote Achilles' speech to them (I've quoted it to several
people here): "It's better to be the slave of a poor farmer, on earth, than
king among the hosts of the dead." This is the one completely apropos
quotation.

You understand, I am really and truly getting along well, as you can tell
from the tone of my letters; but believe me, it's an accomplishment — an accomplishment that I'd certainly like Guy and Herschel not to have to acquire.

I read [Ignazio] Silone's *Bread and Wine*: he is, if I can judge from it,
one of the most overrated writers in the world. It's more a bad book than a
mediocre one, even.

Our gas masks are extremely efficient; you can put one on in about
thirty seconds — they're made of grey rubber, and look pretty Martian.
We've been allowed to smell the various gases, which are supposed to have
surprising poetic smells like new-mown hay, apple blossoms, and gerani-
ums; actually they don't, except for the new-mown hay, which really smells
like green corn. They broke *tiny* capsules, that you could barely smell from a
distance of two feet; but a couple of highly imaginative boys coughed, got
tears in their eyes, and managed to convince themselves they were much affected.

If you'll send me the write-ups (in the Sunday papers) of the Texas
practice football games, I'd like it. Thanks a lot for *Terry* [*and the Pirates*].

I miss you and Kitten so much. I think I've already written more than
6¢ worth [letter postage in 1943], so I'll stop. You're my darling.

Your
Randall

After taking the General Classification Test, Jarrell wrote Mackie, "It was the sorriest excuse for an intelligence test I ever saw. You're supposed to do as many of 150 questions as you can in 40 minutes: ⅓ of the questions are easy vocabulary questions; ⅓ are easy arithmetic questions — easy, but full of cumbersome figuring that takes time if you're not an accountant or an adding-machine; and ⅓ — this is the silliest part — are pictures of many blocks stacked on, around, and behind each other: you are supposed to say how many there are. This is easy for mechanical draftsmen or engineering students, hard for others; and about as sorry a test of intelligence as I've ever seen. The test is really a great mess; the Army Alpha in the first World War was a lot better. It's the only 'intelligence' test I've ever taken that left me angry and disconcerted — not that I didn't do pretty well on it, I fancy."

The Time *review said, "Compared with Shapiro, Jarrell writes like a spoiled darling" but went on to say that "he makes a moving protest against the world of his time."*

*In a letter to James Laughlin, Jarrell had said in part, "Thanks for the qualified praise about my reviews. I've generally been unlucky enough to be given the bad books and deprived of the good: for instance, if I'd been given Warren's book I'd have praised it very much. But I don't think sub specie aeternitas I've been so hard on my books. I'm perfectly willing to answer to God for anything I've said about anybody. I'm willing to bet that my judgments will resemble those of 1960, say, more than those of more favorable critics will." And further along, Jarrell added, "If anybody gives me [Delmore Schwartz's] *Genesis to review I'll certainly review it, and not beg off as is my inclination to do so about any writing now. I fancy I'd like it, too — I'm fond of Schwartz's writing."*

Guy Steffens and Herschel Baker were fellow instructors at the University of Texas. In another letter, Jarrell asked Mackie if she would get Steffens to donate his old copy of Mozart's Prague Symphony *to the barracks record library, and added, "For that matter, you might send our Beethoven Quartet Op. 127 which the Busch Quartet play so badly . . . We'd really be doing a service to any soldiers with classical tastes — classical as distinguished from* Scheherazade *and the* Nutcracker Suite."

In another letter to Mackie, Jarrell wrote, "Yesterday we went through a gas chamber twice; the second time we took off our gas masks for a moment — this was to convince us that the masks were really protecting us. Believe me, they were: the tear gas made us cry like babies; and it stuck to our clothes a little, and bothered us enough — when we went inside for a lec-

ture — to make lots of us put on our masks again. The masks certainly are good."

TO MACKIE JARRELL

Thursday
[March 4, 1943]

Darling:

Gee, you send me so much lovely mail — it's nicer than anything else could be. I was just crazy about the pictures — some are too dark, and Kitten looks like the King of Shades in all (weren't they becoming of the orange cat?), but all in all they're the joy of my life; I can't wait to see the new ones. The cookies were swell — and much admired; I fed most of them, as a farewell present, to the cadets — whom I saw leave with sorrow, I must confess. I'd got quite fond of several. (Incidentally, they were sent, at 2:30 this morning, to A. and M. [Texas A & M]. Isn't that funny?)

Just after I wrote last, later Tuesday morning, I went home to find some Louisianans shipped out (both Rousseau and Gautier we lost), and I got a bed in the farthest corner of the room, the last bed of all and by a window — just a room with two sides, as I think someone called the stage. My new bed's just wonderful. I'm now practically alone in the midst of kids from Chicago — baby cadets who think me a veteran soldier, and old to boot. Are they young! I was making up a parody of [Rudyard Kipling's] "Danny Deever" during a 20-minute wait in the breakfast line; I sang this to one of the new ones, it was as far as I'd gotten:

> "O what are the whistles blowing for,"
> Said Files-on-Parade.
> "It's time to eat, it's time to eat," the
> Colour-Sergeant said.
> "What makes you look so green, so green?"
> said Files-on-Parade.
> "I'm thinking what I've got to eat,"
> the Colour-Sergeant said.
> For we're eating Danny Deever, they've
> been boiling him all day —

Here I broke off, the poor cadet looked so puzzled. "It's a parody," I said. "Of 'Danny Deever.' "

He looked at me inquiringly and said, "Danny Beaver?"

I was so delighted that I hardly ever sing it any other way now.

This week I've been getting trained and trained: drill, manual of arms, much marching, and obstacle courses and silly kid games in the "cowpasture" (there are cows; but fenced away from *us*) where we are forced to go for "recreation" — o bitter word! Almost every afternoon. But today I got off: everyone that had to turn in an income tax was allowed to seek advice, and we got to sit on a curb all afternoon in the pretty sun. Gee, I was happy and felt good — the afternoon off was just what I wanted.

As you can see, I'm getting along awfully well; even the early mornings are better now. I've done no writing but have read several books: Grace Zaring Stone's *The Almond Tree* was the nicest, and a great pleasure — just a nice sensitive book, and a *new* unread, 1 man one, was a great thrill, since I'd found nothing really goodish that I hadn't read. I've heard a lot of music — I think I enjoyed *Till Eulenspiegel* most.

Incidentally, why don't you just open letters from magazines? They'll be fairly fun to read — they're never private, and you should certainly feel free to open them. [Andrew] Lytle said they were printing my article [a review of Archibald MacLeish's *Fall of the City*] in the Spring Issue [of the *Sewanee Review*].

You know, I always (I did in the C.P.T. [Civilian Pilot Training]) talk in a good deal less cultivated way with uncultivated people; but these people are *so* uncultivated I never have the slightest tendency to do that — it would be ridiculous to try to seem even remotely as spotted as these creatures. So I sound calm, clear, and cultivated, and no one seems to mind or think it odd: I count just as a different variety, and one that they tend to be slightly respectful to in a [Dostoevski's] *House of the Dead* way, rather. This may sound odd, but it's all so.

To call this place inefficient wouldn't be justice: we learn in a very long day what could be learned in two hours at most; it's crazy, even the dumb ones think something's wrong.

I must quit and get some dinner; I felt too calm and pleasant to eat at mess, and dressed nicely and came over to the Service Club to write this and eat. I'm surrounded by soldiers full of eager anticipation: they're about to have a show — little children who dance and play the trumpet, local Dinah Shores, and so on.

I love you. You're my own darling. Do keep writing me as much — it's lovely.

Your
Randall

TO MACKIE JARRELL
                                                    Thursday
                                              [March 25, 1943]
Darling:

I was enchanted with the nicest pictures of you and Kitten.

We've had a bad day today — our squadron thought of a new and unpleasant way to eat up a half hour of our time. Not content with having
formations for us at 6:00, 8:00, 10:00, 12:00, and 6:30 (each time marching
us many blocks), they cooked up another for us at 11:00 (it takes almost
half an hour). So now we march in formation to breakfast, calisthenics,
lunch, dinner, to school, and away from school.

I entered into public life in the Army the other day with a great bang.
There's a corporal in our barracks (half of them, almost, are corporals)
who's the most unpopular person there: he was in charge of our bunch on
the way down and caused us a great deal of trouble. He's eccentric, bossy,
detail-worshipping, and authority-seeking to the point almost of insanity —
his face, an extraordinarily ugly one, is drawn into those strange distorted
lines you often see in asylums. He's really strange, a new type to me. He
managed to get lined up for the position of barracks chief when ours a good
one leaves, and meanwhile got put in charge of the upper floor. When the
barracks chief was home for a day Cpl. Maxwell took over; and by 11
o'clock, by means of unremitting devotion to rolls, details, and the utmost
possible army severity, he had managed to get eight people's passes taken
away; details given to them, etc. (I'd not only been very insolent to him in
formation but had disobeyed practically every order he'd given; he'd threatened to get the captain to take away *my* pass for a month, but hadn't had the
nerve to do anything.) He was on the upper floor by his bed as I was going
out a little before lunch; he said just to one of the boys whose fiancée was
coming and whose pass was gone as I passed that he'd done it all for our
own good, that it was our fault. I went up to him and began to make a
speech to him in a voice so loud and so overbearing that he listened helplessly — the rest of the barracks listened helpless with delight. God inspired
me, and I spoke with the utmost fluency. I never even paused in several very
elaborate sentences. First I told him exactly why he'd done what he had;
then I asked him a series of rhetorical questions (*Is it true that* ...) far more
damaging than any "Have you stopped beating your wife?" (I knew one or
two facts about him and made up the rest.) When I finished — he was still
too overwhelmed to try to say a word — I made an erasing gesture, said
"That's all, Maxwell" in a tone like a blow, and walked off downstairs. I
wasn't feeling angry but wonderful, just wonderful. For the whole rest of

the day I saw nobody from our barracks without getting congratulated, having my hand shaken, and being asked to have drinks on pay day; all the ones who hadn't heard had been told, and wanted to know *everything* I'd said. (I couldn't and wouldn't remember.) Well, believe it or not, Maxwell was so dismayed at my and everybody else's actions that he actually *resigned* as our floor chief. I spoke to him far more loudly and far more insultingly than I've ever spoken to anyone in my life: and I've rarely been more pleased with what I said. I was awfully amused at myself, and pleased, too.

Darling, you are *so* clever. You don't know how pleased I was with my *When We Were Very Young* [A. A. Milne] — the *perfect* book for the soldier, this soldier anyway. I love you so much. The brownies were swell. You're my own darling. I miss you more than anything in the world.

Your
Randall

*   *   *

In another letter, Jarrell wrote, "I've made as sure of this weekend as I possibly can; the guy who gives the passes says so far as he knows I can get them Saturday and Sunday. So, you come and stay at the Kemp Hotel." He then requested some money: ". . . say, $40.00 when you come, so I'll have plenty of money; oddly enough, I've never been paid, and it's of course impossible to cash a check — to cash a money order you have to practically see Colonel Claggett. (He's the commanding officer here; he was the general in command of the Air Force at Pearl Harbor.) There's a painting of him in the Red Cross office that makes him look like a faintly mulatto Uncle Tom, say Uncle Tom with jaundice."

After a one-day pass to Wichita Falls earlier in the month, Jarrell had written, "Everything was so green and wet and untouched and unlooked at, even, by any soldiers; and there weren't, yet, soldiers in town." He then parodied some of A. A. Milne's Christopher Robin rhetoric, saying, "Soldiers are the one thing I'd rather not see than, and the Army the one place I'd rather not be than — go ahead Christopher . . . Once, standing in line for breakfast I met a tall, fat cadet from the east who recited almost all of A. A. Milne [during] the fifteen minutes we were in line. It felt so unlikely and pleasant . . . The [Wichita Falls] library is in the middle of a lovely green park, park, full of grass, trees, and buds — I lay on the grass for about an hour feeling weak and sick with joy."

[April 5, 1943]

Darling:

You should see me sorting the mail at 11 and 4; I stand in front of an enormous box with about twenty sub-divisions, and flip the letters in, just as if I were hitting a ping-pong backhand. The turnover of labor in the mail room is enormous; about half the ones who were working when I began have been shipped away, and I was glad to see them go. The head of the mail room, a first-class private, cares passionately about the mail room and is always worrying and exhorting; he is very stupid and rarely can understand anything the first time. All the replacements are dumb driven cattle, who don't talk at all compared to the old gang, and that's a gift from God.

Some parts of the work are moderately pleasant: the names, a tenth of them, are queer beyond belief. Then the places they're being shipped to work on me powerfully, like the Christmas Store Window and the poor child. And some are very odd: the *Sea Search Attack Group* and the *Prov. Engr. Airborne Regiment, Sedalia, Knobnoster, Mo.* Ask me no questions for fear I should reply. One of the funniest forwarding addresses was Corporal So-and-so, Anti-Submarine Detachment, Exeter Apartments, Galveston. I suppose he sits on the roof of the apartment with field glasses and a rifle.

The best thing about the mail room is that it's relatively off to itself and unmilitary. We're little bothered by officers and non-commissioned officers, both of whom I'm growing to dislike more and more. This is an illustrative incident: I got paid for the first time yesterday — it was obviously my first time. I was supposed to salute the lieutenant sitting at the table and say, "Private Jarrell, Randall, sir." I didn't know that and left off the Private; the officer corrected me very unpleasantly and acted as if I'd committed a crime.

Writing the addresses on the envelopes stirs much envy in me: Peabody College, Nashville, and others to San Marcos and all sorts of charming colleges — lucky cadets! What funny names people have: they're a great pleasure to the postal employee. I'm afraid that as long as I have this job, my letters will suffer. Letters about letters (and the outside of letters at that) aren't a rewarding genre.

How I wish I could see Kitten drinking out of the bathtub. I was as surprised as if you'd told me he'd taken to walking on the ceiling.

We had spareribs for lunch, and I was given six — and the smallest was about eleven inches long. There was so much bone I couldn't help thinking of the boy's remark about education — to have gained so little and have gone through so much; except I've forgotten how it went.

Allen's "Ode" ["Ode to Our Young Pro-Consuls of the Air"] was certainly poor and annoying. One stanza is influenced by [Karl] Shapiro's "Scyros." I thought the Dalai Lama almost the only touch of imagination. I feel like quoting when I read such poems, "Because you saw, and were not indignant ..." The evil of the universe is a poor thing to be ironic about.

I think perhaps if I ever have time I can write some good dreary poems about the army, and the war; but they won't be printable while I'm in the army, and they won't be liked by anybody until the '20's — when those return.

Even though my job is hard and long, it's still wonderful not to have the rollcalls, the drill, the aimless waiting and waiting, and all the rest.

I'll write to Lambert Davis and ask him whether Harcourt Brace minds my using "Orestes" and five or six poems for a New Directions anthology (they can reprint them in my second book with them). If they don't want me to presumably it'll only be because they want another of mine fairly soon.

My, what fun it'll be to think about articles and poems and books and things after the war. Maybe I'll even get industrious, any industry will seem so mild compared to the wicked army. And what a paradise of amusements Austin will seem — a perfect Coney Island.

I love you so much, darling, and miss you. I'll write you again tomorrow. You're my darling. I love you.

Your
Randall

On the subject of poems, Jarrell wrote in another letter, "I read the worst poem imaginable in an old New Yorker, *by Harry Brown; the most horrible, flat fake-heroic stuff about some maneuvers he was in. I'd better not write any poems about* my *army experience: after all, nobody but* New Masses *would print them. Of course, I could pretend to be a German soldier writing about* his *army." A brief literary aside in another letter said, "Did you read Allen's poems in* Kenyon? *They seem so childish to me, and I feel so old and responsible as I read them."*

*   *   *

Jarrell made 138 on the Army Specialist Test, and that score, along with his training in psychology, got him transferred from the mail room to Interviewing and Classification.

Friday night
[April 9, 1943]

Darling:

Since I've been working here at Classification, how my horizon has broadened — about things I can get to do in the army, I mean. I used to have that desperate feeling that there was only Link Trainer or perhaps Weather Observer, and that OCS was useless, almost, because I'd have to be transferred to the infantry or something equally unattractive. Now I've learned that:

(1) I can take a cryptography test that I can almost certainly pass. Then if I want I can get assigned to Cryptography School — you go there for *three weeks* and are then made a *staff sergeant.*

(2) I can take an Advanced Army Specialist Training Test. If I pass this (I surely should — it's a general test on college subjects, particularly scientific and mathematical ones) and a board approves me, I'll get sent to a 3 or 6 or 9 months college course — my interviewer friend thinks it would perhaps be for training as an army psychologist — and wind up, almost certainly, as an officer.

(3) I can apply for OCS in Air Corps Administration, practically the nicest branch of the army; if I get approved by the OCS board I can stay here at my nice Classification job till I get shipped off to OCS — after a couple of months.

Doesn't it all sound wonderful, compared to the old days, the not so old days?

I'm so glad you're well again — I wish I'd written you more the last 3 or 4 days, so you'd have had the letters to read; I didn't partly because I was busy with all my new stuff and partly because I was rather sick and slept or tried to most of my spare time.

Tuesday night I played tennis and called you; that night and early in the morning I vomited several times and was most miserable, though I didn't have fever. I went on sick call at 5 that morning and stood in lines or waited around until 8:45, when the doctor saw me, gave me some pills, and sent me back to duty — that is, the mailroom. When I'd been there a few minutes I saw Sergeant Cook, and asked him if he'd been able to do anything about classification. When I told him what I wanted done he said, "Why, I can do that for you right now," and he wrote me out a letter saying I'd completed my Basic Combat and the 301st was willing to let Classification use me. I ran gayly over to Classification (a big clean new building three blocks away — it has the best fluorescent lights I've ever seen) and reported to

Lieutenant McBride; he's in charge of the administrative part. He said that they certainly wanted me and would put me to work immediately; but they'd gotten in trouble once recently over using such a letter from a sergeant, and would I please take it back and get it initialled by an officer, any officer. I would. Cook promptly got it initialled; I told the mailroom goodbye, laughing with joy, and ran, oh really ran, back to the Classification building. Lt. McBride seemed pleased, shook hands with me and welcomed me to Classification, making a couple of jokes and generally being pleasant; he was getting his desk moved back, and he said, "This is your first official duty; help so-and-so with this." He took me over and left me with a typist, who typed some cards showing I was working there and such; then he came back for me and took me down the hall, saying, "I'm going to put you in the most interesting sort of job we have and the one that requires the most intelligence — interviewing." I almost gasped aloud — generally people get put on testing or such, and eventually get put in interviewing, which is by far their best job. He introduced me to the lieutenant in charge of the interviewing room (really two big rooms) and left. The lieutenant's the one I told you about, Rhodes, with the girl at Texas; I heard some of the interviewers using the nickname Flash Gordon, and I knew immediately who it was they meant — the resemblance is very noticeable. He gave me an official book about the interviewing, and told me I could read it; and that's the last official word he's said to me — he talked to me a little at lunch hour, and showed me a big picture of the Texas University girl.

My interview friend (Gassett, but I've spelled it wrong or remembered it wrong or something — you see, I *thought* he was named Ferguson) was much pleased I was there, and introduced me to lots of them; they are a highly picked bunch, as the interviewing book tells you, extremely superior to The Army. There's a big room lit with fluorescent lights; the screens have the interviewers' favorite pictures of airplanes on them, also the government charts of what Air Force people can become.

That day, Wednesday, I mostly read the book and sat in on other people's interviews. — It's getting late, I'm in town and want to get back and sleep enough; so I'll cut this detailed stuff short and go on in my next letter. I slept all I could that night, all my spare time — I had fever, had it Thursday too; but on Thursday I did some practice interviews, with assistance — that helped the day along. It's really *quite* interesting. Immediately work was over I went home and slept. Today, thank goodness, I've been almost recovered; I had a swell day.

Our office is run like a civilian one except better; when we've finished the work we can read, play Battleship (the interviewers' favorite game — I don't mean *I've* been playing it), and so on; no one minds. We even get to go to mess hall in a group and walk directly in between the waiting lines, who howl like angry and hungry animals — literally; you could hear them a block away; they always respond exactly similarly.

I'll tell you all about the interviewing when I write tomorrow. It's really a wonderful job; I feel like six new brownies or something.

My packages were *swell* — also all the nice letters. You're so good to me, angel Mackie, how clever to send the shoes. I wish so much I could see you and Kitten. I love you.

I'll call you Sunday morning, probably earlyish.

Yours,
Randall

TO MACKIE JARRELL

[April 25, 1943]

Dearest:

Have we been working! Knollwood (Knollwood is a noun that takes *they;* they give us all our orders) sent somebody here who made us get rid of thousands of people in two days. We worked till ten o'clock last night and worked like hyenas all today, taking off just a half hour at lunch; we got them all classified and ready to go. I didn't mind the extra work at all, because I could see it was really doing some good — I managed to get a number of people into schools they belonged in, in spite of their grades being a little low (you get McBride's permission), and this pleased me very much. Just as my darling's letter did.

At present *half* the washed-out cadets (literal, not figurative) in the country are being sent to Sheppard; their stories are enough to make you despair of almost anything.

I, of course, haven't written any poetry; I don't think there's even been a game of Battleship played in the office for two days.

I came in early yesterday when only Lt. McBride was there; he said amiably, "Well, Jarrell, I hope we can keep you for six months or so." I explained about Link Trainer and how I was waiting for it and why I wanted to go (he'd forgotten or never known I was Link Trainer); he agreed and said he'd have offered me permanent party at once if he'd been able to, but since he couldn't he quite saw how I felt. So now I know he'll let me go.

I'm getting to be quite a good interviewer: I'm very successful at making people feel good at getting what they're best suited for, and I've been swell at prescribing, with a flourish, VOM to poor people who can't qualify for anything else. VOM means Vehicle Operation and Maintenance (heavy trucks, tractors, derricks, etc.); most of these people have autos in their past, and they're generally happy as larks at being with them and the pretty airplanes at a field — they can be got in without ever having to be told their grades were too bad for anything else. So far I haven't been confronted with the embarrassing problem of glamorizing Cooks and Bakers for someone too bad even for VOM.

Schwartz's *Genesis* is just <u>awful</u>: I wouldn't dare write a line about it anywhere, I'd be too embarrassed. He puts in a page (of the history of a Jewish immigrant family) of prose so flat, abstract, and completely dull as to seem part of that old story ["The Argument"] with the numbered paragraphs in the *Kenyon;* then he has anonymous ghosts of the great dead make long moral philosophical verse comments for two pages; then a page more of prose, two more of verse; and so on for 250 pages, with two volumes more to come. The great dead are, not enthusiastic but *enthused,* about the inane story flat as "The Loves of the Triangles," and act as if it were a perfect gospel, the ideal text for the final endless commentary. It's a sad affair; to read it through you need resolution, just resolution — more than even a soldier has, if I can call myself that. *Le Soldat Malgré Lui,* eh?

I'd better quit, it's really bed time. This letter's all Classification plus a little Criticism, isn't it?

I love you so much, Mackie, and miss you so much. I hope by September you'll be living with

Your
Old Link Trainer

Jarrell's grade on the link trainer test, combined with recommendations from Lieutenant Rhodes and Lieutenant McBride, qualified him for Link Trainer School, and he was posted to Chanute Field in Rantoul, Illinois.

"The Loves of the Triangles: A Mathematical and Philosophical Poem Inscribed to Mr. Darwin" by John Frere and George Canning first appeared in the journal The Anti-Jacobin *in the late eighteenth century and has since been reprinted in a number of anthologies. It is a parody of Erasmus Darwin's "The Loves of the Plants," which formed the second part of his poem "The Botanic Garden."*

*   *   *

In a letter written on the train while en route to Chanute Field, Jarrell said, "Here I am somewhere in Missouri, looking like one of Wordsworth's little girls at the trees, grass and beautiful irregularities of the ground . . .

We left Sheppard about noon yesterday; it was very hot, and we had to wear our woolen uniforms, gas masks, and helmets; my khaki garrison cap was hanging from my shoulder by its strap, I had my briefcase thing (with a little shaving stuff in it) in one hand, and I had hanging from my shoulders about a hundred pounds of stuff packed in my two barracks bags. We had to ~~march~~ totter five or six blocks with all this, load and unload it from a bus, carry it to a train and load it on that; we were very hot and very wet . . . Last night we stopped on the outskirts of a town, and a little girl, in her back yard, about four, kept waving at us and calling excitedly, 'Hello, soldiers!' She had a beautiful big snow-white puppy with her, who jumped up and down and wagged its tail . . . I'm in Illinois, it's 2:30, and it's flat, flat, flat — bad Illinois."

Chanute Field, Rantoul, Illinois,
April–November 1943

*The link trainer was an indoor model airplane that simulated flying condi-
tions on the ground and was used in preflight classes. After graduating
from a three-month course on the operation of link trainers, Jarrell was to
be sent to an air base as an instructor for beginning pilots. Two advantages Chanute had over Sheppard for Jarrell's purposes were that Rantoul was close enough to
Champaign-Urbana for him to use the University of Illinois library when he got a
weekend pass, and that despite the long demonstration classes, KP, and calisthenics,
Jarrell could find bits of time and odd out-of-the-way places for writing poetry.
He finished thirteen poems at Chanute, and, as if being able to write again
restored other normal responses, these letters are more openly complaining, silly,
or bored.*

TO MACKIE JARRELL

[April 29, 1943]

Darling:

I just finished calling you, so now I'll write you (I certainly won't be
able to tomorrow).

We got to Chanute about seven o'clock last night. They met us at the
train with a truck, let us pile our baggage on top of the truck and ourselves
on top of the baggage, and in general were efficient and fairly pleasant. Nobody here has bawled us out at all — the atmosphere's much more business
and much less concentration camp. (Incidentally, I saw, night before last, a
concentration camp for German prisoners; it was some small agricultural

college or something of the sort, surrounded by floodlights, guard towers, and electrified fence.) Rantoul is a small town with big trees, like any other northern or eastern small town — at a glance fairly like the one at Cape Cod, Hyannis, I mean. Chanute is on the outskirts of the town; it's a *very* big field, twice as big as Sheppard. Besides the ordinary Sheppard type barracks (here stained grey with coal smoke) it has a few more imposing ones, some big brick administrative buildings, enormous concrete hangars, and mess halls made of concrete blocks — mess halls 125 or 150 yards long. It was twilight last night and it rained today, so for me Chanute's strictly Whistler, a morbid mechanical one done for a soot-remover advertisement. It has lots of engine blocks where they run tests — when a couple of engines are going full power they sound like a terrific bellowing, something enormous in a tetanus of pain and anger.

We got put in a barracks very soon with very little trouble. (By the way, I believe it's settled that my number is 18201238; they use it up here, so you do too, it's on my paybook and new orders.) I'm on the top floor on the top half of a wooden double decker bed. I say *wooden* with joy; the metal double deckers look like some economical asylum in a slum; somebody has joined two metal, scaly-white-painted, horribly curlicued little beds together, the top one of course with its legs in air. Being up in the air, you're feet up, is nice, since you're private as you please, well almost, so far as the lower world is concerned, in your little Cloud-Cuckoo-Land. Making beds is *very* easy, since we have just blankets and an unbleached muslin mattress-cover; this pleases me, my slogan is *Less Comforts and More Justice for Soldiers.*

We get up at 5:30. This will be my schedule when I start to school: breakfast between 6:30 and 7; calisthenics and basketball — volley ball — or such between 8 and 10; study hour between 10:30 and 11:30; then lunch; school from 12:30–6:30; then dinner; lights are turned out at 9:45. We get a pass once a week, starting week after next: we get Wednesday night from 10:30 until Friday morning at 5:30, i.e., Thursday. Once a month we can go to Chicago; the other three times it's a 20 mile pass, which fortunately takes in Champaign and the University of Illinois.

Chanute is flatter than any pancake; if anyone in Rantoul saw a hill he would be frightened. It's quite cold here, the very beginning of spring; most of the trees are more brown than green, and the rest are only budding.

The last hours on the train I worked on my "Carnegie Library" and got a few new lines. I love you so much, angel. Write me lots and send *lots* of pictures.

Your
Randall

TO MACKIE JARRELL

[April 1943]

Darling:

If there are now 7,000,000 men in the army I'll bet that, on any day you pick, 1,000,000 are a complete waste, so far as any useful training or useful work is concerned. And I bet that if you said that to the soldiers here even *they* would have sense enough to agree. There's a soldier in the laundry room who's permanent party here; he says his only real work, each week, is to type the laundry roster — a day and a half's work at most. And he was a skilled machinist before he got in the army, was sent to machinists' school, was appointed instructor, and now is being used for this. And he isn't even an especially noteworthy case. Many of the non-coms have so little work it's funny. On a field where there are thousands of men free every day they hire women truck drivers, civilians, for *anything*. They send round trucks to get the garbage cans; there are two prisoners who load on the cans, and an MP who does nothing except guard the prisoners — the MP *always* looks much more criminal than the prisoners, who are dressed in conspicuous blue clothes, are in, generally, for minor offenses and have no possible way of getting out of the field and need guarding about as much as I do. But it's no good talking — the whole army's rotten with this waste and idiocy.

The WAACs here are still wearing their winter uniforms; they are mostly pretty sorry-looking, but the uniform's very becoming to them, infinitely more so than our uniform is to us.

The meat situation's gotten very funny; outside of the hamburger the first day, I still haven't gotten any fresh meat here — only ham, ham in varied forms (and sausage twice, for breakfast). They tell me that as late as February they had chicken and turkey three or four times a week, so much so they all got tired of them.

How *glad* I'll be to see the pictures of you and Kitten. If I could go back to Austin and live with you and Kitten I'd be willing to stay there until I looked like the old professor with the red silk tie.

Your
Randall

TO MACKIE JARRELL

Friday, 4 o'clock
[May 1, 1943]

Darling:

Well, my KP wasn't as bad as I thought, though I must confess I've never worked harder for twelve hours. It lasted from three in the morning until three in the afternoon. Most of the time I was the chief operator of an enormous dish-washing machine full of clanks and steam; through it ran, on a sort of conveyor belt, metal or metal-and-wood baskets full of trays, mugs, bowls, knives, forks and spoons. I snatched (and I mean snatched) these out; most I slid on, but the baskets of trays I unloaded and stacked, and threw the basket on. I got so I could pull the basket out of the machine, unload and stack eight trays, and slide the basket on, in only six movements; but, as Blake says, these beautiful rationalized efficient movements are more tiring than you'd think. But it was worse (and not so interesting — the Clipper, as they call the machine, was fun in a ghastly way) between meals; then I helped clean the dishwashing alcove, and mopped a distressingly large percentage of the floor of that mess hall. So much steam comes from the machine that it condenses on the ceiling and rains down gently; also the machine throws drops off just as if it were a wet dog; also everything comes from the machine in a cloud of vapor. So I got *very* wet; my hands, shod in the most inferior of cotton gloves, their fingers long worn through, weighed me down more than I can say — every few minutes I would wring out milk bottles full of water, water not unmixed with steam, water *very* perceptibly diluted with chlorine. I finished the day by being sent on a wonderfully silly errand; another boy and I were sent, with a large iron three-wheeled garbage-can-carrier, to trade the largest garbage can I've ever seen for one equally large but painted grey-cream with a sad green stripe, the only green I've ever seen worse than the green of our fatigue clothes. We went by sidewalk, road, steps, and finally along a gravel path, the garbage-can-carrier bouncing up and down and clanking exactly like the dishwashing machine. The sun was shining, for the first time since I've been here, and that and the errand made me feel awfully good. I was awfully relieved to get off with 12 hours K.P.; the regular allotment, in many camps, is 18. I know a boy that did it 18 hours a day 3 days straight. Here the regular mess hall attendants work only 12 hours a day *every other day* — *very* soft; but that doesn't apply to us.

I forgot to mention the stupendous uproar: the dishwasher, the bangs of thousands of pieces of metal, everybody's agitated cries — it was a very enlivening scene, and half the time I felt fine and sang aloud — though, like the tree in the forest, nobody heard me.

By the way, I'm a PFC now instead of a straight PVT — I've been since Monday, I learned. This means I get four dollars a month more. What else does it mean, mother? Nothing else, unfortunately, my child.

I forgot to say that the atmosphere of the mess hall is very factory-ish: the concrete walls, the big sky lights and windows, the steel girders and steel furniture, and Our Own Production Line, all made me feel that now I've worked in a factory, and thank goodness that's over.

You see this purple ink? Well, Parker calls it V-Mail or Microfilm Black. I hope they choke.

I like Chanute much better than Sheppard — if the school's good, I'll be reasonably delighted with everything. It's too bad about the passes, but that's unimportant.

Your picture looks beautiful — I just looked at it. I love you very much, darling. I guess I can call you fairly often, since we're saving so much money from your not being able to make trips to see me; also, there wouldn't be any sense to coming up in July, just for the four Thursdays of the month, also I can't even leave the field to spend money myself, but with any luck at all I'll be settled at a permanent post by the first or second week of August, and then you can come and *stay,* angel. And with Kitten, the one only one.

About birthday presents: I want all the pictures and letters I can get, and anything small and inexpensive. It's not that a soldier *moi qui parle,* as James would say, doesn't *need* anything; he needs everything, but he couldn't use it if he got it. Get me something cheap, and deposit the rest of the money for Our Future Life, beginning August.

Barnaby is in the *Chicago Sun;* isn't that nice? Nicer than the *Sun.* They're going to have *Desert Victory* here Sunday.

Did you see Roosevelt's statement that military training was doing American young men and young women so much good that something analogous should be — shall we say *offered?* to them after the war. Maybe your guess about what we'll be like in heaven, after de Wah, I mean, was pretty good.

Half the K.P.'s today were V.O.M.'s — from that school, I mean; you could easily, easily tell that their required GCT is only 70.

I'll quit now. I love you, I love you, I love you. I miss you more than anything — more than Kitten, even. I love you so much, darling.

Your
Randall

A note on the envelope read, "Please send me six or eight wire coat hangers right away — we can't buy them."

To have some extra money, Mackie was to stay on in Austin to teach at the summer session.

Jarrell's approaching birthday was May 6, and on receiving the new photographs he wrote Mackie, "I was delighted. Your pictures of Kitten are wonderful. The best one, one of the best photographs I've ever seen, is the one of Kitten walking in the alley across the street. The dark glowing look he shares with the trees makes it look as if it ought to be called Kitten in Fairyland. *I want an enlargement of this one. The one of Kitten eating alone on the front porch has such a patterned texture (with Kitten's fur, I mean) that it's hard to believe it's not a painting . . . Almost all of yours are pretty good and several are swell. You look charming in the one where you are sitting by the car's rear bumper, laughing; in the one where you're sitting at the table in the back yard; and your face is charming in the one where you're leaning against the rear fender."*

* * *

In another letter to Mackie, Jarrell wrote, "I had a wonderfully pleasant day yesterday. They need typists . . . and at 1 they sent me to the laundry room where I might have [found] some laundry lists to type. There in an enormous dark low quiet room, a big coal stove in the middle, I found two privates surrounded by old newspapers; one was reading papers, the other was writing home to his mother. The sergeant was gone, but they gave a glowing tribute to him; he never made them do a thing. *There were tremendous piles of dirty sheets and pillows behind a tremendous pile of cardboard boxes; I went there, lay down and fell asleep. When I woke at 3 the sergeant was back, but hadn't waked me — apparently he was used to strangers coming in and going to sleep in the pile of sheets." After that, Jarrell regularly wrote poems there.*

Jarrell enclosed "The Emancipators" in his next letter to Mackie, saying, "Remember, the end will seem a little odd at first, because you're accustomed to the rest and not to it; I think it's a really good end. It gives me great confidence to be able to write poetry regularly at night after 5:30." In this letter he also wrote, "I have more candy than anybody in the world; yesterday I got candy and cookies from my mother — counting a couple left from your Sheppard Field candy box, I have five boxes of candy. The world hasn't forgotten me; and O how I haven't forgotten it."

THE EMANCIPATORS

When you ground the lenses and the moons swam free
From that great wanderer; when the apple shone
Like a sea-shell through your prism, voyager;
When, dancing in pure flame, the Roman mercy,
Your doctrines blew like ashes from your bones;

Did you think, for an instant, past the numerals
Jellied in Latin like bacteria in broth,
Snatched for by holy Europe like a sign?
Past sombre tables inched out with the lives
Forgotten or clapped for by the wigged Societies?

You guessed this? The earth's face altering with iron,
The smoke ranged like a wall against the day?
— The equations metamorphose into use: the free
Drag their slight bones from tenements to vote
To die with their children in your factories.

Man is born in chains, and everywhere we see him dead.
On your earth they sell nothing but our lives.
You knew that what you died for was our deaths?
You learned, those years, that what men wish is Trade?
It was you who understood; it is we who change.

TO MACKIE JARRELL

Wednesday night
[May 19, 1943]

Darling:

I've been going to school and it's been raining and — but unfortunately there isn't much *and*.

I got given my dog tags, and I wear them around my neck on the glass cord you gave me; when I turn over in my sleep they rattle like a chain. It's very fitting.

Gee, it was fun talking to you Monday.

Thursday noon

I was so tired last night I quit writing and went to sleep; I'm almost as tired now, because of walking 8 or 9 miles very fast, but I may as well write a little now — going to school for the next six hours isn't going to make me any brighter. This school schedule is terribly dreary; you have almost no time for yourself and you're tired for that. I'll certainly be glad when I finish. I've been thinking about the Celestial Navigation school and I believe it's better not to go: it's five or six weeks delay (meaning you'd have to finish the fall term) and all I get out of it is $10 a month more, as corporal, which isn't worth a long sigh, even. This course will finish August 3 or 4, along in there; well, *surely* I'll get sent out to a permanent field in the next couple of weeks after that, and you can come before school ever starts, and not have to teach in the fall term. If it only works out that way! If it were anything but this lunatic Army it would be a certainty.

One of the people from Sheppard, a reliable one, told me about a weird racket there; selling medical discharges. Their lowest price was $200, though they usually got more; there were several people in it, culminating in the doctor who gave the discharge. After you'd paid your money you went on sick call on the prescribed morning, were sent to the hospital to that doctor's ward, and examined (with cries of horror) by the doctor, who then got the discharge. The people in the racket were getting more and more nervous; one staff sergeant took a demotion to plain sergeant just to get away from Sheppard and the eventual blow-up. Isn't this a shocking story? He told me about several smaller rackets, too.

We're allowed to fly the Trainers so long as we keep one side strapped down — that is, the Trainer will dive or climb or turn, but not bank. It's very pleasant to sit under the hood with the instruments, shut away from all the army. Today we used the fake radio apparatus; I was inside, with earphones and a microphone, and pretended to be flying over flooded Evansville, Indiana, and very confused about everything.

Somebody could write a very dull book about Army humor. It mostly consists of practical jokes (anything from pushing the guy ahead of you to shouting into his sleeping ear, *All up for KP*) or invective; it's cruder than anybody would believe, cruder and more monotonous. I've seen a couple of boys who were professional clowns, though, and pretty funny. I wish that I could develop, not an experimental neurosis as Galton did, but an experimental hysterical deafness; gee, it would be wonderful not to be able to hear these people. I really believe I've got to dislike the people in the army more than the army itself; if they were better it would be unpleasant, but quite tolerable; but as it is they're enough to make Rousseau believe in original sin.

I'm sitting in the small service club writing, and a soldiers' chorus is rehearsing loudly, led with great spirit by a little dark lieutenant; one of the singers, on seeing me, rushed over and shook my hand and said he had to get back but would come over to talk as soon as he finished rehearsing; if I've ever seen him before it's news to me — I hope he gives me some hints in his first few sentences. (It was somebody named Morton connected with Arkansas University that knows Lowell. I managed to convince him that I knew him. My only mistake came when he said something about Washington and Anne Marie; the only Anne Marie I know is A. M. Siegel, so I said, "Yes, I knew she'd gone to Washington," but it was some other Anne Marie that *hadn't*. Nuts.)

How deathly still everything is. The chorus is all gone, after singing "The Star-Spangled Banner" with hob nailed boots.

I miss you so much. The last day of the war is going to be the happiest day of my life. How *could* I have ever said Austin was dull? Why, I've been bored more in my army three months than in 3½ years at Austin, 2 at Kenyon, and more too; than in my whole life, almost. One of the worst things is the feeling that there's nobody in your whole barracks, nobody you see at all, that you care at all about; you're completely robbed of any society you care about, and smothered under tons of people you abhor. Well . . .

I wrote poetry night before last — "Dogs at Sheppard Field" — but did only a little; I've got a line or two more for the World War I one ["The Soldier"].

Write me lots, angel, I love you much more than anything; and miss you much more. I'll be so glad to see you at the end of June. I love you.

Your
Randall

The link trainer students had been told about a course in celestial navigation that would follow their graduation from link training if they could not be placed as link instructors. Jarrell, assuming he would be placed as a link instructor, decided against the celestial navigation training, as it would keep him apart from Mackie and Kitten for several weeks longer.

In a previous letter, Jarrell had written, "The dogs are a great delight. There are seven or eight whom one sees constantly; about half of them are pretty fat, furry dogs, who go on our longest walks and cover about twenty miles to our eight, running round and round the columns. Also, when we do calisthenics from the (you'll love this) 'sitting position of attention,' they often sit by us and look gravely into our faces. Sometimes they get excited and chase each other through our hopping ranks, barking so loudly they drown out the instructor." Presumably this inspired Jarrell to write "Dogs at Sheppard Field," but no trace of the poem has been found.

*   *   *

In his next letter to Mackie, Jarrell wrote, "If only I'm lucky I'll get to leave here Sunday night and go to the university for the 24 hours after that. I'm quite afraid I'll get given KP or something on my day off (for missing signing the payroll — the sign said 'disciplinary action will be taken'), but maybe I'm taking too dim a view.

"Oh, one wonderful thing happened. Some men had a quarrel with the people in charge of our barracks (who are surprisingly decent), saying they weren't waking us up loudly enough, etc. So, yesterday morning at 5:30 suddenly a brass band began to play, bang; my eyes sprang open, and there was a BUGLER, about 10 feet away, playing his bugle as loudly as he could. I couldn't stop laughing for about ten minutes; the dissatisfied ones were so stunned they could hardly speak."

TO MACKIE JARRELL

[May 24, 1943]

Darling:

As you can see from my wonderful stationery, I'm once again for a moment in the real world: the library of the University of Illinois, even. How happy I feel! I came over last night, ate a nice dinner, got a room in a hotel, and slept like a human being, not like a soldier; and this morning I took a bath, had my haircut, ate cereal with cream, *cream,* and so on; I bought myself some trousers to go with my shirt (I look beautiful), shopped for fountain pens without success, looked for a decent photographer's shop, and ended up at the library, where I've been reading the *New Statesman* and such. I don't feel at all the same person I was yesterday.

Illinois is the regular northern university. It has that settled old look, grassy, so deeply shaded by the big trees that you observe with surprise that the shade (or perhaps the soot?) has permanently blackened the buildings. The girls most of them dress straight Vassar, the boys almost straight Princeton, though with fewer coats: the regular costume is saddle oxfords, trousers (but *not* grey flannel) sweater and shirt, tan-washed-white rain-coat, and *hat.* The war seems not only non-existent, but impossible to invent. I feel bitterly envious, naturally, but not disapproving; at most I want to say to them, "If you only knew . . ."

KP was just 12 hours, but it felt — when I got out I expected to see rusted shards of helmets in the barrows that were once Chanute. It reconciled me to my daily schedule, almost.

It is — had you guessed? — raining.

I marched to KP with a wonderful barracks, 407; they are wonderful because they all sing, like angry cattle, the best song I've heard in the army. They begin to bawl without warning, crashing like pots and pans and a brass band, to the tune of "The Stars and Stripes Forever" (sing it to yourself),

Three *cheers* for the *Jones* Junior *High*,
The *best* junior *high* in *Toledo*,
The *boys* and the *girls* they are *fine*,
You will *never* meet a *better* groo oo oo oop

(This *group* goes as high as they can make it)
(In measured cadence:)

Rah ... Rah ... Rah ... Rah ...
Jones ... Junior ... High ... School ...

then (said just as you say, *Percy is a sissy*) *"Our* class *won* the *Bible."* Then as
an afterthought: "TWICE!"

The only funnier song I've heard is a serious patriotic one that ends
(after some gush about our being the best country in the universe):

With never a boast or a brag;
Shall auld acquaintance be forgot?
Keep your eye on the good old flag!

I can't give you any idea at all of how wonderful it feels to be away. Gee,
gee.

I got to type in the orderly room yesterday morning instead of taking
calisthenics.

I heard another bunch singing, "When the war is over we will all enlist
again ..." I think I'll use that for the title of a poem; don't you think it
would be a good one?

I'm going to write poetry later in the afternoon and tonight, though it's
hard to tear myself away from the World.

The *Chicago Tribune* is all it's cracked up to be; the *Sun,* except for *Barnaby,* is a pretty sorry fake paper (if the *Tribune* were liberal it would be reactionary, is more or less your feeling).

I love you so much, darling. I'll be so pleased to get some more pictures
of you. *And* pictures of Kitten.

I love you.

Your
Randall

*   *   *

Jarrell wrote the poem "The Soldier Walks Under the Trees of the University" almost overnight, and he sent it to Mackie in his next letter.

THE SOLDIER WALKS UNDER
THE TREES OF THE UNIVERSITY

The walls have been shaded for so many years
By the green magnificence of these great lives
Their bricks are darkened till the end of time.
(Small touching whites in the perpetual
Darkness that saturates the unwalled world;
Saved from the sky by leaves, and from the earth by stone)
The pupils trust like flowers to the shades
And interminable twilight of these latitudes.

In our zone innocence is born in banks
And cultured in colonies the rich have sown:
The one is spared here what the many share
To write the histories that others are.
The oak escapes the storm that broke the reeds,
They read here; they read, too, of reeds,
Of storms; and are, almost, sublime
In their read ignorance of everything.

The poor are always — somewhere, but not here;
We learn of them where they and Guilt subsist
With Death and Evil: in books, in books, in books.
Ah, sweet to contemplate the causes, not the things!
The soul learns fortitude in libraries,
Enduring patience in another's pain,
And pity for the lives we do not change:
All that the world would be, if it were real.

When will the boughs break blazing from these trees,
The darkened walls float heavenward like soot?
The days when men say: "Where we look is fire —
The iron branches flower in my veins"?
In that night even to be rich is difficult,
The world is something even books believe,
The bombs fall all year long among the states,
And the blood is black upon the unturned leaves.

TO MACKIE JARRELL

Saturday night
[May 29, 1943]

Darling:

What an injustice to call me the Laureate of Libraries on the strength of my last poem, which is not about libraries but a University, and a capitalist one at that. (I think I'll call it "The Soldier Walks Under the Trees of the University.") But you are right just the same, and here is the end of my "Carnegie Library" to prove it. Incidentally, about "Of that deep string, half music and half pain" [in "The Carnegie Library, Juvenile Division"]: when notes get down below a certain pitch, they are apprehended by the ear not as sound but as pain — that's the ground for the metaphor.

I worked finishing (the part before the last six lines) the "C. Library" last night; we had a six-hour lecture that afternoon. It's summer and very hot in the trainer room. Today we took the Trainer apart, pleasant unskilled work with no lecture; I enjoyed the volley-ball part of calisthenics this morning (though they made us roll in dust, fifteen minutes, until we were so dirty even showers wouldn't clean us) and have felt good all day. Yesterday I felt good, too, marching to dinner after school — so I sang the Jones Junior High School as loudly as I could. I was a real sensation; the whole column was laughing, and I've had a dozen people ask me about it today (besides *many* requests for an encore, in line tonight).

Just think, tomorrow (unless they restrict us) I'll be going to Champaign.

I enjoy what you say about the poems so much; write me that much or more about all the ones I send. I'm awfully glad you like "Soldier [T.P.]" so well. I hope you like "The Soldier" as well as I do.

I write poetry every night. Even the night we had to G.I. I rushed home, did mine immediately, and had two hours left. It makes my life much pleasanter: I think about the poetry a lot, and I have the beautiful feeling of getting something out of all this. Also I've written enough by now to have regained my beautiful old feeling that I can always write good poems — just give me the time and a subject, any subject; I'd lost it in my last year before I got in the army.

You wouldn't believe how the time from 7:30 to 10:00 goes by every night, and how much I wish for more.

I've made the sixth line of "The Soldier":

"His joys, his reason, and his blood;"

I got summoned to the orderly room the other day; I went not very trembling, as I'd done nothing, I thought. Well, I had a book two days overdue, and the library had informed my Squadron. The sergeant asked me in an overbearing tone why I'd done it; I was so disgusted and amused that I answered airily, "O, I forgot about it." His surprise checked him for an instant; then he went on to say (unsweetly) I must get it back that morning or sign a statement of charges (i.e., pay for the book).

I love my Mackie so much. The only good thing about the Army besides the poems is realizing how much I do. I'll be so glad to see you, darling. I love you.

Your
Randall

As the Laureate of Libraries, Jarrell wrote "Children Selecting Books in a Library," "The Carnegie Library, Juvenile Division," "The Soldier Walks Under the Trees of the University," "A Girl in a Library," and an unpublished address for the American Library Association in which he said, "I rarely feel happier than when I'm in a library — very rarely feel more soothed and calm and secure. Sitting back there in the soft gloom of the stacks, a book among books, almost, I feel very much in my element — a fish come back to the sea, a baby come back to the womb. I like libraries so much it depresses me that my cat can't go to the library and get out books."

TO SARA STARR

[June 26, 1943]

Dear Sara:

I've meant to write you for a long time. I certainly wish I could see you; maybe I will if they give me a furlough in the fall. How do you like Washington? Better than I like the army, I hope.

For about two months, back around Christmas, I flew all the time, sometimes twice a day; then I got washed out because the chief pilot thought I did some maneuvers badly. (I guess he was right, too.) I didn't like flying much because it isn't very thrilling — instead of seeming to move fast you just seem to stand still, with the world moving around you very slowly, as if it were a motion picture. Besides, we always had to fly at *just* so many miles an hour, at *just* such an altitude, in *just* such a direction — it was too much like one long examination.

Then I got sent to the army as a private. It is like being in an orphan asylum in a Dickens story, or in an old-fashioned inefficient jail — in some ways. I sleep in a double-deck bed with a cowboy from Texas, a nice boy who never finished the third grade, just below me; if I stretch out my left hand I can touch a small dark pleasant Italian, about five feet high; with my right hand I can touch somebody who came from I don't know where, but he's just been here two weeks while his wife had a baby boy. I have to drill, or do calisthenics, or stand in line, or go to classes at my school, or fly in the Link Trainers, or eat meals in the mess hall, all the time from 5:30 in the morning till 7 at night; in the evenings I mostly write poetry or letters to Mackie.

I'm at Chanute Field now learning to teach people blind flying; before I was at Sheppard Field, and there I did more things than you'd believe, Sara. I even shovelled dirt and worked in a postoffice. Some of the time I would interview the new soldiers (or flyers who'd been washed out like me) and help decide what school to send them to; I saw lots of my own students that I'd taught down at Texas. Once I was sick in the hospital for two weeks, but that was the nicest time of all; I would read three or four books a day, and play ping-pong at the Red Cross; once, when we were quarantined because they'd by mistake brought in someone with scarlet fever, I won eleven dollars playing poker. I looked very funny, because I was dressed in *very* old grey flannel pajamas and a faded maroon corduroy bathrobe; they were supposed to give us slippers, but they didn't have any, so all the soldiers went *clump, clump* through the wards in their great big army shoes. You know, soldiers hardly ever wear the clothes civilians see them in: they wear cotton clothes, some like mechanic's coveralls and some like convicts' uniforms, but all a very ugly grey green — and they are always dirty because there are only two of them, and it takes a week to get laundry, and at calisthenics we have to roll around in the dirt and crawl on our hands and knees.

I was terribly disappointed when, because I got in the army and you moved to Washington, we couldn't have you visit us at Thanksgiving. Promise you will as soon as the war is over.

I wish I could see your baby sisters, though not as much as I wish I could see you. I'll put in some pictures of myself in my army clothes if you will send me some new snapshots of you, so I can see if you look any older. *I* don't.

Mackie and Kitten are going to come see me about the first of July. They will come to Nashville too, I think, so they'll get to see you.

Write me and I'll write you again — cross my heart and hope to die.

Tell your mother and father and brothers and sisters (*and* your cousins and your aunts, if you see the other Starrs) that I wish I could see them too.

How is your ballet? Tell me some books you've been reading. I do hope I'll get to see you soon.

Love,
Randall

Sara Starr was the ten-year-old daughter of Jarrell's Nashville friends
Milton and Zaro Starr. Jarrell had written "The Head of Wisdom" for
her younger sister, but Sara was his favorite.

In a letter to Mackie commenting on army clothes, Jarrell wrote, "When
I was saying what I think of our little convict's cap a simple acquaintance
answered, 'Why I don't think it's very bad. I think it looks like you was a
fireman on a locomotive or a flour mill engineer.' " This letter was signed
"Your old RAGGLE PAGGLE."

TO MACKIE JARRELL

Tuesday
[July 20, 1943]

Darling:

I have a wonderful present for you and Kitten; I want (I'm serious)
Kitten to wear it round his neck on a ribbon on state occasions. It is — a
medal! Yes, a medal that the United States Army has given us because I am
a (I quote) *Pistol Marksman*. This is, alas, the lowest grade of medal (below
both Sharpshooter and Expert) — like being a Tenderfoot Scout or getting
the Order of St. Nicholas (Third Class) that Chekhov characters get. Incidentally, it's odd that you get [an] Iron Cross (what else could you call it?)
for your feats.

We finished our shooting today about eleven — just two overtime days
instead of four. Today was cloudy, the shooting was fairly interesting, and I
was cheered by my unexpected success (especially since I'd made just about
half as much in the practice shooting, when I had a wretched instructor).
The automatic kicks so hard that after each shot it stands up straight in
your hand; and the triggers are so hard to pull that instead of squeezing
gently you have almost to tug. The noise is deafening; my ears still have big
sea shells covering them (to judge from the hum) and I'm mildly deafened.
The things that were most fun were shooting a Thompson submachine gun
and petting a cute thin orange kitten who lives at the range. The machine
gun makes you think incredible that anybody, anybody, can charge through
machine-gun fire. You aim at the lower part of the target and press the trig-
ger, and before you can take your finger away it has shot four or five times
and the target has a line of holes from top to bottom when the gun has
pulled itself up in your grasp.

Our practice was all *very* safe and easy — and boy, I want it to stay that
way. I hope nobody ever gets to shoot a machine gun at *me* — or an automatic either, for that matter.

In Champaign I read magazines and [Anita Brennan's] *The Wind That Swept Mexico,* heard a Schumann quartet, [Beethoven's] Grosse Fugue, ate an avocado, and saw *The Constant Nymph,* poor but with Joan Fontaine looking very nice in parts. And — gee, gee, gee — I lost my fountain pen. It's hard to keep them in the army. You know at home you leave them in the armchair, at the office, at somebody's house, and get them the next day. Here, one "leave" and they're gone forever.

I think about you all the time, darling. You don't know how much I love you.

Your
Randall

*   *   *

In another letter to Mackie, Jarrell wrote, "I thought of writing a poem asking The State (the principal god in my new machinery) why it didn't call up Kitten and train him to catch mice (in some army warehouse, of course); but I don't want to put ideas in the world's mind, especially as they've done worse than that with dogs — their trainers are instructed never to pet them or be kind to them, since this would make them friendly." Jarrell did make a drafted cat part of his poem "The State."

TO AMY BREYER DE BLASIO

[July 22, 1943]
[Begun June 8, 1943]

Dear A-

It's so wonderful for you to be well again, and doing something you really like. I'm in an institution, too, and I know what they're like. It's easy for me to be cheerful about mine, though: I don't think there's any real chance of my being killed; the war will be over in a couple of years and I'm so much better off than practically everybody else in the world that I feel ashamed. There are just three races: the rich, the poor, and the Americans.

I get more political every year; the army makes you more so, and confirms all your hardest beliefs. This *you* is strictly *me:* 99 of 100 of the people in the army haven't the faintest idea what the war's about. Their two strongest motives are (a) nationalism, pure nationalism (they find it easy to believe that German generals are paid $30 a month — they find it easy to believe anything about foreigners) and (b) race prejudice — they dislike Japanese in the same way, though not as much as, they dislike Negroes. They feel neither gratitude nor affection for our allies — they'd fight Russia tomorrow, for instance. They have no feeling against the Germans — they dismiss all information about them as "propaganda." This *propaganda* is their one response, frightening and invariable, to anything they haven't always known (and they have known almost nothing). The innocent idealism and naive whipped-up hatred (which collapsed into fraternizing when it really encountered the enemy in the first World War) were a good deal better than this. I believe nationalism, so far from dying out as people once believed, is going to reach heights it's only in isolated cases attained before — in the first World War there was a real queer feeling of solidarity between the "workers" of the opposing armies; how little of *that* is left.

Gee, I wrote this last part many days ago. I've been having a crazy, busy time — they've been overworking us, several days we had to go to the rifle range (believe it or not I won a medal for being a "Pistol Marksman") and I've been doing little in my off hours but sleeping. (Like being an interne.)

Isn't the war going well? The Italians are now one of my favorite peoples. If the European war ends this winter I'll believe in Santa Claus, Pollyanna, God, anything.

When you fire a machine-gun and see the bullets tearing up the embankment you're firing into you realize that you don't want anybody to have to be a hero, to kill somebody else or get killed himself.

I haven't written much poetry lately. I have one about a German prison camp I saw from a troop train that ought to be good. ["An Officers' Prison Camp Seen from a Troop-Train"]. I'll send it as soon as I've finished it.

I had some pictures, snapshots, taken of me in the ordinary, wretched fatigue clothes I wear everyday; a couple are good, I'll trade you one for one of you.

I sent a couple of anti-army poems to the *New Republic;* it turned them down on "ideological grounds," but was evidently embarrassed, because it invited me to send a poem to an anthology of "leading American poets" they're having in August. I wasn't mollified by the *leading,* and maliciously sent them "Soldier [T.P.]," much more anti-army than my preceding two. The ones I'm enclosing on green paper ["Port of Embarkation" and "Absent with Official Leave"] are proof from *Poetry;* the editor (who's just got a medical discharge after a few months in the army) was in a good position to appreciate them.

This is a wretched letter, A, but do take the wish for the deed. It's sad not to be able to communicate except by letters, good, bad, or indifferent. I miss seeing you, just as I always do. Write me soon about the poems and I will — will what? Write you back, I guess.

Love,
Randall

Amy was an M.D. specializing in pediatrics, and her job was with the Bureau of Child Hygiene of the State Department of Health in Hartford, Connecticut. She was agonizing over her marriage but began divorce proceedings shortly after this.

TO MACKIE JARRELL

Tuesday, noon
[August 3, 1943]

Darling:

It was so nice talking to you. Your voice sounded just a yard or two away.

We finished our graduation early yesterday, so early we were in Urbana by 9:30. I slept till about one. Most of the day I listened to music; besides the Schumann concerto (which is the national anthem of my own particular war) they played Beethoven's fourth symphony, one of his violin sonatas, and a Brahms violin sonata and overture. Gee, the students at Illinois are lucky.

I'm so glad you like the prisoners poem ["Prisoners"] so well — I felt sure you would. I wrote half Saturday morning and half Sunday morning. It's queer the effect that rhythm gives, isn't it?

I saw, when I was cleaning out my leather case, the royalty statement from Harcourt Brace; up to Dec. 31st they'd sold 300 copies, and they sent me $50 for it. So I'll bet we get thirty or forty dollars for the first half of 1943, in a few months.

It's been raining hard and looks autumnal, a nice change; August 1 was the hottest August 1 on record here.

There are five or six poems by Cal Lowell (original and goodish, though unsatisfactory and queer) in the latest *Sewanee Review;* the nicest is one about a Boston boy dying of cancer — full of local detail ["Arthur Winslow: Death from Cancer"]. They look so much better than Berryman's two printed by their side ["Farewell to Miles" and "Ancestor"] that it's funny.

I believe I'll try to get Harcourt to publish a book of poems — all my army poems, "Orestes," and a dozen or so others — next spring or so. I believe they'd have a real chance of selling more than usual. I could put in (roughly): all the army poems and "Orestes"; "The Difficult Resolution"; "Eine kleine Nachtmusik"; "Scherzo"; "The Boyg, Peer Gynt"; "A Small Sonata"; "The Dialectic"; "Mother, Said the Child"; "The Patient Leading the Patient"; and three or four more — also any new army poems I write in the next few months. That would make an awfully good book, wouldn't it? You make any suggestions you can think of about the ones you'd like in. I

love you. I'd name the book, of course, *When the War Is Over We Will All
Enlist Again*. I bet it would get some awe-inspiring reviews; I hope the *New
Masses* doesn't see it — what a review *it* could do.

The *Chicago Tribune* and the Hearst tabloids and similar papers up here
are so much worse than anything you ever see in the south. They read as if
everybody on their staff were named Westbrook Pegler. His recent line is
that everybody in the government is a Fascist, consequently (since the two
are identical) a Communist. It seems to be the Republican official line, to
judge from things lately.

I'd better quit and mail this.

I love you so. I love you so.

Your

Randall

*Of the poems for his second book that Jarrell named in this letter, he chose to
include only "The Difficult Resolution"; "The Boyg, Peer Gynt, the One
Only One"; and "Mother, Said the Child." Of the poems written at Chan-
ute, he included "The Emancipators"; "The Carnegie Library, Juvenile
Division"; "Soldier"; "Soldier [T.P.]"; "Come to the Stone . . ."; "The Sick
Nought"; "Prisoners"; and "The Soldier Walks Under the Trees of the
University."*

TO MACKIE JARRELL

[August 9, 1943]

Darling:

There's a pretty good story about the army (the best one I've read for
giving you the atmosphere, though it's much too colored and melodra-
matic) in this week's — August 7 — *New Yorker* ["The Invisible Ship"];
it's by the same guy, John Cheever, who wrote that one we both read about
the tough sergeant in the Southern basic camp. I wonder how *The New
Yorker* reconciles his stories with its official rose-colored accounts E. J. Kahn
writes. Probably it figures Cheever's are just fiction, and fiction, *New Yorker*
fiction, as everybody knows, has to be unpleasant. When you read it notice
the captain's speech: well, not one officer in five, ten, fifteen could make that
grammatical a speech — not one in a thousand that effective a one. What
the Captain would *really* have said would be so rambling and abusive and
altogether different it would be funny.

This is my *Army, Army, who's got the Army?* letter.

Another thing, the soldiers' talk is far too correct in the story. And far,
far, far too proper — but of course he was in a spot there. If I wrote an army

story I'd make every third word _____. It would give the reader a suggestion of what it's like. The trouble with writing a story about the army is
this: people expect something to *happen* in a story (Cheever supplied things,
lots of things); but the whole point of the army is that nothing ever does
happen, and putting the things in falsifies everything. Cheever's story is so
eventful, the soldiers are sharp, vivid as he can make them; but really the
events are just like lumps in Cream of Wheat, almost indistinguishable
from the Cream of Wheat, and so are the soldiers, *essentially.* You get that
melting pot, "aren't they all *different?"* feeling about Cheever's soldiers; but
really you're surprised the other way, that men so different, from such different places, can act so alike, and give you such an intolerable feeling of stupid loud dreary sameness.

I'll tear out the story and put it in — I hate to think of your looking
frantically around for a *New Yorker* so the criticism will be fun. Besides,
we'll save 9¢ (6¢ for extra postage compared to 15¢; and believe me, the rest
of the magazine is a joy to miss).

Gee, I'm pleased with my "Prisoners." I never want to change a word,
no matter how often I say it. Shall I send *it* to *The New Yorker?*

This job's made it quite impossible to write poetry — just no time; but I
got off tonight — *but* I wanted to write you, you who are nicer than *any*
poems, even old me's poems. What a sentence! Nobody but old me would
write it *or* leave it. I love you. So much, so much, darling. I'll quit and mail
this and go to bed in my — here a pause like that before the world ends —
ROOM.

Your own own own
Randall

PRISONERS

Within the wires of the post, unloading the cans of garbage,
The three in soiled blue denim (the white *P* on their backs
Sending its chilly *North* six yards to the turning blackened
Sights of the cradled rifle, to the eyes of the yawning guard)
Go on all day being punished, go on all month, all year
Loading, unloading; give their child's, beast's sigh — of despair,
Of endurance and of existence; look unexpectingly
At the big guard, dark in his khaki, at the dust of the blazing plain,
At the running or crawling soldiers in their soiled and shapeless green.

The prisoners, the guards, the soldiers — they are all, in their way, being
    trained.
From these moments, repeated forever, our own new world will be made.

Pfc. Randall Jarrell at Chanute Field,
Illinois, June 1943

The soldiers graduating as link trainer instructors were now told the army did not need them, and Jarrell chose to stay at Chanute six weeks longer and be trained as a CNT (Celestial Navigation Tower) operator. Mackie and Kitten stayed nearby, and when the session was over, all three returned to Nashville for Jarrell's furlough. The letter of August 9 was Jarrell's last letter to Mackie until late October, when she returned to Austin and Jarrell was about to be shipped out to Davis-Monthan Field in Tucson.

TO MACKIE JARRELL

[October 30, 1943]

Darling:

After I wrote you yesterday I did lots of things, little things. I saw a movie named *Princess O'Rourke* — it was funny but embarrassing at the end, when President Roosevelt is seen (unseen, rather) as God and Falla as Mahomet. I read some more of [Christina Stead's] *The Man Who Loved Children;* and got some bedding (I thought I'd sleep *inside* my mattress cover — I've always wanted to sleep in a sleeping bag; it was smooth and comfortable but far too warm, and I wriggled out); and went by CNT and got a temporary job; and unpacked a little and ate some candy and looked at your Kodak pictures. Northrop (The 19th Bombardment man) was waiting to be given his furlough, and we talked a long time. He has the Distinguished Service Cross, the Silver Star, the Air Medal, the Purple Heart, several citations, and something else I forget; he said he wore them once or twice when he was first in this country, but it got him into so much trouble he stopped. The papers giving you permission to wear a medal are big ones on very thick stiff paper, virtually impossible to carry around; so when the M.P.'s at the gate wouldn't let him out without seeing his authorization for the medals, he had to make two trips back to the squadron, one to get them and one to take them back. *Then* the M.P.s in town stopped him and took him to their headquarters, and he had to call up camp, etc. Then the M.P.s in Chicago did the same thing, and he missed two trains.

He was telling me about battles; he said he had swell motion pictures he'd taken of the battles of the Java Sea and the Coral Sea, but they confiscated them before he got home. He said he dropped a 4,000 pound bomb on a transport at low altitude, and the transport broke in two and completely disappeared before the plane was out of sight of her. He saw a rugby stadium (a concrete one holding 35,000 people) in which a 4,000 pound bomb had been dropped; it was completely leveled.

He has 2,000 logged hours as a transport pilot; all the big airlines offered him jobs when he got home, but the army wouldn't release him — still, they won't let him fly because they think something's wrong with him physically; the C.A.A. thinks him in perfectly good shape and has just renewed his license for five years.

There's another man here with all his medals and four more; and he's just a corporal too. They say that abroad promotions for enlisted men are very bad. When you think of all the people who're sergeants or staff sergeants, and have done nothing but be in the army a few months or a year in the United States, it makes you sick.

Northrop says the Colonel commanding them would always ask each man what he was supposed to do on a raid, just before it; after a while he got a stock answer: "The first hour I'll work on my bombing problems; then I'll read magazines and smoke for two hours; then I'll make a run over the target and drop bombs for five minutes; then I'll read magazines and smoke for three hours." The commanding officer would laugh, nod, and go on.

I'm writing this in the CNT office; they're going to have an inspection, so I cleaned up the office for 15 minutes — that's all the work they've found.

The alarm clock wouldn't start when it got here; I'll send it back for you to have it repaired. But before you come on wherever we're going to be get it fixed or somehow, anyhow, get an alarm clock, Mother's if necessary — we'll absolutely have to have one. Probably ours just needs cleaning — the dirt in it got shaken into the works, I suppose.

I feel the way Alice must have when she got back to Wonderland in *Through the Looking-Glass;* everything's just the same, *soo* familiar, and goofy as ever. I even dreamed that I bawled out Maxwell for something, what I forget.

Be sure to read the Christina Stead again.

Now it's about two hours later and I've been reading and eating lunch: the wonderful menu was macaroni, parsnips, spinach and cake but I got all the cheese-off-the-top, left out the vegetables, and didn't do badly. Yesterday was as good as today was bad — lima beans and roast. Yesterday, for the first time in my life I saw Venus in the daytime. I knew where to look and there it was.

I'm much better about missing you today, thank goodness; yesterday I felt aching and empty. I love you so much. It simplifies everything for me — I don't worry about whether my poems are good, whether I'll be lucky in the rest of the war, anything; I just think that after a while I'll be back with you, and that after the war I'll always be with you.

I love you,
Randall

*   *   *

In his next letter, Jarrell wrote, "The Man Who Loved Children *really is one of the best novels I ever read. It's much better on second reading — you see that some of the things you thought extreme aren't really, and you don't have the feeling of dread and complete personal involvement that actually made me rush over some parts the first time. We're going to leave Friday — we'll be put on shipping tomorrow."*

Aboard the troop train, they were told their destination was Salt Lake City but not to mail any letters en route. Jarrell spent about ten days there and was charmed to live in a tent. He said that "at night with smoke hanging above them they [the tents] looked like medieval pavilions — small, ratty ones." He commented, "On Nov. 15 I will have been in the Army 9 months — 4½ in Training, and 4½ waiting, just waiting."

While he waited in Salt Lake City, he read, and wrote Mackie, "Yesterday I had a swell time. I read Voltaire (who seemed wonderfully childish, limited and smug) and Pascal's Provincial Letters, *which I'd never read before. They are awfully good, almost the clearest and most natural polemic style I ever read. I was delighted with them. The examples of Jesuit casuistry he's attacking are extremely funny."*

When his orders came through, Jarrell boarded another troop train, this time headed for Tucson, via Los Angeles.

Davis-Monthan Field, Tucson, Arizona, November 1943–March 1946

The Jarrells could find no affordable apartment in Tucson, and for a year they lived in one room with Kitten. Nonetheless, Jarrell wrote Lambert Davis, "I am very happy here and couldn't ask for anything more than to stay here for the rest of the war."

During their stay Mackie got an agreeable job as a social worker for the Red Cross and Jarrell perfected the poems written at Chanute for his second book and wrote two long poems, "Burning the Letters" and "Pilots, Man Your Planes," that represented a start on his third book.

In late 1945 Jarrell corresponded at length with Robert Lowell, examining Lowell's poems line by line, often word by word, and persuasively aiding in their final revision for Lowell's second book, Lord Weary's Castle.

Margaret Marshall of The Nation *continued to welcome every poem Jarrell sent; and, planning a year off from* The Nation *to edit the papers of Constance O'Rourke, she offered Jarrell — sight unseen — the "Verse Chronicle" column. After he agreed to do the column, she offered him her own staff position as Literary Editor.*

TO MACKIE JARRELL

Tuesday morning, 11
[November 16, 1943]

Darling:

Here I am. I got in about 5:30, and already have a barracks and squadron; we went by the CNT towers (four of them) and they welcomed us and told us to come back at one. Davis-Monthan is a big field and looks good.

The climate's about that of San Antonio, but dryer; there are mountains on three sides of the field. We are on "working quarantine" for the first two weeks; we aren't permitted off the post, that is.

The first thing I asked about, of course, was living off post. One way or another I think it's absolutely certain. Their quota for separate rations is filled up and we may not get that for several months; *but* you can live off post without getting the separate rations for $20, and I think I can certainly arrange that. If I couldn't for a few weeks they still would give me a married man's pass, which permits you to be off the field whenever you're off duty.

This is my address:

Cpl. Randall Jarrell
18201238
32nd Hq and AB Sq.
Davis-Monthan Fld.
Tucson, Arizona

This means 32nd Headquarters and Air Base Squadron — which means that we stay on with the field, and *don't* ship out with the trained squadrons. Somebody said when he knew we were CNT, "Well, you're here for a couple of years, boys."

I think the thing for you to do is to come on just as soon as possible. Drive down to Austin on Saturday and Sunday (say); stay there a couple of days, getting anything you think we'd need for housekeeping. But this is the most important thing to do in Austin: see all the people in the department who could help and see if they can't get you a job at the University of Arizona, which is here in Tucson. If they could only get you one beginning at mid year that would be wonderful. Or if you couldn't get that you might get one with their library; or at the highschool here; or wherever you think best, angel. But do get them to do *all* they can about getting you a job at the University.

I want you to come as quickly as possible because the sooner you're here the sooner I can make arrangements to leave. If you stayed in Austin Monday and Tuesday and Wednesday (or longer if you like) and then came on, the drive from Austin here probably would take only two days. Thank goodness, it will be warm-weather driving down here. Oh, yes, be *sure* to bring our marriage license. If you go into our boxes of clothes at Austin bring my white tennis trousers and two good sweaters.

There's one drawback to Tucson, the usual one: apartments and rooms are supposed to be very high and very hard to get. Since I can't leave post, 8 miles from Tucson; good bus service, I can't do a thing about getting one. You can stay at a tourist camp the first day or two and get the best thing we can; then after that we'll keep looking for something better — and squadrons do move out of here fairly often, leaving vacancies, so it ought to be possible to get something decent.

We left Salt Lake early Sunday but didn't get here till this morning because we went by way of Los Angeles — we changed trains only 40 miles east of it. I was quite sick at my stomach Sunday night and felt bad all day Monday, so I didn't enjoy the trip. I'm all right now.

They run the towers on two shifts — 8 A.M. to 4 P.M. and 4 P.M. to 12 P.M. Getting a university job would be particularly nice because it would let us see each other any time I have to work on the 4–12 shift.

Oh, darling, you don't know how I've missed you. You're all I care about in the whole world. I love you so much and miss you so much. I've often looked at the pictures of you and Kitten — so many of them are just lovely. I love you.

So far no mail has caught up with me; I'll probably get a bunch Friday or Saturday. It was wonderful talking to you — I was so excited I probably did all the talking. I love you so much. The field's very big and rather nice-looking, with some cactus, bushes and stuff — the mountains look fairly nice. People seem much better off here than in schools on basic fields. The CNT operators are not particularly intellectual, though there's one who whistles (very well, too) classical themes and reads Thomas Wolfe, and loves Brahms. If this world were cleverer I'd be happier.

I keep saying to myself, "Thursday, then Friday, and then I'll be with my Mackie." I love you. I love you.

Your
Randall

Oh, I forgot to say the night sky is extremely beautiful, and old Orion, my mascot (I'm convinced God made him for me) looks as H. G. Wells-ish as ever.

TO OSCAR WILLIAMS

[August 1944]

Dear Mr. Williams:

Yes, I'd like to be in the anthology [*The War Poets,* 1945, edited by Oscar Williams]; here are a couple of poems besides those I sent you. "Second Air Force" is being printed in the fall book number of *The Nation;* I think it would be a good idea for you to use it as one of the anthology poems (since you ask me to tell you which poems I favor using); some of the others *I* like best are "The Emancipators," "Port of Embarkation," "Losses," "Soldier [T.P.]," and "An Officers' Prison Camp." If you like unpleasant poems about a war I fancy "The Soldier" and "The Sick Nought" are very unpleasant (those and "The Metamorphoses" are the same sort of poems i.e. economic, and I guess you should use one, anyway, of that sort). I presume you want just war poems, otherwise I'd put in "Carnegie Library."

I'll send you a photograph in uniform. Here is a biographical note:

In October, 1942 I enlisted in the Air Corps as a pilot; I was washed out after about thirty hours flying. I am a CNT [Celestial Navigation Tower] operator now, at Tucson, Arizona. Ordinarily I'm an instructor at the University of Texas.

The Anthology is a good idea: if anybody can write a good poem about *anything,* he ought to do it about a war he's in — or so one would think, but I haven't seen much good about this war — you'd think Shapiro would have written something good about it, but I suppose his goofy ideas about the war as a subject for poetry have kept him from it.

If I haven't sent some of the poems I mention, or if you need anything else, just write me; I hope you have good luck with the book.

Yours,
Randall Jarrell

Karl Shapiro's book of poems V-Letter and Other Poems *won the Pulitzer Prize in 1945.*

TO AMY BREYER DE BLASIO

My address is 2704 E. Drachman,
Tucson, Arizona.
[October 1944]

Dear A-

I've written halves of two long letters to you but I carried them around in my pocket so long waiting to finish them that they wore out. Really, three — I remember starting one, way back at Chanute, to thank you for the Forest Hills program. I've been wonderfully lucky for the past six months — my job and Tucson are swell, Mackie has an awfully nice Red Cross job (so we've enough money), I live off post and get to play tennis, I like the people in my department, I'm even writing poems. My two subjects are: bombing Hamburg and bombing crews — I feel sympathetic and sorry for both of them. I have a longish poem about the Second Air Force almost done — I'll send it later; I'll put any others in this letter.

I wish I could see you. I'm awfully sorry you still feel so bad about things — I know how hard it is not to. Things do get better with time, that is, one gets different with time; but even though that's a true consolation it sounds so niggardly, like a Dickens workhouse, that it's not worth saying. I'm glad your job's so good. I believe the biggest permanent consolation for *anything* is that the world's so interesting. I think they ought to say "What shall it profit a man if he gain his own soul and lose the whole world?" and give that to people along with the other.

I've just seen Red's *Selected Poems* and that's the only real thing wrong with the good ones: the world and everything in it, in them, is so purely Original Sin, horror, loathing, morbidness, final evil, that to somebody who knows Red it's plain he manages his life by pushing all the evil in it out into the poems and novels. All his theory says is that the world is nothing but evil, whereas the practice he lives by says exactly the opposite. That accounts for the really adolescent tone in lots of *At Heaven's Gate:* you're adolescent when you're so unused to things, bad things, that they seem to you absolute, finally fascinating, unrelated to everything else because everything else is blotted out and unimportant compared to them, too unimportant even to act as a qualifier; so you're constantly in bad taste (Red's worst minor fault is his regular unbelievable lapses in taste) because taste is proportion and sensibleness and comes from knowing and being used to things — and how can there be any proportion between black and white, or any knowing or being used to what you've excluded? It's like solving the Negro problem by sending all the Negroes to Africa and then maintaining in all your dreams and writings that they're pure Evil and that the world is Africa — and they never contradict you, because the real mixed-grey ones aren't here anymore, and the pure Blacks of your imagination were formed to confirm you: so your theory is a nightmare; but your practice is too good to be true, and everybody loves you. In other words, if Red were bad to people or Cenina, and lost his temper and made unkind remarks about his friends, his poetry would get to be considerably more cheerful; and not to see the world as Africa (or at least not pure Africa) his poetry is a therapeutic device, the most wonderful one you could want, but the best poetry there is isn't that. There's a dialectical contradictory relationship between Red's life and his poetry, and either is to an extent falsified by the mere existence of the other; in the best art the dialectical contradictory relationship is inside the work of art, and the contraries aren't falsified but complemented, altered, completed by each other.

What I've been saying is the private reason for Red's poetry, but also there's a public one that springs from his political and general attitude toward society. If you see there is a great deal of evil in society (that is, the world) that *demands* you, you are *forced* to do something about it, (but of course, really doing something is hard, unpleasant, uncongenial to your talents and nature) and you feel guilty if you don't; the only excuse you can find for doing nothing is to say that the world is essentially evil and incurable, that anything you did would only be a silly palliation to hide from yourself the final evil of existence; and so you believe in Original Sin, and dislike progress, science, and humanitarianism, and go in for religion and the Middle Ages, and so-on. *This* reason for Red's poems being what they are is the same one you find in thousands of others (Allen's, for instance); but the reason I talked about first is Red's very own, all his own.

Aren't the best poems wonderful, though? They certainly make most other poets look sick and trivial. I'd certainly love to write an article about them — but it would be embarrassing and impossible, so I've just written a little of it in this private form. I don't think anything short of my theory can explain how anybody as intelligent as Red, anybody that can write the best parts of his poetry, can write and be satisfied with the worst parts of his poems and novels. It was amusing to me how few people reviewed *At Heaven's Gate:* they reviewed the sort of book that a man of Red's eminence, intelligence, and connections should have written; and never noticed (or never confessed they did) the real one.

I play a good deal of tennis, there are several nice players here, nice in both senses. I drew a picture of myself the other day that I wish you could see: it's very like, but makes me look so childish, rueful, and tousled that you can't help laughing.

At this point, alas, I stopped writing this letter for three or four weeks. Last week I had to go to 2nd Air Force Headquarters (Colorado Springs) to be interviewed about a job helping write the history of the 2nd Air Force, an awful job. I did everything I could to persuade them not to take me, and got my commanding officer to promise not to let them get me if he could help it; so I guess I'm safe.

I'm playing good tennis — I won the city doubles tournament and got to the finals of the singles.

My brother [Charles] came through, with his wife, on the way back to Los Angeles from Mexico, where they'd stayed about a year. She was very nice and he was much improved over the old days — he's become a wonderful chess player. He wrote me a day or two ago that he'd just met Morey Lewis, who was playing against [Jack] Kramer in the semi-finals of a tournament in Los Angeles.

The War's going well, isn't it? I believe it will be all over in a year and a half, or a little longer. Just think, I've already been in the army for a year and three-quarters. Gee, I've been lucky.

If you get a chance, see a movie (about a little girl) with the inaccurate title *The Cruise of the Cat People*. Parts of it are awfully good.

Have you read Christina Stead's *The Man Who Loved Children*? It's one of the best novels I've ever read.

I'll put in all the poems I've written since the last I sent you — also a photograph of Kitten that I meant to send you for a Christmas card.

I've seen just one person I knew in eight months, one of my students who came through as a pilot. It's queer how seldom I've seen anybody I used to know, in the last three years. I hope we can see each other when the war's over. I miss you and would love to see you. Write me back promptly and I promise to be as good as good can be about writing back. I hope things are better for you.

Love,
Randall

The Hamburg bomber poems were "The Angels at Hamburg," "Come to the Stone . . . ," and "Second Air Force."

Morey Lewis, Jarrell's tennis partner from Kenyon days, was now a tennis professional.

No other letters from Jarrell to Amy have been found, although several more were written, one as late as 1951. Amy remarried in the late 1940s, had children, and practiced medicine in Texas.

TO MARGARET MARSHALL

[January 1945]

Dear Miss Marshall:

I've just finished a poem I've been working on ever since I got in the army ["Siegfried"] and I thought I'd send it to you, mostly because you liked "2nd Air Force" that much.

We're a B-29 base now, and in preparation for a General's inspection we have white-washed all the stones and swept the dirt off the (dirt) streets. This sounds like a joke but it isn't.

I hope you had a nice Christmas. We always give our cat herring roe for

Christmas, but there wasn't any, so we gave him half our veal roast. Did you know we have a cat? He weighs 17 pounds, has hair six inches long, and has travelled 15,000 miles. His name is Kitten.

Yours,
Randall Jarrell

TO ALLEN TATE

[March 1945]

Dear Allen:

At present you're my main debt to the world, and hang over my head like Adam's fall. Since I obviously had to write you a very long letter, one that would take several hours, I've been putting it off, or writing part and putting it in my pocket till it wore out, and so on. I saw from your last letter that you hadn't got one I wrote you when I was still flying: I described what flying was like at some length, because it's so different from the regular romantic accounts.

I had a pretty good time when I was flying, except for being over worked; we'd get up at 5:45 and our last class was over at 10:30 at night. Often we'd fly twice in an afternoon; we got to praying for rain. Half of us were army people and half were kids being trained for navy combat pilots. All my friends were in the navy bunch; they're mostly in the Pacific now — my second best friend there, the best pilot in our whole class, was killed flying a Corsair. I'd flown about thirty hours, most of them solo, when I was washed out. It was a very great piece of luck for me.

As soon as I was washed out they applied for me as ground instructor and I started helping with the classes; but the army (*of course* as I know now) paid no attention and sent me on to Sheppard Field. I was lucky to get there when I did — six weeks later and I'd have been made a gunner. As it was I went through basic and then stayed about six weeks more waiting to go to Link school — during the time I worked as an interviewer in the classification department, and got to talk to a great many washed-out cadets, besides the regular drafted people. Sheppard was an unusual nightmare even for the army: we normally spent over four hours a day *just standing in line* — mostly in darkness, since we got up at 3:30 sun time in the middle of the winter. Your main feeling about the army, at first, is just that you can't believe it: it couldn't exist, and even if it could you would have learned what it was like from all the books, and not a one gives you even an idea. (Even the dumbest people — I've asked them — agree.) Did you read that article in *Politics* about the German concentration camps, called "Behavior

in Extreme Circumstances"? Most of what he says applies (to a much lesser
extent but very specifically) to basic and school fields in the army. Anyway,
summing up, I think the army teaches you more about people and the State
than anything else I know; prison might be as good in a simpler Society —
but not any more. You know, *The House of the Dead* would probably be the
best book for people to read before they get in the army.

I went on to Chanute, where I stayed seven months. The longest I remember — I went to Link Trainer school and then to Celestial Navigation
Training school, besides waiting around before, between, and after the
schools — doing K.P., painting, sweeping, mopping, washing windows,
shovelling dirt, planting grass, and so on — once I made a list of jobs I'd
done in the army and it took two pages. The general atmosphere was very
prison-campish, but what I minded most was just physical pain and exhaus-
tion, since besides all the school, physical labor jobs, and everything else we
did two hours a day of running, duck-walking, crawling on our stomachs,
inventive calisthenics (obstacle courses, oddly enough, were considered a
rest), and anything else the P.T. sergeant we unluckily had could think of. I
felt so strongly about everything I saw (the atmosphere was entirely one of
lying, meaningless brutality and officiousness, stupidity not beyond belief
but conception — the one word for everything in the army is *petty*) that,
stiff, sore, and sleepy, I'd sit up at night in the day room — all the other
lights were out — writing poems, surrounded by people playing pool or
writing home or reading comic-strip magazines.

The army enlisted schools are bad beyond belief. For the first couple of
years of the war the general in charge of all the air corps enlisted schools (all
except the cadet schools) was a man who'd been last in his class at West
Point, missing flunking out by .000, or something like that; consequently
he distrusted examinations, lectures, or anything else normally associated
with education. As a result in our schools formal lectures were forbidden,
written tests for examinations were forbidden, direct questions were forbidden; at one time use of the blackboard was forbidden. *Nobody* was washed
out of any school for being helplessly stupid, not understanding anything,
not doing any work (you could get washed out only for going AWOL or
quarreling with the school officials); everybody sat on till the end of school
and left with the same diploma. I've had crew chiefs tell me that they
couldn't trust their mechanics straight from school to do anything but
wash the planes.

Anyway, at last I left Chanute and went to Salt Lake City and lived in a
tent (I enjoyed that a lot — only five others instead of a hundred); since it
was the middle of the winter all our tent city had thick smoke, a layer,

hanging over the tents — the airplanes landed about 150 yards away over a drainage ditch, and at night it was like a Christmas tree with all the red and green airport lights.

By a wonderful piece of luck I was sent to Tucson (some of the 2nd Air Force fields are a hundred miles from the nearest town); besides its other virtues, it has the oldest and consequently the best CNT department in the country. The people in the department are awfully nice; I get along with them better than any bunch of people I've ever been with. Our officers are returned combat navigators. The department is hardly like the army at all. Besides that the field is good, the best in the second Air Force. Real fields are different from basic or school fields. I live off post with Mackie and Kitten, and (though I *wish* the war were over) keep saying unbelievingly to myself, "Jesus, how lucky you are!" Because whether you're here or in China, alive or dead, is a *pure* accident.

The first few months I had to work from midnight to eight o'clock, which was miserable; we still sometimes work at oddish hours, but not that odd. Our field's just been made a B-29 field.

What I do is run a tower that lets people do celestial navigation on the ground. In a tower about forty feet high a fuselage like the front of a bomber is hung; it flies the way a Link Trainer does. The navigator (sometimes pilots and bombardiers too) sits in it, and navigates by shooting with his sextant the stars that are in a star dome above his head — we move them pretty much as a planetarium operator does. Also we have radio transmitters he can get radio fixes from, and a sort of movie-projector arrangement that he can do pilotage with. He flies a regular four-hour mission; besides running and setting up the tower, we record his fixes and other stuff, correct them if he's made mistakes, and so forth. Nobody ever even comes near the trainers except perhaps one of our officers; it's our job and we aren't interfered with. I like the job very much. It's extremely useful: a navigator improves as much after five flights in our trainer as he would after ten or fifteen regular flights. One trainer in a year certainly saves five or six bombers and five or six crews: there'd be that many crashes in the same number of real flights. We're giving navigators their last three-months training just before combat.

Since I spend a good deal of time on the bus to and from the field, and since you always have a good deal of extra stuff besides your real job (K.P., calisthenics, parades, etc.), I don't have too much time to write — though lots to read. What I've read has been mostly symbolic logic and philosophy — everybody in my trainer starts laughing at the mere sight of a book full of nothing but Capital letters. I played a lot of tennis last year —

Johnny Faunce, the fifth pro in the country, was here, besides some other good players. Also I've played football a lot; our department team won the Base Championship.

Mackie has a good Red Cross job, so we've enough money. A friend of mine here, a boy named Arthur Blair, has an awfully good library — which is lucky, because the University of Arizona library is one more by grace than grammar. I've written quite a lot of poems, enough so that I've a book of army ones. I've been making lots of notes for articles; I wrote a long prose review for Rahv because I couldn't bear not to review Lowell: I knew that I knew how good his book [*Land of Unlikeness*] was, and would say so, and I wasn't too hopeful that other reviewers would do either.

Your first *Sewanee* was very imposing, I thought — not to mention pretty. I'll bet you were surprised at what you got from Gregory: after his remark about James Whitcomb Riley and "Billie Potts" surely nobody will ever again listen to anything he says about anything. I liked Cal's poem; I finished my review of him ["Poetry in War and Peace," *Partisan Review*, Winter 1945] by saying "Some of the best poems of the next years ought to be written by him," and I certainly believe it.

What do you think of Auden's last book [*The Double Man*] and Shapiro's [*V-Letter and Other Poems*]?

Have you ever read the stuff about signs in [C. S.] Peirce that [Charles W.] Morris sketches [in *Foundations of the Theory of Signs*]? — I know you've read the Morris because you write about it. It's confused but good. An extremely good book that you might not have read (it seems well-known in England but I've never seen it mentioned in American magazines) is [Henry H.] Price's *Perception;* it's the best modern book on epistemology I've ever read.

I've been making a great many notes about Auden (I feel as if I ought to put the James–Ford *poor* before his name); I'm going to take them and what I've done about him in the past and write a book about him.

This is an *I, I,* letter, but I'm the only person I know anything about; I haven't seen anybody I know in a year and a quarter, and during the first year I was in the army I had no time to write letters (except long ones to Mackie) and got out of the habit of writing any at all.

As I needn't say, I was delighted about Sewanee and [editing] the *Review;* it ought to be perfect for you, I imagine.

It was funny (but nice, nice) to see the world suddenly become conscious of Red's poetry. Put in any news about him when you write, will you? (This is on the hopeful assumption that you'll forgive me for not writing for so long. I do feel very apologetic for not writing during '44; but I don't feel apologetic for *anything* in '43 that year the lions ate *me*.)

Give my love to Caroline and Nancy. How does Nancy like Sewanee? It's too bad that everybody isn't at Nashville still. Being in Nashville — or for that matter in Austin — seems as far off to me as living by the ocean when I was a child. I can no longer imagine not being in the army. I mean that literally; I think often about being out, and what a dream of joy it will be, but I can't really imagine it. When I think of before the war I always have the feeling, How did they *let* me?

The *Kenyon* has gotten pretty bad, don't you think? When I looked at the last issue I had this feeling: Universities regularly have a quarterly for the professors and a literary magazine for the students, but here they've combined them in one magazine.

But I guess it's pretty hard to get good things: the condition of literature is certainly awful.

We're very gay because we're about to move to an apartment; Tucson is so crowded that we've just lived in a room for the first year. When you get tourists, soldiers' families, aircraft workers, and "health-seekers" all in one town it's rather like the cauldron in *Macbeth,* but more expensive.

I think I have a fairly good chance of being here for the rest of the war; there are almost no CNT towers abroad — they're too complicated, fortunately.

I'm beginning to run down so far as this letter is concerned, though that's just because I never really started on what the army is like. Don't believe anything you read about it in the newspapers and magazines unless you also start believing the Listerine and National Association of Manufacturers advertisements.

Forgive me for not writing for so long — this must be almost a page a month, though I hope you're well and happy; I really am both.

Affectionately,
Randall

At the time this letter was written, Tate was living in Monteagle, Tennessee, and teaching at the University of the South, in Sewanee, where he was contributing to the Sewanee Review.

Jarrell's dismissing sentence about Horace Gregory referred to Gregory's comment, in his "Of Vitality, Regionalism and Satire," in the Sewanee Review, *October 1944. About Warren's poem "The Ballad of Billie Potts" Gregory wrote, "This experiment in verse . . . need not be taken too seriously, but a sober generalization can be drawn from it . . . the writing of 'dialect verse' is always a questionable exercise and it makes little difference whether the author's name is James Whitcomb Riley or an anonymous John Smith . . ."*

[April 4, 1945]

Dear Allen:

I was awfully glad to get your letter. I'll send most of the newish poems I have. I've put stars by the titles of the unpublished ones — you can use any of these that you care for. Tell me as soon as you decide, will you? — I might as well get them all printed in magazines before my book comes out. I just saw yours [*The Winter Sea*], which is about the prettiest poetry book I ever saw — I'm crazy about that type. Dial is printing mine; Rahv arranged everything with them and then asked me if I'd like to do it. When I said yes they stunned me by giving me $250 advance royalties. Incidentally, you might mention it (book, not $250) with me in the contributors column; its name is *Little Friend, Little Friend* (how bombers call in fighters over the radio) and it's coming out early this summer.

You ask if I've any prose I could send you; well, I will have, by late summer anyway, on Auden. I've been making many notes (in time spare enough for note-taking but not for poem-writing) for a book on Auden — I had my *Southern Review* article and old notes for a start; I'm going to make several articles out of different parts, and if you would like one I'll write it for you.

I'll *bet* you're having trouble getting decent short stories. There was once a senator who said about a dime-novel called *Omoo the Huron:* "The man who doesn't like it isn't fit to live"; something very nearly the opposite of this applies to short stories As We Write Them.

I hope you take the six months off for the job in Paris: think of being a *diplomat*! Opera hats and six-inch (wide) red ribbons from Bond Street, ballerinas from the Caucasus, code from the Gold Bug, and all the rest from all the other places. And after the war I'll call you *sir*. But I'd probably do that anyway, I'm so used to saying *Sir* over the interphone to eighteen-year-old navigators so fresh from cadet school that they call me Sir, too. It's surprising how hard it is to distinguish them from most of the ones back from overseas, though. If you met your proconsuls you'd find you couldn't differentiate them from a high school football team, except for the fact that half of them had gotten killed during the season. I knew a girl whose husband, a pilot, graduated from Randolph Field a day or so after Pearl Harbor; out of his class of twenty-five there are just two left alive.

I can't imagine Nancy grown-up, so I obviously can't imagine her married and with a baby. You know, I've just seen her twice since she grew old and thin — so the real Nancy, to me, is a fat little girl who surely can't have ceased to exist, but is waiting sullenly somewhere for you to discover that the other is an impostor.

What sort of ensign is Nancy's husband? I hope very much it's one of the safe sorts.

My cousin, Howell Campbell's son, got badly shot up the third day of the Normandy invasion; he can't move or feel his left arm, though they're grafting nerves and ought to be successful.

Mackie's gone to San Francisco for a week on Red Cross business, so I'm sitting here playing with Kitten trying to console him; he keeps uneasily wandering around.

This letter should put me, so far as letter writing is concerned, in the class of those reformed pirates who testify at temperance meetings.

> Affectionately,
> Randall

Unfortunately I waited about a month to send this till I'd typed some poems. I forget whether you read *The Nation* much; I had a good poem ["The Wide Prospect"] in their winter issue, I'll save typing by assuming you read *The Nation*.

> *During 1945, Tate, as editor of the* Sewanee Review, *published five poems of Jarrell's and one short story of Peter Taylor's, "Rain in the Heart." That same year, the* Kenyon Review *published a poem of Jarrell's brother, Charles, entitled "The Writing Exercise."*
>
> *Jarrell's reference to Tate's being a diplomat was partly on the strength of Tate's appointment as a Fellow in American Letters for the Library of Congress and partly in reference to the possibility of his being cultural attaché at the American embassy in Paris. Both of these honors were recommended by the Librarian of Congress, Archibald MacLeish. Tate remained a Fellow for five years, but he did not go to Paris.*

TO ALLEN TATE

[May 10, 1945]

Dear Allen:

This in haste, as the saying goes, because I don't want you and *Poetry* cutting me up into little repugnant chunks. You didn't notice what I said in my letter, that you were welcome to any of the poems *with stars by the titles* — the others, I was just sending you to read, as you asked me to. "The State," "The Snow-Leopard" (what do you mean where did I get the caravan? It grew in me) and "News" I'm delighted that you're going to use; but *Poetry* already has "Gunner" and "A Pilot from the Carrier," and *The Nation* "Siegfried."

I'm sure that these poems (with the exception of "Siegfried," perhaps) aren't better than my prewar ones, but they, except "Siegfried," aren't by any means the nicest, of my war productions. Wait till you see them all together. Seriously, I do want to give you something "as good as I can do," and I'll send you the best thing I've done in months and months and months: a long poem, almost 150 lines, named "The Märchen." This you can enter in the memorial contest, it's not in my book, but I am sending it to you, and would send it without the contest; if you didn't exist I'd send it to Margaret Marshall just for the virtuoso performance of getting her to print 150 lines — I have worked her up to 75 and feel great confidence.

You know, I guessed you would want "The Snow-Leopard," "The State," and "News," (and obviously "Siegfried"), but I didn't realize you'd want "Gunner" and "A Pilot" — I guess you really *are* interested in airplanes.

I feel grieved about not being able to let you have "Gunner" and "Pilot," and I'll put in two poems to take their place (if you like them). For a guess, you'll like "To the New World" better than either.

You understand that I'm not unsympathetic to writing about airplanes "like Tate"; I thought the part [you had] when they kill the Dalai Lama wonderful, and even more wonderfully characteristic.

Thanks awfully for your book [*The Winter Sea*]; it's the prettiest book of poems I've ever seen. The poems I like best are "Seasons of the Soul" I, II, and III, the Air Corps "Ode," and "Jubilo"; and parts of "Winter Mask"; the first part of III and the last of V, for instance. And "Ecologue" makes *The Waste Land* seem a cheerful moderate poem: the last part is an absolutely kinaesthetic expression of that state of being.

I put in something named "1914" for you to read; but not for the *Review* — I've already sent it to Rahv to console him for "The Wide Prospect," which he wanted but I had sent to *The Nation*. Did you like it?

The only Southern subjects I ever thought of writing about are you, Red, and Mr. Ransom — your poems, I mean; but to really explain what Red's poems are like you need to talk about what Red is like. This is certainly a difficulty one's spared with you. I was awfully disappointed in Schwartz's article about your poetry ["Poetry of Allen Tate," *Southern Review,* Winter 1940]; but I have never read anything smart about your poetry. English writers always seem especially helpless with it, which shows that it is really indigenous. When this 100 Years War is over I am going to write a long, long article — but first you'll have to give me an indulgence signed in blank.

What do you think of Auden's poetry of the last two or three years? I think some of it is rather bad and the rest disgraceful.

If I were French I'd write an article about the influence of Saint-Simon on Proust and Stendhal.

Tell me what news you know about Red; I know that he's in Washington, that Cenina is an invalid (with what?), and nothing else.

Yours affectionately,
Randall

Warren had succeeded Tate as poetry consultant at the Library of Congress. Cenina was suffering from depression.

TO ROBERT LOWELL

[August 1945]
Dear Cal:

I was absolutely delighted when I read the poems you sent, just about as much so as I was with the long *Partisan Review* one ["The Quaker Graveyard in Nantucket"]. I had rather read your poems than anybody else in the world who is writing now. Your *general* level now is getting up to the level of the best six or seven in the book [*Land of Unlikeness*]. I feel very smart to have predicted in *Partisan* that some of the best poems of our time were going to be written by you; I was so sure of it then that I was perfectly willing to stick my neck out. I've already written lots of comments (scrappy and wholly approving ones) on the *Partisan* poems; I'll do the same thing with the new ones.

I'm glad you feel the way you do about "Siegfried"; I think it's the best poem I've written during the war except for one new one ["Burning the Letters"]. I'll now tell you something that will amuse you; of the poems in the *Sewanee* and *Kenyon* that you were reading, you picked to like not only the poems I like, but the only poems in the bunch that have been written in the last year and a half — all the others are old poems which I gave Tate and Ransom mostly because I had nothing more to give — "News," for instance, I actively dislike. Now this shows, I hope (1) how objective our taste is (2) how much better I am than I used to be. I'm glad you like "The State" that much, I particularly love it. Tell Jean that I too "guessed who wrote it when I read the first line"; anyway, if she knows anybody else who would start a poem "When they killed my mother it made me nervous," I wish she'd tell me who he is, and he and I will form a society.

I have written a poem ["Pilots, Man Your Planes"] about the length of "Siegfried" that I hope is as good; I need about two words and then it will be finished — when it is I'll send it to you.

I believe you're right, that this next year will be the last year of the army. If it doesn't end in the next few months I'll be overseas — maybe, even if it does. I'll certainly be glad to see you. I haven't even seen anybody I *know* in three years. You are the only writer I feel much in common with (when I read your poems I not only wish that I had written them but feel that mine in some queer sense are related to them — i.e., if I didn't write the way I do I might or would like to write the way you do; your poems about the war are the only ones I like except my own — both of them have the same core of sorrow and horror and so on) and the only good friend of my own age I have.

I'm working hard on my Auden; an article about his ideas. It has a long section about Paul, and shorter ones about Luther and Calvin — if I had space I'd put in sections about Kierkegaard, Barth and the other Neo-Calvinists, etc. It will shock you to know that for six or eight months I have read almost nothing but theology, the most gigantic quantities of it you can imagine. (After the war I'm going to write a book on Paul.) I don't know whether I need to say that the knowledge hasn't converted me. Judging from your poems, I can hardly believe that you have the orthodox Catholic position about Grace; will you please (*be sure to*) write me a summary of what you believe about Grace, faith, whether works ever *merit* salvation, etc.?

I am filling out lots of junk for a Guggenheim; Ransom wrote me that their guy Moe brought the subject of me up as Somebody he wanted to give a fellowship to. I imagine I'll get one. Now this is a secret. The money part of it: Henry Holt asked me to do a book for their "American Men of Letters" series (just dead ones — I picked Hart Crane) and they're giving me $2,500 advance to write it with. So, if I get the Guggenheim, I'll be able to spend at least two years up East doing nothing but writing. I have plenty of things to write about: General Patton and the three soldiers he kicked and slapped, first of all using this as a sort of archetypal event. I can't wait to get out of the army.

I certainly was sorry about Alexander Kuh [Lowell's cat]. Anything happening to one's cat is the most painful subject in the world, so far as I'm concerned. I liked your story ["The Homefront"] in *Partisan* extremely, Jean (I started to write a separate letter to answer Jean's postcard; then when I was at the field without paper I used the back of the page for my Auden article, so *that* letter's done for), and felt indignant at their giving first prize to Schwartz's much inferior (but ideologically *so* much more congenial to *P.R.*) story. *But* I had the horrible feeling all through the story that so far as I was concerned — it was a subject nobody *should* write about; that's crazy, but, boy, that was the way I felt. Two or three times I dreamed that something had happened to Kitten, about the worst dreams I've ever had; I would wake up and not go back to sleep for several hours; evidently my subconscious has decided that such dreams are too bad for me to have, since I haven't had one in a year.

What you said in the last letter about the typical protagonist of my poems is true and I am quite aware of it. This is not only the way I feel about people in the war, it's the way I judge. Including German prisoners and former air-crew members, pilots, navigators, etc. I've met thousands of people who've killed great quantities of other people and had great quantities of their companions killed; and there's not one out of a hundred who *knows* enough about it to kill a fly or be stung by a fly. Talking about a slaughter of the innocents! And those are the *soldiers,* not the civilians. You should see a diagram of the latest type incendiary (it's literally impossible to put *it* out) they use, on the Japanese cities. What a nightmare!

Doesn't this long letter shame you, you who print out 100-word night letters and then mistakenly send them by mail?

I am eager to talk with you about theology after the war. I am, I have to admit, a born theologian: I can read stuff at top speed, remember it all, and have my eyes light up whenever I think of the distinguishing characteristics of some minor heresy. Best of all I love doing genetic explanations of it — I have some anthropological theories that would surprise many theologians.

I wrote this about two weeks ago, before the atomic bomb and the peace. You can guess how I feel about both — especially about Nagasaki, which was bombed simply to test out the second type of bomb.

God knows when I'll get out — nine months (say) if the War Department has its way, four to six if Congress yells enough.

Please send me any other poems you have. I don't need nice typed copies; any sort will do. Especially send me the new version of the one in *Partisan* ["The Quaker Graveyard in Nantucket"].

I'm working miserably hard on my Auden; the misery has been added to by having to go to work at four every morning.

They'll have *Little Friend, Little Friend* printed early next month — I've already corrected page proofs. I'll send you one as soon as I get any.

I hope you're both well and happy. I wish I could see you.

Affectionately,
Randall

In his essay "Randall Jarrell" in Randall Jarrell, 1914–1965, *Lowell wrote, "Randall was the only man I have ever met who could make other writers feel that their work was more important to him than his own. I don't mean that he was in the habit of saying to people he admired, 'This is much better than anything I could do.' Such confessions, though charming, cost little effort. What he did was to make others feel that their realizing themselves was as close to him as his own self-realization, and that he cared as much about making the nature and goodness of someone else's work understood as he cared about making his own understood."*

TO MARGARET MARSHALL

[September 1945]

Dear Miss Marshall:

The Army's just completed a lot of preparations to send me overseas — though something might still go wrong — so I wanted to send you a poem ["Pilots, Man Your Planes"] before I go. I think it's the best poem I've written about the war; if you like it perhaps you can use it in the late fall, after my book's out.

I was awfully pleased with the arrangements Henry Holt made about the [Hart] Crane book, and feel very grateful to you for asking me to do it.

The proof *The Nation* sent of my "Dead Wingman" had no errors at all, so I made the Freudian error of losing it.

May I use you as one of my literary references in a Guggenheim application? As a matter of fact, this is a hypocritical request, because I've already done it — I was rushing at it before getting sent away, so I guess what I'm really asking is for you to say it was all right.

I'm looking forward to seeing you in New York after the war's over: all the training people who were kept in this country during the war are being sent over to the Pacific, and we won't be back for quite a while, the War Department willing.

I was awfully pleased with all the responses to the little Mauldin review: by the way how did *it* happen? I can't look at the Anzio one — *"My God, we wuz there and they wuz here!"* — without getting tears in my eyes. How any person in the whole world could think that funny or intended to be funny is hard to see.

I feel so rotten about the country's response to the bombings at Hiroshima and Nagasaki that I wish I could become a naturalized dog or cat. I believe our culture's chief characteristic, to a being from outside it, would be that we are *liars.* That all except a few never tell or feel anything near the truth about anything we do. Though even at that we're not bad enough to deserve the end we are going to get.

Have you read the [Abram] Kardiner books connected with the *Plaintown* book you reviewed? They are awfully good.

Yours,
Randall Jarrell

John Senior's "little" review of William H. Mauldin's cartoon book Up Front *in* The Nation *was entitled "Not Funny" and attacked the cartoons for frivolousness and poor grammar. A laudatory review by King Gordon, "W. H. Mauldin's War," appeared in* The Nation's *next issue.*

Abram Kardiner was a psychiatrist trained by Freud.

Plainville, USA *by James West is the book Marshall mentioned in her "Notes by the Way" section in* The Nation.

TO ROBERT LOWELL

[September 1945]

Dear Cal:

We'd love to visit you next summer. I've been processed for overseas shipment, but even if I'm sent (and I might, with great luck, escape) I ought to be back by summer. It would be fun to drive up together if I'm out by then.

I thought what you said about Grace much the most humane and sympathetic Catholic version, about that of Duns Scotus and the late Scholastics which Luther couldn't bear. Although it doesn't seem *true* to me, it is otherwise attractive, as were all your other sentences about Christianity. (I dislike Lutheran, Calvinist, or neo-Calvinist *theology* much more than Catholic, as you'll see from my Auden article which is always dealing with an extravagant Protestant tradition and position.) But I ought to tell you this: there is almost no indication of this attractive Christian attitude of your letter, *in your poems*. But I imagine this is mostly just because you haven't ever learned to put it there, since you were making the poems as grim, immediate, and weighty as possible.

I am surprised and delighted that you like Paul so much (most Catholics don't seem to; the Catholic Encyclopedia, for instance, quite plays him down in relation to Peter). I myself like him more than anybody else connected with Christianity; he was a good and wonderful man and a more-than-wonderful writer — though using the word *writer* in connection with him seems a horrible error of taste. Anyway, this ought to reassure you about what I think of him. I probably won't ever write a book on him, just a long article instead. I regard him as the founder of Christianity, to put it mildly—the common idea that he adapted or perverted a more attractive primitive Christianity is based on real ignorance.

I *am* going to write about Nagasaki. I'm going to write a lot about the war, articles and stories too.

You don't seem to have read my article about Ernie Pyle — a kind of funeral oration. It was in *The Nation* in May.

Yes, we subscribe to *Politics*. It's spotty and extravagant but has things you get nowhere else.

Give me a little précis of Delmore Schwartz in private life. That a person of his taste and intelligence should write the stories he does — half the sentences would serve as textbook models of banal and ingenuous vulgarity — is extraordinary, and must be symptomatic of some queer segmentation of his personal being into an objective part with taste and another part with nothing but adolescent self-absorption.

I enjoyed what you said about my poems and disagreed only with this:

(a) In "2nd Air Force" the rhetoric "pretty well obliterated the mother and her situation." It's a descriptive poem to show what a heavy bomber training-field was like; the mother is merely a vehicle of presentation, her situation merely a formal connection of the out-of-this-world field with the world.

(b) "The Emancipators" is "brilliant lines rather than a poem." This puzzles me so much that I'm inclined to guess that it's a peculiarity of judgement coming from the fact that Western scientific, technological, industrial development isn't as natural and obsessive a thought with you as it is with me. Did you get the parody versions of Rousseau's and Marx's statements and [Giordano] Bruno's and the rest? When I see you I will let you go over it for me; if you understand it as I do and still think it fragments, I'll really worry about it.

About [Oscar] Williams' silly anthology [*The War Poets*]: I thought Empson's "Sonnet" ordinary for Empson, [Richard] Eberhart's poems good imitative Empson, hence extraordinary for Eberhart. I like just the parts of Allen's poems that you do, though there's a petulance and subjectivity that drops them from the rank of serious first-rate poems about such a subject as the Second World war; Allen is writing about *his* second war, a very different thing. Allen's greatest fault is a defect of sympathy in the strict sense of the word, a lack of ability to identify himself with anything that is fundamentally non-Allen. Red's "Terror" has too much of his exaggeration of and obsession with violence — it's interesting that Allen should think it Red's best poem: Allen never feels the need for any *motivation* of violence — violence is to him, perhaps unconsciously, an intrinsic good. "Our Lady Peace" is very good for [Mark] Van Doren, the least interesting of all goodish poets; [William] Meredith's "Transport" starts well and gets nowhere; [MacNeice's] "Jehu" is rather good but not enough; a good deal of [Wilfred] Owen is the best anybody did with the first world war. I thought [Shapiro's] "Scyros" (a beautifully successful *tour de force*) better than [his] elegies, which have too many faults in writing and (which *matters*) in sense and feeling.

Poetry asked me to review the MacNeice [*Springboard: Poems 1941–1944*], but I turned it down because I then thought I was getting shipped overseas that week.

I think you and I were using different standards of judgement on the War Poets, mine considerably more thousand-years-are-but-a-day-in-thy-sight.

If I get a Guggenheim, as I think I will, I'm going to teach one year at Texas and then come up near New York for several years and just write. Mackie's going to the New York School for Social Work for one year and I, if the time-limit hasn't run out, am going to take one G.I. Bill-of-Rights year of psychiatry and anthropology classes from [Abram] Kardiner and [Ralph] Linton. Have you ever read Kardiner's two books?

Rahv said Dial was getting or trying to get your book [*Lord Weary's Castle*], which greatly delighted me; when I wrote them I told them how smart of them it was, that you would probably be or were one of the four or five best poets in the country, etc. Incidentally, they've behaved just surprisingly well about my book — angelic as can be. I was awfully pleased that you're taking plenty of time with it, and leaving out some of the other, and that I'll get to see it before it's a *fait accompli*. I have got to feel that poems are objective existent things which, if they could be improved by having a street-cleaner suggest that you steal one of Shakespeare's sonnets for a conclusion, *should* be so improved. But perhaps this is an excessive statement of the position.

Have you read much New Testament criticism? I read a lot during the last year: it's on a surprisingly good level, much better than "English" scholarship.

By the way, have you ever read all of Toynbee? He is not only wonderful, but has a theological position you'd like, I think.

I finish this letter 10 days later. Our "Project Wonderful" has been "deactivated" — that is, we're not shipping overseas. Things look much better. I might get out in March, for a guess.

I've just written a long poem about a carrier, "Pilots, Man Your Planes," and two short ones about Americans in the South Pacific — "New Georgia" and "The Dead in Melanesia" — having my Auden done made me feel wonderful.

Yours,
Randall

Eberhart had five poems in the anthology, among them "The Groundhog,"
"Dam Neck, Virginia," and "A World War." Tate had three poems,
"Ode," "Jubilo," and "More Sonnets at Christmas." Jarrell had nine
poems — the most of any poet in the selection: "The Emancipators,"
"Losses," "2nd Air Force," "Prisoners," "Soldier (T.P.)," "An Officers'
Prison Camp Seen from a Troop Train," "A Soldier Walks Under the
Trees of the University," and "The Death of the Ball Turret Gunner."
Jarrell did not write a poem about Nagasaki.

TO MARGARET MARSHALL

October 8, 1945

Dear Miss Marshall:

I was glad you liked "Burning the Letters." I know what you mean about the hard section: from "A child has her own faith" on to the end of that part she's thinking about her own earlier very-Protestant beliefs — they're very like Paul in Romans, and "by man came death" is Paul — but thinking about them in images drawn from her husband, a carrier pilot helping burn the Japanese cities. This part about her belief and her gradual loss of it ends with "The dying God, the eaten Life/ Are the nightmare I awaken from to night." Then for an instant she thinks (in the part in parentheses) about the death and burial of the early Christians who completely believed it all, and then thinks about the antithetical death and burial of her husband and those like him: she thinks that he and they literally died for her (that her life came out of their deaths) just as Christ is supposed to have died for her; it's because of this that I used "it is finished" for the climax of what she says. So far as I can see this is all literally true: they died for us just the sort of atoning death, a death not for their own sins but for ours (after all, most of them were kids just out of high school — [I] believe the majority of such people that died were too young to vote), that Christ is supposed to have died.

I not only didn't get sent overseas (our Project Wonderful was "de-activated" just as it was due to leave) but am going to get a furlough; I feel wonderful.

I just sent you a *Little Friend, Little Friend;* I hope reading the short poems will give you as much pleasure as your printing all the long poems has given me.

Sincerely,
Randall Jarrell

TO ROBERT LOWELL

October 15th [1945]

Dear Cal:

I am going to get a 45 day furlough. We'll be in Nashville for two weeks or so, beginning about the 5th or 6th of November. You say in your letter that you'll be at Sewanee early in November: so we ought to be able to see each other a lot and go over the poems [for *Lord Weary's Castle*] in detail. Could you and Jean be in Nashville some of that time?

That wouldn't delay your getting the manuscript to Dial more than a couple of weeks. Anyway, the day you get this please write me back air mail special delivery at 2027½ East Helen, Tucson, Arizona — so I can know that it's all right to keep the poems. (It's too late for that address; write me instead c/o Mrs. Kay Langham, 705 W. 8th, Austin, Texas.)

The poems you're keeping from *Land of Unlikeness* are just those I'd keep, except for "On the Eve of the Feast of the Immaculate Conception." I think there are several reasons for not using it unless rewritten. I'll talk about these when I see you. This will be just a note — I'll talk about *everything* when I see you.

I'll put in this letter the poems you sent me earlier, most of which I've written up. I'm pretty sure "Forest Hills Cemetery" is better without the last stanza, which runs down like a toy.

Things in the army are looking good — I might very well get out in February.

Margaret Marshall has asked me to do all the poetry reviewing for *The Nation* — their Verse Chronicle, I think they call it. Although I'd made up my mind not to do any more separate reviews, I can't bear not to accept, both for selfish and virtuous reasons. You can spend most of your time on the good books when you get them all, and when the same readers read you steadily you don't have to keep repeating your first principles in each new review.

Have you seen my long poem ["Burning the Letters"] in *The Nation*'s Fall Book Number? I think it comes out this week.

I've written another poem about carriers, 100 lines or so, that's really hair-raising — strictly objective descriptive stuff ["Pilots, Man Your Planes"].

I'll stop. See you in November. Give Jean our love.

Yours,
Randall

TO ROBERT LOWELL

[November 1945]

Dear Cal:

Everything went wrong with my furlough — it was cancelled after I'd been in Austin a week and a half, and I had to come back here to be shipped away so they said; but I haven't been. I'll probably get a job in the separation center here and be here till I'm discharged, in two or three months. Everything's been thoroughly upset, so I haven't been able to do your poems.

I was grieved to see the Bayeux Tapestry poem ["France"] (one of your very best short poems) murdered and its injured limb made part of the Old Testament; I wish you'd use it as a separate poem regardless.

I don't think you ought to use the "Immaculate Conception" in your book: Some of the first part is too much like Allen's Short-and-Kimmel poem ["Ode to Our Young Pro-Consuls of the Air"], and "Oh, if soldiers mind you well/ they shall find you are their belle/ and belly too;/ Christ's bread and beauty came by you./ Celestial Hoyden" is pure Hopkins. (Hopkins — with — a redcoat, too.) The last stanza is good but you could use that somewhere else. It's too mannered a poem, both form and content. All this might be wrong, but I'm sure this isn't: it won't impress favorably some of your readers and reviewers. But, as I wrote before, I agree about all the others you're using from your first book; it's the same list I would make, except I'd put in "Christ for Sale," too. (Though certainly most of your readers and reviewers won't like *it.*)

The only one of the new bunch of sonnets I like is "The Soldier": if I were you I'd not use the others ("Pentecost," "Midas," "Babel," "The Benedictines") in this book, but let them lie around awhile and see what you want to do with them.

I certainly am angry that everything went wrong so we couldn't see each other and go over the poems — I was looking forward to it a lot.

"Mr. Edwards and the Spider" is tremendously effective the way it is now. It's an awfully good poem. "As a Plane Tree by the Water" seems to me only pretty good. I like all of the changes in "At a Bible House" except the last two lines, which don't seem an effective ending to me. "Winter in Dunbarton" is better with the changes: it's a very good poem with wonderfully good parts. "The Dead in Europe" is very good. "The Exile's Return" is not only very good but charming and ingenious. "War" is awfully nice. I think "Hooker's Statue" is still in a transitional stage rather than in its last resting-place; if I were you I'd leave it out of this book. (Remember it's almost impossible to have a book of poems too short: the more poems, the more confused the reviewers and readers.) "Colloquy in Black Rock" is an *awfully* good poem, just wonderfully done. So is "Christmas in Black Rock." "At the Indian Killer's Grave" is a beautiful resting-place for all those lines from your first graveyard poem: it's *quite* good and parts are wonderfully clever. But "the hollow noddle" is better than "the hairless headpiece" and the part that's left out helps with the effect and ought to be left in, I think. The *man hole* and *hole* are better. I like *cracks* walnuts better. *Gospel* seems better than *guide,* though the rhythm's more awkward with *gospel. The* wailing valley is better — the *the* just gets assimilated in the scansion, pretty much. *Bone foot* is wonderful with *Death, the engraver.* I think King Philip's original speech much better than the new; it ought to be kept. (It *is* odd to have him referring to his own gashed and green perfection.) As I wrote before, I think the first two stanzas of "Forest Hills Cemetery" make a good poem by themselves, and are hurt a lot by the last stanza, which is a little too personal-reference à la Yeats — you expect him to turn out to be Lady Gregory's sister-in-law. "Where the Rainbow Ends" is one of your very best poems from every point of view: one of the best religious poems in hundreds of years.

About "The Quaker Graveyard in Nantucket": This is your very best big poem, so you ought to be tremendously careful with it. I like all of the new [part] III except "the waters of the proud," which doesn't seem effective enough or very *so:* The Quakers weren't notably proud, were they? I think the new Stanza V with Versailles and Napoleon a *great* mistake: it takes you out of the world of the poem, is too didactic. "Time was ripe to take a broom and clear this room our vestibule to crime" brings in bric a brac that doesn't fit, and generally weakens and dissipates the effect of the whole poem. I beg you to leave it out. *And* to leave out [part] *VII* which seems overwritten, too rhetorical, not really functioning in the poem. "Snaps your spine across Poseidon's shine" seems too calculated to shock, along with the *disgusting* gulls and *debauched* Atlantic. Then look at all this extreme rhetoric: "green-eyed liquefaction"; "fiery deluge, corrosive smoulder of its mould"; "the knock and knowledge of the rainbow's fouled/ and halcyon summer"; "loud-mouthed terror howled"; "time's lubricious feath-

ers." And this seems awfully contrived and rhetorical, a tour de force but
awkward too:

> Descending, harnessed, harassed, huge,
> Horse up the ocean, spun
> In the fiery deluge,
> World-wide?

If you're not convinced about these stanzas 5 and 7 tell me and I'll write
more at length — I'm absolutely convinced myself that the poem is much
better without them.

I think *Lord Weary's Castle* a good private title but a bad public one: it
won't convey anything to most readers. You might get a good title from
Paul — there are dozens or hundreds — and it might get over more to your
readers. But this doesn't matter much, of course.

"Caron, Non Ti Crucciare" is the most Lowellish poem there ever was;
I'm too exhausted to judge it. I fancy it's too extreme to be a good poem as
it is — there are *swell* parts — it certainly is a tour de force.

I myself wouldn't add that new stanza (that you sent separately) to the
"Quaker Graveyard." I think the poem is much more unified than you realize — it's extremely difficult to add parts that really function. You say in the
note with it that you think you ought to leave out "Babel" and "Pollio." I
think so too. Parts of "Pollio" are good, especially the last part, but you can
improve it; *and* it won't get over with most people, certainly.

I hardly know what to say about Allen and Caroline: in a way I think
anything that will violently change Allen's life will be good for him — he's
his own ruts. Just think how little he's changed in the last ten years, and
think how much Mr. Ransom, a much older man, has changed. But I
haven't seen them in so long. I hope it isn't hard on Caroline.

Are you staying up north all winter or what? Give my love to Jean.
We'll be awfully glad to see you.

Affectionately,
Randall

To continue several days later: I've almost been shipped out three times
in a week, always just escaping; but temporarily I'm better off now. They're
releasing men with 42 months service now; when they drop it to 36 I'm
out.

I am extremely eager to get to talk to you about the poems for days or
weeks before you get a final version of your book. If we get out by January
or February do you suppose you and Jean could possibly come down to

Nashville if I arranged for a place for you to stay and things for you to do? Nashville's halfway between us. I think it's terribly important for you to get your book absolutely perfect so far as inclusions, omissions, or little changes are concerned, for this reason: it will be the best first book of poems since Auden's *Poems,* and might, with luck or sense on people's part, be a wonderful success. I think the best nine or ten of your new poems are better than any poem in *Land of Unlikeness;* not only that, I think they are some of the best poems anybody has written in our time, and are sure to be read for hundreds of years. I am *sure* of this: I would bet hundreds of dollars on it. You know how little contemporary poetry I like: if I'm affected this way — unless I've gone crazy — it must be the real thing. I think you're potentially a better poet than anybody writing in English. I think your biggest limitations right now are (1) not putting enough about *people* in the poems — they are more about the actions of you, God, the sea, and cemeteries than they are about the "actions of men"; (2) being too harsh and severe — but this is already changing, very much for the better too, *I* think. Contemporary satires (which you don't seem to write any more) are your weakest sort of poem, and are not really worth wasting your time on; your worst tendency is to do too-mannered, mechanical, wonderfully contrived, exercise poems; but these you don't do much when you feel enough about the subject or start from a real point of departure in contemporary real life. I think you write more in the great tradition, the grand style, the real *middle* of English poetry, than anybody since Yeats.

I hope all this won't make you faint or retire, your work done; it ought to make you spend all your time writing poetry. Nothing is so foolish as doing what Red does; wasting your life on textbooks, criticism, and so-so novels when you are a good poet.

I'm very glad you're using some of the best parts of your old "Protestant Cemetery" in "The Indian Killer"; I always did like lots of it very much. I've gone over the early "Indian Killer" and written down on it the only changes (in the second version) that seem to me to improve it.

From what the Dial people say in their letter to me I can tell they are crazy about the idea of publishing your book. They are awfully nice publishers — you can tell from my book that they'll try to make yours as pretty as they can.

I think your best poems (leaving out the ones in *Land of Unlikeness;* I've already told you which of those I like best) are "The Quaker Graveyard," "Colloquy in Black Rock," "Where the Rainbow Ends," "Mr. Edwards and the Spider," "The Exile's Return," "Christmas in Black Rock," "The Indian Killer's Grave," "The Dead in Europe," "Winter in Dunbarton"; "Forest

Hills Cemetery" (2 stanzas) is almost as good; your *Partisan* Bayeux Tapestry poem ["France"] is easily in your first fifteen poems, I think, and ought to be preserved even if you do use it in "Caron, Non Ti Crucciare" (which I'm not judging — it's good but I don't know how good, and I'm pretty sure there ought to be changes). There are a couple more almost as good but not quite. I'm running out of ink and will stop. Our love to Jean.

Randall

The Tates had separated and were planning to divorce.

In the end, Roman Catholic Robert Giroux persuaded Roman Catholic Robert Lowell to publish Lord Weary's Castle *with Harcourt, Brace instead of Dial.*

TO PHILIP RAHV

[November 6, 1945]

Dear Rahv:

I was pleased and flattered by your invitation to write the Poetry Chronicle [for *Partisan Review*] — and amused too, because Margaret Marshall asked me to do the same thing for her about a month ago. Whether I could or should do it for you I don't know, though I'd certainly review things rather differently for the two audiences. I might try it for three issues and see how it goes — it wouldn't be too much trouble, since I'd be reading all the stuff anyway. *Or* I could do just one for you, and you could get other people to do the other two. You choose. I believe I'd enjoy doing it for three issues: I always have about six times as much to say about poets as I have space, and it would be a pleasure to get the ratio down to three-to-one.

My furlough was cancelled and I'm back at the field; but *really* I ought to be out in the next two months. I might get a job near Philadelphia [at Haverford College] — which would be nice in relation to *Partisan*; anyway, I'll be spending one of the next two years up near New York, so I'll get to see you all.

I'm glad I skipped the [Bertrand] Russell — it's a disheartening book [*A History of Western Philosophy*].

I'll send you to use in *Partisan* — if you like it — the armiest army poem I've written ["The Lines"]. I wrote it last spring. [Martin] Greenberg asked me to do a review, and said my poems thoroughly brought back his army days, so I put the poem in my letter. He wrote back he wanted it for *Politics,* so I politely though rather reluctantly consented (I wanted more people to read it). My reluctance must have shone through my politeness — they never used it. All this happened long, long ago — about VE day. Anyway, I want it printed before everybody's demobilized.

I certainly agree about Dial and my book — they did a wonderful job.

Yours,
Randall Jarrell

The Lines

After the centers' naked files, the basic line
Standing outside a building in the cold
Of the late or early darkness, waiting
For meals or mail or salvage, or to wait
To form a line to form a line to form a line;
After the things have learned that they are things,
Used up as things are, pieces of the plain
Flat object-language of a child or states;
After the lines, through trucks, through transports, to the lines
Where the things die as though they were not things —
But lie as numbers in the crosses' lines;
After the files that ebb into the rows
Of the white beds of the quiet wards, the lines
Where some are salvaged for their state, but some
Remanded, useless, to the centers' files;
After the naked things, told they are men,
Have lined once more for papers, pensions — suddenly
The lines break up, for good; and for a breath,
The longest of their lives, the men are free.

TO MARGARET MARSHALL

[December 13, 1945]

Dear Miss Marshall:

Since I've finished this Verse Chronicle ahead of time, I'm sending it on.

I hope you'll tell me about things you like in the reviews; and, more especially, about things you dislike. I'm an innocent sort of talker: unless the person I'm talking to nods or shakes his head I can hardly bear to go on to the next sentence.

Most poetry reviews hardly notice *what* the poems say: it can be banal, cruel, absurd, or fantastically reactionary and — if the poet uses the right sort of language and images, the fashionable sort — the reviewer doesn't care. It's almost as if the poet were doing ballet steps, absolutely empty technical performances, and the reviewer rightly neglected his politics or morals.

As you'll notice, I am not (usually, anyway) making unkind witty remarks about poets even if they deserve it. It makes most readers, over a period of time, distrust unfavorable judgements that they would otherwise accept.

Saturday I had to go to a border jail, get statements from witnesses about a soldier who fell out of bed and fractured his skull, and measure the bed. It was 4 feet high and 24 inches wide. Also we had to see the American Consul about a brilliant Mexican confidence man, a prisoner in the Nogales jail. He had induced two of the Mexican policemen to bring him two Negro soldiers on a faked narcotics charge — then, pretending to be chief of police, he fined them the money they had (about $300) and their car. A few years ago he induced the city of Douglas, Arizona, to buy lots of arms for protection from the revolutionists; he then bribed the police-chief in whose custody they were, took them away in a trunk, and sold them to the revolutionists.

He and the real police chief of Nogales came to the Consul to pooh-pooh the whole narcotics affair. His first words were: "Come now, Mr. So-and-so — is it likely that *I'd* be interested in that sort of thing?" Earlier this year he'd swindled the city of Buenos Aires out of $10,000, an advance on American equipment he was to buy, ostensibly for the city of Mazatlán. He neglected to buy it.

Your crime reporter,
Randall Jarrell

P.S. I just got your postcard about my *Commentary* review of [*Poems,* by] Abraham M. Klein ["These Are Not Psalms," *Commentary,* November 1945]; I was delighted you liked it so well. It was awfully kind of you to write.

TO MARGARET MARSHALL

[December 23, 1945]

Dear Miss Marshall:

Would you put this letter in your correspondence column, if you're not pressed for space? (By the way, aren't you ashamed for having printed in *The Nation* a poem ["The Wide Prospect"] whose "banal and sentimental thesis rises to hideous absurdity"?)

It certainly was nice of you to run "Pilots, Man Your Planes" all alone the way you did; it looked lovely.

Sincerely,
Randall Jarrell

P.S. Don't run the letter if you think the matter unimportant. I hated to have him say that I write the opposite of what I actually wrote. The universities have neither the power nor the inclination to "transform capitalist society," of which they are a relatively weak but relatively consenting segment.

Believe it or not, my 38 months now make me eligible for discharge, and I ought to be out by New Year's or Ground Hog Day.

The letter Jarrell intended for the correspondence column of The Nation *is unfortunately missing. It was a response to Delmore Schwartz's review of* Little Friend, Little Friend *("The Dream from Which No One Awakes,"* The Nation, *December 1, 1945). In one paragraph Schwartz wrote about "The Wide Prospect" and "The Soldier Walks Under the Trees of the University": "An effort is made to versify Marx baldly, to go from statements about trade and credit to ... mines and mills. Consequently the poem collapses. Twice, and strangely for an author like Jarrell, he permits his emotions about the war to become an anger against books and the university. The thesis of Archibald MacLeish is renewed when Jarrell attempts to say that if knowledge and scholarship were not actually the causes of war, they ought somehow to have been able to transform capitalist society and prevent war. This banal and sentimental view arrives at hideous absurdity in the poem in which the climax is the burning of the university."*

TO MARGARET MARSHALL

[December 1945]

This is just a Happy New Year note: and a poem for a New Year's present, the pleasantest poem I ever wrote ["O My Name It Is Sam Hall"]. For all I know, it's the first pleasant poem I ever wrote.

By the way, just take my letter to the editor as a private letter to you and let it die in your breast (as a poet would say). I had fun writing it, but the day after I sent it I thought "What's the use?" A complimentary review is the only sort I'd ever reply to, out of sheer vanity — you look too foolish when you make even the most sensible objection to unfavorable criticism.

I thought Schwartz's review of Shapiro extremely good; so did other people here.

I'm glad you liked the Verse Chronicle. Usually the language and images, as they constitute a way of looking at the world, *will* be what I analyze. I am going on the assumption that you'll write an angry complaining letter about anything you don't like — this makes me feel a lot free-er, and what is so good as feeling free?

I'll be out in January, ~~surely,~~ maybe.

> Yours,
> Randall Jarrell

Jarrell reviewed H.D.'s Tribute to the Angels *and Alex Comfort's* The Song of Lazarus *in the "Verse Chronicle" column he refers to above.*

TO ROBERT LOWELL

[January 1946]

Dear Cal:

I have half a long letter to you that I've mislaid; Maybe I can find it before I send this. I leave for work everyday at 7 and don't get back till 6, so I haven't been writing letters or anything else much except Verse Chronicles.

I think the ones you picked for the book [*Lord Weary's Castle*] are good choices — and I wouldn't put in the Milton one, since it would give people a little more chance to think of you as a special-case neo-17th-century poet, not a fine clean upstanding American one à la Shapiro. The arrangement is good, too. It might be a good idea to put Louis XVI ["1790"] later on, in the middle of the book; I think right at the beginning it has a little too much shock value. I'm *awfully* glad you agreed about the "Quaker Graveyard," and are using the Napoleon stanza separately. I always liked the title of the book well enough for myself, but thought other people wouldn't't; since they do, good. In your next book you can use the France-Abel-le-bensraum poem ["France"] by itself, maybe; it really is a good poem and it would be a shame to see it sawed in two and buried in a strange land for good.

I'll send you fairly soon the whole manuscript with any little punctuation changes or things like that: sometimes the punctuation is a matter of taste but sometimes you punctuate the way the Irishman played the violin, by main force. But send the manuscript back to me later, will you? Then I can make notes to review it by when it comes out.

The most important part of the letter now arrives: please, please, for goodness sake change "A.W. I, Death from Cancer" [part I of "In Memory of Arthur Winslow"] BACK to what it used to be ["Death from Cancer on Easter," *Sewanee Review,* Summer 1943]. The old ending was one of the best — and the most genuinely mysterious, magical, haunting, good-be-yond-explanation endings you've ever done; the new ending seems a per-fectly good mural in a church, but not a bit more: it's good fairly conventional religious poetry, and the old was *wonderful.* I actually believed in the first; with the second I just suspend my disbelief indifferently. (Also, *coast* in the first version was awfully good, and shouldn't be sacrificed be-cause you have to change a rhyme.) Then, *Procrustes'* bed is the oldest thing in the world — it's been used so much it's a completely dead metaphor by now, even though justly used in this case; the *adjusted* bed was particular, a real piece of the concrete circumstances of sickness — it's not only better, but needed. *Cox's* is worse than the plural because the plural suggests the continuance of all this — that the squeaking of many coxswains many times dwarfs the bells; it makes you feel his sickness and death more as a regular thing like the vernal equinox. (The other way may be more accurate if you think of it happening just once at Easter; but I think the first way's better.)

But the important thing is the ending. I think it's harder for the poet to recognize a "magical" effect than it is for the reader, and the poet may prefer the well-constructed sensible one he builds up to take its place. You com-pare both and think about them and see if you don't feel that way about the two endings.

The poems I like best are in this order: "The Quaker Graveyard"; "Col-loquy in Black Rock"; "Mr. Edwards and the Spider"; "Where the Rainbow Ends"; "The Exile's Return"; "Christmas in Black Rock"; "At the Indian Killer's Grave"; "The Drunken Fisherman"; "The Dead in Europe"; "Salem"; "The Blind Leading the Blind" (though at the bottom of the bunch). Now, about "Arthur Winslow I" (the old version) — I like [part] IV a little less — the changes in the other parts of "Arthur Winslow" I like; the translations or adaptations are two of the best I ever saw (I compared yours of Rimbaud ["War"] with the poor one [translated by Selden Rod-man] in *War and the Poet* [ed. Richard Eberhart and Selden Rodman] — your Rilke poem ["Shako"] is wonderful). "Louis XVI and the Dog" ["1790"] is an extremely successful, efficient, shocking tour de force: I don't think the subject has enough in it to make a poem as good as the ones I like best. "At a Bible House" would be one of the ones I like best except for (1) "For the small,/ Death, where is thy sting?" and (2) "Will serve for anything/ Or stay to break its fall." (1) seems weak and inadequate coming immediately after the long impressive sentence about the tree. (2) is awkward: it seems so badly worded that the reader first takes *anything* or *stay* as coordinates, then sees it couldn't be; then realizes how it's constructed, but he certainly thinks that the second line should be — so far as simple sense is concerned — "Or stay its fall." "Nothing will stay to break its fall" just isn't English, is it? You don't mean it in the sense of *remain,* do you? Besides being awkward the expression just trails off and lets you feel that the poem (also the tree) has died away in mid-air instead of falling to the ground. It really needs a different two last lines. "Napoleon Crosses the Berezina" is a poem like a still-life of a snowy chess-board: beautifully done and impressive and a successful tour de force, but not by its nature capable of being a really "important" poem. (It certainly is a pleasure to read.) Don't you usually find *tumbrels* spelt *tumbrils?*

"The Soldier" is a thoroughly successful poem, especially the last line: it's a small-scale, special-case poem, too. "After the Surprising Conversions" is naturally a very impressive masquerade, but awkward in a few spots, I believe. "Dea Roma" is quite good; maybe I should have put it among the ones I like best, but I believe it's a little too formal and "objective" for that. I think the main trouble is the third stanza, which is noticeably weaker than the others. Its first sentence is all right, but the "Blood/ ran in through pipes of public aqueducts" doesn't have much effect because it repeats two effects that just preceded it: "Blood licks" and "sewers wound to Rome." (Saying blood ran in the aqueducts to Rome has just the same rhetorical effect as saying all the sewers ran to Rome; so the second time it doesn't shock.) "Squatted on the lid" and the rest is just so-so; I don't think anything after *Vandal patricians* (which *is* good) good in the 3rd stanza; the 4th is the best of all. "The inflated pagan" seems awkward to me because I can't understand it; explain, please. "Forest Hills Cemetery" is good and I should have put it in those I like best (towards the bottom).

"Caron, Non Ti Crucciare" has some of your best patches in it: it seems to me rather an extrapolation of your method, Lowell 2 rather than Lowell, but I haven't read it again and won't talk about it till I go over it some.

When I read "Concord" I couldn't help thinking of making the first line "Ten thousand Fords are idling here in search"; or is that a silly rather than serious pun? You judge. Now that I see it I think I like your *idle* better. Why "Whose echo girdles the imperfect globe"? I don't get it. I know that it's a parody of Emerson's "Concord Hymn"; but why *imperfect?*

In "The Quaker Graveyard" I believe I like *Jonas Messias* a little better than "twice-buried Jonas": *Twice-buried* isn't very accurate for Christ, is it? At least I don't remember any account of his once-buried body getting buried again.

Your devil in "The Blind Leading the Blind" ("Satan snored/ By the brass railing") and mine in "The Märchen" ("cringing in the gloom,/ Shifting his barred hooves with a crunch like snow") make a fine pair.

About the only thing I regret about your book is that you didn't save "Caron, Non Ti Crucciare" for the second book (and give yourself a chance to re-write sections that don't seem good after a year or two) and use the "France" part of it in this. But it doesn't matter, since you can always do a second version of it later, then put that in another book. (I already have my next book [*Losses*] finished, and four or five poems for the one after that, so you can understand the book on book on book talk.)

All the part about the child in it ["Buttercups"], the early soldiers, and the later Versailles ones need to be related more clearly, I think. Also the rhetoric in the first stanza is pretty extreme in spots: the "hollow salvoes stripping you with their bluster, cutting your teeth on the barbaric broom-pole's butt churning into your chin." I think the rhetoric will make most people miss that this means the child drilling with the broom. And how, why, does the child have a *thin blue-blooded chin* and *thin-lipped* humor: he's an aristocratic child, judging from this and his family's possessions, but we don't know enough about him, he's not real. Speaking as an old expert on children in poems, I think you need two or three more details about him.

O, how I resent my beloved "Where the ruined farmer beat out Abel's brains" being transferred to Bunker Hill, and *the* ruined farmer Cain changed to *ruined farmers*! For a minute transform yourself into an imaginary normal reader who doesn't know much about you and your views, and then read "Abel"; and see if it doesn't rather puzzle you. The reader reads the title "Abel"; then he sees a *you* addressed as *Brother* — so he decides the narrator is Abel *or* Cain, and the *you* whichever of the two the narrator isn't. After a few lines he decides the narrator is Cain, the *you* Abel; and he is no doubt pretty disconcerted at Abel's having a highboy and a grandfather's clock, instead of a herd of sheep. Also he feels funny about *heir,* which fits in more with *son* than with brother; and how is pushing your brother into some furniture *rebellion*? How has Abel's house a covenant with time? And how did the sharks get there for the narrator to cast Abel howling to? "The dead caught at my knees"; this *seems* some other dead besides Abel (he's already been cast to the sharks), but Abel was the first man to die — by him came death *practically* speaking, though it came by Adam theoretically speaking. Then the reader will certainly think: Why are the ships shouting? *Boston?* How are the dead shelling Golgotha? He sees that Our Lord is like the pendulum in the grandfather's clock, but he is puzzled by the *staid and shaggy* minutes which He *swords.*

Anyway, by then he's completely mixed up; and Behemoth and Leviathan devouring the merchants, and Cain as a successful farmer making very odd contracts, and Cain's bondsmen as ruined farmers at Bunker Hill — all this confuses him more and more and more. But try to make yourself a tabula rasa so far as your life is concerned, and see if you aren't pretty much puzzled by the poem — though certainly the texture and writing are good, and the poem makes quite an impression even if it's not understood, because the reader will get the vague general drift of it. But it sounds too direct and sensible for him to be satisfied with that, as he is when he reads a conceity, more or less surrealist (to him) poem like the "Slough of Despond."

In "The Crucifix" I think "the worldly angels strip to tease/ And wring a world of bathos from their eyes" isn't good: I think its tone is a little too timely and tawdry for the tone of the rest, and it seems to me to cast a little tinsel around it for several lines.

I think the old "bowels of fierce fire" in "Mr. Edwards" better than "bowels of the fierce fire." The regular rhythm makes it sound inevitable and menacing; you don't need — rather, can't afford — the jump of the anapest. Also *fierce fire* is more general, hence more like the generalized fires of hell.

"Mr. Edwards" certainly is a wonderful poem — I guess I should have put it along with the four I like best.

I'll close with a little personal news: we three-year men were supposed to be discharged last month but the field managed to hold us by declaring us all essential; but things ought to blow up in two weeks or a month. I'll surely be out in February. Surely, surely . . .

Write me back about all this stuff; the one thing I'm *very* much concerned about is the old ending to "Death by Cancer" — you really are seriously hurting one of your nicest poems if you keep the new, I think.

We are all well and strong and had a nice Christmas; my mother sent Kitten a stocking containing a catnip mouse, a catnip turtle, a catnip block, and a box of catnip. We fed him a lot of Christmas goose, which he thought a much better present. Give our love to Jean.

Affectionately,
Randall

Jarrell's poem "The Märchen," which Tate had published in the Sewanee Review, *won their John Peale Bishop Memorial Prize.*
    Lowell's poem "Abel," which Jarrell criticized at length, was extensively revised and appeared in Lord Weary's Castle *as "Rebellion."*

*In a letter to Jarrell written in 1955, Lowell said, "I was just rum-
maging through a carton of old poems, envelopes, pictures, etc. and came on
some of my poems all marked up, stabbed, puffed, and dissected by you. You
had such wit and patience and such generosity and justice, at least in your
jokes: 'these divisions roll on square wheels'; 'you generally have one line in a
poem where the rhythm gets, not harsh, but tetanic like a muscle under too
long tension.' The times come back and I feel excited all over again."*

TO ROBERT LOWELL

[December 1945]
[Mailed January 1946]
(Here's the first unfinished letter, which I found at last. It was written
weeks and weeks ago — a month at least.)

Dear Cal:
   I'll answer immediately to show how much I enjoyed your letter. I hope
your appendix wasn't as painful as the Allen–Caroline reconciliation which
certainly moved you to the heights of comic invention in your prose. I
much enjoyed the Raven story and the Goldfish paragraph. I think people
very unfair to call such an earnest writer as Schwartz malicious: anybody
working that hard for immortality wouldn't dare be malicious. Anyway, he
is plainly one of the most conscientious and just critics working now —
though not very brilliant ...
   To get to the most important things first, you might very well be right
about "The Quaker Graveyard"; anyway, if you will send me a clean typed
copy of the latest version, I will think about it hard and often as I can. I
have no conception of the structure of the whole poem, so I didn't make
your judgements about the parts of each part ... I'm sure that you have
private feelings about Napoleon — when I encountered him in that stanza
[in "Napoleon crosses the Berezina"] I was sure it was your childhood and
not the hero's. I certainly agree with you about wanting to have it perfect.
When we see each other we can go over it at great length.
   I am eligible for discharge already, but am being temporarily held as
"essential." I am almost certain to get out by the middle of January. We
could come North late in May. We'd probably be in Nashville half the time
until then; maybe you could come down for a short while. I got asked to
make one of those YMHA poetry readings in New York on May 25; I was
told to suggest another poet for the other half of the program, and I asked

for you — if Kimon Friar consents it will be the first sensible thing I ever heard of his doing. If he does ask you, I hope you can.

At present I'm assisting the legal officer at the base; I take statements, investigate accidents, talk to prisoners, etc. Yesterday you should have seen me climbing through a wrecked and stolen car hunting for bloodstains, and putting stray hairs in an envelope so they could be compared with the prisoner's. Saturday I went down to a border jail: a prisoner had fallen out of bed and fractured his skull. The bed was 24 inches wide. I try very hard to get everybody out of everything, and usually succeed pretty well — the legal officer's very kind-hearted.

I don't believe in determinism in the strict sense. The best scientific arguments against it are in [Hans] Reichenbach's book on quantum mechanics. The scientific opinion at present is that the laws of microscopic phenomena are statistical: you can be sure A will happen in ⅔ the cases, and B in ⅓, but you have no way whatsoever of *determining* what will happen in any individual case. Macroscopic phenomena involve so many millions or billions of cases that they have the appearance of determinism.

But certainly I don't believe in free will in one sense, in the sense that you are *free* to choose: this is like saying that a man who is ignorant of the existence of square roots is free to choose the correct or incorrect square root of a number. Determining experiences in the past may make you (1) so completely ignorant of the nature and conditions of your choice that it is purely random in relation to both the nature and conditions of the choice, (2) partially informed of the nature and conditions of the choice, so that you can, theoretically at least, make a proper choice — if congenital deficiencies or acquired ones don't make that choice actually impossible for you. The (3) case, the ideal one, would have you thoroughly informed and without any such deficiencies; it never exists.

In a war like ours most of the soldiers are, if not completely, at least virtually, ignorant of the nature and conditions of the choices they make; besides this, they are pretty well determined in the passive sense — even if they should choose not to do a bad thing (and they usually do not have the information and training to make it possible for them to make a really reasonable decision about it), they will be forced to do it by the state (which has already misled them about it by giving them as much misleading determining information as it could). Also, most of the things *suffered* in war are entirely determined, the person has no choice to make: who in Tokyo or Hamburg or London chose to be burned to death?

The great feeling you have in the army is that your own knowledge and the other person's ignorance don't differentiate you *at all,* so far as what's going to happen to you is concerned. Whether you're a gunner or a clerk, safe or dead, is random so far as the state is concerned, and completely determined for you so far as you're concerned. But the person who understands what is happening to him is a great exception to the general rule which is the war writer's subject; besides, what happens to the understanding ones is necessarily not so bad as what happens to the ignorant many. (Many people in the armies are bad, really bad, do evil things; but they're exceptions which do not appreciably affect the nature of the war, which would be pretty much the same if these stayed home and killed — or were — policemen, and were replaced by the passively obedient.) If you'll notice, I've never written a poem about myself in the army or war; unless you're vain or silly you realize that you, except insofar as you're in exactly the same boat as the others, aren't the primary subject of any sensible writing about the war.

I agree about your phrase "armor of desired mediocrity."

The main feeling you have about most people in the army — and in the war, too — is that you're sorry for them; everything else comes after. But the next feeling, I imagine, is one of wonder: the size and impossible lunacy of everything in the war and army are beyond anything.

I agreed pretty well with what you said about the best poems in *Blood for a Stranger,* except I believe I'd have left out "The cow wandering" and "On the Railway Platform" and put in a couple of others. I agree that "Siegfried" is the best poem in *Little Friend*; and the other five you put down are certainly five of the best — though I like five or six more about as well. I'm quite pleased you like "Leave" ["Absent with Official Leave"] that much: it's a quiet poem and people don't notice it much, I imagine.

A poem that isn't in *Little Friend* — "Burning the Letters" — is better than any poem I ever wrote except "Siegfried."

After I'm out I'm going to write — besides a great many army poems about the war — some historical poems: one about Crete, one with Marcion talking, and one about Spinoza.

I have a very long review [of A. M. Klein] in the first issue of a magazine named *Commentary* that you might enjoy reading. I've just done my first Verse Chronicle for *The Nation* — mostly about Alex Comfort's books. They've already sent me about ten books. The best are de la Mare, Stevens, and — almost best of all, believe it or not — [Franz] Werfel; I have to guess that some of this book of his is better than their two books, since I know so little German, but it's a pretty safe guess. I think.

I think I'll stop. I'm very eager to see you; give our love to Jean.

                                                              Randall

*Even though Jarrell referred to this as an "unfinished letter," he had ac-
tually completed it and signed his name as above.*

*Jarrell did write a historical poem about Spinoza called "The Place of
Death." He did not write about Crete or Marcion.*

TO MARGARET MARSHALL

[January 4, 1946]

Dear Miss Marshall:

I was awfully pleased by your letter. In the second place I liked the idea
of doing what you suggested: but in the first place, I felt extremely complimented — I can hardly remember ever feeling so complimented. And, to
insert an altruistic note, I'm glad that you're going to write a book, too.

Taking your job [as Literary Editor of *The Nation*] for the year that
you're gone sounds awfully attractive to me. I'll give you my opinion of
myself "as a possible Literary Editor of *The Nation,*" as you ask me to — but
giving opinions of yourself is a tough and embarrassing job. I think that,
right now, I could do the job pretty well — the job, that is, of taking your
place for a year.

As you say, experience in editing wouldn't be too important, since I
could get so much help from Miss Whiteside [copy editor at *The Nation*];
but I have had some experience. I helped Ransom and [Philip] Rice with
the *Kenyon Review* for its first year. Ransom had taken me up to Kenyon
with him, and we three were the only "literary" people there. I was teaching
only two classes, so I had plenty of time. I read the manuscripts submitted,
corrected proof, suggested reviewers, and so on. Before that I'd become
quite familiar with the way things were done at the *Southern Review* — Red
Warren was one of my best friends while I was in college, and I visited him
[at Baton Rouge] a lot. I edited a wretched college magazine [*The Masquerader*] for two years to make money to go to school with.

You can judge for yourself (have judged, of course) whether I have the
general qualifications for doing the work; I imagine my disposition and
ways of thinking are pretty apparent in my letters. It seems to me that the
particular qualification for taking your place for a year is just generally being
sensible, and willing to learn, and accepting promptly the already-existing
conditions of the job. It would be a question of continuing the usual policies and features as smoothly as possible, and of thinking out about the
variations and special features that you yourself would normally think of in
that time — certainly they're what give the life and shine to the whole
thing. After 39 months in the army, it's become easy for me to get along
with people and to get used to proceedings in different sorts of offices or

organizations (I've been in about a dozen). *Any* civilian organization will seem a miracle of efficiency and good sense and humane charm to me. Besides, I'm sure I'd find the staff and regular contributors congenial. I've always particularly liked people like [Bernard H.] Haggin, [James] Agee, [Clement] Greenberg, Lionel Trilling, and [Delmore] Schwartz — their regular use is one of the things that seems to me to make *The Nation* superior to the *New Republic*. You know what my politics are from the things you've printed: they're fairly close to yours.

I believe that my tastes are reasonably wise and "objective," rather than narrow and personal. I certainly don't like, or have connections with, any particular sort of writing or any particular variety of literary opinion. (Several of my best friends have happened to become editors, and it seemed to me that their dogmatic convictions and idiosyncrasies and general sectarian leanings hurt their work a lot. I won't specify, but I'm sure you can guess the three or four I mean.)

By accidents of education and interests, I'm reasonably acquainted with a good many more fields than most potential editors, and this would help me a lot in picking reviewers or judging (and asking for) articles in a particular field. I was educated as a psychologist, with great quantities of philosophy and the sciences — especially physiology; I didn't switch over into English until my last year of graduate work. If I'd stayed in psychology I'd have had to spend most of my spare time on experiments, and I naturally wanted to keep it for writing. I have a lot of funny interests and I've read a great deal in all of them. I read very fast, get year-long crazes about particular fields, and read steadily in them, with big shining eyes. Besides the things that I write about and am obviously interested in — you know what they are — I've been particularly interested in Gestalt psychology, ethnology and "folk" literature, economics (especially Marxist), symbolic logic and modern epistemology, theology and its origins, and a few even queerer things. These aren't of any particular, practical value to me (except that they, like the spirits who came to Yeats, "bring you metaphors for your poetry"). But they are of a certain practical value to an editor.

It's pretty important for you to know what I'm like as a person, in imagining how I'd do your job; but how on earth am I going to tell you? I don't know whether you'd guess it, but I have an even, cheerful, and optimistic disposition: what I write is therapeutically the opposite, I guess. I've always lived with "ordinary" people, so I don't feel separated or essentially different from them, as so many writers seem to. (Once I invented a man who said that he was normal, and said that if other people were more like him they'd be a lot more normal themselves.) Here's a riddle to serve for a description: all my friends in the army say, "You're not a bit like a writer, it's hard for us to believe you write those things —" And I've been having that said about me as long as I can remember. But my old friends write to me "When we read such-and-such it was just like hearing you talk."

Texas would certainly give me leave of absence for a year — after all, I'll have been gone four years anyway. The army swears to me that I'm completely eligible for discharge on the 15th of February, that they can't hold me as essential, critical, or anything else after that.

I'd like to do your job for several reasons, some of them mercenary in character (I imagine it would help induce colleges to let me teach fewer freshmen to punctuate); but mostly I'd like it because it would be something very different to do (nothing changes one so much, and I have a passion for changing myself as much as I can), and something that's *fun*. I ought to celebrate getting out of the army by doing something that's fun — though of course anything will be fun after the army.

I imagine this is more than enough about the Original Editor in me. I've often thought, "If I were an editor I'd do this or that," so I have some specific ideas — I'll tell you about them if this thing goes through. Whether it does or not, I'm pleased that you thought of me. You've certainly been my good angel in the last year or two.

If this does go through I'm going to play a joke on you: I'm going to hire a little old man — like Rumpelstiltskin, but more irascible — to come to your office and introduce himself to you as

Randall Jarrell

The three or four editors with "dogmatic convictions" and "sectarian leanings" Jarrell alludes to were probably Tate, Ransom, and Warren.

TO ROBERT LOWELL

[Austin, Texas]
[February 5, 1946]
Dear Cal —

This is just a note. I'm in Texas being slowly separated from the army — I'll be out in a week or so. My address is 705 West 8th, Austin, Texas. We'll be in New York April 1 — I'm going to take Margaret Marshall's place as literary editor of *The Nation* for a year. So will you please save for me "Colloquy in Black Rock," "At the Indian Killer's Grave," "The Exile's Return," and "Where the Rainbow Ends," if these haven't been printed in magazines. You know the poems of yours I like best — I'd want almost any of them [for *The Nation*] that haven't been printed. Please tell me right away which ones you have. And include your "argument against determinism which everyone overlooks": if it's new and true I'll think you very clever.

I forgot to say in my last letter that I think "green and gashed perfection" better than "green and slashed" [in "The Indian Killer's Grave"].

I much enjoyed your last letter with all the stuff about Allen and everybody.

You and Jean are in New York a fair lot, aren't you? We're very eager to see you. I guess we'll have to put off staying with you till the summer after next — but you can stay with us in New York, if we can manage to find an apartment there, dreadful prospect!

We're going to be in Nashville in March.

I'll write you a regular letter after I'm out. Give our love to Jean. Tell me how your poetry reading goes. Send me the new poems you mentioned. This is a very Kantian finish.

Affectionately,
Randall

TO MARGARET MARSHALL

[Nashville, Tennessee]
[March 1946]

Dear Miss Marshall:

Instead of getting better after I last wrote you I got worse; I've been in bed most of the time. I finally got better and drove up here [Nashville]. I think I'll be quite well in a week or so.

I'm sending a poem ["In the Ward: The Sacred Wood"] which I hope is the best I've written in some time; but I don't know.

I've written down names of reviewers by some of the books on the list, but many of the names and titles don't convey much to me — and many of them (the *Whither Democracy?* type particularly) I'd always have to get help for. The list looked quite as frightening as you said.

I thought the Trilling article would be particularly nice for the Spring Book Number. Trilling is one of the only critics I always enjoy reading. I thought his Shelley review a model of that sort of review ["The Irrepressible Myth," review of R. M. Smith's *The Shelley Legend, The Nation,* February 23, 1946].

I'll certainly be glad to be in New York and settled down: what with being sick and being related to relatives, I hardly know I'm out of the army. We'll arrange to get to New York on the 31st of March. If you'd like me to get there a couple of days earlier I'd be glad to do it.

If you do find an apartment I'll certainly think you Super woman. As I said, anything would do — anything anywhere.

I knew a quite intelligent Major in the army who was the first pilot home from the Ploesti raid — would you like me to ask him to do a review of the two aviation books on your list? He was a lawyer before the war, and taught a year at the University of Mexico — so probably he *could* write a review, unlike all the other pilots and navigators I know.

I'll send you a Verse Chronicle about Werfel and two others in a few days. About [Louis] Aragon: I can write well enough about his ideas, attitudes, and general performance, but of course I don't have the faintest idea just how good he is as a French poet; so how would it be if I wrote half the Chronicle about Aragon, and got a friend of mine to do a separate half of the Chronicle about the poems as French poems? His name is René Blanc-Roos, and he knows more about French poetry than anybody who is ever likely to review it for American magazines.

Will you be around *The Nation* office all the time for some weeks after I get there, or just around New York itself? I've got confused about it — I hope very much it's the first.

I have a (rich) uncle [Howell Campbell, Sr.] who beats your nephew's army friends: he not only didn't know *The Nation* exists, but confused it with *Nation's Business*.

Sincerely,
Randall Jarrell

Postscript next day: I must have sounded vague about being ill: I had influenza and relapses, and the army doctor at my separation center [in Austin, Texas] told me that my X-ray showed fresh tubercular lesions, though they weren't serious. When somebody good examined me here he found that they were calcified, years-ago-healed affairs, and told me the army doctor had just mis-diagnosed the whole thing. This had a very cheering effect on me, as you can imagine.

TO ALLEN TATE
[Nashville, Tennessee]
[March 10, 1946]

Dear Allen:

Your letter was waiting for me when I finally got back from separation center. I'll certainly be glad to see you. We'd like very much to come up for a couple of days — if we came for a week my mother would not think kindly of us or you.

I'd better not do the Ransom — I'd want lots of time at best, and I haven't any now: I had influenza with complications, and am supposed to take naps, not play tennis, etc. I'll be looking forward to the *Little Friend* review — save a carbon copy for me.

I had heard from Cal about you and Caroline. You can infer (from the end of "The Märchen") that this would please me rather than grieve me; and I have the impression that I never got along very well with Caroline; and I could say more — *but* if you should ever be reconciled you'd remember this and the *more* as very foolish things I'd once foolishly said; and, besides, what do I know about what your life's really like, or what's good or bad for you? So I will conclude by saying I know about it, and no more: which is supposed to cancel out anything I said before that.

Will you send me a postcard before you make any Nashville trip? — then I can go around with you as you do errands, quite like the ole days.

Allen, not knowing the New York cliques you mention will grieve and bother me just as much as not knowing the more prominent representatives of the Red and Green factions that bet on the chariot-races in Byzantium. I've never seen anybody on *The Nation* and nobody on *The Nation* has ever seen me; so they'll hardly expect me to be as orthodox as Paul in one of Paul's descriptions of himself.

Isn't a list of new books to be given to reviewers a revolting thing? Every other book is *Whither Democracy?* [by N. J. Lennes] or *A Foreign Correspondent's View of the Atomic Bomb*. I don't give a damn who reviews them, I wish somebody would burn them.

You know, I haven't seen a single "literary" friend of mine (meaning by "literary" somebody who doesn't run his finger along the lines as he reads) since I saw you four years ago. Isn't that queer?

Margaret Marshall is looking for an apartment for us; if it has any room at all I hope you'll visit us when you come to New York. I'll make you scalded hoe-cakes on the hearth.

> Affectionately,
> Randall

Jarrell, Mackie, and Kitten stayed in Nashville with Jarrell's mother after his discharge from the army came through.

Though Tate had wanted an essay on Ransom's poetry for the Sewanee Review, *Jarrell did not write one for him until 1948 for the "Homage to John Crowe Ransom" issue.*

The review of Little Friend, Little Friend *that Jarrell looked forward to reading in the* Sewanee Review *was never written.*

The last words in the last lines of Jarrell's poem "The Märchen" are "to

change, to change!" and echo Jarrell's hope expressed to Lowell that Tate's
divorce might change him.

TO MARGARET MARSHALL
                                        [Nashville, Tennessee]
                                        [March 13, 1946]
Dear Miss Marshall:

I almost cried tears of joy when I came to the apartment part of your
letter. To tell the truth *anything* would do. I've lived with my wife and Kitten (the Persian cat responsible for all the cats in my poems) in one room
for 13 months during this war: few places wouldn't look good to me. As for
the price, you should know about that — it's *your* salary I'm getting. I suppose anything up to $100 a month or so would be all right. If you will just
pounce on anything, and conclude arrangements for it in two minutes, I'll
be delighted and send you a check and a laudatory ode. I don't remember
what a power of attorney looks like, but all this is supposed to be a logical
equivalent.

I was delighted with your using three of Lowell's poems: two of the
poems you took were poems I intended to ask him for. Isn't that a coincidence?

My wife and I were both crazy about your second article on de Tocque-
ville. All the things you say about American culture we have felt or said
ourselves — or should have.

I finally got out. Yesterday I saw a plane sky-writing and I almost expected it to write: *Discharge cancelled. Return immediately.*

Do you want me to do an occasional *ersatz* "Note by the Way" while
you're gone? I can't decide whether it would be strategically superior for
you to (1) maintain your readers' habit of reading *something* called "Notes
by the Way," or (2) deprive them of it for a year in order to let the insane
craving of deprivation reach its highest level.

Wouldn't you like to continue as editor for four or five days after I get
there, and let me be around all the time and observe? In the army this is
called On the Job Training: it may be an army madness.

I'm so pleased you liked the Chronicle.

                                        Sincerely,
                                        Randall Jarrell

New York, New York,
April 1946–August 1947

♥

*J*arrell despised New York for its wealth, its filth, and its tough, crude, mercenary manners. "What a way to speak!" he would say, repelled by any New York accent. Living there was, for him, a hell mitigated by ballet, art museums, and a part-time job teaching at Sarah Lawrence College. In the city he depended on Bernard Haggin and his passes to the ballet; on visits from the Lowells; and on a deepening friendship with Peter and Eleanor Taylor, who were also living in New York.

At a future date Sarah Lawrence would appear in Pictures from an Institution, Jarrell's satiric novel about "progressive" education. In the meantime, it provided him with a pleasant teaching colleague and tennis partner in Robert Fitzgerald, the poet and translator. Fitzgerald described Jarrell at this time as "young and tallish and a bit gangling but with dignity, his long throat distinctly angled, his dark eyes in repose proud and solemn, the lids drooping slightly toward the outer corners. More often they were animated, exceedingly gay and bright, but in conversation they could shadow swiftly with recognition, looking less at you than at some depth in himself that had been stirred, becoming hooded eyes where memory and mockery lurked. He loved his job at The Nation, or at least he certainly loved the game of matching reviewers and books, and he did it so well that in Mr. Ransom's later judgment his editorship deserved a Pulitzer Prize." (RJ)

Summarizing this period of Jarrell's career, R. W. Flint wrote, "To say that he had been a disturbing figure during his years as poetry editor of The Nation would be a rash understatement. Not since Poe had an American poet of his distinction laid down the law in quite such a carnival spirit." (RJ)

Jarrell's first official letter as Literary Editor of The Nation was a plea to Robert Penn Warren to send him reviews and poetry to publish there.

TO ROBERT PENN WARREN

The Nation
[April 1946]

Dear Red:

I've mislaid your letter, so this is less an answer than a letter. I was aw-fully glad you liked *Little Friend* so well. I'm very eager to see your [*Rime of the*] *Ancient Mariner* piece ["A Poem of Pure Imagination," *Kenyon Review*, Summer 1946], which Allen says is wonderful.

I'm out of the army and here taking Margaret Marshall's place for a year. Will you, if you have any time at all, do me a couple of reviews? If you're terribly rushed for time I could give you Briefer Notices: here one reads the book, writes four or five sentences, and gets ten dollars. But if you are too busy even for that please let me see your poems when you do get back to writing poetry.

We are happy, except for not having a permanent apartment. I'm sure you'll be in New York during the next year, at *some* time; and do write me beforehand so we can see you.

Will you write me back to say whether you can do any reviews?

Give my love to Cenina.

We've seen Allen and I talked to Amy: all of them told me about seeing you.

Yours,
Randall

Warren was teaching at the University of Minnesota and awaiting the im-minent publication of his novel All the King's Men, *which won the Pul-itzer Prize in fiction for 1947.*

TO MARIANNE MOORE

The Nation
April 8, 1946

Dear Miss Moore:

I told Margaret Marshall about the translations of La Fontaine that you are doing [*The Fables of La Fontaine,* published in 1954]; and we were both so charmed by the whole idea that we couldn't resist asking for some for *The Nation.* Will you let us see some when you get them perfected? We'd love to be implicated, in even a minor way, in such an auspicious cultural event.

Sincerely,
Randall Jarrell

Jarrell had been reading Moore's poetry since the mid-thirties and had written a glowing review of her book Nevertheless *in* Partisan Review (*Winter 1945*). *Although Moore had been working at Dial Press at the time they published* Little Friend, Little Friend, *she had not met Jarrell and they knew each other only through their poetry.*

TO ROBERT LOWELL

The Nation
[April 1946]

Dear Cal:

When do you expect to come down? We're looking forward very much to having you here, and have prepared a fine warm bed for you atop the oven. Be sure to bring all your new poems. Red was in town this week. Cenina too: we saw them all one evening, though only at a party.

I spent most of last week at the tennis matches, which mitigated New York, for a little, a little.

I have two queer Christian poems — the letter is, but the spirit isn't — which ought to interest you no end ["The Dead" and "The Clock in the Tower of the Church"]. One, I think I can safely say, is the oddest poem about Christianity ever written; and the other won't ever be called orthodox by T. S. Eliot.

I have spells of thinking editing barely tolerable, and spells of thinking it worse than intolerable. My job began on April Fool's day, and that was no accident. Send me a postcard about when you're coming. Is Jean coming here before going to the west coast? We hope so.

Affectionately,
Randall

TO ROBERT LOWELL

The Nation
[May 1946]

Dear Cal:

I was delighted about the Washington job; please spend all your New York time with us on the way down and on the way back. (If you have a friend with an extra room you'd be more comfortable, probably; but our couch is always waiting for you — like the grave.)

Your "Falling Asleep over the Aeneid" is the best title I ever heard, almost. Send it soon. I have just finished my Spinoza poem, oh joy! ["The Place of Death"].

I send the Hawthorne; please do a lovely, lovely article on it. And please send me copies of all the poems I'm going to use in *The Nation* — so I can. I want to use something fairly long in the Summer Book Number, the deadline for which is the 10th of June. Get a poem from Schwartz for it on the way down if you can tear one from him. I have a rather nice W. C. Williams to go with it.

We certainly do miss you. I hope that fire from heaven consumes your Maineish haven, and you have to come back to New York, that awful place.

I wrote a funny poem about a man who was born in New York City and died there.

I've tapped hitherto undreamed-of, incalculable reservoirs of Christian forbearance in my extended but still profitless correspondence with Winters. The reservoirs are in me, I might add.

Write.

Affectionately,
Randall

Give our love to Jean.

Lowell's book Lord Weary's Castle *won him the Pulitzer Prize in poetry, a Guggenheim grant, and appointment as Poetry Consultant at the Library of Congress starting in 1947.*

Lowell did not review a book on Hawthorne for The Nation *but did review Wallace Stevens's* Transport to Summer. *Jarrell published twelve of Lowell's poems during the year he was Literary Editor.*

The Lowells were living in Damariscotta, Maine.

Lowell, as well as Jarrell, had been hoping Yvor Winters would review some poetry, but Winters was not interested.

TO ROBERT LOWELL

The Nation
[May 8, 1946]

Dear Cal:

Tuesday will be swell. Your new printing is nicer than the old — you'll probably end as a geometrician if the invention of cursive doesn't take place and save you. We're sorry Jean won't be down with you in the beginning, and glad she'll be at the end.

I'll go over the poems with you in all the detail I know.

We'll talk about reviewing when you get here. Do you think you'd like to do a long review of, or short article on, [Wallace] Stevens? Please think of the best article you could possibly do, on anything, and we can make arrangements. I'm delighted that Jean would like to do some reviews: with novels there's the difficulty of Diana Trilling doing them all, but there are plenty of other slightly different things.

I greatly enjoyed seeing Peter [Taylor].

The *Nation* party will be too dignified for you to need to drink: Mackie and I will expect you to go with us. I don't drink either.

I'll send this air-mail special. If you arrive during daylight hours call me at *The Nation.*

Everybody's nice at *The Nation,* Margaret Marshall extremely so. Reviews demand an extraordinary amount of re-writing, also we make-up, cut, proof-read, etc.

We can't wait to see you.

Affectionately,
Randall

Jarrell's reference to Lowell's "new printing" means that it was more legible than his usual printing, which in turn was more legible than his cursive.

* * *

Encouraged by Allen Tate, Peter Taylor had come to New York with his wife, Eleanor Ross, to decide if he really wanted to write. He was twenty-nine, had spent four years in England in the army, and had published stories sporadically in the Southern Review, *the* Kenyon Review, *the* Sewanee Review, *and one — as a result of Tate's influence — in the* Partisan Review. *Jarrell was soon saying Taylor was "the best fiction writer around" and "the best company in the world." He would drop everything at* The Nation *for what Taylor called "an expedition" — which could turn out to be nothing more than a subway ride uptown; however, each nudge and whisper of Taylor's could indicate something that would later appear in one of his stories.*

Much of what Jarrell disliked about New York infatuated Taylor in the same way castles and the class structure had infatuated him in England. Jarrell thought it touching that Taylor could be dazzled by the famous literary rabbits Tate pulled out of his hat, or be "in heaven" at dinner at the Rahvs'; but he would say, "It's almost worth going to a party to get to see Peter at a party . . . he's irresistible." While Jarrell stationed himself in one

*spot, wishing he'd never come, Taylor circulated with shining eyes, wishing it
would never end.*

*Taylor attracted people wherever he went — or, as Jarrell said, "had
them eating out of his hand" — and as for landladies, English departments,
and grant committees, he could "charm them in his sleep." He came from the
kind of Southerners he wrote about — lawyers and Episcopalians, with a
governor here and a senator there — and had in his veins the blood of ladies
and gentlemen with land, faithful servants, and all the social graces.*

*Taylor wrote about Jarrell in New York, "It was then that we became
really close friends. I doubt if I could have ever got started again after the
war if I had not had Randall to talk to or to listen to." (RJ) When Taylor
joined the faculty at the Woman's College in Greensboro, North Carolina,
in the fall of 1946, he charmed the English department there into granting
Jarrell a job interview.*

TO MARGARET MARSHALL

The Nation
[May 1946]

Dear Margaret:

Nothing has changed, we are all running around like quiet good-humored squirrels in our nice quiet whatever-you-call-it-that-squirrels-run-in.
Wouldn't Mrs. Whiteside love to get to work on that sentence? We've
been on good terms except over Diana Trilling's use of the word *scruplings;*
Mrs. Whiteside was pretty angry: "Who does she think she is to make up
words? *Good* writers can make up words." Then she told me just how bad
Diana Trilling seemed to her; I am getting awfully sick of having people do
this to me — pretty soon I'm going to develop a conclusive formula like
D.T. is the great modern critic, which would at least shut them up.

[Arthur] Schlesinger is doing Eisenhower's aide's diary [Harry C.
Butcher's *My Three Years with Eisenhower*] — he asked for it specially;
[Ralph] Bates had done nothing but read the book, and amiably turned it
over: *amiably* since I (a) gave him three more books (b) asked him to make
his Ingersoll review [Ralph Ingersoll, *Top Secret*] longer, to be featured
more (c) asked him at great length all about his Stendhal article (d) let
him keep the diary, which he had "annotated" (e) listened to 35 minutes of
telephone conversation. But let me say that he was very nice and that his
conversation was good — I don't want to produce an unpleasant impression
with my little comic recital.

Schlesinger says that [Paul] Sweezy will be glad to do us a Toynbee article [on Arnold Toynbee's *Study of History*]. I asked Schlesinger to do [Bernard] Brodie's book on the effect of the atomic bomb on world affairs [*The Absolute Weapon: Atomic Power and World Order*]. [Carl] Withers will not only do reviews for us (he turned out to have read in Portuguese the book I asked him to review) but was seeing [Ralph] Linton the next day and is arranging for Linton to do something. [Arthur] Mizener and [Wylie] Sypher are glad to do things. Nobody has refused except [Yvor] Winters; he said he'd decided long ago (*he* said 15 years) that reviewing is a waste of time. I could hardly argue, since *sub specie aeternitatis* he is right all over; so I gave him a soft answer that might get us an article to look at.

I saw [Herman] Eberling and talked to him at length; he re-wrote, I did — much, much, much — then he did a little more, then I did, and it turned out beautifully, everybody says (I hope truly). [Reference to Eberling's review of Saul K. Padover's *Experiment in Germany* and Julian Bach's *America's Germany*.]

We had to go to parties for two days after you left; since then we haven't seen anybody or done anything, and we're so much better and happier that we almost fly from room to room.

We had a night staff meeting that was very exhausting but very interesting too: only King, Bendiner, Freda and me — I mostly listened, but thoroughly sided with the other two against Freda's position — though the positions weren't too different so far as practical policy goes.

I am taking to make-up like a duck — if ducks can make-up.

The wicked Camus reviewer sent in 1,000 words on the psychology of the hero of *The Stranger,* and not one lonely little word of criticism or review.

All the regular features are going well — Haggin and Agee have been particularly good; I enjoy talking to them about their things when they call.

I miss you a great deal; all the things I would say I don't say at all, or else run to Caroline's office and say — and one morning she was away, I was laughing wildly over Agee's piece, and I could find nobody but Mrs. Whiteside to hand it to; she didn't laugh, and barely smiled.

I wrote an editorial paragraph for the issue that will come out May 3 or so; see if you can guess which one it is.

We have a permanent apartment — small, expensive, with ingeniously horrid furniture; but with clean walls and shiny kitchen and bathroom — it's just four years old. We got it through a letter Mackie wrote in answer to a newspaper advertisement.

I asked [Bill] Mauldin to do [Ernie] Pyle's last book [*Last Chapter*]; I hope he will.

There's a charming Brief Notice from [Albert] Guérard about Gide

[Gide's novel *Thésée*]. But I'd better not go into details of what's come in, or this will be a magazine and not a letter.

I am going to write some poems about New York and its poor inhabitants.

I think I will quit writing this reasonably endless letter, though. I hope that you're having all the luck you need with Constance Rourke's papers.

I like Caroline very much, so naturally that makes working very pleasant. So far I've been too harried to get any work of my own done; but when I'm all settled — we're all settled, that is — in our new apartment I ought to get a lot done. We are going to buy some plants to remind us of the existence of the natural world; you and Judy [Marshall's daughter] can come to see them and Kitten, we can serve a picnic supper, and it will be almost like Nature: i.e., Central Park.

Yours,
Randall

At this time the editorial staff at The Nation *included Freda Kirchwey, editor and publisher; J. King Gordon, managing editor; Gladys Whiteside, copy editor; Caroline Whiting, assistant literary editor; Diana Trilling, fiction reviewer; Bernard Haggin, music critic; James Agee, film critic; and Robert Bendiner, associate editor.*

Diana Trilling had invented the word scrupling *in her review of Eleanor Clark's book* The Bitter Box.

"The wicked Camus reviewer" is unknown, since no review of a Camus book appeared in The Nation.

Jarrell's "editorial paragraph" was commentary on the action of the president general of the Daughters of the American Revolution to permit the Tuskegee Choir to sing in Constitution Hall. The D.A.R. action was the result of Clare Boothe Luce's public protest after they had prevented Marian Anderson from performing there.

TO ALLEN TATE

The Nation
[May 1946]

Dear Allen:

Some of my best poems are "Siegfried" and "The Wide Prospect" in *Little Friend, Little Friend*: and "Burning the Letters," "The Dead Wingman" and "Pilots, Man Your Planes."

I'll call you next week and we can talk about the anthology [*A Southern*

Vanguard, ed. Allen Tate, 1947]. I doubt that it could be made into a text-book sort of anthology without spoiling it, but maybe not.

The book section, getting new reviews, and people at parties almost drove me crazy here; but everything is pretty quiet and pleasant now. We have an apartment — small and expensive, but permanent. New York is certainly no place to live.

Yours,
Randall

The businesslike, straight-to-the-point tone of this letter was a complete departure from the expansive, literary, confiding, and affectionate tone of Jarrell's earlier letters to Tate. Jarrell may have been vexed by Tate's request for "the best poems you can write" — as if some of what he had sent to the Sewanee Review *was second-rate — and he may have been irked that Tate had ignored his repeated requests in letters for a response to the Auden article, which was his major critical work to date, had been ten years under construction, and was comparable to a second master's thesis. Tate, on the other hand, had undoubtedly been hurt by Jarrell's brief comment on his book* The Winter Sea *that "It is about the prettiest book I ever saw."*

Obviously it had been hard for Tate to watch Auden's influence surpass his own in Jarrell's thinking (just as it was hard for him, later, to relinquish Lowell to William Carlos Williams's influence). Jarrell was moving with the times but Tate was not, and this is what Jarrell had meant when he wrote Lowell, "Allen is his own ruts." This is the last letter from Jarrell that Tate kept.

TO ROBERT PENN WARREN

The Nation
[June 11, 1946]

Dear Red:

I thought I ought to write you a fan letter about *All the King's Men*. It's an overwhelming book: I, and my wife, and four people I lent it to, and several people who've talked to me about it, were all like people in a movie advertisement — we'd had an "experience," and still felt stunned. It seems to me very much the best thing you've ever written: it's really quite out of the class of the other novels, I think.

I've just read two extremely stupid reviews of it, one of which is going to be in *The Nation*. All the fiction goes to Diana Trilling, automatically, and she really surpassed herself on yours. I think that she will suffer a good deal more from it than you will, though, in fact, I can say in a grim tone that I'm absolutely sure she will.

Your *New Republic* Faulkner article ["Cowley's Faulkner," August 12, 1946] was awfully good. I haven't bothered you about doing articles or reviews because of your being so busy. If you ever have time I'd like for you to do either — like it awfully much.

I imagine that the Huey Long tie-up will make reviews of your book stupider than even reviews usually are; I thought at first — judging from the readers I'd talked to — that it would have so much effect on reviewers that they'd be beaten into sense.

I hope we'll get to see you if you come east. New York is the worst place to live I've ever seen.

Yours,
Randall

TO ROBERT LOWELL

The Nation
[July 10, 1946]

Dear Cal:

We miss you very much still. We're in our new big apartment now. Kitten loves it. I've written two poems and finished my Spinoza ["The Place of Death"]. One of them ["A Camp in the Prussian Forest"] is in the summer number [of *The Nation*] that the "Indian Killer" [Lowell's "At the Indian Killer's Grave"] is in. Oh, where is "Falling Asleep over the Aeneid"? And the other new poems, where are they? You won't have any readers if you don't send out your work.

Say hello for us to the Taylors; we miss them. They were the only people we saw here.

I wish you'd got to see the Old Vic; though what they did to *Uncle Vanya* was terrifying.

Anytime you want to come down we can give you a lovely room looking out over a lot of trees, with a brand new desk to write poems on, and the same old me to try them out on.

Affectionately,
Randall

The Old Vic had been performing in New York.

The Taylors were visiting the Lowells in Damariscotta before driving to Greensboro, to Taylor's teaching job at the Woman's College of the University of North Carolina.

TO ROBERT PENN WARREN

The Nation
[August 1946]

Dear Red:

Would you review Jean Stafford's *The Mountain Lion* for *The Nation?* It's a good book and wouldn't be much trouble to review, I imagine. I'd like awfully to get some good fiction reviews while Diana Trilling is vacationing; also, I'd like to get something by you before I finish here.

Yours,
Randall

Warren did not review The Mountain Lion, *but Robert Fitzgerald did. His review, entitled "The Children," appeared in the April 5, 1947, issue of* The Nation.

TO JOHN BERRYMAN

The Nation
[September 1946]

Dear Berryman:

I sent you the book [*A Critical History of English Poetry*, by H. J. Grierson and J. C. Smith]; I'd like to give you lots of space but I'm so far behind on space it's pathetic — can you keep it down to 600 words? or about that? Can you have it done reasonably soon? 2 or 3 weeks.

Thanks a lot for what you say about the book section — I've had so little space, and most of the reviewable books are so bad, that I haven't been able to do a great many things I meant to do.

I didn't know about the Little Treasury, though I could have predicted it — I knew that my reviews meant never being put in another Williams anthology, but I didn't know he'd even get to work on the old ones. Poor thing, he doesn't know any better — it's such an innocent response.

Do call us up when you come to town; Mackie was awfully sorry to miss Princeton and I was awfully sorry to be such a comically sick visitor.

Yours,
Randall

"Little Treasury" refers to Little Treasury of Modern Poetry, *an anthology edited by Oscar Williams, who also wrote poetry. Reviewing Williams's book of poetry* That's All That Matters, *Jarrell had made his often-quoted remark about Williams's poems "seeming to have been written on a typewriter by a typewriter." This, plus other slighting witticisms in the review,*

*prompted Williams to delete Jarrell's poetry from reprints of old anthologies
and exclude him from his future ones.*

*Jarrell's allusion to being "comically sick" at dinner in Princeton was
more fully described by Berryman himself, who later wrote that Jarrell "had
a hangover, and that was very amazing because Jarrell did not drink . . .
He'd been to a cocktail party the day before in New York and had eaten a
poisoned canapé." (RJ) While everyone else dined, Jarrell reclined on the
couch looking at a book of photographs of the Russian ballet and calling out
witty remarks.*

TO WILLIAM CARLOS WILLIAMS

The Nation
[December 1946]

Dear Mr. Williams:

I'd like to do the introduction [to Williams's *Selected Poems*]. Shall I
write to Laughlin about when, how long, and how much? And I'd love to
make some offhand suggestions about things to include — but not *entirely*
offhand; I'd want to read everything over and think a while. Can Laughlin
send me whatever of yours he's printed? And is there a bibliography of
things printed by other publishers or only in magazines?

Writing the introduction makes me feel rather like Little Lord Faunt-
leroy introducing Henry Wadsworth Longfellow into Heaven; but I'm very
much pleased to be asked.

We'd like to come out to see you and are sorry about the hospital.

You promised to let me see future parts of *Paterson* for *The Nation;* are
any suitable sections done yet?

Yours,
Randall Jarrell

*Jarrell had been an interested reader of Williams since 1940 and a self-
proclaimed enthusiast for* Paterson, Book I, *so that he seemed an obvious
choice to introduce Williams's* Selected Poems (1949). *Jarrell published
three of Williams's poems in* The Nation.

TO JAMES LAUGHLIN

The Nation
[January 1947]

Dear Mr. Laughlin:

Williams had mentioned the introduction to me; I'd like to do it, I
think. I'll need to take some space — so let me do the long one at $100, not

the short one at $50. How long is long? and when does it *really* need to be finished? (I'm busy until April 1.) Will you send me all of Williams' poems that New Directions has printed? And does anyone have a list of poems published by other publishers or only in magazines?

I'll be glad to make suggestions about poems to include. I suppose you're going to ask Winters to make suggestions? It would be a good idea.

Empson is reviewing your Thomas book [Dylan Thomas's *Selected Writings*]: he lost the first copy I sent, with all the notes he'd made, and is now working away at the second.

Yours,
Randall Jarrell

*   *   *

Shortly after this, Laughlin, as Kenneth Patchen's publisher, wrote The Nation *protesting the assignment of Delmore Schwartz to review Patchen's* Selected Poems. *Laughlin wrote, "This is awful. Those two hate each other and each other's works fanatically, and neither could humanly be capable of an impartial judgement of the other." He closed, "Of course, Schwartz is one of the best critics in the USA. That is a fact. With his command of rhetoric this would just be a massacre, I'm sure you don't want that." And in a postcard to Jarrell Laughlin wrote, "If this is your idea of a joke, I don't think it's a bit funny. It may be amusing to you to stage affairs of this kind, but I think it is damned unfair to your readers who are entitled to an unbiased judgement. If you want Patchen panned I'm sure you can find plenty of people who will do it on the basis of literary criticism and not personal jealousy." Schwartz's review appeared in the February 22 issue of* The Nation *under the title "I Feel Drunk All the Time."*

TO JAMES LAUGHLIN

[January 1947]

Dear Mr. Laughlin:

Schwartz wrote a good objective-seeming review of Patchen, with which almost any good critic would agree. Patchen isn't a commercial writer, but I should never dream of calling him a *serious* writer; anyone who, through ignorance or innocence, praises Patchen as a good poet is doing real harm to poetry and criticism. I dislike New York and am not very gregarious, so I don't move in any "literary circles" here — but when I did see people I never heard them talking about any enmity between Patchen and Schwartz; I never heard Patchen mentioned at all, except as a bad poet Greenwich Village circles were fond of.

I've been reading over all the Williams I could find, and I'll talk to him about things to include when I see him next. Many of his best things are well-known, but some aren't at all. I was grieved by all the dumb short reviews of *Paterson*. Lowell is reviewing it for *Sewanee* and ought to be good — he's very fond of the poem.

Ransom wants to use my Williams piece, when I write it, for *Kenyon;* is that all right with you?

Yours,
Randall Jarrell

TO MARGARET MARSHALL

[April 1947]

Dear Margaret:

Caroline [Whiting] has been telling me all about Jamaica and has given me a couple of your letters to read; it sounds awfully nice — and it must seem wonderful to have written a lot of the book. Did you know that Joseph Szigeti [the violinist] is a faithful reader of "Notes by the Way"? He mentions it twice, very approvingly, in his autobiography.

We've been seeing the ballet — and Bernard [Haggin] too — all the time. We put an advertisement in the *Times* and got several offers of apartments for you. Mackie's seeing them today; it's nice to know the *Times* is good for something.

I'm trying to have everything fixed for you — about reviews and articles — so that it won't be any trouble for you your first four or five weeks. I have a lot of things coming in that I think you'll like; there should be more than enough for the book issue, so you'll be able to pick and choose. This unless all the writers lose their minds — which reminds me of what Hannah Arendt told me about Simone de Beauvoir: that twenty-four hours after a *Partisan* party for her she was still in a highly nervous state, and said that William Barrett had behaved to her like a crazy man. He had asked her what American writers the French liked, and while she was making the standard response he shouted at her, "You think we're nothing but savages — nigger sculpture!"

I made a seeing-and-being-seen, two-day trip to the Woman's College of the University of North Carolina; if I didn't meet your relative there she's the only one I didn't meet. I was impressed with the campus, which is large enough to have an abandoned golf-course and a pine forest on it. But New York makes you a sucker for anywhere else.

I got Eleanor Clark more or less to take Diana's place while she's vacationing. Schlesinger is doing [James] Burnham's *The Struggle for the World* — I'll save it for the book issue. And there are articles by Auden (on D. H. Lawrence) and Delmore (on American poetry) which may be ready by then — should be, but you know how reliable such things are. But I'll bet all this sounds fantastic in the sunshine.

Mackie sends her love and so does Kitten.

Yours,
Randall

William Barrett was an assistant editor at the Partisan Review, *under Philip Rahv and William Phillips, who wrote on philosophy and literature. In his book* The Truants, *Barrett said of Jarrell: "[His] persona . . . was to come on as the individual with the most glittering IQ you ever met . . . one would be unlikely to take him for a poet at all, so intensely cerebral did he appear to be. But perhaps this impression was intensified by the nervousness he felt in the New York milieu. He was uneasy with New York intellectuals, as if he felt perpetually challenged, whereas he in his nervousness was the challenging one . . . Had he relaxed for a moment, he would have been feted, both for his own considerable talents and for his temporary position of literary power." Though Jarrell had not felt uneasy with Edmund Wilson or Hannah Arendt, there is some truth in Barrett's observation.*

*   *   *

Peter Taylor had sung Jarrell's praises to the English department at the Woman's College of the University of North Carolina and had arranged for the interview that resulted in Jarrell's teaching job there at the end of his one-year stint at The Nation. *Taylor wrote, "At lunch, on the day of Randall's interview with the six senior members of the English Department at Greensboro, he behaved very well, except that he insisted upon talking about books instead of letting us ramble on about whether we preferred the fish cakes or the roast pork." (*RJ*)*

Along this same line, Lowell wrote, "He could be very tender and gracious, but often he seemed tone-deaf to the amenities and dishonesties that make human relations tolerable . . . Although he was almost without vices, heads of colleges and English departments found his frankness more unset-

tling and unpredictable than the drunken explosions of some divine enfant
terrible, *such as Dylan Thomas." (RJ)*

*In the departmental files at the Woman's College, a reference letter from
Ransom said, "Jarrell is the best young all-around writer and critic that I
know; he is sure to be a power in the land before he goes much further. I have
known him a long time, of course; my first year at Kenyon he lived in my
house ... Perhaps I should go on a little further, to say he is a chap of the
very first integrity and loyalty."*

*Jarrell was hired as an associate professor and Mackie as an instructor.
Before driving south to Greensboro, the Jarrells and Kitten spent part of the
summer in a small run-down house on Long Island.*

Greensboro, North Carolina,
August 1947–September 1951

So congenial were Jarrell and Taylor that they pooled their GI loans, and their working wives' salaries, and bought a duplex together. While it was being finished, the Jarrells stayed in the spacious home of Marc Friedlaender, of the English department, and his wife Clara May, who were on vacation. The Friedlaenders were a cultivated, well-to-do Jewish family with a tradition of Southern hospitality, and they added the Jarrells and Taylors to their clique of faculty friends that included Frank Laine, who taught Greek and Greek mythology and could whistle Chopin; Malcolm Hooke, head of the French department, who played tennis and followed the Redskins and Yankees; and Hooke's wife, Lucy, an accomplished storyteller who made superb lemon meringue pie. The friends gathered at the Friedlaenders' to play croquet, picnic by the lake, or pantomime charades before a crackling fire. None of this is mentioned in the letters, but it played an important part in Jarrell's contentment with what he called "pastoral" Greensboro.

TO BERNARD HAGGIN

108 Kemp Road East
[August 1947]

Dear Bernard:

Mackie and I have both meant to write you ever since we left. Can't you come visit us? — any time up until September 1. We have a tremendous modernist house — 15 or 20 rooms — in a pine-forest, twenty yards from a lake; it's very cool and pleasant, quite summer-resortish and there's plenty of room. It's very easy to get down here: you catch a train at Pennsylvania Station at 10:30 at night, sleep all night, and get here at 10:30 the next morning. Think how excited your *Herald-Tribune* readers would be to read about Southern programs in your column — Southern programs would inspire a toad to flights of invective, and you'd probably feel like the Old Haggin reborn.

Your Berlioz overture conductor [Willem van Otterloo] sounds wonderful; we get the *Herald-Tribune* about noon, so read you every Sunday. We've arranged for a good place to live in the fall, but are already making plans for New York ballet trips.

I shan't make this much of a letter, on the supposition that you'll come down and make writing unnecessary. I've just been in Indiana [at Indiana University] teaching a criticism class for a week — I gave a Frost lecture which I've designed for periodic use, like your Mozart concerto one.

Have you ever seen Diana Trilling's pieces in *Junior Bazaar*? I read one which told girls what to read during the summer — the mixture of a Y.W.C.A. improving tone with Diana's usual one gives an amusing effect. The article began by recommending [Isabel Bolton's] *Do I Wake or Sleep?* and finished with Berlioz — is this the influence of B. H. Haggin?

Have you made your final selection of columns for the book [*Music in the Nation,* 1949]?

Mackie and Kitten are well and happy, and send their love. We miss seeing you and hope very much you can come down.

Yours,
Randall

In The Nation, *December 17, 1949, Jarrell would write that Haggin the music critic "spoke of the Good with transfigured, self-forgetful eloquence [and] of the Bad with helpless, incredulous indignation . . . consequently, he was a sort of exemplary monster of independence, of honesty, of scrupulous and merciless frankness." Haggin the dinner companion was a superb raconteur and in appearance was anything but monsterish. Tall, handsome, masculine, and youthful, his sartorial standards required a Liberty tie, hand-sewn buttonholes, and, when the occasion warranted, a silk shirt. Haggin was friendly with Toscanini, Balanchine, Tanaquil LeClercq, and — when they were in New York — the Jarrells. Since he did not like trains or airplanes and did not drive, arranging any visit from him outside of New York required a lucrative lecture fee and much psychotherapy. Haggin did not come to Greensboro.*

TO ROBERT LOWELL

[August 1947]

Dear Cal:

I've been meaning to write ever since your letter came.

A Winters review of mine ["Corrective for Critics," a review of Yvor Winters's *In Defense of Reason*] ought to be in this or next week's [*New York*] *Times;* and I wrote a Frost lecture for Indiana, where I had a good time and met somebody extremely nice named Brendan Gill.

We ought to be moving into our house — I'm sure Peter's written all the details — in the first week in September. We'll have two extra bedrooms; you'd better come and stay a lot — we'll put a cot in the doorway between the two, so you'll get full value from both. This is a nice tennis town, and I've been playing a great deal. We really are getting to feel prewar, non-New-York, just one more version of pastoral.

We are delighted that Yaddo turned out to be such a good place to work. I'd write you about the poem ["The Mills of the Kavanaughs"] but I lost or mislaid it when we moved: I thought the writing was very good but that it needed more story or argument — but this is a first impression.

After Austin Warren's review of you [in *Poetry,* August 1947] don't you feel like writing a verse history of New England, à la Wordsworth's ecclesiastical sonnets? But, I forgot, you already have: *Lord Weary's Castle,* minus those foreign sonnets in the middle.

Auden's new book [*The Age of Anxiety*] is sad; and Jean Garrigue has turned into something so bad that most of her book [*The Ego and the Centaur*] is a perfect primer of poor rhetoric — I'm going to use some of the poems with my classes, for that.

We've had three extra cats — a mother and two kittens — here at the Friedlaenders' all summer.

Send me the poems you've written this summer (won't lose them), Peter says you've written a lot. His play [*The Death of a Kinsman*] is excellent, the nicest thing he's ever written.

Even the slow or ordinary train gets here from Washington in a little over seven hours, and I think there's a fast one to some neighboring city.

I've been surprised at *The Nation* — I thought that Margaret would keep most of my people and that it would go along pretty much as usual. I certainly was wrong.

I believe we'll like it here. School doesn't start till September 22.

Have you seen Delmore's story ["The Child Is the Meaning of This Life"] in *Partisan?* The end is the crudest effect, almost, that I've ever read. Can you read an effect? Golly.

Randall Jarrell at Greensboro, North Carolina, 1948

Elizabeth Bishop had a long poem ["At the Fishhouses"] in *The New Yorker* that wasn't one of her best but was nice to read, with some lovely parts.

What is Berryman doing next year? Give him my regards, if you see him.

Did you see *Time* the week it had a big literary section? I thought it interesting that, in an article on the state of American literature, no poet or dramatist or critic was mentioned: nothing but fiction.

We play a lot of croquet; we all feel that croquet is just your game.

I made a lot of notes on Gray's "Elegy," going to Indiana; added to the ones I already had, they're enough for an article. I wish articles grew from notes.

I've done lots of rewriting and gap-filling and such on poems — I have ⅔ of another book after *Losses*.

I was asked by a magazine to do a review of translations of German poems; they told me that the German was there too, so that I'd be able to criticize the translations as translations. You see how my fame as a German translator spread; whereas the "notable inaccuracies" — such was my friend Teufelsdröckh's characterizations of them — in *your* translation of Rilke have soured the Germans on you. A little learning ... Better none.

I have read some funny things in Friedlaender's library — *Tom Brown at Oxford* [by Thomas Hughes] and *The Ring* [the Richard Wagner libretto] were the oddest, I guess. The last one made me yearn to write a poem in which somebody gets to say:

Woe's me! Woe's me!

Write soon, not as I did. Mackie sends her love. Kitten says (here I do an imitation of R. Lowell being a cat): "Where's that man that ate up all my pancakes?"

Randall

As Poetry Consultant at the Library of Congress, Lowell was living in Washington, D.C. By this time he had separated from his wife, Jean Stafford.

Berryman was teaching at Princeton and awaiting the publication of his book of poetry The Dispossessed.

Because of Lowell's influence, Jarrell left Dial Press and returned to Harcourt, Brace, which published his third book, Losses, *in March 1948.*

Jarrell did not review the book of translations of German poems.

He used "Woe's me! woe's me!" in the first of his poems entitled "Hope."

TO HANNAH ARENDT

[October 1947]

Dear Hannah (Arendt):

We never did call each other any name that I remember, so I hardly knew how to start the letter. I felt extremely foolish leaving New York without getting to have lunch with you a last time — I had forgotten about the Memorial Day weekend, and couldn't get you at your office, and we left early Monday morning.

I wanted to send you the concentration camp poem we talked about ["Overture: The Hostages"] — tell me how it sounds to you; and I've just written a poem ["Money"] about the greatest of all poetic subjects, that no one ever conceivably writes a poem about — tell me how *it* seems to you.

We are pretty well settled here — we had a nice summer. You know how it is here: few people and lots of trees, and peace comes dropping slow, as the poet says. I miss having lunch with you; and I miss the ballet and the classical music on the radio — but outside of that . . .

I've never seen your "Dark Side of the Moon" piece in *The Nation,* and I feel guilty but extremely surprised: naturally I was certain that Margaret would use everything I'd left her, just as I'd used what she left me. It was long, but I'd gone over it carefully and cut it as much as I could without hurting it; I understood she was going to use it for a book issue. (She did the same thing (i.e. didn't use) with Empson's review of Sartre.) Of course Freda [Kirchwey] would have made a tremendous row — maybe that and the length and God knows what else added up into one big Gestalt.

Do you know Corbière's poetry well? I've just translated "Le Poète Contumace." He is a *wonderful* poet — good beyond belief.

I have several good students in modern poetry and writing — poetry classes; the first day one of them, to my great amazement, turned in a faithful imitation of Robert Lowell. But the only thing to do with the freshmen here is to write a ballet with a Chorus of Peasant Girls for them.

We are planning to come to New York in the winter when the Ballet Russe de Monte Carlo is there. Can I make a date for lunch with you, a long time ahead, and could you go to the ballet with us some evening?

My address here is 1924 Spring Garden — Can you beat *that?* The number's even more attractive than the name, these days.

I wish I could see you; do write me about the poems.

Yours,
Randall (Jarrell)

Hannah Arendt, forty-one, was a Jewish social philosopher and refugee from Germany. Jarrell met her in New York, where she worked for Schocken

*Books. After reading Jarrell's poetry she asked him to translate some Ger-
man poems for Schocken's book* The Ghetto and the Jews of Rome. *They
had frequently lunched together in New York, ostensibly talking about the
book but actually to talk about Goethe, Marx, Wittgenstein, Hölderlin,
Heine, Rilke, and others. Arendt so bolstered Jarrell's beliefs about the supe-
riority of European education and culture to American that he made this
the underlying theme of his novel* Pictures from an Institution *and mod-
eled his character Irene on Arendt.*

Jarrell inscribed the copy of Losses *he gave Hannah Arendt in the same
manner as this letter — i.e., "To Hannah (Arendt) from her translator,
Randall (Jarrell)" — to tease her about using his first name, which she, as
a German, was slow to do.*

*"Overture: The Hostages" never satisfied Jarrell, and though it was
printed in the* Kenyon Review *that fall, Jarrell never included it in any of
his books.*

TO ROBERT LOWELL

[October 1947]

Dear Cal:

We'd love to have you come at Christmas. Come as soon and stay as late
as you can. How much vacation do you get?

I think the Aeneid ["Falling Asleep over the Aeneid"] and the nun
poem ["Mother Marie Therese"] are two of your very best ones — the
other's good, but not quite *as* good. The new stuff quite transforms the
"Falling Asleep." And the nun one is as good a poem about people as
you've ever written — better in some ways than any. I wonder what the
Church will think of it? The ending's particularly marvelous, with the quotation.

The new stanza helps "The Kavanaughs" — the poem stands at the side
of the story it tells a little too much, I think. Parts are extremely good. We
can talk about it Thanksgiving — we ought to be there [Washington,
D.C.] three or four days.

I'm glad you like "The Breath of Night" so much. In "The Clock in the
Tower of the Church" there is something wrong with the poem toward the
end; on the other hand, it would be absurd to have it direct like [W. B.
Yeats's] "The Second Coming," since the poem is *about* things slowly and
very gradually wearing away into meaninglessness — hence the Jarrellish
around and around. "The Hostages" ["Overture: The Hostages"] is a very
slight affair, put into fairly good shape when I gave up on it as a serious
poem.

I have written a poem ["Money"] I think you'll be envious of, what with reading Chaucer. *Miss Tarbell* in it is Ida Tarbell, the most famous of the muckrakers at the time; *Ward* is Ward McAllister. The poem's said during the early 20's when that *Service* stuff was everywhere; it's supposed to be exactly like real speech. If I only had a good place to print it I believe hundreds of thousands of readers could get a lot out of it — but there's no such place, and I'll probably give it to *Partisan* or such.

During August I translated "Le Poète Contumace" — I worked on it week after week, living in the largest-sized French dictionaries. Haven't you even a copy of that Corbière edition [*Poems,* by Tristan Corbière, translated by Walter McElroy] I reviewed? I have two, and will send you one if you want it.

I've just finished about seven or eight typed pages on Frost ["The Other Frost"] for *The Nation* — it ought to be printed in the next three or four weeks. All about "my" Frost; maybe it'll get a few people to change their minds, at least it would if they'd read the poems.

My, *Paterson* is wonderful. I reread it yesterday.

I was rereading some Chaucer too. Did I ever show you the effective-as-later-poetry-is-effective descriptions in the temple of Mars part of *The Knight's Tale?* Nobody ever seems to quote or notice this section, though it has "the smiles with the knife" embedded in it.

I have seven girls in my writing–poetry and fifteen in my modern poetry, Jean Farley, one girl is rather promising as a professional poet, and two have done nice slight poems, one a very clever imitation of your couplets — I'll bring it when I come up. The classes are better than I thought they'd be — quite serious and overjoyed with the poetry; we've been doing Frost, Hardy, Hopkins, and Yeats mostly. Though in the writing class we've done *Uncle Vanya,* Chekhov's stories and [Katherine Anne] Porter's; "Prufrock," "Gerontion," some [Emily] Dickinson, etc.

Wouldn't you like to come next year to take my job for a year while I do the Guggenheim here? (Rhyme, Rhyme!) You'd have a job with the rank of associate professor, a good bargaining point from which to arrange for another job; there'd be very little work and $3,600; they leave you to yourself extraordinarily; and a number of the girls you'd have to teach would be ones I'd already done for a year, so it wouldn't be starting in a desert. I think it could be arranged without any trouble, if you'd like to. I believe it would be a good way to spend nine months — you could get a great deal of writing done here.

Have you read Peter [Taylor]'s *Death of a Kinsman?* It's the best thing of his I ever read — ever so nice.

Did you see Eliot as you meant to this summer? How was he? Have you read his piece on Virgil ["What Is a Classic?"]?

It took me a long time and ever so much work getting settled — we are fairly much. The house is good except for truck and train-noises.

Besides my "Money" poem I've written a short queer one on Sears-Roe-buck ["Sears Roebuck"] and a pastoral one about a class of girls and falling asleep while they write a quiz ["A Girl in a Library"] — all made up of course. I've translated, respectively but not too well, Corbière's "Paris." (Anybody who could translate the "Rapsode" ["La Rapsode foraine et le pardon de Sainte-Anne"] is the best translator there ever was.) Have you noticed the changes in some of Ransom's poems in *Selected Poems?* I'm going to mention some of them in my article — they're great or small improvements, almost always. Are you writing a piece for that issue [of the *Sewanee Review*]? Also I have to do this Williams introduction; and shortly say what is wrong with about ten poets for *The Nation.* Too much.

Did I tell you that I got a fan letter from René Clair about my first Cor-bière review?

We ought to have a pleasant easy life here and get a lot done. I'm not playing any tennis — I hurt my elbow quite badly playing and will feel lucky to have it well by spring.

Write about how long you can get away at Christmas. Later, in the spring, let's arrange a reading so as to have an excuse for another visit. Is your job much work? Don't let it be whatever you do. Kitten and Mackie send their love.

Randall

Hope the silly *Time* paragraph didn't make any trouble.

Jarrell's question about what the Church would think of Lowell's religious cynicism in "Mother Marie Therese" was soon answered by Lowell's break with Catholicism.

Jarrell's suggestion that Lowell take his place teaching in Greensboro the next year was as close as he would come to acknowledgment — in writing — of the Lowells' pending divorce. Even with this good friend, Jarrell was disinclined to "enter in" (as with the Tates), and in his letters to Lowell he continued to write in his accustomed way about literature and ordinary life.

"Getting settled" was the Taylors' idea of a good time, but not Jarrell's. Eleanor Taylor later wrote that "He had no use for work in the sense of toil or duty. And while he had boundless energy for tennis and didn't know

what it was not to find time to write, he must have had some hard moments
that spring as we got the duplex into shape." (RJ)
    René Clair was a French film director.
    The Time paragraph had sneered that while Lowell had won the Pul-
itzer Prize, a Guggenheim fellowship, and a National Institute of Arts and
Letters grant, nobody had ever heard of his book Lord Weary's Castle.

TO ROBERT LOWELL

[November 1947]
Dear Cal:
    The letters and postcard — and divine Justice clashing her scales in my
ear — prompt me to write astonishingly soon; "you little know how surprised you ought to be to see me here" as Robert Bridges said (just like
Bernard Haggin does) to begin a lecture. What a *rich* sentence! A little
richer and I'd have never found my way out.
    Can't you stay longer at Christmas? Perhaps you can get conveniently
sick here in Greensboro.
    I'm eager to see the prison poem ["Memories of West Street and
Lepke"].
    I'm not a French expert, alas! Or journeyman; or apprentice; mais non!
(Though it's very gratifying to have deceived you so thoroughly.) Just a
Corbière enthusiast; I'm gradually getting a largish Corbière vocabulary,
which isn't much used for any other French poets — I say this to their
shame. If you look up all the words in a *large* dictionary you can find some
strange and wonderful things in a Corbière poem — he makes Shakespeare
look like [Wordsworth's] "Lucy Gray" when it comes to plays on words.
I'll send you the extra copy I have. Can you buy *Les Amours jaunes* there in
Washington? Or get it through the Library? I'll pay you and be very grateful. I'll enclose a translation, in almost final form, of "Le Poète Contumace," but please *send it back when you're through reading it.* There are six or
seven things that had to be changed because there's no English equivalent
that's bearable; in general it's extremely close — some of the things that
look as if they aren't, actually are, because Corbière's using a queer idiom,
slang, or such.
    I saw a milk-weed in a hot house with a great white beard: the after-
image looked like Ernest Hemingway. These sentences are written in poetic
prose; it's not a thing you (want to) come on every day.
    Pound ought to like the content of "Money," anyway; and at least the

blank verse is a third hexameters, an irregularity that might engage. Tell me what he says. How is he?

My classes are surprisingly good in many ways. My modern poetry class all wrote paraphrases of "Of Nature Considered as a Heraclitean Fire" [Gerard Manley Hopkins] and, to my bewilderment, every person understood it and did a creditable job. We had spent much time on other Hopkins, but I hadn't said a word about it. This is still hard for me to believe.

I wrote a long piece on Frost that'll be in *The Nation*'s Winter Book Number, I suppose. I named it "The Other Frost."

You remember Empson's "Just a Smack at Auden" in which every line ends with *Boys*: I discovered he got this particular effect from a lovely early parody of Lewis Carroll's, quite worth reading.

Did I send you "Sears Roebuck"? I guess not. I enclose it — send it back with the Corbière translation if you will. Don't bother to send it back; but do send back the translation.

Peter's doing well on a new play; we're all getting settled after all our planting and painting and pounding.

Greensboro leaves one alone just wonderfully — we've had to go out to dinner only once, and in six weeks of school we've had one meeting of any kind. At Sarah Lawrence they wanted you to go to some meeting every other day. I confess I didn't *go* to any.

Shapiro's new book [*Trial of a Poet and Other Poems*] is pretty bad: the first third, "Recapitulations," is a bobby-soxer's ["Hugh Selwyn] Mauberley"; the middle section of lyrics has a few goodish and a lot bad; the last long dramatic poem or argument or something, "Trial of a Poet," is awful. I wonder if he's ever going to grow up any. And stop depending on Auden.

These people that think *Paterson* mediocre or bad would bewilder me if I weren't used to such fools. Did you see that unexpectedly dumb *Sewanee Review* article ["William Carlos Williams: Imagery, Rhythm, Form," by Frederick Morgan]?

A guy named [Peter] Viereck sent me his *Atlantic Monthly* article ["Poets versus Readers," July 1947] which thought [Dylan] Thomas, you, me, and — surprise, surprise! — Howard Nemerov the best recent poets; lo and behold, in the next issue he discovered two other wonderfully good poets: Robert Hillyer and Oscar Williams. Don't you think in the end he's going to take the place of Untermeyer?

Gee, you must be a grief to O. Williams; I'll bet every little prize was a big nail in his heart.

How (and where) is Berryman?

Peter Taylor, Robert Lowell, Robert Penn Warren,
and Marc Friedlaender in Greensboro, 1948

Mackie sends her love and Kitten sends you a Kieffer pear out of the yard — there've been between a thousand and two thousand.

Margaret would like to have you send her a poem; *The Nation* readers must be famished for one, God knows.

Yours,

Randall

The Hopkins poem Jarrell had his modern poetry class paraphrase is actually entitled "That Nature Is a Heraclitean Fire and of the Comfort of the Resurrection."

Taylor's new play was an early version of Tennessee Day in St. Louis. *Living next door made it easy for him — as in New York — to talk over what he was writing with Jarrell. Eleanor wrote of their visits, "[Jarrell's] voice could express more affection and welcome than anybody's. Peter and I were there often and long. If we made as if to go, saying, 'You're working on your writing' — for he did write down things in the course of our visit — he would always insist he could write and talk at the same time —* liked to." (RJ)

Jarrell painted and pounded on his side of the duplex and joined Taylor in planting a Ligustrum *hedge around the property, but when the Taylors wanted grass in front Jarrell objected, since it would have to be cut. The wily Taylors persuaded him to allow rye grass, which they told him didn't require cutting. When it did, they took their turn first. Jarrell did not follow suit but mischievously quoted their own words back to them, saying, "It doesn't need to be cut."*

Oscar Williams had vindictively dropped Lowell, too, from his Little Treasury of American Poets *anthology because of Lowell's unkind reviews of him. When Lowell was heaped with prizes for* Lord Weary's Castle, *Williams looked foolish.*

Berryman was an instructor of creative writing at Princeton but was not writing anything himself.

TO ROBERT LOWELL

[January 1948]

Dear Cal:

I should have written long before ... Peter says you've written a lot more on the Kavanaughs — I can't wait to see it. I've been making lots of notes on [Eliot's] *Four Quartets* and grading papers.

Allen wrote congratulating me on my Ransom essay ["John Ransom's

Poetry," *Sewanee Review,* Summer 1948]: there were two parts he was particularly interested in, the two sentences with his name in them, and he wrote a paragraph about each. He said at the end of his letter that he was glad you and I were back to writing about "the really good poets" after Williams and Frost — that we made too great claims for "Bill Williams." My paraphrase hardly does justice to his tone.

I've been rereading a lot of Elizabethan plays. Were you conscious, in "Her Dead Brother," of echoing a phrase from [John Ford's] *'Tis Pity She's a Whore?* I've got two more for you: I think you know where "It all comes back" (in "Falling Asleep," which looks swell in *Kenyon*) comes from; but have you ever compared

> Where is the end of them, the fishermen sailing
> Into the wind's tail

[T. S. Eliot, "The Dry Salvages," from *Four Quartets*]

with

> This is the end of them, three-quarters fools,
> Snatching at straws to sail
> Seaward and seaward on the turntail whale?

[Robert Lowell, "The Quaker Graveyard in Nantucket"]

The way the *sail* and *tail* survive is particularly interesting.

I've found lots of places things in the *Four Quartets* come from. Have you ever read a book named *John Inglesant* [by Joseph Shorthouse]? I believe Eliot must have read it when he was young; just as he read [Sir Edwin Arnold's] *The Light of Asia.*

Does the Library of Congress have any books by Nicholas Ferrar, the Anglican more-or-less saint who ran the whatever-you'd-call-it at Little Gidding? I *fancy* that the "Sin is Behovely" and "All Manner of Things Will be Well" are from him or somebody similar; do you know anything about them or the line "With the drawing of this Love and the voice of this Calling"?

You'd be surprised all the things (in the Krishna part) that come from the *Bhagavadgita.*

I want to correct something I said to you: the epigraph of "Sweeney Agonistes" comes from the *Maid's Tragedy* [by Beaumont and Fletcher] and I told you it came from [Thomas Kyd's] *The Spanish Tragedy.*

I think I'll write a long appreciative critical paraphrase of the *Four Quartets.*

I'd better quit this all-too-professional letter. We're delighted with the rhymes and the picture of the cat. And thanks *very* much for the dust-jacket quotations [for *Losses*]. Send me the new parts of the Kavanaughs.

All my lamentable haste over the Ransom was unnecessary — it didn't really have to be there until April, but they didn't tell me that until after they got it. Golly. We all send our love.

Randall

Jarrell repeatedly spoke of writing about Eliot or his poetry; and though he admired the poetry and taught it every year, he could not get beyond the stage of making notes for an article or a book on it.

TO ROBERT LOWELL

[February 1948]

Dear Cal:

My girls have been arranging about the Lowell Poem-Reading: we are going to have tickets, posters, lady-book-club-members, and are going to scare up a hundred or so come what may — at 50¢ a head this will keep you alive and well, though hardly happy. Time: Tuesday night, March 9. (Wednesday night there's a lecture by Gropius or something.)

I have just learned — I called you last night but couldn't get you — that I can take somebody else to Salzburg, technically as an "assistant." He'd get room and board — in a Castle — and travelling expenses just as I will. Could you possibly get away, if you wanted to? It lasts from July 15 to August 31st. Some other faculty people are Margaret Mead and Reinhold Niebuhr. The students are European teachers or graduate students, a very picked bunch of about a hundred. It's called the Salzburg Seminar in American Civilization. It's much approved of by the American government there (it gets its expense-money from the Harvard Student Council) — and the Library of Congress might look with approval on your going as helping international relations or something. I have a lecture course and a seminar — all you'd have to do would be help with the seminar, it's going to be about Eliot, Frost, etc., i.e. talk some, no lectures required. It's six weeks in all: I know you get at least two weeks vacation — couldn't you get leave to do it for the rest of the time?

All this so you won't get to feel sad at my seeing Europe first.

Write or call me about it right away, won't you?

How about having Frost over for an evening party — or dinner and a

party? If you'll write him — *we* don't know him — we'll arrange the party.
If this isn't a good suggestion you make a good suggestion.

Yours,

Randall

*Jarrell and Taylor had invited Lowell and Robert Frost to the Spring Arts
Forum on campus at the Woman's College.*

*Lowell could not go to Salzburg, since, because of his prison record as a
conscientious objector, the State Department would not issue him a passport.
Instead, he went to Yaddo writers' colony to write.*

TO WILLIAM CARLOS WILLIAMS

[April 1948]

Dear Dr. Williams:

I should have answered your letter the day I got it, since it was certainly
the most interesting thing anybody's ever written about my poetry, and I
was extremely grateful for it. But I didn't get it until it was two weeks
old — I was away from home — and I wanted to send with my answer a
long poem I've been working on for six months, which was almost finished
then and is finished now ["The Night before the Night before Christmas"]. I hope you'll like it — I think some of the rhythms (I think you'd
count them as organic metre) and details will please you.

I was *extremely* pleased that you thought "Burning the Letters" and
"Lady Bates" two of the three best poems; "Burning the Letters" seems to
me the best and "Lady Bates" the next best. My wife and I are quite fond of
"Sears Roebuck," and never read it without laughing aloud; it made me
laugh with joy to have somebody like it so well.

I feel guilty not to have finished the *Selected Poems* introduction long
ago: it's very hard for me to write (*Paterson*'s not being part of it is the great
difficulty) and I want to do a good job. Also, I got mixed up in a long
string of poems, from "Lady Bates" to the new one I'm sending; I really
don't like writing prose, and love to write poems.

I'm sure that, *sub specie aeternitatis,* what you say about the best poems
having a "return" from the losses must be true; but when you write about a
war, really write about it, you haven't that much choice, and feel a direct
responsibility to the facts i.e., people in it (most of which have no "return"
mixed in at all) that makes writing such poems quite different from writing
peacetime poems. I'm not talking theoretically but just saying what it was
like. I think what you say applies much more to peacetime poems when

you're representing a whole reality and not that particularly awful selection of it that's a war; with these you almost always need the return.

I think you're right about the regular ballad forms, usually. I rarely write them any more except for special-case poems; the regular way I write now — forms I use, that is — is that in "Lady Bates," "Moving," and the new poem I'm sending with this letter. I find that by having irregular line lengths, a good deal of irregularity of scansion, and lots of rhyming, not just perfect regular rhymes, musical forms, repetitions, "paragraphing," speech-like effects, and so on, you can make a long poem seem a lot shorter and liver. But of course you know this better than I do.

Mackie and I had such a wonderful time, the evening we spent with you, that we still feel ashamed for not having you and Mrs. Williams to dinner; you know you said you'd be busy during March, and by the end of the month we were way out on Long Island about 2½ hours from you, in a tiny ratty place, and felt that it would be intolerable to make you come so far.

Cal Lowell told me about your angina; I was sorry, and am glad that you are able to write while you're convalescing.

I was very much interested in what you say about the phantasy parts of the poems: I think there are a number of places in this new poem that are like that — but *you* say.

When I was in Washington I went with Cal to see Pound; he [Lowell] talked about your poems with real love. I've just been rereading *Paterson* before having some of my students read it, and I was overwhelmed all over again at how perfect many of the parts seem, so that you wouldn't want to change a word. I was indignant, unbelievingly indignant, at that extremely stupid article in the *Sewanee Review* about your poetry.

Yours,
Randall

"The Night before the Night before Christmas" was Jarrell's longest poem to date, 300 lines; and it was the first of his lengthy semiautobiographical poems that culminated in the three-part Lost World.

TO MARGARET MARSHALL

[May 20, 1948]

Dear Margaret:

Here's the Aiken letter with a polite answer. He must not have any wife or family, or they'd never let him mail letters like that one.

The Hart Crane book [Brom Weber's *Hart Crane: A Biographical and Critical Study*] is so bad that it would be absurd to review it separately; I'll put a paragraph about it in a Verse Chronicle. I'm going to do Tate, Berryman, Brecht, and a couple of others very briefly, in one chronicle — or if it gets too long you can split it.

I'm in the middle of exams, and will write at more length later.

For some reason I never got Richard Wilbur's book [*The Beautiful Changes*] if it's supposed to be good; could Caroline get the publisher's to send it?

Yours,
Randall

The "Verse Chronicle" Jarrell mentions was his last for The Nation *and included reviews of Shapiro, Berryman, and Brecht only.*

The Aiken letter and Randall Jarrell's response to it were prompted by the following paragraph that he wrote for The Nation's *"Verse Chronicle" for May 8:*

> Conrad Aiken's The Kid (*Duell, Sloan, and Pearce, $2.50*) *is one of those manufactured, sponsored, "American" epics: a surprisingly crude hodgepodge of store-bought homespun, of Madison Square Garden patriotism, of Johnny Appleseed and Moby Dick and Paul Revere and the Grand Canyon, all banged out in conscientiously rough rhymes, meter, and grammar — "just like a ballad." There is something a little too musically ectoplasmic, too pretty-pretty, about Mr. Aiken's best poems; but one longs for them as one wanders, like an imported camel, through the Great American Desert of* The Kid.

Conrad Aiken's reaction to this review appeared as a letter to the editors in the June 12, 1948, issue of The Nation.

The "Irresponsible" Critic

> Dear Sirs: *Randall Jarrell once before left me for dead on the dueling ground which he likes to make of reviewing, and I for one am damned if I will let him get away with attempted murder again (in his Verse Chronicle of May 8). It has come to a point where poetry needs a Public Defender against this self-appointed judge and executioner — and it is certainly time that his credentials were examined.*
>
> *Everybody knows of course that he can be very witty, and at times very funny, and he gives signs of becoming perhaps a good poet: but I*

suggest that these are not the only or the best qualifications for a good critic....

One begins to wonder, in fact, whether Mr. Jarrell is not the victim of some sort of Private Predicament: as if for some reason in himself — perhaps he will take us into his confidence — he is condemned in advance to condemn in advance, and therefore to look with glee for faults about which he can be funny rather than with love for virtues which can be praised.... The result is a kind of review which is not only wholly unreliable but wilfully misleading: it is simply not Mr. Jarrell's aim to see, or tell, the truth: he is completely irresponsible.

Luckily for his victims, and unluckily for Mr. Jarrell, the truth is in the end objectively ascertainable in these matters, and his exercises in malicious preciosity and highbrow autointoxication will be recognized for what they are: the attempts of one who is himself insecure to keep up intellectual appearances. It is the prevalence of this sort of smart-alec and pretentious parti-pris reviewing that still prevents our having a single good critical paper in the country, one that can be relied on in advance for criticism that is informed without being bigoted or personally biased, which combines an ordered sense of the past with a knowing gusto for the contemporary, and is based on trained perceptions and disciplined taste. And Mr. Jarrell is by long odds the worst example.

> *Conrad Aiken*
> *Brewster, Mass.*
> *May 14*

TO THE NATION

May 20, 1948

The "Serious" Critic

Dear Sirs:

In the last few years I've written favorable or admiring reviews and articles about Robert Frost, Marianne Moore, William Carlos Williams, William Butler Yeats, Dylan Thomas, W. H. Auden, Elizabeth Bishop, John Crowe Ransom, Tristan Corbière, Robert Graves, Walter de la Mare, Robert Lowell, R. P. Blackmur, and others; I'd have written similar reviews of T. S. Eliot, Wallace Stevens, William Empson, Louis MacNeice, and Allen Tate if I'd been given their poetry to review; and there are at least a dozen other contemporary poets who have written poems that I admire very much. Some of the earlier poets that I love or admire are Wyatt, Chaucer, Campion, Raleigh, Marlowe, Middleton, Jonson, Webster, whoever wrote the additions to *The Spanish Tragedy,* Shakespeare, Donne, Herbert, Marvell, Milton, Pope, Blake, Wordsworth, Coleridge, Keats, Tennyson, Arnold, Whitman, Dickinson, Melville, Hopkins, and Hardy.

I have had people write unfavorable reviews of my own poems, so I know how Mr. Aiken feels; my readers may have had people make unfavorable remarks about their wives or children or cats — if they have, they will know how Mr. Aiken feels. But there is a kind of scope and vigor, of *poetry,* in Mr. Aiken's description of me that I'll bet my readers couldn't match — I certainly couldn't myself. Like most reviewers, I found little of this scope and vigor in Mr. Aiken's last book; but there is a good deal in some of his earlier poems, and there ought to be a good deal in his future poems — as you can see, Mr. Aiken is no extinct volcano. I may be mistaken about his book; I *may* be wrong in admiring the poets I've listed; but I don't think so — and if there's any mistake, it's a perfectly serious, disinterested, good-hearted mistake. (It is always hard for poets to believe that one says their poems are bad not because one is a fiend but because their poems are bad.) Reviewing poetry is hard work — I read *The Kid* three times; if Mr. Aiken isn't more charitable toward my mistakes about his work, I shall have, in the end, to give up reviewing his poetry altogether.

When we read the criticism of any past age, we see immediately that the main thing wrong with it is an astonishing amount of what Eliot calls "fools' approval"; most of the thousands of poets were bad, most of the thousands of critics were bad, and they loved each other. Our age is no different. Pope says that when he wrote unfavorably about mediocre poets they would indignantly aver that he didn't like *any* poetry: "How did they fume, and stamp, and roar, and chafe! And swear not ADDISON himself was safe." The two dejected, matter-of-fact sentences I wrote about *The Kid* have made Mr. Aiken write a letter that would do credit to any of them; the many enthusiastic and admiring pages I have recently written about Frost and Corbière and *Paterson* and *Lord Weary's Castle* have made so little impression on him that he doesn't even remember their existence. These were the wrong poems, the wrong poets, for this particular poet to notice praise of.

Randall Jarrell

Regarding this exchange, John Berryman wrote, "He [Jarrell] was a terror as a reviewer ... He was immensely cruel, and the extraordinary thing about it is that he didn't know he was cruel ... That rather sweet-souled man, Conrad Aiken, wrote a letter to, I think, the New Republic *... saying that Jarrell's reviews went beyond decency — that he was a sadist. I was* *very fond of both Conrad and Randall. Jarrell's reviews did go beyond the limit . . . Conrad was quite right. But, on the other hand, Jarrell then wrote a letter in a rather aggrieved tone . . . He himself hated bad poetry with such vehemence and so vigorously that it didn't occur to him that in the course of taking apart — where he'd take a book of poems and squeeze, like that, twist — that in the course of doing that, there was a human being also being squeezed." (*RJ*)*

*　　*　　*

Late in June 1948, Jarrell packed his tennis racket, cable-knit sweater, and some poetry books and crossed the Atlantic by boat, then crossed Europe on the Orient Express. Arriving in Salzburg a few days early, he played tennis when it was not raining and wandered through the marbled and mirrored Schloss Leopoldskron, whose deer park and statues served as the setting for his poems "A Game at Salzburg," "A Soul," and "Hohensalzburg: Fantastic Variations on a Theme of Romantic Character." Two other poems from this period were "The Orient Express" and "An English Garden in Austria"; and two of Jarrell's poems with psychological roots in Salzburg were "Seele im Raum" and "A Quilt-Pattern." As Jarrell himself wrote to James Laughlin in a letter that fall, "Europe had about as much effect on me as the Coliseum had on Daisy Miller."

Jarrell was always selective about friends, and those he chose at the Seminar were the Leontiev family — Vassily, a Harvard economist, his wife, Estelle, and their young daughter, Svetlana — and a talented Viennese ceramist in his poetry class, Elisabeth Eisler.

Elisabeth Eisler, twenty-eight, was half-Jewish, charmingly feminine, and more of an artist than a student. With her short red curly hair, pink-and-white complexion, and round-eyed, round-cheeked face, she resembled the madonnas and angels in Stefan Lochner paintings. In 1939, her father had owned a commercial tile factory, which the Nazis allowed him to keep but put under military surveillance. Elisabeth, then twenty, was forced to leave the Akademie der Kunst and withdraw from student clubs and even friendships. For five years she lived in seclusion with her parents and her brother and his family, enduring the bombings of Vienna, the starvation rations afterward, and the imposition of a Russian officer in the household.

Somehow the old yellow Akademie buildings survived, and when they reopened — without heat or electricity — Eisler went back to earn her Diplom in decorative ceramics and painting. By 1948, her bowls and vases, or "shapes," as she called them, had been exhibited in a group show and were being sold through Hagenauer's, a fashionable shop on the Opernringstrasse.

*Schloss Leopoldskron, with
Hohensalzburg in the background*

Elisabeth Eisler

The Seminar at Salzburg was the first time she had been away from her family and work since before the war. She attended J. J. Sweeney's lectures on American painting and Jarrell's lectures on American poetry, and she and Jarrell soon became friendly. They liked to look out over the city from the parapet at Hohensalzburg and have Kaffee mit Schlag *and pastry at Est, Est, Est, or to walk along the Salz talking about Barbarossa (the corsair reputed to have accompanied the Turkish siege of Vienna) and Austrian folk tales. At the Schloss they read in the rococo library or sat by the lake, or Jarrell "posed like an apple" while Elisabeth sketched him in the English Garden. They loved their six weeks together but (out of deference to Jarrell's marriage) were not lovers and made a pact to return to their usual lives at the end of the summer, imagining they could write each other simply as "friends." In Jarrell's first letter to Eisler (printed in full) he observed their agreement; but after a few days in Greensboro he wrote her, "I can't be anyone's husband but yours."*

Of the seventy love letters that followed, only the most literary and autobiographical portions have been excerpted.

TO ELISABETH EISLER

[Salzburg]
September 8 [1948]

Dear Elisabeth:

This is Monday night; Sunday and Monday have been so different that it hardly seems Salzburg. Nothing at all has happened to me: I have gone to bed early, played tennis (but it's raining), shopped, and felt vacant.

Only about eight people eat at Leopoldskron now: a meal is like a very dull person's dream. Last night's dessert was a cake like chocolate stucco; when I saw it I thought, "Architecture is the mother of the arts." Tonight there was cake baked from a ready-made American biscuit-mix, but flavored with licorice. I haven't been back to Café Est, Est, Est.

I'll try to send you some linseed oil, and some books, from Paris — otherwise I'll send them from the United States. Also, I'll send you my book, some pictures, and some poems, as soon as I get home.

On the Seminar list of addresses your name is given as Lisbeth — but this is a nickname, isn't it?

It felt very strange when we left each other at the Arlberg station: as if we were bombing a city or signing a treaty; but it was like everything else I have ever seen you do — good, and without anything to change.

TO ELISABETH EISLER:
*"I send you a picture somebody had taken of me
at Salzburg, teaching. My mouth is wide-open,
curled in an odd way, as if I were Mowgli
calling to some wolves."*

When you write tell me what you draw and paint and what ceramics you are making. Tell me what the room you live in is like; and the garden there. And please do, *do* write me about the poems. Everything you think to say I want to hear — you mustn't be shy and not write about the poems.

Yours,
Randall

Jarrell sent Elisabeth Eisler a postcard from Paris reporting that he could not get the linseed oil and that he and Svetlana Leontiev had gone to the ballet. In a short letter after he got home, Jarrell wrote, "The boat trip back was very dull, though Svetlana and I played as much as we could. The boat, the 'Washington,' was terrible and I enclose a photograph of us that Vassily [Leontiev] took. The ones you won't recognize are a French girl and a preacher. Svetlana looks so unexpectedly grown-up that I almost feel I should apologize for holding her hand; but considering that thirty seconds before she'd been pleading with me to jump off the boat, 'You're a coward if you don't!' I won't."

* * *

In another letter to Eisler, Jarrell said, "What you wrote about 'A Game at Salzburg' is all true; and some of it — the part about the change between the American among the things he just knows by seeing, and the last of the poem — I had not realized, at least not in that way. The point of the end of the poem (I think that you know, but I want to be sure) is that when the world says in anguished, longing acceptance, Hier bin i' *there is no answering* Da bist du, *ever, though the world feels that there is just about to be: this is meant to express our longing, worshipping, painful acceptance of things, a sort of question-and-waiting that has to be its own answer." In his Selected Poems, Jarrell explains that Germans and Austrians play a little game with very young children in which the child says "Here I am," using a little rising tune, and the grown-up answers "There you are," in a resolving, conclusive tune.*

A Game at Salzburg

A little ragged girl, our ball-boy;
A partner — ex-Afrika-Korps —
In khaki shorts, P. W. illegible.

(He said: "To have been a prisoner of war
In Colorado is a *privilege*.")
The evergreens, concessions, carrousels,
And D.P. camp of Franz Joseph Park;
A gray-green river, evergreen-dark hills.
Last, a long way off in the sky,
Snow-mountains.

Over this clouds come, a darkness falls,
Rain falls.
                    On the veranda Romana,
A girl of three,
Sits licking sherbet from a wooden spoon;
I am already through.
She says to me, softly: *Hier bin i'*.
I answer: *Da bist du*.

I bicycle home in my raincoat
Through the ponchos and pigtails of the streets,
Bathe, dress, go down four flights of stairs
Past Maria Theresa's sleigh
To the path to the garden, walk along the lake
And kick up, dreamily, the yellow leaves
Of the lindens; the pigeons are cooing
In the morning-glories of the gardener's house,
A dragonfly comes in from the lake.
The nymphs look down with the faces of Negroes,
Pocked, moled with moss;
The stone horse has sunk in marsh to his shoulders.

But the sun comes out, and the sky
Is for an instant the first rain-washed blue
Of becoming: and my look falls
Through falling leaves, through the statues'
Broken, encircling arms
To the lives of the withered grass,
To the drops the sun drinks up like dew.

In anguish, in expectant acceptance
The world whispers: *Hier bin i'*.

TO HANNAH ARENDT

[September 1948]

Dear Hannah:

I got back from Salzburg yesterday and found your letter — it hadn't been forwarded. It's certainly a letter I'd have answered on the day I got it. What you said about the poems made me happy. And there was no need to explain about not writing: in the first place, I'm bad enough about writing to forgive any delay whatsoever from somebody else — and I'm always pleased with you, letters or no.

Salzburg was wonderful, the nicest place I've ever been. I wrote one long poem about it which I'll send you ["Hohensalzburg"]. Also, there are a lot of my poems in the current *Poetry,* most of which you haven't seen.

I am supposed to go up to Harvard for a day or two, in early November [Salzburg Seminar Conference]; I'll write you two or three weeks ahead of time and we can see each other really, in the evening, and not simply at lunch.

Nothing but the army had ever made as much impression on me as Europe.

Tell me what you think of "Hohensalzburg" reasonably soon and I'll be more pleased with you than always.

Are you teaching any class now? I'm teaching only one — one afternoon a week — and taking my Guggenheim this year. I'm going willingly to write poems and reluctantly to write a book about Hart Crane. I think if I were wiser I'd never bother to write any more criticism, and would write only poetry.

Nothing anyone has said about my poems has pleased me more than what you've said.

Yours,
Randall

TO ELISABETH EISLER

[October 1948]

Thursday afternoon I took my class outside and we sat under some trees by a lake — a pond, really. We analyzed ballads and a longish poem of Tennyson's named "Ulysses," full of Faustian yearnings for knowledge, a great believer in science and progress and evolution, miserably bored with Ithaca and Penelope and Telemachus, and full of *good* reasons for leaving — but oratorical like Ulysses.

A college named William and Mary — its main distinction is being the oldest college in the country — asked me to be their Phi Beta Kappa poet in

December. Phi Beta Kappa is a sort of honorary society for the best students in a school — when they're accepted as members there's a sort of public ceremony at which somebody makes a speech or reads a poem. Being asked to do this made me feel very old. I refused, at first, because I thought they wanted me to write a didactic, improving poem just for them — but it turned out I can read any poem I please. I think I'll read a war poem and "Lady Bates." Alas, I will have to wear a dinner-jacket, and I haven't worn mine since 1941 (you can see how my social life is) and it is fairly tight. I will tiptoe.

I'm writing you from the music room, but, alas, there wasn't any letter from you this morning. The sunlight's very beautiful — in a little I'll go and play tennis.

I think I'll tell you about Greensboro. It is as large as Salzburg, larger, and is pastoral, with trees and pleasant country around. The campus of the college is very quiet, mild and pleasant, too. It is a wonderful place to write. The house I live in is about a kilometer from the college. It's a large brick house with a fairly large back yard. Downstairs on our side is a living-room, a dining-room, a kitchen, and a small back porch. Upstairs there's a small bedroom, a large bedroom, a bathroom and a library room. The walls are nice colors — soft greys, yellow, and such — because I painted them myself. It's a rather pleasant house to live in, though the district it's in is rather too cityish and sometimes the trains make a lot of noise.

The faculty of the college are very much like the city of Greensboro — though this is doing an injustice to several trees which are cleverer than several of this faculty. But there are four or five pleasant ones who are quite fun, and usually there are several students who are fun, too.

I'm going to see a football game tomorrow, so I will have an "American face" then — but not a critic's face, an innocent enthusiastic face, the sort I have when I read the funny-papers.

I am looking now at some leaves from a red-leaved tree which sparkles like gold in the sunlight. I wish we could take a walk together here. I have found a beautiful walk far out in the country.

TO JAMES LAUGHLIN

1924 Spring Garden
Greensboro, N.C.
[October 1948]
Dear Mr. Laughlin:

I can do nothing but apologize over and over about the introduction, and say that — now that I'm back in this country — I'll get it to you in a couple of weeks. Europe had about as much effect on me as the Coliseum had on Daisy Miller — I didn't get anything written except a long poem about Salzburg. I'm really awfully sorry about it — I'm generally reliable enough about such things, but this is once when I went to pieces. You forgive me, and I'll forgive you when you do something equally foolish, if you ever do.

Yours,
Randall Jarrell

In a note to Elisabeth Eisler, Jarrell wrote, "I am miserably writing away at that same Williams Introduction I put off doing all summer — I have it half done. I wish my prose style were fast asleep in Barbarossa's cave in the mountains, or grinding salt at the bottom of the sea, or doing anything but making me write it. I used to think that when I grew up my prose would get easier and easier for me to write; but really I hate to write it more and more. Writing criticism is too much like raining in the ocean; you're wasted, and the ocean's as salty as ever. Well, this isn't quite true, but it's entirely too near to being true. I want to live like the immortal gods and write nothing but poetry; I suppose they write nothing else, at least I'm sure they don't write critical prose. I think that later I'll write a different sort of prose criticism, more like notes or letters, just to please myself. But mostly it's better, really, to make things yourself, not to write about what other people have made — if you can make anything yourself."

TO ROBERT LOWELL

[November 1948]

Dear Cal:

I meant to write all summer, but I had such a good time that I didn't write anybody but Mackie. Salzburg is wonderful, the nicest place I ever lived. In fact, Europe is wonderful — you ought to see if you can't get a passport and go next summer on your Guggenheim; I guarantee, *guarantee,* that you'll be glad, glad, glad as Pollyanna. The final judgment on Mary McCarthy is that she was disappointed in Europe.

I bought you an awfully nice translation of the *Duino Elegies* [by Rainer Maria Rilke] — I'll send it as soon as I know where you are.

I wrote a long poem ["Hohensalzburg"] at Salzburg about Salzburg.

How has the very long poem ["The Mills of the Kavanaughs"] been going? Even [R. W.] Flint liked the New Brunswick nun poem ["Mother Marie Therese"] very much.

The students at the Seminar didn't know enough English or enough about poetry, mostly, to be any real good; but I made several good friends and had a wonderful summer.

Mackie and Kitten are well and strong.

I expect to be in Washington for four or five days — about the 15th; will you be anywhere near there? I wish I could see you. I was hurrying home so fast — my boat was late — that I didn't even stop in Washington.

My reaction to Europe was roughly this: Had I actually not been there my whole *life*? Why, how'd I get *along*? (Voice is supposed to rise in incredulous wonder.)

Somebody on the boat told me about a woman who met Delmore at a party and said: "I've *always* wanted to meet you, Mr. Schwartz. I think you have the second worst prose style in English." Apparently he could think of no reply. I keep wondering who had the worst, according to her.

Write me.

Yours,
Randall

TO ELISABETH EISLER

[November 1948]

I am writing from home and Kitten is curled up on my students' examination papers.

I think I'll tell you some things about myself as a person. I work hard at poetry but put off, or don't DO, many other things; I hate even the feeling of having lots of little duties, even if they're quite easy ones — so, I'm not as much help to my wife as I should be, though I may be up to the European average; I don't know. I doubt it. You know how I am about people — rather cold to and bored by a great many. I am sympathetic and don't get angry, but I do get cross and make little automatic critical remarks. I guess this crossness usually accompanies nervousness, when things are unpleasant and get on my nerves, but that doesn't make it any better for the people I'm around. I am a good patient (few demands, no groans and complaints) but a bad nurse, since I want *my* patient to make few demands and no complaints. As you can see, I'm pretty selfish in many ways, especially about writing poems. I argue hard; and though I'm perfectly *willing* to be persuaded differently (I like the feeling of changing my mind because of evidence) it's pretty hard to persuade me, I guess.

I lead an odd, independent, unsocial life remarkably unlike most other people's lives, the life of someone whose principal work-and-amusement is writing, and reading and thinking about things. And this isn't nice for one's wife unless she has some great interest to take up most of her time.

I like the feeling of being taken care of, of having decisions made for me, of being saved bother. I'm quite optimistic, mostly in order to save bother: I accept, dismiss, and forget about bad things that happen as quickly and well as I can. I guess one great principle of my life is: *O, don't bother, forget about it; I should worry.* (Probably this is because I have a quite emotional nervous temperament, and naturally tend to do the opposite.) The reason I'm so silly about having lots of little duties hanging over my head is partly this: for ten years I've been (1) teaching, or being in the army, or being on *The Nation*, (2) writing poetry, and (3) writing criticism, answering letters from magazines, etc. Having all these going on at once means one feels distracted, and harassed, especially if one is lazy and easily gets feelings of guilt.

Proust says that intelligence and sensibility are rarely accompanied by will; and this (if I may immodestly give myself intelligence and sensibility) is sadly true of me. It's very hard for me to force myself to do anything unpleasant or dreary. (If I'm forced to, as I was in the army, that's different.) I guess I can sum up my bad points by saying I can't, even if I try, be dutiful and make my life careful and methodical and unselfish and self-sacrificing. Even if I tried, I wouldn't succeed.

O, and I forgot to say, I am childish in many ways, but this is as much good as bad.

I miss you. I wish we could put the blue bench by the window in that hall and look up at Hohensalzburg as we used to and talk.

TO ELISABETH EISLER

[November 1948]

Yesterday afternoon I drove with a friend out in the country about forty miles, to see some potteries. One lady was very arty (Juliana Busby) and named all her dogs after characters from Wagner; copied old American or Chinese pottery (some quite nice); and talked about the shapes of her pots as "having authority"; she rather embarrassed one, poor thing. But a thoroughly uneducated native potter there (Ben Owen) was awfully nice. He talked in a strange Southern mountain English and said "hit" for "it" and "thar" and "whar" for "there" and "where." He was so mild and gentle and polite that you not only liked him but were afraid the wind would blow him away. His little boy, about seven, had made a cream pitcher and mustard jar (in the shape of a churn) that delighted me and I bought them.

I was so sorry your letter sounded tired and lonesome. Please, please don't be depressed about things. I think there is less and less chance of a war coming soon. There have been no troop concentrations, the railroad to Berlin has never been double-tracked as it would be if war were intended; trade between the West European countries and the satellite states has much increased in the last few months. I know you have been through terrible and dangerous things in the past, and were very brave; you mustn't be afraid now. It's generally believed here that when Dewey becomes president he'll take a more conciliatory attitude.

TO ELISABETH EISLER

[November 1948]

Now I am going from New York to Boston and I'm still on a train.

I had a good time in New York. *Life* took our pictures (with Auden sitting on top of a ladder) at a bookstore called The Gotham. There was a party there afterwards and I saw quite a few friends. That night I went to the Balanchine ballet and yesterday I saw Sara Starr and met a very modest, honest, individual poet named Elizabeth Bishop, and saw Hannah Arendt and her husband [Heinrich Blücher] in the evening. She is a German woman in her forties, a historian and philosopher who's done some literary criticism; I've always liked her very much.

It turned out that "The Olive Garden" is her favorite Rilke poem — she knows it by heart. She was delighted that I'd translated it. Hearing the two of them occasionally say something in German made me very homesick. The atmosphere of their conversation was so genuinely cultivated and literary, so different from the atmosphere of ordinary "intellectual" circles in America, that I thought of those with more distaste than ever — if that's possible. This morning I had breakfast with Margaret Marshall, the old friend whose place I took for a year as literary editor of *The Nation*. Didn't I do a lot in a day and a half?

Hannah Arendt said something last night that gave me the feeling of being talked about by posterity. She, I think, finds my poetry more congenial than any other contemporary poetry in English. She said to her husband about me, "He has affinities with Rilke, you know." Then, she added, "His face is a little like." Her husband looked at me and said quietly, in a surprised way, "Why yes, that is so." I sat, rather awkward and silent, and finally remarked what an odd man Rilke had been; they both laughed, and I did, too.

I evidently was quite successful in writing "The Face" in a style quite different from my usual style for she said she would never have recognized it as mine. She liked it and "A Game at Salzburg" quite a lot.

When I look at your last letter while I write my own it is much more like talking to you. When I read them it is quite as if we were still at *The Marriage of Figaro.*

In another letter to Elisabeth Eisler, Jarrell wrote, "They compared me to Rilke because they were Europeans and cared for poetry more — you can't imagine how few Americans care for poetry, and in what a bad way most of the ones who do care about it, read it. I think that someday quite a lot of people will like some of my poems, but it is a day that is far away. One has few and bad readers — still, because of the poetry and criticism I have a pleasant easy job and plenty of time to write poetry and criticism, so I won't complain, though I will look wistful."

TO ELISABETH EISLER

November 16, 1948

I'm about an hour away from Washington. I've been riding on the train all day, keeping myself drugged, more or less, by reading magazines and newspapers. I left Boston at noon — I spent the morning reading poems to Estelle Leontiev; she was feeling sick and welcomed it particularly.

Henry [Nash] Smith made an extremely fair, pleasant and amusing chairman of the Seminar meeting. But there was one student who talked for an hour during the day — he was worse than any of the "talkers" at Leopoldskron, if that's possible. I got along well with [F. O.] Matthiessen, who seemed awfully well-behaved. I read part of his book that described Leopoldskron [*From the Heart of Europe*] — it wasn't our Leopoldskron. Or our Europe, either. The faculty for next year should be much better than this year's, if the ones invited accept.

The Leontievs are in good health and good spirits. Svetlana went to her first dance last night, and told us for a half an hour at the top of her voice what each girl wore and what each boy did; she was so excited she almost exploded. Their house is nice, with many Mexican things, most of them selected with extremely good taste.

I saw many photographs of all three Leontievs in their younger years. Vassily looked younger, more vulnerable, and very nice; Estelle looked plumper, and prettier, not exactly in her present style. I liked Vassily particularly this time; he's very intelligent and sympathetic when alone. As a matter of fact, when he's with people he has a kind of veneer and gaiety not too unlike my own.

My temperament amuses me: when I'm alone (or with people who bore me) I'm so indifferent and reasonable, and when I'm with lots of friends and interesting people I'm gay, excited, and say things I'm proud of or regret. In other words, when you're asleep on a desert island the most moral (or at least equable) behaviour is easy.

I saw Barbara and Herschel Baker in Boston — they've been two of my best friends for years. It was wonderful to see them. My good friends are scattered all over the country and I rarely see them.

Your letters are so wonderful to me. Your phrase, "the unknown, unwanted life" is very beautiful in English; and, "but sometimes at dusk all that questionable precariousness would come over me" sounds awfully good. I think you'll quite enjoy getting to know English thoroughly so that it will be another language all your own. And "a path through a wood full of lives" is just beautiful, too, in English. I think I will get you to become a writer, or else take the phrases for a poem.

*   *   *

A letter to Elisabeth Eisler written shortly after this begins: "I don't know whether you believed me when I said I'd put what you wrote in a poem, or thought I was playing; but here is the poem. Write me a lot about it because after all it is partly yours."

IT IS LIKE ANY OTHER

One looks from the train
Almost as one looked as a child. In the sunlight
Things still seemed to me plain,
I was safe; but sometimes at dusk
As the world darkened, a questioning
Precariousness came over everything.
XXXX XX XX XX XX XX XX XX XX
XXXX XX XX XX XX XX XX XX XX XX XX XX XX XX
XX XX XX XX XX XX XX XX XX XX
XXXX XX XX XX XX XX XX XX XX XX XX XXX

Once after a day of rain
In the winter evening
I lay longing to be cold; and after a while

I was cold again, and hunched shivering
Under the quilt's many colors, gray
With the dull ending of the winter day.
Around me there were a few shapes
Of chairs and tables, things from a primer;
Outside the window
There were the chairs and tables of the world.
I saw that the world
That had seemed to me the plain
Gray mask of all that was strange
Behind it — of all that was — was all.

When the bud has uncurled
It sees that there was, within it, space —
And it is a leaf.
That is all.

But it is beyond belief.
One thinks, "Behind everything
An unforced joy, an unwilling
Sadness
(A willing sadness, a forced joy)
Moves changelessly.":
                              One looks from the train
And there is something, the same thing
Behind everything: all those little villages,
A passing woman, a field of grain,
The horse with his head on a gate,
The man who says goodbye to his wife —
A path through a wood all full of lives, and the train
Passing, after all unchangeable
And not now ever to stop, like a heart —

It is like any other work of art.
It is and never can be changed,
Behind everything there is always
The unknown unwanted life.

*"It Is Like Any Other" was a poem in progress. It had moved beyond its
prose beginnings but more changes were to come: "dusk" became "evening";
"I was safe" grew into "I am safe"; and the pallid title and bud-and-leaf*

imagery in the fourth stanza were sloughed before "The Orient Express"
was achieved in final form and Lowell claimed it "a sequel to 'Dover
Beach."
    The X's in the first stanza of the poem indicate lines Jarrell had crossed
out.

TO ELIZABETH BISHOP

[November 1948]

Dear Elizabeth:

    May I call you Elizabeth? — I think we're at that stage of acquaintance
when one doesn't call the other anything, and it would be a shame to go
back to Miss Bishop and Mr. Jarrell. I wanted to send you the Rilke translations I talked about. Also I send the long poem I told you I'd written
["The Night before the Night before Christmas"], but I wish you'd send it
back when you're through with it, if it's not too much trouble — I haven't
any other copy, though it will soon be in *Kenyon.* I hope you'll send me
your new poems to read; I'll send them back.

    It was a great pleasure to get to talk to you in New York; I'm sorry you
won't be there when I go next month, though goodness knows you're better off in Florida. I hope you'll make a lot of notes for your Marianne Moore
posthumous piece — it would be a shame to forget anything.

    I've just been reading Turgenev's *A Sportsman's Sketches* and can hardly
bear not to conclude by saying: "Don't believe evil of me." It's a pity we
don't have the expression — we could use it.

    How was Eliot? Peter Taylor once heard him lecture on Poe in Lon-
don — Peter had met him, dressed all in black, thoughtful and melancholy,
in the hall outside the lecture-room; when he came to *ungainly bird* in "The
Raven," he remarked, "A rather graceful bird, *I* have always felt," and Peter
thought with joy, "Why, you look just like a raven yourself."

                                                                    Yours,
                                                                    Randall

Whenever Jarrell taught Marianne Moore's animal poems to a class, he
cited Bishop's anecdote about Moore's treasured elephant-hair ring. When a
strand or two of the hairs on the ring broke and came off, Moore conceived
the idea of replacing them the next time she went to a circus. All went well
until an elephant keeper noticed her approaching a standing elephant with a
pair of nail scissors and intervened. Bishop said that Moore's explanation

was so innocent and irresistible that the keeper gallantly snipped off — and presented her with — a lifetime supply.

*   *   *

Elisabeth Eisler had asked Jarrell for a reading list, which he included in the following letter.

TO ELISABETH EISLER

December 1, 1948

It's all grey and rainy this week, so I miss you more — even more — than when the sun shines. I wish that I were in different rain, Salzburg rain.

Here are the names of some books; they'll probably have some at the American Library — but I'll put down some other names of English and European books, too. If I mention things you read long, long ago, forgive me. (To tell the truth I don't like a great many American books in prose.) Mark Twain, *Huckleberry Finn;* Katherine Anne Porter, *Flowering Judas* or *Pale Horse, Pale Rider* or *The Leaning Tower* — all are good; Henry Adams, *The Education of Henry Adams* (first half); Margaret Mead, *Sex and Temperament in Three Primitive Societies;* Henry James, *Daisy Miller* or *The Aspern Papers;* Thomas Hardy, *Tess* or *Far from the Madding Crowd;* Emily Brontë, *Wuthering Heights;* Isak Dinesen, *Out of Africa;* Christina Stead, *The Man Who Loved Children;* Evelyn Waugh, *Decline and Fall;* Dostoievski, *The Idiot;* Chekhov, *The Cherry Orchard, The Three Sisters, Uncle Vanya,* and most of the short stories; Jane Austen, *Pride and Prejudice;* Dickens, *Great Expectations;* Hawthorne, *The Scarlet Letter;* Bemelmans, *Hotel Splendide;* Karen Horney, *The Neurotic Personality of Our Time;* Yeats, *Autobiography* and *Collected Poems;* Robert Graves, *I, Claudius* and *Claudius the God;* Proust; Stendhal, *La Chartreuse de Parme;* Tolstoy, *Master and Man, Hadzhi Murad, The Death of Ivan Ilyich* (these are novelettes); Gogol, *Dead Souls;* Saltykov-Shchedrin, *The Golovylov Family;* Turgenev, *Fathers and Sons;* R. B. Cunninghame-Graham, *Rodeo;* Shaw, *Pygmalion;* Kafka, *The Castle;* Maugham, *Of Human Bondage;* Ibsen, *Peer Gynt;* Wilde, *The Importance of Being Earnest;* Shakespeare, *Antony and Cleopatra* (the best of all his plays, to me); *Lay My Burden Down,* edited by Botkin (stories by slaves); Huxley, *Brave New World;* William Blake, *Songs of Innocence* and *Songs of Experience;* some of Hemingway's short stories — "A Clean Well-Lighted Place"; Malraux's *Man's Fate* (*La Condition Humaine* is the French title); Céline, *Journey to the End of the Night;* and there are lots more, but I'll quit here. Some are better than others, but all of them are at least fun to read.

I think of our forest and our castle and the hill where we sat in the day-
time — and everything else. I am lonely without you.

*   *   *

*During the Christmas holidays Jarrell decided — out of deference to his
marriage — to give up Austria and Elisabeth. In another letter to her he
wrote, "When I was at Salzburg I really forgot the United States existed —
that my life here, and people here, and my responsibilities and feelings for
them, even were. That made me behave very badly toward them. Because I
let myself feel what I shouldn't have, I made things so that anything I did
made someone suffer. You know how everything was for us, so you won't believe it was something I felt lightly and lightly forgot; I've had to do what I
have done because I felt I couldn't do anything else. I want to write to you,
and help you in any way I can, and be your dearest friend, but it mustn't be
more than that now. We can write normal friendly letters, if you think it
would be a good thing for you and not make things more difficult for you."*

TO WILLIAM CARLOS WILLIAMS

[December 1948]

Dear Dr. Williams:

Your letter about the introduction made me very happy. I can't tell you
how glad I am that you liked it that well. I'd had such an awful time
putting off writing it and slowly writing it — why I don't know — that
I almost cried tears of joy at the happy ending of the whole thing, your
letter.

What you say in the middle two paragraphs is all true, and I was much
impressed with your seeing it so plainly. The attitude behind most contemporary writing scares and horrifies me, and I was writing about you (and the
others I mentioned or didn't mention) most of all as people who didn't
have it, who had just the opposite attitude. (I haven't even tried to say this
well, since you already know what I mean.)

I hope *Paterson* is going well; have you done much of the third part? I
was awfully sorry, last spring, to hear of your illness.

I don't want to finish without thanking you all over again for your wonderful letter. It made a lot of difference to me.

Yours,
Randall

TO ROBERT LOWELL

[January 1949]

Dear Cal:

I should have written before — there are so many letters I'm supposed to write, and the Hart Crane, and so forth, that I've been putting off things more than usual. I finally finished the Williams — it's O.K. but not too good; Laughlin liked it all right, but was disappointed that I didn't have a lot of metrical analysis — he said that the interest of Williams' poetry is "mainly metrical."

I saw Elizabeth Bishop for several hours in New York. I certainly do like her.

Peter has a copy of my long poem "Hohensalzburg" — I haven't, or I'd send one; I'll tell him to send it to you instead of sending it back to me.

I liked Auden when I met him in New York. Berryman seemed very nervous and harried, because of his wife's illness I'm sure. I made up a description of Edith Sitwell: a skull fattened for the slaughter — she really does look so.

That's all right about *Losses* — but send it back to *Sewanee* and maybe they'll get somebody else to review it.

Did you see Peter's story ["Middle Age"], about three weeks ago in *The New Yorker*? I thought it very good.

When I was in Washington the Starrs [Milton and Zaro] and I went out to see the statue [Daniel French] on Marian Adams' grave; the face, seen close up, is rather unfortunate but quite interesting — we spent a long time trying to say what we thought of the face.

When you get your long poem ["The Mills of the Kavanaughs"] finished you'll have to get the *Atlantic Monthly* to print it as a serial, like [Auden's] *New Year Letter*.

I saw Jean [Stafford] for a moment at that silly party where I saw all the others; she seems in good health and humor.

It's amusing to compare your poem ["Shako"] with Rilke's ["Letzter Abend"]; they're so thoroughly and characteristically different it's as if he were representing the South Wind and you the North in a pageant.

Did I tell you that I went over [your] "Between the Porch and the Altar" with my seminar at Salzburg? They liked it a lot. They liked Ransom a lot; Frost was really hard for them, more than Eliot, he (Frost) was so different from their expectations of any poet. A hard English poem is hell on wheels for a foreigner; and most of them, the French excepted, just hadn't read any *modernist* poems — there were none in their language.

Did Elizabeth Bishop tell you about Marianne Moore and the Reptile Farm? I will next letter if she didn't.

Are you coming to Washington any this winter? I could probably come up there and see you.

This is a very scrappy, spotty, low-pressure letter but fairly long, I can't think of anything else in its favor.

I'm feeling better; I was sick quite a bit, off and on, in October and part of November. I hope your poem's going well.

> Yours,
> Randall

Jarrell was sending poems to Taylor in Bloomington, where Taylor was teaching at Indiana University.

Berryman seemed "very nervous and harried" not only because of his wife Eileen's illness but also because of personal stress from being in analysis, as well as from (as Berryman described her in Berryman's Sonnets*) "an Excellent lady, wif whom he was in wuv."*

Jarrell had assumed Lowell would review Losses *for the* Sewanee Review, *but Lowell, too, was nervous and harried. Writing Jarrell from the Yaddo colony in Saratoga Springs, New York, he hinted at how wounding his divorce proceedings were. Also, he had become the spokesman for an investigation of the morals and politics of the directress at Yaddo. Elizabeth Hardwick, Flannery O'Connor, and Edward Maisel supported him, but when news of the investigation leaked to the literary community, angry accusations were sent to the board. As Sally Fitzgerald wrote in her introduction to* The Habit of Being: Letters of Flannery O'Connor, *"The kind of injurious attack launched, chiefly against Lowell, by people he had thought were his friends, was a profound shock to him . . ." For these reasons he felt he was in no state to write a review of* Losses, *and this was borne out by his nervous breakdown a few months later.*

The "Reptile Farm" anecdote referred to the time Bishop and Moore, two animal lovers, were driving to the cemetery after the funeral of Moore's beloved mother. Bishop said that they were riding in silence and that Moore was lost in grief when she (Bishop) noticed a sign at the side of the road and couldn't keep from saying, "Oh, see the little reptile farm!" For an instant Moore's face lighted up with the intention of stopping, then clouded over as she remembered where they were going. But she did say, "Oh . . . oh . . . maybe on the way back."

TO LOUIS UNTERMEYER

January 8, 1949

Dear Mr. Untermeyer:

I came home from Christmas vacation to find your letter, and it certainly was a pleasant one to read. I'm awfully glad to have you like the poems so much. About the selections: you write, "Let's say that your group must include 'A Camp in the Prussian Forest,' 'A Country Life,' 'Pilots, Man Your Planes,' 'The Refugees,' 'Jews at Haifa,' 'The State.' " This would be thoroughly satisfactory to me, goodness knows, if you'd substitute the other double-checked poem in *Losses,* "Burning the Letters," for "The Refugees." "Burning the Letters" is a lot better poem (William Carlos Williams and quite a few people think it my best poem), in the first place; in the second place, I've partially rewritten "The Refugees," haven't finished and would hate to have it in the anthology just as it was. I don't think it matters a bit not having something from *Blood for a Stranger;* as you say and as I think, the later poems are better. And quite a number of the *Losses* poems were written during or just after *Little Friend,* so it matters even less which of these two a poem comes from. Nobody knows or cares which book a poem comes from, really; and I'm not a venerable figure with periods that need to be represented.

Several people liked "Hope" as you did — better than I expected it to be liked, really; I guess the mailman is everybody's tutelary deity — the only one left for most or many people. I can never see a mailman without thinking he's mine, or an envelope without thinking, "Maybe it's addressed to me." Either "Hope" or any of the others you mention would be quite all right with me, if you do turn out to have more space (they're all poems I like); but I'm sure the six you mention, with "Burning the Letters" instead of "The Refugees," would be a quite adequate and representative sample.

I don't suggest any brand new poems because the best two I have are too long, 200 and 450 lines; the long one, "The Night before the Night before Christmas," is in the Winter *Kenyon,* and the other's named "Hohensalzburg" and will be in *Poetry* this spring. I imagine you'll like the second, judging from what you've written about Heine. He's one of my favorite poets — I could recognize the linden trees in Salzburg as lindens just from having read about them in Heine.

"Lady Bates" doesn't seem to me like Ransom but it is a little like Corbière's *Rondels pour après* — if you ever come on my translation of them you'll see what I mean.

What you say about the poems in *Losses* is *extremely* gratifying. By the way, since you're using "Pilots, Man Your Planes," it will amuse you to know that I've met five or six carrier pilots who talked to me about it; they say it really brings back the old days, you can always tell when somebody's really served on a carrier, etc. The funny thing is that I've never even been on one for a minute.

Cordially,
Randall Jarrell

TO SISTER BERNETTA QUINN

[January 8, 1949]

Dear Sister Bernetta:

Thank you for sending me the [Hart] Crane essay — I very much enjoyed reading it. I agreed with a great many of the things in it; I heartily disagreed with what you quoted from Shapiro: that a poem is written with "not-words," that a word in a line of poetry is completely different from a word in a line of prose. This false and silly theory is borrowed from Sartre (it appeared in this country in an article of his in *Partisan Review* ["What Is Literature?" January 1948]) — I could see that you disagreed with it yourself, and I hope nobody will ever believe it.

Yours sincerely,
Randall Jarrell

Sister Bernetta Quinn is a Franciscan nun, poet, and scholar who corresponded extensively with Pound, Warren, William Carlos Williams, Jarrell, James Dickey, Robert Bly, James Wright, Berryman, Flannery O'Connor, and other writers. Although she met many of her literary correspondents, she never met Jarrell. She is the author of The Metamorphic Tradition in Modern Poetry; Ezra Pound: An Introduction to the Poetry; *and* Randall Jarrell.

TO ELISABETH EISLER

[January 1949]

Dear Elisabeth:

I'm so late in answering your letter because I've been away in the North between a week and ten days and I didn't get it until I came back.

Next letter I'll send a couple of poems — but not new ones, I haven't written any. Mostly I've been writing prose about Auden, when I've written anything. There is an Auden line, "We are lived by powers we pretend to understand," that seems to me very truthful, even if he did take it from [Georg] Groddeck.

In Washington I saw a big exhibition of the paintings and drawings of Kokoschka. I'd seen very few of his things before, and was much impressed with what a good and interesting painter he is. Some of the ones I liked particularly were *The Tempest, Lyons,* and a painting of two lovers and a cat. Are there any of his paintings in Vienna? Is it easy to get reproductions of his work? Some of the landscapes are good in such a queer way — not what you expect from a landscape at all. Do you like those lithographs called *Columbus in Chains* or *The Bound Columbus?* Naturally I can't remember the German for this.

I've been reading an enormous amount of anthropology and Freud; if you say that the unconscious reason for this is to convince myself that everybody else acts as unreasonably as I do, I won't deny it.

I've just been playing [Richard Strauss's] *Don Quixote* on the phonograph, and noticing that its sub-title is *Fantastic Variations on a Theme of Knightly Character.* I'd been correcting proof on "Hohensalzburg" (I'll send it to you in print next month) and I thought, "A good subtitle for it would be 'Fantastic Variations on a Theme of Romantic Character.' " I tried to imagine what a reader would make of it who knew nothing about Salzburg or me, and I couldn't; in fact, when I read it, I think, "What does it *really* mean?" And this I can't answer, though usually I know exactly what my poems mean. It's like a dream that needs analysis to be plain.

Do you like *Don Quixote?* I do. But not as well as some Mozart Sonatas for Violin and Harpsichord that I've also been playing.

I'll send some poems ["A Sick Child" and "A Perfectly Free Association"] in this letter.

Yours,
Randall

TO ELIZABETH BISHOP

[February 1949]

Dear Elizabeth:

I should have answered your letter weeks and weeks ago; I've been generally putting off writing letters. I was glad you liked the "Night before Christmas," and interested in what you said about it. I'll send you a *small* child one ["A Sick Child"] and see how you like it.

Rilke certainly is monstrously self-indulgent a lot of the time, but the good ones are so good it makes up for it. Really one expects most of a good poet's work to be quite bad — if that isn't so it's the 30th of February; it's amusing to have reviewers complain that some of the poems in a poetry book aren't good, because that applies to every book of verse there ever was.

Your German man sounds very typical. Have you learned much German by now? Mackie learned quite a bit, but I'm too lazy.

When are you going North this year? Couldn't you visit us for a while on the way? We have a great deal of room. Mackie said we must ask you, the other day when we were talking about Cal; if you'll come she'll write you an invitation with illustrations and things.

I haven't written any poetry, and I've written little enough prose; but I've read lots of anthropology books, and now amuse myself by looking at the North Carolina faces and deciding they're full of Paleolithic survivals or else fell against a wall early in life.

Do you think you'll go to Yaddo this summer? Cal was talking about getting different people; it might be fun.

I thought you said you'd send me some of your new poems to read. Please do; I'll return them promptly, so it won't be a matter of losing copies and having to type more. Have you ever read the Turgenev novelette about the two friends who systematically visit all the households in the neighborhood to find a wife for one? It's a very funny charming one.

Yours,
Randall

I still haven't your address; it wasn't on the postcards and I can't find the letter. I wrote this letter five or six days ago and still haven't found the address, so I'll send this to your publishers.

I bought your *North and South* to give somebody the other day, and read the clean new one instead of my dirty old one. The best poems in it — quite a lot — are really just wonderful; they seem perfect, especially for the tone and moral attitude, or whatever you'd call it.

TO MARGARET MARSHALL

[February 1949]

Dear Margaret:

Here is a thoroughly negative, useless letter, except for two poems. I finished the MacLeish review [of Archibald MacLeish's *Actfive and Other Poems*]; when I read it and thought about it I just couldn't bear to publish it — it would depress and vex the poor guy and do no *good* at all, since nobody needs to be told it's a bad book. It's all the truth, but the whole thing would be like digging up a corpse to tell it it wasn't any good when it was alive. So I send it to you to read but *not* to print — just send it back, if you will. I'm sending back the book and you can give it to Rolfe Humphries.

As for Tate, I found I just couldn't do a short review of all his poetry —

it would be hard enough to say what I think in a long article. I made notes, notes, notes, I had old ones, I was lost in notes. It's been so long since it came out [*Poems 1922–1947*] I'm sure you'd rather not print a review of it anyway. Please just say *That dumb Randall!* and forgive me.

Yes, I'll have a long biographical chapter on Crane, influence of life on poetry, etc. But alas, I couldn't possibly have it done by May. You remember when I saw you last I talked about doing the last writing and rewriting over the coming summer? Well, after I saw you I lost even more time being sick than I had earlier in the fall. I was in bed a lot and actively nauseated a lot of the time I wasn't. They thought I had gallstones and X-rayed me and so forth; but I didn't, so they just gave me medicine. I'm lots better now — I've felt fairly decent for the last three or four weeks.

Don't you want to take some days off early in the spring and visit us? Think of sitting knee-deep in violets and whine-y Southern girls while *The Nation* is still snowbound. Seriously, we'll probably be going north next year (we're sick of North Carolina — the average North Carolina girl talks as if she were an imbecile with an ambition to be an idiot) and then won't be able to offer you any weather but your own.

When I find out the exact date I'm going to read at Wellesley I'll write you. Danilova's going to be here tomorrow, oh joy!

One of the poems is very poetic and the other very prosaic; if you don't like either just send them both back and I'll send one half-way between.

Yours,
Randall

No one reviewed MacLeish's book for The Nation.

The possibility of going north the next year may have been related to the reading (and an interview) at Wellesley. However, no offer from a northern university was forthcoming.

The two poems Jarrell sent Margaret Marshall were "A Soul" and "A Perfectly Free Association," and she published both.

TO ELISABETH EISLER

[February 28, 1949]

I'm awfully sorry you couldn't get the French visa, but Italy may turn out to be almost as good, and you can stay longer, I imagine. Are you going to see the paintings at Florence? You can really see a lot of the Donatellos I sent you in the book.

Dear Elisabeth, I'm so sorry about everything. I hope so much that Italy will be nice for you — that you can paint there, yourself, and see all the paintings and meet people you'll enjoy meeting. Write me all about what you do and I will write you what I do. Last week I went to Detroit to read poems and make a lecture. It is a hideous city, 8 miles wide and 20 miles long, like a parody of America. In every direction there are immense factories, each worse than the last.

You remember I once said, scornfully, that *I* wasn't going to the symphony to hear Mahler? Well, I now feel terribly foolish to have said so, and he's become one of my favorite composers. I've got some of his symphonies from the record library at the college, and bought two more. By now I know the First, Second, Fourth, Fifth and *Das Lied von der Erde* well. He seems wonderful to me, and his neglect in this country seems particularly strange. I'm sure that in the end he will be thought a great composer by everybody. I've heard four or five of his Songs and they seem wonderful, too. Did you ever meet his wife, or his daughter? I read his wife's biography of him (and his letters), and she seemed a mixed blessing. His letters always seemed so much more reasonable than her picture of him.

I'm sending this letter the next morning after getting yours, so I hope it will get to you as soon as possible. Tell me how you liked the poems I sent in the last one. Tell me what Italy's like, and what painting you like best. I hope so much that Italy will be nice for you.

TO ROBERT LOWELL

[March 1949]

Dear Cal:

I was delighted you liked "A Game at Salzburg" that well. Peter writes that he's sent you "Hohensalzburg" which is *really* full of German scenery — Austrian, that is.

We're not going to Europe this summer but are next (and next and next, if we have the money). Why don't you get people to use influence to get you a passport by then? I'm sure they could. Europe's out of *this* world.

All the stuff about the poetry consultant and the [Bollingen] prize was very interesting. I didn't know it was given for all one's work, not just a book. They had plenty of courage to give it to Pound — and if they lose their nerve and give it to Williams, that's good too.

Williams was (I quote Laughlin) "wildly enthusiastic" about my introduction and wrote me a lovely letter; so in the end I felt good about it also.

I can't wait to see the Kavanaughs.

During the next five or six weeks I'm going to read poems at Wellesley — I think I'll stay in Boston several days with the Bakers (Herschel and Barbara Baker). Why don't you come there? I'll tell you when I get the exact date.

I've been getting some Crane done: it's hard work . . .

I don't think I'm ever going to write any more reviews. I wrote a last one for Margaret — MacLeish — and it seemed perfectly true but so crushing that it was like digging up a corpse to demolish it, and I decided not to print it. We live in a reviewing criticizing age that doesn't give a damn for works of art, mostly — why should I help it along? I'll write articles occasionally about what *I like* and all the rest can just die quietly without any help from me.

Mackie sends her love. What are you doing this summer?

Randall

TO ROBERT LOWELL

[March 1949]

Dear Cal:

I'm not sure when the Wellesley thing is; I'll write when I know. Maybe you could come to Boston for a couple of days and I could come back to Yaddo with you for a couple. Coming to Yaddo this summer might be fun, if you could arrange it; Mackie's done about half of a translation of Stendhal's *Lucien Leuwen,* and might finish it there.

Going to Rome to see Santayana would be awfully nice — and the rest of Europe too. Why don't you come down and see us some week early this spring, while Yaddo is still bathed in glaciers?

Tell that wicked Peter to send you the poem as he wrote me he already had.

I haven't been writing much but have been becoming learned; I've read more anthropology than anybody but an anthropologist or some wild eccentric. Some other wild eccentric, that is. Would it interest you to know that Auden doesn't have a true Nordic face, but a combination of Nordic and Brünn man, a late-Paleolithic survival? If I come on a picture that looks like *you* I'll write. I've decided I'm Atlanto Mediterranean, but it wasn't easy.

I think I'm writing this letter just to escape from my real problems, which are, so far as I can see, that I don't like to write prose. I'm just like *The Cherry Orchard,* half of me keeps saying to the other half, "You must work, my friends, you must work" and the other half does any thing to keep from it, although the *idea* sounds lovely to it.

Maybe your colleague Alfred Kazin thinks the Catholic church is the root of all evil, but I don't: to me it's just one more horrid thing.

I had a MacLeish review hanging over from my discarded verse-chroniclership; I at last reluctantly did it and then decided it would be too hard on the poor dope and that I wouldn't print it at all: it wouldn't do any *good* — nobody thinks anything of him any more. So I'll just send it to you to read, in this letter — send it after you read it.

I hope the poem's going well.

Randall

"Wicked Peter" had written Jarrell from Bloomington of the emergency Caesarean-section birth of the Taylors' daugher, Katherine Hillsman, and that it had cost three times what they had put aside. The salary at Indiana University was not worth the price of leaving the South, he said, "especially if my friends are not going to be brought here, too." Taylor had recommended Jarrell to teach poetry at Indiana University, but they had chosen a Mr. Yellen instead. Reporting this, Taylor had written, "I'm afraid our New Yorker Poet Yellen is too slick and fast-moving for a backwoods Tennessee politician like me. He made an alliance with all the young Yale Ph.Ds. We really do live in a wicked, wicked world." His letter went on to say that he hoped to get his old job at the Woman's College back again, which delighted Jarrell, except that the Taylors wanted to dispose of their half of the duplex and find a house in the country. Taylor wrote, "There is one thing certain, you won't want us living there again, not with Katie, and not with the one we are hoping for within the next two years."

TO ELISABETH EISLER

[April 21, 1949]

I'm *so* glad you're getting to go to Paris! The pictures you can see there are more closely connected to what you do yourself. What you've written about the Italian paintings is wonderfully interesting.

I've been playing tennis a lot, and unusually well — but I hurt my hand so that it's very stiff and sore. I can't play for a week or ten days and probably won't be able to hold the racket tight and play normally for several weeks more. The silly hand hurts when I write, type, or do nothing at all.

I'm crazier than ever about Mahler. Some of his Songs have just been issued on records, sung by Desi Halban; they're so beautiful. Do you know *Das Lied von der Erde*? He really is one of my favorite composers; it seems weird that I hardly knew he existed.

I've been reading Dickens novels I hadn't read before: the best is *Little Dorrit.* Mostly you feel, "Never were such gifts so wasted." A book that begins wonderfully, full of imagination and brilliant and accomplished writing, then goes off into a perfect swamp of sentimental, oratorical, optimistic lies and commonplaces, stuff his readers and his own baser self just couldn't do without.

The poet who was my particular friend among poets — Robert Lowell — has had a bad "nervous breakdown" and is in a mental hospital. I had a pathetically irrational letter from him last week. You have such a helpless bewildered feeling when something like this happens.

I think you'll love Paris and the Paris paintings. Tell me about all you see.

TO SISTER BERNETTA QUINN

[May 11, 1949]

Dear Sister Bernetta:

I'm delighted that you liked "Hohensalzburg" so well. No, there's no reference to Kafka's castle: Hohensalzburg *is* a big castle, the best I ever saw, on the hill above Salzburg — I lived under it all last summer. Germans (some of them) really think that ghosts, if you meet them, change you into something else, just like the *Wizard of Oz. These,* at the end, refers first to "our life, our death, and what came past our life" just before; second, to all the varied and opposed things in the poem, many of which have been mentioned in the ten or fifteen lines before.

I really shouldn't, in politeness, have expressed myself so forcibly about Shapiro: I thought that you, as a nun, would have a more or less Thomist position, and automatically disagree with him. He seems to have such a limited and naive view of what words do that when words do something besides that he calls them non-words: but if there's anything modern authorities on language agree on, it's that words were always doing all these things he thinks special to poetry, in prose, speech, or anything else. Calling words non-words because they're performing a usual and essential function of language, whether in a poem or in prose, confuses everything, cuts off poetry from prose and speech in general (and many of the most wonderful poetic effects in English are of course in prose — look at the Bible), and makes me impatient and despairing.

Sartre's piece ["What Is Literature?"] is in the January 1948 *Partisan.* He makes an absolute gulf between poetry and prose: prose uses words as meaningful signs, but poetry "does not use them in the same way, and it does not even *use* them at all." Poetry "is on the side of painting, sculpture,

Richard Wilbur, Peter Taylor, and Jean Stafford,
Greensboro, 1949

and music." Poets "do not speak, neither do they keep still; it is something different." The poet's words aren't normal words at all: "they become things themselves ... The word-things are grouped by magical associations of fitness and incongruity, like colors or sounds" (into "the veritable poetic unity which is the *phrase-object*"). He calls the language of poetry "language inside out." Plainly these word-things of Sartre's, these ordinary words turned inside-out, that poems are made of — these are Shapiro's non-words that poems are made of.

But really this is like showing that Sycorax was Caliban's mother: I wish that the mother had been childless and the son an orphan.

Yours sincerely,
Randall Jarrell

There's lots more to say about the Shapiro, but it's not really worth it; I imagine we'd agree well enough if we went over it sentence for sentence.

TO ROBERT LOWELL

[May 1949]

Dear Cal:

Mackie and I were terribly sorry to hear that you'd been sick. As soon as you're better we want you to come for a long visit with us, as long as you want — we've got plenty of room and have missed seeing you ever so much. Kitten says *Meow, meow,* meaning *Do come.*

Here at the college they gave Katherine Anne Porter an Honorary Degree — I was her sponsor, which meant that I whispered jokes to her to keep up her spirits, made her stand up, put a hood over her head, and so on. She likes Peter's stories very much, she said.

I haven't written much poetry this spring — mostly one medium-length poem, a child's Hansel-and-Gretel poem ("A Quilt-Pattern"); but I've improved several old ones. Mackie has been gardening a lot, and I've been transplanting hedge plants to the front yard — I began with feeble little things and ended with ones about five feet high, all of them growing like Tannhäuser's staff.

Next year's Pulitzer Prize will go to Cole Porter, I bet.

Have you ever read *Little Dorrit?* I just read it — it has extremely good parts. I've been reading a good deal of Dickens, and I read or reread all Turgenev this winter. Have you seen my Williams introduction? I, at last, got it done, in November. But mostly, all winter, I read anthropology and psychoanalysis in the greatest quantities.

A very nice poet was down here for the Arts Forum — Richard Wilbur. You'd like him a lot, I think.

We're going to be on Cape Cod in August, and I'll come to see you, if you'd like for me to — I certainly do want to see you a lot; so does Mackie.

Peter's coming back down here as you know, I suppose. It'll be nice.

There was a young man in the Arts Forum who wrote carbon copies of your poems — and I was sent a little magazine with another faithful imitator in it; but *he* was influenced by the Fugitives too, and wrote a religious poem with the word *escheat* in the second line.

We'll see you soon; get better fast, come stay in Greensboro and pretend to be Orpheus in Thrace.

Love,
Randall

The remark about Cole Porter winning the Pulitzer Prize was inspired by Peter Viereck's winning it in 1949.

TO ROBERT LOWELL

[June 11, 1949]

Dear Cal:

We can't tell you how pleased we were that you're well and can come to stay with us some; if you'll send us Elizabeth Hardwick's address *right away,* Mackie will write to ask her to stay too. If you could come on the 5th of July that would be a good time for us; we get there on the 3rd. It's at Nag's Head, about forty miles from Norfolk. It's about a mile from the post office — if you inquire there they can tell you where it is.

We're delighted that Elizabeth Hardwick can come too — but be sure to send us her address right away i.e. air mail special delivery or such, so that Mackie can write her a nice formal invitation.

We haven't seen Peter yet, but ought to in a couple of days. He went to Missouri for a week — a writers' conference. Doesn't it seem justice that *writers' conference* and Creative Writing should be such awful names?

See you soon.

Affectionately,
Randall

The Jarrells spent the early summer on the North Carolina coast near Nag's Head. On the subject of this vacation, Jarrell wrote Elisabeth Eisler, "I had a miserable time, since I was typing and writing eight or nine hours a day. I was trying to finish a prose book made up of mostly old articles about Auden, Frost, Ransom, Corbière, and so on. I got two hundred and forty pages completely finished — but O, it was dreary!"

Lowell and Elizabeth Hardwick did not visit, as they were planning to be married in July.

The Jarrells spent the last part of the summer on Cape Cod, not far from the Starr family.

TO BERNARD HAGGIN

[September 1949]

Dear Bernard:

Although we spent a month on Cape Cod, we never got north of it at all — we'd thought we were going to Boston, and meant to try to see you then. We were crazy about the Cape, and rented a rather large house — Colonial, too — for next summer. Won't you come and visit us for a couple of weeks or longer if you can? Any time from June 20 to September 5. We asked Margaret to come too, and thought it would be especially nice if you could both come at the same time. If you don't come I'll start telling everybody that *really* your favorite composer is Shostakovich. No, Howard Hanson.

I've been buying some records recently, and read your *Music on Records* over, and enjoyed it very much. When will *Music in the Nation* be out?

I don't know whether we'll be in New York any this winter. I do have to read poems there early in April, so I'll see you then, at least.

I've just been playing on the phonograph the *Rosenkavalier* "little Resi" speech [Marschallin's monologue, Act I] — it sounded lovely. I certainly do agree with you about *Don Quixote*'s being much Strauss's best orchestral piece — and that the Victor recording is a million times better than the Piatigorsky one. The two recordings hardly sound like the same piece.

One thing I don't agree with is that Prokofiev's second violin concerto is "completely uninteresting"; it's not extremely good music, but some of it really does seem to me charming, pretty, delightful. I heard the Philadelphia play it just after Virgil Thomson's Battle March of the Alligators, and oh, it did sound lovely!

What do you think of the *New Statesman*'s record critic? I usually quite enjoy him from week to week, but when I got the bound volumes and read or reread him in quantities I was disquieted by some of the things he liked, and his style seemed too florid.

I hope you're well and happy and had a nice summer. The ballet ought to be fun this fall — do write a lot about the English, how it compares with ours; it's your *duty*. I think that we'd come up and see it except that we're saving money to buy ourselves a pretty new car for Christmas.

It's so sad, reading your record book, to see [Artur] Schnabel's Opus 109 and Schubert's B Flat Major promised soon, "soon," by Victor. Gee, they're wicked people.

Yours,
Randall

I read Virgil Thomson's last critical book [*The Art of Judging Music*] up at Cape Cod, and I was astonished all over again that anybody who could say the best things in it could say the hopeless things too. How I wish I were a French composer under the age of 79, so that Virgil Thomson could write about my music! You feel like saying "Who will deliver us from these Franks and Franco-Americans?" And the really patronizing style in which he talks about Prokofiev and Toscanini! Well. He's lots of fun in the good parts, but by the time you read any book of his you don't *trust* him at all. I was much amused by the finest compliment he could think up to pay Mahler's Ninth — that it was really quite like a French impressionist work, must really have been influenced by them.

"Battle March of the Alligators" was Jarrell's spoofing title for Thomson's Louisiana Story Lyric Suite.

TO ELISABETH EISLER

[October 1949]

I've put off writing you for ten days because each day I would think I'd have this poem ["An English Garden in Austria"] finished to send you, I mean, and I didn't finish it until today. Finishing it made me feel wonderful, the way Goethe felt when he said, "You know, I'm a born writer." I almost never feel like a born writer and I particularly didn't this fall — I hadn't written a poem for six months.

But I'll look at your letter and write about the things in it before I write about the poem. (One thing you'll like about the poem — that I liked about it — is that it has *Der Rosenkavalier* in it.) The things I won [in Cape Cod tennis tournaments] were *fairly* out of my style: a silver card tray, bread dish, a leather photograph frame, cigarette box, and bill-fold. The cigarette box looks particularly odd: it has on it, in bright gilt letters:

RANDALL JARRELL

MIXED DOUBLES

I was particularly interested in what you say about Paris seeming such a grim and merciless "Big City" to you, because — to an American, compared to *any* big American city — Paris is almost like Salzburg, so beautiful, odd, pleasant, and civilized. You would hardly believe how ugly, violent and over-whelming a big city like Detroit is; and in New York, looking at crowds waiting underground in the subway stations, I've often thought, "This *is* Hell. Hell must be exactly like this." If you saw one you wouldn't think I exaggerate.

I love Braque, too. (I think late 19th and early 20th century painting gives one more of an immediate thrill — is easier and more congenial to one — than any.) I've seen a number of other Brancusis. They're generally carried to the same degree of abstraction, seem thoughtful and pure, and have beautiful surfaces. Shall I try to find you some photographs of his sculpture or a book on him? Did you like him that well?

Have you ever heard the Lotte Lehmann records of *Dichterliebe*, the Schumann song-cycle? It's really my favorite song-cycle, and she sings it just wonderfully. She's my favorite singer, I think.

Now I'll write some about the poem. Since it's a poem about the "cultural past," so to speak, it has about a million allusions in it; often the allusions are made by faintly parodying or echoing things people said or wrote. I took "English gardens" as a symbol of Romanticism spreading across Europe: they were the very first big sign — it's wonderful to think of people carefully *building* a Ruin in a garden and grottoes and all the rest. Milton called Adam and Eve "our first great parents." Racine really did write *Athalie* for Madame de Maintenon's convent school. And Strauss called Baron Ochs "a rustic beau of thirty-five or so," — one who'd have been behind the times and have expected it to be Metastasio when it was really Rousseau. Have you ever read anything about Farinelli? I read a book about him, as is evident. After I finished the poem I looked him up in the encyclopedia and they treat him at moderate length: he really did half-cure the King of Spain of his madness, by singing the same four songs to him, every day for ten years; as the books say, he was "prime minister in all but name." All the great writers, composers, singers in Italy belonged to the Arcadian Academy, and had pastoral names: Goethe actually belonged, and was called Megalio Melpomeneo. Faustina Hasse and her husband [Johann Hasse] were the other greatest singers of the day and her husband, the composer of the operas Metastasio wrote the libretti for and Farinelli sang in. Then I have all the stuff about Voltaire and Frederick the Great, and the French Revolution, and *Figaro* and Mozart, he did write Masons' Funeral Music; the Revolutionists, to take the place of religion, once had a ceremony in honor of Raison, it being acted by a French actress. Napoleon really did read *Werther* seven times; criticized Werther, to Goethe, as being too ambitious (he should have felt only love, according to Napoleon). He did carry *Werther* to Egypt, when he fought the Mamelukes under the pyramids, and told his soldiers that History was looking down upon them; he told them that every French soldier carries his Marshall's baton in his knapsack. He would delight his favorites, show favor to them, by leaning forward and pinching one of their ears, vulgar man! At Jena, of course, he did say "Voilà un homme!" to Goethe; and said to him, "Politics is Destiny." "Others have understood the world; we change it" is a parody of what Marx said; "Truth is what works" is roughly what the most famous American philosopher of this century [William James] said; "I have seen the future and it works" is what a fairly famous American writer [Lincoln Steffens] said when he first saw the New Russia. I wanted a collection of revolting statements to express Our Present World. Then all the stuff at the end is stuff you'll remember from *Der Rosenkavalier*. There are really a hundred or two hundred allusions or echoes in the poem. Don't think of it unkindly, even in part, as the work of the "American critic," because it's not that, as you can see from the end, which I hope you'll like. Aren't you surprised at my knowing that many German words? Once I knew none, now I know almost none. Anyway, don't tell me if you don't like the poem, because it will break my heart; I still feel in a happy daze from writing it.

I wrote another poem before this, a mocking, fairly funny, fairly long poem about Ireland ["A Rhapsody on Irish Themes"]; I'll send it next letter. Earlier in the fall I finished, really finished after long labors, a translation of Corbière's longest poem ["Le Poète Contumace"].

I had to interrupt writing "An English Garden" for two days, to write a review of the criticism of Bernard Haggin, a music critic whom I like very much. I'll send you a copy of the review [of *Music in the Nation; The Nation*, December 17, 1949] to read — I think it will be some fun for you to read, not as though it were something unkind about some bad American poet you don't know.

I'll write soon. I think of you; I hope you're well and that your work is going well; I hope very much you do get enough done for an exhibition of your own. Write me how you like the poem.

AN ENGLISH GARDEN IN AUSTRIA
(seen after *Der Rosenkavalier*)

It is as one imagined it: an English garden ...

Mein Gott! — as all the little girls here say —
To see here the path, the first step of that first path
Our own great parents took! Today, *le Roi Soleil* shines
On his mistress's nuns' orphans' *Athalie;*
Saint-Simon, Leibnitz, and some wandering stars
Murmuring for joy together ... and in the night
A Ruin, a Prospect, and one blasted tree
Lour on their progress, and the next day where are they?

On such a path as this, a "rustic beau
[Or bear; one's doubtful, with this orchestration]
Of thirty-five" pauses to hear a man
Reciting in a big fur hat, with feeling —
And growls politely, "Metastasio?"
They whisper: "Quiet! That's J. J. Rousseau,"
And bear him off to the measures of a *Ländler.*
Helped to his coach, the Baron exits grumbling
About the "luck of all us Lerchenaus."

... It was not thus that you sang, Farinelli!
By graver stages, up a sterner way,
You won to those fields the candelabra lit,
Paused there; sang, as no man since has sung —
A present and apparent deity — the pure
Impossible airs of Arcady: and the calm
Horsehair-wigged shepherds, Gods of that Arcadian
Academy, wept inextinguishable tears.
Such power has music; and the repeated spell
Once a day, at evening, opened the dull heart
Of old mad Philip: all his courtiers wept
And the king asked, weeping: "Why have I wept?"
And Farinelli sang on; Ferdinand
Buried his father, ruled —
　　　　　　　　and heard, paused, heard again:
The years went on, men withered, Farinelli sang.

You are silent now: you, Faustina Hasse,
Her husband Johann Adolf, the Abate

Metastasio . . . very silent.
They float past; seem to whisper, to the oat
Of a shepherd wintering very far from Weimar:
"We also have dwelt in Arcady."
                              — So Death.

The shades of your Grotto have encompassed me.
How can I make out, among these ruins, your Ruin?
You went for this pleasing terror to the past
And built it here, an Image of the Possible:
Well ruined, Ruin! . . .
                              But I come late.

In those years Europe lived beneath the lightning
Of the smile of that certain, all too certain spirit
Whom Almighty God —
                     whom *le bon Dieu* sent for a rod
To these Philistines; he held out sixty years,
Gentling savage Europe with his Alexandrines,
Submitted, went up to Switzerland, and perished.
One spends one's life with fools, and dies among watches.
But see him in flower, in a Prussian garden.
He walks all summer, yawning, in the shade
Of an avenue of grenadiers; and a Great Person
In a tie-wig walks with this monkey, tags his verses,
And — glancing sideways, with suspicion — speaks of *Götz*
Von Berlichingen mit der eisernen Hand.
Said Frederick: "Here's the hand, but where's the glove?"
Or words to that effect; and next year jailed him
For having gone off with his (Pharaoh's) flute
In a sack of corn upon a baggage-camel.
Or words to that effect . . . Then all the world
Shifts to another gear: Count Almaviva and his valet
Shake hands, cry *Citoyen!* are coffined by a sad
Danton; assisting, Anacharsis Clootz —
To the Masons' Funeral Music of their maker.
And one might have seen, presiding among drummers,
An actress named *Raison* (*née* Diderot).
Meanwhile Susanna and the Countess sigh
For someone not yet on the scene; their man of tears
Retires, is rouged as Destiny: Rousseau

Comes in as Cain, upon a charger . . . Instead of his baton
This corporal carries *Werther* in his knapsack.
He reads it seven times, and finds no fault
Except with Werther: he was too ambitious.
The soldier nods — these buzzing Mamelukes
Have made him drowsy; shadows darken all the East
And over his feeling shoulder, as he sleeps,
Die Weltgeschichte peeps down upon his Sorrows.
(He wakes, smiles sleepily, and tweaks its ear.)
At Jena he shows his gratitude, says: "Here's a man!"
(What were the others? . . .

                  Dead men. He'd killed them every one.)
A vulgar demon, but our own: he still prepares us
"Plays worthy of the savages of Canada" —
Up from the floorboards soars the infernal
Everything that is deserves to perish,
And actors, author, audience die applauding.
Then he whispers, winking: "Politics is Destiny!"
And some *Spiessbürger,* some *aquarelliste,*
Some *Spielverderber* from a Georgian seminary
Echo him — higher, higher: *"Es muss sein!"*

"Others have understood the world; we change it."
"Truth is what works." "I have seen the Future and it works."

No Lerchenau was e'er a spoilsport,
A ghost sings; and the ghosts sing wonderingly:
Ist halt vorbei! . . . Ist halt vorbei! . . .

Then there is silence; a soft floating sigh.
Heut' oder morgen kommt der Tag,
And how shall we bear it?
                  Lightly, lightly.

The stars go down into the West; a ghostly air
Troubles the dead city of earth.

. . . It is as one imagined it: an English garden.

[December 1949]

Dear Cal:

We opened the Christmas present before Christmas and played it. We liked it very much especially one of the German songs, all except the *Richard* [*Coeur de Lion*] — never again will I believe Henry Adams or such about him. It's the sort of song a fullback would write if he weren't musical.

I've just finished a longish poem which I send in this letter ["An English Garden in Austria"]. I wrote a sort of longish Curse on Ireland ["A Rhapsody on Irish Themes"] — not too good, but fairly funny — earlier in the fall, but mostly I've been finishing up older poems or translations. I finally got "Le Poète Contumace" done so that it's smooth.

We were crazy about Cape Cod and are going to spend the summer there, at Dennis.

Peter told us about your going to Iowa: we hope you and Elizabeth will like it. It ought to be quiet and peaceful, and I'll bet you find teaching a great deal less trouble than you imagine. So far as I'm concerned, it's the next thing to hereditary wealth.

How nearly is your long poem done? Half or two-thirds?

Have you ever read Goethe's aphorisms at much length? They certainly are good: so far as truth and not poetry is concerned — leaving out Blake and Heraclitus and such people — they're as good as everybody else put together. And some of them are almost as good so far as the poetry's concerned.

It certainly is fun having Peter and Eleanor back next door: but they're moving to Hillsboro in the spring and I imagine we'll sell the house.

Trilling (L.) and Blackmur are the visiting critics this spring at the Arts Forum (silly name!): would that [Henry] James were here to write it up in his own inimitable style. Seriously, though, it will be fun to see Blackmur; and though I don't like Trilling or think too much of his taste, he certainly is an intelligent man, a really intelligent man: His comments in that great string of Statements by Jewish writers (in *Commentary*) made all the rest sound like Paul Goodman — especially Paul Goodman. I've often wondered: in bed at night, alone, "What does Trilling think about his wife's reviews?"

Which — by way of K. A. Porter's (favorable) review of Edith Sitwell — reminds me that she, Katherine Anne Porter, was here last spring, and was notable more for being a niceish *eccentric* partially outmoded *Southern* belle than for being a profound (or superficial) thinker.

You read Eliot's piece on Pound ["Ezra Pound"], the one in *Poetry* [volume 68, 1946] several years ago, didn't you? It certainly is nice. I was rereading it the other day.

It was a shame you couldn't come to Nag's Head: it's nice, and the sand dunes are the next thing to the Sahara. I guess: I *know* they're the next thing to Death Valley, I've been there.

Would that you could meet the old lady in charge of Jug Town, the place your candlesticks came from. She's named her dogs after different characters from Wagner's *Ring,* is a sort of anthropological Lady Bountiful to the peasants gathering faggots nearby, and says "All the shapes have Authority. Not one thing was invented." I'll bet she was invented.

A cloud has just come over the sun and dampened my spirits (which are extraordinarily high what with finishing my poem); I will stop. I met Merrill Moore, who said that you and I and Peter must start a summer writers' conference on Cape Cod, because Breadloaf was full of Philistines and sent me a book of clinical sonnets [*Clinical Sonnets*], one of which Mackie used to illustrate a lecture on Freud and literature. We should wind up at some crowned head's bedside.

Write and tell me all about Iowa when you get there. It's pretty much unchanged, here — but what with Peter's being back, our no longer noticing the dull features, and making lots of money, it's quite pleasant. Say hello to Elizabeth for us; Mackie and I both send you our congratulations; and we hope we'll get to see you this summer. Where will you be? In New England?

Yours,
Randall

Ben Owens was the master potter at Jug Town, and the Jarrells had sent a pair of Owens's candlesticks to Elizabeth Hardwick and Lowell as a wedding present.
Allen Tate had helped arrange a teaching job for Lowell at the University of Iowa, and Lowell was to begin in February 1950.

TO JAMES LAUGHLIN

[December 1949]

Dear Mr. Laughlin:

Delmore Schwartz told me — after I'd said that I wasn't going to send my next book to Harcourt — that he'd mentioned that to you and that you were interested in publishing it. I could send the book of poems [*The Seven-League Crutches*] to you immediately; and I could send in two or three months a critical book on modern poets that is finished except for the last thirty or forty pages [*Poetry and the Age*].

I'm not sending them to Harcourt because Harcourt always seemed so grudging and dreary — they made me feel that publishing the poems was a minor cultural duty that they performed without the slightest enthusiasm. (Also, they sold out *Losses* quickly, promised bookstores a new edition on different definite dates, and never printed one.) What I want is a publisher with a Happy Smile — your ordinary advances and advertisements will do, whatever they are, but I do want that look of joy, or mild pleasure, or *something* — I got the feeling at Harcourt, that a window-dummy made out of ectoplasm was publishing those poor poems.

I'll be in New York at Christmas, and could talk about the type and so forth; I'd like to have the poems come out early next fall, if that's possible. Write me about them and I'll send them on. And thanks very much for the Valéry you sent me.

Yours sincerely,
Randall Jarrell

Harcourt, Brace did not keep their word to the bookstores because they had melted down the plates for Losses *and did not want to go to the expense of setting the type again.*

TO ROBERT GIROUX

[February 1950]

Dear Bob:

As you know I wrote to James Laughlin about his publishing a new book of poems and one of criticism. He talked to you about it, and asked me to think it over for a while, in order to "avoid anything that might smack of any taint of stealing authors" and he goes on to say that "I don't want you to have false hopes that we would be able to do much better for you than Harcourt, Brace. They do a very fine job at all times." He really does quite lean over backwards, as you see.

I wrote him because I decided, some time ago, that Harcourt has a rather perfunctory interest in my books. Laughlin writes that Harcourt's "feelings are rather hurt at the thought that you would want to make a change." But consider it from my point of view: you sold out *Losses* fairly quickly, without any advertisements to speak of, promised bookstores a second edition, and didn't print one; you didn't write me about this, about printing my next book, or about anything else. I thought, "No, this isn't the way an *ardent* publisher behaves." Wasn't it a reasonable thought? —

But I don't want to give the impression of stalking away like an offended statue: if you're really interested in my new books write me about them, and we can talk them over before I do anything else with Laughlin. His letter made me think that writing you immediately would be the simplest and quickest way of moving things along.

Yours,
Randall

Giroux won Jarrell over, and he stayed on with Harcourt, Brace.

TO ROBERT PENN WARREN

[February 1950]

Dear Red:

Thanks ever so much for the book [*World Enough and Time*]. I've read part of it already and have got full of primitive narrative suspense, wondering exactly what's going to happen. It's most engrossing to read.

You know Peter and Eleanor have bought a very old house in a small town near here: the room where Peter has his books, typewriter, and such reminds me so strongly of one of the rooms in your place in Nashville — the country one where Amy and I used to come so often — that it always gives me a queer homesick feeling, and I can hardly believe that you aren't in that house anymore and that I'm not going out to see you there ever again.

We're going to spend this summer on Cape Cod, at Dennis. I've written three medium-long poems and finished a translation of Corbière's longest poem; but I did it during the winter, so I already have an "I don't *do* anything in this world" feeling.

I was recently teaching your "Original Sin" and "Pursuit" to a class of mine. They certainly are good poems, with your whole feeling about the world, almost, condensed in them; I don't believe that anyone who knew them well would be surprised by anything in your other books.

I hope we'll get to see you someday before we're all old and dead. Give my love to Cenina.

Yours,
Randall

The Taylors had bought the first of many run-down houses that they would restore charmingly and sell. Taylor was again teaching at the Woman's College, and Eleanor was riding to campus with him to attend Jarrell's writing class.

TO ELISABETH EISLER

[February 1950]

Your studio looks nice though *fairly* odd in shape: once in Mexico City when I was looking for apartments I saw one with a narrow triangular room made half of glass bricks.

I knew, found out later, about having *Götz* wrong [in "An English Garden in Austria"] and had corrected it: but it's no wonder I got it wrong, since I wrote it from memory and I don't know *any* grammar. But I am getting to read *easy* German pretty well: I can read Grimm's Tales quite fluently (a lot of the time) and am reading virtuously along in a second-year German reader. And I've read quite a lot of *Des Knaben Wunderhorn* and [Edward] Mörike and assorted lyrics and no end of Heine. The best story I've read is a lovely one (I was just fascinated by it) named "Das geheimnisvoll Dorf" — by Friedrich Gerstacker. I imagine it's a quite well-known story — is it? — but I've never seen an English translation of it. Some poems I liked a lot were "Strassburg, O Strassburg" and "Waldgesprach" and "Schön-Rohtraut."

The *feel* of German delights me. It has such a folky, old, primitive, poetic feel compared to English: it really is *the* language for fairy tales and folk-poems and all sorts of things. I often wonder what the feel of English is: since it's my own language, I naturally haven't any idea at all. How does it feel to you, compared to German?

I wrote an absurd poem about learning German, full of jokes and German phrases I like and fairy-tale furniture; when I get it really finished I'll send it to you, even though I'm not sure it will be much fun for you to read — since naturally the German things won't seem to you the way they would to an English-speaking reader. The poem is named "Deutsch Durch Freud" or "German by the Aesthetic Method": alas, it's not likely to add to my fame as a poet, but I certainly did enjoy writing it.

I'll send two poems in this letter: "An English Garden" in a somewhat improved version and a new poem ["Seele im Raum"]. I don't know whether you'll know the English word *eland* in the new poem; an eland is a big African antelope — almost as big as a horse — with spiral horns. I don't know what he's called in German.

In my other poem Baron Ochs and Rousseau meet not because they have anything to do with each other but because they're opposites: Ochs, as typical of the 18th century, the *ancien regime,* is walking in the garden, or in such a garden, when he meets (in the person of Rousseau) the beginning of Romanticism, of the 19th century, of everything that was going to destroy the old way of life and feeling. Unless I remember incorrectly, Rousseau did make several visits to Vienna — and he recited, with feeling, everywhere he went.

Tell me some German poems you're *particularly* fond of — some of your real favorites — and I'll read them. Really do, I'll be grateful.

The weather here is just the opposite of yours: I played tennis yesterday, and there are flowers and fruit-tree-blossoms outside. It gives one rather a superstitious feeling — there hasn't even been a real winter.

At a party someone took a picture of me that made me feel like a dwarf or Rumpelstiltskin, very inferior: he had climbed up on a ladder with his camera and one had to sit still for ten seconds. The top of my head looked very big, like a dark cloud, and the bottom was very thin, thinner than an El Greco; also I'd moved. I looked as if I'd been grown, like a carrot.

Write me a nice long letter — your last didn't have much news, except for the studio part; I think you felt guilty for not liking the poem more. But that's my fault, not yours. (In my new poem the eland is a symbol for lots of things, not for any one definite thing.) I hope you like it, but if you don't write me soon reproaching me for not having written a better one. I hope you feel well and that your work's going well.

Elisabeth Eisler's studio was in the Grinzing district, next door to Bee-thoven's house. She had given up serious painting and returned to ceramics and glazes.

TO SISTER BERNETTA QUINN

[April 1950]

Dear Sister Bernetta:

I should have answered you weeks ago. I was extremely delighted to have you like "A Girl in a Library" so well, and I certainly wish you would write about your impressions of the other.

"Many a dolphin curved up from necessity" means: many people have, like dolphins, leaped for a moment, from the world of what Leibnitz calls "brute and geometrical necessity," up into the purer world of — oh, art, mysticism, philosophy, love; from actuality to potentiality; but the poor girl sleeps placidly in the trap, and has never even felt the need to escape.

Tatyana is the heroine of Pushkin's *Eugene Onegin*; I'm fond of it and quite fond of the opera.

I'm glad there was no need to make suggestions about *Paterson*; you know a lot more about metamorphoses in it than I do, since you're a conscious specialist in metamorphoses and I an entirely unconscious one like a butterfly.

I've just finished a longish piece about Stevens ["Reflections on Wallace Stevens"] for *Partisan* [volume 18, 1951]; my deadline was yesterday, and I didn't get it finished until midnight the day before, after doing nothing else for three or four days. Did most of my "Obscurity of the Poet" [*Partisan Review*, January–February 1951] seem true to you? — it's such a sad truth I wish I were mistaken; but I'm afraid I'm not.

Have you ever read anything by Ludwig Tieck? He wrote a fairy-tale called *Fair Eckbert* that's unimaginably haunting; and a very tender and funny story named "Life's Luxuries"; and a play with charmingly funny parts, *Puss in Boots;* and about 30 volumes more I haven't read, since they're in German that isn't baby's German. And, since I'm recommending books, let me tell you about a wonderful book that nobody else knows about (except a hundred people I've got to read it), *The Man Who Loved Children* by Christina Stead; it really is one of the best novels in English, I think. And do you know a poem of Hardy's named "During Wind and Rain"? — I think it's one of the best poems anybody ever wrote. But I will stop — telling things to read is something I can hardly make myself finish.

Yours,
Randall Jarrell

A GIRL IN A LIBRARY

An object among dreams, you sit here with your shoes off
And curl your legs up under you; your eyes
Close for a moment, your face moves toward sleep . . .
You are very human.
                    But my mind, gone out in tenderness,
Shrinks from its object with a thoughtful sigh.
This is a waist the spirit breaks its arm on.
The gods themselves, against you, struggle in vain.
This broad low strong-boned brow; these heavy eyes;
These calves, grown muscular with certainties;
This nose, three medium-sized pink strawberries
— But I exaggerate. In a little you will leave:
I'll hear, half squeal, half shriek, your laugh of greeting —
Then, *decrescendo,* bars of that strange speech
In which each sound sets out to seek each other,
Murders its own father, marries its own mother,
And ends as one grand transcendental vowel.

(Yet for all I know, the Egyptian Helen spoke so.)
As I look, the world contracts around you:
I see Brünnhilde had brown braids and glasses
She used for studying; Salome straight brown bangs,
A calf's brown eyes, and sturdy light-brown limbs
Dusted with cinnamon, an apple-dumpling's . . .
Many a beast has gnawn a leg off and got free,
Many a dolphin curved up from Necessity —
The trap has closed about you, and you sleep.
If someone questioned you, *What doest thou here?*
You'd knit your brows like an orangoutang
(But not so sadly; not so thoughtfully)
And answer with a pure heart, guilelessly:
I'm studying. . . .
    If only you were not!
Assignments,
   recipes,
     the *Official Rulebook*
Of Basketball — ah, let them go; you needn't mind.
The soul has no assignments, neither cooks
Nor referees: it wastes its time.
       It wastes its time.
Here in this enclave there are centuries
For you to waste: the short and narrow stream
Of Life meanders into a thousand valleys
Of all that was, or might have been, or is to be.
The books, just leafed through, whisper endlessly . . .
Yet it is hard. One sees in your blurred eyes
The "uneasy half-soul" Kipling saw in dogs'.
One sees it, in the glass, in one's own eyes.
In rooms alone, in galleries, in libraries,
In tears, in searchings of the heart, in staggering joys
We memorize once more our old creation,
Humanity: with what yawns the unwilling
Flesh puts on its spirit, O my sister!

So many dreams! And not one troubles
Your sleep of life? no self stares shadowily
From these worn hexahedrons, beckoning
With false smiles, tears? . . .

                              Meanwhile Tatyana
Larina (gray eyes nickel with the moonlight
That falls through the willows onto Lensky's tomb;
Now young and shy, now old and cold and sure)
Asks, smiling: "But what is she dreaming of, fat thing?"
I answer: She's not fat. She isn't dreaming.
She purrs or laps or runs, all in her sleep;
Believes, awake, that she is beautiful;
She never dreams.
                        Those sunrise-colored clouds
Around man's head — that inconceivable enchantment
From which, at sunset, we come back to life
To find our graves dug, families dead, selves dying:
Of all this, Tanya, she is innocent.
For nineteen years she's faced reality:
They look alike already.
                              They say, man wouldn't be
The best thing in this world — and isn't he —
If he were not too good for it. But she
—She's good enough for it.
                              And yet sometimes
Her sturdy form, in its pink strapless formal,
Is as if bathed in moonlight — modulated
Into a form of joy, a Lydian mode;
This Wooden Mean's a kind, furred animal
That speaks, in the Wild of things, delighting riddles
To the soul that listens, trusting . . .
                              Poor senseless Life:
When, in the last light sleep of dawn, the messenger
Comes with his message, you will not awake.
He'll give his feathery whistle, shake you hard,
You'll look with wide eyes at the dewy yard
And dream, with calm slow factuality:
"Today's Commencement. My bachelor's degree
In Home Ec., my doctorate of philosophy
In Phys. Ed.
            [Tanya, they won't even *scan*]
Are waiting for me. . . ."
                        Oh, Tatyana,
The Angel comes: better to squawk like a chicken

Than to say with truth, "But I'm a *good* girl,"
And Meet his Challenge with a last firm strange
Uncomprehending smile; and — then, then! — see
The blind date that has stood you up: your life.
(For all this, if it isn't, perhaps, life,
Has yet, at least, a language of its own
Different from the books'; worse than the books'.)
And yet, the ways we miss our lives are life.
Yet ... yet ...
         to have one's life add up to *yet!*

You sigh a shuddering sigh. Tatyana murmurs,
"Don't cry, little peasant"; leaves us with a swift
"Good-bye, good-bye ... Ah, don't think ill of me ..."
Your eyes open: you sit here thoughtlessly.

I love you — and yet — and yet — I love you.

Don't cry, little peasant. Sit and dream.
One comes, a finger's width beneath your skin,
To the braided maidens singing as they spin;
There sound the shepherd's pipe, the watchman's rattle
Across the short dark distance of the years.
I am a thought of yours: and yet, you do not think ...
The firelight of a long, blind, dreaming story
Lingers upon your lips; and I have seen
Firm, fixed forever in your closing eyes,
The Corn King beckoning to his Spring Queen.

TO ELISABETH EISLER

[October 1950]

I didn't write to you for several months because I was feeling rather bad and felt it was better not to, somehow: then, when I got feeling better I, of course, felt extremely guilty for not having written, and put it off some more. I'm sorry to have been so dumb; I won't say, "Forgive me for this once," because it isn't once, but do, anyway.

For three or four months I drew and painted most of the time; I even painted a landscape with a tree, in an ingenuously *pointilliste* way. At the same time I was virtuously reading German readers and stumbling through

German poems: I wrote a poem about it, a silly heart-felt poem, named "Deutsch Durch Freud."

I met a French poet named Pierre Emmanuel who came and stayed with us at Cape Cod for about a month. I wish you knew him; he's so witty and spontaneous and good-hearted and generally overwhelming that he makes one more dissatisfied than ever with most people one sees every day.

I painted a picture of myself, in a condition of summer brownness, shaving; it looks as if I had a beautiful snow-white beard. This somehow reminds me that Svetlana [Leontiev], now, is supposed to be very thin and beautiful.

There was a very enthusiastic article about the Salzburg Seminar in a recent *Nation;* it made me wonder whether it had got better or whether it was the same thing being given the same old enthusiastic treatment.

Pierre is an extremely accomplished handwriting analyst — he does it in a quite Proustian or Stendhalian style. Have you ever had someone good analyze your handwriting? It's a quite bewildering experience — you wouldn't believe that anyone *could* know so much about you.

I saw a wonderful Klee exhibition in Washington this summer — more than a hundred paintings and drawings; they were so good, so incredibly imaginative, that you felt quite lost in him, as if other painters had for a minute stopped existing. Later I saw some paintings from Vienna that I knew you must often have seen — the Velásquez portraits of Margaret and Maria Theresa were particularly beautiful.

Have you ever read a story by Ludwig Tieck named "Life's Luxuries"? Do read it if you haven't; you'd like it very much.

I don't usually send you critical things I write because I don't want to vex you with "the American critic"; but what I wrote for [a] Harvard [lecture] about poetry in the modern world ["The Obscurity of the Poet"] is rather different, and I do want to send it to you — I think you'd like it.

I think of you, as you know, often — sometimes too often; this spring and summer I felt complicatedly guilty and remorseful — it's even more complicated because I can't help thinking of you as standing for Europe and the past and whatever is the opposite of the actuality one lives in. Many things remind me of you. I hope so much you're better off now, that your painting is doing well.

Thanks so much for the anthology you sent me. Are there any books I could send you? Are there good German translations of Proust? I don't know how much of him you've read. One can get all of *Remembrance of Things Past,* in a wonderful English translation, in two big volumes; is this better than the German situation? He's really my favorite writer in the whole world — it's the nicest book to *have,* year in and year out, that I know.

I've recently been reading all Rilke's letters — many parts of them are wonderfully interesting. Have you ever read Turgenev's *A Sportsman's Sketches?* You'd like them a lot.

I played tennis a lot this summer; I won a singles tournament at Cape Cod in a very long match, the most satisfying I ever played. When one does what one *should,* beyond one's expectations, it's a queer feeling — one gets as much used to one's own faults as to the world's, and yet they are an obsessive grief in a way the world's never are. Forgive me for the crazy notwriting — since I've worked away from tennis to important things; and forgive me for everything else — I feel endlessly guilty toward you. But I won't talk about it anymore, and certainly not, next letter.

Pierre Emmanuel, a French writer, was the author of The Poet and His Christ, Sodom, Babel, *and critical books on Baudelaire and Saint-John Perse.*

This was the last letter of Jarrell's that Elisabeth Eisler saved, and they never saw each other after Salzburg. In the 1950s and 1960s she became known as "EE" and her work was widely exhibited in Austria. In Vienna there are EEs in churches, parks, schools, and government buildings, as well as in private collections. When presenting Jarrell's letters she commented, "I always wished that something would come out of our contact, and now, because of Randall Jarrell's Letters, *something will." Animated and still pretty, she spoke of other romantic attachments, but she never married and continued to live at home with her parents until her death from cancer in 1975.*

TO HANNAH ARENDT

[November 1950]

Dear Hannah:

Thank you very much for the book [*The Origins of Totalitarianism*]. I read it the day I got it. It's one of the best historical books I've ever read — if it doesn't make you famous, at least *moderately* famous, this is an unjust world. From the start of Chapter 9 to the end is the part I like best of all: from there on it really does seem a sort of crushing unbearable poem, quite homogeneous, something the reader feels and understands at the same time. This part is notable for imagination and empathy, I think; you never once say, "But this is inconceivable," or "But nobody could feel so." Many of the earlier parts I liked almost as well, in a rather different way — and of course they had to be quite different; I particularly liked the part about the Jews and the State, in part I; and 5 and 6 and the South Africa part of 7, in part II.

Both your facts and your machinery of interpretation, your reasoning, really do make the reader feel he's understanding how and why it happened; and the tone, the writing itself, make him feel that he's making a commensurate emotional response to what happened — not wholly commensurate, of course, but what could be?

You really do have such an imposing *amount* of reasoning things out — and so much of it new or quite different from what most other people say; this, even more than all the facts, gives the book a sort of imposing *This is a lifework* book.

The only things I remember that I didn't like — I put these in to show you I did have my wits left, and wasn't in a wholly ignorant transport — were the rather abstract Hegelian attitude toward Negro tribes (Chaka and the Zulus were about as atypical as Genghis Khan and the Mongols, I believe) and the attitude toward evolution that seems to be implied (I'm not sure) in several remarks.

It really is a wonderful book. It's a model of dispassion where it needs to be. After one has read it one never will think of most of the things in quite the same way one did — that's what readers will feel, I'm sure.

To descend to the almost-ridiculous: the photograph has succeeded in making you look like a shy, sincere, serious schoolgirl; you ought to be wearing a dark blue uniform-blouse with *Koenigsburg Gymnasium* lettered on it. It's very touching, but I'll never dare make an unkind remark to you: you would, plainly, burst into tears. I feel as if I'd seen the other side of the moon.

I've written half a poem about "The Knight, Death, and the Devil" — but just a little poem, not very good — but otherwise I'm well and happy. Thanks again for the book.

Yours,
Randall

TO HANNAH ARENDT

[February 9, 1951]

Dear Hannah:

As soon as I got home I cut out of *Poetry* the poems I promised to send, put them in a safe place, and after a couple of days started to send them. It was *really* a safe place; I never found them until yesterday — they were in an envelope marked *Household Papers,* along with the 1951 Income Tax blanks. No, this isn't allegory, it just happened so.

I'm going to be in New York May 25 and 26; let's plan to go on a picnic or something. You know you said I must tell you beforehand so you could invite people over for me to meet — but I'm telling you beforehand so you won't. Don't you know Freud's story of the man who was cured of blindness by stopping drinking? — when they met him being led along the street by a little boy, he said: "Nothing I saw was as good as the whiskey."

The nicest thing I've been doing is playing [Verdi's] *Falstaff* over and over on the phonograph. What was the Bach record you liked so?

I loved seeing you; do write me.

Yours,
Randall

TO ROBERT LOWELL

[April 1951]

Dear Cal:

I should have written long ago to thank you for the Donatello book — he's all in all my favorite sculptor, so I was more than delighted. I'm glad you're having such a good time; Europe is wonderful, to an American humiliatingly wonderful.

I don't know much news. Red's going to be here this week at the Arts Forum; Peter's written an extremely good story, one of his best ["What You Hear from 'Em?"]; I like Robie [Macauley] very much and am much impressed at how well read and seriously interested in literature he is; I've just finished a poem called "The Knight, Death, and the Devil," a translation of Dürer's engravings. I've put in "A Conversation with the Devil," but will you send it back next letter? It's the last copy I've got.

And I wrote a piece, half review and half article, about Stevens; it will be in *Partisan.* Here's another poem I just wrote:

A WAR

There set out, slowly, for a Different World,
At four, on winter mornings, different legs . . .
You can't break eggs without making an omelette —
That's what they tell the eggs.

You ought to get Harcourt to give you Hannah Arendt's book, *The Origins of Totalitarianism;* it's really good.

We were in New York at Christmas; we saw Delmore several times. He's now a convinced theist — but not a Christian. He feels sure that God wouldn't have picked an out-of-the-way ridiculous little spot like Palestine. Did you know his wife [Elizabeth Pollet]? — she certainly is nice. Margaret Marshall is well and writing good drama reviews: she wrote in *The Nation* that a good deal of Tennessee Williams is a level beneath criticism, an elementary truth no one else writes. But, alas, she liked Christopher Fry [*The Lady's Not for Burning*], her only mistake.

It will interest you, anthropologically, that is, to know that *South Pacific* is a remarkably crude job, written by people without shame or much skill.

If you ever get a chance to see [the film] *The Blue Angel* do.

The Taylors are awfully well and happy. Their place is lovely. Elizabeth Bishop has written a charming poem about the prodigal son ["The Prodigal"].

One sees lots of criticism by William Carlos Williams these days, but very little by Baby Snooks; it's an unjust world. I thought the two infinitely long pieces on "the principles of my criticism" by [Leslie] Fiedler ["Toward an Amateur Criticism," *Kenyon Review*, Autumn 1950] and Richard Chase ["Art, Nature, Politics," *Kenyon Review*, Autumn 1950] things to make the devils in heaven envious. Did you read Blackmur's wonderful review of Trilling ["The Politics of Human Power," *Kenyon Review*, Autumn 1950]? And an even better piece on *Dr. Faustus* ["Parody and Critique," *Kenyon Review*, Autumn 1950]?

I guess many people have told you about Allen's "as a Catholic" letter. Peter said, "He should have written, 'As a Catholic of many months.' " I haven't heard what Cardinal Spellman thought of being called a heretic, but he may as well get used to it.

There was a nice article in the London *Times* (by Spender, plainly) about American poets; it spoke well of both of us, especially so of you. Viereck quite moves Spender to wit.

We're going back to the Cape this summer, to the same house, that is.

Is it possible to get large colored reproductions of that Uccello *Rout of San Romano?* Preferably the most jousting one of the two. I have never seen one over here. If it is I certainly would like to get you to buy one for me.

I'm eager to see the re-written long poem ["The Mills of the Kavanaughs"]. I thought the last half needed rewriting — it seemed too nightmarish and arbitrarily obsessed. I thought several parts of the *Partisan* poem ["David and Bathsheba in the Public Garden"] smoother than way back in

'47 or so when I saw it last: it's an extremely effective poem. But the New Brunswick one ["Mother Marie Therese"] I like best of all — I think it's the best you've ever done.

If they have good opera productions of *Falstaff* you ought to go whenever you can; it's one of the summits of human creation, make no mistake.

Mackie sends her love to you both. Guess who called Gide and Eliot "a little stupid, as both realize themselves"? Kant? No. Aristotle? No. Paul Goodman? You've guessed it. Have you done any European poems?

Affectionately,

Randall

Robie Macauley, thirty-two, was another graduate of Kenyon who had been taught by Ransom, and a friend of Taylor and Lowell. He was teaching fiction at the Woman's College in Greensboro.

Baby Snooks was a character invented by the comedienne Fanny Brice, who played the part wearing a baby bonnet and licking a lollipop.

Tate wrote the New York Times *on February 1, 1951, protesting Cardinal Spellman's attempts to suppress Rossellini's film* The Miracle *and saying he did not wish to deny the Cardinal's right to try to do so but that such action was unnecessary, because bad art does not endure.*

TO SARA STARR

[April 1951]

Dear Sara:

Would you like to do something stuffy but imposing, like seeing a bust of General MacArthur unveiled? I'm getting given a thousand dollars by the National Institute of Arts and Letters, and they are having a ceremony in which I am an unimportant part, one of many people getting [a grant for] a thousand dollars. You'll probably never see more prominent-authors-sculptors-painters-and-musicians all together; and you'll also get given refreshments and have to listen to an organ prelude by Henry Cowell, a speech by Mark Van Doren, and an organ postlude by Virgil Thomson. All this occurs at Five o'clock, Friday, May 25. If you can go and have dinner afterward with Margaret Marshall probably, I think she's free then, she's coming to the thing — write me: 1924 Spring Garden, Greensboro, N.C. We might meet each other at the Museum of Modern Art at four, say; or you suggest a place.

We're going to Princeton next year to teach, on a year's leave of absence — you can come out and see us, or we can go to ballet together.

I've been writing a lot — I've written a whole book that I think you'll enjoy reading. How is school going? Are you going to be at the Cape much?

Love,
Randall

Writ by hand, in haste.

Sara Starr, the daughter of Jarrell's longtime friends Milton and Zaro Starr, was a student at Sarah Lawrence College.

TO HANNAH ARENDT

[May 1951]

Dear Hannah:

I write to remind you that I'm going to be in New York next week-end: I hope that you will tell the world, so far as Saturday and Sunday are concerned, that you are going to be encouraging American Poetry, and will have no time for anything else.

You can imagine how delighted I was to see your chubby girlish face on the front of the *Saturday Review.* Inspired by your example, I too have written a prose book [*Pictures from an Institution*], and I'll bring it along for you to read. I'm not joking, I really have.

What you said about my "Obscurity of the Poet" was a great pleasure to me because of the way you put it: that you were "intoxicated with agreement 'against a world of enemies.' " I always feel this way when I see you. Someone said about somebody that "while that man is alive I am not alone in this world"; I guess I feel that way about you.

If you'll tell me the telephone number of that place where you work I'll call you Friday afternoon.

I've done a great deal of work this spring and feel wonderful. I enclose a poem ["A Quilt-Pattern"]: I won't tell *you* what it's a — so to speak — translation of ["Hänsel and Gretel"].

Several people here have read your book — one a historian — and they were all crazy about it.

I'll bet *you* don't know that I'm going to be away from here for a year, next year — at Princeton; so we ought to get to see each other more than twice a year.

Do write and tell me how you like the poem and how much time you'll have free Saturday and Sunday: if it isn't a lot I will — I will — well, I don't know what exactly, but something awful, surely.

Yours,
Randall

Peter Taylor wrote of learning about the "prose book" when Jarrell drove to Hillsboro to visit him for a day: "When he got out of his car, he was carrying a briefcase. He didn't often carry a briefcase in those days. My wife and I eyed it without comment until at last he said, 'Guess what! I've written a novel!' 'You're kidding,' I said. He burst out at me, 'Are you crazy? You know I don't kid about things like that!' And of course he was right. He didn't kid about things like that. It was Pictures from an Institution.*"* (RJ) *What Jarrell had written — though he did not know it — was not a book but a start on a book that would not be fully written for another year and a half.*

On the subject of Jarrell's visits, Arendt wrote: "For some years he came at regular intervals . . . He read English poetry to me for hours, old and new, only rarely his own . . . He opened up for me a whole new world of sound and meter, and taught me the specific gravity of English words . . . Whatever I know of English poetry, and perhaps of the genius of the language, I owe to him." (RJ)

TO HANNAH ARENDT

[May 1951]

Dear Hannah:

I sent you a *Little Friend, Little Friend* today. And I wrote another page of my book [*Pictures from an Institution*] to give Irene your "Just call me *you*" story — it looks lovely and later on may make me famous, who knows?

I bought a lovely bottle of 1937 Deidesheimer Herrgottsacker Riesling — but alas — that wasn't all the name: it ended *spätlese,* and I didn't notice that till I was on the train; it was like a raisin's day-dream.

I had a wonderful time in New York. I am always going to tell you many months before I get there.

After you get used to *Little Friend* tell me which you like best. Address: Dennis, Mass.

I am going to do something rather notably absurd Saturday; instead of going to a matinee (ballet) I am going to Bridgehampton, Long Island, to see the sports car races — all sorts of strange and wonderful and exotic cars.

(Sometimes I don't think I'm getting older.) It seemed providential that this should occur the only day I'll be in New York: it was a Sign, don't you think?

Princeton seemed pleasant and we're going to have a nice big house to live in — [Donald] Stauffer's: he's going to Oxford for the year.

I'll say all over again what a wonderful time I had, and what a pleasure it was to get to see you so much. I'll call you Friday.

Yours,
Randall

After diligent research in car magazines Jarrell bought a "sea-foam green" Oldsmobile 88 with a 200-horsepower Kettering engine, only to discover he had acquired a taste for sports cars and the unshakable habit of reading Road and Track. *Bridgehampton, Jarrell's first sports-car race, was one of the stops on a racing circuit that included Monza, Monte Carlo, Pebble Beach, and Watkins Glen, and it initiated him into a world of Ferraris, Jaguars, Allards, and Mercedes-Benzes contesting for the Neuerburgring, the Mille Miglia, the Mexican Road Race, and Le Mans. The driver Phil Hill was the Danilova of the track and General Motors the village idiot. This enthusiasm, which Mackie did not share, absorbed Jarrell to the exclusion of croquet and charades, and he often preferred staying home with* Road and Track, Autocar, *and* Motor Trend *to accompanying Mackie to faculty evenings of drink and chat. What he had written Elisabeth Eisler about himself was as true as ever: He led "an odd, independent, unsocial life remarkably unlike most other people's lives ... and this isn't nice for one's wife unless she has some great interest to take up most of her time."*

*   *   *

In June, the Jarrells and Kitten drove to Cape Cod. Mackie fished while Jarrell played tennis, and together they planned a series of house guests for August that included the Taylors, Elizabeth Bishop, Margaret Marshall, and Hannah Arendt.

In July, Jarrell once again packed his tennis racquet, cable-knit sweater, and poetry books and left — not for Salzburg but for Boulder, Colorado, and the three-week Rocky Mountain Writers' Conference there. Reminiscent of Salzburg and his postponed Williams introduction, he had a long article to write for Partisan Review *that he put off day after day to play tennis with a student, Peter Arendrup, talk poetry with*

Mackie and Randall Jarrell at Cape Cod, 1950

another student, Dee (W. D.) Snodgrass, and be friendly with a student named Mary von Schrader, who was there with her mother, Irene MacAdams.

Mary von Schrader, thirty-eight, was a Californian with a degree in philosophy from Stanford. Fourteen years earlier, she had married a Naval officer turned architect and had accompanied him on a trip around the world, including a 5000-mile bicycle tour of the castles and cathedrals of Europe. When she met Jarrell she had two daughters, Alleyne, eleven, and Beatrice, eight, a half-finished novel about a Nisei family in a relocation center during World War II, and a divorce. She had resumed her father's German name (which had attracted Jarrell's attention), and Jarrell was intrigued by what he called in a letter "the astronomical coincidences" of their two lives. On learning Mary was enrolled in all the writing classes but poetry, Jarrell said, "Why don't you just wash them out and come to mine?" Boulder became an idyll like Salzburg, and they walked in the woods near the campus and waded in a nearby stream, where Jarrell found a chunk of obsidian and Mary found a porous rock they called a meteorite. On the grass by the bandstand in the park they proofread the galleys of Jarrell's Seven-League Crutches. *In his poetry classes he introduced her to Lowell, Frost, and Williams, and at the library to Taylor, Chekhov, and Dinesen. On the tennis court, Mary — no player herself — watched. On a day trip to Denver hunting for* Remembrance of Things Past, *they rested in record shops with listening cubicles where they played* Das Knaben Wunderhorn *and* Der Rosenkavalier. *In the warm evenings they haunted the magazine racks in the Boulder drugstores, where Jarrell read the write-ups of Le Mans. Mary finally had to ask, "What's Le Mans?" And Jarrell said with amused condescension, "Le Mans, child, is the most famous sports-car race in Europe, that's all." Mary said, "Never heard of the races. Of course, I was there for the cathedral, you know. You don't? Well, Le Mans cathedral, child, has the most famous flying buttresses in Europe, that's all." Jarrell tousled her hair and said, "Words fail me!"*

At the end of the conference Jarrell had not written his article for Partisan, *but he had asked Mary to marry him. As they parted at the airport, she said, "When you get back there to your real life and all this seems a dream, Randall; and if you don't want to go ahead with it . . . I'll understand." But Jarrell clapped his hand over her mouth, saying, "No-no-no! Re-dikkl-us! You are my real life. I'll write you every day. And you write me. I love you, cross my heart, and I'm going to marry you."*

Mary von Schrader and her daughter Beatrice, 1951

TO HANNAH ARENDT

[Cape Cod]
[August 1951]

Dear Hannah:

My plane went through New York during the small hours of the morning — so I didn't see or call you. Instead of, as always, writing to ask you to come to the Cape I'm doing just the opposite: this is because of what I believe *The Three Musketeers* calls "a family matter" and what *Kim* calls "urgent private affairs." I'll be at Princeton about the fifteenth of September; I'll come in to town to see you and tell you about it.

Did I tell you that I've written fifty more pages for *Pictures from an Institution?* Lovely pages, many about Art — tell your husband; if he isn't crazy about [the chapter] "Art Night at Benton" I'll die of chagrin.

I had a wonderful time in Colorado: among other things, I played tennis all the time with a charming Danish Davis Cup Player named Peter Arendrup — you'd really like him, he is gay and witty as can be. To tell you the truth, I liked Colorado as well as Salzburg (this is the most subjective judgment I ever made; I hope it hasn't caused you to drop dead with astonishment). As you can see, I'm well and happy.

I'll see you soon; it will be such a joy to live near New York and get to see you more than our usual twice a year.

I believe by the terms of our contract (about *Little Friend, Little Friend*) you owe me a letter about it. Send it or I'll sue for repossession.

Affectionately,
Randall

Writ by hand during manic state.

"A family matter" and "urgent private affairs" were Jarrell's euphemisms for his divorce. Writing about it to Lowell in Amsterdam, Jarrell said, "I know how fond of [Mackie] you were (so was I) so it's sure to be a grief to you; but we'd been getting further and further apart every year, we had almost none of the same interests . . . it was bad for us and getting worse, and I know we'll both be a lot better off apart. This sounds like the sayings of Spartans, but you can't write about such things very well." (Houghton Library, Harvard University)

In his reply to Jarrell, Lowell wrote, "Robie and Peter had written us about your divorce, and I was surprised enough not to believe it. I can understand, perhaps, what brought it about, but you and Mackie seemed to discount your differing enthusiasms and indifferences. You mustn't mind my saying that we all envied you and Mackie because your difficulties seemed to have nothing in common with the difficulties of other marriages, none of the open deliberate unkindnesses, scenes, etc. Well, one mustn't say anything about the wisdom of divorces or proposals, except that your friends feel the same toward you and know they know less than you do about it." (Berg Collection, New York Public Library)

As with the Eisler letters, only the most literary and autobiographical portions of Jarrell's nearly one hundred love letters to Mary von Schrader have been excerpted and presented, with occasional small deletions made silently.

TO MARY VON SCHRADER

[Cape Cod]
[August 1951]

You should have *seen* the foreign-car advertisements in the *Times* this week. For $2900 we could have gotten an Alfa-Romeo super-sports, convertible, body specially designed by Pinin-Farina for a famous film star, so it said, only three years old. Car, not film star, I guess — maybe it's really his kiddy car; I thought the price low.

Peter and Eleanor Taylor (she's the one who's a good poet and nice but who's never managed to recover from her country upbringing) paid us a nice visit, *planned that way,* of a day and a quarter. Did you ever hear of driving 850 miles north, staying one day and a quarter, and then driving 850 miles south, home?

We spent several hours persuading, all in vain; it was particularly funny (and helplessly neurotic of Eleanor — Peter would have stayed a year) because they *love* Cape Cod. Had never seen it before — and plan to rent this house next summer. I've never been funnier and more appealing — my two high points were saying to Eleanor, laughing lovingly, "Eleanor, you're a dope! Eleanor, you dope!" — and grabbing her by the arm (as if I were proposing) and appealing with fervent warmth for her to stay: she upset her (fortunately empty) coffee-cup, blushed all over, and actually had to get up and go sit in another chair. But, no soap — she'd made her plans and she *knew* it would be too much trouble, be an unbearable imposition, to stay for another day.

You certainly will like them; they're *very* nice and very interesting; and Peter is as original, odd, and attractive as anybody you ever saw — you never saw anybody at *all* like him. Though, now that I think of it, Red Warren's speech and bone-formation are like his, rather.

Peter read all the new parts of my novel and was crazy about them. He said that the book was so good that he was sure *The New Yorker* wouldn't be able to use it now. He quite fell in love with Gertrude after "Art Night." When they left I said to them (about their visit) "Why, I'll be dining out on this story for a year."

I'll enclose "Deutsch Durch Freud" with this. I miss you so *much*, Mary. Living has never been at all like living with thee. The more I think about you the more unbelievably happy I am. When I think about you at any time I feel a sort of warm yearning surge of trust. I'm thinking now, "In a couple of hours I'll have a letter from Mary, and it's like the live foot print in the sand on Robinson Crusoe's island."

Tomorrow I know, I *know*, I'll have a photograph, photographs; then instead of reading over and over I'll read over and over and look again and again. Remember how I'd knock on your door at Regent's Hall and say, "I'll be by the Coca-Cola machine," and you'd come out all beautiful and we'd go to breakfast? And how we'd sit on the parapet and look into the woods? And take our books and read in the cool theatre, and then go back to lunch, and then go walking by our stream? Or to that park where they fished in boats? I remember Boulder as Adam and Eve must have remembered Paradise. And I keep thinking of all the astronomical coincidences! Our Oldsmobiles and both of them in "Sea-Foam Green," and both of us in Long Beach at the same time and both of us born in 1914, both of us in early May. Truly we are one and were always one. *As* you know, there is no difference between us, we are each other's completely. Be mine forever as you are mine now and were always mine.

My piece of obsidian is on the dresser — how's your meteorite? To think, that big rock not only journeyed from outer space to our Boulder but has traveled in your company and Proust's on the Union Pacific to California, and by Oldsmobile to Laguna. O star, sister, breathe on me!

TO MARY VON SCHRADER

[August 30, 1951]

Six-thirty of a rainy morning, but the prospect of letters at 8:30 makes every little rain-drop like a star-sapphire.

I trimmed my moustache yesterday and got a hair cut. I look *young,* so children tell me. Did you know that Mrs. Disraeli cut Disraeli's hair and saved it all for twenty years and stuffed a pillow with it? True.

You won't believe how many hours I spend looking at those beautiful photographs! I love the one of you on the sofa with your mother. And the ones at Laguna on the beach with those beautiful children! They are! And — and — Tell your mother how lucky you are to have such a nice mother; and I'll write her and tell her how lucky she is to be Mary's mother — not that she needs telling!

And what you wrote about the poems was such a great delight. You like best in *Seven-League* just the ones I do. And I was pleased with what you said over the phone about "The Märchen."

This is one of those written-sideways-in-bed letters. What a world! And how one comes down in it. Once I wouldn't have dreamed of writing a letter in bed.

Elizabeth Bishop left last night — nice, but unhappy and not knowing what to do with her life. She left a typewriter, a large box of Eskimo baskets and sculpture (she'd been in Labrador) and a sweater — I look in corners occasionally, for *her*.

The tennis tournament starts tomorrow. Somehow I haven't felt like practising and really getting into shape for it this year — LIFE has distracted me; I decided to see whether I couldn't coast through. After all, a bowl is a bowl, a vegetable dish is a vegetable dish — they're not like LIFE.

It's almost 8:30 and just think I may have a letter from that old letter-writer Mary von S. (There used to be a man in Austin with a sign in front of his house that said THAT OLD SAW-FILER IS BACK AGAIN.)

In another letter, Jarrell wrote, "Today I play the best quite young player in the quarter-finals. He's fair, tall, handsome, swell strokes — NO EXPERI-ENCE — oughtn't to be too hard — and then two doubles matches."

TO MARY VON SCHRADER

[September 1951]

I've already played three matches today and won them — semi-finals and finals of men's doubles at Dennis, semi-finals of mixed doubles at Wianno — play finals in 45 minutes. Won both men's doubles 6–1, 6–0, mixed 6–2, 6–4.

Pierre [Emmanuel]'s here for several days — he flies back to France Saturday. We went for half an hour to a children's puppet theater showing *Hansel and Gretel*. Believe me, those puppets didn't have their feet on the ground. They were like captive, spastic balloons. How they shook, and flew! It amazed you that the audience and the chairs in the audience managed to stay down. And, believe me, it wasn't Grimm's *Hansel and Gretel*. For instance, the father in it told the children the story of *Peter Rabbit*. Famous old

Mediaeval German story *that* is! Hansel had a heavy New England accent and Gretel had a heavy New Yorky one. They all said *Deah* and *Dere*. The puppets kept getting tangled with one another or with bushes or the witch's house and a giant hand would descend from Heaven, and then go back but, sometimes, not quite far enough to be out of sight. In your letters you always write happily so that it looks like hoppily — first two times I thought it was; well, hoppily is the word for that puppet-show.

At the Starrs' for dinner last night, with Pierre I did a handwriting analysis from a torn-off hand written postscript to a letter, two lines: I said that was hardly enough to analyze, but then I saw that it was. I talked for twenty minutes about it, everything I said turned out to be right. For instance, I said *pathological instability* and the guy's actually been in sanatoria and under psychiatric attention lots of the time. Well, it turned out to be their *South Pacific* friend, Josh Logan.

In *Holiday* I saw a picture of the State Capitol in Denver: the caption under the photograph said (so to speak, so to speak) "The two bronze recumbent figures on the lawn represent Randall Jarrell reading *Pictures from an Institution* to Mary von Schrader. This husband-and-wife team are best known for the recent novel *The Ladies*."

I had to play a first round doubles match yesterday and we won 6–1, 6–1. Today and tomorrow and the next day lots of matches, two or three a day. Wish me luck — after all, it'll be your vegetable dish, if we win.

The Ladies *was a Proustian novel Jarrell and Mary hoped to write together. It was to be based on the lives of Bertha and Susan, two New England spinsters who were relatives of Mary's. Having visited in their home for weeks at a time since her childhood, Mary knew intimately their household, their servants, and the enclave of Jamesian Bostonians who were their friends in Pasadena. In another reference to* The Ladies *Jarrell wrote, "I can't wait to sit with thee under Clarissa Baxter's sampler. Clarissa is a real antiquity — no wonder her relatives wanted to preserve her needlework. And we'll preserve it, too, in* The Ladies. *That long, rosary-like necklace you said Bertha always wore is a good detail for our book. I've been reading some Proust and thinking competitively of* The Ladies. *Oh, darling, we're going to make Bertha's death better than Aunt Léonie's, wait and see: though we won't be able to do it as well as the death of his grandmother. We will do a good job, a really good one; I know it, I know it."*

In his next letter to Mary, Jarrell wrote, "No vegetable dish this year. Just a candy dish. Oh well."

TO MARY VON SCHRADER

[September 9, 1951]

I've been sorting thru things here and will wrap a little package for thee and send it later today. It is a reproduction of that big Kokoschka *Tempest* that I told you about, he is the man and the woman is Alma Mahler and I think you will like it as it is in some way akin to us. I am alone here with Kitten. He, wanting a cool place to lie has cleverly chosen the lower shelf of a glass tea-cart we have and is in a sort of cool glass cave. I wish *you* knew Kitten, best beloved — he is *very* sweet and loving and in emotional ways like a person; and so cute and funny and characteristic. You'd love him. Hardy wrote a *beautiful,* just wonderful poem about his cat; it's called "Last Words to a Dumb Friend" ... I'll read it to you at Christmas. I'll write, here, a beautiful Hardy for you:

WAITING BOTH

A star looks down at me,
And says: "Here I and you
Stand, each in our degree:
What do you mean to do, —
      Mean to do?"

I say: "For all I know,
Wait, and let Time go by
Till my change comes" — "Just so,"
The star says: "So mean I —
      So mean I."

I was awfully interested in what you said about the poetry in that an-thology. I have several better anthologies that I will show you at Christmas. The Untermeyer [*Modern American Poetry,* 1950] has a great big and really well selected bunch of my poems, and the *Oxford Book of American Verse* has a big and abominably selected bunch — old Matthiessen didn't even know I'd written *Losses,* everything's from the first two. I will bring my Hardy and Yeats as I will have them in the Princeton library and won't need my own, and I'll read them to you and look into your eyes and see them change.

Packed all afternoon and did I do a loving-crushed-newspaper job on the breakable objects! And the most breakable — my Lotte Lehmann *Rosenkava-lier* and Mahler's 9th Symphony — I will take along in my own hands so as to keep them unbroken for us. As one has eleven records and the other 17 or 18, I will be very muscular by the time I get to Princeton.

Aren't I good to write you such long letters? It feels good to write them — it's the nearest thing to being with you. Though not nearly near enough. I'm going to Hillsboro tomorrow and stay with the Taylors before I travel on. Oh, Sunday, Sunday! Lovely-phone-call-day. I'll stop now since Kitten is standing on the letter paper rubbing his head on mine. I love thee. Hier bin i'.

Jarrell enclosed the following poem with the letter:

THE METEORITE

Star, that looked so long among the stones
And picked from them, half iron and half dirt,
One; and bent and put it to her lips
And breathed upon it till at last it burned
Uncertainly, among the stars its sisters —
Breathe on me still, star, sister.

In the divorce settlement, Jarrell agreed that Mackie should have the duplex in Greensboro, the Oldsmobile, Kitten, and half his Princeton salary. When their sorting and packing was done Jarrell left for New Jersey and Mackie for Austin to complete her Ph.D. at the University of Texas, where they had first met.

Princeton, New Jersey,
September 1951–May 1952

*L*ike the letters Jarrell wrote while in the army, the Princeton letters resemble a diary, densely describing the thoughts and activities of an uprooted intellectual again separated by miles and time from the person who loves him. On rereading his army letters, Jarrell wrote Mary, "There are some terribly funny parts, and some rather well-written ones. I was struck with how (relatively) cheerful and determined I managed to stay, at least in the letters. Sometimes I'd be amused at what the letters didn't say — I never said how bad a lot of it was, naturally." Those sentences could be said about the following letters as well, except that in the army, Jarrell managed to write almost two books of poetry, while at Princeton he was barely able to finish one poem, "The Lonely Man." Scrambling to pay the rent and fuel bills, Jarrell took on every review, article, and speaking engagement he was offered — and accepted every free meal.

Mary, Alleyne, Beatrice, and their dachshund, Schatzel, were living at Laguna Beach but making frequent trips to Pasadena so Mary could see Irene and the girls could visit their father.

TO THE <u>PARTISAN REVIEW</u>

[September 1951]

Dear Miss Carver:

I'll get you the piece on October 5, Special Delivery; I was just writing to Delmore last night to make sure that was the date. I'm *very sorry* about August 5; I'd thought I could make myself finish it in Colorado, and I was having such a good time in Colorado I couldn't bear to waste three or four days on Criticism.

Yours,
Randall Jarrell

Miss Carver was one of the office staff at Partisan Review, *and the "piece" referred to was "A View of Three Poets," which appeared in the Novem- ber–December issue, 1951.*

TO MARY VON SCHRADER

[September 1951]

When Posterity asks, "What did Mr. Jarrell do during the second half of 1951?" it's going to froth at the mouth when it gets told, "Oh, that was the year he wrote letters to California."

I spent all day in Boston with the Leontievs and we had a lovely time. Vassily is just finishing an article for *Scientific American.* They'd asked him to write one, almost the first he'd ever written for a "popular" magazine. He's supposed to be the best mathematical economist in the world; and is in charge of a big, very important Air Force thing, so complicated it has to be done with "mechanical brains" and it is about how to arrange industry in the country in the next war.

He had to buy a conference table for his headquarters here, and we were all much shocked to discover that an ordinary price for a good conference table is $5,000. When I asked him what *Scientific American* had asked him to write on, he replied simply, "My work." It will be in the October issue.

We really had a swell time and all agreed that we ought to go back to Salzburg and Leopoldskron summer after next. I said to Vassily, "If you get me an invitation I'll go and bring my wife." He seemed sure that he could and (since he's very important in the Salzburg administration) there's nine chances out of ten that he can. That would pay our steamer fare, food, room in Leopoldskron, everything. Wouldn't it be *wunderbarschön?* That's a word the Americans at the Salzburg Seminar were always saying.

About that car you saw in Pasadena: that was the normal 120, not the XK-120 we've talked about. No one in this country will be able to buy "ours" till next year, if then. Only the Jaguar factory has it: to point up the difference I enclose several beautiful pictures of it. Aren't they dovey? (Kindly return to owner for files.) I hope they don't change it very much when they put it into production. We'll be very happy in that Jaguar.

The sports-car advertisements in the *Times* are really something today: A Simca convertible, an MG-TC '49 roadster for $1250, and an Alfa-Romeo with a Cadillac engine and *Hydromatic.* Even the Hillman Minxes advertise a special customized convertible, the only one of its kind. Wonder how much that Alfa is?

I've been reading *Pictures from an Institution* and thinking about changes and additions; 'speck I'll do quite a few things to it this fall. I liked some of the narrative parts well enough to think, "No, Homer was right — it *is* better to have narrative with digressions rather than digressions with narrative"; I'll remember next time. Man is the animal that likes narration.

How I want to listen to Mahler with you and talk about Proust, and read poems to you, and play with those little girls. I know I've said so, but I want to write so: you do for me exactly what Irina in my novel does — push out the boundaries of the world. Just think, beloved, six weeks ago we were walking over the grass, just touching each other, to that blue spruce and our world and our lives were about to get something like another self, but better — someone we could say anything to, could trust, could possess and be possessed by.

I sent you a couple of little books, *Faust* and Corbière and I am about to mail you some Moonlight marked Fragile.

The "Moonlight" was an LP recording of Schönberg's Verklärte Nacht.
Between this letter and the next, Mary's stepfather died after a long illness.

TO MRS. IRENE MACADAMS
[September 1951]
Dear Irene:

I want to write to you what Mary has already said for me, probably better: my sympathy for you in your loss. Mary has often said to me what a good and delightful man your husband was, and how happy the two of you were; I know that nothing anyone could say can mitigate the grief you feel, but the memory of your years together must surely do that, in a sense.

I am looking forward more than I can say to visiting you at Christmas; I'm looking forward more than that to migrating to California in June. I am extremely glad that we got to know each other in Colorado, so that I won't seem to you, for Mary, a more or less unknown quantity. I could tell from the way you looked at Mary how you felt about her, and I hope you can tell from the way I looked at her, and write about her, how I feel. I *do* know, and know well, how good and sweet and wonderful she is; and I hope you know that I am more concerned for her happiness than for anything else in the world.

Thank you *very* much for your sweet letter about *The Seven-League*

Crutches; I was so pleased to get it that it was only a little tiny disappointment to have a letter from 880 turn out to be — it never had before — not a letter from Mary at all. Besides, I had two Mary-letters to make my mail Maryish enough, if mail *can* be Maryish enough.

I wish that you had been televised, Proust and Mahler and all; I'd have been willing to buy a set to see it.

Mary says that you are known for your original photographs, mostly of headless torsos; if you send me some of your own taking I'll love them, headless or not. Besides, photographically speaking, Mary doesn't *have* a head, as I've told her — why, she's managed in 3½ weeks only to lose the camera. If you send me some nice colored photographs — even if only of her leg or arm — I'll bless you till the day I die.

Affectionately,

Randall

Mary had mentioned reading passages from Proust aloud to her mother and enjoying Das Knaben Wunderhorn *with her on the weekends in Pasadena.*

TO MARY VON SCHRADER

[September 1951]

Here, Bottom and his band are running the mail system — I've been to the English office, the Princeton mail room (where a mild old gentleman with grey hair and a brown toupee told me, at 10 minutes' length, everything about mail so as to prove I *couldn't* have any) and the main postoffice where "the mail carriers don't sort mail until after they come back at 3:30 and you would have to have the postmaster's consent to intercept mail." Well, I'll call thee tonight and probably tomorrow have two or three letters. What fools these mailmen be! Grey daemons my eye — grey idiots. What Princeton needs is an Institute for Advanced Postmen. Well, send me all at 14 Alexander Street and if that's too slow I'll get a postoffice box. I did get a letter from *Poetry* saying I'd won their $100 [Oscar Blumenthal] prize and, walking home, I saw two cats — and both, though rather wild-looking, came up to me and let me pet them and purred and purred so that seemed lucky, too.

Blackmur has been very nice, shown me everything and gone on errands with me, everybody has been very nice to me; and yet I look at them, all critics and English professors and such, and give a sort of impatient sigh and feel, "That's not the *point*!" They're all so satisfied with their world, even the ones that are most dissatisfied with it and the World; even while they're not believing They Believe.

Can't wait for the honey-dew melon and avocados. I love melons and avocados. In the best Princeton shop I saw four or five Ancient Madder ties but none so beautiful as the one you sent. I'm wearing it now.

Oh, I almost forgot to tell you I saw a beautiful black Simca with red leather seats driven by a touring French couple. Good old Gottfried!

I'll stop and make sure this letter gets to thee — please God they haven't been messing up the out-going mail the way they do the in-coming. Let's get J. Edgar Hoover to denounce the Postoffice.

Gottfried Knosperl Rosenbaum, a character in Pictures from an Institution, *was a twelve-tone composer who drove a Simca.*

TO MARY VON SCHRADER

[September 1951]

Was it Alleyne that answered the phone? It sounded remarkably like you; and Oh, how *good* you sounded! If I am not given some letters tomorrow morning I'm going to have a Nasty Interview with the Princeton postmaster. Of course they may be holding them to set up a National Shrine around them — but just the same . . .

Thank God, I had an evening with somebody not professor-y or writer-y — Eileen Berryman. She was eating dinner at the restaurant where I was — John Berryman had played tennis all afternoon and was so tired he had eaten some cold soup and gone to bed. She's a sort of child psychologist. We talked, I did a handwriting analysis for her, and she's going to do a Rorschach test of me sometime. She is a *nice* girl and you'll like her very much; John's nice, too, but thoroughly neurotic.

One of those cats — the one who lives a block away — not only purred tonight but accompanied me for a hundred yards and then, seeing a dog, walked home. Children love me, too — the dog, a giant collie, was sitting in the rectory yard by an old church down the street. He was looking the other way but when I said something friendly to him and indicated I wanted to pet him, he was so delighted that he looked at me wide-eyed as if I'd been a giant steak, and jumped on me and almost knocked me down. After a couple of minutes of petting I started to leave and he ran eagerly to the rectory door apparently expecting me to pay a call on Master.

I'm awfully pleased you are reading the girls *Moby-Dick,* it's the best book ever written by an American, I think: the nearest thing to an Epic anybody's written in a hundred years.

This house certainly is nice — it even has boxwood in its little side yard. I'm sitting in My Library; the walls have windows, doors and bookshelves and not one inch of anything else. And talk about "varied": two books directly before my eyes are two volumes of *Zoroaster and His World,* by Herzfeld, whoever he is; a few inches away a biography of [Ernst] Hoffman, a history of Norway, and *Auden's Collected Poems,* and so it goes.

For a couple of weeks will you write me even more and longer letters than you do? I've no real friends here and not even a routine, as yet, and I feel lonesome and depend on the letters completely.

TO MARY VON SCHRADER

[September 1951]

Gee, I'm looking forward to being all unpacked and settled into this dovey house. For a house on an ordinary street it is still well apart from the others and you can even play music late at night and not worry.

The radio is just full of music here. I can choose practically any kind I want to hear. Right now (and I'll be changing this) it is playing an overture by Jean Jacques Rousseau. Talk about light music! — it makes "Morning, Noon, and Night in Vienna" sound like the "Dies Irae." And now "with a turn of the dial" I'm about to hear Mahler's *Kindertotenlieder.* I've only heard it once or twice and am not very fond of it; maybe it's better than I think. We'll see.

I've been getting along well with Blackmur. He's been very agreeable, and is very intelligent and *very* well-read. Our offices are side by side and we talk a fair amount and eat lunch together, usually. There's something wrong with him all right, but it's less conspicuous as you know him better and doesn't affect him too much in ordinary conversation. I think he likes our daily conversations because I'm always good-humored and listen interestedly besides talking — which is rarer than you'd think among intellectuals. He works really *hard* — but because he wants to — his lectures and his critical articles (and a few partly fairly good, much-labored-over poems) are his life, poor thing.

You should see me cooking and eating my dinner. It's a fairly good dinner, "what there is of it, such as it is" — *not* in courses; the kitchen table where I sit is within reach of the icebox and the toaster. Now, don't laugh too hard if you're laughing; it's all very Functional. Oh, well, laugh as hard as you please — it's Funny, you should see me.

The trouble with the *Kindertotenlieder* is that it sounds as if those children had always been dead; and it's just enough like *Das Lied von der Erde* to make you think the children must have been half-Chinese. All the songs sound as if they wanted to stay on one note all the time but didn't quite have the nerve. Even Mahler nods.

Poor Peter [Arendrup]! He's a familiar type to me, though with much more charm than the regular examples. It's tough luck that he got married, otherwise I think he'd have a (superficially, at least) good time among the Southern Californians. Really complete egotism is so hard on you because you feel that everybody else is, *essentially* is or should be, like you — so you're alone, really alone. It's Gertrude's war of all against all. I've never heard it stated more baldly and pathetically than when Peter said, "Nobody's *loveable*." He really did think this self-evident — he knows that people make a mistake to love him, and feels it would be exactly the same mistake to love anybody else. You can't be much more mixed-up than he is.

At the present moment the radio has a poor choice, either Hindemith or Milhaud. You can see how spoiled I am.

Gertrude Johnson was the main character in Pictures from an Institution.

TO JOHN CROWE RANSOM

[September 1951]

Dear Mr. Ransom:

I'd got mixed up this summer about deadlines: I thought you'd said September 6, and a few days before August 6 (when I was in wildest Colorado far from critical thought) I got a letter from the [*Kenyon*] *Review* saying *that* was it. All I could do was curse God and die, figuratively speaking. I've been working on a first piece (4000 words or so); if you'll tell me the deadline I'll have you the article there airmail special delivery. Sorry to be such a nuisance to you. (Something in me doesn't *want* to write criticism.)

Some of my students here are good and I'm enjoying it. Just had a letter from Cal, all settled down in Amsterdam. Did you get the *Seven-League Crutches* I sent you? I was harried and distracted and sent one family of dear friends two copies—they thanked me elaborately for the second copy, an unprecedented event.

I hope you're well and that things are pleasant at Kenyon. The classical music on the radio is wonderful here.

Yours,
Randall

TO MARY VON SCHRADER

[September 24, 1951]

Did I work yesterday? From about two in the afternoon until one in the morning, with an hour off for dinner. Worked on my *Kenyon* piece ["The Age of Criticism"] — did well, too, except alas! alas! I'm afraid they may think it an unkind tactless piece more or less directed at them, among others — as it is. It's about the Age of Criticism — takes a dim view of it. You know, once someone told me she overheard a man in the audience say, about my lecture, "Whatever he says has an edge to it," and it's kind of true, but it's also a kind of Midas-blessing. It's *so* hard for me to write prose sentences so that they don't, even if I'm trying to be mild. I suppose that wit is a good slave and a bad master, but I'll stop complaining about my blessings — if God had wanted me to be different he would have made me different, I guess.

If you and your mother do come here in the spring, a lovely time, re-mind me to show you the pictures in a book called *The Margery Medium-ship.* Believe me, *the hairs of my flesh stood up straight:* you see this nice, sympathetic-looking, really charming sometimes, woman dressed in a ki-mono, lying in deep trance in the darkness, and the flashlight photograph shows extended from her the strangest half-formed hands or, worse still, strange huge projections like brains with thin coiling tubes to the mouth and ears; and if these photographs — taken under rigidly controlled circum-stances — were faked, a number of perfectly reputable people were in on the conspiracy. I've never seen anything like these photographs, for instance in some of them a strange whitish mass is covering her face like pale seaweed and makes you almost tremble with fear. There are dozens and dozens of these photographs. I just happened to come on the books (the *Proceedings of the American Society for Psychical Research*) in the philosophy-psychology sec-tion of the library. When I'd finished looking and reading in them and went to bed I lay there alone *and surprised to be alone* — I was ready for Other Things. Don't worry, old Randall hasn't become a medium. But I haven't those firm prejudices which dismiss anything as impossible unless it fits in with everything you've always believed; and in the case of those pho-tographs I think I'll just feel, Can such things be? — and let it go at that. But if such things *are,* how senseless they are; and this, alas, agrees with reality, which goodness knows doesn't make sense to *us*. Goodness knows this is a queer letter. Makes me feel very young somehow — it's the sort of thing one did as an adolescent.

I just heard a piece over the radio guaranteed to seduce anyone who says he doesn't like *any* modern music. It was Poulenc's Concerto for Organ, Strings and Tympani — and though neither heavy, nor original, it was really charming — on first hearing, anyway.

I'm really ⅗ done with this piece and doing it isn't so bad; but making myself do it is awful. When we're married and living together in Laguna I'll say to you, "Beloved, if I get up from this chair push me down and say, *You dope, finish that piece!*" Then it'll be easy — but so will *everything*.

TO MARY VON SCHRADER

[September 26, 1951]

This is one of those — certainly there is no need to say after looking at this writing! — one of those written-in-bed letters. The radio's playing *Tales from the Vienna Woods*.

Have I fixed up my bedroom! It was a rather noticeably dreary scholarly mess, very odds-and-endsy; now I've put up photographs of Donatello sculpture, photographs of Mary von Schrader, two of Elisabeth [Eisler]'s drawings, a map of Salzburg on the door, and a big, *big* picture of Kitten. I've changed some things downstairs, too, in fact if Stauffer saw his library he'd faint. I now have on the table where I write many of my own favorite possessions; my piece of fossil-Alaskan-mammoth-ivory, my obsidian from Boulder, the cut-metal Salzburg bull I gave to Gottfried Knosperl Rosenbaum; and a small lead casket with the signs of the Zodiac on it, a mermaid with two tail-like legs, for instance. On another table I have my plover and snipe decoys from Cape Cod and a blue-and-gold tooled leather book cover from Florence that Amy gave me in 1935. What a pleasure! It does help to look around at things in one's own style and not just Stauffer's sometimes-tasteful-and-more-often-not-quite academic style. I also have my own Proust, and Rilke and Hardy and Grimm's Tales, and since-boyhood-Bible on the shelf before my eyes, two feet away. They're playing Dvořák waltzes. I wish my favorite waltzer were here.

On top of the phonograph, four feet to the left, is a strange, large wooden hub-like thing that was washed ashore from a wreck and that's to me wonderful-looking and to everyone unidentifiable; there is also a Mexican bird-embroidered bag full of chessmen. Oh, I'm well-protected from *this* world (Princeton University) which would say in wonder at such a remark: "Who could want to be protected from us?" Now, they're playing dopey old Hindemith and I'll bound out of this bed and put him out of his misery.

Later.

I've just put my Salzburg painting up on the wall by the Donatellos. It's a painting on glass that I got from Leopoldskron by paying for it and saying it was broken. It's mostly gold, silver, blue and red on an opaque background. It has St. Florian, who puts out fires, pouring a silver stream from the pitcher he holds; he's dressed like a somewhat Oriental 18th century ballet dancer, and has just behind him, practically leaning on him a stag with four stars inside his antlers, just the way I sometimes put the Little People [Alleyne and Beatrice] stars and yours and mine inside the crescent moon.

You call me Sunday the same time I always call you; I'll be Waiting By the Phone, Mother, Waiting By the Phone. The number is 2019, I believe; yes, I remember your saying that after I read it off to you. You said, "Twenty nineteen." I can remember that. Now they're playing Haydn and I've just shaved. Outside, just next to one of the big trees I can see Sunlight.

Boy, this sure is a blow-by-blow account of my morning; it's like what the first publisher that read *Swann's Way* said, "Why, he takes seventy pages to tell you he couldn't go to sleep when he went to bed!"

I can remember that exact page of *Moby-Dick* — I used to have the same Rockwell Kent edition; the stars are certainly on our side, beloved.

I *liked* Alleyne's drawing. Ask her to send me more.

How do you like my drawings of the crescent moon and two stars? I think it is a pretty emblem for us. I like it's being physically impossible though spiritually *so*.

After this, Jarrell frequently drew a crescent moon with two stars inside its curve on his envelopes or letter paper. Some emblems had shaded sky in the background, or clouds, and some were framed inside a square. He continued to draw them on birthday cards, at Christmas, and for anniversaries the rest of his life. Once in a while he put four stars in, to include Alleyne and Beatrice.

TO MARY VON SCHRADER

[September 1951]

Well, last night I finished the house — now everything's straight and settled but the maid's room, which is full of dirty clothes and old poems.

And I admit, yes, that the kitchen sink's full of dishes, but what's wrong with that?

You should see me gravely buying eggs and lettuce and jam and stuff at the grocery; buying it I'm used to, but I feel masqueradish when I go home and cook it. So far my cooking's been better than Gertrude's because I've only cooked breakfast; later on, when it comes to dinner, who knows? It was the first good breakfast I've had up here and, as there was no egg-beater I just mixed the eggs and cream together in the skillet and it worked like a charm — and since this saves washing and drying (a) the egg-beater and (b) a bowl, I'll go along with it a while longer.

I have all together (have never looked at them since writing them) about a hundred letters I wrote Mackie during the time I was in the army. Well, I have been reading them and enjoyed it *very* much, I have to confess. There are some terribly funny parts, and some rather well-written ones. I was struck with how (relatively) cheerful and determined I managed to stay, at least in the letters. Sometimes I'd be amused at what the letters didn't say — I never said how bad a lot of it was, naturally. But how I did write poems! The circumstances under which my earlier war poems were written were really absurd, about like writing them during the time-outs in a football-game.

Now I'm sitting in Blackmur's office more or less pretending to be Blackmur-signing-students-for-Creative-Writing. He had to go to a Graduate Conference or something. Tomorrow I'll have to sit in my office most of the day for my students to arrange conference dates. I'm looking with some interest at Blackmur's handwriting and meditating on Analysis, though not, believe me, of Blackmur. It's a notably unspontaneous handwriting.

Oh woe, I'm really going to have to work some the next seven or eight days — the *Partisan* piece is due October 5, and I just got a postcard saying they're expecting it. Well, it will be very character-building. And then my lectures, my lectures. *And* my letters. Above all my letters. Goodness, if Posterity ever prints our letters it will have to furnish a book-case with them à la the *Encyclopaedia Britannica*.

When I got home ole Bottom had left me a Princeton weekly bulletin, a Princeton alumni magazine, and an advertisement from Princeton — nothing more. Am I philosophical! I have a pale smile and an Oh-well-telephone-and-Special-Delivery-tomorrow air.

The "Gertrude" Jarrell referred to was, again, Gertrude Johnson in Pictures from an Institution.

TO MARY VON SCHRADER

[September 1951]

Well, I've just seen ¾ of a *bad* football game — poor NYU didn't have a team. How longingly I wished for you. Do you like Football? One cute thing happened when a pass-receiver had been knocked down in the end-zone, he protested indignantly though not very hopefully to the referee; and when pass interference was allowed the boy was so delighted he actually jumped up and down and clapped his hands. The best thing there was a tiger: I don't *think* he was a real tiger, since he did the Charleston, led cheers, and walked upright half the time; on the other hand, he tried to eat the cheerleader *and* the cheerleader's straw hat, so he may have been real after all. He certainly had a real tiger's head and a splendid furry, baggy body. If there had been more tigers and fewer football players I'd have been happier.

In reply to your offer of doing without my letters while I'm so rushed for *Partisan* all I can say is: Anytime I don't write you because I'm preparing lectures they can tan me and use me to bind books with. Still, as you can imagine, I didn't do much beside work yesterday. My *Poetry* prize check [Oscar Blumenthal Prize] came ($100) and I am putting it in escrow for a flight to California.

Oh, oh, OHH! I don't like to write criticism. Here I sit surrounded by unkind remarks about the last three parts of Williams' *Paterson;* but the worst part of it is, half of them are still in my head. Let's be Critics of To-morrow living in the House of Tomorrow and just Grade poems: "*Paterson Part IV* is a 6-B poem and gets a 72 on examination."

I'll bet Williams will want to murder me. Shaw said about the critic, "His hand is against every man and every man's hand is against him." There's some truth in that: Favorable remarks seem Only Right on your part and unfavorable seem Original Sin.

Oh, writing *criticism!* Booooh! Let's be novelists. How about it? Why should we go around telling Posterity what is good and bad? — Let it stay asleep. Or as Goldwyn or somebody said, "What's Posterity ever done for us?"

I've left myself so little time to finish my *Partisan* piece that I'm doing everything else — well, it, too — at top speed. See where the first paragraph is smeared? I put my head down on it for a moment's rest and now you can read five or six words from it on my palm, they came off so clearly.

Herbert Read arrives today — he's giving the first part of three bunches of lectures the third of which I give in the spring. Wish it were someone less dopey.

Better quit and get this off and not give Bottom a chance.

TO HANNAH ARENDT

[September 1951]

Dear Hannah:

Your letter, besides delighting and astonishing me as much as any letter from my favorite non-correspondent always does, was especially dear to me as my first real letter about *Seven-League Crutches* and my last and nicest letter about *Little Friend, Little Friend.* I hope very much that what you say about *Little Friend* is true. A lot of the nakedness and directness comes from where and under what circumstances and with-what-feelings I wrote the poems, I imagine. This sounds as if I were saying Heredity and Environment did it — but I really meant specific things, too long to be said except in a whole book. But in those days I wasn't thinking of anything but what I saw and knew about, and putting it into the poems — the other day I read a lot of letters I wrote at the time and it was queer to think about it all.

Princeton is *much* more Princetonian than — Princeton, even. Writing to someone about getting settled in Princeton, I decided that when I get completely settled I won't even wake up in the morning.

I'm getting settled by myself — Mackie and I are being divorced. We've been getting more and more different in every way for a long time, and I'm sure (she is, too) both of us will be better off. It almost happened three years ago and is a well-considered affair. That's why I didn't want you visiting us in August.

On the other hand, I have a very different sort of news, connected — as you can easily guess — with the lyrical–Colorado portion of my last letter. This news I haven't told anybody, and will tell to you as my own special friend. Could I come see you weekend after this, or are you busy then? You could enter in your engagement book *Sat. Oct. 6, Sun. Oct. 7* — American Poetry Weekend.

I can't resist telling you one part of my news that will make you, surely, laugh aloud, remembering my "Deutsch Durch Freud" poem and all the rest; her name is von Something. On the other hand, I know more German than she does, so this will show you that she couldn't be German, no, not if she were two years old.

I'll never make a real novelist — I haven't a bone of Suspense in my body. By now you can say about my news, in a calm accustomed tone: "Well, what comes before and after *von* and when are you going to be married?"

Reply to this in longhand and I'll do a handwriting analysis for you (of my own amateurish variety). Probably the effect of this ingenuous sentence will be to make you type even the signature. (But see, I write to you in this most Revealing handwriting.)

I'm *awfully* sorry you had a bad summer; everything connected with [Hermann] Broch's death must have made it particularly difficult to get any of your own work done. And your "Othello's occupation's gone" feeling must have made new work very hard — I remember how queer it felt to be no longer writing poems about the war.

I've met several people who've spoken of your book with the greatest admiration.

I'm very eager to see you; do write me right away (*only a line or two —* this to placate the non-corresponding Cerberus in your heart) whether next week's end will be all right.

Affectionately,
Randall

Hermann Broch was a Viennese novelist who came to America just before World War II. Among his books are The Sleepwalkers *and* The Death of Virgil.

TO MARY VON SCHRADER

[September 1951]

I've been — you won't believe this — writing to someone else, to Hannah in fact. I had one paragraph so silly that I can't resist copying it for you:

"So far I'm a better cook than Gertrude [Johnson] because I cook only breakfasts and Picnic suppers, and any fool can cook breakfast; and if you can shuffle cards you can make sandwiches, the principle is the same. I'm a housekeeper of the Functional School — they're going to exhibit me at the Museum of Modern Art next spring. (Next summer the Museum of Natural History gets my bones.)"

I don't know whether this was worth copying, but I know that if it's good you'll like it and if it's not you'll love me just the same.

In her letter Hannah thanked me for 7-*League Crutches* (I've written that so much lately I feel like the 7-Up Company) and also for a last-spring present of *Little Friend* (as you can see from that "last spring" she's not much of a correspondent normally). She wrote about *Little Friend* what I want to copy for thee, to make thee proud for our book (this is my copying-letters-letter): "This has a quality of nakedness and directness which none of your later work has. There is no other book on the War, poetry or prose, which comes even near to this almost unbearably striking, whipping impact (I don't mean impact, but don't know any better word)."

The next time I see her I'm going to tell her about thee; just think, I haven't told anyone about you. And at Christmas I'm going to tell the Little People about you; they only know you as a Friend. I wish I could have heard Beatrice say, "You love him, don't you?"

I've now registered and arranged conferences for all my 22 students. Alas, they don't seem any different or any better than the girls at Woman's College.

Oh, I don't know what I'd do without you. This pretty grey stone ivy-clad world of Princeton is like an absurd costume-ball set, I walk through it looking for you to make it real.

In another letter, Jarrell wrote, "I had two very good students and one strange in my conferences today, so it was an interesting day. I did them an injustice — their level is higher than at Woman's College."

TO MARY VON SCHRADER

[October 1951]

Got ⅘ of that old review done — tonight I type it and tomorrow, in nooks and crannies and by crook, under high students and low, I'll finish the rest and type *it*.

Thank God, I found that letter I'd written to Cal about his book that I thought I'd lost; it was — surprise! — in the book. And I was able to use lots of it, with hardly a word changed, for my piece — that must be something unprecedented in criticism, don't you think?

Guess what I had today? A sweet letter from Amy. We haven't written in three or four years. She'd happened to meet my mother and learn about my divorce (she lives in Texas but was visiting in Nashville); she plainly didn't know whether it was something I'd wanted or not, so she wrote a nice letter all about her children and Texas and a little about what poems of mine she'd seen. Wasn't that sweet of her? I hope we get to see her someday; I haven't seen her myself since '42. You would like her and she'd like you. And I like you!

I loved your letter about *Little Friend* and like to think of it on your coffee table. What I want to see on that coffee table is *The Ladies*. Don't look forward to much in *Blood for a Stranger*. About ⅔ are poems I wish my worst enemy had written, or anybody else, just not me. But a few you'll like.

I wish I could have heard the seals that day and seen Catalina in the sunset. Won't our long Christmas vacation be wonderful? Really the seals are saying: "We want Jarrell." They say it in Seal.

I had a very nice time with the Berrymans at dinner at their house: stayed till late. Berryman was very complimentary about my (long past now) Auden pieces; he said that if anybody knew *him* as well as I know Auden he'd murder them right away, it would be too embarrassing and disquieting to know that such a person existed. I agree with what you said about Berryman's poems. But, he's very intelligent and nice and Disinterested: and believe me, *that's* rather rare among Our Intellectuals. One thing that ought to endear him to you and me: he's almost the only poet I know of who has written one or two poems influenced by mine.

Blackmur's making four or five lectures on Stendhal's *Charterhouse of Parma.* The first was extremely good, one of the four or five best (and most difficult) I ever heard. He doesn't talk down (and hardly to) his audience. If you can get that book out there why don't you read it? I know you'd enjoy it — it's a *scream,* a charming book.

I had a nice postcard from Hannah — I'm to go there on the weekend; but boy, that postcard was like the Rosetta Stone if the Rosetta Stone had nothing but hieroglyphics. I can see why she always types her letters. When I tell her about thee and show her the pictures she will say, "Oh, you lucky Randall!" If she doesn't, I'll — ah, but that's impossible, nobody could resist those photographs and that smile; but if people do I'll throw them out the window.

If everybody in the world told me marrying you was a bad idea I'd say to you with a confident, indulgent smile, "Aren't people silly?" It would be like telling Adam not to marry Eve but one of the rabbits.

TO MARY VON SCHRADER

[October 1951]

Here I am in wicked old New York. It has rained all afternoon and half of New York was stained all over and coming out of its sodden clothes. I went to the Museum of Modern Art in the afternoon. Before one painting, a distorted one of a dark girl, I heard a boy say to his date: "She looks just like Beatrice Lillie — or Hitler." I saw some cadets in military uniforms — ages 13, 14, and 9, say — sitting eating lunch with two very dressed and peroxided girls of 25 or 27, all talking the most animated Spanish. I never managed to find a hypothesis for *that* group.

There was an exhibition of 8 foreign cars there as an Example of Design and I looked at another ten or so at dealers'.

I'm slightly dazed and sleepy — I didn't finish typing the last of my *Partisan* piece till 2 in the morning. I'd finished writing it about ten and went over to the Berrymans for two hours. They'd called me earlier. I had a good time with them and listened to some good music — the Berrymans certainly are nice.

I'm getting quite to like Blackmur. We eat lunch together almost every day with a couple of friends of his, a woman about 50 and one about 40, both nice and the last quite attractive. We're usually quite gay and make jokes — well, I make most of the jokes, but the atmosphere is jokey. I was originally disquieted about the little queer or horrible or sadistic-seeming things that would come up from time to time in his conversation, but I guess they're just an unpleasant idiosyncrasy.

I send in this letter Cal's review [of *The Seven-League Crutches*]. Hannah and her husband [Heinrich Blücher] both read it and were delighted. She was particularly interested in it because she had in the past said several of the things herself and felt, so to speak, proud of having done it for poetry in a language not her own.

I really do like her husband. He's a very intelligent man, a wild enthusiast (more than I — imagine!), *echt* German; he really does say good things about paintings. He's a *most* individual man. They're a scream together, sometimes — they will have little cheerful mock-quarrels, and they have an odd matter-of-fact sharing of dishes and little household duties; she kids him a little more than he kids her. They seem a very happily married couple.

Pictures from an Institution now has a pretty, dark, heavy Spring Binder for a cover with *The Origins of Totalitarianism Volume II* marked on it; Hannah gave it to me, it's left over from her book.

Hannah said many complimentary things about you when I showed her the pictures and then she added, "That's all one can tell from little snapshots like these." I said, "You're blind!" and she laughed and laughed. Did you know that I LOVE YOU, you funny, dear, good, beloved thing?

In a letter about the review, which was entitled "On the Seven-League Crutches" and appeared in the October 7, 1951, New York Times Book Review, Lowell wrote, "Harvey Breit asked me to review your book saying he thought you needed a push or something of the sort. Then he wrote through his secretary that I should keep to 500 words. I've gone to about double that length and, though no critic, think I've done a fairly good job." In the review, Lowell said, among other things, that Jarrell had "gone far enough to be compared with his peers, the best lyric poets of the past; he has the same finesse and originality that they have, and his faults, a certain idiosyncratic willfulness and eclectic timidity, are only faults in this context . . ." He concluded by saying that his favorite was "A Girl in a

Library" and that it was "an apotheosis of the American girl, an immortal character piece, and the poem in which Jarrell perhaps best uses his own qualities and his sense of popular culture ... 'Belinda' was once drawn with something of the same hesitating satire and sympathy." (RJ)

TO SISTER BERNETTA QUINN

[October 10, 1951]

Dear Sister Bernetta:

Please forgive me for not having written when I should have several months ago; my life has been complicated both with griefs and joys, and I've put off doing many things — I've lost your last letter, even. If you will send me a sort of questionnaire about any puzzling things in the poems (or anything else in them) I'll scribble answers and send them back.

I'm sending you a copy of *The Seven-League Crutches* — naturally, as one of my two or three special readers, you make one of the books simply gravitate to you; however, parcel-post-gravitation is pretty slow, so it probably won't get there for several days.

I'm working here at Princeton this year, mostly with students who write; several are extremely good, a great pleasure to work with.

Won't it be nice when Marianne Moore's collected poems come out? Do you know "The Pangolin" very well? I think it's a wonderful poem, a morally beautiful poem.

I hope your work is going along well and that you're having a good year.

Yours,
Randall Jarrell

TO HANNAH ARENDT

[October 29, 1951]

Dear Hannah:

Thank you so much for your kind and dear letter; you can't know how delighted I am that you like the pieces on Wallace Stevens that much. I'd had a wonderful time in New York with you and was going to write you anyway about that. I have much the best reason in the world for being late about writing — Mary (*my* Mary, the one I said "you're *blind!*" about) has been in the East for two weeks, and just left. She's going to be here in the spring, too, and I'll bring her to see you then. I'm going out to California at

Christmas — there's a long Christmas vacation here, and I can arrange my schedule to give me an extra week. So I feel, as an Austrian (don't turn up your Prussian nose) acquaintance of mine always used to say, "rather good."

Thanks so much for the Hölderlin; it has that pure grave exact tone (as if it were his duty to say only what was really true, no more) he always seems to have. Would that I could know what it's really like.

Your "awfully simple" translations are just what I need.

I'd love to come up and see you in a couple of weeks, two or three; would come up sooner but I am living as far as I can like Diogenes — I go along the street and say scornfully to the squirrels, and ants too, "You spendthrifts!" Of course, they're not saving up for an airplane trip and can afford their modest luxuries, so they say, leaning back in their fur coats.

It was a great joy to spend the time with you and talk as we did; you are a true friend to me — believe me, I'm glad *you* exist. And it's always so much fun to see and talk to and listen to your husband — he's a *really* interesting man. And it's always awing (for an enthusiast) to see someone more enthusiastic than yourself — like the second fattest man in the world meeting the fattest.

Don't Germans always make Autumn excursions to the Free Forest? *Lots* of Free Forest (and free beds and free picnic lunches, I'll make a blue one for your husband and a pink one for you) around Princeton. Think — it's only an hour on the train. A nothing!

Affectionately,

Randall

TO MARY VON SCHRADER

[November 2, 1951]

I was so tired at lunch today (Blackmur and Edward Cone, the composer, and an old acquaintance of mine, named Robert Fitzgerald) that it made me feel very irresponsibly and hysterically funny; I had everybody laughing and laughing. It amuses me to more or less kid Blackmur (in a nice way); I think I'm the only one who does.

Last night was Herbert Read's lecture about free verse. He just loves free verse and "organic form" — meaning by that any special happen-only-once form that the subject matter imposes on the poem; if he had his way there wouldn't be any other kind. I was polite but argued a good deal; rather enjoyed it. One English professor actually said in the after lecture discussion, about William Carlos Williams: "Well, of course his poems are bad; how could anyone write good poems dashing them off in between writing prescriptions?" His voice was so full of complacent ignorance and prejudice that it made me tremble with aversion.

I didn't do any work last night because when I got home the lights were out; and of course, I didn't know where any candles were, didn't even know if there were some. I watched matches and candles and flashlights flickering up and down the stairs of other houses; played the piano a little and then went to sleep. When the lights came on at midnight it woke me and I read a book I've always meant to read, de Vigny's *Splendors and Miseries of Military Life* [*Servitude et grandeur militaires*], was disappointed, listened to music awhile and went back to sleep. I'll quit this. I'm too tired and dopey to be a letter-writer worthy of you.

TO MARY VON SCHRADER

[November 6, 1951]

So many of the leaves are gone that much of the sky shows from my upstairs windows. How much the damned advertisers do talk on day-time WQXR programs; I heard one fifteen minute program that had only two short pieces on it, the rest was talk about Zenith Hearing-Aids, everything said two or three times.

One of my students has invited me to eat with him at his — well, I think they're called eating-clubs. They're the Princeton equivalents of fraternities (or, as *they'd* put it, fraternities are the world's equivalent for eating-clubs). I accepted partly à la Gertrude, something a novelist ought not to miss, but partly as an economical man delighted with a free dinner: I thought, "Yes, that's a third of a trip to New York." The simple pleasures of the poor! I got a check for $12.50 from the publishers of *Little Friend, Little Friend,* half of it the permission money for a poem used in an anthology, and it seemed so important, such a delight; and before it would have been like a returned postage-stamp. I know I shouldn't talk about money; but you and I talk about everything. And believe me, I know how rich I am (because of you) with a warm dovey life I can sink into like a quilt; and without you I would be like a rubber skeleton sitting on a glacier without even a white fox to look forward to being eaten by.

Last night Blackmur was pretty bad — very mannered, and he does so enjoy talking about awful or unseemly things in a relishing-in-his-mouth way. He quoted this sentence, "What if my breath does smell bad? The dead smell worse," and he then repeated it *twice.*

He loves to shock people as much as Gertrude did. I've now heard his first and second lectures on the *Charterhouse* and his first and second on *The*

Brothers Karamazov: in each case the first more general one was *extremely* good and the second bad or mediocre with an occasionally good part. He does so love to show off to people and his way of showing off is unattractive. About the best things in our life he has no modesty or shame or gentleness or forbearance, nor does he have any about the worst; he talks about both as if they were the same, almost. He's a queer man: if he traded a little intelligence for a little goodness or sweetness he'd certainly be better off. But he wouldn't like that because either goodness or sweetness hampers you, you can't do what you please then, and he wants (again like Gertrude) to be free to do anything he pleases. To him everything is something you can manipulate.

He thinks he's really good, really hot, and this isn't so good. You ought to realize that even if you're really good it's just in comparison to other people, that really you're practically a joke compared to what you might be and what somebody could be. *What is man that thou art mindful of him* is just so.

TO MARY VON SCHRADER

[November 1951]

You will laugh: my twelve hours' work is all wasted (temporarily), because I decided I couldn't possibly do justice to the criticism piece ["The Age of Criticism"] in the time I had, and all would be a mess — *so* I'm doing an appreciation of Whitman instead; his sensitivity, originality of language, good details, etc. Oh, criticism! Would that I were a poet or novelist, and not a critic. I finished the first page and a half and have 3½ days to do the next ten more pages, with quotations taking up some of the space — hah, a nothing! The age of criticism piece would have taken twenty or more pages, *Kenyon* wouldn't have had room, etc. But now, I have a good start and lots of notes and will do it later. *Partisan* would want it, I imagine. So t'will all be well.

Margaret Marshall says Spender is reviewing me for *The Nation* and she's asked me to review a dictionary. No kidding, it's that tremendous $50 *Dictionary of Americanisms* [ed. Mitford M. Mathews] she gave it to me more or less as a piece of wit and said, "How novel to have it reviewed by a poet."

I think I'm going to write a poem rather like "Deutsch Durch Freud" called "The Poet-Cook"; at least I've been thinking about it. I'll have a mermaid in it that comes to live with the Hero. I've already thought of some details like the little pools of water where she stands, the flop of her tail on the stairs, as she comes up the stairs. In some ways she's going to be like another mermaid I know — I bet nobody's ever written a poem about a poet-cook with a mermaid. Ah, originality!

The next few days are going to be all Whitman and no play.

Jarrell never wrote "The Poet-Cook" as a poem, but he used the idea and some of its details in a prose children's book called The Animal Family.

TO ROBERT LOWELL

[November 1951]

Dear Cal:

I'm a wretch not to have written you long, long ago. I did write you a long letter about your book and thanking you for the Uccello: lost it, found it just before I reviewed you in *Partisan* (and copied many sentences from it for the review); it's somewhere here in my extraordinarily messed-up — like Kenyon — house. I've looked for half an hour and can't find it. I'll send it later whenever I find it.

First let me tell you what a *great* pleasure your review was to me ["The Seven-League Crutches," *New York Times Book Review*]. You said such *interesting* things — it was so different from those old Reviews the Reviewers write. I read it while spending the weekend with Hannah Arendt and her husband; they were much impressed with it, and she said with delight, "He says many things *I've* said to you about it — I am proud." She really had, too. It was far and away the best things anybody's written about my poems. I've seen only two other reviews — one, the usual somnambulistic one by Babette Deutsch, and another almost as favorable as yours. I saw a typical [Dudley] Fitts review of you in *Furioso* — almost fawningly respectful and impressed but taking little pretentious digs here and there among the Latin tags.

I hope my review ["A View of Three Poets"] — I'm assuming *Partisan* gets to Amsterdam; this right? — wasn't a displeasure to you. Everybody knows, from past reading, that I think you a wonderful poet, so I spent more time on what seemed to me wrong than I otherwise would have. (By the way, Fitts' judgment of the reality of the heroine [*The Mills of the Kavanaughs*] was the exact opposite of mine: he said that she was the most appealing female character since — I *think* it was Tess, somebody about then. Honest, he did.) Anyway, if I said anything you didn't like forgive it me, it was honest if nothing else. I was writing so fast for a deadline and under such odd circumstances that I didn't get it as balanced and smooth as I might have otherwise. (It'll all be the same 100 days from now.)

Jesus, have you *seen Paterson IV?* Golly, golly.

I guess you know from the Taylors that Mackie and I are being divorced. I know how fond of her you were (so was I) so it's sure to be a grief to you; but we'd been getting further and further apart every year, we had almost none of the same interests . . . it was bad for us and getting worse, and I know we'll both be a lot better off apart. This sounds like the sayings of Spartans, but you can't write about such things very well.

I've been leading a very quiet industrious lonely life here at Princeton; I've a big house (it was already rented, worse luck), read, write (a Whitman article, surprise, surprise!), listen to classical music over the radio, sleep. I see Blackmur and a composer, Edward Cone, and a couple of friends of theirs at lunch most days; see the Berrymans and Robert Fitzgerald every couple of weeks. I'm awfully broke, so I've been in to New York only twice this fall. I do all my school work on Thursday and Fridays — it's mostly talking to boys about their poems and stories. They're nice, one is really good, two rather good.

Did you know that I've written a — well, not really a novel, but a prose comedy about 200 typed pages long? Has Peter described it to you? It's named *Pictures from an Institution* — I won't make any very pretentious claims for it, but I'll bet you a dollar against a penny that you enjoy reading it, poor vain mortal that I am. I *loved* writing it: Cal, you ought to write a — prose book of some length; I still don't want to say *novel*.

I was delighted that you liked the Stevens [review] that well; Hannah Arendt did too ["Reflections on Wallace Stevens"].

Do you want a low-level compliment? Your printing is now *wonderfully legible*. The World's Great Age Begins Anew.

I felt that Europe would affect you as it does; there's nothing like it. I'll bet in the long run it's awfully good for your poetry — I can't help thinking it was for mine: the army and Europe really happened to my poems in a big way.

About "repeating (oneself)" or the "void and formlessness of not repeating" — take a chance, Cal; let things work for you, if you've changed it will change the poems and in the long run change them for the good. I don't know whether this advice is right but I do know it's sincere, I go by it myself. I think you, less than any poet alive, need to worry about losing your style, your old way of doing things — enough of it will always be there no matter what you do. And I think not having written, having lived in Europe instead, will be good for your poems — they *surely* come out of one's life, not out of one's work and industry and good intentions.

I had a boy last summer at Colorado who was good (did an excellent Rilke translation) and most of his poems were excellent though unconscious imitations of you. You'd had him in a class at Iowa, I think — De Witt Snodgrass, poor ill-named one! When you influence people — when your poems influence theirs, that is — you really mow them down: they're like Charcot's hypnotic subjects.

I stayed with Peter and Eleanor just before I left Greensboro; they're in fine shape in every way. Robie and Anne talked a lot about their travels with you. I like them very much.

I saw Red for several days this spring — he was *so* nice. What a pleasure to see him again!

I'll repeat a Caroline Tate story you may not have heard. Edward Cone got her a medal from St. Teresa's birth- or deathplace, and she wrote thanking him: "It has already brought me luck! Today I was asked to teach a special class at the College of St. Teresa. I'm so glad: to tell the truth, I'm a little tired of teaching Protestants."

I spent this summer on Cape Cod except for three weeks at Boulder, Colorado — I was crazy about it, and played tennis all the time with a Danish Davis Cup player [Peter Arendrup]. Peter [Taylor] and Eleanor came up to the Cape for a day and a half; we kidded them a lot, said it was the longest journey for the shortest stay ever made.

Herbert Read gave six lectures (dopey, but he's a nice man) in this Princeton Seminar in Literary Criticism series. I give six on Auden in the spring. A Dominican monk named du Menascas, or something like that, one of the smartest and nicest men I've ever met, is giving three now: small audience — 35 or so — invited: Auden, [Jacques] Maritain, Oppenheimer (who talked quite brilliantly and much too much). [Robert] Fitzgerald, Blackmur, etc. Auden came over and said *Seven-League Crutches* was "frightfully good"; then he said that he'd told a friend he was coming to my lectures and the friend had said, "They're *on* you." I said politely that I'd love to have him at them.

I've been the worst of correspondents, but you write soon and I promise faithfully to answer promptly. Give my love to Elizabeth — I hope she's well and happy and enjoying Europe. When you get one of your poems finished do send it.

Love,
Randall

Lowell answered from Amsterdam that Robie Macauley had told him about "a novel that you read aloud to yourself between tennis sets, and that Peter admires and thinks (as a veteran novelist) you had no right to write."

TO MARY VON SCHRADER

[November 1951]

How it's raining — all yesterday, all today.

Edward Cone took me to hear a pianist play her last rehearsal at home before a concert; she played an awfully good, late Schubert sonata, but not too well — Edward, himself, is a much better and much more powerful pianist. Surprisingly good. When he was illustrating points about the way some of the symphony or sonata is and ought to be played, he would (just out of his head, with great spontaneity and power) play it the wrong way and then the right or unusual way; it was so impressive to hear somebody doing it — and he did it with as much easy power as if he'd rehearsed it for weeks.

Last night Father [Jean] de Menasce gave his first lecture; alas, he's only giving three, not six, as Read did. He was just *wonderful* — one of the most intelligent, modest, sensible, perceptive, acute, *right* men I've ever heard. Never have heard anybody with such a gift for clear expression.

He was talking about poetry and language and translation and so forth. He's a linguistic expert, translated *The Waste Land* into French, very international (a Hungarian count to begin with but partly French and a professor at a French university) — you couldn't even be sure he was a foreigner, his English is so good. Very witty — when Maritain said (after conceding you could translate, really, French into German) "But, could you really translate a Chinese poem into English?" Father de Menasce replied, "No, I don't know Chinese that well." Wasn't that clever? Maritain's comments were mostly commonplace, Oppenheimer's were almost too good: well-phrased (phrased to dazzle) and he talked rather too much; but he was good, really good. Auden said almost nothing: his face has got *so* heavy and wrinkled and powerful and old (he's only 44) so that he looks like a disenchanted lion, almost ... He was awfully nice — he quite hurried over to me after the lecture and talked (he knew I was going to give my lectures on him — he said that before he knew this he'd already replied to someone, "Oh yes, I'm going to them"). About my book he said it was "frightfully good."

Blackmur talked too much and in an idiosyncratically personal way at the lecture and, poor man, got very drunk at the party afterwards at Cone's and (as he always does when drunk) talked very pessimistically, egotistically, and obscenely, a bad combination. Edward Cone played the wonderful Liszt "Vallée d'Obermann" again and one called "After a Reading of Dante" that's wonderful, too. Good old Liszt! If I were a music critic I'd write an article about his good pieces à la my Whitman article.

I'm about ⅗ through but from now on must work, work, work on it and nothing else.

Help, help! The rain is turning to snow!

TO SARA STARR

[November 1951]

Dear Sara:

I'm leading a sort of quiet industrious lonely life here; my students are nice, a few quite good. I certainly would like to see you: could you come out and spend the day sometime, or could we meet each other at the Central Park Zoo some weekend? We might see Garbo.

I hope you're having a good year. There was a wonderful picture of Harold Taylor in the *Herald-Tribune* — entirely *true* but otherwise libellous. You know, he really isn't a bit older than he was in 1946. He's like that wheat from Egyptian tombs — I'll bet if they buried him for three thousand years and then exposed him to limelight he'd begin to make a speech on civil rights.

Write me a nice letter and I'll bless you.

Affectionately,
Randall

Harold Taylor was the president of Sarah Lawrence College from 1945 to 1959, and Dwight Robbins, the college president in Pictures from an Institution, *shared certain traits with him.*

TO MARY VON SCHRADER

[November 1951]

All continues as before — I've got ten pages typed and finished now, four or five more will do — tonight and tomorrow will see me done, all done. I'll send the carbon of the Whitman article when I finish and you can send it right back when you finish — I'm sure you'll enjoy it, fond as you are of both subject and writer.

Old Whitman sure is a wonderful poet at his best. A really sizeable one — the size of a person and the world. I think "Song of Myself" and "The Sleepers" are the best — ⅔ of his best poetry seems to me in "Song of Myself." I'm not as good in it as I am in some articles, but *those quotations!* I quote a lot in it. It's funny.

It's funny that Whitman could say both the wonderful things and the goofy junk (though that's true of so many good or great writers). I've noticed, though, that to be a good poet in 19th century America you had to be *very* eccentric and entirely on your own, otherwise you were just provincial, like Longfellow and Poe and Lowell and Bryant and the rest. The good ones, Whitman and Dickinson and Melville are like nothing else — though Melville in his poems is often so completely amateurish that you positively wriggle around in your chair. Even the "provincials" aren't as bad as the bad parts, worst parts of *Pierre.* I've never read worse dime-novel rhetoric anywhere; and he wrote it right after *Moby-Dick!* It's a strange world.

Later

I'm through, through! And with an hour and a half to spare — the last air-mail leaves at 7:30. My God how I've worked. And I'm still well and strong, can almost walk, almost talk, even — thinking, though, I fear, is beyond me.

I have a horrible feeling that they'll say, "It's too long, we won't have space till next issue." If they do! *If they do!* I send you the carbon, and as soon as you've read it (and written lots of immediate comments in a letter to your dear Brother) send it back, will you?

In just a minute this letter is going to be Over; I can scarcely sit up, and I have to write a letter to Ransom, to go with the article, get stamps, go to post office, put flowers on Whitman's grave, etc. I'll bet if Whitman is looking down from Heaven and reading my article he's *pretty pleased.*

Did I tell you that my mother said Whitman was her mother's favorite poet?

Oh, happy Sunday telephone call!

TO JOHN CROWE RANSOM

[November 1951]

Dear Mr. Ransom:

Here's my article — a piece about Whitman over which I've labored like a hermit horse; for a number of days I've eaten, slept, and written my Whitman article, and done no other thing, not one.

As I said in my other letter, I was very sorry not to have the article ready for the last issue — the *Review*'s note reached me in Colorado only a few days before the deadline, a deadline much earlier than I'd supposed.

It's sad but true that intellectuals and academics know next to nothing about Whitman — of the last four critics of poetry I asked about Whitman (two of them excellent critics) three answered what amounted to *I hardly know him.* "Our" sort write day and night about Melville and never even mention Whitman.

Yours,

Randall

The two critics Jarrell alludes to were probably R. P. Blackmur and Del-more Schwartz. Leslie Fiedler wrote that, thanks to Jarrell, "With Whit-man we have come to feel at home once again, forgetting that only a couple of decades ago he had been declared officially dead by . . . Tate and Black-mur and Yvor Winters and all the small fry they spawned . . ." (RJ)

TO MARY VON SCHRADER

[November 15, 1951]

It's all cold and sunshine-y and blowy — Winter, but with her best complexion on.

I just read a saga in which there was a man called Hallfred Troublesome Poet; if I ever say anything that you don't like, just say, "You're hampering my personality, Hallfred Troublesome Poet."

In another saga there was a poet who came to the King of Iceland and sang a poem in his honor. The King said touchingly: "I've never had any-body make a poem about me before." Then he asked his chief counsellor, "Suppose I give him two ships — would that be enough, you think?" The counsellor (old spoil sport) said that gold rings and some costly coats and smaller treasures of this kind were the customary thing, really quite enough; so the King gave him lots of those. They did things differently in those days didn't they? When we're married and live together in Laguna, the envy of all who behold us, I'll read you some sagas; the best few are wonderful.

Made a dovey guess in our music-guessing game, there was this early ro-mantic piano concerto I tuned in on: not Schumann or Chopin, like Liszt in parts but different, not Weber; finally I thought, "There's a *Wanderer Fan-tasy* of Schubert's for piano and orchestra, orchestrated by Liszt, that I've never heard; this must be it." And lo, lo! it was.

Your [identification of] Glinka was certainly a triumph! As for getting Chopin wrong at the last moment, that's the kind of defeat that's as good as a victory — and whenever there's an orchestra with Chopin's music, he does sound more like the others. Don't lose heart over your latest set-back: I don't think anybody can tell Mozart from Haydn *all* the time — or even a great majority of the time; that error was quite creditable, I think. How I love your letters — you're the best letter-writer there ever was — I wouldn't trade you for Madame de Sévigné.

I'm as dazed as I usually am at this time on Thursdays: I've been talking-about-poems-and-stories since 9 and didn't get much sleep last night because when I came home about 12 (from hearing Edward Cone play, Chopin and some more lovely Liszt pieces I'd never heard before — you'd be nuts about them), I was so wound up from my Whitman that I couldn't get to sleep.

I saw Berryman and met John O'Hara at Edward Cone's. O'Hara was polite enough and uninteresting enough. He looked quite middle-aged, you could see his face about to break up and reform in an old man's face, so that you felt rather sorry for him in spite of feeling that he wasn't a likeable soul.

When I finish conferences tomorrow I'm going to give a long sigh and say, "My God, I'm through!" I've been working quite steadily except for the football game last Saturday all week since last Thursday morning.

The "music-guessing game" was played by turning the radio on at a classical music station and trying to identify the composer.

TO MARY VON SCHRADER

[November 1951]

It was *so* wonderful to hear thy voice; I'm *so* glad you called. (Every other sentence, lately, I say *so* or underline something or capitalize it — a writer really does have complete trust in someone when he writes her in *this* style. It seems a fine example of what perfect love casteth out.)

Well, I've seen a football game in a snow-storm. The Brown game was one of the easy-to-get-tickets-for games (50¢ ticket in fact). It was *fun;* everybody was dressed *so* oddly (parkas, jungle-camouflage raincoats, blankets, umbrellas, Scotch tartan tams, stadium boots, etc.), the field was a quagmire with icing, and late in the game the sun came out and the yellow-and-red-leaved woods and trees shone out at you. I was well got up: two pairs of wool socks, Stauffer's rubbers, one scarf around my neck and one scarf around my ears, two sweaters, ordinary coat, raincoat and my rain-hat. This had only one drawback: part of the time I was too warm. Glad Stanford won, that was a close one; and good ole Texas won, too, it did, it did!

Last night I worked for about five hours, very successfully, on *Pictures*. I was working on the long Gottfried-Irene-Constance part that begins Book III. I think I've cut out anything too favorable or sentimental-seeming, and I've written 30 or 40 new sentences to bring out different things here and there. I believe I've got that part just right now, and it was the only part that needed much going-over. It's surprising what a few cuts and a few new sentences can do. This afternoon when I finish typing my altered pages I'll send off our sweet *Pictures*. May it have all the luck it deserves and much more too!

TO HANNAH ARENDT

[November 1951]

Dear Hannah:

I've just finished a piece about Whitman that I think you and Heinrich might like to read — I'm sending the carbon copy in this letter. I'm going up to Boston on Saturday and I wanted to stop on the way to see you, if it's a convenient time for you. Could I come out late Friday afternoon and spend the night with you?

Art News printed my "Knight, Death, and the Devil" on one page and the Dürer on the opposite; it was a thrill to see them so.

Am leading a quiet lonely life — worked *hard* on the Whitman, though there's lots more I want to say about him.

Yours,
Randall

In his New York Times *review of* The Seven-League Crutches, *Lowell wrote: "'The Knight, Death, and the Devil' is a careful translation of Dürer's engraving. The description is dense; the generalizations are profound. It is one of the most remarkable word pictures in English verse or prose, and comparable to Auden's 'Musée des Beaux Arts.'"* (RJ)

TO MARY VON SCHRADER

[November 1951]

Wasn't "The Knight, Death, and the Devil" fun to see right there beside the Dürer? Now you can see how truthful I was. About the dog — perhaps a Bedlington? — most scholars think, I think, that he's the Knight's; and one had a rhapsodic sentence about what a fine highly bred court dog of a certain kind he was. Poor court, to have such dogs in it!

I got a letter from my nun saying how much she liked Cal Lowell's review of me, but that she thought I rather overpraised his poetry — this was a mistake on her part, I felt, but rather an appealing one. It was really a sweet and intelligent letter of thanks for my having sent back her article about me with comments and bits of information about poems. Her second sentence was this: "The simple, gracious and — please understand — child-like spirit of what you wrote brought me great pleasure." I thought, well, it's a good life when you get as queer and nice a sentence as that written about you.

Later

Late this afternoon I arrived in New York — I'd made a date with Robert Linscott to talk about *Pictures* (he's one of the main Random House people); he said I'd definitely have a letter in my mailbox about it when I got back from Cambridge. He took me to lunch at the Plaza with guess who? Truman Capote. He is such a poor, little, tiny, fat, dowdy, spectacled, commonplace creature, who talks like an incredibly effeminate maiden aunt with a lisp and asthma; he was dressed in a dark, smoky, chartreuse velveteen jacket, a beige knitted double-breasted vest, and a cravat tie. He seems so pathetic and absurd that you don't dislike him too much. The head waiter practically proposed to him; he got them to fix him his special chicken hash with strawberry jam on the side. I'm going to the ballet tonight on a ticket Sara couldn't use. Then I'll take a cheap fairly fast bus to Boston and try to get a nap in the afternoon.

Jarrell's trip to Boston was to visit Herschel and Barbara Baker for Thanksgiving.

TO MARY VON SCHRADER

[Cambridge, Massachusetts]
[November 1951]

It's cold as ice and bright and sparkling as ice, too — the sunshine's *so* pretty.

How I wish you'd seen *La Valse* with me! It's danced to Ravel's *Valses nobles et sentimentales* and is Balanchine at his best. It has a wonderful, very sinister finale which is half Death and the Maiden and half the Decline of the West or World War I coming to Europe.

I'm having a very domestic time with the Bakers with plenty of talk with Barbara or Herschel or the children; and as this is just what I wanted, I'm enjoying it. They have a smallish separate house attached to a tremendous thing all chimneys, iron grille work, spires and courtyard called Dunster House; it's full of Harvard students and sits with a half dozen others beside the sparkling (I almost wrote Cam) Charles. Herschel is more or less the head of the thing.

He is very intelligent and wonderfully educated: knows Greek, Latin,

French, German, Anglo-Saxon, plays the piano and organ, etc. I think he's
fairly emotional underneath, but has a kind of 18th century manner (dry,
urbane, ironic) that covers this. He's extremely well-read and has better
taste than any scholar I've ever met — and better than any but a few critics.
He's very industrious, methodical and energetic. I like him a lot and he's a
good friend, but not a *great* friend like Peter Taylor or Hannah or Barbara.
Barbara is much more emotional and spontaneous and helter-skelter,
though very shy and sweet and grave and ladylike and thin, now. When I
first knew her back in Austin she looked like an essay on the advantages of a
nice upbringing and sheltered life: she had such a pure, clear, beautiful,
this-is-the-way-people-ought-to-look look. I've known Barbara for so long
and I'm ever so fond of her. She's truly a nice and dear person. But now as I
look at her face I think life has not been easy for her. Not that I'm complaining about how hard life is but still, when you see what happens to
people's faces and to your face, you are not inclined to believe that life *is*
easy. You and I are lucky beyond belief! How I bless the crazy chance that
brought us there to Colorado from the Atlantic and the Pacific.

One evening looking in their photograph album I saw three photographs of me with them in 1940: I looked so slender, gay, slight, innocent,
and about-to-blow-away-in-the-wind that for a moment I felt sorry for myself and thought, looking at my picture, "Poor dear, rash, young creature,
what's become of him?"

Harvard is an odd place, not a bit normal or spontaneous. Some year in
five or ten years we'll probably get invited there and find it most odd and
interesting *for a year;* more would be too much, I imagine.

TO MARY VON SCHRADER

[November 1951]

Had dinner on Park Avenue with A Reader and it turned out pretty
well. In the first place, Paul Engle, the director of the Creative Arts Program
at the University of Iowa was there and he asked me to read poems at Iowa
this spring and make some money! I'll go when I go out to Michigan.
And — this will kill you — the Poetry Editor of the *Ladies Home Journal*
was there (doesn't that title sound like Queen Victoria?) but really she was
a nice-enough girl with a professor husband (both readers of *Partisan* and
Kenyon and such), and *she* said wouldn't I send some poems to the *Ladies
Home Journal!* She said it would be such a thrill to her if any were suitable
for them and she could print them; she said this rather timidly, since many a
poet would have replied, "I'd rather die." I said modestly (or immodestly)
that I was afraid I didn't have any that would do, but that I'd look thru

things or perhaps send a translation. Wouldn't it be wonderful to be published in the *Ladies Home Journal!* Oh Life!

My Reader was a strong rugged man of 55 or so; he'd been a flyer in the first world war; a lawyer with many writers or artists for clients — *quite* liberal (more than I) and nice, actually. His wife is a nice-looking woman with a bit too much of that smooth-dressed, reasonable, hard look of lady executives; she's non-fiction editor (or, more especially, How America Lives editor) of the *L.H.J.*

There was a portrait of her by Vertès over the mantel. It had a green background (the same as the walls of the apartment) and showed two pastoral cherubs holding between them the portrait.

To my surprise, two people whom I know fairly well through the Starrs were there. They're both highly professional writers in the Make Money Out of Writing Way and are quite nice. She's a pleasant-looking (all faint shades of pink and white and gray that run into each other) middle-aged woman who writes detective novels under her own name, Dorothey Cameron Disney, and her husband is Milton Mackaye and writes articles for the *Post*. They were intimate friends of Ernie Pyle and his wife and reminisced a little.

About half of these people had read my poems and were very complimentary — it felt funny, I'm not used to it. My Reader didn't much care for Eliot; or, I found later, for Yeats; though, oddly, he liked Marianne Moore a lot. He liked for poems to Say Something to Him, and I was lucky enough to, but Eliot and Yeats not to — I'll bet they're crying.

Went by the Nash-Healey show window and saw the one that's been custom-converted for Wheaties (or something like that) to give to Ted Williams; it's cream-colored with air-intakes above the headlights and a queer radiator grille; nice but, all in all, excessive.

Wicked old California to beat Stanford.

Gee, I lead a queer lonely life in Princeton — it's odd to come back here after a visit to know that in the whole city, there's nothing better than an acquaintance or two — no good friend or child or relative waiting for me. If I had a lion I'd be just like St. Jerome.

TO MARY VON SCHRADER

[November 1951]

Here I am somewhere in Connecticut looking out the train window at seagulls, a lighthouse, marshes full of light brown weeds, and the sea.

Barbara was so nice about you. I didn't have to say, "You must be blind" about what she could see from your photographs. She wants very much to meet you. What a joy it was to talk about you with one of my two or three best friends.

I went over to see the Leontievs before I left and Svetlana has become very grown-up and dazzlingly pretty. She's delivering a lecture on Picasso (she chose the subject) at her school; she said discontentedly, "Imagine having to talk to the fifth grade about Picasso!" I said, "What a shame! Why the fifth grade?" She answered, "Oh, all the grades will be there, but the *fifth* grade!" Scorning something fast, is Svetlana's stock in trade. It used to be startling when she was only 12½ and would express her scorn of some poor grown-up at Leopoldskron in swift, well-turned and generally unjust sentences.

This gives her an odd manner that maybe *sounds* worse than it is. But she constantly scolds or makes fun of her parents in a clear, light, clever, rather loving way. I was mocking her for this and said it was plainly a defense against her Overbearing Parents — who were sitting there looking lovingly at Their Svetlana — and we all laughed. Then she said, "Huh, I suppose I ought to have had a parent like you?" I said, "Well, I was practically your parent for three months in Europe," and Svetlana said, "You certainly were. It took me two years to recover." She is a cute girl. She was a fat and pretty one then and a thin and mighty pretty one now.

When I re-read *Pictures* after getting it done I was delighted with most of it, don't see how I did it so well.

When I think of you I feel so steady and trusting about my life as if it were built on the rockiest of rocks without one grain of sand. Oh, everything is so so wonderful — Constance is right, "It's a wonderful world."

Constance was a young student in Jarrell's novel.

TO MARY VON SCHRADER

[December 1951]

I was just re-reading a little of your letter that had at the top: *Sunday, My Quiet House*. Both when I read it now and when I first read it I felt such a surge of tenderness and delight in you; there are many such phrases in your letters — I love your whole spirit and way so devotedly.

I learned from Dick Blackmur of a — a Phenomenon. A publisher who thinks me a great poet and "A Girl in a Library" a great poem; this dovey creature [Harry Ford], may his tribe increase, is one of the people at Knopf. So I got Dick to write him a note saying he understood I had a novel and critical book and was interested in changing publishers. May something Good come out of it!

I laughed with delight at the handwriting with which you addressed your letter from Pasadena. It was so firm and spontaneous and gay that I thought, How *lucky* I am to belong to somebody who writes like that. Think of it, *think* of it: a week and a half!

Blackmur's lecture on *The Brothers Karamazov* (a part about the children) was good *and* very mild and pastoral, not a disquieting thing in it — couldn't believe my ears.

I got a sweet long letter from Sara Starr and a sweet long letter from Elizabeth Bishop, written on a Norwegian freighter going to Rio de Janeiro or Buenos Aires, I forget. She says the captain spends half the time on deck hammering on what seems to be a raft! His wife sits by and embroiders.

My, my bedroom's mussed up: it looks as if the cyclone that blew Dorothy to Oz had stopped off and spent the weekend here.

Think of seeing *thee,* and California, and the little girls, and Pasadena, and your mother — can it be? It's like going to a live Louvre. Probably for months after I'll go around dazed and feebly.

By the way, in a couple of days I'm going to send a big express package to you at Laguna, partly presents but also books and tennis racket and different junk; I'll probably stuff it all in one of the fibre barrels I sent things up here in. Do *not* open till Santa Claus arrives. Are A and B [Alleyne and Beatrice] much excited about Christmas? I'm not about Christmas, but about Christmas vacation, baby doll!

Harry Ford was a book designer at Knopf.

TO ELIZABETH BISHOP

[December 1951]

Dear Elizabeth:

You really are just like Livingstone; and Stanley too. I read a wonderful book (long autobiography) about Tierra del Fuego, I'd like to go there too. I expected to see your letter postmarked *Captain's Raft, South Atlantic;* he should have had more faith, it's evident his ship was sound.

I wish I'd got to see you before you left, but probably you'll be back before I leave Princeton. It was tough luck that you came to stay with us just after Mackie and I had decided to be divorced and were feeling at best polite and constrained. I'm settled here at Princeton all alone in the big house we'd already rented; mostly I read, write, and listen to classical music over the radio; but let me say hastily that I'm well off and, for several reasons, happy. Since you knew mostly me (and Mackie hardly at all) I won't talk at length about it but simply say that we'd got rather unhappy about our marriage and it was bad for us — I think we'll both be better off apart.

I think one letter of yours to me must have got lost — this was the first one since the Cape. But maybe you wrote it to Mackie?

I'm glad you liked the review ["A View of Three Poets," *Partisan Review*, November–December 1951]. I was probably a little too kind to Wilbur, though maybe not; God knows he and his friends didn't think so. I wanted to make him think about his poetry without making him so angry he couldn't; it was a hard job, and I moved to Williams and Cal with a sigh of relief.

Just wrote a long piece about Whitman for *Kenyon;* but I'll bet it never gets to Tierra del Fuego.

I'm going to write a piece à la "The Obscurity of the Poet" called "The Age of Criticism" and saying, roughly,"Brothers, if you write enough criticism like this, in the end nobody will even want to write a limerick." The boys who write poetry and stories here say that they're a small minority now, most students never think of writing anything but criticism. Two professors lead a great war, with many impassioned adherents among the students, about whether Melville was a complete Atheist or believed that there was a malevolent God — I *think* I've got it right, something like that.

I hope you're having a good time; and feel sure you are. I'm going to California for three weeks at Christmas — haven't been there, except in an air force plane, since 1927.

I've got along well with Blackmur and in many ways quite like him; some of his lectures have been *excellent.* I see John Berryman sometimes — I really like him. There was a lovely Dominican monk here to make lectures, born a Hungarian count, of Jewish blood, in Cairo, he first translated *The Waste Land* into French, is an expert in ancient Persian, Aramaic, dozens of others, and is one of the smartest and nicest men I ever heard lecture. But I haven't any real friends here, just close acquaintances. If you get back in the spring come out and stay a few days — it's a lovely place; a great big nice house, and I promise not to be about to be divorced from myself. I can cook scrambled eggs and toast, with reluctance; it's more room than board. I *do* hope you're getting along well.

Love,
Randall

TO HANNAH ARENDT

[December 1951]

Dear Hannah:

Where's the letter that was following the telegram? And I answered the telegram with a letter, you're so far behind you'll never catch up. Ah well, don't you mind. (Did you like the Whitman?)

If I came late Saturday afternoon and stayed through most of Sunday would that be a convenient time for you and Heinrich? It's the only time I could until the middle of January; on the night of Dec. 14, oh joy, I leave for three weeks three days in California. Isn't Christmas a wonderful thing?

Yours,
Randall

Arendt described these visits while Jarrell was at Princeton thus: "The moment he entered the apartment, I had the feeling that the household became bewitched. I never found out how he actually did it, but there was no solid object, no implement or piece of furniture, which did not undergo a subtle change, in the process of which it lost its everyday prosaic function. This poetic transformation could be annoyingly real when he decided, as he often did, to follow me into the kitchen to entertain me while I was preparing our dinner." (RJ)

TO MARY VON SCHRADER

[December 1951]

If my writing looks unusually large, clear, and awkward don't be surprised, I've just finished writing a letter to Alleyne.

Your voice sounded so good and live and *Maryish,* as poets say. I closed the door to the bedroom tight, hope no sound filtered through the floor to my baby student downstairs. This student endeared himself to me by not only knowing my poetry well but by saying that when he'd read "The Truth" aloud to people they'd practically cried. I feel like the Dickens *de nos jours,* a very lovely feeling.

I've just finished my review of the big dictionary ["To Fill a Wilderness," *The Nation,* December 29, 1951], a very poetic performance mostly about our Past (America's, not yours and mine — didn't even *mention* it).

Gee, I'm getting to be a spontaneous soul — I just talked and talked, and listened and listened, my eyes flashing, till the student must have thought, "Why he just pours out his soul to *everybody.*" If he could have seen me sitting politely or impolitely silent and reserved at many a party, he'd have thought, "That's his older brother — or father, maybe life has embittered him." I vary between Reserve and no reserve at all — not that *you'd* know, I've never had one milligram of reserve with *Thee,* my own sister.

Forgive the rotten writing — when I write fast and enthusiastically with this pen it's a gale not a zephyr. None of the stores have a new inside for my ballpoint pen — however, insides cost 50¢ and so do pens or ones like them. I might as well get a new pen and will.

What do you know, they're starting *two* new sports-car magazines, delighting me, as you know.

Gee, it will be fun to see A and B — imagine seeing little people that look quite like you and even partly behave like you! Dear mermaid, *my* Ingrid Bergman, I feel so good about you and us. So far as I'm concerned jobs are just to get us enough extra money to live on. All I really want is you and the little people and our life together, everything else will take care of itself.

TO MARY VON SCHRADER

[December 1951]

Just cleaned up my bedroom — it looks as if it had had a long beard and been shaved, I'm afraid it will catch cold now.

At lunch I heard a professor complaining because he'd sent an article on Boileau to one of the highbrow literary quarterlies and had it turned down — thought this indicated a fatal narrowness on their part. He was so full of complaints he sounded like *Götterdämmerung* (transcribed for flute). Cocteau said he wasn't a poet but wrote poems, I'm glad I'm not a professor, but teach in a college. I also heard a cute thing quoted from [Henry] James: a man is looking at the (*he* thinks) tigerish young woman he is in love with, and thinks: "What if I should bore this magnificent creature?"

I forgot to tell you, I was mentioned in both the lists of best books of the year that appeared in the *Times* and the *Herald-Tribune* Sunday. The *Times* had all the eight or ten best poetry books but the *Tribune* had only about four, I was lucky to be in.

And I got a letter from that publisher at Knopf's that likes my poetry so much. I'll copy it because it will be a pleasure to you and may mean some money (please God) and a pleasant publisher (and what I'd give for one!).

Dear Mr. Jarrell:

This afternoon I received a letter from R. P. Blackmur indicating that you are dissatisfied with your present publishing arrangements. I gather from the letter that he was kind enough to indicate my interest in your work and enthusiasm for it.

I would like to tell you straight off that nothing would give me more pleasure than to be able to consider for publication anything you might care to write. In saying this, I'm quite certain that I speak not only for myself, but for a good many other people here.

Blackmur speaks of a finished novel and an almost finished book of critical work. To hear of a novel is startling and pleasing; as for the other, I must report to you a strange coincidence of several of us (after discussing your first-rate piece on Williams and *Paterson IV*) trying very hard to think how we could get you to do such a book for us! To add a personal note, I'd like to take this chance to tell you that I've been reading your poems since before *Blood for a Stranger* with more admiration than I can easily indicate, but *The Seven-League Crutches* hit me very hard indeed. It seems to me that poetry is running pretty thin now, but I venture to say that not even the richest climate could have produced a better poem than "Girl in a Library," which I would like to claim to having read silently and aloud more times than any man alive.

Should you care to submit any of your work to us, I think I've made it clear that it will have more than sympathetic attention. We *do* know what you are doing, and we *do* care.

I look forward to hearing from you.

Sincerely yours,
Harry Ford

Isn't that a *nice* letter? The tone's really awfully nice, I think I'm going to get my book back from Random House Friday (they've said nothing about it) and let this guy read it. Please God, all will work out well. They sound as if a critical book and a *Selected Poems* were in the bag, don't they? It'll be so *wonderful* to have a decent publisher — I've felt I'd give anything for one.

Probably the express package won't arrive till a couple of days after I get there — they say it takes five days. I'm going to send it Monday.

TO HARRY FORD

[December 1951]

Dear Mr. Ford:

Your letter was a great pleasure to me; I feel I ought to thank you as a reader before saying a word to you as a publisher. I'm particularly glad that you like "A Girl in a Library" so well — except for my Dürer engraving poem, it's the last poem I've written.

I have two books that I'll give you to read. One is finished and I'll bring it by on Friday afternoon, if that will be convenient for you — I'll be in New York on the way to a California Christmas vacation. The name of this one is *Pictures from an Institution,* and is different from poetry and criticism in that it might sell pretty well. It is a prose narrative that isn't exactly a novel, more a comedy; it's quite a funny book, I believe, and might interest a good many readers in other ways.

The other book is 9/10 done now; I could give it to you slightly unfinished in January, quite done in February. It's criticism mostly of American poetry: articles on Whitman, Stevens, Ransom, Marianne Moore, William Carlos Williams, Robert Frost, Robert Lowell, and one or two more; that general article called "The Obscurity of the Poet" and one on the development of modern poetry; shorter pieces on Corbière, de la Mare, Elizabeth Bishop, and four or five more, all Americans, I think. (In February I'll have a piece analogous to "The Obscurity of the Poet" called "The Age of Criticism.")

All my poems (except the new book, of course) have been out of print since the end of 1948; Harcourt sold out *Losses* very fast, gave bookstores two definite dates for a second edition, and then didn't print one. This is a good situation, so far as (after a year and a half or two years) bringing out a *Selected Poems* is concerned, but it's been a bad situation for the poems — no one could get them except by paying double to some book-dealer who'd hunt out copies. But the real reason I want to leave Harcourt is they're no fun to publish things with — they have at best a sort of perfunctory pious interest in my poems and criticism.

I am writing a good deal and probably will be writing more so I'd like to get settled with a publisher who enjoys me and whom I enjoy. I'm looking forward to talking to you and to bringing you the book; I'll come at three or so on Friday if that's possible for you.

But let me say over again, before I finish, what a pleasure it is to get such a letter from a reader; I don't see too many readers, and tend to think of the Reader as an abstraction with a discouragingly blank face — the real ones make me want to write more poems.

Yours sincerely,
Randall Jarrell

TO SISTER BERNETTA QUINN

[December 1951]

Dear Sister Bernetta:

I meant to write you this afternoon and got your "A Quilt-Pattern" this morning; it's lucky I didn't write yesterday as I started to.

You have the feel and general significance of "A Quilt-Pattern" per-fectly. Some of the details you don't get as I meant them to be, but of course I may not have managed to make it mean what I wanted it to. (I *thoroughly* sympathized with what you said about "La Belle au Bois Dor-mant"; if I'd realized that people wouldn't take the first line and a half liter-ally I'd have put a sort of quotation, a newspapery one, at the start of the poem as an epigraph — I'll do this in a *Selected Poems*. Other people have had exactly your difficulty, though some didn't. It seems to be accidental: if the reader takes "She lies, her head between her knees, in their old trunk" as the wife's (or *lover's*) dead body in the husband and wife's (or *couple's*) trunk everything is easy; if not, not. I only wish I'd known about your difficulty earlier, I'd have put the explaining epigraph in the book.) Back to "Quilt-Pattern": you know, the mother in *Hansel and Gretel* is the real mother, not a stepmother — so in my poem, when I say "the dead mother" in the dream that's because the boy's made her dead in the dream; she is demanding and completely possessive and awful to him and he hates her. Many psychoana-lysts and psychiatrists say that many children habitually divide themselves into Good Me and Bad Me — they'll even say, "It wasn't *me*, it was Bad Me that did it." (This split doesn't have anything to do with the conscious Ego and the Unconscious Id; it's a conscious split between the parent-approved, conscience-approved, superego-approved "Good" half of the child and the "Bad" half that does (or wants to do) what the parents and superego disap-prove of.) Henry [Harry] Stack Sullivan wrote a lot about this and said that sometimes both Good Me and Bad Me, the child's normal "explainable" conscious self, are aware of something that they call the Other, this is more the Id, if we use the Freudian terms, the unexplainable Unconscious that makes them do things, they don't know why. (Incidentally, Good Me and Bad Me have somewhat the relationship, in the poem, of a child and the child's imaginary companion; at a certain age most or very many children believe they have one, then they're not alone against Authority.)

What the poem is, in its simplest terms, is the child's redreaming of *Hansel and Gretel* (presumably it was one of the many tales he got told that afternoon) *in terms of his mother and himself.* There's nobody else in the dream; everything is either himself or his mother (presumably there is no father in this family). Many commentators on *Hansel and Gretel* say that the wicked mother *is* in some sense the witch; after the witch is killed they come home to find the mother dead. The mother is the house (a common symbol for women in dreams, all psychoanalysts say) and the witch too; and partly so in the fairy tale — the witch can tell when somebody nibbles on her house just as though it were part of her. The fact that the house is the mother who used to nurse him is alluded to in "house of bread," the finger he sucks at, and the "taste of the house/ Is the taste of his" — he won't admit this to himself even in the dream, but thinks, "No, I don't *know!*" Later (*very* unexplicitly — I wanted to have it far under the surface, uneasily present) there is a sort of sexual symbolism, since the child does at first conceive of sexual things in terms of his mother, and his mother has made this child her whole emotional life.

Your way of taking *the Other* is perfectly possible; if I made a dream that could be interpreted, plainly, in only one possible way, that would be the undreamiest of dreams. But when I have a *Selected Poems* with notes I believe I will quote a little sentence from a psychoanalyst like Sullivan about Good Me, Bad Me, and the Other.

I believe almost any divergence in your understanding of it came from thinking there was a stepmother — I think it's easy to do this but not at all inevitable, for you're first introduced to the mother in the phrase "and the humming stare/ Of the woman — the good mother — / Drifts away." You *can* think her the stepmother and the next reference, "The scaling face/ Of a woman — the dead mother," a reference to the dead real mother; but you can just as well take it as being a second reference to the same woman, made dead now in the child's dream.

Even in the dream the child cannot bear to know, to be conscious of and face the guilt of, his feelings toward his mother; after he pushes her into the oven and kills her both parts of him deny that it's anything of theirs that they've done it to — *and* they deny they've done it, say, timidly smiling at each other, "It was the Other." Of course the child is completely helpless in reality, triumphs only in the dream to which he escapes, and has a most pathetic tiny triumph (pretending to be asleep and "willing" her away) to be a tiny happy ending for the poem.

Now to answer your earlier letter. I can't tell you how pleased I was by your "simple, gracious and — please understand — childlike spirit." I know I *am* childlike in one sense (since I can do handwriting analyses, I can see it even in my handwriting) and I'd like very much to be in the other more important sense, that of the Gospels.

I talked to Father de Menasce at a sort of party after the last of his lectures — I liked him *very* much. He likes American (the language) better than customary English, said that it was like the Latin of Saint Augustine compared to that of Cicero; he'd said this to a young mathematical physicist at the Institute for Advanced Studies, who had replied that he thought American *was* English — was there any difference?

I know what you meant by Little People, but the ones in "Hohensalzburg" don't seem that, are more mysterious and general. I hardly know *what* they are.

I used quite to dislike and underestimate Freud; but now that I've read about ⅚ of what he wrote I think him extremely good — some of his writing is very good as writing, too. A lot of his most interesting things are in the *Collected Papers*. *Civilization and Its Discontents* is an attractive book that occurs to me.

You're the only person I know who knows "A Ghost, a Real Ghost." I will put it in a book. I'm very glad you like it — it's one of the most personal poems I ever wrote.

Art News printed Dürer's *The Knight, Death and the Devil* and mine on facing pages, and sent me two copies; I'd like to send you one of them as a sort of Christmas card. I hope you have a very happy Christmas.

Yours sincerely,
Randall Jarrell

A QUILT-PATTERN

The blocked-out Tree
Of the boy's Life is gray
On the tangled quilt: the long day
Dies at last, after many tales.
Good me, bad me, the Other
Black out, and the humming stare
Of the woman — the good mother —
Drifts away; the boy falls
Through darkness, the leagues of space
Into the oldest tale of all.

All the graves of the forest
Are opened, the scaling face
Of a woman — the dead mother —
Is square in the steam of a yard
Where the cages are warmed all night for the rabbits,
All small furry things
That are hurt, but that never cry at all —
That are skinned, but that never die at all.
Good me, bad me
Dry their tears, and gather patiently
Through the loops of the chicken-wire of the cages
Blackberries, the small hairy things
They live on, here in the wood of the dream.

Here a thousand stones
Of the trail home shine from their strings
Like just-brushed, just-lost teeth.
All the birds of the forest
Sit brooding, stuffed with crumbs.
But at home, far, far away
The white moon shines from the stones of the chimney,
His white cat eats up his white pigeon.

But the house hums, "We are home." Good me, bad me
Sits wrapped in his coat of rabbit-skin
And looks for some little living thing
To be kind to, for then it will help him —
There is nothing to help; good me
Sits twitching the rabbit's-fur of his ears
And says to himself, "My mother is basting
Bad me in the bath-tub —"
                              the steam rises,
A washcloth is turned like a mop in his mouth.
He stares into the mouth
Of the whole house: there in it is waiting—
No, there is nothing.

He breaks a finger
From the window and lifts it to his —
"Who is nibbling at me?" says the house.
The dream says, "The wind,
The heaven-born wind";
The boys says, "It is a mouse."
He sucks at the finger; and the house of bread
Calls to him in its slow singing voice:
"Feed, feed! Are you fat now?
Hold out your finger."
The boy holds out the bone of the finger.
It moves, but the house says, "No, you don't know.
Eat a little longer."
The taste of the house
Is the taste of his —
                          "I don't know,"
Thinks the boy. "No, I don't *know!*"

His whole dream swells with the steam of the oven
Till it whispers, "You are full now, mouse —
Look, I have warmed the oven, kneaded the dough:
Creep in — ah, ah, it is warm! —
Quick, we can slip the bread in now," says the house.
He whispers, "I do not know
How I am to do it."

                "Goose, goose," cries the house,
"It is big enough — just look!
See, if I bend a little, so — "

He has moved. . . . He is still now, and holds his breath.
If something is screaming itself to death
There in the oven, it is not the mouse
Nor anything of the mouse's. Bad me, good me
Stare into each other's eyes, and timidly
Smile at each other: it was the Other.

But they are waking, waking; the last stair creaks —
Out there on the other side of the door
The house creaks, "How is my little mouse? Awake?"
It is she.
He says to himself, "I will never wake."
He says to himself, not breathing:
"Go away. Go away. Go away."

And the footsteps go away.

TO MARY VON SCHRADER

                              [December 1951]

    I told Blackmur I'd read half of *The Brothers Karamazov* on the train coming back from Cambridge: I said, "It was very like your lectures — sunnier, though." He laughed and laughed. I think I kid him more than any of the others do and I think he rather likes it. I am getting to like him, and felt quite sorry for him at one of the parties where his former wife was; he was very noticeably silent and depressed. The French have some proverb, based on Prometheus, that says "Each of us has his vulture" (eagle). Well, each vulture has his vulture, too.

    He said something very complimentary, particularly coming from *him*. He said he'd read my *Partisan* review of Cal and agreed completely — he was supposed to review it for *Poetry* but thought he'd just tell them he agreed with mine and didn't see any point in doing one himself. I tried to persuade him (I hope with success) to do it just the same so that Cal would have approval expressed by so prominent a critic — more or less said I thought it his duty to do so.

I had a good time in New York! First I called up Margaret [Marshall] and she was going to the ballet, too, but asked me to come to dinner. Then I went out to Hannah's to leave my things. Heinrich, her husband, had such a cold you couldn't look at him even without Feeling, being very conscious of, your own sinuses and nose. But we had an awfully good time. They took me to lunch at a Chinese restaurant near Columbia. I got to fancifully describing the confusion of my housekeeping and cooking and they laughed so hard that I'd make every sentence more extravagant than the last. Heinrich then said three very funny German poems (translating along the way) by Christian Morgenstern.

As I was going to the matinee as well as the evening performance I barely had time to get there after lunch. I had to *run* five blocks to the subway, get off near City Center, and *run* five more blocks to City Center. I arrived in breathless triumph 1½ minutes before things began. It was ever so much fun being with Bernard [Haggin] and Margaret; and the best of the ballets were wonderful. The very young dancer I'd seen last year and am so crazy about, Tanaquil LeClercq, was just wonderful, *wonderful!* In *Baiser de la Fée* she was better as the bride than Danilova used to be. Counting the ballet that night I saw 8, 7 by Balanchine, 4 wonderful, 2 good, 1 nice. Gee, gee! I almost died of bliss at Tanaquil LeClercq's best moments (she's so young that when you see her a year later she's much better).

There was a young English girl staying with Margaret and she was at dinner, of course. Tennyson dreamed that Prince Albert gave him a prize and embraced him — and T. thought in his dream: "Very nice, but very German." And I thought at my dinner: "Very nice she was, but very English!"

I came back on the 11:55 train thinking, "I've somebody waiting for me, my Letter! Haven't the mails been smooth, lately. Bottom is in full rout. A week from this moment I'll be in New York breathlessly waiting to go out to the airport."

TO MARY VON SCHRADER

[December 1951]

This is one of my train-to-New-York-letters — written in the station actually; I'm going to that funeral I told you about yesterday. I just heard a queer remark; one man said to a girl as we left the train, "This smells just like the ship I was on, in the hold. We used to stand in a long line for chow. But we never got chow, we got —" and curses, at that moment, he got out of earshot.

I got a letter from Random House saying they're very much interested in *Pictures,* even "one of our partners" has read it — nothing definite. I hope the partner wasn't Bennett Cerf who would steal all the crudest jokes. I wrote them that I wanted it back on Friday to show to another place that was interested in publishing all my stuff — that they needn't say anything definite by then but that I'd like to have it back. Then, I'll pick it up in New York on my way to the plane, give it to Henry Ford (as I think of him) at Knopf's, and then — if I can keep from dying of bliss — I'll go out hours early and wait for that plane. *That* plane is one I don't want to take any chances on missing.

Blackmur had a cute and quite good poem in the last *Poetry* called "Mr. Virtue and the Three Bears." It's "based on a true story"; there was a man named Virtue, in Blackmur's section of Maine, who ran a filling station and had a pet bear (a young one that drank soda-pop); one day the bear ate Mr. Virtue, who "left no living kin."

The poem is a sestina, a very complicated Italian form: you take six words for "rhyme" words, put them in one order in the first six-line stanza, and then put them in prescribed order in the next five stanzas: the last — seventh — stanza is three lines, two of the words to a line. I've written sestinas, but I hate that last three-line stanza and don't use it.

I think Blackmur was quite pleased that I liked his poem so well — he *knows* it's better to be a poet than a critic, and would probably trade ten first-rate critical articles for one not-quite-first-rate poem. As for calling him by his first name, I've done that for months and months. I just hadn't happened to use his first name in a letter. I really do like him pretty much, queer creature that he is, and have decided, reluctantly, not ever to put him in a novel; but boy, *could* I!

Father de Menasce made his last lecture and it was very good — I had a very nice long talk with him at the party afterwards, and John Berryman and I were talking with Robert Fitzgerald about poems (mostly Frost and Housman) and Berryman astonished me by saying he thought and had thought for many years that I was the best reviewer of poetry alive. Was I dazzled and grateful!

The funeral was for Sara Starr's grandmother.

The following week Jarrell flew to California on a bargain-fare, nonscheduled airline called North Star. He spent the next three weeks with Mary, Alleyne, Beatrice, and Irene.

TO MARY VON SCHRADER

January 10, 1952
11 AM New York time
8 AM REAL or Pacific or
my heart and watch time

We flew here from Chicago in two hours and a half — GEE! There was snow at Chicago — nothing but freezing rain here, so they told the passengers to watch their steps. This is a stupid place — I can shut my eyes and see the rocks at Emerald Bay. There's a seal on them — How *can* people who live in New York make remarks about Southern California? They ought to be put in asylums, which would at least be a change from New York City.

You and the children and Laguna seem so much more real than all this that I'm surprised it doesn't vanish under my denunciatory stare. But soon I'll be in that other species of unreality, Princeton, there to write and tell others how not to write. I'm in good spirits considering everything — everything meaning you, Mary, dear sister, I miss you as much as I always miss you. Everything I think about — the waves and the boysenberry pies and getting the pictures framed and running out of gas, and dinner last night — all, all the things are so sweet and lovely and such fun, exactly like you. I want to live with you always, all our lives, and never leave you anymore . . .

TO MARY VON SCHRADER

[January 11, 1952]

When I got home from conferences and classes I had your letter, the one you wrote me while Beatrice and I were looking at the Breughels. Dear Mary, you've never written me a nicer letter — tears of joy came into my eyes. I love you so much, sister; it doesn't seem to me that I could have been really alive and had a real life before I knew you. I've told you thousands of times all I could tell, but it was never nearly enough — you're everything there is for me, all that I could possibly want or imagine. *Ich dich so lieb, so lieb.*

The three weeks and two days with you were so much better than any other time in my life. You're the dearest and nicest and sweetest and best and funniest and gayest and best-humored and Mary-est being in the whole world; if you were any better I'd die of bliss. Oh, there was never anything like you — compared to you Florence Nightingale was a perfect bitch.

Do you know that that imbecile Viereck sent me not only the *Atlantic* article, but three others and answers-to-letters-to-the-Editor he's written, all lovingly underlined? He's the only man I know who *couldn't* write an anonymous letter — he even signs bombs.

My best student had saved a little review of *Seven-League* from an old-fashioned newspaper reviewer in Philadelphia. The reviewer was fairly respectful and very uncomprehending, but ended triumphantly: "Mr. Jarrell is not so original as he thinks: he is influenced by Browning and Edgar Allan Poe." That Poe is the best yet! Would Poe be mad!

Blackmur, Berryman and Delmore Schwartz were all there for lunch today — two literary little boys at the next table stared at ours in awe.

Delmore carries such a petty, personally involved, New Yorkish atmosphere around with him it's almost unpleasant for me to see him. He thinks that Schiller and St. Paul were just two *Partisan Review* editors. John Berryman has such a nice feeling of dis-interestedness and consciousness-of-the-centuries-and-other-lands, in comparison.

Beloved, I miss you so much that I don't know what to do or say. How I wish I could wake up and look at the cliffs and rocks and sea, and finally get up and have pancakes with you and walk on the beach and sit on the deck and read poems to you, and drive to Laguna with the top down and shop for the next day — and have the whole day go as our days went.

Tell Alleyne Old Grey Matter sends his love and will answer her letter soon. And give my love to your mother if she's still with you.

I tried to call Laguna for a surprise but kept getting a busy signal. Operator tried for fifteen minutes and I said, like the Merman in [Matthew] Arnold's "Forsaken Merman," "Long prayers they say in the world above." After an hour still busy, they verified and told me triumphantly, "No wonder it's busy. Someone at the number has left the phone off the hook." I said, "It's Schatzel! He's so little he can barely phone at all — he loves poetry, though."

Schatzel was Mary's pet dachshund.

TO MARY VON SCHRADER

January 12, 1952

I just looked at myself in the mirror and said sadly, "It's not my California face." And now, I've been straightening up. My room looks so much better and more cheerful straight that I'm going to try to keep it that way. I'd never seen the rug, swept — it's *much* prettier, not nearly so dusty gray and cobwebby.

I'm bogged down in my translation of the [Eduard] Mörike Girl-making-the-Fire-at-Dawn poem. It's called "The Forsaken Maiden" ["The Forsaken Girl" was the eventual title] and it begins:

> Ere the cock has crowed,
> The least star dwindled,
> I kneel here at the hearth
> Till the fire has kindled.
>
> The warm light is beautiful;
> The flames flare up eagerly,
> I gaze unseeing,
> Sunk in my misery.

There are two more stanzas in which she tells about dreaming of the one who's deserted her. It's very difficult to get things right; I want things to sound sincere and emotional, but with a faint archaic formality (to go with the past time) — the last stanza is bad for rhyme words, and the third says one thing that can't come over into English and takes twice as much room to say the rest as English does. Translation is hard — it reminds me of Blake's "A little flower is the labor of ages."

One of my students is — quite seriously — exactly like a saint; I've never seen anybody so much so. He's so young and kind and gentle and completely self-forgetful of self that you feel quite inferior to him. For instance he goes for hours and hours a week to a home for mentally deficient children, to play with them and do little things for them. (He's going into the "institutional ministry" which means ministers at such places apparently — there are few, as you can imagine, in this field.) He's quite a good poet — recognizable style — in a gentle-, old-fashioned, wistful way. You know Alyosha in *The Brothers Karamazov* is a young, saintly being, immediately charming to everybody; well, this boy quite beats Alyosha. Honestly, goodness and sweetness just beam from his face.

Writing this about his face reminds me so much of the look on yours that I particularly long for you. Dearest, my own sister, I want so much to be married to thee, to never leave even for a day. I miss you far more than I can say, and I miss Beatrice and Alleyne and Schatzel and the house and the car and the sea. This is queer: I know your face so well now, that the photographs are much less satisfactory to me than they used to be. They're good and lovely souvenirs, but they don't really look like my Mary.

(Later)

Wicked Bottom not only delayed your letter today, but got *all* my mail; when I got home at two there was nothing, so I thought cheerfully, *He's late,* and walked up the street to meet him — the postman, that is. Then I saw with a pang of horror that the mail-basket next door was all full. I steadied myself, breathed or tried to breathe calmly, and went home and re-read your last three letters. Aren't I the most stoical thing since Marcus Aurelius? But really I wanted to leave this damn town and go spend the rest of my life in Laguna Beach at Emerald Bay.

Tonight I'm going for three-quarters of an hour to the President's Reception — which means going in, being introduced, and then talking to my regular acquaintances for three-quarters of an hour: not bad, not good, just University Life. Which reminds me of a sentence of Emerson's: "Today I saw two snakes gliding back and forth in the sunlight — not to eat, not for love, just gliding." Somebody used that for an epigraph for a novel about Harvard.

Tell Alleyne and Beatrice I miss them. Oh, if only I could be with the three of you and Schatzel I'd be willing to sleep under the car in the carport — and maybe Trixie would come out and sleep with me if I went *Meow, meow.*

Later, after "The Forsaken Girl" had been published, Jarrell wrote, "I just received my check for 'The Forsaken Girl' — it came to $96 — I'd forgotten that it's 16 lines, not 12. Never thought I'd get a hundred dollars for being crazy about that sweet Mörike poem. I did it so much for love that I hardly thought they'd print it. Good ole Ladies Home Journal — *it'll spoil me for other magazines."*

In another letter, Jarrell wrote: "The President [Harold Dodds] was a right pleasant, home-spun type; his wife was Doing her Duty and not revelling in it one bit. She had a signal triumph with me; when I said good-bye to her an hour later after being introduced briefly (there were 150 there) she said, 'Goodbye, Mr. Jarrell.' I looked at her in awe. The President's house is a big Southern barn-y mansion with high ceilings; the little cakes and sandwiches were very good, varied and ornamental, and the coffee-and-tea-services big and blinding. No word of interest was said, so I ate quite a bit. So you see: no love, no gliding, just to eat."

TO HARRY FORD

[January 1952]

Dear Mr. Ford:

Your letter, the reader part, was a *great* pleasure to me, and the publisher part wasn't unexpected. During my vacation I thought of a way in which I could make the book have much more of the superficial form of a novel: by pretending that it's more the story of Gertrude's year at Benton, and of how she gets the material for her novel; there are several parts of Benton and Gertrude that I've decided to write some more about. So suppose you tell anybody reading it or attach a memorandum to it that this is an incomplete form of the book, that in the end it will *look* considerably more like a novel. You often have books shown to you in unfinished states, masses of pages in a suitcase, don't you, which you then make into Thomas Wolfe? (*You* meaning publishers.)

I had a wonderful time in California: I could hardly bear to come back at all. People said to me when I got back, "Why, you're brown!"

I really haven't got poems just now to give that New American Library thing — though I'm in a very good humor from having sat up until three writing both a poem of my own ["Dreams"] and a translation of Mörike's poem about the forsaken girl who makes the fire at dawn and cries, if English only had some usable words rhyming with *over!* It's almost as bad as *love.*

Yours,
Randall Jarrell

TO MARY VON SCHRADER

[January 1952]

I'll probably have an awful or at best mediocre review in the *Saturday Review.* Insofar as they know of me, they dislike me. They like for people to be very namby-pamby and old-fashioned and romantic, they're quite down on Eliot and Auden and such. But *we* should worry, *we* should care.

The class and I did James' *Aspern Papers* today. I remembered it as good but, read again, it is better. It has two maiden ladies, one very aged, in Venice; you'd like it.

Believe me, I haven't been gay or funny without you. I often was in the fall, in a sort of desperate way. I missed you so much and was so lonesome; now I'm calmer, and no matter how much I do miss you I do manage to feel that you're *there* and are completely mine as I am completely yours. Hier bin i'.

Tell Beatrice I am still grieved over not getting to kiss her good-bye and send her ten bonus kisses X X X X X X X X X X. How I want to lie on the sofa listening to records and lie on the sundeck petting Trixie and reading

Eliot to you. Your voice sounded so good Sunday. It's the one thing I want to hear most. I'm working on a poem for thee ["Dreams"].

TO MARY VON SCHRADER

[January 1952]

Now it's 8 of a blowy-about-to-rain-or-storm morning. I'm writing in bed on a book.

Last night I saw [Jean Renoir's] *The River*. Although the rhetoric of the narrative is poor and so English, it's really worth going to see. The Hindu or half-caste girl is lovely, just beautiful-looking, and so is the little English boy whose hobby is playing flutes (and putting out bowls of milk) to attract cobras. Many of the scenes are very beautiful — it made me want to go to India and spend several months buying cloth, just cloth — I wish you had some of Melanie's saris. You could dance on the beach in them.

I've been working on a couple of translations ["The Forsaken Girl" by Mörike and "Childhood" by Rilke] and a poem for and about thee ["Dreams"]. I saw a *Kenyon* at the library with my Whitman piece — Mr. Ransom, dear sweet idiot that he is, had *changed* the title without telling me. My "Some Lines from Whitman" had become (a quotation from later in the article) "Walt Whitman Had His Nerve." As you can imagine, I felt right distressed, but I reasoned myself into being philosophical about it and not really caring. He meant well, but gee, gee! Oh well —

I'm so glad you took your typewriter to Pasadena. There's nothing like a type-written love-letter, I always say. And I like the new pictures of our own dear house in Emerald Bay and our own dear children. I can just see the car port and that trail we go up and down to get the driftwood from the beach, and the grassy lot where — I believe I can see one mushroom we didn't get. And surely that's that charming cat from next door in the eucalyptus tree. Yes, that's Trixie.

The sweet saint-like boy I wrote you about gave me a poem of his that the children might like that I now copy:

> Walking through a dusky lane
> I met a man with a dove-white beard,
> And he had frost-white cakes to sell.
> Following him was a duck or two
> And a few pale children,
> A little white horse,
> And a goose.

And when they passed by
It was like the winter wind
And the snow which fell all about . . .

Isn't the man like Death playing the Pied Piper with all his white prisoners? — But a gentle delicate Nice Death.

TO MARY VON SCHRADER

[January 1952]

I'm *so* sorry about your mother — it's such a shame, especially since she
won't get to take the trip she'd been looking forward to so much. I was
sadder about it before I called, because with your so close voice in my ears I
still feel so warm and happy it's hard for me to think of anything else. You
tell her how awfully sorry I am, and that she mustn't do a thing, but let you
do everything for her, and how much I wish I were there to help. Probably
it's only slight and she'll be completely over it in a few weeks. But, dearest,
if you should need to stay with her longer or if we'd need to be with her a
lot in the future, or *anything else,* you know how I feel about that, and about
everything else in the world, don't you? You are everything in the world to
me — anything with you is wonderful and anything without you is what
we always say. You know I'm yours completely, that all I want is to be your
life and have you mine.

Sara [Starr] and I ate breakfast over at the restaurant — she came back
and listened to about half of *Falstaff* and then left, having an ice-skating
date in New York. She's certainly a quiet, abstracted, dreamy-eyed girl, with
a sort of gentle enchanted manner. Sometimes I feel half at a loss for something to say to her and can't think of anything for us to do — but I guess
nieces and uncles, especially adopted ones, haven't too much to say and do
together.

This next week is going to be Grim. I'll have to work all day and every
day on my *Partisan* article. Ah well, how good I'll feel when it's over!

Dearest love, I do hope things aren't too difficult for you there and that
your mother gets better fast; I wish very much I were there with thee. You
are mine and I am thine, and beloved, dear sister, I'm *so* sorry I'm ever not
there with you.

Tell Cute Mother, our Cute Mother, that I'm terribly sorry about her
heart attack; that she must stay in bed and let you lift soup spoonfuls to her
mouth. Tell her that if I were there I'd freeze a Mint Julep for her. I'm awfully concerned but am so relieved you think it is not too serious — and do
make her do nothing but just rest.

*Irene had been industriously tending to her business affairs and her house-
hold in order to take a South American cruise when she suffered a mild
heart attack.*

TO BEATRICE GARTON

[January 1952]

Dear Beatrice —
            or should I say, Dear Beezie?
I've thought about it till my voice is wheezy,
I've thought about it till my stomach's queasy,
I've thought about it till my toes are freezy —
No use! My poor gray matter's in a fog.
No wonder I've cold feet, with no warm dog —
And no warm Mommy, warm Alleyne, warm you
To snuggle by me as you used to do,
Or all bounce on me till you squashed me flatter
Than any pancake, cooing: "What's the matter?"
I never said; I hadn't any breath.
I think that you'd have snuggled me to death
If you'd had one more heel of bread for dinner.
And yet, dear Beezie, *you* were six tons thinner
Than your Grown Mother or your Growing Sister.
But tell the fair Alleyne how much I've missed her:
The imprint that she made upon my tummy
Is almost gone — and say the same to Mummy.
I miss you, Beezie: all my lipstick's worn away
And no one says now, as they used to say,
"Look, look! It's Randall the Red-Nosed Reindeer!"
How I miss you! Wasn't I insane, dear,
To leave my three girls for three thousand boys?
I'm sick in bed of them. A big sign says: NO NOISE!
SILENCE! *NO WHISPERING!* They feed me soup and rice,
The nurses scamper in and out like mice,
Sometimes the undertaker tiptoes in
And thinks about me with a sunny grin.

But it was all different when I got your letter.
The doctor murmured, "Why, this patient's better!
But he has Princeton — *no one* has recovered
From *that*, you know." When I'd read every word,

The nurse said, "Why, a miracle's occurred!"
"Quick," I cried, "my trousers and my fountain pen!
I've work to do — oh, I am well again!
What if I *do* have Princeton? I should care!
In just four months they're shipping me (by air)
To California! Brother bear! Oh, Sister Bear!"

And so I've shaved my whiskers, combed my hair,
And made this letter for my real friend
Beatrice Garton. This poem has reached its end.
Well, almost has. But here's a great big kiss
For Alleyne and Mommy and my Beatrice;
And one for Nonny — I hope she's *much* better.
I miss you, miss you, miss you.
                                        End of letter.

P.S. Dear Beezie, I wrote you your letter like a poem. Get Mommy to read
it aloud to you. I loved your letter — you *did* know just the things to say.
I'll be glad when it's May. Oh gee, I'm still rhyming.

                                                              Love,
                                                              Randall

TO MARY VON SCHRADER

                                                        [January 1952]
    I had a crazy train of thought the other day; I thought, "Yeah, A and B
will finally get married and have children and I'll be their stepgrand-
father — poor little things, they'll have three grandfathers: I'll be one, their
father will be one, and the other — let's see, who'll be the other?" I tried
gravely to figure out who the other would be, had no luck (I was wandering around vaguely in the neighborhood of your father), and then burst
into laughter at myself as I realized what I'd done.
    There's a psychologist named [Karl S.] Lashley who is, roughly, the
T. S. Eliot of physiological psychologists. When I was In That Field I admired him no end. He is giving four lectures here, I went to one yesterday
afternoon — on brain localization — and much enjoyed it. He was a quick,
modest, intelligent, completely-absorbed-in-his-work man, rather funny at
times.
    He more than anybody else has proved that there isn't nearly as much
brain localization as people had supposed: that memories and functions —

most of them — aren't stored up in some particular place, but are functions of the whole. There's an area called Broca's area that, ever since 1860, has been supposed to control speech; when it goes, speech goes, so they said. Finally, in searching for a better operation for insane people than prefrontal lobotomies, they cut out Broca's area in both lobes of the brain of two mute catatonics: after the operation both just talked and talked. (The audience burst into laughter; they were a nice bunch and loved Lashley.)

I've just taken a Rorschach test for Eileen Berryman — I am about the twentieth poet she's done. It took three hours; apparently I see five or six times as many things as most of the others. You know what Rorschach tests look like, don't you? They're made with blots on folded paper, so that everything is perfectly, bi-laterally symmetrical; as a result there are lots of things that look rather Suggestive. About once or twice I was honest enough to say what they looked like, but not thereafter, and after I stopped saying I more or less stopped seeing. But aside from the sexual things I saw animals in the greatest quantities; airplanes; things like things in paintings and in fairy tales. There was one particularly dull one, almost no interesting details, that I said I didn't like. It turned out it is usually interpreted as two old women arguing or gossiping, and is called The Mother Card. Do you suppose I accidentally didn't like it? Or that I didn't like it because of the Feminine-motherly side of my mother, even though I didn't "see" the women in it?

I've got on the black fur hat. Just put it on when I came downstairs.

It must be hard to make your mother slow down to a standstill on the sofa — lie still, that is. Gee, I hope it'll make her take things easy in general. Tell her I hope she is so much better now. Say that I started to write a letter to her but it was too exciting and when I tried to write a quiet, sobering one the words wouldn't come. As soon as she's well enough to have a silly letter, I'll write one.

TO MARY VON SCHRADER

[January 1952]

I bet you don't know why your Monday letter is late. Because I wrote you a poem — for you and about you, with 148 Emerald Bay, seals, dachshunds, children, see for yourself. Here it is and as soon as you read it send me a Special Delivery letter to reward me: if you do that, maybe such a reward will condition me to write other poems. I'm *serious;* do, please do. I can't wait to hear.

DREAMS

It is already late, my sister.
Out from the door the sea is snoring,
He dreams all night of thee.
The moon looks over the hill like a leopard
And rubs his silver fur at thy feet.
The dachshund whines in his sleep.

It is already late, my sister.
Out from the cliffs the seals are sleeping,
They dream all night of thee.
The white stove burns with a hissing purr,
The darkness puts to its lips its finger.
The children spell in their sleep.

It is already late, my sister.
Up over the roof the stars are turning,
The world dreams of thee.
Close thy lids, sewn together with lashes
Of starlight, tight around me —
I sleep all night in thy sleep.

TO HANNAH ARENDT

[January 1952]

Dear Hannah:

Forgive me for not writing — I guess you've corrupted me. I'm awfully
well — well, awfully bored, too, with my lonely existence in this silly
Princeton, but I had a *wonderful* time in California. I got back two weeks
ago; first I had to do a good bit of school work, then I had to write, worse,
try to make myself write a long article — *had* to do it since I needed the
money. I'll get it done the middle of next week, then I'm going to Greensboro for four or five days to make arrangements for next year (if they'll let
me stay away next year too I can teach at the University of Illinois during
only the last half of the year for quite a lot of money — that way I can be
with Mary and the girls in the girls' accustomed surroundings for five or six
months before we go to very different ones). That following weekend or,
perhaps better, the one after, I could come up and spend with you. As for
my dishes, all they say is, "Why doesn't Hannah Arendt come and wash
us?" They've heard about that *Kinder, Kirche, Küche* motto up on the wall in

your house; oh, I have one in mine too, but the *Kirche* and *Küche* are crossed out.

I didn't know you were going to Europe during the last half of March; I'm glad for you but sorry for me. Where are you going, for how long, what to do?

Many things and the feel of every thing in California were familiar to me from childhood days; just being what you knew first is an almost final recommendation for a place.

I just *couldn't* have got along better with the girls (they're *very* pretty) and everybody; and Mary I couldn't not get along with; I could hardly bear to come back here. My face looked so different it was funny; but after I'd been here a week I looked in the mirror one morning and my California face was gone.

I had a crazy time going out on a non-scheduled plane; it landed everywhere, almost froze us, took 24 hours, and was a delightful experience *once* — I came back TWA Air Coach, fast, smooth, and scheduled.

Write a letter answer to my answer as promptly as I wrote this answer to your question. I hope you got a lot done at Yaddo. See you soon as I'm back from Greensboro.

Yours,
Randall

In early December of 1951, Jarrell had received a query from William Rogers, head of the English department at the University of Illinois, asking if Jarrell would come there and teach for the academic year 1952–53. During the semester break he rode the bus roundtrip to Greensboro to talk in person with the head of the English department and the Chancellor to secure the extended leave of absence.

TO MARY VON SCHRADER

[February 1952]

Look, look, we've bought us a ball-point pen! So I thought the first words I write with it will be to my own Mary. And here they are.

You must make me teach unusually industriously and well next year at Illinois; they will be looking me over (as Blackmur reminded me today) for a big eight or nine thousand dollar a year job that they're considering mostly me or Mark Schorer for — and Blackmur and I doubt that Schorer is interested. With that job we could go to Europe every summer, if we wanted to. But this is just idle talk, like talking about what sort of

car we'll get; as you know, my one *big* ambition is to spend my life with
you.

The radio just played Boccherini's *School for Dancing;* isn't that the one
you liked?

You're sweet to praise me for having been so good about my "sentence"
at Princeton. I can bear it easily enough because of the letters and Thee, and
because I know that very soon I won't be alone again ever, ever; but thank
God I have all that! It's awfully lonesome otherwise.

Guess what, old sugar plum, the Special Delivery man just came with
the proofs of "The Age of Criticism"; and I just went over them, correcting
little errors to send to you. Send the proof back as soon as you're through
with it, will you?

Tell Bea I wish I'd had a piece of that chocolate pie! Bea is the best
speller alive, a real Creative speller. I'll have to make this letter a short one,
to catch the one o'clock mail.

TO MARY VON SCHRADER

[February 1952]

Last night I spent a long Happy time making you a Valentine — hope
you enjoy getting it as much as I enjoyed drawing it. I didn't do much else,
I have a sort of sinus infection, ought to be better soon. Joy, joy, in two
hours I'll have a letter from thee. When one doesn't come for a day I just
yearn for the next. Letters are a drug like opium, I'm surprised the government allows one to get them without a prescription.

Yesterday I was bored enough to buy not the good science fiction magazine, which I buy every month, but one of the bad ones. There were twenty
pages of *Letters to the Editor* (plus editor's comments, some quite witty),
and they were absurd and funny and strange beyond belief. There was even
(I have to judge from the Editor's veiled euphemistic account) a discussion,
very tongue-in-cheek, about whether sexual intercourse would be possible in
space ships under conditions of free fall. I really must save the magazine and
read you the funniest letters and comments — they're far more fantastic
than the stories.

Apparently there's great controversy about whether you should have ill-
clothed girls and space-ships on the cover, or just space-ships. The purists
say: *No Sex;* the impurists say that the purists are immature and use bad
grammar and that there's nothing like the female form; one lady said that
she wanted ill-clothed males on the cover with the space-ships; and the reasonable majority say that they realize the girls have to go on the covers to
sell the magazines, but for God's sake keep them out of the stories.

Oh, my Bergman, I feel quite as if I'd been talking to you. You're such a *blessing* to me. I love to talk to you about anything, you're my sister. I meant to buy you a *To My Sister* Valentine, but the only ones I saw were too depressing. The ones I got Alleyne and Beatrice are like a pastel amoeba's version of *Gone With the Wind.*

When you talk about 148 and the beach and everything else I see it all so clearly: it's *our* family and *our* house and *our* beach. I never have felt a hundredth so family-ish and part of a separate private tribe.

TO MARY VON SCHRADER

[February 1952]

It's been warmer and sunnier yesterday and the day before but today all is icy again. I hate winter! People are crazy to live up here on Hudson's Bay; if I hadn't sunk all my ready capital in the blanket trade I'd move South.

Last night they broadcast recorded versions of Mahler's First and Fourth and played a tape of the Second done at some Dutch Festival. A few years more and Mahler's going to be a Great Composer — ahh, yes.

It always surprises me at lunch with these Princeton Intellectuals how many petty or sordid or faintly unpleasant or improper subjects come up. Me for Queen Victoria, as far as Public Life is concerned. I don't think these people make much distinction between them — lunch with acquaintances is Private Life for *them.* Somebody in one of Shakespeare's plays says to his acquaintances, "You have but mistook me all the while" — and what sort of life is it if you can't say *that* to your acquaintances? You're *my* Real Friend. Gee, I'll be glad to move away from this society into Ours. (This Society could probably say, "Move away! You see us about an hour a day"; and I'd reply, "Yes, that hour is what is getting me down.")

Can't wait to hear how you like "The Age of Criticism." I quite feel that it's the sort of piece you'd write yourself if you wrote such pieces. See how *that* sentence goes round and round.

I've — Guess what? — written a poem; almost done. It's called "The Lonely Man" and is a dramatic monologue as he goes along looking at all the animals in the block. He's *not* me; he hasn't any Mary, poor thing. It isn't going to take the place of Gray's "Elegy" or "Trees" either, but I think you'll enjoy it.

Edward Cone (the one that's the composer) had bought a little painting, and used its unveiling as an excuse for a party last night. I went, though I left rather early; mostly I talked to John Berryman, some to his wife. I certainly do like him. He's a quite touchingly modest person under the surface.

[February 1952]

I just got two letters from you, my Valentine tie (bad Randall, he couldn't resist opening it. What a tie! I'm wearing it with my grey shirt. Boo-ful!) and valentines from A and B, and a letter from B. Tell B I'd rather see *her* spell one word than see anybody else spell a hundred. Isn't it awful to think that she'll eventually be educated out of it? Yet, who knows? with education becoming what it's becoming maybe she's safe. Tell A I love her dearly; tell B so, too.

In a photographer's window here there are the usual boys, fathers, mothers, blooming young girls and one old man: Einstein. I enclose "The Lonely Man." Now *don't* cry, it's all right. It's just a dramatic monologue, that poor "I" in the poem hasn't a single von Schrader, he's not *me*. But, I have to confess, sometimes I feel that he is, the times that I miss you most. But you've given me such a happy day today. Oh, I'd rather be yours than President.

I had the odd experience of seeing myself (well, my name only, thank God) in a novel. In Mary McCarthy's *Groves of Academe* there are some people at a college arguing about what poets should have been invited; and there are eight or nine names, mine among them. Gee, it felt odd.

I am a bad writer to have phrased my remark (about being rich enough to go to Europe every summer) so ambiguously: I said it the way one would say, *rich enough to buy a new Jaguar every year*. It would be awful to go to Europe every summer — I didn't mean we *would*. I meant we'd have enough money (with that job). I imagine we'll go to Laguna most summers, don't you? I'd half taken it for granted. I *love* Laguna, wish they'd move Woman's College, or Illinois there. After we've been back at Woman's College two years (or wherever we are) we can say, "How about a year's leave of absence at Laguna?" You can go to Laguna whenever you need to, or want to, as you know — but O do take me with you. I want to be with you always.

Did you see the photographs of the Duke of Windsor leaving New York for the funeral? All his individuality had left his sad strained face, and he looked like his family, no more, no less. I've always much sympathized with him, too. When I thought about King George's life, ordinary dutiful humdrum respectable life seemed at once so touching and awful that I practically wanted to get him canonized as a martyr. Oh, I'm so glad we're both free of that awful labyrinth in which there isn't even a Minotaur but just yourself sitting dully with someone, both of you admired and envied by the people on the outside.

This weekend I must start on the undone half of my Auden lectures. How I hope having made myself write "The Age of Criticism" will carry over to making myself write the Auden! Surely the Will gets better with exercise.

TO BEATRICE GARTON

[February 1952]

Dear Beezie:

I enjoy your letters *very* much; you're a wonderful letter-writer and my favorite speller in all the world. I miss you and Alleyne and Mommie and Schatzel. It's *cold* here — at the moment it's way below freezing. I'll be glad when it's May and I can come out to Sunny California.

I opened my Valentines a day early; thank you, thank you for mine.

What does your boy friend look like? Is he gray, fat and furry like Trixie or is he tall, thin and brown like Schatzel? Does he go *Meeow* or *Bow-wow-wow?* Tell me All.

Send me a picture of yourself in your new dress. Can't wait to see it. I *liked* your Modern Art drawing.

There is a cat near here that just sits in the middle of the pavement; I've never seen him doing *anything* else, he just sits there. I think he must have caught a mouse there once and just as he was about to eat it, and closed his eyes dreamily, thinking *yum-yum,* an owl flew down noiselessly and grabbed it and flew off; and ever since, as soon as he finishes his breakfast or lunch or dinner, that cat goes and sits there and hopes the owl will come back and bring him the mouse for dessert. It was a catnip mouse too.

I miss you very much, Bea, and love you very much; I'll see you in May.

Your friend,
Randall

TO MARY VON SCHRADER

[February 1952]

I'm *so* glad your mother is getting better. Give her my love. Is she really talking about that South American cruise again?

And Oh, I'm so glad you liked "The Age of Criticism" that much — you're my Real Reader. I'll tell you why I eased up in the last paragraph the way I did. (1) This attack will *horrify* many people who'll need a sort of frame of modest doubt; (2) many people will think "That cannibal's a Wild Man if there ever was one"; (3) I am genuinely doubtful about whether I said the right things, whether my sense of proportion was right, whether I did justice to the critics and the situation — I finally got to feel that I had, but I was awfully uneasy about it when half through the article. I didn't want to end it on that high note in the next to last paragraph, but wanted to put in a little doubt and deprecation, ironically phrased to be sure, and then a quiet little inspiring end. I may well have not done it right. I'll read it really carefully months from now when it's cold, and if it doesn't seem good I'll re-write it.

You know, the article seems obviously common-sensical and justified to you and me, but to many people it will seem as radical, self-assured, and heretical as an attack on the Pope and all the Cardinals by some little Monsignor would. And then, some *awful* anti-highbrow people will welcome it and quote remarks (torn from context) made about the bad highbrow critics and will apply them to the good highbrow critics. That's another thing that made writing the whole article hard. Other people *could* have said lots of what I said: they didn't because they were afraid of this and were uneasy.

Hope you had a dovey time up in the snow. I bet you looked lovely in your ski clothes. How I long to see you and the children when I read about everything in your nice letters, your lovely letters. California was much, *much* the nicest time of my life, *as* you know. Gee, I wish I could have seen all of you and Schatzel walking the mile thru the snow to the cabin.

It's such a joy to me that you like Proust as much as you do.

Blackmur made a lecture on Henry James that was just excellent — wish you could have heard it.

I enclose a review of 7-*League Crutches* by Spender [*The Nation,* February 23, 1952], it has a nice tone and some of the things he says are gratifying, but isn't it difficult to even believe that he's read much of the book? Imagine thinking "La Belle au Bois Dormant," "Black Swan," and "A Sick Child" the best ones! It's particularly puzzling to me because he was nuts about the satiric parts of "The Obscurity of the Poet," and said that if I ever put such things in poetry the poems would be masterpieces — and "Conversation with the Devil" and "Girl . . . Library" are full of such satire and he never even noticed them, or all the funny poems, or . . . several hundred other things. Ah well, I'm sure glad I'm not a Great Poet, imagine how hard my things would be for them, then; it could take them forever to get used to me. It's not his fault, though; he's not very smart and the English have great difficulty with our poetry — he plainly meant well and was doing the best he could. Willing but wanting. We bless him.

Reading your letters and writing to you are much the best parts of my day. I don't know any news to report — one of the nice car magazines was on the newsstand today, I ate a waffle for breakfast, I learned that *Elektra* is going to be broadcast Saturday afternoon from the Metropolitan (listen, if you can, you'd love it) and I read my two letters several times.

Tuned in on the middle of Mahler's "Sentry Song," our own beloved song. It made me feel Lucky. And now, I can't *believe* it, when I changed stations (when they'd finished and were about to play some dreary Sibelius) I got another Mahler song, the one that keeps saying *Adeh, Adeh,* or however you spell it; we'd played it once at that music shop in Boulder. Now they're playing one I've never HEARD before! Sounds like [Alfred] Poell. Easily recognizable as Mahler, all right ... Now another of the ones we heard in the little listening room, but this time with orchestral accompaniment, not piano. Oh the wonders of the earth! They just identified them — songs to Rückert's lyrics: now two more are coming, the third one is "At Midnight" that I've always wanted to hear, Lotte Lehmann specialized in it. Boy, it was overwhelming! And then they played three more.

Irene MacAdams recovered from her heart attack and went to South America for a month.

TO MARY VON SCHRADER

[February 1952]

I got a good review in the Princeton Alumni magazine; got a bad one (but I'd have bet my bottom dollar that it would be bad, since she's always heartily disliked my poems) from Louise Bogan in *The New Yorker*. She said that, though my translations were some good, my own poems were so indistinct and dark and vague that nobody could get interested in them (or words to that effect). Just wait till they put up a statue of me as the Bad Black Poet of Laguna Beach, she'll be sorry!

In the intervals between my conferences with students I have been reading the last volume of Freud's *Collected Papers*. He certainly was a good writer, besides all the other things he was.

There was a charming continuation (in another psychoanalytical book) of a famous patient of Freud's called (because of his constant dreaming, when he was four, that he was in a tree surrounded by wolves) The Wolf Man. He stayed cured for about 12 years, but then under new strains and stresses (he'd been a Russian millionaire, and Lost All) he went to a different psychoanalyst with new problems. He had had much trouble with his nose, and there was a scar on it (imperceptible to the naked eye) which he thought ruined him forever, he said — it's lovely in German — *So kann ich nicht mehr leben,* So can I no more to live. And he was having his wolf dreams all over — grey wolves now, not white.

You'll be relieved to know he completely recovered (Psychoanalyst wasn't sure why) and married a nice, modest woman.

There was another case of a man who went around Swindling and Imposing on All because he wanted a good, kind rich mother to take care of him; after years all gave him up, and rightly so. But he recovered completely having met a good, kind, rich mother who married him.

I figure I've always been so difficult because I wanted a perfect sister named Mary von Schrader; now that I have her everybody'll say, "Why he's like a lemon chiffon pie, wouldn't hurt a fly."

TO MARY VON SCHRADER

[February 1952]

I'm going to write a long, rhymed "Curses on Bottom": after delaying my Friday's letter till Saturday, my Saturday's letter till Monday, and my Sunday's letter till Monday, he ought to really be proud of himself. Ah well, when I get up in the morning I'll bet there's a lovely Special Delivery in the mail slot.

Thanks for the sympathy about old Louise Bogan. When she reviewed my last book she said (I forget how she worded it) that since I, myself, hadn't been in a concentration camp, poems like "A Camp in the Prussian Forest" or "Jews at Haifa" were wickedly exploiting these situations, were a sort of making money out of topical situations — it sounded as if I should have been put in jail for writing them. As you can imagine, that really got me. But there's nothing to be done except wait for her to die, and she's a hefty-impressed-with-herself lady in the flower of middle age. We should worry: when she's dead and we're famous we'll quote what she said and people will shake their heads and say *Can such things be?* And when her ghost comes around whimpering thinly we won't give it any blood to drink. And ere she perishes may her girdle burst! There we've done for her.

You're *some* car-critic. Yeah, I hate having the little parking lights there, too; don't like parking lights. We'll get Farina to take ours home for Christmas-tree. Don't worry, almost none of the Nash-Healey-Farinas are domestically made — just the engine and such things, and then they can be serviced here more easily. But it does take away some of the glamour, all right. I read that in the future Ferrari intends to make in some volume medium-priced sports cars, maybe; as theirs now cost at least $10,000, they may not mean what we mean by medium-priced. I'll put in this letter a pretty sports-car body that I'll bet will please you — isn't it simple and sleek? If you bought a chassis you liked and put that on perhaps changing the grill a little, you'd really have a pretty (and *fast* — the body only weighs 185 pounds) sports car. There are several others that are going to be manufactured in Southern California. And I've read that the next model MG is going to have a streamlined Italianish body like that. By the time we buy a sports car there'll probably be so many pretty ones we won't know what to do.

I have three or four eensy-teensy changes in "The Lonely Man."

L. 4 Long shadows *lengthen* instead of are *lengthening*

" 9 *Soft* instead of *bottle-tailed*

" 10 Cancel *thin*

" 14 and 15 are now:

A fat spaniel snuffles out to me

And sobers me with his trusting frown.

L. 16 *That* is changed to *it*

Did I ever tell you, O Real Friend, that you're my Favorite Reader? It terrifies me to think I might never have known you, that we might have gone on in our poor old lives!

THE LONELY MAN

A cat sits on the pavement by the house.
It lets itself be touched, then slides away.
A girl goes by in a hood; the winter noon's
Long shadows lengthen. The cat is gray,
It sits there. It sits there all day, every day.

A collie bounds into my arms: he is a dog
And, therefore, finds nothing human alien.
He lives at the preacher's with a pair of cats.
The soft half-Persian sidles to me;
Indoors, the old white one watches blindly.

How cold it is! Some snow slides from a roof
When a squirrel jumps off it to a squirrel-proof
Feeding-station; and, a lot and two yards down,
A fat spaniel snuffles out to me
And sobers me with his untrusting frown.

He worries about his yard: past it, it's my affair
If I halt Earth in her track — his duty's done.

And the cat and the collie worry about the old one:
They come, when she's out too, so uncertainly. . . .
It's my block; I know them, just as they know me.

As for the others, those who wake up every day
And feed these, keep the houses, ride away
To work — I don't know them, they don't know me.
Are we friends or enemies? Why, who can say?
We nod to each other sometimes, in humanity,
Or search one another's faces with a yearning
Remnant of faith that's almost animal. . . .
The gray cat that just sits there: surely it is learning
To be a man; will find, soon, *some especial*
Opening in a good firm for a former cat.

TO MARY VON SCHRADER

[February 1952]

There was sunshine outside the window at seven this morning, and it was still light last night at six; it's coming, Spring, coming! (Better not mention that there was ice on the puddles of water outside at seven — and I doubt if any of it's melted.)

Blackmur lent me Auden's first book of poetry (I've lent mine once too often, to some unknown student, and don't have it anymore); inside it was a review he'd written of Auden's first book [*Poems*] and Spender's first book [*Twenty Poems*]. It carefully, reasonably, impressively showed that Spender was a better poet than Auden and wrote a better *kind* of poetry — you couldn't tell what those Auden poems meant, he said. Now, *there* was a good critic getting things exactly backward, and in such an authoritative-seeming way. It read as if it had been written as an exhibit for my "Age of Criticism" article.

Just a little ago I read *that* over carefully to make up my mind what I thought of it: I was relieved to have it seem true and moderate enough, the tone seemed what it should be. What you said about it (and what you said about the poem and the Valentine) was such a great pleasure to me, sister, beloved. You're a joy to give things to, my own dear favorite Reader and Listener-to-Music-With.

You know, I bet I've written as many words in the last six months (words in letters) as Balzac or Dumas or Arnold Bennett.

TO MARY VON SCHRADER

[February 1952]

I've been doing an Adaptation — quite free translation — of Rilke's poem named "Childhood." I send you the first two stanzas; they were hard, but the last two will be harder, alas, since they're not quite as good in some ways and have several key-words there's no very good English word for. But something may come, and if it doesn't I'll make up something: what I want to do is a sort of transcription into English (as from orchestra to piano) of Rilke's whole German poem, and if I have to make up and leave out I do it cheerfully: what I want is something that's a real poem in English, and I do think that if a reader came on these two stanzas in a book he'd think them an ordinary English poem, not a translation.

Heard the *Elektra* yesterday afternoon over at Edward Cone's; quite a few people listen to operas there, Saturday afternoons when there're good ones. It sure was good: one of the two best parts is when Elektra, after many years of living like a dog in the courtyard, whipped, fed on scraps, realizes that it's actually her brother come at last. She has a beautiful long passage full of joy and love, with a very touching part saying she knows how ugly and old she must look to him. Do you know that one of those *pigs* listening kept talking about incest and said an accompaniment was "positively lewd," and half the people laughed appreciatively? I didn't say much more than 2 cold disagreeing sentences; but I happened to leave at the same time as the girl who'd been looking at the libretto with me and we burst out indignantly about it. How I hate such people as that man — they spoil everything they touch with little nasty jokes; and, worst of all, he's an intelligent and in many ways nice person.

They're playing selections from *Otello* now, on WNYC.

You know, I do feel very lonely here, but I'm usually fairly contented when I don't see people; when I do see them I'm dissatisfied and long for you; and otherwise I think of thee and read and write and listen to music and all goes well except for those Tasks — articles and lectures — that keep awfully recurring from time to time.

Lashley's lecture was good again today. Darn it, I'm going to have to miss the last one because it comes at the same time as my class comes.

Did some work on my Auden lectures; I do with Reluctance. Oh, Criticism!

I just had a note from Hannah inviting me to spend Saturday and Sunday with her and her husband. Just think, I haven't seen them since my Journey to California — I wonder whether they'll be able to recognize me?

TO MARY VON SCHRADER

[February 1952]

I had a wonderful experience: I woke about five-thirty from a nap, and turned on the radio into the middle of an unbelievably good and moving performance of *Elektra,* a thousand times better than yesterday's — it was so good it really made you shake all over with emotion, I was in another world for hours. I'd have given *anything* to have you listening with me. It was a tape recording of an Italian performance directed by [Dimitri] Mitropoulos, who'd also directed a wonderful performance of it I heard two years ago on Christmas day. It was far and away the most powerful and moving and shattering opera performance I ever heard, in spite of the fact that the Elektra needed a bigger voice. I wished *so* for thee. I've meant for many years to write the best verse-play I could on a big serious subject, and I thought, "I really will do *Elektra.*"

I went over to the library to get von Hofmannsthal's libretto — and this will delight you — they had it only in Hungarian and Russian! The German was out, and there was no English. But I got something I've always wanted to read, the letters [Richard] Strauss and von Hofmannsthal wrote to each other while they were working on the last of *Elektra,* all of *Rosenkavalier,* and two later ones. Lots of passages in von H's letters are wonderfully good and most encouraging to any serious artist.

I think the brother and sister part in the myth will particularly help me with an *Elektra* of my own — and you, O my own sister, you help me and encourage me; late this summer and next year we will write *The Ladies —* we can work on it — I'll read things to you as I write them and we can talk about all the action and everything. It will be so good to have somebody to work with, to be a real companion to me; I never have had. I really am far more a dramatic poet than a lyric one, essentially: if I can write a play with speech as good as "Seele im Raum" or my other best dramatic monologues, it will be really good. Of course, probably nobody will produce it, not for many years at least, and then they won't like it — but we should worry. Von Hofmannsthal has several passages on that, too good not to copy out for you; I'll copy them and three or four more — when I read them I longed for you to be here so I could read them aloud to you.

> That which is essentially poetic in a poet's work, its real meaning, is never understood at first. Only that is understood in which there is nothing to understand — the higher, the essential element, remains unrecognized, and to this *there is no exception.*

Then he tells how all the critics found the libretto of *Rosenkavalier* vulgar and dull and silly, kept talking about "blood" and "decadence" of *Elek-*

tra, actually asked of *Lohengrin* and *Tannhäuser*, "What are they *about?*"

He says, "I believe that only a unique creation with a peculiar style of its own has either the right to exist or the power to survive, and that every success which is achieved by compromise and the obliteration of special characteristics is sure to be discounted somehow by a postponement or diminution of the *real* success to which the work is entitled."

He says about the opera they are working on: "Even should this pass muster now, we have to reckon with time, which robs aging features of all but the inward light." That's quite like Proust, isn't it?

Strauss tells him he's thought of a lovely idea for a libretto, about "a really aristocratic female spy" who becomes "a traitor for love's sake" and "is made use of by a secret agent or something else really amusing." Von H, for once not a bit careful, bursts out: "I had to have a hearty laugh over your letter! The subjects you propose are, from my point of view, so shocking that they well might frighten one off from ever writing another libretto as long as one lived—though by *one* of course I mean *me!*" Then he goes on and explains why he couldn't and sweetly suggests something else. (Incidentally, he's usually very good about accepting Strauss's changes when they're good, and they often are, in *Rosenkavalier*.)

Strauss has a good letter telling von H how some of his ideas about opera have been essentially changed by him, and von H replies: "It is fine when a man like you is not content to stick in a rut . . . fine, too, that you and I are able to learn from each other. In a world where all the rest rush madly along, stupid, stubborn, self-opinionated, impatient of instruction or any sort of discipline . . . a real collaboration between two men of mature experience must always be extremely rare. Ours, it is true, is but a shadow of what it might be, but we both have good will, earnestness, and consistency, and that is better than the god-forsaken 'talent' with which every blockhead nowadays is so well equipped."

And he has this magnificent paragraph: "Publication has only a secondary interest for me, stage production merely a tertiary one—all that is quite irrelevant to the real value of my works and to the chances of their survival. The work of a lifetime, as mine is, will either be self-evident and justify my very definite pretensions, or it will *not* do so — the stage, the printed book, the thing they call Success, etc., these things have nothing whatever to do with it; I know my proper course and must follow it."

All these are fortifying words, aren't they?

Blackmur at lunch today was so amiable and good hearted about the world, and so disquieted by writers who see life all horror and nastiness, that he seemed an entire Man of Good Will. God keep him so always.

I've about finished my Rilke translation — I'll send it along tomorrow.

How pleasant it is to write translations and poems and stories, no matter how hard they are — how different from writing Articles and Lectures!

I typed out "The Lonely Man" with the changes and it really did seem smooth and well-organized and nice, as if it were a good poem. I hope, hope, hope so.

With von Hofmannsthal's assistance I've written you a perfect rock-python of a letter. LONG.

TO HARRY FORD

[February 1952]

Dear Mr. Ford:

I should have answered before — I've been in the middle of writing an article, and put off anything else. Yes, I'd like the manuscript back, to work on this summer: I'm so thoroughly covered with lectures and articles that I can't till then. I haven't yet seen which pages you meant (my carbon's not numbered) but I'll be very interested. The suggestions sound very reasonable. The narrator has a wife (to be treated a little more at length in the new version) so readers won't say, "Why doesn't he marry Constance?" or words to that effect. The present conclusion of the book is going to be followed by thirty or forty pages.

I decided to take a little more time putting together my critical book — I wanted to have some extra stuff on Moore (I'm doing it for a summer *Partisan*) and on Frost. Meanwhile I've done another piece for the book that you've probably seen in the new *Partisan* ["The Age of Criticism"]: it makes three general articles besides all the specific ones.

That Whitman sounds better "out of context" is new to me: *I* thought that people always said it's the monumental sweep, grandeur, and range that does it, even though the details are pretty crude or simple usually. I'm glad you're reading Whitman again; that's what the article was for. The "Song of Myself" and "The Sleepers" are the best two I think.

I'm glad the readers enjoyed *Pictures.* I was a little disappointed to have only the assurance of a warm rereading of its later state, but I can see how an odd book's an odd problem; after all, if I'd wanted it easily acceptable I shouldn't have given it two heads. It was a great pleasure to have you yourself enjoy it so much.

Yours,
Randall Jarrell

Pictures from an Institution *is subtitled "A Comedy," and the chapter titles are proper names, like the cast of characters in a play, except for the* last chapter, *"They All Go,"* which was a Shakespearean stage direction. It was not a play, however; it was a work of fiction that was — in this very early stage — just barely a novel. That the readers at Knopf had faulted it for being so *"odd"* provoked Jarrell's exaggerated description of it as a monster with two heads. This also provoked him to do a great deal of work on the book until it conformed more to the requirements for a novel; odd, still, but a novel.

TO MARY VON SCHRADER

[New York City]

[March 1952]

A cold rain is falling, the wind is howling and New York City lies grey and nasty beneath me. Ah, Laguna Beach! How I wish I were in the sea with you! How I wish I were walking in the eucalyptus grove with you!

I got here in the middle of the morning yesterday. Hannah was just leaving, covered with regrets — there was some unexpected urgent stuff to be done at her office: her husband and I talked and talked. His name is Heinrich Blücher; he's a *very* nice and smart man. He read my article (I had the proof because you'd so cleverly sent it *right* back). We had a nice long lunch consisting of Spanish bread, German smoked meats and wurst, and Darjeeling tea, all very good. Hannah got back late in the afternoon when we were taking a nap, and later on she read the article while we talked. She would hush us up when she got to some crucial part. They both said it was just right (and that lots of people had mentioned my Whitman article to them). Hannah said she thought it — "The Age of Criticism" — would get me a lot of concerted antagonism from critics, that I'd attacked a great Vested Interest but that fortunately they wouldn't be able to *do* much to me. After dinner we read poems and talked, and generally had a Constance-and-the-Rosenbaums evening.

Now I've eaten breakfast and it's 10:30 or so. Heinrich is still fast asleep; Hannah and I talked about translation, and I told her that you and I meant to learn German together, and she said that was good, that I was a wonderful translator and if I translated a lot of German poetry probably would, in the long run, have my own poetry broadened and given odd, un-English virtues by it. If you and I do learn German well enough to talk to each other in it and read things I will give you some tremendous reward like an epic called *The Mariad,* or 16 Jaguars — you will really have transfigured me. Oh, do, do!

Heinrich was away for half the evening and I described California and A and B and Thee to Hannah — Anybody hearing would have said, "My, that poet's lyrical!"

The Ford Foundation is sponsoring a magazine supposed to represent American Culture to Europe and the world; Laughlin (the head of New Directions, the publishing firm — and a dope, alas!) wrote asking me to review Williams' *Collected Poems*, said I'd be paid 7½ *cents a word*. That means if I write six typewritten pages I'll get $150. Isn't that dovey? We can buy ice creams whenever we feel like it.

TO MARY VON SCHRADER

[March 1952]

I just turned on the radio and — incredulous with joy — heard Elektra's first *Oreste!* when she recognizes her brother. I immediately turned out the light, settled myself in bed, and prepared to hear the last half hour of the opera. After ten minutes, just as the being-murdered-Clytemnestra screamed horribly, the program abruptly ended, leaving me almost weeping.

You know when Orestes finally comes (in the opera) Elektra looks at herself and is ashamed for him to see her, she's so old and haggard and not what his sister ought to be: I almost feel that I look that way now, compared to my California self. But a few days of being with thee in late March will transfigure me, I know.

I read the whole libretto of *Elektra* in German, looking down for much, much help to the English below. It's *good* — when they make long speeches, believe me, it's because they've got a lot to say, and everything mounts up just the way it should; the emotional and actual organization of the whole thing is wonderful.

I'm certainly a sucker for German; if I knew German really well I'd even write some poems in it, I'm so crazy about it. And I'm not talking romantically and exaggeratedly just for fun (though often I do about it); there are a lot of *wonderful* things about it, would English had kept them! Though of course, the most wonderful thing of all is the flavor of the common, ordinary words, and that you'd never taste if it were your native language. You're my von Schrader. Remember how amused you were and amazed I was when you first told me your name dancing at the Tulagi? How would you like *Elektra* for a wedding present? I think we need it for a Family Jewel like *Das Knaben Wunderhorn* and the Proust.

Heard Dylan Thomas read to a large audience supposed to be at 5, but he arrived late on the wrong train. He began with a long, mannered, wordy, poetic, funny in spots, brilliant in spots, vain and self-obsessed performance in prose, read (plainly for the thousandth time) off typed pages. Then he read poems by modern poets all of which (except for serious ones by Yeats and Hardy) were slight, funny, or satiric ones — Oh, no, there was an *awful* grandiloquent one, "Still Falls the Rain" by Edith Sitwell. Nothing by Eliot but a parody of Eliot which he read in a parody of Eliot's voice. Nothing by any American poet, in fact. Then he read his own poems, three *excellent* ones and four or five others. He reads poems half-well-and-half-abominably; he has a wonderful voice and fine sense of rhythm, but he reads most things just alike, intones them, quavers his voice like Sarah Bernhardt, puts in hushes, silences — the same sure fire stuff — no matter what the poem is. He actually read "What shall I do for pretty girls/Now my old bawd is dead?" in a heartbreaking, hushed, pause-y, tragic voice at the end. Generally if I'm crazy about the poem I'm angry at his reading, unless it's one of his poems, and sometimes he spoils that.

The audience lapped it up, they couldn't have loved it better. Sometimes I think the only thing to do with this world is retire from it. But Thomas read "Fern Hill" beautifully—it sounded good. Wished for you. Worked on my Williams.

TO MARY VON SCHRADER

[March 1952]

My Monday letter got here right on schedule. Marshal [Andrei] Zhdanov said once, "There's a great big hole in the middle of the foundations of Soviet literature." Well, My Day is just like that when old Bottom gets my letter.

Blackmur's concluding lecture on *The Ambassadors* was *good*. He's far and away the best novel-critic I ever heard — I sat there feeling contentedly inferior. He's been unusually plain, serious, idealistic and unmannered the last two times. He was good to begin with, and has worked on great works so much that he really knows how to go about it — *fundamentally* knows how. He's good at poetry but he's wonderful at novels.

While I was listening to him I felt ashamed of having worked no longer than I did on *Pictures from an Institution*. I was excited with my new toy, if that's excuse enough: I made up my mind to work hard on it and have it as good as possible before printing it; more plot and organization, more school, more dark side of Irene and Gottfried, more dark side of narrator, more Constance, more lots of things. More relation between Gertrude-and-Sydney.

My goodness, I forgot some nice though far off news. Blackmur's been down to a meeting of the Fellows of the Library of Congress — Ransom, Warren, Auden, Cleanth Brooks, etc. He said that the pay of the Poetry

Consultant has been raised to $7,700 a year, regular office hours no longer exist, you can keep the job two years now; not one. *And* they have a sort of permanent list to pick from (I'm on it); so inside the next six or eight years that's something we're almost certain to get.

When I woke this morning there was 8 inches of snow, and more's coming down. There were drifts up to the porch and over the smaller bushes. Late this afternoon everybody dug out their sidewalks — me, too, with a shovel I found in a tremendous cellar, half as big as the whole house, which is there underneath and all unknown to me. Then the moon came out and all the houses looked pulled up under the bedclothes waiting for Christmas. I looked pretty exotic dressed for shovelling in my black fur hat, heavy wool scarf, German leather coat, sheepskin gloves and high galoshes; very like some officer in a combination German-Russian army.

Having lunch with Blackmur is such a let-down after his lectures; I can't help thinking about him, no matter what his good qualities, "He's so much *part* of this whole literary-academic, semi-fashionable, established accepting-things-at-their-own-valuation world." Believe me, I'm glad I'm marrying a wild tribe and am not institutionalized myself.

In a note to Mary just before her spring visit, Jarrell wrote, "I didn't feel much like writing Auden so I straightened the house and washed some dishes. Now don't worry, I didn't clean. I didn't do a good job. There are still some dishes stubbornly soaking in soapsuds. Mostly it was picking up pieces of paper with my handwriting on them and throwing them down in the middle of a sheet and finally carrying it to the back porch until there wasn't any more room there: I had three sheets full." Many of these papers with Jarrell's handwriting on them were early drafts of poems and lectures. There were also letters from his mother, friends, editors, students, and the like. Often when these writers referred to the contents of their letters, Jarrell had forgotten about them, and he would have to ask them to write him again. He told a young English instructor at Vanderbilt, "I'm bad about keeping letters, I guess. But really, if I'd kept everything people have written me over the years I'd have been buried under paper long ago."

TO JOHN CROWE RANSOM

[April 1952]

Dear Mr. Ransom:

May I put off giving you my piece until the next issue? I've got myself into such a jam for time, what with doing these Auden lectures here and making some lecture trips for the money, that I don't see how I can do a good one in time. I'll try to do really good ones for the next two issues, in *plenty of time.* I'm awfully sorry.

Giving six two-hour (written out beforehand) lectures on Auden is making me wish that Auden had never existed.

I enjoyed your piece on Cleanth's book very much.

Yours,
Randall

In the end, Jarrell did his Kenyon Review *piece on Robert Frost. It was entitled "To the Laodiceans" and appeared in the Autumn 1952 issue.*

TO MARY VON SCHRADER

[April 1952]

I had a nice letter from Cal Lowell: he wasn't angry about the review [of *The Mills of the Kavanaughs*] at all, virtuous boy. Wants me to come and live with them in September — I'll politely refuse but not say *just* why. We might stay with them some, some summer, you'd like Cal a lot, and goodness knows he'd like you.

Oh, I think one of us should mention the Tuberculosis Cure; isn't that extraordinary? Pretty soon *The Magic Mountain* will be as out of date as *Ghosts.*

I copied down two things you'll love. The Duke of Wellington, on first seeing his troops in the Peninsular War, said: "I don't know what effect these men will have on the enemy, but by God, they frighten *me.*"

And the Friesland national anthem (it's a Dutch province with a language of its own) is, "Friesian Blood, Rise Up and Boil!" Isn't that wonderful?

You never know how much you loved your grandma until she dies: I'm referring to my old ball point pen. Apparently that cartridge was a mutation caused by the atomic bomb tests, and this is the normal kind — woe, woe!

The letter from Lowell that Jarrell refers to was saved, and in it Lowell quoted R. W. Flint: "Dear Jarrell, he annihilates us all and by our stripes he is healed." Lowell went on to say, "I was expecting ugly treatment in your review . . . I agree with most of what you say, except the heroine is very real to me and in a freakish way the poem has much more in it than any of my others. Anyhow, I am delighted . . . and have read it many times out of vanity. Perhaps I agree with it all, but since I've still written nothing new, I go on over-rating the Kavanaughs." Further along, Lowell wrote, "A cold comfort compliment but your divorce seems to be the most calmly and humanely conducted of any that I know of."

TO MARY VON SCHRADER

[Columbus, Mississippi]

[April 1952]

Here I am in an old hotel room with a ceiling sixteen or eighteen feet high. But how I suffered to get here! It was a rough day: as the stewardess said when she brought lunch, "It's too rough to serve liquids": A number of people were sick; I wasn't, objectively speaking, but boy, I *felt* sick. And we stopped at Washington; Richmond; Raleigh; Charlotte; Atlanta; Birmingham and Tuscaloosa. Most of the time I was too nauseated to read. I recovered while waiting an hour and a half in Birmingham (changing planes). From there on the weather was good and the plane, a little DC-3, was smooth — before it'd been a DC-6 at its worst. The waitress in Birmingham looked a little like you — your cheekbones especially; it was very disconcerting to hear her talk with a broad Southern accent, but I stared at her lovingly just the same.

The airfield here is way out in the country at a revived Army Air Base. I was met by the Southern head of the English department and his Southern wife. How familiar and different it all was! I felt as if I'd fallen into a machine which ran like cold molasses, was full of the best and sleepiest of intentions, and began every sentence by telling you where it was from. After being delivered at the hotel I walked around relishing the wonderful Here-we-are-out-in-plain-old-*America* feeling of everything; the college itself looked so just-yawnily-there, so small time, that you felt it wasn't an institution at all, just a dumb private citizen.

As I walked by the girls' dormitory one of the girls was standing by the window with her hands and elbows above her head almost, drying her hair; she looked so pleasant and romantic, like an illustration to a novel of 1905.

Ha-ha, old Katherine Anne Porter called them up last Friday and said she wouldn't be able to come; so they have Eudora Welty. When told about all this I laughed knowingly; and the English professor knew immediately what my laugh meant. He said, "Has she done that at your school, too? Several people have told me that; they said Miss Porter just isn't a very reliable person."

I just read over my "Age of Criticism" to see if there were any words I didn't know how to pronounce. Besides my hour-long speech I have to talk for two hours about the children's poems, eat lunch and dinner formally and stand in — honestly — a receiving line; I'll bet I have to finish by washing the dishes. And all for nothing! My expenses are going to come to $145.00; so I'm going to refuse the extra $5.00 and say, "This lecture is on me; I did it for the girls of Mississippi."

Jarrell was attending the annual literary festival at the Mississippi State College for Women.

TO MARY VON SCHRADER

[April 21, 1952]

Friday was some day — it began at 9:30 and wasn't over until 10 that night. Eudora Welty gave a shortish speech in the morning, I followed with the "Age of Criticism." There was the most tremendous crowd for her — soon as she was over about three fifths of it got up and rushed out; the school had given all the girls cuts to hear her *because she was an alumna,* then they had to go away to class. My own audience (the more literary, and all the visitors) laughed and laughed and were most engrossed, though the piece was about ten minutes too long and I had to fret and worry and leave out sentences. Miss Welty was crazy about it. She is certainly one of the three or four nicest writers I've ever met — somewhat homely, but so sympathetic, natural, and generally attractive that you quite forget it, particularly since you feel you've known her always. She's like Peter Taylor in some ways. She and I got along together just wonderfully; sometime when we're living in Greensboro we'll have to get her to visit us.

Several hundred people to lunch; the president's wife, and an old fanatic who looked and dressed like Gandhi (honest, no kidding, practically a sari) spoke on modern literature compared to the literature of her youth. She said something pleasant about Eudora Welty and me, and that was the end of any pleasantness. She thought *Time,* the *New York Times,* Harvard, and *The Saturday Evening Post* communistic or very radical. She compared modern literature very unfavorably with the dime-novels of her youth (E. D. E. N. Southworth was her favorite), which Had Standards, believed that man was created by God, etc. There was one wonderfully funny touch: she said that in these novels you could always recognize a villain because he wore a black *moustache.* I was sitting four feet from her; everybody just laughed and laughed, and I gently put up my two hands and covered the bottom half of my face, and they laughed harder, *much* harder.

It was the most violent and senseless attack on the modern world I've ever heard. Most of the audience, I think, bitterly resented it. She'd particularly insisted on happy endings, poetic justice, and nice, uplifting subjects. That afternoon, criticizing a raw-slice-of-life poem, I summarized the plot of *Oedipus* ("somebody who kills his father, marries his mother, and finally tears out his eyes with his own hands," I said) and added cheerfully, "I guess Sophocles didn't have Standards." Well, the whole class not only broke into laughter, ten or fifteen of them *clapped.*

I then talked about a few of their poems, answered questions, and talked about writing poetry in general; they were a particularly nice and sympathetic bunch (not one false note) and I had a good time and thought of lots of funny things to say, none of which I can remember. Oh yes, there was a cat in a sonnet-sequence that got called *it, he* and *she:* finally, I said in despair "which makes it like the Holy Trinity." I think they really did enjoy it and the guy in charge of the Literary Festival thanked me later that night and said lots of people had talked to him about it; and Miss Ransom, John Crowe Ransom's sister, said it certainly was going to be a pleasure to write him and say how splendid I'd been.

Now I will stop Boasting to My Big Sister and get down to Real Business: *The Tea.* Would you believe that we had to stand in line for an hour and meet about three hundred people filing by? Each shook my hand, said "I certainly enjoyed your speech, Mr. Jarrell" — and went on. Except for one fat girl, a far-worse-than-Girl-in-the-Library type, who giggled and said, "Oh, you're the man who read that *long* speech." I laughed and said gaily and forcefully, "Why you can't open your mouth without putting your foot in it. You're supposed to tell me how much you enjoyed it." She was only momentarily taken aback and recovered with, "Do you *really* believe all that stuff?" I said, "Sure do." And we each said an amicable sentence and she went bumpity-bumpity on.

We had about 45 minutes free before dinner. I sat and talked with Miss Welty and some friend of hers, a pleasant professor from Jackson, Mississippi. Dinner was Even as Lunch, down to the Speech. The Dean of the Graduate School of the University of Mississippi made a speech defending that Forgotten Man, the reader, and took about 40 minutes telling all the crimes against him committed by Faulkner, Hemingway, Fitzgerald, publishers, modern poets. It was about as vicious, spiteful and completely patronizing a speech as I have ever heard. He said all the great writers of the past had made their experiments without being difficult for the reader, *ever.* He was particularly sore at writers for not writing as well when they got old: publishers shouldn't print them then, it was "just asking alms from the public" for them. Then he went on to inform the students that of course there was a statistically negligible chance that any of them would ever "become a professional writer." Miss Welty got white with anger as he proceeded; so did I; we looked at each other occasionally. He was even pleased at the possibility that soon all books would just be published as paperbound books, and have to sell 250,000 copies to break even — the writers would *have* to give the readers what they wanted, then. But he also pretended to dislike "slick" or "popular" work. It was the nastiest, pettiest, most ungenerous job of trying to make everybody proud of his ignorance, determined to get more ignorant, that I have ever heard. Miss Welty said to me later, "What would it have been like if we hadn't been here?" And yet most of the students were nice, and were delighted with anything good said to them.

Miss Welty's speech was good: quite sincere, imaginative, serious — it had an unusually direct appeal to the audience; she wouldn't believe it, though — it was almost the only one she'd ever made, apparently, and she was afraid she'd been awful.

I see the collie lots these days, and the cat that just sits there, too. Eudora Welty and I petted the cutest big furry dog, a real Colorado one, he was just the color of a lion, and gentle as a lamb.

TO MARY VON SCHRADER

[Princeton]
11:45 P.M.
[April 1952]

Here I am on the choo-choo train going to New York; I'll arrive at the hotel about quarter till one, sleep till seven, and then go out to the airport and leave for Iowa.

My lecture was successful enough last night but Blackmur practically drove me crazy. In the discussion period he talked more than everybody else put together, and he did his usual stunt of completely misunderstanding what the speaker said and talking about his own version of it. I was giving examples of Auden's use of a particular kind of extended metaphor, treating a person as if he were a country, a piece of geography; and I used one example from Auden's poem about the death of Yeats ["In Memory of W. B. Yeats"]. I'll copy the sentence: "The provinces of his body revolted/ The squares of his mind were empty,/ Silence invaded the suburbs,/ The current of his feeling failed:" That was all — every word. This was just part of a list I was making. Well, would you believe it, Blackmur said that this poem about Yeats was a fine poem, and I'd said the metaphor was bad. I said I hadn't said that it was either good or bad, that I was just using it as an example. He then said that it was my duty to commit myself; I replied, laughing, that nobody had ever accused me of not committing myself. Then he said that I'd implied by the tone of my list that it was bad, and that it was my duty as a critic when something as good as this came along to pay homage to it. I said in despair that I hadn't even mentioned the *poem* itself, that I couldn't talk about every poem of Auden's; and he went on and on.

Robert Fitzgerald made some *good* comments, he knows Auden's poetry well; and an old German named Erich Kahler made a good one and talked to me afterwards and said he would appreciate it so much after I got back from Iowa if I would spend some evening with him, and really talk about Auden and poetry. And Francis Fergusson's remarks were entirely agreeing, too. Blackmur was really practically rude, and just hopelessly dumb and irrelevant; it was one of those *absurd* situations.

I got an "Age of Criticism" fan letter from Newton Arvin, a pretty well-known critic who won the National Book Award last year for his book on Melville. He said I was performing, in that piece, the same function that Pope's *Dunciad* performed in its age, and said nice things about how necessary, brilliant, and good-tempered the piece was.

Four weeks from now — one hair cut away and one issue of *Road and Track* away — I'll be on my way to you. Think of being through with these lectures; and then Princeton; and then My Old Life. Bernard Haggin used to make jokes about the Old Haggin and the New Haggin — O joy to be the New Jarrell entirely surrounded by daughters and dachshunds, California and you.

Jarrell was going to Grinnell College in Iowa to judge student poems and read his own. Also, as a result of seeing Paul Engle, director of the Writing Workshop at the University of Iowa, at the dinner in New York, he had been invited to read poems and discuss students' work at the University of Iowa.

TO MARY VON SCHRADER

Iowa City
April 29, 1952

Just got my letters at the Post Office. What a dream of Bea's. Tell the little people I'll answer theirs as soon as I get back to Princeton. Oh, how glad I'll be when we're together for good — when I'm your husband and their Randall and there's no need for letters.

Well, I've had a wonderful time here at the University of Iowa! I never saw such a pleasant, unspiteful, un-nasty-intellectual bunch of poets as here. Eleanor Taylor's sister's husband, Donald Justice, is one, and of course Snodgrass. He's done some lovely Rilke translations and a good Rimbaud. I talked to them and some others about 2½ hours yesterday afternoon about their poems and poetry. Last night I read "Childhood," "A Sick Child," "Knight, Death, and the Devil," "Black Swan," "Lady Bates," "Lines," "Transient Barracks," "8th Air Force" and "A Girl in a Library." I've never in my whole life been so successful with an audience; by the time I was ⅔ through, there was such rapport that we were like mother and long-lost child, in "A Girl in a Library" you could *see* the audience sway and be changed at every big change in the motion of the thought of the poem. I've never, almost, felt more strongly what a wonderful thing it is to have made the poems and have moved people so.

Guess what? I got *my* handwriting analyzed. She was the wife of a graduate student here; an odd, silent, quite attractive girl who is a physiological chemist. She was almost a professional at it; far better than I. It turned out that she was a poet, too, and I saw some of her poems — very strange ones, full of a queer way of looking at a quite personal, quite different world. Her name is Meryl Johnson.

She was much impressed with a tremendous change which occurred right in the middle of my life, and said that after it I'd be well-off and have a very happy, fortunate rest of my life. She said she didn't know how old I was and couldn't say exactly when the great change would occur, but it was soon. I laughed and said, "You're right, it already happened just a few months ago." She went on to say I was extravagant (not with money so much as doing things extravagantly), very emotional, sensitive (had been miserably so as a child), impulsive, open, was good at art but not nearly as good as at writing, would have been a good ballet dancer, very enthusiastic and infatuated with things, very generous but with unexpected little carefulnesses about some things; she said that I had an extraordinarily gay and happy temperament, and that I was simple, *not* complicated. She said that in the last few days I'd been very much upset by something that had offended my sense of justice. Imagine — wasn't that clever about the Blackmur thing?

This was really the most successful criticism-poetry reading-talking to people I've ever done; the people were so *nice* to me, and seemed to like me and what I said so much, that I felt childishly embarrassed and happy. After

Parker Tyler's review ["The Dramatic Lyricism of Randall Jarrell," *Poetry,*
March 1952] and these readers I feel like saying, "Lord, I'm sorry I ever
complained."

I hope the little girls are well and happy and that not too many silly duties have piled up for thee; do them very sloppily, so everybody will say,
"She's in love."

I miss you so much my best beloved, Real Friend, sister. But I feel so
fortunate, too; and happy beyond belief. Really, when I think of what's behind me and what's ahead I feel like a walking Happy Ending.

TO MARY VON SCHRADER

[May 1952]

Everything looked so beautiful landing at New York; we came to the
shore twenty or thirty miles south, and then flew a little over the sea, seeing
all the islands and rivers and geometrical new apartment buildings and tall
buildings and slums. Sometimes in the middle of the miles of brick tenements and apartments where people lived, you'd see a beautiful spot many
blocks long, all grass and trees — and *that* was where the dead people lived
. . . I had to wait in Penn Station for an hour and a half to get back here but
I was proud of myself. I wrote on the Auden lecture and the time flew prof-
itably by.

At home I had my letter from Thee and various nondescript mail. This
morning Princeton was so beautiful I could hardly believe it. All the leaves
are perfectly new but almost perfectly full, there are fruit-tree blossoms, the
sun's as brilliant as can be but the air is cool and clear. I had twenty minutes
free between conferences and walked down to the Prospect Garden by the
president's house. It was so beautiful, the flowers perfected by man, so fresh
and wonderful, that I couldn't help thinking that — regardless of all the
awful things he does — man is the glory and wonder of the earth. There's a
chorus by Sophocles that begins by saying that nothing is so wonderful as
man, who's done this and this and this — He's so much righter than the
Original Sin people. To fly across the country in the day time is to think a
lot about the Works of Man.

TO MARY VON SCHRADER

[May 3, 1952]

My lecture last night was a *great* success, and this time I wasn't long-
suffering but just demolished old Blackmur (quite politely, most of the
time); he was incredibly rude both to me and two members of the audience.

I felt *so* good when it was over; the audience was excited and had a wonderful time; Robert Fitzgerald said all the lectures had been good and this one was best of all. Louise Keeley (that girl who is the graduate student's wife and who had been so angry that day at Edward Cone's when people talked about *Elektra*'s being lewd and obscene) said that almost the whole audience had been vexed and shocked at the last couple of lectures at Blackmur, and that even in the first ones his attitude had been apparent to them; she said she'd talked about it with several people including Edward Cone and they'd all thought it was simply jealousy on Blackmur's part.

I really felt so gay-serious, competent, and inspired while I talked, and was able to think of long elaborate sentences, lovely phrases, attractive informalities, etc. — so that the impromptu parts were better than the written ones.

I was so glad to learn from this girl that the audience had known all along how long-suffering I'd been, and was pleased when I finally acted.

Fergusson just dropped by — I'm in my office — and told me how much he enjoyed the lectures and talked for a while about Auden. And now, Blackmur has just dropped by; he was very polite, as was I; apparently the combination of jealousy, someone else having the center of the stage, and having too much to drink was too much for him.

Life is so *commonplace* without you — with you I feel like a Rilke poem; maybe in the end this will make me write them. Seriously, he's got to seem to me a sort of symbol of the real poet of our age — what to write like to be the opposite of the Others.

I've just been reading part of a book about the first few weeks of the South Pacific War, so far as the Air Force was concerned. They're *so* touching; they had nothing, were just shot to pieces, tried so bravely to do what they could. I had practically my old feeling of wanting to write poems about them immediately.

I think I'll try to telephone you this instant. I *miss* you.

Afterwards

Wasn't that a wonderful connection? I felt as if our ears were touching.

John Crowe Ransom described the kind of demolition Jarrell used on Blackmur, saying, "More than once I had seen him rising in the academic forum when the official speaker had finished, and . . . ruining him with three or four perfect satirical sentences uttered in that high and piercing voice." (RJ) Jarrell wrote in another letter, "Gee, I was pleased to get it all obvious in the last lecture. I don't know how I did it so well, Pallas Athena certainly came to my aid, good grey-eyed one."

[May 6, 1952]

When I got home from dinner there was my Liebfraumilch (well-named) and the cute bottle of beer, too. You're so sweet to me — it was a lovely surprise on top of all the others that came this morning. I put them in the ice-box immediately. All I needed was you to drink them with me, especially since the radio, told it's my birthday, is playing *Das Lied von der Erde* — just started.

At noon it became a wonderful day, I took a long walk over by the big estate and by most of our favorite houses. You remember the old dog that growled at us one day? Today he was lying there just as ever, growling at the postman. Later I saw a cute, half-grown dachshund, a beautiful light red, long-haired, very affectionate one. Our big estate is prettier than ever with all the leaves; there was a tremendous tree all of whose leaves were a beige-brown-violet; with the sun coming thru them they were so pretty and strange you could hardly believe it.

I've been sorting out papers and books and beginning on packing. Isn't that thrilling? I found this poem which I thought I'd send you. I wrote it about a year and a half ago. In it I have the Sphinx ask a queer mocking riddle of Oedipus (instead of the real one), one he can't miss because She's the answer to it and stands for the life he gets by answering: killing his father, marrying his mother, and finally blinding himself with his own hands. And it's all supposed to stand for the fate of the superior person (Him who sees) isolated from his kind.

The first stanza means that the ones who didn't guess and died reluctantly like ordinary mortals, killed by me (the Sphinx) are luckier than you, who in the end will be alone, will blind yourself, will wish for death and not die for a while. The poem's supposed to have a grim enigmatic sound like something one of the oracles would say.

THE SPHINX'S RIDDLE TO OEDIPUS

Not to have guessed is better: what is, ends,
But among fellows, with reluctance,
Clasped by the Woman-Breasted, Lion-Pawed.

To have clasped in one's own arms a mother,
To have killed with one's own hands a father—
Is not this, Lame One, to have been alone?

The seer is doomed for seeing; to understand
Is to tear out one's own eyes with one's own hands.
But speak: what has a woman's breasts, a lion's paws?

You stand at midday in the marketplace
Before your life: to see is to have spoken.
— Yet to see, Blind One, is to be alone.

It's funny — in one way this is a lonely birthday, since there's nobody
here; but really I don't feel one bit alone, because of thee. And my California birthday-to-come is my real birthday this year.

TO MARY VON SCHRADER

[May 1952]

Old Tom's free. Free! Lectures all done, all done. The last lecture was a
great success, considerably more of one than I expected it to be; I finished
by reading them three Auden poems, one a new hard wonderful one, and
the audience just *bubbled* with delight. It's fun reading somebody else's
poems quite well so that an audience is much affected — you have a sort of
objective powerful actor-ish feeling that's very different from the Sincere
feeling you have with your own. Even old Blackmur behaved properly, i.e.
sat there expressionlessly and said hardly a word. Later Fergusson said how
splendid the lectures all had been; that this was what they'd meant such lectures to be, *about* the poems, and that it was plain I really knew Auden.
There was the usual party afterwards, I stayed until 12:30 and Bob and
Louise Keeley took me home. I gave them some of the Liebfraumilch to
drink and they told me some unimaginably funny stories about John Berryman as The Great Unappreciated Theoretical Lover; I'll tell them soon as I
get to California. They're too long to write.

That German who admired so much turned out to be a pretty well-
known writer named [Erich] Kahler, and a good friend of Hannah's. I'm to
spend part of the evening with him and his Austrian wife on Tuesday.

Well, as you see, these last two days have been Fine Rewarding Days for
the Public Me, as for the private me, it misses you. I was delighted to learn
from you about Goethe's saying *Dear Sister* — I'd completely forgotten
that; or rather, when I read it it must have made no impression on me, I
didn't have a sister then.

Got my official Leave of Absence for next year from Woman's College.

Read my small class "The Witch of Coös" and they were carried away.
One who'd heard Frost read it told me I read it better. I beamed modestly.
Frost reads it as a comic New England dialogue poem and pretty well kills
the serious poem it is.

Between doing all these things I read an advertisement that amused me.
It was for an Austin and I copy it for Thee:

AUSTIN (We sell 'em by the carload)

When it's loving you would get
There's nothing like the Somerset,
Big wide seats, front and rear,
Safety door locks, — You needn't fear.
Man, it's the thrill of your life
Guaranteed to please your wife.

What will they advertise next?

Gee, I'm going to work peacefully and well on Writing this fall in Laguna: poems and *Pictures from an Institution* and we can do early work on
The Ladies. I'm not even going to read silly magazines, but live in Ewigkeit
with thee.

Can't wait to see your reply to the handwriting analysis letter, wasn't it
uncanny?

TO MARY VON SCHRADER

[Northford, Connecticut]
[May 19, 1952]

I didn't go to bed until two, alas, and woke up at seven, alas. I've been
having a good time with Cleanth and Tinkum. They live in a dovey house
on top of a hill all covered with lovely forest. It is a 1720 salt box that was
moved there plank by beam. There are floor boards 14 inches wide, two
fireplaces where you can bake bread in the ovens, a big brook, a view across
the valley to a village, and so on and so forth. It is really something — few
and simple furniture.

Red got here in the middle of the afternoon, with Eleanor Clark — you
remember the one who wrote that book about Rome [*Rome and a Villa*]?
She's in her forties; really quite nice looking, intelligent, seemingly very
nice. She occasionally says words or has intonations quite like Delmore
Schwartz, and as he is a man with a heavy slablike face, this is disquieting.
Red looks and sounds wonderful — you don't see any tension in his face at
all; being divorced has certainly worked wonders for his spirits. Divorce is a
wonderful thing — think I'll write an article called that for the *Ladies Home
Journal.*

Have you ever seen anybody playing Diabolo? With two sticks, connected by a string, you spin a grooved rubber doughnut rather like a yoyo:
and Eleanor Clark can throw it about thirty feet in the air and then catch
it — looks extraordinary.

TO MARY VON SCHRADER

[May 20, 1952]

I'm on the train to New York. I certainly had a good time! Red was as gay as could be — he, Eleanor Clark, Cleanth, Tinkum and I even had a soft ball game in the afternoon, using a piece of tree limb for a bat and a tennis ball tied in a handkerchief for a ball. We read some Hardy poems after that, Red and Cleanth and I are all crazy about his poetry. Red and Eleanor left for New York in the afternoon and Cleanth and Tinkum and I had such a nice evening together. I couldn't resist telling them about you — they were delighted, and very eager to meet you, and want us to visit them whenever we're in the east. I have a really homey feeling with them.

Eleanor Clark was right nice and surprisingly athletic, but oh, that slight Delmore Schwartz–New Yorkishness! Red's almost finished a very long poem — a narrative several thousands of lines about Jefferson. When I woke up Sunday morning I had such a strong hunch that he'd win the Pulitzer Prize that I told Red about it. I hope I turn out to be a prophet.

Cleanth told me a wonderful dream he had: that Colonel Sartoris, one of the cats, had come to him and said he wanted to take him out in the forest to meet a friend of his, a coon; they went, and pulled themselves with some difficulty into a hollow tree, and there was the coon — Cleanth could remember how nervously Colonel Sartoris looked into his face, as they talked, to see whether his two friends liked each other. Cleanth had forgotten this, but Tinkum remembered that the coon had turned hand springs in his elation at having a human friend. You're *my* Human Friend!

It was such a wonderful place for cats and human beings to live — their cats had a little square hole cut for them in the cellar, and they could get outside and in whenever they pleased. One of their cats has 28 toes — his front feet look as if he were wearing boxing gloves.

I tore a hole in the seat of my trousers (really their dog did it) and Tinkum mended it surprisingly well. Once how vexed I'd have been at having to spend a day in New York, seeing different people, with patched trousers — now the New Jarrell has the comfortable feeling, "Why not? It's the same me, isn't it? What difference can a patch make?"

Look at those "a's" and "o's" aren't they a scream? They're so open (indicating an Open Nature) that I had to close one up because it was a "u". This is really my Old Friends weekend. I'll be seeing Bernard and Elizabeth Bishop today and then back to pack. To PACK!

You really appreciated that handwriting analysis in a big way. It *was* extraordinary, wasn't it? I don't believe any of my friends could have done as well in describing me. I think all you said about her ability is true — I wonder if I could ever do that well, though. She's better than Pierre [Emmanuel]. We'll see how I improve. It amuses me how my handwriting has changed in the last seven or eight months. Wonder how my old would have been analyzed?

Gee, I'm impatient for these last days to be over. I'm like somebody in the midst of *Get ready, Get set, Go!* having to eat and sleep and cook and write, when all I want to do is crouch there tense all over waiting for that *Go!*

Good-bye for a little, I'll phone you tomorrow. O Laguna! O California!

Warren's narrative poem about Jefferson was entitled Brother to Dragons *and was published in 1953. In his review of the book in the* New York Times Book Review, *August 23, 1953, Jarrell described it as "Warren's best book ... an event, a great one." It did not win the Pulitzer Prize.*

Bloomington, Indiana / Laguna Beach, California, June 1952–January 1953

🍂

*T*he break between the end of Princeton classes and the start of Jarrell's summer teaching job at the Indiana University School of Letters gave him a month-long holiday, which he spent in Laguna Beach, playing tennis and taking long walks along the beach. In Laguna Beach, Jarrell stayed in an apartment on Sunset Terrace and his hi-fi stayed with Mary in Emerald Bay. Many hours were spent sunning on Mary's deck, translating a few lines in a few Rilke poems, "customizing" her Oldsmobile in his head, and watching the waves lap the rocks where the seals were barking. Beatrice and Alleyne were with their father, which left Jarrell and Mary free to listen to Strauss and Mahler and read Moore, Thomas, and Ransom. There was an occasional weekend in Pasadena with Mary's mother; a day at the Los Angeles County Museum to see the Henry Moore miniatures; and another day with Mary's friends Marjorie and Woody Dickinson to see the Post-Impressionist paintings at Edward G. Robinson's home. Sundays were devoted to the sports-car races in Inglewood at the Carroll Speedway, and other days they loitered in racing-car garages, straining to catch what drivers like Ted Coppel, Stirling Moss, and Phil Hill were telling their mechanics. Jarrell self-consciously avoided staring at the drivers and wouldn't have dreamed of speaking to one of them.

The only letter Jarrell wrote during this month in Laguna Beach was to Harry Ford at Knopf, accepting the advance they had offered for Pictures from an Institution and Poetry and the Age. Jarrell wrote that he wanted the advance because "I'd love to get a secondhand MG to fool around with and improve my sports-car driving in."

Toward the end of June, Jarrell flew to Bloomington, Indiana, to join the faculty of the School of Letters for approximately one month.

The Indiana University School of Letters was founded by John Crowe Ransom as a school of literary criticism to "teach it to those who teach it." Among the previous faculty members were Jacques Barzun, R. P. Blackmur, Alfred Kazin, Lionel Trilling, Delmore Schwartz, and Allen Tate. The current faculty included Kenneth Burke, Francis Fergusson, Robert Fitzgerald, Leslie Fiedler, Jarrell, and Ransom.

TO MARY VON SCHRADER

[Bloomington, Indiana]

[June 1952]

Beloved:

It's plain to me that people get paid $1500 for *living* here for six weeks, not for teaching. I taught for two hours this morning and that was fun — but the rest, oh boy! It's so hot that when you take a drink of iced coffee sweat breaks out all over you. It was 102 yesterday and no expected change today.

They very sweetly met me at the airport; but they'd done nothing about getting rooms for the faculty who are rooming in the dormitory — we get what was left. Robert Fitzgerald had come pretty early, got a good room, and then been moved out of it because they were vacating that wing — was he sore!

I'm in a room that looks exactly like three closets in a row, with a double-decker cot, two desks, two bureaus and (after you come in thru the main door) three doors all in a row — one to a closet, two to a closet, and three to a little closet with a washbasin that is shared with the person next door. My new room has all this; but a washbowl of its own and two feet more width. To think that 48 hours ago I was in the guest room in Pasadena. How art the mighty fallen! To your tents, O Israel! Wish I *had* a tent, this campus is very wooded and green and cool-looking.

I'm writing this in an air-conditioned Education Library; as I came up the steps I heard a *big* Negro in striped gabardine trousers, T-shirt, and a white linen cap say: "I said, 'They're too fast for ends, what you want to make 'em is guards.' "

I've found a giant, deserted, air-conditioned classroom and this is where I'm going to write you and my articles; the weather's lovely *here*.

I played some ping-pong in the afternoon and evening (there are two good players) so I didn't have too bad a day. The papers are full of accounts of heat victims, heat suicides, heat fights, heat remedies — the cartoon on the editorial page was about the heat, too. And added to the heat are, for me, quite a number of insect bites. I suppose I got them while walking on the grass at the cocktail party "welcoming" us. While I was outside I got into a long, enthusiastic conversation about science fiction. I talked a lot. When I don't have a good time at such things I go home feeling that parties aren't much, but that I've behaved admirably; when I infrequently *do* have a good time I go home feeling guilty, guilty for talking too much and showing off. It's pathetically easy for me to feel dissatisfied with myself and generally guilty. I'm so glad to have *you,* you make me feel good and like the Golden Age's favorite brother.

Everything we did last month was such *fun* — the swimming and the cars and the Carroll Speedway and the Golden Gate Races — oh, wasn't Phil Hill marvelous? All that gearing-down without a clutch — and then winning! And all the drives we took, and eating at the Mexican place, and dancing in the kitchen, and reading poems. Life without you is so *commonplace* — it wouldn't attract a tree-frog.

Thy
Randall

TO MARY VON SCHRADER

[June 1952]

I feel awfully cheered: yesterday was a couple of degrees cooler and less humid, there's about to be a thunderstorm (if we're lucky) this morning, and Mr. Ransom's public lecture last night was awfully good and interesting. Afterwards, at the party Ransom said that in 1930 or so Frost came to Nashville and that he entertained Frost and all the local poets one evening. He said that Frost pretty much started a monologue, and kept on, and the hours went by, and the poets went home one by one, and finally Frost was left there all alone with Mr. Ransom; Frost said, "Well, I guess I'd better be getting home. My wife told me not to stay out late." So Mr. Ransom drove him to his hotel; as they got there a winter dawn was breaking, and Mr. Ransom had just time to get breakfast before driving out to his eight o'clock class. It's been lots of fun seeing Mr. Ransom — I'm ever so fond of him. I'm going to sit in on one of his classes tomorrow.

Yesterday afternoon I went swimming in a wonderful limestone quarry with Robert [Fitzgerald] and Francis Fergusson and his little girl. I spent most of my time paddling around on a beautiful big log. A neighboring quarry had an island of great blocks that looked like Agamemnon's palace at Mycenae. Floating in the water holding onto the log is the most bearable thing you can do in this heat. I wish we'd stayed longer — so far as I'm concerned we left much too soon.

This is so dull and academic compared with Boulder that it's funny. The

School of Letters *feels* like a summer school, not like some special literary thing — and it does nothing but go to classes and, once a week in the evening, attend a public lecture; it has no social existence, no live or individual peculiar existence. It's just supernaturally boring, really, except when one is teaching; still, I should count my blessings — today's only about 90.

I feel just as you do about being apart. All the reality and joy go out of everything. I feel as if I were enchanted into being an unhappy, inconsequential, unreal Other Self and couldn't even be my real self till I get back to It where It stays with you. Oh, sister, I love you. I love you. Let's not ever be apart again — not ever, EVER!

Randall

Fitzgerald described Jarrell swimming at the quarry "coming up for air, his hair plastered over his forehead, his line of mustache dripping, eyes shut tight in the delicate sallow bony face that at those times and at others had what I thought of as a Confederate *look — old-fashioned and rural and honorable and a little toothy or hungry. Once up and paddling and often laughing, he would talk about what had crossed his mind underwater . . ." (*RJ*)*

TO MARY VON SCHRADER

[June 1952]

Nobody here wears shorts but it is the best shorts country I ever saw — though, what you really need is a sort of air-conditioned birthday suit. It was 98 degrees official yesterday. This had the additional disadvantage of making people talk about it just endlessly.

Mr. Ransom is as cute and sweet as ever. The Hudsons had him to dinner, and *moi qui parle* (as James says) and alas, the Ubiquitous Critic, Leslie Fiedler. Mr. Ransom told a story that would go right into "The Age of Criticism" did not friendship forbid. It was about this wonderful freshman student he had who wrote him a *50 page* typed essay about Eliot's 32-line poem "Burbank with a Baedeker." All about its allusions, sources, etc. He told it entirely seriously and praisingly as an example of how wonderful students could be nowadays — didn't see a thing incongruous or disproportionate about it. I said gently that it was like Tristram Shandy, who took a year to write the story of the first day of his life.

Mr. Ransom has a brother who is an engineer with Bendix and who's invented a new shock absorber with which he drove Mr. Ransom over dirt roads at 70 miles an hour, in and out of ruts and ditches, etc. Mr. Ransom says this one will surely make his fortune.

There's a red MG (TC) parked every day by the Education building and I went and walked around it lovingly and looked it over for many minutes. How happy we're going to be when we get our own TC!

Well, the day passes. I'm sitting here sweating and soon I'll go out, mail this, buy a couple of cheap towels (linens not furnished) and lay plans to telephone you.

Richard Hudson taught in the English Department at Indiana University and was acting director of the School of Letters.

Leslie Fiedler, thirty-six, was a promising poet and critic just back from Rome, where he had been a Fulbright lecturer.

TO MARY VON SCHRADER

[June 1952]

I've found some lovely new Rilke poems in the library, plus a prose book of his I'd always meant to read; some of the poems are honeys. And when I got to the English office there were two letters waiting for me. I took them into the forestiest part of the campus and read them. I loved all you said about me, and about "the good, sweet years we have ahead." I felt so entirely yours, had hardly separated from you at all, and this bun-oven or double-boiler of a place disappeared and I was in Laguna or Boulder or Pasadena or all Our places.

Robert Fitzgerald and I ate dinner together and talked "Age of Criticism" talk about the literary-academic world and quite cheered ourselves up. He wants to go home to Connecticut as much as I want to go home to California.

Have to go to Kenneth Burke's public lecture at 8:15, have to sit on the platform with the rest of the Fellows, be introduced, help in the discussion later, etc. — worst part of *this* is, I'll be bundled up in a coat and tie. And 90 plus today.

Later

Burke's speech was just like a parody of everything in "Age of Criticism"; Robert and I looked at each other in mute awe. The audience shifted and yawned and half of them, even, saw how bad it was. It was so bad it was almost feeble-minded; so extravagantly mechanical and verbose and senseless and full of absolutely irrelevant free association that you felt a band of robbers had made up the speech and were *making* him deliver it, to his own disgrace, with a machine-gun trained on him.

Another dull party afterwards — all faculty husbands and wives, most homogenous. This morning I saw a Hindu girl in a sari, and I decided that was what the party needed — or a polar bear, or a Venus fly-trap, or *something*. I'd have been terribly bored except that Leslie Fiedler was very interesting and amusing. You really would like him — he's awfully nice; very appealing, looks so warm and human when he talks about his children.

I've gotten all the *Motor Sports Worlds* — you clever thing — both air-mail and regular mail. Weren't the pictures of Le Mans good? And Phil Hill's account? *Poor* Levegh, ahead for 23 hours! No wonder "even the mechanics cried."

I'm going swimming in the marble quarry again. About twenty or so people from the School of Letters go there, too. I can swim at least twice as far as when I came to Bloomington — and that's not far, either.

They're hopeful that this June will break the all-time heat record for days over 90, *but* a cold front has come as far south as Minnesota. Pray for that cold front. The heat has moved me to such desperation that I made funny jokes all thru lunch so that everybody laughed and laughed. I can't remember anything now except saying (in a note of despair) when the waitress brought us bread and butter plates with a little shallow circular spot of cherry jelly on each: "They've shot my plate."

Kenneth Burke, formerly a music critic for The Dial, *saw literature as "symbolic action" — that is, he viewed language as a haze of symbols. He was the author of* Counter-Statement, Attitudes Toward History, *and numerous other books. Jarrell's lecture "The Age of Criticism" followed Burke's.*

TO MARY VON SCHRADER

[June 1952]

[The lecture] went pretty well — lots of people seemed impressed by the speech and a good many seemed influenced by, or sympathetic to, the discussion afterwards, though lots of that was on such a low level it was funny — and bewildering. People would say that I'd said all criticism was bad and useless, say that I'd said the opposite of what I'd said, etc. The mediocre ones who love the present situation, want to become Critics, see in the way things are . . . their own personal treasure and salvation, were very upset — with them, it was as if, to a bunch of junior executives, I'd questioned Free Enterprise. I was rather emotionally effective and vivid and witty in the discussion, but had too much sense of dramatic excitement to talk with calm good sense as in a quiet conversation. I always get Carried Away, being a poet rather than a quiet discusser. Leslie Fiedler was much shocked at how elementary and absurd much of the discussion was . . . and he said to Dick Hudson, in a grim tone, "I'd better make *my* talk *very elementary."* I like Fiedler — he's very intelligent and much more restrained and pleasant than what he writes.

All in all I had rather a sense of how lonely you are when you come out on the side of life and risk-taking and thinking works of art are live and mysterious and unaccountable; on the side of everything that can't be institutionalized and handled and graded by Experts. Most academic highbrow people really do go along with the critical abstract categorizing mind, not the artist's, since that's the way things naturally seem to them.

TO MARY VON SCHRADER

[July 1952]

This will be rather a fast letter. Just spent 3½ hours giving two oral examinations for M.A.'s; sat on a sofa between Leslie and Robert. One guy was unspeakably bad about everything, hadn't read almost anything you asked about so that you were just *embarrassed.* The other was good, very good about modern literature but hadn't read anything *else,* was worse than a good sophomore. Burke was as bad as ever and all of it was sort of interesting in a gruesome way. But would you believe it, they passed them both, just telling them to read some old stuff. Robert and Leslie and I were sick about it, it was such a farce. Robert's voice trembled and his face got red he was so angry. It really was shocking, particularly since they're the first two to get M.A.'s in Criticism from the School of Letters. The three of us felt our despair and vexation at the Older Generation back in full force. One of the two candidates was so bad that his hour and a half was like a complete, shameful, abject, final exposure of his absolute non-existence. Dick Hudson felt about the orals exactly the way we did.

I've got to feel like the Three Musketeers or something when with Robert and Leslie. I noticed on the list of Fellows on the School of Letters stationery that Fiedler, Fitzgerald and Jarrell come in alphabetical succession, in a Little Group, and it's been like that this summer. You'll be crazy about Leslie and Robert — they are really *fun* to be with.

These are Busy Days: last classes, last papers, final grades, Leslie's lecture, and more cocktail parties — ugh, ugh! Mortal men, man, mortal men!

(Later — another day later)

Leslie gave the most incredibly wonderful lecture on Criticism last night. It was very like "The Age of Criticism" in some ways (we took exactly the same line, I agreed with *every word* he said) but he made his general and reasoned-out and an explicit, sensible, absolutely convincing Statement, not something so poetic as mine. Everybody, practically, was over-whelmed. And his answers to questions would have done credit to Aristotle, Dr. Johnson, and Lenin rolled into one — never *saw* anybody so good at Reasoning, Convincing, and Stating in Wonderful Form right while standing there thinking about it.

Robert and I were so happy we could hardly go to sleep. This conference has really been a triumph for the Light and Right, for those with Feeling Hearts and Seeing Eyes. (But a few, of course, have Seeing Eye Dogs.) I'm really awfully glad I happened to be at the School of Letters, in spite of this heat and the misery of being separated from thee. I really have learned some things and learned to feel good about the possibilities of the new generation of critics and writers, the ones that'll finally take the places (some of the places) of the Old Monuments.

If any of us could ever Get Power Over a creative-writing set-up at some school we could try to have Leslie and Robert and *moi qui parle* and Peter Taylor. Well, these are just innocent hopeful dreams, but someday something like them might well happen.

TO MARY VON SCHRADER

[July 1952]

At last my translation's done ["Requiem for the Death of a Boy"] and I send it to thee; I read it to Robert last night and he was overwhelmed — said hearing it was a mesmeric experience, or words to that effect. He said that after hearing it and seeing how like it was to the Rilke and how unlike [J.B.] Leishman's was, he couldn't understand how the Leishman could have had such an effect on him, and have seemed so good. Incidentally, almost *always* when mine's different from Leishman's it's the same as, or much closer to, the Rilke.

Yesterday it was 103 but by swimming in the afternoon I survived. Last night I heard recordings of *Don Quixote* and some Beethoven and Mozart. I miss you so much when I listen to music. Oh, my best beloved.

Knopf said (in reply to my letter) that I could tell — since they were publishing my critical book which would sell decidedly less than the novel — that they'd almost certainly print the novel unless something went badly wrong. So I think I'll just go ahead with them — let them give me the $500 advance on the critical book when I give it to them in late September, and then the advance on *Pictures* later. I haven't managed to write any articles here. It's just too hot and dormitory-ish; I got *Partisan* to postpone that one for two months, have made notes for the Frost one for *Kenyon,* and will write it out during the first ten days I'm home with my Mary.

Were there some good foreign car advertisements in the *Times?* Somebody wanted to sell that Bugatti we saw at the Auto Sports Show in New York for $3,000; and somebody in San Antonio wanted to sell a '49 TC (new tires, excellent engine, mint) for $950. I'll put the whole page in my suitcase for us to read together.

Just think, this is the last letter and three days from now I'll *be* there never to leave your side again, oh bliss. Oh, mermaid. I'm coming on TWA's flight 17, the one leaving Chicago at 6 and arriving at Los Angeles Thursday at 11:00 P.M. Pacific Time. How I want my welcome kiss and to be in your arms again. You do know, don't you, darling Mary, how different you are from everyone else? How different you've made me? All I want is to be with you and have the little girls with us. Be mine always. Don't ever change. I think you and I had better burn our letters some Midsummer's Eve when we're about 102 and think we might die. People will be able to see the flames for miles.

TO JOHN CROWE RANSOM

166 Sunset Terrace
Laguna Beach
August 10, 1952

Dear Mr. Ransom:

This is a letter from a really exhausted man, but from one that feels awfully good; I'm hopeful that I've really done the best I could with Frost ["To the Laodiceans," *Kenyon Review,* Autumn 1952]. I hope that this will arrive on the afternoon of the 12th, I'm mailing it on the evening of the 10th, and sending you a telegram at the same time, so that you'll know it's on the way if it doesn't get there till the morning of the 13th. I'm quite eager to have proofs, as you can imagine — would you send me two copies if it's convenient? My address here in Laguna Beach is, until the 22nd of August, 166 Sunset Terrace; from the 22nd till the end of the month it's 880 South Arroyo Boulevard, Pasadena, California.

I had a wonderful time at the School of Letters, and am looking forward very much to being at it two summers from now, when you'll be there again; I'll write more at length when I get a little less dazed — I've been working on this almost all my waking hours for quite some time.

Yours,
Randall

TO HANNAH ARENDT

[September 1952]

Dear Hannah:

I've meant to write for months, but really do now because I've a poem to send you, one that I hope and believe you'll think one of my best ["Woman"]. (It's in a new kind of verse — you use either pentameter or hexameter lines, varying for different effects. I like it better than straight blank verse.) And I've translated no end of Rilke — "Requiem for the Death of a Boy," "The Great Night," "Death," four more. Will send some of them later.

I'm getting along well — I taught for six weeks at The School of Letters in Indiana and liked *very* much Leslie Fiedler — was surprised to, otherwise I've been out here.

Mary and I will be getting married any week now, i.e. soon as we can: i.e., last week in October. I lead *such* a different life out here — it will feel funny to be back at a university in February, with Mary, Alleyne, Beatrice, Schatzel (dachshund) and Kitzel (kitten).

I've done all but the last two or three days' work on my criticism book — Knopf is going to publish it and he's already given me an advance; they also want to print *Pictures from an Institution* when I get it done — I'm going to do this during October and November.

I certainly do miss you; you'll *surely* need to come out to Illinois this spring, won't you? to give the Ark of the Covenant to a library in Cairo, Illinois, or such. I had a letter from Alfred Kazin saying what a good time you were having in Europe, and when I, astonishingly to me, answered it, I asked your address but didn't get it. Tell me about Europe.

I hope Heinrich likes "Woman" too; tell me what he thinks of it. Do send me a *fast* scrappy appreciation.

Love,
Randall

I'll send you my translation of "Requiem for the Death of a Boy" next letter; I'm very eager for you to see it. It's the best translation I've ever done, I think. What are you writing or doing, and where are you, and tell me all about Europe, and so forth.

TO JOHN CROWE RANSOM

[October 1952]

Dear Mr. Ransom:

I'm delighted that you liked the Frost, and was pleased to have it first in the magazine; and I *loved* the little typographical error about the spider web, *a sudden passing pullet* (bullet) *shook it dry* — it delights me to think of most of the readers laughing and a few knitting their brows.

I was really much flattered to be asked for part of my prose book — a comedy, I call it, since it's hardly a novel. I've copied out for you, and send, the first book, which I think does pretty well by itself; there are two parts which would do as well or better: one, a little shorter, is a general treatment of Benton College in (quite particular) terms of an old teacher of Creative Writing named Camille Turner Batterson (this part's almost like a short story); the other part is the story of Gertrude at Art Night, a yearly event at which the painting and sculpture and drama departments have an exhibition and a writer makes a speech. One is considerably more serious than Book I and the other is considerably funnier (Peter's read both and can give you an idea of them). I tell you about them because I don't want to print the first book by itself unless you think you'd have room for them later on, *if* you liked them of course. You see why this is: as long as I have the first book for an introduction I can arrange some of the other parts and print them in a magazine, but without the first part I'd be rather at a loss.

I have the whole book done except for thirty or forty pages here and there. I'll have it entirely finished by the first or second week of January, I think. I could send you the whole thing to see and select from. If you like this part and want to print it you might just say that you expect to print other portions later.

Peter [Taylor] sounds very happy to be there [Kenyon College]; I'm certainly going to miss him at Greensboro when I get back next year.

I don't want the sight-unseen part of this *Pictures from an Institution* deal to be in any way troublesome to you: if you feel it would be a lot better to see them now, the other two parts, I could send one of them complete and the other 9/10 done — write me airmail Special Delivery here at Laguna Beach if you'd like that. I just don't have proper copies of them.

I can't wait to see Red's long poem [*Brother to Dragons*]. I'm awfully glad you're printing that much of it in *Kenyon*. I think it makes so much

difference to do things like that; it would take a magazine like *Partisan* a
couple of years to find room for a couple of pages since it's poetry.

I am just about to be married again (on November 8, to Mary von
Schrader), my mother's out here to be at the wedding and I'm more or less
In the Midst of Things. I hope you'll let Mary sit with me at your class at
the School of Letters summer after next, if we're all there; she is crazy about
your poetry, and would very much like to.

Affectionately,

Randall

*On the subject of the wedding, Jarrell said, "Just think, pet cat, we're proba-
bly the only people in the world getting married on the eighth so we can be at
Madera [California] on the tenth." In her memoir "The Group of Two"
in* Randall Jarrell 1914–1965, *Mary wrote, "It was a fine, bright, smog-
free eighth in Pasadena, as dry and glittering as California used to be in the
twenties. That, and being able to see Mt. Wilson Observatory, seemed the
main topic of the guests and Randall muttered to me, 'One touch of weather
makes the whole world kin.' But it was* Gemütlichkeit *with my friends of
thirty years perpetuating us in Kodachrome in front of portraits and brasses
in my mother's home. Randall's dark eyes lingered on mine above our cham-
pagne as we toasted* ewig Freundschaft *to each other, ewig, ewig.
Ländlers on Helen [Dengler's] accordion ebbed and flowed in the rooms,
and it was dark when our last goodbyes drifted off into that eucalyptus-
scented air. Im augenblick Madera, and two Jarrells perched on a rail
fence oblivious of all save ourselves and Phil Hill racing the first C-Jag in
this country."*

*Greetings and gifts came from the Taylors and the Ransoms in Gam-
bier, the Leontievs in Cambridge, and the Lowells in Amsterdam. A Liszt
recording came from Edward Cone, and a tray from the Fitzgeralds, accompanied by Eliot's line "For lingering in the chambers of the sea."*

TO JOHN CROWE RANSOM

[November 1952]

Dear Mr. Ransom:

I just got home from a trip Mary and I took to Northern California
(Southern California talks of itself as the Southland, and is hardly even a
part of the Union — when you mail letters to the rest of the country you
drop them into a post-office-slot marked *The States*) and found your letter

John Crowe Ransom

waiting for me. But before I answer it I want to thank you for the telegram from all of you, which was a *great* pleasure to us.

As for the relation of Dwight Robbins to Harold Taylor [president of Sarah Lawrence College], I'd better talk at length. *My* President is a Molière-esque type, the type of all such presidents, and is pretty different from Taylor, but he's also like him in some notable way. The real trouble here is this: *any* character who's a curly-haired young president of a progressive college will seem (to people in the world of colleges) to be Harold Taylor because there's only one curly-haired young president of a progressive college, Harold Taylor. I'll talk some about differences and similarities. Mrs. Taylor is an ordinarily unpleasant Englishwoman, not within a million leagues of my fabulous South African; the Taylors have two ordinary children, no growling Derek; they have an ordinary English sheepdog, no Afghan twins; Taylor himself is a Canadian; a philosopher not a sociologist; was never an Olympic diver or anything of the sort; didn't hire lots of Rhodes Scholars; isn't a sort of *idiot savant* of Success like Robbins, but is much shrewder, more pretentious and hypocritical, more intellectual, etc., was an Assistant Professor metamorphosed into a President, not a professional educator like Robbins. He didn't come from the Lower Depths à la Gatsby, and has perfectly ordinary manners. But my Dwight Robbins' appearance, perpetual youngness, perfect adjustment to his surroundings, are modelled on Taylor's (Taylor's conversation is quite unlike Robbins', Robbins talks ordinary President-banalities, Taylor likes to sound as cultivated as possible, as versatile as possible, like Renaissance Man being pals with Stephen Spender.)

In other words, I think Taylor is like my Dwight Robbins (except for a few particulars like curly hair, ingenuous sincerity) only insofar as he's like the general type of such Boy Wonder executives, he was mostly a point of departure for me, but I did take several steps before departing.

But this is all different from the question: *will* this part of the book get me or *Kenyon* into trouble as being too like Taylor? I just don't have the knowledge or training to judge. Knopf seems sure it wants to publish the finished book, and no fears about libel have occurred to it, but *The New Yorker,* when Peter showed it to them, was afraid (though it's famous for being afraid of anything of the sort) — they wanted to print most of the book, and kept it a long time, but couldn't find any way to divide it into installments complete in themselves. I would be more than glad to make any changes you and Phil [Rice] think necessary; I couldn't make essential changes like having Pamela Robbins come from Independence, but I could, with tears, change smaller things.

This is the only section of the book that would raise any Problems of this Nature. My lady writer, Gertrude, reminds people violently of five or six lady writers, whichever one they happen to know, but there are many deplorable writers of the sort, just as, alas, there's only one young president of a progressive college.

I've taken it for granted that all this will delay the piece to the next issue (assuming that the piece seemed safe or that we can make changes which will get it safe); probably I'll have the new parts of the book finished by then, and you can look at it in its completed form and pick whatever parts you like.

Benton College is completely synthetic, fanciful, typical; its education is like the education at Sarah Lawrence, but there is no teacher or student at Sarah Lawrence with *any* resemblance to my people at Benton — Dwight Robbins is the only human resemblance. My Dwight Robbins is so different from Taylor that as you'll see later in the book I rather like Robbins, and think about him, "Poor creature, if he could only become human!" But Taylor seems to me a smarter, more disingenuous, more unpleasant man, a real differentiated individual — Robbins is just a type, inhuman because he's no more than a type.

I do hope this hasn't been a trouble to you; whatever you think best, and if you think some changes are essential, write me and I'll make them. I'd even sacrifice the curly hair, though with as many tears as a princess in a fairy tale.

Affectionately,
Randall

TO HANNAH ARENDT

[December 3, 1952]

Dear Hannah:

I feel as if I should begin, *Loved Reader!* after your loved letter about the Frost article. I've made you an extra copy of Book II of my Benton book (about ¾ of it is new, just written in the last month) and send it as a Christmas card. Book I is in the winter *Kenyon Review;* this'll be in Spring. Also, I'll tell you where two other articles are: one about Marianne Moore ["Thoughts about Marianne Moore"] is in *Partisan* [volume 19, 1952] and a short one about Williams ["The Situation of a Poet"] is in that new magazine *Perspective.* There is also a German version of the short article, in the German edition of *Perspective.* Oh, what a writer I am in German: I can't read me, even. Did you know that I am an "Amerikanischer Flieger-Soldat" who was "in Nashville, Tennessee, einer alten Stadt der Südstaaten-Aristokratie, geboren"? I was disappointed with my German: it's very *German* German, doesn't look a bit like Rilke.

Here — if I get it typed off this morning — is the best Rilke I've done ["Requiem for the Death of a Boy"]. Alas, my German isn't a *bit* better: if I translate, how can I find time to learn German? if I don't translate, I forget about German.

I couldn't be happier or better off. We'll be here until February, the first week — then at Illinois.

I hate to think of Heinrich's going to Bard four times a week. Tell him how much I miss seeing him; and you know how much I miss seeing you.

The parts of your letter about Germany and England were especially interesting: 1500 people at that lecture! I was amazed to see, from this morning's Gallup Poll in the newspaper, that even Australians read more than Americans.

If you ever send me another poem-without-English I will weep like a child. I have a vague dictionaryless impression of it, and when I get to Pasadena where my little blue dictionary is I'll have a clear dictionaried one.

I think you could do a better article on my poetry without English than other people with. I *was* lucky enough last spring to have a quite good though quite strange one written (in the March 1952 *Poetry*) by Parker Tyler. It's almost entirely about the fairy tale subconscious subjective side of the poetry, and is sometimes exaggerated, worst about Freudian puns, but it's surprisingly good, a real labor of love and I learned from it several — more than several — things I had no idea of. (If you read it read it with a kind heart, making allowances.) It felt strange and lovely to me: as if I were named, like that [fictional] Danish family, Night and Day, and somebody had written a long detailed piece about Night, not knowing the Day existed that *I'd* been paying more attention to.

I will start typing the Rilke. I hope you have a *very* happy Christmas, and that everything goes as well for you as it does for me — I couldn't wish more.

Love,
Randall

P.S. Proverb: Let not the Old year go down upon the order of thy writing! (Found in a goatskin bag, all covered with bitumen, beside the Dead Sea.)

* * *

Becoming more objective about California, Jarrell called it "the world of the future," and what he had observed during the past few months became the basis for his first mass-culture piece, "The Taste of the Age." What he learned from interviews with fifth-grader Beatrice and eighth-grader Alleyne informed his illustrative section on current grammar-school education. Jarrell wrote:

Sitting in my living room by the nice warm fire . . . I thought of some samples I had seen just that winter [when] I had occasion to talk with some fifth-grade students and some eighth-grade students. I had gone to a class of theirs; I had even gone carolling, in a truck, with some Girl Scouts and their Scoutmistress, and been dismayed at all the carols I didn't know —

I was not dismayed at the things the children hadn't known, I was overawed . . . Half the fifth-grade children — you won't, just as I couldn't, believe this — didn't know who Jonah was; only a few had ever heard of King Arthur. When I asked an eighth-grade student about King Arthur she laughed at my question, and said: "Of course I know who King Arthur was." My heart warmed to her "of course." But she didn't know who Lancelot was, didn't know who Guinevere was; she had never heard of Sir Galahad. I realized with a pang the truth of the line of poetry that speaks of "those familiar, now unfamiliar knights that sought the Grail." I left the Knights of the Round Table for history: she didn't know who Charlemagne was.

She didn't know who Charlemagne was! And she had never heard of Alexander the Great; her class had "had Rome," but she didn't remember anything about Julius Caesar, though she knew his name . . .

But all these had been questions of literature, theology, and European history; maybe there are more important things for students to know. . . . She had been taught, I found out, to conduct a meeting, to nominate, and to second nominations; she had been taught — I thought this far-fetched and truly imaginative — the right sort of story to tell an eighteen-months-old baby; and she had learned in her Domestic Science class to bake a date-pudding, to make a dirndl skirt, and from the remnants of the cloth to make a drawstring carryall . . . I felt a senseless depression at this; and thought, to alleviate it, of the date-pudding she would be able to make me.

Champaign-Urbana, Illinois / Laguna Beach, California, February–September 1953

*I*n mid-January of 1953, Mary readied the house at Emerald Bay for renters and Jarrell drove alone in the heavily packed Oldsmobile to meet his classes on time at the University of Illinois. Mary, the girls, Schatzel, and Kitzel arrived there by plane ten days later.

Jarrell's leave of absence from the Woman's College had been extended to enable him to teach the spring semester at Illinois, and it was a busy four months. The cultural events were hard to resist, and the social events seemed obligatory, as he was being considered for a permanent position in the English department. For once in his life, Jarrell had hardly any time to read, and there was no time to write, except to finish "The Taste of the Age" for his formal lecture to a large evening audience.

During the first weeks in Illinois, Kitzel, the cat, was hit by a car and killed, but Maggie Stoddard, the wife of the president of the university, found a handsome tortoise-shell Persian to console the grieving Beatrice. Jarrell named him Elfie after a pet cow belonging to Miss Batterson, a character in his novel.

Jarrell cried for joy when Mackie telegraphed that she could not keep Kitten and Jarrell could have him back. Kitten, ten years old, petted, praised, and always "included," knew he was not merely one more pet in the house, like Schatzel or the new cat, Elfie; he was Kitten, Randall's Kitten. They played a game of wits and reflexes something like tennis, where Jarrell flicked the end of a necktie just out of Kitten's reach — if he could. They ranged over rugs and furniture after the flicking tie with the easy grace and skill of two matched players who had never been clumsy at anything. When Kitten wanted a game and thought Jarrell had been writing too long, he would stand in the middle of the room and make a long, drawn-out wail of vexation that brought Jarrell to his feet; or he would take a *stance in front of Jarrell's chair, where Jarrell was reading, and, with his ankles together and his tail floating, would stare up at him giving off rays of invitation. Soon one could hear Jarrell's melodic refrain, "Little ambassador, are you bored? All right, we'll play. Come now, we'll laugh and play. Oh yes, oh yes." At a cocktail party on campus, an elderly professor began drawing Jarrell out about Kitten, and, delighted to escape general conversation, Jarrell became animated and voluble. To get a laugh, the professor teased him by bringing up a story he had heard about Jarrell using his meat-ration coupons for the cat during the war. "Why of course!" Jarrell snapped, flashing sparks. "What would you expect? He's only a poor cat, and has to eat what he can. People can eat anything. What an absurd remark!"*

Jarrell was not only too busy but too happy, with his new family, seeing Lowell, and having Kitten back, to worry much about not writing. And yet, as the end of the semester approached he canceled plans to visit the Taylors in nearby Ohio to return as soon as possible to the privacy of Laguna Beach, where he could perfect his novel at leisure and write at whim.

TO BERNARD HAGGIN

604 Hessel Blvd.
Champaign
[February 1953]

Dear Bernard:

I got your letter only after it had been tossed from place to place for a week; I'm new and strange to them here. I believe it would be better for you to ask the music department for the answers to the questions about the equipment. I don't know anybody in the School of Music, and am very much a foreign writer just visiting here: it would be rather as if you conducted negotiations with the Russian government through the Bolivian ambassador at Moscow.

Oh, that *wicked* Freda Kirchwey! I hope very much you don't resign: Margaret and everybody else can tell how you feel about it all, and it'll be really sad and dreary for so many people, not to get to read your weekly column. I wrote Margaret at length and she replied with a very sweet and cheerful letter about Yaddo, her book, and so forth. I hope very much you don't stop being a music-ballet-record critic, it would be a disaster. What does Margaret think about it? (I think I can guess, but might be wrong.)

It'll be great fun to see you here; Mary's very eager to meet you. We hope you'll have dinner with us and do anything else you've time for. Tell

me how long you're going to be here and so forth. I've already met an
English professor who knows your columns by heart.

I never would have believed that Freda and the Front Part of *The Nation*
would have that much nerve — wretched things. See you soon.

Yours,

Randall

*Jarrell's letter to Margaret Marshall about Haggin's quarrel with Freda
Kirchwey has been lost. Haggin did not resign from* The Nation *until
1957.*

TO HANNAH ARENDT

[Champaign-Urbana, Illinois]

[March 1953]

Dear Hannah:

If an Austrian composer named Gottfried von Einum comes to see you
and gives you a note from me, written on the back of a blank check, and
sending you fondest greetings, love, kisses and I don't know what else,
don't be surprised; this was the impulse of a moment — a moment at a
party, during a hailstorm with thunder and lightning. He seemed nice and
knew your work well and was delighted with the prospect of meeting
you.

I miss you and wish I could see you. Mary and I like it very much here.
My classes are awfully nice and I made a big public lecture on "The Taste of
the Age" which, to my astonishment, got me more praise than anything
I've ever done; if a policeman came up to me it wasn't to give me a parking
ticket but to tell me that he had laughed until he cried, and that our age *was*
just as I'd said it was. It was queer.

Indeed I *don't* read Greek — it's a wonder I can read English. In my earlier lives I couldn't read anything, but just sang songs so that people put
gold bracelets on my arms or threw big bones at me.

I'd send you my lecture to read but most of it is still handwritten; part
of it was written to be in *Pictures,* a long part about Charlemagne — or
rather, about eighth-grade students who don't know who Charlemagne was,
but have been taught to hold elections, to make dresses, and thousands of
other things. And I'm a fine example of it myself — but, as a *poet* I need to
stay as naive as if I'd been taught Greek in high school or grammar school.
Maybe naiver, who knows?

I didn't leave California till February 1 — I drove back, and Mary and the children and the pets came by airplane. We now have Kitten back ... who's happy as can be, and I was already that happy and am even happier. This part of my letter must be rather like the part of the "Grecian Urn" where Keats keeps saying how happy the boughs were, and I wouldn't blame you if you felt like saying to me, "Boughs, stop telling me how happy you are!" — but you've got to admit that it's an unusual complaint to need to make.

I got *Pictures* roughly done before I left, and now need two or three months to get it smoothly done. I wrote on it steadily for two and a half months — it was wonderfully enjoyable to do.

I wish you were going to come out here with Bernard Haggin when, in April, he comes to make a Mozart lecture. Can't you come and pretend to be the *Coronation Concerto* and let him point to your first movement and coda and so on?

Katherine Anne Porter just made a lecture; it was as if one had a grandmother who was a vulgar, extravagant, coquettish, self-obsessed, denunciatory great lady à la Mary Garden, and who said anything that came into her head (i.e., anything that she'd already said in conversation and lectures a thousand times before) for an hour. Fortunately, almost everybody felt it was like that. I had to talk to my class for a class period about the difference between the artist and his work, and so on; they were upset.

My new publishers (the two people at Knopf who take care of me) [Philip Vaudrin and Harry Ford] are awfully nice to me: they write me Appreciations, ask me which English publisher I'd prefer — one sent me a little book of Rilke's; I have to pinch myself.

They have lots of music and a wonderful orchestra here. They also had an exhibition of paintings — which — oh, nothing could do it justice! Mary and I go to lots of things together: we've even been Behaving Properly and Accepting Invitations — for a purpose, that is, now that we've worked our way through most of them, we stay home sighing luxuriously.

I hope you're well and happy; do write soon.

Yours,
Randall

The Jarrells were Behaving Properly in deference to Blackmur's counsel that the University of Illinois was looking for a permanent poet- and writer-in-residence.

Shortly after Haggin's Mozart lecture, the Jarrells attended a Scarlatti recital performed by the sensitive — and much-overshadowed-by-his-father

— Soulima Stravinsky of the music department. On the way to a party for him afterward, Jarrell cautioned, "Let's not bring up his father, ever." Stravinsky was aristocratically thin and wore pale silk ties in the European tradition. His French wife, Françoise, was chic and intelligent, with a welcome touch of tendresse. They had a three-story wooden house from the 1890s with a cork-lined practice room on the top floor for Soulima and a completely white downstairs like a many-roomed gallery for displaying their Max Ernst originals. The Stravinskys were cultivated in the arts and amusing in several languages, and their best local friends were the Stoddards — George, the president of the university, an educational psychologist and friend of Piaget, and Maggie, his wife, a generous, outgoing person who could be warm and at ease with one guest or one hundred. Such was the nature of this friendship that George counseled the Stravinskys on their son's adaptation to America and Françoise cut Maggie's hair. Both couples entertained the Jarrells intimately and informally and were largely responsible for Jarrell's liking the University of Illinois as much as he did.

TO ROBERT LOWELL

[March 1953]

Dear Cal:

As soon as I got here I said, "Did you know that Robert Lowell is back in this country and that we might be able to get him to read poems?" Their eyes widened, naturally — or unnaturally, I didn't know enough about how their eyes look normally to be able to tell; and they told me that they'd used up all their money for lectures and readings, a lot of it for Eliot in June. But — they have a little culturalish Englishy club which meets once a month, and if you could come over and just read poems and say anything you please about them the club could raise $75. This is a poor amount, but would be a pretext for a visit with expense-of-visit paid and some over . . . (If you do in April I do in May, or vice versa. I'm talking free — just to enhance the $75 in your eyes) — the last speaker who spoke on Elizabethan eschatology, didn't get a cent either, thank God! It's rumored that he's going to be forced to pay every listener ten dollars.

I guess they'd either furnish a Student-Union room for you and Elizabeth or somebody would jump at the chance of inviting you; we'd jump at it but you'd have to sleep in the basement — a magnificent one, heated, floored, walled, full of washers and dryers and irons, but still the basement.

Unless there's some giant obstacle, do come — it'd be a great joy to see you, and I've described you at great length to Mary (she knows a lot of your poems well and is crazy about them) and she's looking forward to it a lot.

And wouldn't you like to see me in a household with (besides me and Mary) Kitten, as ever, a dachshund named Schatzel, a 13-year-old-daughter named Alleyne, and a 10-year-old named Beatrice? And the house is a German professor's house with more than 70 Steins and Things to Match.

This seems quite a nice place. I got here February 7 and have been working hard, partly on classes and partly on a big public lecture on "The Taste of the Age." You can imagine lots of what I said: Queen Victoria first, the next nowhere; but they didn't get mad but loved it.

I haven't seen Peter and Eleanor since last spring — wish I'd been with you all at Kenyon.

I've done a tremendous lot of writing since August 1 — it was wonderful having no classes, and living at Laguna Beach so close to the surf I could hear the seals barking every night, and putting off Duty, Business, Letters, and all the stuff they find for writers to write. I got a criticism book all finished (it's named *Poetry and the Age* and Knopf's bringing it out in September) and got *Pictures from an Institution* almost done and wrote a tremendous long poem called "Woman" (nobody'll have to read Pope's *Characters of Women* anymore) that's in the new *Botteghe Oscure* and four or five shortish poems and some Rilke translations and Frost and Moore articles. If you say you don't believe it I don't blame you.

I'm now looking at the Uccello [print, *The Rout of San Romano*] you gave me — it's hanging in the living room over the sofa, all beautifully framed; I can't tell you how much pleasure it's been to me.

I was delighted and overawed by Leslie Fiedler last summer; he's a *highly* intelligent man, with awfully unusual qualities, I think — more of a Critic and Thinker than Writer, but really both. Robert Fitzgerald and I went around with him all the time.

You and Cleanth ought to have lots of fun with your course. I certainly do like Cleanth — I saw him a couple of days, along with Red, at Yale last spring; I hadn't seen him for ten years.

I can't wait for you to read all of *Pictures* — the first book is a generalized introductory picture, mostly of a type, and the other books are slower and have characters, sympathetic ones even.

How's Iowa? I thought, last spring, that the students and climate of feeling were really unusually good.

I'm awfully happy and well off, as you can certainly tell from this millrace of a letter. I'm teaching a Mod. Poetry and a writing course here and have delightful classes. This place has enough Cultural Events — music, painting, movies, etc. — to kill a horse; they've got a wonderful student orchestra, the best college one I ever heard.

How are your poems — subjects — the ones you told me about, half-worked-out ones getting along? Iowa must feel strange after 2½ years of Europe; how does it feel to Elizabeth? Or did she like Europe as completely as you did?

I'll stop, since I'll surely get to see you pretty soon. Do you suppose there's any chance of our, i.e. you and Elizabeth and Mary and me, working out something like going over to Kenyon just after school ends in June, and seeing Peter and Eleanor and Mr. Ransom? We could get two tents and — but *I* don't need to tell *you* what to do with tents when visiting writers. When does Iowa end?

I forget whether (when I was writing you after I'd reviewed *The Mills*) I told you that, O woe, O shame to my judgment, I was all wrong in thinking "Mother Marie Therese" a little better than "Falling Asleep"; it's just the opposite, JUST THE OPPOSITE. Hundreds of years from now little boys will be cursing you as they memorize "Falling Asleep over the Aeneid"; and thousands of years from now people will suppose that it was written by Virgil himself, Virgil the Magician.

Affectionately,
Randall

On Allen Tate's recommendation, Paul Engle had given Lowell a half-year writer-in-residence position at the University of Iowa. After Lowell's European trip, he and Elizabeth Hardwick returned there for the spring semester. Cleanth Brooks made a short visit and introduced Lowell's students to New Criticism.

The joking allusion to the tents was a reference to the summer when Lowell was about nineteen or twenty and went to visit Tate in Clarksville. Since Tate's house was already full of family and guests, Lowell pitched a tent in the back yard and lived there.

TO ROBERT LOWELL

604 Hessel Blvd.
Champaign
[April 1953]

Dear Cal:

How will Thursday the 7th of May be? And there's a choice of arrangements: either just read poems, plus slight random comments, to the Journal Club, all literaryish people, for seventy-five dollars; or else part read poems and part give more extended and impressive comments — making it like a lecture — to a more general audience for $125. This would be for the

Humanities Division, which has lectures, not poem-readings, as a usual thing.

Your comparisons and nice sayings for *Pictures from an Institution* were as winning as comparisons well could be — I love being compared to Pope and Arnold and now Cocteau, by you, instead of to the people one ordinarily gets compared to. It's quite a long book now — seven Books, and most of them twice as long as the part you saw. It's almost done — about two or three months of final smoothing and cutting and inventing of extra incidents here and there is all that's left. I was *delighted* you liked the first part so well.

I certainly am glad that you're (probably) going to be here for a year or more. They [Iowa] will ask you in the end, but public things like telling other people just necessarily have to — life is like that — come before private things like asking you: it's part of the burden of being a public figure. (This is how We Novelists talk.)

I'm glad you've so many good students — last year when I was there I thought them and their general atmosphere awfully good. Yes, I thought Mrs. Johnson a good poet in an interesting Graves-ish or Graves-characterish way. Eleanor's sister's husband — why didn't I just say [Donald] Justice? — had written a Stevensish poem that was very graceful and accomplished, and there were at least five, then, whose poems were enjoyable to read.

I liked your two longer ones better than the (ah, familiar Hellish country!) Stuyvesant Square Elevated one ["Inauguration Day: January 1953"]. The black prisoner poem ["A Mad Negro Soldier Confined at Munich"] is a very successful concentrated nightmarish one; the longest ["The Banker's Daughter"] is like a violent, hallucinatory surrealist picture made from heads and arms of statues, square feet of canvas cut from museums, pages of a *Companion to European Literature,* all of them acting out a frightening charade — the best parts were *extremely* effective. The parts varied considerably more than those in the Prisoner poem, though that's natural. I'm awfully glad you're getting whole poems done again — I imagine this country *is* better to write in. I never wrote anything in Europe but "Hohensalzburg."

I'll — since you've cast your bread upon the waters — send a tremendous loaf back to you, a poem ["Woman"] I wrote late this summer: one designed, roughly, to make readers throw down Pope's *Characters of Women* in discontent. It's going to be in the next *Botteghe Oscure.*

Will you have time to stay a couple of days? We have a sort of garden room, conservatory, glass house, what shall I say? that we can fix into a perfectly possible bedroom for May weather — why don't you stay there *unless* (there's one *unless*) that's the week Mary's mother is visiting us from California. Then you could sleep at night at the Student Union, a thing like Mount Vernon, and spend your waking hours with us? I have no classes at all on Thursdays and Saturdays, only some on Friday afternoon.

They've had some *wonderful* concerts here: the best playing of the Bartok [piano] concerto I ever heard, and [Guiomar] Novaës, and two really good — I couldn't believe it — compositions by an American composer, a man named Elliott Carter. Last week we went to concerts for four straight nights.

I have some good writers and intelligent people in my classes, and like both classes a lot. This is a nice place.

I haven't seen Robie's book [*Disguises of Love*] — I've meant to read it but haven't come across a copy. I imagine I'll think what you do about it.

I had a swell letter from Peter yesterday. I think Mary and I'll go over to Kenyon to see them some weekend in May.

You've no idea how much fun writing a novel — my sort of a novel, anyway, I'm just calling it a comedy on the title-page — is. It's not at all a wearing *job,* like criticism, and you don't have the helpless possessed exhausted feeling you have with poetry even when that is most fun: all the playful, inventing, noticing, organizing, knowledge-y side of you can really go to work.

Send me a note — or better still, a letter — about whether that date is all right, which sort of reading you want to do, and so forth. You've certainly been away a long time; I can't wait to see you again.

Affectionately,
Randall

Jarrell's be-patient reassurance to Lowell about his probable reappointment at the University of Iowa reflected Jarrell's feelings about his own appointment at Illinois. In Lowell's case, Iowa's indecision proved to be the University of Cincinnati's gain, and he accepted the Chair of Poetry there for January through June of 1954.

TO ROBERT LOWELL

[April 1953]

Dear Cal:

We'll meet you at the train. We've got a hotel room reserved for you: Mary's mother (*not* mine; Mary's mother is very pleasant and easy to get along with) is arriving Saturday and is going to occupy the conservatory or garden room, to freeze in your stead. I had just about got from the Naval ROTC a pup tent to put in the backyard, but Mary said it wouldn't do for you. Little did she know!

I'm just finishing correcting proof on my prose book [*Poetry and the Age*], and I am delighted that you're going to write a prose book, for of course it would be foolish not to make those lectures into a prose book. That's swell about the Cincinnati job. I'm really quite glad it'll make you do the prose writing — I was crazy about your *Sewanee Review* Bishop — Williams — etc. piece ["Thomas, Bishop and Williams"]. Doesn't it seem long ago?

Can you stay through Friday? — The more days the better, of course. We thought we'd give a party for you Friday night if you can be here then.

How I wish I could have heard you and Peter! Peter and Jean [Stafford] once did a criticism-of-stories-duet, at Woman's College Arts Festival; Jean was so scared she said almost nothing, and that merely to establish her cultural status, and Peter acted as if he were Disraeli charming Queen Victoria down from a Tree — he was *wonderful* — He began one criticism: "This is a story about an old lady" — then, eagerly and confidingly interrupting himself — "*I love stories about old ladies!*" I've just about never enjoyed a lecturer more.

I'll quit since I'll be seeing you so soon. Send me a postcard saying whether you can stay for several days, will you?

Affectionately,
Randall

Lowell's "prose book" was to have been a collection of his poetry lectures at Cincinnati, but it was never completed.

Taylor's visit to Iowa to judge fiction represented one of the numerous occasions on which Lowell, Taylor, and Jarrell arranged to cover the expenses for a private social visit with each other by means of a speaking or teaching engagement.

*   *   *

Between this letter and Lowell's appearance was the visit of T. S. Eliot, Nobel Prize winner and international literary figure. In the United States to attend a family reunion in nearby St. Louis, Eliot had agreed to come to Urbana for an early dinner and poetry reading, after which he was to return immediately to his family. One hundred guests came to President and Mrs. Stoddard's home for cocktails and a reception beforehand. Eliot, tall,

*genteel, and formal in his dark suit, was prominently placed where guests
were presented, received a polite "How do you do," and moved on. At Jarrell's introduction, Eliot smiled to attention and said with warmth that he'd
wanted to meet him, and added, "We must have a chat." Unpredictably,
Jarrell was so overwhelmed by Eliot that he immediately left the circle
around him and sought refuge among strangers in the furthest corner of the
room.*

*Thirty guests had been invited to stay for dinner, but there were place
cards at the table and Jarrell was seated at one end, Eliot at the other, and
Mary placed at Eliot's right. Eating less than he smoked, Eliot was engag-
ingly conversational but made no attempt to monopolize. Tilting his satin-
smooth head to one side and resting his yellow-brown eyes on a guest, Eliot
spoke and listened with remarkable absence of self. Any initial sense of strain
at his end of the table was soon replaced by keen interest. He spoke of being
more of a playwright than a poet in recent years, so that returning to his
poems that night made him see them somewhat as he was seeing his relatives.
He said, "For instance, I'm rather surprised to find them so different from
what I remembered. Some of them seem quite harmless now." He smiled
sweetly. "Some, of course, are more eccentric. Above all, what I mostly feel
about them is . . . is how old they seem to me. And a bit alien, even. Still,
though, we are related."*

*Eliot read to an audience of several thousand, with another thousand
listening over loudspeakers outside on the grass. After many bows and much
applause, he was spirited away through the back to a car waiting to return
him to St. Louis, and there was no chance for his great humility to overcome
Jarrell's qualms and make possible their chat.*

TO JOHN CROWE RANSOM

[June 1953]

Dear Mr. Ransom:

We're leaving here on the 10th of June and will be at 906 van Dyck
Drive, Laguna, California, all summer. How I long for all my classes to be
over, so I can be there with nothing to do but finish my book. Fiction gives
one odd feelings.

Cal was here two whole days. We had a swell time. He certainly seems
happy and gentle and equable. We'd been looking forward very much to
our Kenyon visit to see you and were grieved when it blew up: as Peter may
have told you we are going to come in September on our way back to
North Carolina.

Aren't you glad you aren't going to be roasting in Bloomington this summer? Just the thought of what the air felt like fills me with wondering terror.

Affectionately,

Randall

The Jarrell-Lowell reunion after more than three years was fond and playful to such an extent that after Jarrell's introduction at one of Lowell's appearances, an elderly professor commented, "Mr. Jarrell seems to have partaken of too much before dinner" — an indication of the heights of silliness Jarrell could reach simply by self-intoxication.

Lowell, thirty-six, was taller than Jarrell, and with his fresh haircut and shy smiles seemed much younger. He had something of the Kenyon College magna cum laude about him, as if he weren't as familiar with the world as Jarrell. Lowell's clothes — in contrast to Jarrell's Brooks Brothers West — were dowdy, durable, old-gentleman-of-Back-Bay clothes straight out of Arthur Winslow's closet. Driving or walking on campus, they talked about Mallarmé, Williams, Eliot, and Whitman, and, quietly seated at home, they continued. Lowell spoke in long, halting sentences that Jarrell darted in and out of but that Lowell, unperturbed, perfected as he went along, choosing just the right, most exact, precisely descriptive word. He accompanied this with a downward-pointing forefinger that he revolved in a circle like the needle end of a tone arm. It was a familiar gesture that Jarrell described as "Cal stirring his porridge," and as their interest mounted, Jarrell responded by working his jaw as if he were chewing on a straw.

By the time he left, Lowell had charmed Irene and the girls and petted the pets, especially Kitten, and he wore a pleased expression on his face, as if he were happy because Jarrell was happy. After warm goodbyes to all, he telephoned Mary from the airport to say thanks again.

TO PHILIP RAHV

[Laguna Beach, California]
[August 1953]

Dear Philip:

As soon as I read your letter I could see that you were quite right, that people would think what you said. Since Gertrude is my principal character and mortar-for-Bricks-of-Books I can't send you a chapter in which she doesn't figure more or less, but there's not too much of her in Book II, and most of that is un-McCarthyish as can be — and in Book VI she, so to

Robert Lowell with Beatrice and Schatzel, May 1953

speak, does cadenzas for the whole time, and won't seem to anybody anybody but Gertrude. So I'll send those two parts and let you pick. Book III is the longest and least Gertrudish part, but Ransom is using it.

I'm delighted that you liked *Poetry and the Age* so well. It feels strange to have written a prose book, even stranger to have written two — I've had *Pictures* done for ten days now, and play tennis, fool around; wrote a review of *Brother to Dragons*, even ["On the Underside of the Stone, *New York Times Book Review*, August 23, 1953].

Gertrude is so large and real to me (I can make up in my sleep a sentence for her to say about anything) that it seems funny to have her confused with Mary McCarthy, whom I know slightly and don't know too much about: but she *is* the same general type as Mary McCarthy, her books are like, and I got five or six happenings or pictures from M.M. But the readers who know Jean Stafford best think *she's* Gertrude, and the ones who know — but I won't go on with this list of Lady Writers. I hope (this is said in a grandiloquent tone) that Gertrude will survive when all of them are forgotten. One of the other characters says about her, "She is one of the principles of things — a naked one," and I hope this is right too.

If you should want to cut Book II in two, at the end of the party at Gertrude's, that would be quite all right with me. Let me know as soon as you conveniently can, will you? I've promised to give a part to *Accent*. I believe these two books are the best for you to pick from: Book IV is a long, serious, sympathetic, more or less, section about the Rosenbaums and Constance, and Book VII, the last, is full of Happy Endings, and wouldn't do to print by itself.

Yours,
Randall

The fact that Rahv knew Mary McCarthy more intimately than Jarrell enabled him to see more resemblance between her and Gertrude than Jarrell could. Rahv apologetically returned the manuscripts, and though Jarrell made light of this, Partisan *was not offered his poems or reviews in the future.*

TO ROBERT PENN WARREN

[August 1953]

Dear Red:

I was about to send you a copy of *Poetry and the Age* when Knopf wrote me that they'd already sent you and Cleanth and Mr. Ransom one; so I won't, but will just write instead.

Mary, Randall, Alleyne, and Beatrice, 1953

Brother to Dragons is a wonderful poem — I don't see how people could be live-r or speak more naturally than Laetitia and Isham and Lilburne and Aunt Cat and Laetitia's brother; and the whole action is just as real and truthful. I reviewed it for *The Times* — but in only 650 words; I had to spend considerably more time cutting than writing. I think it's the best narrative poem anybody's written for many years; if people won't read *it* because it's modern poetry they really are through with poetry for good. I didn't like Jefferson and that part as well as the rest; it seems to me you crucify him upside-down, so to speak. But I hate letters which tell you what a wonderful book you've written and what's wrong with it, so I'll stop. It's one of the best long poems I've ever read, and everybody I've seen that's read it thinks so too.

Harvey Breit says that you're a father; well, I'm a step-father, though not a very wicked one — Mary has two daughters, one 14 and exactly like a movie star, and the other 11 and fairly like a little girl in a fairy tale. We've been living out here all summer and are going back to Greensboro in September.

Will you be at Yale next winter when the Bollingen-judging-people come? I'm going to be in New York, reading poems at Vassar, late in October. I'd certainly like to see you one of the times.

Yours,
Randall

Warren and his second wife, Eleanor Clark, had recently become parents of a baby girl, Rosanna.

Jarrell was not so much a father to Mary's girls as an affectionate encyclopedia.

Jarrell was to be a judge in the 1954 competition for the Bollingen Prize in Poetry, awarded annually by Yale University Library.

Lucy and Malcolm Hooke

Greensboro, North Carolina,
September 1953–August 1956

*W*e have a dovey house here," *Jarrell wrote Robert Lowell about a rental Jarrell's long-time friend Lucy Hooke had found them that had a screened porch, a sizable strawberry patch, and a fenced and shaded yard for the pets. In his commemorative essay "Randall Jarrell: The Last Years," Robert Watson — then an instructor and unpublished poet — described Jarrell at the college gymnasium on registration day as reading* The Wind in the Willows *while he waited for students and laughing aloud from time to time, exclaiming what a wonderful book it was. When Watson asked him what the college students were like, Jarrell told him to read his poem "A Girl in a Library" and then added, "Gee, I'm glad to be back here. This college is like Sleeping Beauty." (RJ)*

The Jarrells took to dropping in on the Hookes the way the Taylors had once dropped in on the Jarrells. There was always Lucy's homemade pie on hand, and, for Jarrell, her homemade milkshakes and homespun observations that began with something like "Well, Randall . . ." and led to something like "She was as homely as a rich girl ought to be . . ." It was a long, mild fall, with tennis for Jarrell, Jarrell's classes for Mary, and, on weekends, the World Series, Forest Hills, and the Redskins on the Hookes' TV. At home, Jarrell played the pianists Schnabel, Lipatti, Novaës, and Rachmaninoff on the phonograph; and in the first year he translated Chekhov's Three Sisters, *reviewed Malraux's* Voices of Silence, *planned an anthology with Lowell, and wrote the poems "Cinderella" and "Nestus Gurley."*

                                        September 9, 1953
Dear Margaret:

I was pleased with all your nice news and grieved at the Provincetown apartment and the [Harold] Strauss opinion. I know nothing of him except a piece by him (on American writers) in the *Saturday Review:* it was one of the nastiest, most complacent pieces I ever read — said that American writers were ignorant escapists, that they should go to New York and become part of the world of Business and publishing, which is Life, and then they'd be like the great writers of the Past, who lived in London and Paris and knew life. He later was very sore at Robie Macauley (who'd had some connections with Knopf) because Robie hadn't given Knopf his novel, and wrote indignantly "Why? Why?" Robie wrote back that it was mostly because of this article, and the man was more indignant than ever.

I don't know anybody at Knopf except Vaudrin and Ford, and they couldn't have been nicer to me.

I want *very* much to get to read your book — the contrast between your early life and *The Nation* and such ought to be wonderfully effective. I've always thought you were one of the funniest and most naturable (supposed to be *natural,* but *naturable* sounds nice, doesn't it?) writers. I thought your dramatic criticism decidedly the most *sensible* of any of the New York critics of American writers. If old Strauss had happened to *me* I'd certainly have been just as vexed and bothered, but heaven knows it doesn't mean *anything* except practically.

Judy's baby [Margaret Marshall's grandchild] sounds as charming as can be. Imagine having a son-in-law working at Los Alamos!

We had a swell summer at Laguna Beach. The girls live with their father in the summer, so we were alone with Kitten, a little cat named Jason, and a dachshund named Schatzel. We had a gardeny house on a hill and an MG and even got to see the New York City Ballet up at Los Angeles.

We were lucky and got a nice house here and are very happily settled down. Mary and I are going to be in New York late in October and want very much to see you and Bernard; we'll write sometime before to tell you the exact date.

Poetry and the Age has been very lucky and already is having a second printing. Having a prose book published is *very* different.

I read sentences from both you and Bernard about the *Nation* review ["New Books in Brief," *The Nation,* September 5, 1953] before I read it — they had prepared me for something so much worse that the real thing felt like a fan letter. *The Nation's* book section is just pathetic these days. *The Nation* really is a wonderful subject for you to write about; there was something at once absurd and Archetypal about it: as one looked at it one felt how everything it stood for was embodied in it. Its motto could have been: Every Other Week a New Rubicon — and the Rubicons were all moral as well. And in spite of the hair-raising oddities there was never anything that *surprised* one or was different from what it should have been: it was a most logical *reductio ad absurdum* — everything was what you expected but unbelievably more so.

But I mustn't reminisce to *you*.

I hope you're getting along well — hope that the hot weather's gone. I'll write a note soon, when I know the exact date we're coming up. It's the last weekend in October, I think.

Yours,
Randall

Harold Strauss was editor-in-chief at Knopf and had rejected Marshall's book.

TO HARRY FORD

[November 1953]

Dear Mr. Ford:

The sample pages [*Pictures from an Institution*] are *extremely* good-looking, I think — almost better than *Poetry and the Age*. The print's beautiful and plain, the proportions of the page nice, the chapter numerals and page numerals unusually nice, and so on: and the big "Constance and the Rosenbaums" somehow makes the book look beguiling and easy, as if it were Angela Thirkell or a box of candy. I can't wait to see the whole thing, title page, etc.

This is my year for doing odd things — I'm at present translating *The Three Sisters*. Not from Russian, which I don't know a word of, but from Constance Garnettese — a grammatical, organized, shapely tongue — into speech, an altogether different affair, and some Russians are translating literally for me anything she didn't. One day after working all day on it I read [Giovanni Verga's] *The House by the Medlar Tree* that evening, and I really felt very sad, and had trouble going to sleep. Oh, I'm translating it because a visiting English play-director [Giles Playfair] wants to give it at the college, and I fell into it as a sort of Homage to Chekhov.

We had a wonderful time seeing all of you at Knopf's, and am looking forward with delight to our next visit.

Yours,
Randall Jarrell

*Angela Thirkell was an English novelist who wrote light romances about
the upper classes.*

*Harry Ford, in his mid-thirties, was fair, of medium height, and had
elitist tastes and elitist professional standards that Jarrell valued. Ford wore
a gold collar pin under his tie, carried a pencil-slim umbrella, and made
gastronomic tours of France with the* Guide Michelin. *In New York, Ford
knew what each of the best French restaurants did best, and at lunch he ordered Pouilly Fumé — not Fuissé — and told the steward how it should be
chilled; and at the taste-testing Ford meant business. According to Jarrell,
he was decisive about the "right things" but also defensive and prickly —
though never with Jarrell. His worst fault in Jarrell's eyes was in naming
his family of cats after the Sitwells, which was, Jarrell said, "mighty unfair
to those cats."*

*When Ford and Philip Vaudrin escorted Jarrell to the stately eigh-
teenth-century room where the Knopfs held court, the petite Blanche sat behind one desk flashing her rocks and nuggets and interrupting anyone who
spoke. The monumental Alfred sat behind another desk, encased in a bolt of
gray flannel and wearily condescending to Jarrell, who, unimpressed, went
into a silence. The "wonderful time" at Knopf's was not in that room, but
behind the scenes in the editorial office of Vaudrin and in the cramped, me-
ticulously ordered space given to Ford.*

TO MARIANNE MOORE

[November 12, 1953]

Dear Miss Moore:

If I've put off answering your kind and pleasant letter for so many
months, you can see with what trepidation some part of me thinks of writing to you — I suppose it feels that you are poems to write about, and not a
mortal woman to write letters to.

I'm delighted that you liked Gertrude Johnson and Derek. They have a
conversation later on, mostly about snakes. I've asked Knopf to send you
one of the early copies of the book — I hope that it can give you a couple of
hours of pleasure, in return for the thousands that I've had in reading or
teaching or writing about your poems.

My favorite saying about criticism is Goethe's "Against criticism we can
neither protect nor defend ourselves, we must act in despite of it, and gradually it resigns itself to this." Your regarding my criticism of you as a trouble
of mine that you can feel sympathetic toward, and not simply as a necessary
trial, is a joy to me. I noticed that several reviewers said that my articles

about your poetry were "almost lyric" or "quite lyric," and I hope that this is true.

Your constant and grateful reader,
Randall Jarrell

TO HARRY FORD

[January 1954]

Dear Mr. Ford:

I was *extremely* grateful to you for the Rilke — I figured it must have been from you, nobody else has ever given me a copy of Rilke. Since I've sent word by Mr. Vaudrin how dazzled I was by the continental copy of *Pictures*, I won't repeat all that. I was spending the weekend with Peter Taylor and his wife, and he showed me proofs of his new book [*The Widows of Thornton*], and I felt *so* sorry for him, the printing looked so ordinary — the book looked as if it had won its format off a punchboard.

I want very much to read all of (Erich Auerbach) *Mimesis* — I was crazy about the part in *Partisan*. I have a request for it at the library, and as soon as it gets catalogued I'm to get it. I'm particularly eager to read him on Saint-Simon, one of my favorite writers — I've never read anything good about Saint-Simon except in Proust.

I thought that I'd send you, as a sort of thanks for the Rilke, two or three poems I've written in the last year or two, and a re-writing of "Glückel of Hamlin." Will you send back the Glückel? I can't find an extra copy of it.

It certainly felt strange to be finished with *The Three Sisters*. For two months and three weeks I'd worked on it almost every day — even our children were saying *You're a joker, Vassily Vassilyevich* ... or, as one of them put it, *You're a joker, Vesuvius, Vesuvius.* They've also picked up two lines from *Pictures* — they're fond of saying something about Gertrude's garter belt and they constantly say, *One feels that.*

Yours,
Randall Jarrell

The poems Jarrell sent Ford were "The Meteorite," "The Lonely Man," "Windows," and "Aging."

In his next letter to Ford, Jarrell wrote, "I've had the intense pain of seeing The Three Sisters *acted exactly as if it were a soap opera or television program. The Russian friend and I stopped going to rehearsals, they made us so sick. All I can do is look forward to the second produc-*

tion of the translation — even if a nursery school does it next, it will be better."

TO HANNAH ARENDT

[January 12, 1954]

Dear Hannah:

Your letter was a real joy to me. Not writing to you is the only way to get a letter from you. Wicked Knopf not to send you a paper-bound book [*Pictures*] immediately so you could walk around in it barefooted! But of course I don't count this one as the *real* book at all — as soon as I get those I'll send you yours first thing of all with a loving inscription.

I'm awfully glad you liked it that well. I really did work hard on it, though all the work was a pleasure. And how nice to have you know, because of Heinrich at Bard, that some of the most exaggerated things are true.

Although the Rosenbaums aren't too like you and Heinrich as individuals, I hardly could, hardly would, have made them up without knowing you. I think I made them very like you in some of the very big general things — in most of the medium-sized things they're quite different. I first got the idea for Gottfried from a man different in almost every way from Gottfried, with whom I spent some summer weeks at the beach house of a family I used to be very friendly with [Milton and Zaro Starr] — he was Freud's friend and disciple Hans Sachs. Then I used a lot of things from myself for him, just as I did for Gertrude. After I'd written a little about Gottfried he seemed real and wrote himself; Irene was a vaguer, nonromantic, partly contradictory idea, and I had to think a lot about her, work and change, before she got to seem real. I think she's a little more like you than Gottfried's like Heinrich — but it's only part of her that's like part of you, and there's almost nothing in her that corresponds to the historian-philosopher part of you. But the Rosenbaums' relation to this country is very much understood in terms of you and your husband — and the sentence about Gottfried and Irene "quarreling" fiercely about Goethe and Hölderlin, etc., applies even better to you two than to the Rosenbaums.

Thanks so much for the pictures, and I send back one of me, one of Family Group, in grateful exchange. Partly I was just delighted to have yours, partly I thought sadly, "She looks so thoughtful" — I thought of how hard and steadily you work and think. (This "she looks so thoughtful" is what Kulygin says about Masha in *The Three Sisters* — for two months and three weeks I spent all my time making a new translation of it, with much help from a nice Russian and somewhat less help from seven already-existing bad English translations.) But even without the photograph I'd have felt that from your new articles, which are simply wonderful — the best parts of them seem to me the best-thought and best written things you've ever done. I always say to people, with pride, that I'm a friend of yours, but now I'm sure I'll be doing it to pale ghosts in Hell.

We're going to be in New York, I'm certain, on Saturday the 20th and Sunday the 21st of March. Don't faint, I'm really telling you this far ahead of time. How about our coming to see you late Sunday afternoon and taking you out to dinner? Heinrich's there on Sundays isn't he? We'll regret the missing of a chance to eat your red fruit dessert — Mary's made it twice — but we want to take you to dinner, since you never leave New York for wild buffalo-ridden America, where you could visit us.

Did you see my piece about Malraux in the December *Art News?* If not, pray do — I hope you like it.

Your sentences (in one of the articles) about we're all "members of a society that's ceased to exist a hundred and fifty years ago" was wonderful, wonderful, if we ever go mad and write The Story of Our Lives we ought to put that on the title page.

Love,

Randall

Pictures from an Institution was dedicated "To Mary and Hannah," and in Mary's copy Jarrell wrote "To my Mary from her Randall" and sketched two stars inside a crescent moon.

TO JAMES AGEE

[January 1954]

Dear Jim:

I can't tell you how much pleasure I got from what you said about *Pictures* — and it wasn't just your liking it, but the exact thing you said, that made me so happy. And I was just as much overjoyed at what you said about the Whitman piece and "The Obscurity of the Poet."

I certainly miss the old days when I could read you every week or every other week — I always thought you the funniest-wittiest writer writing, and seeing the occasional bigger things you write, or you yourself in [*The Bride Comes to*] *Yellow Sky,* is consoling but doesn't take the place of the continual things in the old days (and your *Time* pieces too, since they were always easy to recognize). How *Time* has fallen! It's hard to believe it used to have you and Robert Fitzgerald and Really Literary people.

I saw Bernard and Margaret in January. How *The Nation*'s changed! I wish I could think of some good changes to match all these bad ones — I guess I'd better think about The Long-Playing Record.

When you do get the novel [*A Death in the Family*] finished, I guarantee I'll be one of its eagerest readers.

I've just spent three months translating (with much Russian assistance) *The Three Sisters*. Mostly I'm basking in the sensation of having become visible after having been invisible for so long — that's the way you feel when you have prose books published after nothing but poetry. I've written a fair amount of poetry in the last three years, but I was working on *Pictures* so much of the time that I wrote less — and, too, when you write poetry you're writing both against the current of the world and the current of the World of Poetry, a small world much more interested in Wallace Stevens than in Chekhov, Homer, and Wordsworth combined. Not that this *really* matters, but it's a surface vexation in a big way.

I don't know where you are, so I'll send this to some magazine or publisher with a *please forward*. Thanks all over again, very much, for the letter.

Yours,
Randall

Agee's letter to Jarrell has been lost, but a quotation from it was used on the dust jacket of the hardbound edition of Pictures from an Institution: *"It is best of all to see how deeply all the fun and insight are rooted in humaneness and in angry and tender loyalty to every achievement, our only way of reconciling ourselves to the brevity of our moments of authenticity, and the foolishness of all the rest."*

*   *   *

In April a totally changed Robert Lowell visited the Jarrells on a weekend away from Cincinnati. He had an oddly swollen look, as if from gaining weight, which was accentuated by his wearing Jarrell's "Ferrari-red" sweater that was much too small, and Jarrell's English tweed cap that was much too tight. Lucy Hooke said he looked like "the bully in the 'Our Gang' comedies." He was chain-smoking and chain-beer-drinking, and his conversation was not literary, as he seemed obsessed with details of his mother's recent death in Rapallo, Italy, his decision to divorce Elizabeth Hardwick, and his plans to marry Giovanna Madonia, whom he had met in Salzburg in 1951 and had looked up during his recent week in Italy. Elizabeth Hardwick was not Jarrell's type, and he even congratulated Lowell for leaving her, but after that he wanted to talk about Malraux and Chekhov.

Lowell could only talk about Rapallo, and this got on Jarrell's nerves. Calling on the Hookes (in quest of beer, which was not sold within the city limits), Lowell infuriated them with tactless Yankee comments about Southerners.

Before Lowell left, the Jarrells noticed that the cats ran from the room whenever he came in. At breakfast on the last day of his visit, Alleyne observed that her daddy had a seal ring like the one Lowell was wearing, but Lowell said, "Oh, I'm afraid not, Alleyne. You see, this is my father's Naval Academy ring." "My father went to the Naval Academy," Alleyne said. "Perhaps so," Lowell said, disgruntled. "But this ring has the Lowell crest on it." "My daddy's ring has the Garton crest on it," Alleyne continued. Lowell turned his attention to her fully then, and said, "Well, Alleyne, what is the Garton motto? The Lowell motto is Occasionem cognosce. *Do you know what that means? That means 'Know the occasion.'" "Know the occasion, indeed!" Jarrell expostulated. After insisting on the immediate return of the Ferrari-red sweater and the English tweed cap (that Lowell wanted to borrow and send back from Cincinnati), Jarrell rather hustled him off to the railroad station and bade him a surly goodbye.*

Shortly after this, Jarrell's vexation turned to chagrin when Lowell telephoned to say that he had been hospitalized for mania and to ask Jarrell if he would write Giovanna Madonia an explanatory letter and, in fact, receive her letters to Lowell. When the call was over, Jarrell sat staring at the telephone half-stunned. Shaking his head from side to side, he said ruefully, "So that's what it was. He was manic . . . As any fool could plainly see . . . but me . . . Oh, Randall, you're so dumb . . . How really stupid of me . . . Poor old Cal."

Jarrell found it distasteful to be even minimally involved in this crisis of Lowell's, but he did write Giovanna at least one letter and perhaps two, and he wrote Lowell at least one letter informing him that he had written her and reassuring him that he would be better off without Elizabeth Hardwick. Soon, however, relations with Madonia were terminated and Hardwick was reinstated. Lowell recovered after four months at Payne-Whitney, but it took Jarrell much longer, and he invited Karl Shapiro to the Arts Forum in 1955 instead of Lowell.

Except for this one instance, Jarrell had no direct involvement in Lowell's abnormal states, and he wanted it that way. Not only did he decline to listen to Tate's accounts — which further wounded Tate — but he would only endure the barest reference by Taylor before changing the subject to literature. When Lowell was manic he often telephoned or wrote Jarrell,

but it was Blair Clark, an old family friend, who ultimately took the re-
sponsibility of helping him. Lowell wrote knowingly that all "coarseness"
grieved Jarrell, and he took care to shield Jarrell from the romantic or pu-
gilistic behavior that accompanied his affliction.

TO LOUIS UNTERMEYER

148 Emerald Bay
Laguna Beach, California
[June 4, 1954]

Dear Mr. Untermeyer:

I want to thank you both for your letter to me about *Poetry and the Age*
and for your letter to Knopf about *Pictures.* I'm delighted that you liked
both books, and I'm sure your quotation about *Pictures* made lots of people
want to read it.

It's very interesting being a prose-book-writer, after having been a po-
etry-book-writer for so long; it's like wearing a Visible Cloak. What I'm
working on now is a *Selected Poems,* so soon I'll be as invisible as ever.

I'm in very poetic surroundings here — there are three swallows' nests
within ten feet of my window, and two rocks covered with seals in the bay
below. But these are very unliterary surroundings in general. Still, I just saw
a very nice paperbound anthology of yours at the drugstore.

Thanks again for your letter.

Yours sincerely,
Randall Jarrell

Untermeyer had written that Pictures from an Institution *was "A won-*
derful blend of wickedness and sheer fun . . . a continually bubbling witches'
brew . . . it combines the quick play of the wit, the imagination of the poet,
and the spellbinding charm of the half-ironic, half-whimsical and wholly
detached story-teller."

TO KARL SHAPIRO

[June 1954]

Dear Karl:

I should have written long ago, but I've been putting off typing neat
copies of the poems ["The Lonely Man," "Meteorite," "Windows," and
"Aging"] and putting off letter-writing, I've so many letters I ought to
have written.

I had an awfully good time at Chicago and hardly minded the unfinancialness of the trip. All they did was send me a check for $75 and my air and airport-bus expenses were $102; if *Poetry* can fix up the difference, or get them to, that would be nice.

I'd like to send greetings to *Poetry*'s secretary and to tell both her and you that *Vogue* asked me to write an article on sports cars and sports-car racing ["The Little Cars"] — isn't this a case of Heaven smiling on one's vices or hobbies or sillinesses or whatever they are? And we really are going to buy that Mercedes — *Pictures* has been doing pretty well.

It was a lot of fun seeing you after so long, and talking about everything and Rilke. I met a young German-Englishman at a party who told me he was helping MacLeish translate Rilke, and whenever I wake up in the middle of the night this keeps me from going back to sleep again.

Yours,
Randall

Shapiro, forty, was editor of Poetry *and on the faculty at the University of Illinois in Chicago, and he had spurred them to finance Jarrell's reading there. He was handsome, hale, humorous, warm, genial, and (as Jarrell said of Shapiro's poetry) "fresh and young and rash and live." About his poetry and criticism, Jarrell said, "Shapiro loves, partly out of indignation and partly out of sheer mischievousness, to tell the naked truths or half-truths or quarter-truths that will make anybody's hair stand on end; he is always crying: 'But he hasn't any clothes on!' about an emperor who is half the time surprisingly well dressed." (RJ)*

Shapiro's enemy was the Emperor of Hi-Cult, his coverall word for Eliot, Pound, Yeats, Joyce, Lowell, Partisan Review, *and literary institutions. Once, after reading Jarrell's review of one of his books, Shapiro wrote Jarrell, "I felt as if I had been run over but not hurt." By the same token Shapiro ran over Hi-Cult, but it survived unhurt and unoffended. When Hi-Cult awarded Shapiro the Pulitzer Prize in poetry in 1945, Shapiro called it "kissing Fame's ass-hole," but he kept it; and when the Hi-Cult Library of Congress invited him to be Poetry Consultant, he accepted. However, when the Hi-Cult priests of the Institute of Arts and Letters elected him to membership, Shapiro refused once, then twice; but after their graceful insistence, he, in his own words, "chickened out and joined." As a war poet, Jarrell saw Shapiro as a rival to whom he had lost, but in peacetime, Jarrell felt he was pulling ahead and found Shapiro quite likable.*

Karl Shapiro

TO ROBERT PENN WARREN

[July 1954]

Dear Red:

Your letter about *Pictures* was such a joy to me that it's a wonder I didn't take less than two months to answer it. I was especially happy about what you said about Gertrude. About the first part: I see what you mean and you may be right, I can't tell — I meant that part to be a sketch, introduction on a more superficial level, since the movement of the book is one of getting-down-to-a-deeper-layer this new time around. But maybe it's too superficial and essayistic.

It's hard, *very* hard, to write a book in which the main structure isn't a plot or story — I don't think I ever will again.

I've just finished a long poem ["The End of the Rainbow"] I wrote on for my first six weeks out here — I think it's one of the best I've ever written so, as you can imagine, I really feel good.

Your paint method with a broken leg sounds like Jack Sprat and his wife painting a house. I sprained my ankle twice and fractured my wrist once playing tennis this spring, so I can sympathize. This is a bad year for arms and legs.

Mary and I were extremely disappointed that the ice-storm kept us from getting to see you and Eleanor more and Rosey-Posey at all. We'll be up for the Bollingen thing again early next January so we'll certainly see you then if not before.

Wasn't Peter's book [*The Widows of Thornton*] good? I really miss him in Greensboro; I can see that Gambier's a lot nicer for them, though.

I spent last winter translating *The Three Sisters* and Cheryl Crawford is going to produce it with the Actors' Studio. I want to write a play myself but it's rather like joining some church — I need to believe in plots first.

I've spent the summer not shaving and have a big black beard — when I look in the mirror it's just as if the fairies had stolen me away and left Odysseus in my place.

I've been reading [Robert Browning's] *The Ring and the Book* but haven't liked it as well as *Brother to Dragons*. I'm still sore at its not being Book of the Month Club and so on.

Yours,
Randall

Warren had written about Pictures: *"Only you could have written it . . . the real fun, the incisive satire, the closeness of observation, and in the end a kind of sympathy and human warmth. It's a remarkable book . . . sadly, and funnily, true."*

Rosey-Posey was the Warren's baby daughter, Rosanna.

Jarrell's poem "The End of the Rainbow" was the ultimate outcome of the lists and pages Mary had compiled about her New England relatives in Pasadena. She had written the opening chapters of The Ladies *when Jarrell still thought he would write it with her; but, in the end, she preferred time with Jarrell and her daughters to time at the typewriter, and decided to give the novel up.*

TO JOHN CROWE RANSOM

906 Van Dyck Dr.
Laguna Beach, Calif.
[August 1954]

Dear Mr. Ransom:

I hope you're having such a cool summer that nobody goes out to the quarry except to skate on it. It's so cool here that I've just finished a poem three hundred and thirty-four lines long ["The End of the Rainbow"]. I've spent June and July on it, and I send it to you for *Kenyon* instead of the Yeats piece — I believe it's considerably better than the Yeats piece would have been. Anyway, it was considerably more welcome to me, as you can imagine. The thought of your perhaps no longer running the *Kenyon Review* was so dismaying to me that I wanted to give you the best things I had while I had them.

I was delighted with what you said about *Pictures.* That a book of its sort should be a best-seller seems the oddest sort of miracle to me; I certainly enjoy being the beneficiary. Another nice thing has happened to me. Cheryl Crawford is going to produce, with the Actors' Studio, that *Three Sisters* translation I made last winter.

Alleyne and Beatrice are living here in Laguna with their father, so we see them quite a lot. We've got the same house upon a hill over the Pacific that we had last summer. We go to Los Angeles every week to see the New York City Ballet, but otherwise lead a working or doing-nothing life.

The inhabitants of Southern California — those who make their presence felt — are so uncultivated and McCarthyesque that it's pretty depressing.

What have you heard about Cal in the last few weeks?

I hope you're having an especially good School of Letters; I hated to miss it, but I couldn't resist a whole summer of writing in a cool climate.

Affectionately,
Randall

Cheryl Crawford and the Actors' Studio produced The Three Sisters *in June of 1964.*

Ransom's letter has been lost, but in a later essay, he wrote that Pictures from an Institution *"might be his great masterpiece . . . It is one of the merriest and wittiest things of our age, and Randall's metaphors are bold and almost innumerable. He equates his characters and their behaviors with stunning figures and figurations from literature. There must be many scholars who know as much literature as Randall . . . But scholars are not artists. Outside of Pound and Eliot and Joyce . . . I think there must be precious few of literary artists in our time and tongue who have had so wide a range of reference."* (RJ)

Lowell was still at Payne-Whitney.

TO PHILIP VAUDRIN AND HARRY FORD

[August 1954]

Dear Philip and Harry:

I thought I'd write a combination letter, because I wanted to send you my new poem — what I've done with this first half of the summer. Fear not, I'll have the *Selected Poems* ready September 1.

Thanks a lot for telling me about the sales. I'm about a million miles from disappointed: they delight me no end, and being twelve in this week's *Times* was a real surprise and joy. The readers of America — 8,000 of them, anyway — are out of their minds.

I read Anthony West's review in *The New Yorker* ["The Sacrosanct Groves of Academe," June 19, 1954]. He's a progressive left over from the '30s, the sort who thinks that *Madame Bovary*'s helping to bring the Revolution: and, since Gertrude = Flaubert, he's for Gertrude. He doesn't realize that Gertrude = Madame Bovary. Still, though, I love Gertrude so much that I got a queer kind of thrill at having somebody spring to her defense — as he said that the book "sprang to the defense" of Benton College.

Joseph Henry Jackson, out here in the San Francisco and Los Angeles papers, had a swell review of *Pictures,* it must have sold quite a few.

This is certainly an uncultivated part of the World — you get the impression that the inhabitants, at breakfast, spell out *Little Nancy* with their fingers and their reading for the day is done. Thank goodness, they support the New York City Ballet, though, which we go to every week.

About the *Selected Poems:* I'd like a title page as much as possible like the early 18th century tombstones Gottfried saw at Stanhope — really they are the Moravian ones I saw at Winston-Salem near here. I notice sometimes you have little designs pressed into the front of the binding instead of the author's name. I wonder if you could put one instead of my name: a little crescent moon with two stars inside the crescent? This is our family symbol, and I'd like to have it there as a surprise for Mary.

Send me a second edition copy of *Pictures*, will you? I want to see it with my own eyes. Send the *Saturday Review* one and maybe they'll review it again — they reviewed the second edition of *Losses*. (First request serious though foolish, second request in play.)

Mary sends her regards to you both. We're both brown as can be and — how could I have forgotten? — I have a black beard six weeks old and look remarkably different, like some minor Greek religious figure; little children look at me distrustfully in the street, though if I were they I'd come up and let me pat them on the head.

Yours,
Randall

Pictures came out *in May* 1954 *in an edition of* 6000, *followed by a second printing in June of* 1500, *and a third printing in late August of* 1500.

*   *   *

In September the Jarrells moved to 1200 *West Market Street in Greensboro, where they stayed for the next two years. It was a white two-story house with shutters and canvas awnings, and it had a small, grassy, unfenced yard graced by a towering deodar tree. Market Street was a busy thoroughfare, but Jarrell's stereo blocked out the traffic sounds; however, the traffic itself was a threat to the pets, and Schatzel had a near-fatal brush with a car but, luckily, rolled to safety only bruised. Sometimes Jarrell would say, "If only Greensboro had a river," but even without a river he liked it. He wrote Ford, "We have a big house we're crazy about, here; we've never been so well settled in our lives — we have the MG too. My life is so happy and blissful . . ."*

The social gatherings of Jarrell's old friends were now entirely at the Hookes' house instead of at the Friedlaenders'; and absent were the Taylors, who were at Kenyon, and also the Friedlaenders. After making an inspection of General Education in California, Friedlaender had enlisted a group of younger faculty members and the susceptible chancellor, Eddie Graham, to instigate a General Education takeover at Woman's College, at the expense of funds and faculty in art, music, and the humanities. "How can Marc fall for that?" Jarrell said; but Friedlaender did, at the cost of his friends — Hooke in French, Frank Laine in classics, Jarrell in English, and others. Soon Friedlaender and his young allies were in active combat with Hooke and the curriculum committee. Jarrell sided with Hooke, but he was preoccupied with his Selected Poems *and did not involve himself in the controversy at that time.*

TO KATHERINE GAUSS JACKSON

[January 1955]

Dear Mrs. Jackson:

I've wrestled with myself over your more-than-attractive offers, and finally virtue — anyway, I hope it's virtue — has triumphed all over again. I really think I'd better refuse about the book-reviewing: it would mean that those months I'd hardly write poems or stories or long pieces about poets, and I know that's what I ought to be writing. Four or five months ago the *Yale Review* asked me to do a long piece about poetry for them, every issue: some about current books, some about old poets or general things, just as I choose. I said that I would, since I thought this would make me write that much criticism every year, almost all of the criticism I could later use in a book. But if I added to that the six months of general reviewing it would take a tremendous proportion of my time — I'd better not, much as I liked writing for *Harper's,* and look forward to doing the Marianne Moore piece.

I'll be seeing her early next month — we're both on the committee that makes the Bollingen Award — and I'm going to ask her to talk to me ("as much as her natural reticence will allow") about her early life, the *Dial* days, and so on; she may not want to, but maybe she'll feel like it.

Let me thank you all over again for the extremely gratifying offer — I was very much pleased that you liked the review well enough to want me to do others.

Yours sincerely,

Randall Jarrell

Katherine Gauss Jackson was the literary editor at Harper's. Jarrell did two reviews for her: "New Books: 'Very Graceful Are the Uses of Culture,'" November 1954, and "The Year in Poetry," October 1955. He did not write anything more on Marianne Moore for Harper's, but he did review her book Predilections *for the* New York Times Book Review *in May 1955.*

In her memoir of Jarrell at the Yale University tribute to Jarrell in February 1966, Marianne Moore said, "At first meeting, and always to me, Randall Jarrell was the embodiment of triumphant anticipation, gratitude

to life, naturalness. He said, 'At a distance, friends — and now we ex-
change books. Can I believe it!' He wrote about me what was claiming much
more for me than I deserved; and one might say here something about the art
of appreciation that does not estrange the beneficiary from the giver . . . Al-
ways when parting he had some confident word about 'next time'. Abound-
ing in nutritive allusions, always growing, with no revenges . . . I cannot
think of anyone who gives me more incentive than Randall Jarrell, as I read
about him or think about him."

TO ROBERT LOWELL

[February 1955]

Dear Cal:

I've been meaning to write ever since Christmas — I'm getting more
and more case-historyish about putting off letters. I sent you and Elizabeth a
Selected Poems several days ago, but I'll send this air mail and maybe it'll
catch up with the book.

We have a big house we're crazy about and are very well settled: it's already been spring for two weeks. We shipped our MG back from the coast
and drive around in the country a lot. I did a long piece for the *Yale Review*
on Stevens' *Collected Poems* ["The Collected Poems of Wallace Stevens,"
Yale Review, volume 44, 1955] — maybe you've seen it, it ought to be out.
For my next piece I've got many delightful things like Van Doren's and
Sitwell's *Collected Poems,* all the stuff I put off writing about when I did
nothing but Stevens. Auden certainly is becoming a sit-by-the-fire-do-my-
embroidery and to-hell-with-the-muse poet, isn't he? He makes the slightest
demands imaginable.

Are you going to be in Duxbury this summer? We're going to spend
most of the summer on Cape Cod, I think. We're going to get a Mercedes
sports car early in July (going to name it Gertrude Johnson) and, as you
can imagine, are really looking forward to early July.

Wasn't it lovely getting the National Book Award for Stevens? Oscar
Cargill liked Stevens and the new poems as well as I do and we managed to
get it through. Eberhart wanted to give it to any (*or* any two) of six young
poets — Merwin, Moss, Hoffman, etc. When it was settled he said with a
modest smile that he'd thought it might be either Stevens or Cummings, so
that he'd written out little announcements, award-acclamations, manifes-
toes, for each; then he read them to us.

Tell me what you're writing and do send me any poems you've finished.
How does it feel to have spent a whole winter in Boston?

I spent about a month reading nothing but Wordsworth — variants, letters, biographies, everything — and like him much better than ever, even. What a poet!

Have you read Stevens's new poems, the section named "The Rock"; some of them are wonderful.

Affectionately,
Randall

Lowell was teaching at Boston University and industriously trying to break out of his early didactic, classical style that had been encouraged by Allen Tate and develop a more relaxed and direct style currently encouraged by William Carlos Williams.

*   *   *

After their summer vacation in Cape Cod the Jarrells, Kitten, and Elfie drove back to the house on Market Street, and Alleyne, Beatrice, and Schatzel flew in from California. As usual, there was Jarrell's tennis for Mary to watch, and his classes for her to attend; and there were televised sports events and campus politics on the weekends with the Hookes.

The power struggle between the administration and the curriculum committee had become a nightmare. The campus was split in two, friend was pitted against friend, and both sides frantically recruited from the uncommitted while the uncommitted frantically scuttled to avoid them (only the librarian maintained his neutrality). Week after week, the fat faculty members got fatter, the thin got thinner, and stress-related ills swept the ranks. Hoping to halt this, Gordon Gray, former Secretary of the Army and now president of the consolidated university, called a meeting and drove in from Chapel Hill to address not the issue but the situation. Taking what he called "the malcontents" to task, he advised any and all who were not happy with current administrative policies that they "were free to go elsewhere." Where they went after the meeting was to the Hookes' living room. Outraged by what they called this "slap on the wrist," malcontents from the psychology, philosophy, music, history, and English departments chose Jarrell for their spokesman, knowing he would not be intimidated by institutional authorities.

In time, they hammered out a petition to Gray for formal and confidential hearings to present the positions of tenured faculty for and against Chancellor Graham and Friedlaender's vaunted General Education. The petition was granted, the hearings were set, and a fight to the finish began that jeopardized promotions, departmental grants, staff jobs, and, in the case of classics, a whole department. The major depositions from Hooke's side were scrutinized by Jarrell: nothing was left to chance. At Hooke's, Laine, bellig-

erent but defeatist, stirring his ice cubes with his forefinger, kept saying, "But you can't fire a Graham in North Carolina." Thus it was Jarrell's strategy to pair Laine with himself on the day of testimony. That Laine (Jarrell said) spoke scarcely a word was more than made up for (Laine said) by Jarrell, who, in that menacing "high and piercing voice," attacked Friedlaender and Graham with all the logic, ridicule, and brilliance for which he was known.

Friedlaender and Jarrell never spoke to each other again (which was awkward later on when both were associated with Atheneum Publishers). Graham and Jarrell never spoke again, or met; though before the academic year was over, Jarrell (in another context) was forced by the FBI to seek a character vindication from Graham, and, depending on what Graham said, would — or would not — be in some political difficulty. Meanwhile, the tension over the hearings subsided and there was a lull in the winter while the administration in Chapel Hill considered who was to stay on and who would be "free to go elsewhere."

TO IRENE MACADAMS

[January 1956]

Dear Irene:

I wanted to thank you very *very* much for the Mercedes vacuum cleaner — it's a wonderful present, and will keep the car beautiful as can be. I'm awfully glad you liked the skirt. We had a lovely Christmas and a nice luxurious vacation — it felt strange to get up early for the children's school this morning.

Your Christmas sounded awfully nice and awfully eventful. I hope you'll be coming back to sunny (I can't say snowy, since this winter it doesn't snow) North Carolina to see us all.

With lots of love,
Randall

*   *   *

In February of this mild winter Kitten was killed, and Jarrell was crushed by grief. Kitten had spent thousands of hours at Jarrell's side while he read and wrote and had spent years playing, napping, and traveling with him, so that Jarrell was his as much as he was Jarrell's. Kitten had loved him as his own. When Jarrell stretched out on the sofa, Kitten perched on the arm by Jarrell's head and washed his hair with the same purposeful strokes he used on himself. When Jarrell relaxed in the tub

*after tennis, Kitten often stood with his paws on the edge giving him
"kisses."*

As Mary Jarrell wrote in "The Group of Two":

*Anyone holding Kitten on his lap had, as the girls said, King's X. If
the music on the FM "went bad" while Randall was holding him, I'd
hear him in the other room saying, "Away, away, base Menotti." (Or
Sibelius, or Hindemith.) And in another instant, "Help! Help! Someone
come change the music. I'd do it myself but I'm holding Kitten . . ."*
        *On many clear nights, back from the library, we'd put the car in the
garage and be looking up to find Orion's belt . . . when a downy, faintly
warm, almost invisible presence wound itself in and out between us,
leaning lightly on us. "Isn't that polite?" Randall said. "To want to
come and meet us!" One night he didn't come. Kitten was hit at the side
of the road by a car . . . One blow on his skull killed him instantly . . .
The beautiful eyes and face, and the graceful body were not hurt in any
way.*

On finding him, Jarrell moaned and sank down on the grass by the curb.
Mary's arms were around him, and his arms were around his cat, as he
cried, "Kitten. Oh, KITTEN . . . poor, poor Kitten." In the dark, Jarrell
dug his grave under the deodar tree, and Mary lined it with fern. Then
Jarrell curled Kitten's body in a circle "like a little fox."
        The following days were difficult, as Mary explained in "The Group of
Two":

*Randall could scarcely teach and we decided to drive to Charleston for a
few days. When we came back to Greensboro, people spoke so kindly to
Randall. Alleyne and Beatrice were so loving; and I did all I could to
comfort him, but in the end he had to suffer by himself all the zigzag
work of mourning, with the guilt and the longed-for dreams and the
dreaded fading and the reluctant giving up.*

TO QUINCY MUMFORD

March 7, 1956

Dear Mr. Mumford:
        Thank you for your letter. It gave me a quite comprehensive idea of
what the work of the Consultant in Poetry has become; it is a position in
which someone can be of real service to poetry in our country. I am very

much interested in the position and would, I believe, be available for it —
the college here would give me leave of absence for the two years I am sure.

If Monday and Tuesday, the 12th and 13th of March, are convenient
dates for you, I'll be glad to come up to the Library then, and we can discuss
the whole matter at more length. My home address is 1200 West Market,
my telephone number 39540.

With all best wishes,
Yours sincerely,
Randall Jarrell

*Quincy Mumford, as Librarian of Congress, was spokesman for the Fellows
of the Library who chose the Poetry Consultant.*

TO ROY BASLER

[April 1956]

Dear Roy:

Thanks very much for your letter. I trust the forms were complete and
the fingerprints clear — the police lieutenant seemed very professional. The
big NON-SENSITIVE on the forms made me feel good, as if I'd at last
made the football team and in the line at that.

We're arriving in Washington early Friday evening (April 27th); Robert Richman wanted me to read poems at his Institute then. Mary and I
thought we'd come over to the Library Saturday morning, mainly just to see
everybody, but also to do anything that might still need to be done.

I'm delighted that the general reaction *was* one of approval; as you say,
you never know. Miss [Mary] McGrory was very pleasant over the telephone, and made the interview easy for me.

I just had a letter from Karl Shapiro — he was here for a couple days last
month; he wrote how much he liked the job when he had it. I'm very much
looking forward to it myself.

With all best wishes,
Randall

*Roy Basler, head of Reference, was major-domo of the Library of Congress's
cultural activities, which included the office of the Poetry Consultant. Jarrell's allusion to Basler's "you never know" was curiously prophetic in that
shortly after the media announced Jarrell's appointment in Washington and
Greensboro, a perturbed Basler telephoned Jarrell that an unnamed infor-
mant had reported to them that Jarrell was a Communist. He cited the re-*

sults of a McCarthyesque investigation that turned up (1) *numerous poems and articles in such "pinko publications" as* Partisan Review, *the* New Republic, *and* The Nation, *and* (2) *certain Marxist friendships at the University of Texas. Basler added that this was extremely embarrassing and could be a threat to Jarrell's appointment. What was needed at once, he said, was Jarrell's sworn oath that he had not been a member of the Communist party, backed up by a letter of character recommendation signed by Chancellor Edward Graham.*

Jarrell revealed nothing of his own embarrassment, nor that now his appointment was doubly threatened, but went so far as to assure Basler he had not been a member of the Communist party and to presume that the vindicating letter would be in the mail. It was, and on examination proved to have been drafted by a dean and entrusted to the chancellor merely for signature.

*   *   *

During the summer, the Greensboro newspaper announced Graham's resignation from the Woman's College and Friedlaender's leave of absence. Jarrell was rereading Eliot's poetry and taking notes for a possible book. While Mary packed, Jarrell returned a year's accumulation of books to the university library; and after a farewell dinner at the Hookes' — with Lucy's lemon pie — they drove with Elfie in the Mercedes to Washington.

Alastair Reid, Robert Graves, and Randall Jarrell
in Washington, 1957

Washington, D.C.,
September 1956–June 1958

✇

*T*he house at 3916 Jenifer Street, N.W., was in what the natives called "the
third alphabet," and what Jarrell said was "like an address in science fiction." (The first-alphabet streets were A, B, C, and so forth; the second-al-
phabet streets had two-syllable names, such as Ashby, Benton, Calvert; and the
third-alphabet streets had three-syllable names such as Albemarle, Brandywine,
Chesapeake, Davenport, Ellicott, Fessenden, Garrison, Harrison, Ingomar, Jenifer,
and on through Wisconsin.) Jarrell wrote Elizabeth Bishop, "I've always loved
Washington, and when you live in it, it is best of all."

For Jarrell, living in Washington meant season tickets to the Redskins' games
and the Washington Opera Society, and evenings with the Budapest Quartet. It
meant knowing an antique dealer on a first-name basis, being friends with a waiter
at the Colony who raced a kayak on the Potomac, and feeding liver to a lynx at the
zoo who reminded him of Kitten. It meant living in a city that had a southern accent, a river, mockingbirds, and a vast wooded park to get lost in on summer nights
in the Mercedes with the top down. Furthermore, Washington was an easy run to
Cumberland for the sports-car races. When Jarrell was quoted in the newspaper as
saying that Washington would be ideal if he just had a good singles partner, a
good singles player named Larry Jaffe obliged him with a call. They divided their
tennis time between the Sheraton courts and Jaffe's Jewish country club, where, on
the first day, the bearded Jarrell was overjoyed at being asked by one of the members
if he was the new rabbi.

The Poetry Consultant at the Library of Congress is not a government employee.
He, or she, is chosen by the Fellows of the Library (formerly with the able assistance
of Allen Tate). Although the consultant's office is in a government building, the
salary is paid by the Isabel and Archer Huntington estate, the poetry readings that

are arranged by the consultant are funded by the Whittall estate, and the special programs are often financed by the Bollingen Foundation. Prior to Jarrell, there had been no consultant for four years, and he conscientiously set himself the task of learning what was available or might be made available not only to reactivate the position but to enhance it.

It was Jarrell's idea to solicit writers' original manuscripts in exchange for tax benefits; and it was Jarrell's idea to interview and record poets in conversation. In his first year, he spent many hours listening to previously recorded readings, and it was his idea to select the best of those to make a series of LP records (funded by the Bollingen Foundation) to be sold to the public. As his appointment became more widely known, he was asked to read poetry locally to audiences at Howard University, Sidwell Friends School, and the Faculty Wives Club of the United States Navy, as well as to the congressional pages and others. And after his formal lecture ("The Taste of the Age") in the Coolidge Auditorium received news coverage in Washington and in Time *and* Newsweek, *more speaking engagements and much correspondence followed. In addition to this, Jarrell met with visiting poets who might come from as far off as Finland and who could be as far out as the Beats. He also regularly took phone calls asking for the identification of poems or parts of poems to settle arguments or to adorn congressional rhetoric.*

The side of Jarrell that loved to teach and to bring poetry alive for congenial audiences enjoyed the coast-to-coast appearances and the intellectual pace during his two years in Washington; but the side of Jarrell that needed calm and quiet to write poetry was neglected. Though he wrote an hour-long tribute to the Peruvian poet Gabriela Mistral, it was merely an official assignment. He managed to write two essays while in Washington, "Against Abstract Expressionism" (Art News, *Summer 1957) and "About Popular Culture," an address given for the National Book Award ceremony in 1958 that was published as a monograph by Paleamon Press of Winston-Salem, North Carolina, in 1981.*

For the most part, translating seemed best suited for the scraps of time between Jarrell's official duties, and he finished eleven Rilke poems and "The Archangels' Song" from Goethe's Faust. *At times he was troubled and slightly despondent at having written only four new poems: "The Woman at the Washington Zoo," "The Bronze David of Donatello," "Jerome," and "Jamestown."*

TO ELIZABETH BISHOP

[September 1956]

Dear Elizabeth:

I've been meaning to write a long letter for so long, a long one like *Paradise Lost,* and never even starting, that I despair of it and am just going to write a scrappy one. I was awfully glad you liked my review and what I said about Vuillard and Vermeer ["The Year in Poetry," *Harper's,* October 1955] — I've been meaning to write a regular article about your poems; all the new ones are such charming, sympathetic, happy-sounding ones. I was crazy about your village story ["In the Village"] in *The New Yorker* too — Peter Taylor said that it was the best thing that had been in *The New Yorker* for years.

I'm here in Washington being the poetry consultant; it's very nice, especially since Phyllis Armstrong [Jarrell's assistant] is so pleasant. We have a pretty house out past the zoo, near Chevy Chase; I've always loved Washington and when you live in it it's best of all. We have a Mercedes 190 SL, a white one; before we had an MG just like yours. The Mercedes is all it's supposed to be — we couldn't like it better, though we miss the MG.

I was delighted when you got the Pulitzer Prize and the *Partisan* fellowship. I (I guess because of my grey and black and white beard) was made one of the Chancellors of the Poetry Society of America, silly people; I nominated you about three weeks ago for that $5,000 prize they give, but it probably won't do any good — the only time they ever gave it to anybody under the age of Edgar Lee Masters they gave it to Rolfe Humphries. I was one of the judges, for two years, of that Lamont Poetry Selection; there were four or five good poets applying, but those wretched judges gave it one year to Constance Carrier and one year to Donald Hall, and I resigned in despair, and they put Richard Wilbur in my place. The world of the younger poets, at present, certainly is the world of Richard Wilbur and safer paler mirror-images of Richard Wilbur — who'd have thought that the era of the poet in the Grey Flannel Suit was coming?

I feel very guilty and apologetic not to have written for so long. I've got worse and worse about writing real letters, and I got started not writing to you when (I blush to say it) I was vexed at your letter about *Pictures,* which to me is a serious book not about Mary McCarthy. But I soon got over that, and after that not writing was just ordinary or extraordinary neurotic behavior.

I haven't written too many poems lately — I wrote a long one about Donatello's *David,* the bronze one, I just wrote a poem about "The Woman at the Washington Zoo," and I've done eleven or twelve Rilke translations. I've done most of the notes for a book about, so to speak, the psychoanalytical foundations of Eliot's poetry, writing it will be very hard, because I have enough for six or eight hundred pages and don't know what to leave out or how to organize the whole thing. I have about three-quarters of another book like *Poetry and the Age* — have you seen the six or seven pieces I've had in the *Yale Review*? I've even written a piece about sports cars ["Go, Man, Go!" *Mademoiselle*, May 1957] — when it comes out I'll send not you, Elizabeth Bishop, but you the MG owner a copy.

I'll look for a picture that has Mary and the girls in it. Alleyne is 17 and Beatrice 14. We've been spending most of our summers in Laguna Beach or at Cape Cod. We have a lovely dreamy childish cat named Elfie; he has more fur than any cat I ever saw. Kitten lived with us until this spring, when he was killed by a car; he was almost sixteen.

All I had to do was start the letter and it turned into a long one.

Brazil certainly sounds nice — it must be *much* better for you than this country. I don't know where I want to live — somewhere in the 19th century, I know that much; here it's almost the 21st.

Have you ever read Giraudoux's *Electra*? I've read it about ten times. And have you ever heard Richard Strauss' *Ariadne auf Naxos*? There's a wonderful Angel recording of it that we play almost more than any other records.

We've been going to the zoo a lot here and taking pieces of kidney to the lynx and two wolves; they come right up to the edge of the cage and almost eat from your hand. They're so beautiful, and look at you with such life and intensity; the wolves are tremendous white ones.

I've had to do lots of newspaper and radio things and, worst, a television program; they came to the house and took seven hours to make six or seven minutes of film — they had incredibly arduous complicated technical procedure and not the tiniest bit of imaginative or dramatic knowledge; as they tried to make up an interview they were like children trying to improvise a play. And all this was supposed to produce five natural, unrehearsed, spontaneous minutes. But the professional football games are wonderful.

I see very little of Cal. When he was in love with that Italian girl he wrote that he was going to be divorced and wanted to visit us; he did, fairly along in a manic stage — then while he was in the hospital I had to do quite a bit of difficult corresponding with the Italian girl, since he'd named me, in letters, as the American friend to correspond with; also he'd shown Elizabeth Hardwick my letter saying I was glad he was being divorced — presumably also saying to her, "Yah, yah, you see what he thinks of you!" We saw them a little last summer; she was very cordial, poor disingenuous thing! and Cal was joylessly being good, good, the properest Bostonian imaginable, saying what a nice man MacLeish is, everybody is.

I've bought many hundreds of records, read hundreds of books by Freud and anthropologists, and written a little and thought a lot about paintings, since I saw you last. (Down in North Carolina you couldn't get any real

Randall, Beatrice, and Mary at the Washington Zoo

music on the radio.) Alas, Peter Taylor moved up to Kenyon from North Carolina — I don't have any really literary friends here, though several good ones of other sorts.

We've bought a fair amount of old furniture and that was a lot of fun; aren't you going to revisit the United States next year, just to see what's missing you? — You could stay with us here. Mary would like awfully to know you; she admired your Houghton Mifflin picture very much. With many ashamed heartfelt apologies from your worst correspondent, and most inveterate reader.

Love,
Randall

The year Jarrell nominated Bishop, the Poetry Society of America prize went to Joyce Horner.

Lowell, recovered from his last manic swing and stabilized on tranquilizers, was teaching Sylvia Plath, May Swenson, and others at Boston University. He and Elizabeth were happily reconciled, which accounted somewhat for the recent distance between him and Jarrell. As usual, it was Lowell who reached out to Jarrell, and, after accepting Lowell's invitation to visit, Jarrell braced himself to face Elizabeth. The tension was eased when she partnered him to victory over Lowell and Mary at darts, and whenever she said the word "Massa-toosetts," Jarrell's features softened visibly. After lunch that day, Lowell escorted the visitors to historic Winslow House, where he bought their tickets but went in free himself. "Member of the family, Randall," he said airily, which somehow grated on Jarrell.

Later that day, Lowell brought out a prose memoir of his childhood (originally written for his analyst) that he called "91 Revere Street." He waited expectantly as Jarrell speed-read it in his accomplished way and when finished made no comment. Lowell volunteered that he was going to use it with several poems in his next book, and Jarrell was still noncommittal. "Why not?" Lowell asked him. "What's wrong with it?" And Jarrell said, "But it's not poetry, Cal."

Lowell stared at him in pained and angry silence. He described these feelings later when he wrote, "I have never known anyone who so connected what his friends wrote with their lives . . . This could be trying: whenever we turned out something Randall felt was unworthy or a falling off, there was a coolness in all one's relations with him. You felt that even your choice in neckties wounded him." (RJ)

When normal, Lowell was indeed vulnerable to Jarrell's disapproval and was touchingly attached to his friendship. Throughout Jarrell's life-time, Lowell had a sweet readiness to make amends with him and a contin-ual willingness to apologize and thank.

TO KARL SHAPIRO

October 18, 1956

Dear Karl:

I'm just back from two and a half weeks on the West Coast, otherwise I'd have sent the poems long before. The Rilke translation is for your maga-zine, if you like it, and the "Woman at the Zoo" is just for you; do write me how you like it.

I just had a long letter from Elizabeth Bishop, in reply to a long one of mine. She sounds wonderfully happy and well settled.

I fairly often, on the Coast, read Rilke, Yeats, Hardy, Hopkins, Stevens, Bishop, Auden, and so forth to audiences; I read your "The Leg." It cer-tainly is a wonderful poem.

I met a really good (and wholly delightful) new young poet named Gregory Corso. He's all that the tea-party or grey-flannel or World-of-Richard-Wilbur poets aren't. Not that I don't like Wilbur, but one is enough.

I hope you like Nebraska a lot. We flew over it yesterday, but whether or not we saw you I don't know.

Yours,
Randall

Shapiro was teaching at the University of Nebraska and editing their liter-ary magazine, the Prairie Schooner. *He published Jarrell's translation of Rilke's "The Grown-Up" in the winter issue, 1956.*

Before leaving San Francisco the Jarrells had been invited to a Chinese restaurant by Kenneth Rexroth and his wife. Jarrell enjoyed both Chinese food and reading Chinese menus, but Rexroth had preordered the meal, in-cluding, he said, "really authentic" dishes. Nothing looked familiar, and when the lid was lifted off one unsightly conglomeration, Jarrell said, "What, pray, is that?" Rexroth then discoursed at some length, peppering his speech with Chinese phrases, until Jarrell could stand it no longer and burst out, "And they scoop it out of hollow trees?" Rexroth served himself, saying nothing, and Jarrell ate rice.

Gregory Corso was the only Beat poet who interested Jarrell. He had the appeal of a streetwise naïf with perhaps the potential of a Villon. With little more than grade schooling, he was so "wholly delightful" that someone made it possible for him to audit classes at Harvard, where he wrote his first book of poems, The Vestal Lady on Brattle. *Inscribing a copy for the Jarrells, Corso wrote, "For Randall and Mary Jarrell in return for that wonderful, gentle evening in San Francisco."*

The Jarrells had taken the vegetarian Corso to Fisherman's Wharf, where he ordered a fruit salad and impressed them with his hopes for loving the world and living his life for poetry. Later they met with Lawrence Ferlinghetti, Allen Ginsberg, and William Burroughs, who challenged Jarrell to demonstrate "excellence" in poetry. When Jarrell read Frost's "Home Burial" aloud to them, Ginsberg leaped up in the middle shouting, "Coupla squares yakking!" Jarrell finished the poem and was finished with Ginsberg.

Later, Corso left San Francisco en route to New York and stopped off in Washington to see Jarrell. He arrived in his Harvard chinos and tennis shoes and wearing a black Shetland sweater over a white Arrow shirt. He was medium height and Mediterranean-looking with a jutting brow, heavy jaw, and thick, black, blown-about hair. He was coatless, tieless, sockless, and penniless — all of which Jarrell gladly supplied. Then, remembering his own hard times as a beginning poet, and what the hospitality of the Breyers and the Starrs had meant, Jarrell invited Corso to stay indefinitely and work on his poetry.

He stayed six weeks, writing a poem a day, in the language of Whitman, Williams, and Cummings, celebrating such subjects as the yak, the needle, the penis, and cosmic love. Though Jarrell's long talks with Corso kept him from his own poetry, he obligingly took on Tate's role as mentor. Corso, however, was committed to the Beat principle that spontaneity was all, and he refused to revise but would simply throw out the old poem and write another. "Failure to select, exclude, compress, or aim toward a work of art," Jarrell wrote, "makes it impossible for even a talented beatnik to write a good poem except by accident." Disenchanted with Corso, Jarrell was relieved when he finally resumed his trip to New York.

TO BERNARD HAGGIN

[October 1956]

Dear Bernard:

Influenced by the music critic B. H. Haggin, I started to write this letter on a postcard but after two sentences I ran out of postcard. Dear Bernard, we are *very* eager to see you; now that we live in the northeast section of the universe, we're coming to New York and we can see you, and I can perform for you, if you'll accept a queer invitation for the night of Wednesday October 31st (I'm scared stiff the ghost of Schnabel will be giving a recital that night, or something of the sort.) I'm going to be making a lecture (very much in the style of *Pictures from an Institution*) at Barnard, and the Dean of Barnard is going to invite you to have dinner at the "Deanery" — truly! truly! — and then hear the lecture. Do come, do come. Mary and I really will burst into tears if you can't. And, now that we're in Washington, we really will cry or nurse a smouldering resentment if you don't *some* time during the next year come down and stay with us: it's *very* close to New York, there're concerts, we've a new Renoir lithograph, the National Gallery (and the Phillips) are full of new acquisitions, and so on.

I didn't have a carbon copy of the review ["Harmony, Discord and Taste," review of Haggin's *Listener's Companion, New York Times Book Review*, June 17, 1956] so I couldn't send you the sentences those wretches cut out: I say *wretches* because I'd scrupulously stayed inside the prescribed wordage and then they cut out my peroration, which told everybody to be absolutely certain to buy *The Listener's Musical Companion* and *Ariadne auf Naxos*.

We've got a nice house and are crazy about Washington: I am particularly because I've written three poems since I've been here. Our address is 3916 Jenifer St., N.W. If by some awful bad luck you can't get free the night of October 31st let's all three of us have lunch that day — in fact, let's have lunch whether or not.

We've just been on the West Coast for two weeks; several people at colleges mentioned your criticism to us, and one man talked for a long time about how much in your debt he was so far as his whole taste in music was concerned.

Yours,
Randall

TO ELIZABETH BISHOP

[February 1957]

Dear Elizabeth:

I like the Pound poem ["Visits to St. Elizabeths"]; it gets all the ways one feels about him and the poor contradictory awful and nice ways he is, and it's more varied and specifically live, than I'd have thought it possible for a House-that-Jack-built poem to be. Changing it to *wretched* at the end certainly is right.

Gee, it was a joy to see you again, Mary was so glad to get to meet you. I hope you'll be down here before long. We're going to be gone April 25–27, May 2–5, May 10–13, and here all the rest of the time.

I like all of your new poems *so* much, you seem to me to be writing nothing but good poems, something theoretically and practically impossible. I ought to explain my rather funny and personal remark about your sestinas: I like your poetry better than anybody's since the Frost-Stevens-Eliot-Moore generation, so I looked with awed wonder at some phrases feeling to me a little like some of my phrases, in your poems; I felt as if, so to speak, some of my wash-cloths were part of a Modigliani collage, or as if my cat had got into a Vuillard. I think too, that all people who really remember childhood and do it at all right sound alike in some ways.

I'll send you the "Jerome" and "The Woman at the Washington Zoo": I've just been typing them.

We had a swell time talking to Meyer Schapiro and looking at paintings at the Metropolitan; every time I look at five or six Goya portraits I like him better — It's hard to see how anybody could respond over and over to the specific essence of each new person.

Your house looked like fairy-lace-modern on the moon. You remember how (I think this is right) in the [H. G.] Wells *First Men in the Moon* there'd be sixteen or eighteen moon-men all alike, buds from the one plant; well, that's what your three Melanie Klein psychoanalysts are.

I've got copies of the "Manners" poem, the sestina I think, and the last one in *The New Yorker;* if you could without too much trouble give me copies of the other poems after your book [*Poems*], it would be wonderful. I want to write a very long piece about all your poetry. The new *and* the book; if I could have them all around together, to look at over and over, then I'll be able to say not only what I know but lots more I now have no idea of.

I always have a queer feeling when I talk to you — I don't know whether I can describe it. It's as if what you said — even when it's uncongenial to me, something I'd never think or say — were in another way always congenial, direct, easy for me to see and feel; as if we were very different but *did* come from the same planet, so that it's easier for me than something from somebody just like us from another planet. It's a feeling I never have with anybody else: I'm not saying this as a vague intensive but as a precise observation. It's as if you were a color I see so easily I hardly have to look.

I've just been writing, mostly on the airplane coming home from Texas, a poem about a Picasso picture. It's all too inspired; most of it, that is, just comes, and isn't enough like my regular way of writing for me to know whether it's good; when I go along with the poem it all feels wonderful, and when I don't I don't even know whether it will ever be even a mediocre poem. All in all, though, I'm so overjoyed to be writing a poem that I don't care.

Yours,
Randall

Jarrell had met the art historian Meyer Schapiro earlier at an arts festival in Dallas, where Schapiro lauded Cézanne and Jarrell compared abstract expressionism to the work of Betsy the finger-painting chimpanzee at the Baltimore Zoo.

The Picasso poem was never finished.

THE WOMAN AT THE WASHINGTON ZOO

The saris go by me from the embassies.

Cloth from the moon. Cloth from another planet.
They look back at the leopard like the leopard.

And I. . . .
           this print of mine, that has kept its color
Alive through so many cleanings; this dull null
Navy I wear to work, and wear from work, and so
To my bed, so to my grave, with no
Complaints, no comment: neither from my chief,
The Deputy Chief Assistant, nor his chief —
Only I complain. . . . this serviceable
Body that no sunlight dyes, no hand suffuses
But, dome-shadowed, withering among columns,
Wavy beneath fountains — small, far-off, shining
In the eyes of animals, these beings trapped
As I am trapped but not, themselves, the trap,
Aging, but without knowledge of their age,
Kept safe here, knowing not of death, for death —
Oh, bars of my own body, open, open!

The world goes by my cage and never sees me.
And there come not to me, as come to these,
The wild beasts, sparrows pecking the llamas' grain,
Pigeons settling on the bears' bread, buzzards
Tearing the meat the flies have clouded. . . .

                                        Vulture,
When you come for the white rat that the foxes left,
Take off the red helmet of your head, the black
Wings that have shadowed me, and step to me as man:
The wild brother at whose feet the white wolves fawn,
To whose hand of power the great lioness
Stalks, purring. . . .
                    You know what I was,
You see what I am: change me, change me!

TO ELIZABETH BISHOP

                                                    [April 1957]

Dear Elizabeth:
    I've meant to write every day, and now at last it's come — how's it dif-
ferent from the other days? How is it that now my hand's going over the
page instead of just being meant to go? There must be some kind of dyke
inside me and every day that little boy brings a bucket of water and pours it
into the water and finally the water spills over the top and floods everything
and wonders why it waited so long to flood it.
    Gee, your poems are wonderful. I'm like you, I don't much like the last
one, but every other one is really good, just beautiful. If my little foxes
poem helped you with your armadillo poem ["The Armadillo"] I'm awfully glad, because yours is ten times as good. They're all so good I hate to
quote parts, I have many dozens of favorite lines or parts. Your poems seem
really about real life, and to have as much of what's nice and beautiful and
loving about the world as the world lets them have. I've quite got to like
your poems better than Marianne Moore's as much as I do like hers — but
life beats art, so to speak, and sense beats eccentricity, and the way things
really are beats the most beautiful unreal visions, half-truths, one can fix up
by leaving out and indulging oneself. That, too, is just half the truth about
her, but I've written the other half at great length and don't need to do it
all over again. I often think of Wordsworth's "I have endeavored to look
steadily at my object," and your poetry is so much like that — often it's as if
you were allowed just one light — slightly off, like Debussy or Bartók or
Berg melodies — fixing phrase for an object or part of one. I liked your
dream poem very much — I'm always particularly interested in the second
kind of poem you write, the more subjective, personal interior-life kind, not
that I like them better than the others at all, but there're fewer of them, and
I have a kind of *What are these going to come to?* feeling about them that I
don't have about the others.

I'll send you in this letter my Donatello *David* poem, incidentally, you can't see all the things I talk about in an ordinary small photograph, but if you'll look at the ones in the big Phaidon Donatello, they're all there. I don't imagine you saw a poem named "Nestus Gurley" in *The Virginia Quarterly* — surely it doesn't get to Brazil — so I'll send it. And I've just written a queer, nay, weird, poem and can't resist sending it. I was asked to write a poem about Jamestown (390th anniversary) and said that I doubted that I could but if one came I would. I imagine the magazine [*Virginia Quarterly Review*] will turn pale when it sees what came.

I'm awfully glad you're coming. I'd like to ask a favor of you, if you can bear to do it. Would you stay till Monday morning and read some poems aloud to me (in the process getting them recorded)? I can arrange to have the engineer stay out of the way and never say a thing. I'd like to hear you read them, all the new especially, and I'd like to have a recording of them exist: probably both of us will live to be eighty-three. I have a serious feeling about that particular age, but the world is full of bombs and airplane crashes and you really ought to read them. I haven't recorded anyone since I've been here, and I'd like so much to do it with your poems and then be able to have them on a record the public can buy when this silly place gets the money to bring some out.

What you said about "Jerome" was a great pleasure to me — I hope it really is that way. That's the way I wanted it to be.

I have ten, I'll put in four or five, Rilke translations done now; from short ones to big ones like "The Great Night" and "Requiem for the Death of a Boy." It took many, many hundreds of hours, though — and you never can tell till late whether you can really do one. "Strange violin, are you following me?" is one that I can't do in English, but I couldn't believe it and I had many dozens of versions before I finally quit. Sometimes when you finally realize that a translation of some line is impossible, that you'll have to imagine an equivalent, that helps; it's queerest of all when you get everything but two or three lines done, and these take fifteen or so hours spread out over three or four years. I've got quite a few poems of his half or a third done — I'm hopeful that I can get six or eight finished in the next couple of years.

Let's plan to do a lot together while you're here. Mary'd like very much for you and your friend to have dinner with us and we can arrange some other things. Our telephone number is WO-6-4651.

I feel like *Lord Lundy* where it says, "Let's cut the poems in half," let's stop the letter. I'll see you next week.

Yours,
Randall

In his review of Bishop's book Poems *two years before, Jarrell had written that it was "one of the best books an American poet has ever written . . ." After citing thirty-one poems as "musts," he said, "This is a ridiculously long list. And have I not one fault to find? Some of the later poems are too exclusively descriptive — and there are fifty-four poems in the book not several hundred."*

TO HIRAM HAYDN

[April 18, 1957]

Dear Hiram:

Yes, I've definitely made up my mind to leave Knopf, and I think it would make me very happy to become one of your authors. I have three books mostly done. The first is like the general sections of *Poetry and the Age* only more general and about the United States; there's one long essay about the arts, the public for the arts, and education in the United States ["The Taste of the Age"]; one long essay about the poet and his relation to real critics and ideal ones ["Poets, Critics, and Readers"]; a piece on the intellectual in the United States ["The Intellectual in America"]; one on progressive education ["The Schools of Yesteryear"]; a piece about love and poetry in our day here ["Love and Poetry," *Mademoiselle,* February 1956]; short pieces about the United States in the style of that "Dictionary of Americanisms," of [John P.] Marquand's books; a piece about art (especially Abstract Expressionism) in this country; a piece (it's not done yet — it's for *High Fidelity,* the magazine) about listening to records; a sort of half-lyric half-mocking piece about sports cars and their drivers in the United States ["Go, Man, Go!" *Mademoiselle,* May 1957]. Most of these pieces are, roughly, in the style of "The Age of Criticism"; all are supposed to be, primarily, little anomalous works of art, fun to read; I mean to call the whole thing *The Poet in the USA,* or something of the sort. It's almost done — by the end of the summer I'll be through.

The other prose book is one like the poetry sections of *Poetry and the Age:* a *long* section on Auden, and a long one on Graves; a long essay about Stevens; shorter pieces about Cummings, Spender, dozens of American and English poets. It's about three-quarters done. And the third book is a book of poems, which is just about done: I haven't published any new poems in books since 1951, so by now I have plenty for a book.

I'm doing a short story anthology for Anchor, and I have a table of contents for an anthology of modern poetry that I'm interested in getting somebody to do; permissions might be too expensive for a paper-backed book. Anyway, there are the things I'm in the middle of; besides these, I have half the notes for a very long book on the (so to speak) psychoanalytical roots of Eliot's work, but it will take me years to write and I don't know whether I could print it while he's alive.

It was a great pleasure to meet your wife; and Mary had a wonderful time talking to you, and felt she'd known you for years. If only she'd got to hear Margaret Mead and Harlow Shapley *be,* be their own wonderful selves, instead of — how could they — just sitting there eating like other mortals!

Yes, you can certainly clear this with Pat Knopf, and we can move on to a contract. What I seem to myself to want from a publisher is simple: interest, real interest; I like Harry Ford and Bill Cole very much, but I really don't even have an editor at Knopf's any longer, and there's nobody in the literary end who, so to speak, knows me from Billy Rose.

We're looking forward very much to seeing you in May.

Yours,
Randall

Hiram Haydn, forty-nine, was a bald, tall, fit midwesterner with a Ph.D. in Renaissance literature. He wore owlish round glasses professorstyle and brisk hard-finish suits Madison Avenue style. He had taught in Ohio and at the Woman's College in Greensboro (before Jarrell was there) and was a favorite with the Friedlaenders and the Hookes. Haydn had met Jarrell through them on one of his return visits to Greensboro. With his energy and enthusiasm, his powerful managerial skills and drive, Haydn could have been chairman of the English department, dean of humanities, or president in the college of his choice, but he chose to work in publishing. Starting out in New York as executive secretary of the United Chapters of Phi Beta Kappa and assistant editor at Crown Publishers, Haydn went on to become editor of the Phi Beta Kappa quarterly, The American Scholar, *and later — on leaving a top spot with Bobbs-Merrill — became Bennett Cerf's right-hand man at Random House. His personal warmth, bodily vigor, and generous candor about himself magnetized Jarrell. Haydn seemed a man securely in his prime — a winner winning — and Jarrell was not only pleased to serve on* The American Scholar's *editorial board but thought he had found a friend and editor for life.*

The meeting in New York that Jarrell refers to was for an American Scholar *dinner at the Biltmore. Others on the editorial board were Richard Rovere, Washington correspondent for* The New Yorker; *Roy*

Wilkins, president of the NAACP; Senator Paul Douglas; and the two rival scene-stealers, anthropologist Margaret Mead and astronomer Harlow Shapley.

*   *   *

The Jarrells and Beatrice spent June and July on Cape Cod in an eighteenth-century sea captain's house. In August, the family — including Elfie — drove to Antioch College in Yellow Springs, Ohio, for a writers' conference. The main attraction for Jarrell was that the chairman said, "Peter Taylor is coming, too."

By this time, Taylor had written one novel and started another; had written one play and started a dozen; and had two collections of short stories and — besides teaching — was a regular contributor to The New Yorker. *Though the two friends were as congenial as ever, their lifestyles were worlds apart. The time Jarrell devoted to tennis and ball games Taylor employed tracking down vacated houses in the country, usually stuffed with hay. The money Jarrell poured into sports cars and stereos Taylor spent on shoring up foundations and traveling. Jarrell still craved ballet, music, and art museums (in this country), and Taylor still craved "expeditions" — but to Paris, London, and Rome. Taylor gossiped with Tate, played bridge with Mr. Ransom, and drank with Lowell; but with Jarrell, he talked about Lawrence, James, Tolstoy, Ibsen, and Strindberg — in a word, literature.*

Something of a drawback at Antioch were the cramped graduate-student apartments provided for the two professors and their families; and a special drawback for Taylor was the Lemon Drop Café in Yellow Springs, instead of some swaybacked clapboard house in the country where two sisters served "marvelous meals." On the other hand, their classes and conferences were not demanding, and the small, grassy campus swarming with friendly dogs had, as Jarrell said, "a kind of innocence." In the hot afternoons, little Petie napped with his mother while the others explored the dirt roads; and in the evenings, by lamplight, the men talked, the wives listened, and little Katie and Beatrice read Louisa May Alcott.

In recent years, both writers had declined invitations to summer conferences, preferring to write, and Jarrell wondered why Taylor had wanted to come to this one. On their last night together, he asked him, and Taylor answered, "Why we *wanted to come? We only came because the summer-school dean said* you *were going to come."*

TO ROBERT LOWELL

[November 3, 1957]

Dear Cal:

I thought I'd make this just a note so you'd get it immediately. I've been quite sick for several weeks and didn't get in to the Library of Congress and your letter till today. I like the poem ["My Last Afternoon with Uncle Devereux Winslow"] *very* much. The motion really has changed and is much clearer and easier. Do send me the others right away.

I was just delighted with what you said about [Philip] Larkin — I'm crazy about him. Say what one will, there's a surprising amount of objectivity in taste.

That Donatello poem is going to be in the next *Art News* along with, I hope and think, several photographs of David and Goliath's head.

I've been sick most of September and October and haven't any real news. We're delighted that you're coming down in December. We saw Peter and Eleanor for four or five days late in August.

It's wonderful to have you writing poems again. I can't wait to read the others.

Yours,
Randall

Jarrell's "sickness" was a painful sacroiliac injury he suffered over Labor Day in the tennis tournament at Larry Jaffe's club, when he leaped to smash a lob, crying, "Mine! Mine!" and fell onto the court.

In his letter, Lowell said he'd been writing poems again and added, "I want to try them out on you. Are you in the mood?" He wrote that he had been reading a new English poet, Philip Larkin, whom he liked better than Dylan Thomas and thought was "by far the most interesting of the Amis, Wain bunch and, unlike our smooth younger poets, says something." He also wrote that he thought Jarrell and Bishop were "worlds better than anyone else" and that Shapiro was next, "mostly in early poems, though there have been some good ones in the last year. He has a really Donne-like smash and something very racy and Jewish added to Auden's wit."

While Shapiro never saw this letter sifting the wheat from the chaff on both sides of the Atlantic, he had seen Lowell and Jarrell do this often enough to accuse them of playing a game he called Who's First: "The idea is to grade the poets until the downgrading wipes most of the competition off the board." (RJ) As usual, Shapiro was half or three-quarters right, except that it was not so much a game to them as a conversation of agree-

*ments and disagreements over who was first — never mind the competi-
tors — of all the European and American poets of each age since Homer:
an ongoing conversation that had begun years before, when they shared
Ransom's attic.*

TO ROBERT LOWELL

[February 10, 1958]

Dear Cal:

It certainly was fun talking to you for so long. Mary and I would like
very much to come for a visit in May — May in Boston ought to be just the
thing to get the blood boiling in Henry Adams' veins. I was delighted that
you're writing some new poems, just as I've been delighted (for about six
weeks) to be writing one myself; I say it to myself in the middle of the
night — about four pages of it — and wonder how it's going to end.

I've been meaning to write you about your manuscripts. The Library of
Congress is very much interested in getting for its archives the manuscripts
and papers of some distinguished American men of letters. The printed page
I enclose gives most of the details, but it doesn't go into detail about the
income tax deduction: the papers are valued by the Library when they are
deposited here, and an amount equal to 20% of your income is transferred
outright to the Library each year, making 20% of your income for that year
tax-free. This is the first tax-provision I've heard of that treats a writer almost as kindly as if he were an oil-well owner; it's odd that most writers
have never heard of it.

It would be a very great pleasure to us to have you decide to deposit
some of your literary papers and manuscripts here.

I'm hopeful I'll get my poem done while I'm at Cincinnati; I'll send it
to you when it's finished. And I'll send you the last Rilke translation I've
done — that "Washing the Corpse" poem I told you about.

Mary and I talked to Auden for about an hour and a half and enjoyed it
extremely; he certainly was fun. He had read his new poems beautifully —
several from *Nones* and several not yet in a book; they are better heard than
read.

We expect to spend every other weekend with Peter and Eleanor while
we're in Cincinnati.

Yours,
Randall

*Jarrell's new poem was his second poem entitled "Hope," and it was not fin-
ished until 1963.*

In March and April, the Jarrells, Beatrice, and Elfie spent six weeks in Cincinnati in a suite at the Alms Hotel. During this time Jarrell lectured and taught poetry classes at the University of Cincinnati as the Elliston Poet. At the same time, he completed an address to be delivered at the National Book Award ceremonies called "About Popular Culture," which was the forerunner of his long-projected mass-culture essay, "A Sad Heart at the Supermarket."

During their visits to the Taylors in Columbus, the Jarrells made plans to spend the summer near them in Italy.

TO WILLIAM COLE

[Cincinnati, Ohio]
[March 1958]

Dear Bill:

Here it is — I finished typing it about three o'clock and am sending it airmail special delivery, so it ought to get to you Friday morning.

I had a million things more to say or to quote from [Ernest] van den Haag, but these few are better than none. If you haven't seen his book [*The Fabric of Society*], do read the part called Popular Culture — you'll love it.

That letter the National Book Award office wrote me asked whether or not we'd like to go to the dinner afterwards; yes, we would. Our plane gets in at 12:40 and we'll come right to the hotel.

Yours,
Randall

Bill Cole and Jarrell met at Knopf, where Cole was publicist for Pictures from an Institution. *Later he worked for the National Book Award committee and asked Jarrell to deliver the annual address for 1958. "About Popular Culture," Jarrell's address, was a nervy attack on the publishing business for serving both God and Mammon that began, "If it is Mr. Cerf's id that publishes* Don't Go Near the Water, *it is his superego that publishes Mr. Warren's poems; and it is Mr. Warren's superego, or muse, or daemon, that makes him write poems like* Brother to Dragons *and* Promises, *when he could be writing best-selling novels. We are safe as long as these men's superegos survive." In another paragraph, Jarrell said, "In an ideally good society there would be no conflict between God and Mammon:* Swann's Way *would make Proust and his publishers twenty or thirty million dollars, and Elvis Presley would be the favorite of a few eleven-year-olds. In an ideally bad society* Swann's Way *would not be published at all, and Proust would have written Presley's autobiography for* The Saturday Evening

Post." *This was followed by penetrating revelations about our culture quoted from van den Haag's book, with further twists of the knife such as, "Santayana said it was worth living in this century to get to read Proust. Is it worth it to get to read* Peyton Place? . . . *We ought to say what we know: It's better to read Proust or Frost or Faulkner . . . better in every way; and we ought to do all we can to make it possible for everybody to know this from personal experience. When we make people satisfied to have read* Peyton Place *and satisfied not to have read Proust we are enemies of our culture . . . and are doing what we can to make the new America something Jefferson and Franklin and Adams would look at not with puzzled respect but with disgust and despair."*

During the talk the audience stirred and whispered and Ayn Rand said audibly, "Ach, thiss man, mein Gott! He should not be allow-ed. Vhy don't ve leaf?" At the conclusion there was mild and brief applause, and three persons came forward to congratulate Jarrell: Ernest van den Haag, Ralph Ellison, and James Jones. Dinner followed at Toots Shor's.

TO JEAN STAFFORD

Library of Congress
[April 1958]

Dear Jean:

It's really astonishing that *The New Yorker* hasn't told you, Peter, or A. J. Liebling about the tax provisions for literary manuscripts: maybe its Unconscious (I can't make up my mind whether or not it has one) wants to keep you slaves of a benevolent overseer.

You say that for years you've been sending your manuscripts to the University of Colorado. I ought to make some comments about this, the first formal and the second as an old friend of the family. (1) The Library has — nay, wishes — to be like Caesar's wife as far as the gifts of manuscripts are concerned: the giver should keep on giving to the old recipient unless, quite independently of anything we say or do, he decides that, so to speak, the Library would be better off with his manuscripts than his old home town would be. (2) Have you made a legal gift to the University of Colorado of all those manuscripts? Unless you've legally transferred title each year when you sent them, you may be able to regard them as simply a deposit there, and can each year transfer title of an appropriate amount (up to 20% or 30% of your income for the year). This is what they should have had you do — *should* means that this is what any of the libraries or universities that go in for collections would have done. So far as current procedure goes,

Delmore Schwartz and Randall Jarrell, 1958

your manuscript deposits are as incomplete as if you'd given a number of stories to a magazine and never received any checks for them.

We wish you could come down some weekend — I'm afraid we're not going to get to New York till next fall. We're going to Italy this summer — to the same town the Taylors are going to.

"Full of Roman Catholic whimsies" really does describe those two you mentioned [Allen Tate and Caroline Gordon]. Blake said, "The sleep of Reason produces monsters," and the wish-fantasies of Authority are monstrous to begin with, like Pekingese dogs the size of dinosaurs.

Aren't the Twenties clothes fun? It's the nearest thing to a time-machine available to mortal man.

Love,
Randall Jarrell
Poetry Consultant

Jarrell sent similar letters from his office to Léonie Adams, Louise Bogan, Ludwig Bemelmans, John Berryman, Cleanth Brooks, Katharine Hoskins, Wolfgang Köhler, Alfred Kroeber, Clarence Lewis, Bill Mauldin, Vladimir Nabokov, Karl Shapiro, and Peter Taylor.

*   *   *

Alleyne, on finishing her freshman year at the University of North Carolina in Chapel Hill, married a medical student, Charles Boyette, and they spent the summer in Mexico and California.

In June, the Jarrells, Beatrice, and Elfie sailed on the Cristoforo Colombo *for Genoa. Robert Fitzgerald met the ship and took them to Levanto, a small seaside resort in northern Italy that was far off the beaten path of American tourists. Fitzgerald, his wife Sally, and their six children had a farm-style house and had found the Jarrells a roof-garden flat with an English library and a daily maid. The Taylors were in the next town, in a villa with French doors and oleanders and palms. Texan Sally's northeastern accent disquieted Jarrell, but he and Fitzgerald picked up their Rilke discussion where they had left off in Bloomington and were soon amiably comparing the translator's lot, with Jarrell speaking for* Faust *and Fitzgerald for* The Odyssey.

Before Fitzgerald left for three weeks in the Greek islands, he and Jarrell enjoyed some doubles matches with two Pirelli tire men, from whom Jarrell, scrambling for points, learned to cry out, "Il mio! Il mio!"

There was the customary exchange of dinners among the three couples, but the Jarrells and Taylors tended, as of old, to form a private social unit and — *after the daily swim with the Fitzgeralds — might go off on their own for tea at the* pasticceria *in the park and then to their accustomed evenings by lamplight. On a typical afternoon at the beach, Sally dealt out rewards and punishments in Italian to her children, Ughetta, Michael, Benedetto, Maria, Barnaba, and Caterina. Petie Taylor stuck close to his mother, positioning toy reptiles in the sand and crooning, "The brontosaurus goes here . . . and . . . the tyrannosaurus goes there." Katie Taylor gamely plowed the shallows in her water wings, and Beatrice played lifeguard.*

Once, Jarrell chose the beach as the place to go over Eleanor's poems for her book "one last time." Bare to his waist in his batik swim trunks, he sat in the bright sun analyzing a poem far-sightedly at arm's length, finding yet another symbol from the unconscious that the poet denied and insisting fondly, "But it's so, Eleanor. Oh, yes . . . Oh, yes." Jarrell was oblivious of the stares from the families sprawled around them, deaf to the vendor's cries of "Co-co! Co-co Bell-o!" and blind to the advances of wet dogs and diaperless babes, but Eleanor was cruelly embarrassed. Retreating into the shade of the umbrella, she tucked her legs under her chambray skirt and looked down at a dinosaur or out at Sardinia, but never at Jarrell — though she was listening with all her might to his every word.

Jarrell was used to her scruples about "imposing on your good nature, Randall" and her distress over accepting presents, hospitality, or praise, and though he teased her about it, he also marveled at her "Calvinism." In his introduction to her first book of poetry, A Wilderness of Ladies, *he wrote, "So much, still, is sin! . . . a character in one of the poems says hotly, 'You talk so much of rights, now;/ You ask so seldom what your duties are!' The poet knows too well for asking what her duties are, and has no rights except the right to do right and resent it . . . Some of [her] world is grotesquely and matter-of-factly funny, some of it is tragic or insanely awful — unbearable one would say, except that it is being borne. But all of it is SO, seen as no one else could see it, told as no one else could tell it."*

Writing about their sessions, Eleanor said that sometimes he would tell her, "I think you might make this better," or, "I think I'd just throw this one away — it's sort of cooked-up." But then all at once he would say, "Gee, this is magical!" (RJ) That is when, suddenly, she would look at him fully, her face pinking, her eyes sparkling, her smile radiating joy and gratitude. But she would never say a word; speaking would have been intolerable. Comparing Eleanor's writing to Peter's, Jarrell once told Lowell, "Peter's is like a glass-bottom boat and Eleanor's is like going to the bottom — touching and clutching the slimy green grass and murk." Lowell laughed and said, "Yes, Eleanor is a Protestant Flannery O'Connor."

*   *   *

In August there were forlorn goodbyes when the Taylors departed for their winter in Rome, the Taylors wishing the Jarrells would join them and the Jarrells wishing they could.

Although Sally, regrettably, had been in that category of persons Jarrell felt "cold or indifferent to," Fitzgerald kindly insisted on driving the Jarrells — in an equinoctial storm — to the railway station for their train to Genoa. Beatrice, with three straw hats stacked on her head, sat in back with Mary, half-buried in tote bags, and Elfie, meowing in his carrier. The men were in front, and as the windows steamed and the rain pelted the car, Jarrell — patting a worn red volume on his lap — said blithely, "Robert, in Homer's honor, I want you to have my thesaurus . . . a little going-away present. I can buy another when I get back . . . It's really a dovey thing for translating. Or just to look through. You run across the queerest words." Jarrell laughed happily and added, "Believe me, I know, now, where some of Marianne Moore's come from."

At the station, the women fled through the torrents to put Elfie inside, the porters hustled the bags, and after Fitzgerald and Jarrell said an abrupt goodbye, Jarrell ran for shelter. Back with the family, Jarrell knelt to comfort Elfie through his grid, saying, "Poor little dear . . . Don't you mind . . . Such a clever cat! I know it's hard . . ." Gently stroking the carrier and looking worn, he said, "People, people! Words fail me . . . Robert wants me to write Sally a note of apology." Beatrice, awed, said, "Are you going to?" And Jarrell said, "Huh, tell me!"

Greensboro, North Carolina,
September 1958–October 1965

🙟

*T*he Jarrells returned to a peaceful campus that had an interim chancellor.
*Once again, Lucy Hooke found a rental house for them, and they moved
their Georgetown and Florentine antiques into a prim old upright white
frame house at 123 Tate Street. It had a high-ceilinged upstairs room with good
light that they called "the studio," where Robert Watson's wife, Betty, painted
Mary's portrait; and it had a high-ceilinged kitchen with room for a rocker, where
Jarrell sat and read the mail aloud.*

*In his first letter to Jarrell after their parting in Italy, Taylor wrote, "How we
miss you. I guess you know that when we turned away in the street in Levanto we
were all on the verge of tears. We had to talk about other things fast. If I'm not
careful this will sound like a love letter, so I'll talk about other things now." He
wrote about elegant Roman dining with the Macauleys, driving to Naples with
Warren, and reading* I, Claudius *to the children; of visits to the zoo with Petie; of
Katie's room, where snapshots of Beatrice were spread over the dressing table; and
finally, of their apartment, which was so beautiful that "the only change we have
made is to remove one picture in the living room and to hang our Uccello [a gift
from the Jarrells] there."*

*   *   *

*Jarrell was often quoted as saying, "I'm crazy about teaching. If I were a rich man,
I'd pay to teach," and, after two years of doing without, he was starved for classes.
On arrival in Greensboro he was promoted to full professor, put in charge of the
Arts Forum, and given a class of 300 on what he called "The Narrative." Reading
furiously, he invented the class as he went along, delighting in the discovery that he
preferred* Crime and Punishment *to* The Brothers Karamazov, *in the redis-*

covery of his enchantment with The Great Gatsby, *and in teaching Taylor's story* "What You Hear from 'Em?" *from his own just-published* Anchor Book of Short Stories. *Jarrell continued to translate Rilke and Goethe and write criticism in the absence of poems; but he wrote few letters (except to Taylor) and agreed with Lowell that he had a "note-block."*

The white Mercedes was painted a shiny black that set off its red leather interior. There was tennis as usual, and television weekends around the nut bowl at the Hookes', with Lucy saying, "Every peanut has a little devil inside saying 'Take another! Take another!'" Jarrell had too little time of his own, and, expressing his feelings to Karl Shapiro, he wrote that he was "part happy and part worked to death and generally distracted."

TO KARL SHAPIRO

[November 1958]

Dear Karl:

I've meant to write and to send some poems for many months. Here are some Rilke translations and a Goethe translation for the *Prairie Schooner* — and I thought, too, that I'd wish you luck at Cincinnati and congratulate you beforehand on what a nice time you're sure to have and what nice lectures they're sure to get. We really had a wonderful time there — it's a most unusual city. Say hello for us — to it and to everybody.

Since last spring I've been translating *Faust,* the first part that is; I'm about a third through and am part happy and part worked to death and generally distracted — it's too hard and too long really, but I'm hopeful that in the end I can get it done.

When we were there at Cincinnati we went to a number of psychiatric things and met a *wonderful* psychoanalyst — we couldn't have enjoyed it more. Professor Crockett arranged it all, and may very well be arranging something of the sort for you, if you want it.

I wish all the San Francisco poets would eat all the University poets and burst, so that Nature, abhorring a vacuum, would send one plain poet or cat or rat to take their place: it's pretty awful to look at Mass Culture, and at its side High Culture, and hardly know which you like less. There are *some* times.

Get somebody to show you the Music Museum Director's house — it's just three or four blocks from the Alms. To think that you're living in the Alms!

Yours,
Randall

Shapiro published four of Jarrell's translations in the Prairie Schooner: *"The Archangels' Song" from* Faust *and three Rilke poems — "The Child," "Childhood," and "Washing the Corpse."*

TO ROBERT LOWELL

[February 1959]

Dear Cal:

I guess I have a note-block, too. It'll be good to see your poems, and I'm delighted that you're coming to the Arts Forum. I was going to send you an *Anchor Book of Stories* (I didn't get all the copies till I was back from Europe) but if you're already using it in your class I guess there's not much use.

We had quite a good time in Italy; I worked fairly hard on *Faust* and liked the Donatellos better than anything else I saw. We went to Florence a lot and once to Arezzo. I was crazy about the van der Goes triptych in the Uffizi.

I'm still sick after reading [Archibald MacLeish's] *J.B.* It's really as vulgar, exaggerated, and completely awful as the worst things in the mass media — what they would do if given more freedom.

I spent about five weeks teaching *The Great Gatsby;* gee, it was fun! The only book of that size that's organized just like a short story or poem.

Didn't Samuel Johnson say, "He who is sick of Boston is sick of life"? Well, no, now that I think of it.

We can't wait to see you.

Yours,
Randall

Archibald MacLeish had won two Pulitzer Prizes for his poetry and won another in 1959 for his play J.B.

In his most recent letter to Jarrell, Lowell had written that they were sick of Boston and were "going to Brazil or West Berlin, or somewhere. The only unconventional people here are charming screwballs who never finish a picture or publish a line. I'm dying to see you . . . I really miss you terribly. Love to you both, Cal."

*   *   *

In an exchange of letters with Peter Taylor at this time, Jarrell learned that McDowell and Obolensky were to publish Eleanor's book A Wilderness of

Ladies *and that Peter had been given a Ford grant that not only provided him and the family with a year in London for the 1960–1961 season of the Royal Court Theatre but also afforded him a welcome release from the prospect of editing the* Kenyon Review. *On Ransom's retirement, Robie Macauley became the editor.*

TO HIRAM HAYDN

[February 1959]

Dear Hiram:

I've typed six or eight sections of *Faust* for you to read, about fifty pages in all. There isn't any verse translation of *Faust* in English that will give a reader a real idea of *Faust,* make him feel at all as he feels when he reads the German — and this is a tragedy, since there's nothing in the literature of the world that takes its place, is at all the same sort of thing. All the verse translations except MacIntyre's are doggerel — and they're not in English at all but in translationese, that strange language that makes everybody talk like everybody else in the play, but talk as nobody outside a translation ever could talk. MacIntyre's often tries to be more natural — but it's so eccentric, leaves out so much, has such hopeless rhythms, that it's almost as troubling as the others: besides, he just isn't a good poet.

This translation of mine is, I think, quite different from any of the others. If it's what I want it to be, it's in natural dramatic English to be said aloud; moves; changes from scene to scene; is a play — is, sometimes, really poetry. But that's for you to judge: I hope you will compare it with some other translations and with Goethe. Normal translations (partly in order to preserve the rhymes) are almost fantastically inaccurate, and put in a great many things Goethe never says; my translation is, normally, quite close. I hope that when it's finished it will be (however far below the German) a homogeneous work of art.

I have a third of it done; I believe that I can finish it in two and a half years. Normally I don't have much interest in advances, but this is different, I find: it takes all my writing time, just about, so for several years I won't make anything from what I'd otherwise write. And I want to spend all my summers on it and a half-year or year off.

I'm eager to find out how you like it, and how Jess [Stein] and Jason [Epstein] like it; do send me a note whenever you've read it yourself. As I said, I've left occasional blanks for unfinished lines — I hope they won't bother you.

I think a good translation of *Faust* — one that's a pleasure to read, a work of art in English — might create a lot of interest if it were well brought out, and might in the long run be read instead of the miserable things people dutifully read now.

I was extremely sorry to miss the meeting of the *Scholar* Editorial Board — the snow finally stopped late in the afternoon, though it's still lying around like broken bathtubs. I'll see you in two weeks.

Yours,
Randall

Haydn was at this time leaving Bennett Cerf at Random House to found Atheneum Publishers with Michael Bessie from Harper and Row, Harry Ford from Knopf, and Pat Knopf. While Jarrell's projected books of poetry, essays, and translation of Faust *were easily affordable at Random House, young Atheneum needed moneymakers. They contracted for* The Woman at the Washington Zoo *and* A Sad Heart at the Supermarket, *but Haydn was hesitant about* Faust *and reluctant to invest the money. His response was ambivalent: He wrote "I salute you!" but he also wrote that the Bayard Taylor translation was not as bad as Jarrell thought and that perhaps Goethe, too, was doggerel; and in conversation he revealed the same negative mindset most Americans have about* Faust — *that it is not "relevant" to our time. This did not seem to Jarrell the "interest, real interest" he wanted from an editor, and a certain disenchantment with Haydn began. What ultimately made the* Faust *contract and advance possible was the acquisition of a financial backer and new member of the firm, Haydn's old friend and Jarrell's old foe, Marc Friedlaender.*

TO THOMAS DICKINSON

[March 1959]

Dear Tom:

I enjoyed reading your poems. They give a good feeling of the natural world and of someone's emotions. I've written some comments on them here and there mostly where there's something awkward. One can go over poems much better in conversation — in an hour you can talk thirty or forty pages. We're going to be in California this summer; I'd love to talk about all the poems you have then — I can talk about the scansion and sounds and little shadings of the words, and the way the subject builds up or doesn't, and so on. If you're going to be there too why don't you plan to come talk about them some time?

Why don't you look around at magazines in the library and pick three
or four that print poems you like? Then you can send each of them several
of yours. All you need say is *Dear Sir: Would you care to print these poems in
your magazine,* or words to that effect, and enclose a stamped self-addressed
envelope. Sending poems to magazines, to begin with, is about like a lot-
tery — nobody has too much chance of being accepted (Frost, for instance,
had almost no poems published before he was thirty-eight) but it's fun if
you're lucky and ought not to bother you if you're not.

I think your poems have a nice natural feeling, as if poems were a good
thing for you to write, yours go together well, though I don't think you've
written poetry long enough to have a quite personal style yet — it's like
learning a game, a really individual way of doing it comes with a lot of experience. I'm glad you sent them to me and any time we're in the same
place I'd be delighted to talk about them or about new ones.

With all best wishes,

Yours,
Randall Jarrell

*Tom Dickinson was the son of Mary's friends Woody and Marjorie and
was a distant relative of Emily Dickinson. Jarrell ranked him favorably
with his own best students and felt he would develop into a good poet, but
Dickinson died at nineteen.*

Dickinson had enclosed this stanza, among others:

> Blasting blow the winter winds;
> Whipping dust on tarnished trees;
> Sweeping round in writhing reels
> As time teems with wasted weeks.

*Jarrell wrote beneath it: "When you use this kind of alliteration it calls a
lot of attention to itself, so it ought to pay for itself by a really good effect, by
a sound or look or feeling you couldn't have got without it. Roughly, Hopkins' or Rilke's alliteration is good most of the time (it really does something) and Poe's and Swinburne's is bad, usually — theirs is just there for
its own sake." Jarrell liked the lines:*

> The agony of death is pain:
> Felt by one,
> Known to another,
> It hurts two times.

TO BERNARD HAGGIN

[May 1959]

Dear Bernard:

I'm awfully sorry not to have written right away about the book [*Conversations with Toscanini*] — I did read it right away, and enjoyed it *extremely*. I was finishing a long piece about Mass Culture and the arts in this country, and read the book, since that was pleasure, and put off the writing, since that was work.

I got nowhere with [Robert] Evett [editor of Books and Arts at the *New Republic*]. He answered my letter asking to review your book with a short, in every sense unfriendly, note saying that he always tried hard to avoid even the appearance of log-rolling when it came to books that the contributing editors wrote; that if I wanted to write a review of the book I'd better make arrangements with some other magazine — that the most he could run was a brief note. It was such an unfriendly letter I didn't even answer it. He certainly is an unlikable man.

I thought your book gave a wonderfully vivid and glowing and exact picture of Toscanini — the conversations were so interesting that I longed for them to keep on indefinitely. Dramatically, I thought, the best single part was the one where he asked you what you'd like for yourself — it was wonderfully marvellously surprising and stood for *so* much. Some of the things he said were quite surprising and all of them were extremely interesting both in themselves and in what they showed one about him. And it was such a pleasure to have a different picture from that "official" one. The writing of all the scenes was smooth and pure and had a beautiful motion or carrying force. And of course the whole part about the records will be wonderfully good both for people who haven't bought many Toscanini records and for people who want more or less to complete their Toscanini collection.

All your quotations from him had very much the sound of somebody talking with a particular accent in a particular way: it made everything extremely live, as if one were really listening to the conversations.

I've been working hard on *Faust* and we've been getting ready to move into a house in the forest in the country; we're going to be here all summer. Are you going to Maine as usual?

Mary sends her love.

All the best,
Randall

About the time Mary finished decorating the house on Tate Street, the owner sold it to a motel, and the Jarrells decided to buy a house of their own and avoid the upheaval of moving every two years.

The Jarrells spent the summer of 1959 settling into their rustic, board-and-batten house on a red clay road in a wooded area of Guilford College near a pre-Revolutionary graveyard. There were squirrels, rabbits, and owls in their woods, as well as rarities such as tanagers and cowbirds. The nights were so quiet a dairy cow could be heard mooing on a farm two miles away, and Jarrell liked to tell the Hookes and the Taylors, "We are living out where the fox says good night to the hare."

* * *

Beatrice spent the summer in Hawaii with Irene, seeing Gerhard Hofer in Chicago on her way across the country. The Jarrells went nowhere, but through a spate of postcards tried to arrange a visit from the Taylors, which resulted in nothing more than their stopping by for an afternoon on a hurried trip to see relatives in Albemarle County.

* * *

For the remainder of 1959 Jarrell wrote permissions letters to publishers for the anthologies he was doing, and letters arranging interviews for candidates for head of the English department. There was the usual tennis, TV football at the Hookes', and the joy of buying a secondhand MG for Beatrice and teaching her to drive it.

Haydn's letters to Jarrell about A Sad Heart at the Supermarket *and* The Woman at the Washington Zoo *lacked any enthusiasm and tended to niggle about production costs and minimal sales. Since Jarrell needed literary companionship and interest from an editor, he stopped writing Haydn and returned to Harry Ford, his genuine admirer.*

TO ROBERT LOWELL

[March 1960]

Dear Cal:

I'm translating too, just like you. I've got *Faust* about ⅔ done — in the last few weeks I've done Brecht's "Plum-Tree" and "Pirate Jenny" and most of Mörike's "Forest-Idyll." Living out here in the forest with two big snows and hundreds of birds is pretty like the Mörike.

Your publisher sent me all the reprinted statements about your book

[*Life Studies*]; gee, they were good — they hardly *could* have been better. I hope you get all the prizes this spring to wind it up properly.

I was certainly grateful to you for the National Institute election; I know that you had much more to do with it than anybody else. I was pleased and amused to get it just as Mary McCarthy did (I liked her Florence book [*The Stones of Florence*] very much) — and I was more than amused to accompany Harry Levin and Richard Eberhart. They should wear placards saying: *Just to Remind You What World You're In.*

I've got a very good poetry class this year — and had, first time, a good class for *Crime and Punishment, The Great Gatsby,* and so on; the writing students aren't too many or much, except for Eleanor's niece, Heather Ross, who's extremely good.

Some of my class were writing haiku and I read some books and several thousand or billion, who knows? haiku, twenty or thirty of which I liked or loved. That Auden book's nice [*Homage to Clio*]. A nice witty hell for me would be to write — read too — nothing but French haiku.

Some of the *Faust* scenes I thought would be hardest — Mephistopheles and the student, for instance — I've enjoyed doing and got quite smooth; and I've finished the Easter hymns, that I didn't see how I could ever do. The "Midsummer Night's Intermezzo" is something that stands before me like 28 hours in Education before you can get your Teacher's certificate.

Do you and Elizabeth ever come down to National Institute meetings? Mary and I are going to the one in May — maybe we could all see each other then.

Have you ever seen the two-volume Princeton University Donatello book? It really is a wonderful one.

I should have written months ago — forgive, forgive.

Yours,
Randall

Lowell had nominated Jarrell for membership in the National Institute of Arts and Letters, saying, "I think of Mr. Jarrell as the first man of letters of my generation." This was seconded by Elizabeth Bishop and — surprisingly — R. P. Blackmur.

Heather Ross Miller later wrote The Edge of the Woods, Tenants of the House, Wind Southerly, Gone a Hundred Miles, *and* Horse, Horse, Tyger, Tyger.

In his next letter to Jarrell, Lowell said how much he wished Jarrell were teaching with him at Harvard: "Maybe they can be coaxed into giving you MacLeish's job whenever it falls vacant. The trouble is, none of them know how you really differ from say, Richard Chase, or worse ... I hope we and our families will find some way of living near each other. We can play the parts of Faust and Mephistopheles. But who is which?"

TO HARRY FORD

Sun Valley, Idaho
[June 1960]

Dear Harry —

This certainly was correct, pretty proof — I could find almost no errors. It's a beautiful-looking book [*The Woman at the Washington Zoo*], as pretty as the dust-jacket.

I've never corrected proof in such odd places — all over the Rockies, in Yellowstone, and now at the skating-rink at Sun Valley, with many little girls pirouetting and skating backwards.

Lots of the country we've seen was as wonderful as the animals — going out early on back roads at Yellowstone we've seen a moose and her baby sitting by a stream, a grizzly bear (along with four elk) eating tubers and stuff in the middle of a tremendous meadow, many deer and such, at least sixty or seventy bears, of every size and color. And osprey-nests on pinnacles several hundred feet below in a canyon, the mother-osprey just sitting on the nest, a four-foot pile of grey weathered sticks.

I'll quit writing the letter and get this off air-mail. Mary sends her love — we certainly enjoyed seeing you and certainly are grateful for the beautiful book.

Yours,
Randall

*   *   *

The Jarrells and Elfie spent the summer of 1960 in Montecito, California, between the Sierras and the sea. They had a rambling Spanish-style house (formerly the Polo Club) with a colonnade and a vine of Banks' roses trained over it. Irene MacAdams came to visit, as did the Dickinsons, Alleyne, Beatrice, and her friend Gerhard Hofer.

Bernard Haggin, who was giving a series of music lectures at the University of California at Santa Barbara, came for a candlelight dinner outdoors in the colonnade. Cooking for him was easy — "Nothing but steaks, Mary. Raw." — but conversation was not, as he quickly detected that Jarrell was not reading him as faithfully as before. For some time Jarrell had said, "Bernard's tastes are so predictable . . . and each year he likes less." Still unshakable were Haggin's pillars — Mozart, Beethoven, Berlioz, Schubert, and Stravinsky — and equally rigid was his disdain for Liszt. As for Mahler, only the First and Fourth symphonies held Haggin's interest (because they had Berlioz's "fastidiousness, precision and originality"); and each year he jettisoned more of Brahms, finally citing him as "a small-scale artist" whose large works were "labored and pretentious" and many of whose shorter works betrayed "a cloying sweetness and archness."

About Strauss, Haggin had passionate feelings for Don Quixote *and nothing else.* Don Quixote, *he said, was "inspired in its invention; unflawed by a single Straussian excess or error of taste; every note in the complex texture counting for something; every detail making its programmatic point brilliantly." Otherwise, Haggin complained of Strauss's "inferior musical substance" and that his "prodigious technical virtuosity and garrulous facility" produced "endless pages of empty tonal luxuriance" — especially in "the vastly overrated* Der Rosenkavalier." (Quotes from The Listener's Companion, *by Bernard Haggin.) Two years earlier, at a dinner in New York, Haggin had allowed it "one moment of inspired creation and beauty" in the first exchange of Octavian and Sophie in the "Presentation of the Rose." At dinner in Montecito, that, too, fell into what Haggin termed the "deterioration" and "opulent daubing" of Strauss's later work. Jarrell heatedly defended one part after another of* Der Rosenkavalier *as subtle or brilliant or making its points, but Haggin — above arguing or reasoning — maintained on each count, "I don't hear that." In response to Jarrell's protests about the "Presentation of the Rose," he smiled but said inexorably, "No, Randall. No. All sugary sevenths. I'm sorry." Their friendship did not end in a Grand Finale but entered into an indefinite suspension.*

A pleasure to Jarrell during this time was the completion of his first poem in two years, "In Montecito."

* * *

During August, the Jarrells followed the presidential campaign on the radio, but Jarrell wanted to see Kennedy (of whom he said, as he said of Ted Williams and Kitten, "every part of him had a clear, quick, decided look"). So a television set was rented, and the Jarrells watched the assembling of the Kennedy clan, the nomination, the seconding by Governor San-

ford of North Carolina, and Kennedy's acceptance speech delivered in the high flinty voice that by Inauguration Day had lowered so perceptibly that Jarrell quipped, "Kennedy is the only man over forty I ever heard of whose voice 'changed.' "

In Greensboro, the newly political Jarrells subscribed to the daily Washington Post and installed a large antenna and a large television set for Kennedy-watching.

TO ROBERT LOWELL

[November 1960]

Dear Cal:

Thanks so much for your letter about the book [*The Woman at the Washington Zoo*]. I'm awfully interested in your doing the [Johann Peter] Hebel father and son dialogue — I like it very much and thought that the nearest equivalent might be two Negroes (or very Faulkner or Eleanor Taylor southerners) talking outside Richmond or such. I can't wait to see your *Phèdre* [translation].

I'll bet New York and the opera are fun for you. The Taylors are crazy about Kensington — have you read his "Miss Leonora When Last Seen"? One of the best allegorical stories since Hawthorne.

I'm away, way, way ahead on the *Faust* — over two-thirds through. What you say about being a hand not a soul when translating, certainly is so. You're the soul of somebody else's hand or the hand of somebody else's soul; anyway, the cares of being a soul all fall away.

We'll be up in New York late in January and can see you then. Did you see a piece of mine in *Daedalus* named "A Sad Heart at the Supermarket"? It rather goes with your *Atlantic Monthly* poem ["For the Union Dead"]. I liked it.

Lots of love from all of us,
Randall

The Lowells and their young daughter, Harriet, had left Marlborough Street in Boston and moved to an apartment at The Dakota in New York City.

*   *   *

Jarrell had recently received a letter from Peter Taylor in which Taylor said that Petie and Katie loved Miss Ironsides' school in London and he and Eleanor loved their house "on a little square with a garden (to which we

have the key)." Taylor was attending all the rehearsals and three perfor-
mances a week at the Royal Court Theatre. At the end of the letter he wrote,
"Be sure to let us know your plans for the summer. We might stay on here if
you all are really going to be in France, or better still, England." On the
other hand, the house they had bought in Monteagle, Tennessee, the year be-
fore was calling them, and he suggested, "Perhaps we would all meet there."
Jarrell answered this with a ten-page letter praising "Miss Leonora When
Last Seen."

TO ROBERT PENN WARREN

[March 1961]

Dear Red:

Thanks a lot for the check from Holt. This was a better time for me
than an earlier one. I've just been writing some new poems and thought I'd
send you some and see how you liked them. I certainly did enjoy your last
book [*Understanding Poetry*] — what you said about some of the poems in
mine was a great pleasure to me.

We've been living in the country now for almost two years and can
hardly believe we could ever bear to live in town. Our house is in a pretty
forest, enough of it so that we don't much mind the houses that are getting
built around. We've counted fifty sorts of birds that have come at one time
or the other; there's a downy woodpecker hanging on the suet ball now —
you can say that half the time, though.

I'm about three-quarters done with *Faust* and have been writing a good
many other things; my classes are the best I've ever had, too. Beatrice, our
younger girl, is a freshman at Woman's College this year, and just comes
home on weekends — she's crazy about college.

I thought I had that five thousand dollars prize (the Academy of Poets
gives) for Mr. Ransom this year — I nominate him often — but the votes
got tied, six for him and six for Jesse Stuart, and then it went to Jesse
Stuart. I think I'll nominate Baby Snooks next year. Four or five years ago
William Carlos Williams and David Morton were tied, but that time it
ended happily.

Mary and I recently drove fifty miles south to see a student [Heather
Ross Miller] who's got married to a forest ranger and lives just outside the
state forest in a small, old, country house. They weren't home, but we could
see their books through the windows, paintings, and so forth — it reminded
me *very* much of the house you used to live in outside Nashville. I felt very
nostalgic, as if I'd seen a real live doughboy. But I guess the point is that

one *is* a real live doughboy. I often think when I hear Frost talk that his voice has several more layers of moss or atmosphere than regular voices.

— I got this far in the letter before I went to New York and before I got your letter. It certainly was nice of you to write about the award [the National Book Award for *The Woman at the Washington Zoo*]. I have wanted to write you about your Civil War piece in *Life* — Mary and I both thought it was the best essay on the Civil War that we've ever read. The amount of knowledge in it, the amount of attention you paid to the noblest and basest things in the war, and the thoroughly live and thoroughly dignified style were all just extraordinary.

Yours,
Randall

The check from Holt was a permission fee for Jarrell's essay on how he wrote the poem "The Woman at the Washington Zoo."

In addition to translating Faust, *Jarrell was writing about Frost's "Home Burial" and working on "On Preparing to Read Kipling," his introduction to* The Best Short Stories of Rudyard Kipling, *a book he was doing for Doubleday. He had also written three new poems — "Washing," "Well Water," and "The One Who Was Different."*

The judges for the Academy of American Poets award given to Jesse Stuart instead of Ransom were J. Donald Adams, Witter Bynner, Henry Canby, Max Eastman, Robert Hillyer, Jarrell, Marianne Moore, and John Hall Wheelock. Ransom won the award in 1962.

In his acceptance speech at the National Book Award ceremonies, Jarrell thanked Atheneum, his publishers, and Harry Ford, his "favorite book designer," but not Hiram Haydn, his editor. He went on to say, "Sometimes a poem comes to me — I do what I can to it when it comes — and sometimes for years not one comes. During these times the only person who helps much is my wife: she always acts as if I'd written the last poem yesterday and were about to write the next one tomorrow. While I'm writing poems or translating Faust *I read what I have out loud, and my wife listens to me. Homer used to be led around by a little boy, who would listen to him; all I can say is, if Homer had ever had my wife listen to his poems, he would never again have been satisfied with that little boy."*

Continuing, Jarrell said, "I think all of us are grateful that for the first time in the history of the Republic, a great poet was invited to help inaugurate the president of the United States [John F. Kennedy]. The president made his invitation not as a friend, not as a politician, but as a reader: any of us who heard the president talk about Frost's poetry, on television . . .

will remember that he spoke as only a real reader of Frost could speak, and read the lines almost as Frost himself would have read them. It is good to have Fred Waring in the juke boxes, but it was sad to have Fred Waring, nothing but Fred Waring, in the White House, too. It is a pleasure to think that for the next four or eight years our art and our government won't be complete strangers."

Jarrell went on to say that he couldn't help "feeling unhappy that, because this award was given to The Woman at the Washington Zoo, *Eleanor Taylor's* A Wilderness of Ladies *will not be read by people who might have read it if it had been given the award. I assure you that in heaven or hell, or wherever it is that good poets go, Hardy and Emily Dickinson are saying to all the new arrivals, 'Did you really get to see Eleanor Taylor?' — just as Blake and Wordsworth used to say, 'Did you really get to see Hardy and Dickinson?' If you would like to read a true, a unique American poet, read Eleanor Taylor's* A Wilderness of Ladies."

Peter Taylor sent congratulations from London, saying they wished they could have heard the speech, "but with Eleanor hiding under the platform," since when she read Jarrell's words about her she "literally blushed." Jarrell answered this with an ecstatic response to Taylor's story "Reservations," and Taylor answered with another letter saying, "I suspect that you two are the only ones who really got it." Further on, he wrote, "I wish you could have heard Allen give his reading at the Royal Society! I felt that it was really a dream that I might have had about Allen Tate when I was in his freshman English class at Southwestern. He was introduced by Lord David Cecil, and there was the grandest collection of English creatures I've yet seen." Tate had been accompanied by his new wife, Isabella Gardner, also a poet.

*   *   *

In October 1961, Jarrell was honored at a tribute in Chapel Hill sponsored by the North Carolina Historical Society and the University of North Carolina Press, instigated by Jarrell's first editor, Lambert Davis. After a dinner for two hundred, an audience of two thousand heard the tribute address given by Jarrell's first teacher, Robert Penn Warren.

Warren opened his speech by saying, "Time has passed and the skinny young man is not quite so young. His tennis game has slowed a little, only a little ... and his severe passion for high standards of intelligence and reason have turned inward into a self-demanding scrupulosity in his own writing that is seasoned by humor with an undertone of pity for human failing and human feeling, especially in his poems about women."

Robert Penn Warren, Randall Jarrell,
and Lambert Davis, 1961

TO ROBERT LOWELL

[November 1961]

Dear Cal:

It was fun to see you — we really are looking forward to January. I saw that stupid review [of *Imitations*] in *Time* — *Time*'s the cheapest magazine in the world and Dudley Fitts the cheapest poetry reviewer; I can imagine what he was like when he had a chance to hurt a real poet in *"his* special field," translation — as if he had once in his life translated a line of poetry into a line of poetry. Translations are done by real poets or pure accident, nothing else. Your *taxidermists* is just right.

I certainly did enjoy *Imitations*. It's all live English, a real book to read from beginning to end. The Hebel, Hugo, Baudelaire, Rimbaud — all the 19th century French poems, really — and the Italian ones, especially the Montale, are some of the ones I like best. All your readers will like the book just the way they'd like a book of your own new poems, since this is, really, a book of your own new poems.

It certainly has a beautiful cover — your Marshall Lee was quite inspired.

I loved hearing you read the Boston poem ["For the Union Dead"]. I feel about the world, now, just as you do: it's heartbreaking. Who would believe even people could get things to this point?

I read something Luther said that, by now, I remember as two lines; well, actually I've made it into a little poem for the start of my new book [*A Sad Heart at the Supermarket*].

THE AUTHOR TO THE READER

I've read that Luther said (it's come to me
So often that I've made it into meter):
And even if the world should end tomorrow
I still would plant my little apple-tree.
Here, reader, is my little apple-tree.

It's queer to have had Luther's imaginativeness changed into plain fact.

Yours,
Randall

In his last letter, Lowell had written, "I seem to be getting a rain of mangling reviews. Time *magazine and now Dudley Fitts, who says my poems should be read in a salt mine with grains of salt. I must know something about what I'm doing. I'm sure I do … The world is very much under my skin and really seems like a murderous nightmare when one looks around … I am sick of nations armed to the teeth. It can't be*

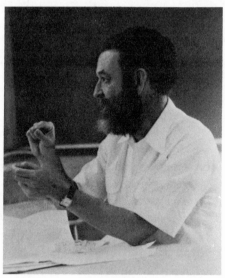

*Randall Jarrell teaching at the
University of North Carolina, Greensboro, 1961*

true. We must lift a finger or whisper!" In another letter Lowell said,
"You are one of the very few people I feel deeply enough in with to talk
deeply with."

*   *   *

*In November 1961, Jarrell was presented with the Oliver Max Gardner
Award for "that member of the entire faculty of the University of North
Carolina who, during the current scholastic year, has made the greatest contribution to the welfare of the human race." When the new and permanent
chancellor, Otis Singletary, asked Jarrell for a list of people to invite, Jarrell
said, "Gee, Otis, I don't know . . . we know more chipmunks than we know
people."*

At the ceremonies, Jarrell said:

Being given the Gardner Award means more to me than I can say.
What people at home do for you is far more important than anything
strangers can do, and this is my home.

. . . Because of the service to humanity of which the award speaks, it
would take a very self-confident or complacent person to feel that he
really deserved the award. I certainly don't feel that I do. But I've got to
admit that it's nice to get something you don't deserve; even if it's all a
mistake. I can't help feeling: "What a fine mistake for people to make!"

To have your own friends and colleagues approve of your work
makes that work even dearer to you — and, to me, there is no work so
dear as teaching . . .

Teaching is something that I would pay to do; to make my living by
doing it, here at the University of North Carolina, with the colleagues I
have and the students my colleagues and I have, seems to me a piece of
good luck I don't deserve but am immensely grateful for.

*   *   *

*During the Christmas holidays Jarrell lacked the energy for tennis and
watched the bowl games at the Hookes' in a listless state. Admitting he "did
not feel so hot," he consulted a doctor, telling him that he felt "blurry" and
that "something in my middle is sort of Aaaaagh." Tests proved he had hepatitis, and the New York plans were canceled.*

*While hospitalized, Jarrell received a letter from Michael di Capua, a
junior editor in children's books at Macmillan who knew his poetry. From
reading "The Märchen," di Capua had gotten the idea of asking Jarrell to
choose and translate some of Grimm's tales for a series of children's books*

that included translations by writers such as Jean Stafford for "Arabian Nights" and Isak Dinesen for Hans Christian Andersen. Jarrell thought this quite imaginative, "especially using Jean for the 'Arabian Nights.'" When he selected "Snow-White" and "The Fisherman's Wife" to translate, he began to feel better.

TO ROBERT PENN WARREN AND ELEANOR CLARK

[March 1962]

Dear Red and Eleanor:

Thanks *ever* so much for your Brittany letters; for you to go to so much trouble for us is extremely kind. Alas, we can't go to Brittany or anywhere else; I've been extremely sick and still haven't recovered. I had hepatitis and, after that was done, all sorts of duodenal and neuralgic complications; so, aside from teaching two classes, all I do is diet, take medicine, lie down, and wish I were well. The places in Brittany really sound beautiful.

I'm delighted that Red enjoyed my book [*A Sad Heart at the Supermarket*]; I'll send you a real one with a cover. As you can imagine, I'm short of any news except health news, the dullest kind for everybody but the invalid. About all I've done is translate some Grimm's Tales to make a children's book with Italian illustrations; it and my classes are a blessed relief from time spent just to spend time.

I think we'll spend most of the summer here and then go over to Monteagle for a while, where the Taylors are; by next summer I'll be in ordinary shape and able to go to Europe, please Heaven.

With all best wishes,
Yours,
Randall

TO HARRY FORD

[March 1962]

Dear Harry,

The book [*A Sad Heart at the Supermarket*] just came from Kingsport and it really is beautiful — I can't help thinking it's the prettiest of all the books of mine you've designed. Thanks so much for making it so really delightful-looking.

When Mary and I were talking about people to give it to, including doctors and nurses, I realized that I ought to ask you to send me thirty (not twenty, as I said before) charged to my account, besides the ones I'm given.

I really am improving a lot — sometimes the pain is just discomfort and sometimes the discomfort slips away for an hour or so. I've been teaching my classes since the start of last week (just two hours on Monday, Wednesday, and Friday afternoons) and it helps to be doing something for its own sake and not just to get through the time. This doctor has me on a good diet, with various medications and injections, and I'm improving as steadily as, under the other doctor, I got worse.

As I often say to Mary, "O, how wonderful when I'll be through saying a word about *health!*"

I've been reading lots of Dostoievsky and made up this definition for you: Man is the animal that has brain fever.

Yours,
Randall

A Sad Heart at the Supermarket was dedicated to Mary, and in their *copy Jarrell wrote, "To my nurse, Mary, from her patient, Randall, with so much love."*

*   *   *

On receiving Jarrell's translations of the Grimm's tales, di Capua not only sent a handwritten letter but telephoned his excitement and pleasure. Further letters and calls proved him to be thoroughly grounded in all Jarrell's writing. Perceiving the overtones of Der Rosenkavalier *in Jarrell's poem "The Face," di Capua proposed an opera evening at the old Met; and just as he had associated "The Märchen" with Grimm's tales, he saw in Jarrell's children's poems the possibility of a children's story. Intrigued again, Jarrell stationed himself outdoors in a hammock under the pines, among the cardinals and chipmunks, and, with the stereo volume turned up, wrote* The Gingerbread Rabbit *and started on* The Bat-Poet.*

When Quincy Mumford at the Library of Congress invited Jarrell to deliver the first evening address at the first National Poetry Festival, Jarrell was himself again.

TO QUINCY MUMFORD

[May 1962]

Dear Quincy:

Your invitation was a real delight to me; Mary and I look forward with great anticipation to the three days at the Library. I'll plan to write my little speech this summer, and will be delighted to read poems and participate in the discussions. The Poetry Festival will be a fine thing for poetry — and an especially fine thing for former Poetry Consultants, who'll get to see their old Washington friends again.

With all best wishes.
Yours sincerely,
Randall Jarrell

The National Poetry Festival was instigated by the current Poetry Consultant, Louis Untermeyer. Funded by the Bollingen Foundation, it was open to all poets in America. There were to be three days of panel discussions in the morning, poetry readings in the afternoon, and a formal address each evening. The first night, Jarrell gave his speech entitled "Fifty Years of American Poetry." Robert Frost gave a reading of his poems the next night, and the last night Sir Herbert Read delivered an address entitled "American Bards and British Reviewers."

TO IRENE MACADAMS

August 1, 1962

Happy Birthday from Monteagle! We often think of you and wish you were here with us. We're leading a quite old-fashioned life and loving it.

Love,
Randall

On the Fourth of July, Jarrell gave the bride away at Beatrice's marriage to Dr. Gerhard Hofer, and the Jarrells and Elfie spent the rest of the summer in Monteagle with the Taylors. The two households wrote in the mornings. Jarrell was at work on another Kipling anthology, an introduction for his anthology Six Russian Short Novels, *and his speech for the National Poetry Festival. There were picnics and drives in the Cumberlands to the Old Stone Fort and Rutledge Falls; and there were evenings with lemonade on the Taylors' porch swings behind the vines. The most interesting outcome of the summer was Taylor's decision to leave Ohio State the following year and — if the English department were willing — return to the University of North Carolina at Greensboro. Jarrell, overjoyed, told the Hookes, "Just think, old Peter Bell got me my job here and now I'm getting him his job here."*

TO ROBERT LOWELL

[September 1962]

Dear Cal:

I'd heard about all that trouble with the "Y" [YMHA] but then had forgotten it; it certainly would be incorrect for you to do anything for them like introducing me. I'll get them to send you some tickets, though. We'd already made arrangements to stay at the Plaza; since I have to go direct from the airport to Channel 13 and record things till just after midnight, we'd better go ahead with that arrangement and see you in normal daylight hours. How would you all like to have lunch with us Sunday? — and then we could go back to your apartment.

I was so touched and pleased with what you said about my critical essays that I've arranged, by magic, for a new critical essay, ending with you, which I send in this letter ["Fifty Years of American Poetry"].

I have a new poetry book just about done; I mean to read all new poems that I've written in the last three or four months.

I have a long critical essay that's an introduction to an Anchor book, *Six Russian Short Novels*. I'd send you one but I don't have any yet, though I believe it's just come out.

I feel pretty young myself but I must admit there're two houses near whose children call, "Santa Claus! Hi, Santa Claus!"

We'd love to stay with you some other time. I'll call you Saturday morning. There's one thing I wanted to arrange with you: for us to nominate Peter for one of those new National Institute nominations this year. Imagine Harry Levin's having been one for several years and not Peter?

See you next week.

Love,
Randall

Lowell's "trouble" at the Young Men's Hebrew Association (YMHA) in New York occurred when he read there from his book Imitations *and got some applause, some booing, and a cry from someone in the audience that he'd paid his money to hear new poems and these were merely translations. In place of Lowell, Eric Bentley introduced Jarrell's reading at the YMHA.*

To cover fifty years of American poetry in a one-hour speech, Jarrell singled out fifty-seven poets to mention. Who got the most space was significant, and who placed at the finish line was significant. In his conclusion, Jarrell gave Wilbur 230 words, Shapiro 250, and Lowell 700. Downed

*by depression and unable to attend the festival, Lowell read of himself in
the copy Jarrell sent him: ". . . the subject matter and peculiar circumstances of Lowell's best work — for instance, 'Falling Asleep over the
Aeneid,' 'For the Union Dead,' 'Mother Marie Therese,' 'Ford Madox
Ford,' 'Skunk Hour' — justify the harshness and violence, the barbarous
immediacy, that seem arbitrary in many of the others. He is a poet of
great originality and power who has, extraordinarily, developed instead
of repeating himself. His poems have a wonderful largeness and grandeur,
exist on a scale that is unique today. You feel before reading any new
poem of his the uneasy expectation of perhaps encountering a masterpiece."*

*Although Jarrell said he had a book of poetry "just about done," he
had written barely half the poems that would appear in the book eventually called* The Lost World *and published more than two years later,
in 1965.*

*Jarrell and Lowell did sponsor Taylor's election to the National Insti-
tute of Arts and Letters.*

*   *   *

*On October 22, 1962, the National Poetry Festival began with a Library of
Congress reception in an exhibition gallery where working manuscripts from
all the poets were displayed under glass. Among the guests who greeted Jarrell, Ransom was fond, Shapiro was sunny, newly met Ogden Nash was a
friend at first sight, and wily Frost was playing the Grand Old Man. Wilbur was mannerly, and Muriel Rukeyser and Eberhart ungrudging. Untermeyer's two former wives, Jean Starr and Virginia Moore, both poets,
were sociable, but the Tates were aloof. Léonie Adams and Louise Bogan
were civil, but Oscar Williams refused contact with Jarrell by hand, word,
or eye. Elizabeth Bishop, in Brazil, had declined because of the distance.
Lowell was too depressed to attend; Roethke and Williams were in failing
health; Warren was hospitalized for tests; and Sandburg, rumor had it,
would never share honors with Frost. Viereck had missed his flight from
Lisbon, someone said; and Aiken, MacLeish, Patchen, and Winters were not
accounted for.*

*The poets who were most gregarious and hilarious, and who were
having the best time, were Snodgrass, Berryman, and Schwartz, all in
varying states of inebriation. When Snodgrass sidled up to Jarrell, who
was engaged in a sober discussion of Ingmar Bergman, Jarrell, including
him politely, asked, "Have you ever seen* Through a Glass Darkly?" *To*

which Snodgrass, in a fit of giggles, answered, "Doesn't everyone?" and reeled off to join his pals.

For all the events the women dressed fashionably, and there were several fur coats among the cloth. Unable to restrain himself, Jarrell lightly touched one finger to the current Mrs. Untermeyer's fur sleeve and murmured half to himself, "What a splendid mink coat!" Mrs. Untermeyer, beaming, said good-humoredly, "There are three splendid mink coats here, and Louie bought all of them."

Formal greetings from President Kennedy were conveyed by the Special Consultant on the Arts, August Heckscher; Mrs. Kennedy invited the poets' wives for sherry; and buffet suppers for everyone were planned at former Attorney General Biddle's and Senator Udall's.

At a luncheon one day Jarrell was seated between a glowering Blackmur, saying nothing, and a gruffly condescending Rexroth. When Jarrell inquired, "How did you happen to learn Chinese?" Rexroth replied, "Oh, Jarrell, everyone knows Chinese." The whole table was struck dumb until Ogden Nash (quietly studying the individual menus provided) broke up the log jam, crying out, "Backfin-lump! Backfin-LUMP! Oh, I must remember backfin-lump!"

Shapiro wrote that on the night of Jarrell's lecture, "All of the poets sat on the edge of their seats while Jarrell . . . put together the jigsaw of modern poetry in front of our eyes." (RJ) All the poets, that is, except Bogan, who went to bed early and missed hearing herself paired with Adams as a poet in the "Elinor Wylie and Edna St. Vincent Millay tradition of feminine verse." Bishop and Moore, on the other hand, were "poets in a very different tradition who seem . . . the best women poets since Emily Dickinson, [and] an extraordinarily live, powerful and original poet, Eleanor Taylor, is a fitting companion of theirs . . ." Jarrell's summation of American poetry continued for the allotted hour, but as the author, his own contribution to the past fifty years was naturally not mentioned.

The next morning, Mrs. Kennedy's sherry party was canceled and the National Poetry Festival found itself competing with the Cuban missile crisis. Though Jarrell wrote Warren afterward that the panels and programs in Washington "gave one no time to worry much over Cuba," he was speaking for himself and his own absorption in poetry. Rexroth rebooked on an earlier flight to San Francisco, and Ogden Nash holed up in his room with the television, not to be seen again until his own reading. Frost spent the day in bed with the curtains drawn, his companion, William Meredith, reported; but rumors flew that this was not from fear of

nuclear attack but from grief at losing the Nobel Prize to Steinbeck.
Rousing himself sufficiently for his reading that night, Frost seemed
touchingly broken, and Jarrell was irate at the disrupting late arrival
of Snodgrass, Berryman, and Schwartz, who were full of spirits and rude
remarks.

Afterward, Snodgrass went to the party at the Udalls', but Schwartz
retired to his hotel room and smashed the furniture. As he hurled the tele-
phone out the window the police arrived. Berryman came to his aid, and
together they battled the foe through the lobby and into the paddy wagon.
Jailed for the rest of the festival, they missed hearing Sir Herbert Read's
lecture, which was also missed by a number of others, who felt that if
this was the END, they preferred to meet it at home. Jarrell, inside his
poetry bubble, felt no cause for alarm and stayed to the last, his opinion
of Read unchanged since hearing him at Princeton: "a nice man —
but dull."

TO ROBERT PENN WARREN

[November 1962]

Dear Red:

We'd like very much to get to meet Max Shulman. We'd have liked
even more to get to see you at the National Poetry Festival. It was a shame
your being sick. I'm a lot better now; I don't eat some things and take a
little medicine, but play tennis and feel fine.

Actually Washington gave one no time to worry much over Cuba and
this was a blessing. I liked getting to talk about American poetry. It was
interesting hearing what the poets said and what they read, and how the audience responded; in general I just sat dully through the bad conventional
poems, and was affected by the good ones. This may sound too good to be
true, but it is true.

We spent almost two months at Monteagle; Peter and Eleanor were
there the whole time.

I've written a lot of things lately — some about Kipling and different
Russian writers; while I was sick (and sick of reading as I've never been be-
fore — I longed to have something to do besides that) I translated some
German fairy tales for a nice children's editor, Michael di Capua, and before
I knew it I'd written a children's book too [*The Gingerbread Rabbit*]. Now
I've written half of another [*The Bat-Poet*]. It feels queer and entertaining
to write a sort of thing you've never written before.

I certainly do know the way you feel about the classes. The two years I spent in Washington without classes made me want never to be without them again.

Do tell Mr. Shulman that we'd be just delighted to get to see him; I hope he'll have dinner with us or anything else he has time for.

With all best wishes,

Yours,

Randall

Max Shulman was unable to come to Greensboro.

TO MICHAEL DI CAPUA

December 2, 1962

Dear Mr. di Capua:

I wanted to tell you that, after getting to see nine or ten Sendak books and five or six more Garth Williams books, I feel as you do about Sendak. He's better — Sendak, that is — at lyric or quiet or thoughtful or imaginative effects, and his people are much better than Williams' people; his general taste is better, too. I liked many of his animals — his bear family, for instance — very much. He would probably be better for the tone of *The Bat-Poet* than Williams, though we might wait to make up our minds till we've seen Williams' illustrations for *The Gingerbread Rabbit*.

Oddly, I saw the best Williams book I've seen, Margery Sharp's *The Rescuers.* They're mice or small furry animals in good *black* pen and ink drawings. If you could tell Williams how much I liked the pen-and-ink style of *The Rescuers,* and that I would be enchanted to have *The Gingerbread Rabbit* somewhat like that, perhaps he'd feel like it.

If I'd known about Sendak I'd probably have suggested going ahead with him for *The Rabbit,* but Williams is wonderful at rabbits, squirrels, foxes, and such, and we may be quite glad.

I hope you have a nice Christmas — we'll see you soon, with a typed out *Bat-Poet.* With all best wishes,

Yours,

Randall Jarrell

Maurice Sendak was the final choice as illustrator of The Bat-Poet.

*   *   *

During the Christmas holidays Jarrell finally met the young man he had known only from the clear, firm handwriting and the empathetic voice in the

leisurely long-distance phone calls. Di Capua, twenty-six, was neither hand-
some nor homely. He was short, wore glasses, and had thinning hair and a
mouth whose corners pointed up and made him look even younger when he
smiled. The Jarrells immediately noticed his selfless deference to them, con-
trasted with his city-tough skills in getting a cab, getting a table, and get-
ting a waiter's attention. His disarming willingness to listen and to put
himself at Jarrell's disposal was combined with a marked editorial keenness;
and it seemed as if he and Jarrell were just what the other needed and were
meeting at just the right time in their lives.

TO ANNA REGAN

[January 1963]

Dear Mother:

I do hope you're feeling a lot better now. School's started again for us and I'm mainly trying to finish *Crime and Punishment* before the end of the term. It was a great pleasure for us getting to talk to you Christmas. I got a pretty striped English shirt from Brooks Brothers with my half of the Christmas check you sent us; Mary got a beautiful pink blouse at Bergdorf Goodman. Thank you so much.

There was a nice mention in *Time* of *A Sad Heart* we cut it out to send you, so as to be sure you'd see it.

Did I tell you that I've just finished another children's book? It's named *The Bat-Poet* and has several poems inside the story. I really enjoyed writing it a lot, and felt almost as if I'd written a grown-up story.

Little Marie [Boyette] certainly has grown; she looks more like a small girl than a big baby. I gave Mary a little Georgian child's chair for a Christmas present, and little Marie liked sitting in it.

Bea has fixed her apartment awfully prettily; she and Gerhard are happy as can be.

Your Christmas sounded awfully nice, both for all the visits and all the presents. We didn't have much snow compared with yours; so far this has been rather a warm mild winter here — sunny, too.

Write and tell us how you're feeling now; I hope very much you're beginning to feel like your old self.

With lots of love,
Randall

Anna (Jarrell) Regan was hospitalized for chest pains in 1960, and
before and after that she suffered from arthritis, headaches, "nerves," and
weakness. She still bought a new outfit for every wedding and sent the

society columns to Jarrell, along with news of his cousins Bitsy and Candy, and whether she'd heard the opera on the radio the previous Saturday or missed it.

TO MAURICE SENDAK

[February 1963]

Dear Mr. Sendak:

What you wrote about *The Bat-Poet* made me feel wonderful; I'm awfully glad that you like it that much. I meant to write you right back and put it off because I was in the middle of another book — for the last week I've been writing an owl's bedtime story in terza rima. It's more or less the climax of the book. This new book — it's a sort of dream book, all in the present tense, named *Fly by Night* — will be so easy for you to illustrate that I've laughed over the thought again and again. I think as you do that *The Bat-Poet* will be hard, but believe me *Fly by Night* will make up for it; when you first read it I'm sure you'll get to laugh at how, paragraph by paragraph, it divides into pictures, and pictures thoroughly in your style.

When you start on *The Bat-Poet* I'll write you about it, though really I've almost no suggestions and want you to do it just as it comes to you. The animals like the mockingbird and chipmunk are very much the same as the real ones, so color photographs or watching the real animals might help with them. That particular sort of little brown bat, on the other hand, has too much a devil's face to use; other sorts of bat, just bats for instance, have faces more like squirrels or mice's, and you could invent a face for him more like theirs.

It must be awful not to be able to get the sort of thing you really want to illustrate — it is such a waste. We've looked at your Parson Whackwell pictures [in *Schoolmaster Whackwell's Wonderful Sons*] over and over; they have a beautiful, lyric, individual feeling to them — the brother who goes to the birds and the hermit bird-teacher are my particular favorites.

We had an awfully good time at your house after the opera; I hope you can come and visit us sometime. In the spring the bats, the chipmunk, the mockingbird, and the cardinal are all right here.

With all best wishes,
Yours,
Randall Jarrell

Sendak, thirty-four, had illustrated the popular Little Bear *series by Else Holmelind Minarik (Harper and Row) and had written and illustrated the even more popular* Nutshell Library *and* Where the Wild Things Are. *It was typical of di Capua's acumen to match Sendak's lyric drawings to Jarrell's lyric writing; and from the day illustrator and author met, their love of music and wit and childhood drew them together. In* The Art of Maurice Sendak *by Selma G. Lanes (Harry N. Abrams, 1980), Sendak is quoted as saying, "I've worked with many writers, but he [Jarrell] was probably the most extraordinary of them all, because he was a poet and had a visionary sense. But, oddly for a writer, he had a graphic sense, so that he knew what a book could look like. Randall conceived of the book from its binding to the quality of paper, so working with him was an amazing experience."*

TO MICHAEL DI CAPUA

[March 1963]

Dear Mr. di Capua:

I'm delighted with the [Garth Williams] drawings: the gingerbread rabbit's *very* cute and touching. The fox is wonderful, and the old rabbit in the colored sketch makes me want to be adopted by him. Since the big rabbit in the black and white drawing is so big that his ears come to the mother's eyes, I believe everybody will take it as just perspective — also, his ears come up to the chimney, and the mother's head goes over the roof.

Do send Garth Williams back the sketch for the cover so that he can get the old rabbit *exactly* the same in the finished drawing for the cover.

I'm sending everything back to you, including my letter to Garth Williams — I don't have his address. Read it and see how it sounds to you.

You described the gingerbread rabbit well — I was all prepared for him. I like him very much. He's plainly made of dough. Poor innocent thing! I believe Williams is getting quite inspired and will make a charming book.

I certainly did enjoy talking to you about everything; I was enchanted that you liked the idea of *Women* so much.

Will you make one change in the biographical note about me in *Gingerbread Rabbit;* my school here is called The University of North Carolina at Greensboro.

With all best wishes,

Yours,
Randall Jarrell

Women was the title Jarrell had chosen for what was to have been his next book of poetry.

TO ADRIENNE RICH

[April 29, 1963]

Dear Adrienne:

They gave me your check a couple of hours after you left, and here it is. Mary and I were sorrier to see you go than anybody we've met in many years; instead of feeling that we were in the sands of age in which nothing grows, where all our friends are old, we had the feeling that the world is full of new ones, if we only knew them. Do send me your new poems, and I'll write you about them and these in your new book. I'll send you a poem I got from your "Roofwalker." After I'd read that, early in the morning, it somehow made me think of gleaning. As a child in California, the families coming back from their Sunday picnics would stop in the already harvested lima bean fields and glean, and my poem ["Gleaning"] has a woman remembering this.

Yours,

Randall

(P.S.) I did want to say about Frost and Williams that I feel it your way just about as much, but I was just saying it the Frost way. To me, Frost is a wonderful but tragic character like Oedipus, like the king who says he's conquered everybody but stands here among graves; whereas Williams is a happy ending, even the plainest and flattest of his lines has a kind of dumb unconquerable happiness welling up underneath.

At Jarrell's invitation, Rich had taken part in the Arts Forum in Greensboro.

*   *   *

The University of North Carolina at Greensboro had granted Jarrell a four-month sabbatical and he decided to order a Jaguar XK-120, for delivery in Coventry, and tour Europe. The model he chose had a metallic beige finish called Desert Gold and an orange leather interior he said was "the color of a brand-new football."

Jarrell had the comfortable feeling of having enough poems for The Lost World *and two or three for* Women. *Michael di Capua had become an invaluable New York friend, attending all Jarrell's readings there, obtaining opera tickets, introducing him to unusual restaurants, and keeping himself free to spend unlimited time talking about everything, especially books. Jarrell, who had always longed for an editor who would be his friend, suddenly realized that this friend could be his editor if he left Atheneum,*

*and he resolved to do so. Haydn's interest in Jarrell had been short-lived,
and he was currently occupied with a power struggle in the firm and with
his psychoanalysis. Jarrell had felt neglected and had turned to Harry Ford.*

TO MICHAEL DI CAPUA

May 2, 1963

Dear Mr. di Capua:

Here is *Fly by Night;* I'll send it airmail special delivery, and do call me
and tell me how you like it.

We had an awfully good time having dinner and going to the opera
with you; and I enjoyed making plans about the books even more. I have a
good friend at Atheneum and told him, in confidence, what I mean to do.
He [Harry Ford] feels that Atheneum will let me go right away, since
they've made such a big public point of saying they'd never hold an author
against his will. He tried to persuade me for about an hour to stay with
Atheneum; he said that he'd be my editor from now on, and personally
guarantee they'd do as much — twice as much, he said — as Macmillan
would. He'd only partially realized what things were like for me at Atheneum; he said that the amount of advertising or other measures depended
entirely on an author's editor, at Atheneum, and that was why there'd been
so little. As a friend, he was worried about my going to so big a firm as
Macmillan; he felt I'd be lost in it. He said he'd heard a number of things
about you, and without exception they'd been favorable. We had a *long*
conversation; I'll tell you all about it over the phone.

I think I'd like to make partial arrangements with you over the telephone and by letter, and then come up to New York in two weeks and talk
to you and Mr. Gross [Gerald Gross, editor-in-chief] about everything. I've
enjoyed everything about the children's books too much not to want to
have it just the same with the other books. I have pleasant impressions of
Macmillan's but I'm doing this just as a personal thing with you; if you
weren't my editor and didn't manage everything about my books, I
shouldn't dream of transferring to Macmillan.

Mary sends her best along with mine.

Randall

With Atheneum's release, Jarrell took his book of poetry, his Three Sisters
translation, and his half-finished Faust *translation to Macmillan. Describing di Capua to Lowell, Jarrell said, "He's like nutrient broth and makes it*

easy for me to write in all the ways Haydn made it difficult." When Lowell inquired, "But isn't he a little young?" Jarrell answered, "He's Providential, Cal . . . And just think; Yeats' publishers!" Di Capua's golden rule for success with Jarrell was to do one-third of the talking and two-thirds of the listening, and to keep the talk away from himself and on Jarrell's writing, present and future, and how to make as many books as he could out of it. His silver rule was to make himself indispensable. His final estimable quali-fication, Jarrell thought, was that di Capua himself did not write.

TO ADRIENNE RICH

[June 1963]

Dear Adrienne:

I've taken a long time getting used to your new poems. I really do think that at the moment you are writing the best poems you've ever written [*Snapshots of a Daughter-in-Law*]. Your poetry has changed a great deal and has lost the qualities that were most a weakness. What hurts the poems most in *The Diamond Cutters* — and there are some beautiful ones, and others with beautiful parts — is something faintly conventional, traditional, orthodox about the things you say, the style you say them in, the rhythm and form, even; they still have some connection to "my praised and sedu-lous lines" — your new poems have none. The earlier ones are a little like beautiful 18th century pieces of music that sound first of all like the 18th century and only second like a particular composer on a particular subject. You write, in them, like a young, trained, skillful being who has her own way of doing things but a way that's a little too much influenced by the right way of doing it, the common denominator of the poetic practice of good poets — occasionally one can see the particular good poet that's hav-ing some effect on you. One reason I like "Autumn Equinox" so much is that you were quite carried away by that woman and situation and made things bare and minimal, sometimes — "I thought that life was different than it is" and "Even autumn/Can only carry through what spring began" and "We finish off/Not quite as we began." I know that it's a young poet's poem in a certain manner and it must feel queer and wrong to have it liked (what must seem to you) too much, but the whole thing has real force and truth and quite overcomes small weaknesses. I think you're right in believ-ing she wouldn't have thought of "vague Arcadian longing . . . Some incor-ruptible myth that tinged the years/With pastoral flavors"; if it moved from "Why Satires, I have wondered?" to "What in that bitterness can speak to

him" it would probably be better. I *love* "And yet he seemed superb in his
refusal/To read aloud from Bryant to the ladies/Assembled on the board-
ing-house piazza/Among the moth-wings of a summer evening." I don't
much like "what quirks of vanity"; in "Static as figures on a mantelpiece."
The *static* seems deadly, conventionally, unnecessarily to say what the lines
are showing. The steel engravings you picked for her to notice certainly are
good psychoanalytically. Most of their conversation is very good; in "babble
things I never thought" the *babble* doesn't sound to me like a word she'd
really use there — it sounds more like your descriptive word about it. I like
the end of the sentence that begins "Young lovers talk . . ." but not the first
three lines. "Loss of leaf/And rain upon the boughs?" seems a slightly weak,
expected carrying out of the conceit after the wonderful sentence before.
"The irritable gust of youth/Stopped turning every blade of grass to find/A
new dissatisfaction" is troubling to the reader because he's thinking of the
two, *hard,* as trees, and suddenly one of the trees starts turning over the
grass blades. (I didn't mean to write so much about "Autumn Equinox"
but I like it lots and want to use it in an anthology. Other people I've got
to read it like it very much — Mary's crazy about it; it really is worth
changing a little in the spots you're dissatisfied with, like the Ovid pastoral
part.)

Some other poems I want to use in the anthology, if I may, are "The
Roofwalker," "Thirty-three" [later entitled "Necessities of Life"] and one
of the other new ones, I'm not quite sure which now. I like "At Long Last"
very much. An old one I'd like to use (I guess you'll give the same groan I
do when I get "Death of the Ball Turret Gunner" letters) is "Living in
Sin." I don't like it as Cal does, but "a pair of beetle-eyes would fix her
own — /envoy from some black alley in the moldings . . ." really is wonderful. I feel like a child who has broken one plate and can't resist breaking
another: have you ever thought (this is bad of me, but I like the rest of the
poem so much I can't resist) of changing the sentence in "Pictures by Vuillard" "But we, the destined readers of Stendhal,/In monstrous change such
consolations find/As restless mockery sets before the mind/To deal with
what must anger and appall"? If you really meant and liked this sentence
would you have had such abstract rhetoric in it? It seems to me that instead
of inventing or imagining something to make "we" as vivid as the Vuillard
women you use a convenient ostensive phrase for them and then give them
some rhetoric, quite stock rhetoric. To me this is the only thing wrong with
the poem, but it hurts it so.

Well, now to talk a lot about your new poems. As soon as one starts
Snapshots of a Daughter-in-Law one feels you've changed, that your rhythms,

word-style, general decor, and attitude toward the world are different. The rhythms are so many strokes of a paring-knife instead of so many measures of a *ländler,* and have Williams behind them instead of Palgrave. The words are much more precise, hard, like prose in particular instead of poetry in general; the decor is the furniture and intellectual furniture of a specific life rather than the museum-properties and cultural scenery of a tourist in Time; the attitude is serious and, like Wordsworth, tries to look hard at its particular subject, which is final for it — the poems seem life first and poetry second, and have entirely lost any conventionally or traditionally poetic attitude. I think it was an easy change in one sense: you had to make it to get the poems expressions of what you'd become and what your life had become, but it seems rather a hard change so far as getting your new style to make poems that would be just right as poems. A lot of the poems in *Snapshots* are, so to speak, ways of learning to write "The Roofwalker." I really don't think you've ever written a better poem than it: I can't see one word that has anything wrong with it. When your laconic exact statement that seems understatement bursts for an instant into something like "and due to break my neck" it's marvellous; and when the exact description crystallizes, so to speak, into the antithetical aphoristic conclusiveness of "A life I didn't choose/chose me" and of the last sentence, which is a conclusive aphorism in the image-language of a dream, it's best of all. The poem has that real heart-breaking quality that your new poetry has.

Some of the others in the book that I like best are the second half of "The Loser" — I'll interrupt to say, interestedly, that the last two lines of "The Absent-Minded" are Rilke lines, good ones. Number 3 in "Snapshots of a Daughter-in-Law" is particularly witty and nastily exact, 4 and 6 are good and effective. It's all a pleasure to read but it's a little more tersely, and wittily allusive, a clever person being dry and exact and flatly laconic for other clever persons, than your best new poems are. I like most of "Merely to Know," a lot of "Antinoüs: The Diaries" — "winced and hopped and limped" is so good. "Juvenilia" is slight but just right, a real Kodak picture; in "Double Monologue" I liked very much "A puzzle/for the maker who has thought/once too often too coldly," but I thought the whole poem was a conceit too exhaustively worked out — a reader gets tired of a dry, terse, allusive style pretty fast, compared to a style like that in the "The Roofwalker," and "Thirty-three." In the next poem ["Readings of History"], if I read to you "I skulk here leafing ancient copies/of LIFE from World War II," wouldn't you laugh and say, "Funny old Cal!" The words *skulk* and *leafing,* the present tense, the prosaic historical properties like *LIFE* and *World War II;* these are pure Cal. I think it's an echo of some specific lines,

almost [from "Grandparents"]: "There/half my life-lease later,/I hold an illustrated *London News* — ;/disloyal still,/I doodle handle moustaches on the
last Russian Czar." If you ask "Where's the doodle gone?" I'll reply, "Oh, it
spilled over into 'Juvenilia.' " If you ask "Why are you writing this?" I'll
have to answer "Isn't it silly?" I just got carried away — it's not anything
that has anything to do with your new style, which is entirely original. I
think "Readings of History" seems part of an interesting diary of ideas
compared to a real poem like "The Afterwake," one of the best in the book.
I don't like "Artificial Intelligence" as a whole poem exactly, but "You
never had a mother,/let's say? no digital Gertrude/whom you'd as lief have
seen/Kingless? So your White Queen/was just an 'operator.' "/(My Red
had incandescence,/ire, aura, flare . . ." is marvellous, so witty and with such
original charm; just the r's in ire, aura, flare, seem a triumph.

"That face — /part Roman Emperor, part Raimu —" [from "A Marriage in the 'Sixties"] seems to me the kind of description that depends on
looking at the thing described and seeing how just description is. "Stale as a
written-out journalist" [in "End of an Era"] is Cal. "Rustication" gives an
excellent drawing of the woman and makes the reader feel about her as you
do; to me it seems to stop short, compared to your last poems. "Peeling
Onions" is one of the best, I think; but "yet all that stayed/stuffed in my
lungs like smog" seems not quite strong or climactic enough, so that you
wish the poem went a little further. "Ghost of a Chance" seems to me one
of the best or better ones; "Well in Ruined Courtyard" is a good one; "Novella" is appealing — "separate as minds" is good about the stars; "The Lag"
is nice and the end of "Peace" is beautiful. I've written rather little and at
random about the book because seeing "The Roofwalker" and the typed
poems makes one feel the book mostly a working up to them, no matter
how good parts or individual poems are.

I'm crazy about "Thirty-three." "A dark-blue thumbtack" is so good, as
is "a hard little head protruding"; these are perfect as objective phrases in a
poem by an unknown author, but they're even better when one knows
you — one thinks, "That's *exactly* right for her as a little girl!" "The
dot/begins to ooze. Certain heats/melt it" is so witty and exactly truthful;
gee, *certain* is nice. It gets so magical and beautiful, but remains entirely accurate and truthful, at the end. One feels it's your own emotional and spiritual development made into a real poem; it's wonderfully appealing. The
image transition from "thumbtack" and "hard little head" to "Scaly as a dry
bulb" to "solid/as a cabbage-head" is extremely good; the end fills the world
with sensible life.

"Old Partners" and "At Long Last" are beautiful poems; there's something so touching about "At Long Last." It's interesting, in it, to see you getting away from your short specific Williams-imitated lines (I'm talking just about rhythm) to a longer motion more like all English poetry but not a bit like your old *Diamond Cutters* rhythms. I have a hunch that lots of the poetry you write in the future will have rhythms more like it than (to talk of an extreme) the rhythms in the fish-climbing-from-the-sea evolution poem ["Ghost of a Chance"]. It seems to me that in both your rhythms, your words, and your statements you had to make everything bare, exact, concise, photographically true to the subject because in your early poems you'd been too much the opposite — it was your real way of escaping from your old style, and you're certainly right to be so grateful to Williams for helping you to do it. How glad I am that you're never influenced by Auden any more. He was bad for you, I thought.

"Like This Together" is a good and complicated poem with a lot in it, the beginning (I mean this entirely as praise) certainly does feel like *Wild Strawberries* or some similar Bergman scene. The only thing I don't like about it is "grip earth and/let intuition burn" — this, to me, comes right out and *says* it in a rhetorical way that doesn't seem entirely fresh imagination, particularly not since it's so much a carrying out of the conceit about the tree and roots. Imagine someone who's unsympathetic to your poems: he'd say, "Oh, that's one of these inspiring rhetorical endings that tell you about life," and unjust as this would be, it would be partly true, I *think*.

I admired so much "A Latinate Word." It's an almost impossible sort of poem really to succeed with, to do right — you do, though. You really do get the feel of the old America into it. The end is beautiful. I like a lot of "For Kin," but I wish parts of the second and third divisions were more like the good "sun-and-moon clocks, Balzac in forty-volume sets, riding boots, still like new." I thought "arrows of light striking the water" maybe not as striking as it ought to be. "Science-fiction tragi-comical" certainly is good.

Most of this is written too scrappily and at random, but I hope it will make you feel how much I like the new poems and how different they are from the old. As you know from that long old review, I liked the old very much, but the best of your new ones are quite out of their class; you've become a different and better poet, you really have.

We're leaving for England on Tuesday. Do write us — American Express London would do for July, American Express Munich do August.

We often mention you and wish we could see you again soon. With all best wishes, yours,

Randall

Rich did in fact delete "grip earth and/let intuition burn" from the poem "Like This Together."

TO MICHAEL DI CAPUA

[June 1963]

Dear Michael:

The Munich operas look lovely. I think we'd like to go to *Der Rosenkavalier,* August 21; *Intermezzo,* August 22; *Ariadne,* August 24; and *Elektra,* August 29. We don't like *Arabella.* That's why we're leaving it out. We thought we could drive down to Innsbruck and some of the places along the South Bavarian border, between the 24th and 29th.

It's *awfully* nice of you to get the tickets in New York; tell me how much they are and I'll send you a check. This reminds me to thank you for the check for my New York trip.

Since we'll be seeing each other so soon in Munich, I don't think we'll wait until the 17th to see you at Amsterdam, but will go on into Germany about the 12th; that will let us do the part of our trip through Lake Constance, before we drive over to Munich.

I was delighted you liked "Gleaning" that much. Here is the whole *Lost World.* Two of the poems I'd just written and meant to save for *Women,* I decided to put in this book — they're "A Well-to-Do Invalid" and "The Lost Children."

The Government sent me a letter asking me to send them nine hundred dollars as part of my unestimated income tax for next year — the part that withholding doesn't cover that they're covering with this new withholding — so I think I'll ask you to send me the advance for *The Lost World,* since I have such a good, indeed inescapable, use for it.

I think Vienna will be lots of fun for you, and the opera does start at the beginning of September. We won't get to Vienna until the 15th of September, I imagine.

We're enchantingly flooded in maps, passports, steamer and airline tickets for us, a steamer ticket for the Jaguar, guidebooks, European picture books, the biggest Donatello book so we can list all the Donatello places, two waterproof blue shoulder-strap bags Alitalia sent us, foreign driving licenses, etc. We've got plans all made to see the paintings in London, Paris, the Belgian and Dutch cities, Munich and other German places, Florence, Venice, Rome, and other Italian places — among other things, we're going to list possible illustrations for *Women* in a little notebook.

Mary sends her love.

With all best wishes,
Randall

Women was to be published after The Lost World, *and "Gleaning," "A Man Meets a Woman on the Street," and two Rilke translations, "The Widow's Song" and "A Lady on a Balcony," were intended for it.*

Because of his distaste for Stephen Spender and other British intellectuals, Jarrell planned to give England short shrift. He wanted to see the Turners and the Blakes at the Tate, the Donatellos at the Victoria and Albert, and Sir Kenneth Clark's Italian acquisitions at the National Gallery. At Mary's insistence he agreed to see Durham Cathedral; but that was all. On hearing this, Peter Taylor proclaimed, "That won't do," and, as Mary wrote in Randall Jarrell, 1914–1965, *"he and Eleanor (such a . . . castle-combing, monarchistic, Anglophile pair) forced Somerset, Goathland, Doncaster, etc., on Randall with the same sweet unreasonableness he'd used to force Freud,* War and Peace, *and Bosch on them."*

Before the Jarrells left for Europe, the English department — prompted by Jarrell — reappointed Taylor to the faculty. Atheneum had equally released Jarrell and their option on his poetry anthology, and di Capua was urging Macmillan to bring the anthology out in hardback. Finally, after a nine-year delay, the theatrical producer Cheryl Crawford had definite plans to open The Three Sisters *on Broadway in the summer of 1964, with Lee Strasberg directing it for the Actors' Studio. After depositing Elfie in Raleigh for safekeeping with the Hofers, the Jarrells left from Idlewild Airport on what a gentleman they met later in Bamberg called their "secondt vedding moon."*

TO MICHAEL DI CAPUA

Park Court Hotel
Lancaster Gate
London
July 10, 1963

Dear Michael:

We love London and are having a splendid time.

I have a delightful English tailor who's making me two suits; I meant to go to Adeney and Boutroy but by accident went to Bryant and Burleson in the same small building. Mr. Bryant is worthy of Kipling or Wilde — every word pleases.

Our address here — it will work for the next 8 days or so — is Park Court Hotel, 75 Lancaster Gate, London W.2. England.

We're in a nice shabby hotel with ridiculous furniture and two big windows looking out into the park, that looks just like a Constable. We admire the way the English use their park; they're awfully pleasant, and do they love cats! We pet one at a bakery, and it's plain no one has ever done anything but pet him; one evening he didn't even open his eyes.

We certainly did enjoy getting to see you at the airport. Alitalia's jet was the most beautiful plane I've ever been in; it was finished in two shades of brown leather, so that Mary said it was like being in a Gucci suitcase. The sun rose over the Atlantic at 2 o'clock Eastern Daylight Saving Time; we didn't get much sleep.

I got some slacks made out of riding trouser material so thick that the slacks will stand in the corner by themselves.

We enjoyed very much but were slightly disappointed in the National Gallery; it's more like Philadelphia than the Metropolitan or National. The Seurat *Bathers* and the Pieros [Piero della Francesca] were wonderful; I couldn't believe it, but the Mantegna *Agony in the Garden* is better in black and white reproduction than in reality.

Mary sends her love. See you in Munich.

Yours,
Randall

TO ANNA REGAN

[July 1963]

Dear Mother:

We're crazy about England — the people in the streets and parks are awfully good-humored and polite and nice. Is it cool! They really just have no summer, but a kind of spring they call summer here. We've seen a great many paintings both here and in Paris — we saw the Bolshoi Ballet here. If you're a man and like to buy clothes London is almost as good as it's supposed to be. We start driving in the country tomorrow.

I do hope you are feeling lots better; you sounded a great deal better the last time I talked to you. Mary sends her love. I'll write again soon. With lots of love.

Randall

*   *   *

In "The Group of Two" in Randall Jarrell, 1914–1965, *Mary wrote:*
"Randall couldn't get over his astonishment at the way London looked com-
pared to New York . . . Everything cozy and well made and stable that had
fallen out of America in this century seemed . . . there in England. He still
liked Germany but it was hard on him to be cut off from magazines and
newspapers, even menus. 'Oh, I'm so ill-educated,' he complained. 'Imagine
knowing one *language!' . . . More and more, England seemed the fulfill-*
ment of Randall's wish for a foreign country where they spoke English. And
more than once, over his game pie at Fortnum and Mason's, he said, 'We
ought to get a flat here some summer.' "

TO MICHAEL DI CAPUA

Park Court Hotel,
Lancaster Gate
London
July 21, 1963

Dear Michael:

I've been working over *The Three Sisters* a good deal. I think any additional changes are going to be rather easy, but I'm very much looking
forward to going over the whole thing with the literal translation. I got
Hugo's *Russian Reading Made Easy,* the familiar old textbook that has half
of *The Three Sisters* in completely literal English between the lines of Russian — if only they had it all!

We've been having an extremely good time. I really think the most
striking single thing we've seen is the Romanesque inside of Durham
Cathedral; it was even better than the Pieros at the National Gallery, the
Seurat *Bathers,* and the Turner *Fighting Téméraire.* We mostly saw paintings
in Paris while we were there, but we also saw *Giselle* and *Tannhäuser* at the
Opera — we saw the Bolshoi do *Romeo and Juliet* in London, and Struch-
kova was the best dancer I've seen in years.

The Lake Country and the Yorkshire moors are all they're supposed to
be. So's the car — we love it. Driving on the left turned out to be easy and
English drivers are good as gold, but oh the roads! oh the traffic! There must
be *three* by-passes in the British Isles, one for England, one for Scotland, and
one for Ireland.

The Delacroix exhibition at the Louvre certainly does convince you
that, except for a couple of portraits, he was a second-rate painter. I'd have
given everything else in it for his portrait of Paganini and the beautiful portrait of himself.

You know, it's queer, but there're more good paintings in the New York museums than in the Paris ones, and our National Gallery is so much better than London's that there's no comparison.

American Express, Amsterdam, would be a good place to write me — we go over to the Continent Saturday. We certainly are looking forward to seeing you in Munich — going to the operas together ought to be delightful.

With all best wishes,
Yours,
Randall

Di Capua had arranged with Paul Schmidt to make and send a literal or "word-for-word" translation of The Three Sisters *that Jarrell wanted to apply to his own for possible refinements. Somehow Schmidt took longer to do this than was expected, and the delay became a maddening frustration to Jarrell.*

Although the Jarrells extended their stay in London to watch Wimbledon on television, they did not see the Tower of London, the Poet's Corner, or the haunts of Dr. Johnson or Dickens. Jarrell had a horror of being a tourist among tourists submitting to a guided tour. When this was unavoidable, he hung back, pretending not to be with the group, and was then made more conspicuous by the guide calling out, "Kindly keep with the group, sir."

*   *   *

Robert Lowell had passed through London and spent a few hours talking with the Jarrells on a park bench in Kensington Gardens. In "The Group of Two," Mary wrote, "Cal was for Plath that day, and Gunn — and Larkin. Randall was for Larkin, Larkin, and Larkin: that was normal. Cal's and Randall's temperaments . . . were about as opposite as some of the poets they compared. But the two friends' intelligences were complementary. At each visit they roused each other up once or twice, whether they meant to or not; and then, like two physicists on different hemispheres who advance their own knowledge on each other's papers, Cal and Randall (when their initial resistance passed) often pushed with their paws and found something palatable in each other's latest Enthusiasms. 'Cal's right,' Randall might say. 'I was dumb about X ———. He's better than I thought.' Or he might say, 'The people Cal likes!' "

Though Lowell's intelligence and wit were a match for Jarrell's — and they often matched them — Lowell was almost as considerate of him as di

Capua was. He took care to mention, repeatedly, Jarrell's help with his po-etry; took care not to quarrel with him as he did with Taylor; and took care not to use the fashionable four-letter words with Jarrell that he used with others, even to the point of refining bullshit *to* bull.

TO BEATRICE HOFER

The Mermaid
Rye, England
[July 1963]

Dear Bea:

Your darling letter was so clever that I'm helpless to think of any suit-able answer — I weakly thought of having the Jaguar write back, but even the best car's a very mechanical letter-writer. I'm *so* glad Elfie's getting along so well. He'd like seeing cats — or anyway, the status of cats — in England; they're all fat, happy, and petted, and the newspapers are full of advertise-ments of cat-goods and vitamins to make your darling kitten grow up into a big strong cat.

We're in an Elizabethan bedroom with a canopied bed with a carved statue-encrusted roof, not to mention pillars and an Elizabethan-lady-statue playing a lute on the headboard, flanked by two bearded men with their arms in slings.

If you took one very narrow blind road, full of sharp curves and steep grades and filled it with doubledecker buses, trucks, cars, motorcycles with sidecars, three-wheeled cars, Boy Scouts, Girl Scouts, dogs on leashes, and somebody on a horse — and then put some roadworkers to work repairing the road, that would be English traffic. It's lucky the English drivers are so careful and phlegmatic.

England certainly has been fun. I think I liked the inside of Durham Cathedral, the big arches at Wells (to support the tower) and some sheep-dogs gathering together a flock in the Lake Country best of all.

Thanks *so* much for taking care of Elfie for us. With lots of love to all three of you.

Yours,
Randall

Pet Elfie for me.

Beatrice Hofer's letter had been written as if it were from Elfie.

*　　*　　*

The Jarrells drove to Grasmere to see Wordsworth's Dove Cottage, to
Hurst Green to see Kipling's Batemans, and to Rye to see James's Lamb
House, but only to look at them from the car, not to go inside. At Lydd
they boarded a plane for France, taking the Jaguar with them. From
France, they drove via Belgium, Holland, and the Moselle valley to Mu-
nich.

In "The Group of Two," Mary wrote about their stay in Munich:
"Mornings there started with a frantic routine: the Jarrells half through
their breakfasts and urging on the half-asleep Michael di Capua with his,
so we could be first at the box office for the turned-back opera tickets of the
day." By ten-thirty the crisis would be passed: either all were going to the
performance that night, or some, or none. At any rate, it was settled, and
the Jarrells could relax, and di Capua could wake up, at Café Luitpold.
Then, di Capua — drawing on his years of following opera — became that
rare kind of good company Jarrell so often longed for: "Someone who knows
more than I do about a subject I'm interested in."

In Munich, di Capua brought news that Sendak was on fire over The
Bat-Poet, *that all was well with Garth Williams in San Miguel, and that*
Paul Schmidt's literal translation was in the mail and Jarrell should have
it any day.

After two joyful weeks in each other's company, di Capua flew to New
York and the Jarrells drove on to Salzburg. Paul Schmidt's literal transla-
tion of The Three Sisters *had not come and Jarrell hoped to find it waiting*
for him in Vienna.

TO MICHAEL DI CAPUA

Kaiserhof Hotel
Vienna
September 10, 1963

Dear Michael:

Yesterday the Royal Hotel on Singerstrasse told us they'd received a letter and forwarded it to the Kaiserhof Hotel, where we're staying now; I said
to Mary, "It just seems too good to be true — tomorrow morning *The
Three Sisters.*" It *was* too good to be true, alas! it just turned out to be a note
about the copyright of *The Gingerbread Rabbit.* I really am feeling the force
of destiny about that literal *Three Sisters:* "Maledizione!" as they kept saying
in *Die Macht von Schicksal,* our second night here. We're leaving tomorrow
and will hope that the manuscript gets forwarded to us. Perhaps if you mail
another copy to me at American Express, Florence, that will reach me in

time. I'm about to give up on the Munich copy, which will probably be returned to its sender any day now.

The *Bat-Poet* manuscript looks splendid — the type size for the poems is quite all right. I return it with this letter. I was enchanted with the drawings for *The Gingerbread Rabbit,* making the rabbit so small, in the walking-into-the-moon picture, was a wonderful idea.

We've seen operas every night except two — one of those nights had none and the other was a duplication. Last night [Teresa] Stich-Randall sang about the best Violetta I ever heard; she was *marvellous.* Claire Watson sang a *beautiful* Sieglinde in *Valkyrie,* much better than her Munich *Così;* [Otto] Edelmann was an awful Wotan. [Anton] Dermota is the fairly ever-present curse of Vienna opera; he helped spoil *The Magic Flute,* along with everybody else except a *good* Papageno. You see why Strauss felt as he did about German tenors. We saw a wonderfully acted, live, rather well-sung *Figaro.* The principals were so happy about it they kept kissing each other at the last curtain calls. With [Irmgard] Seefried as the Countess, a big young excellent American, Robert Kearns as the Count, Taddei excellent as Figaro, Hanni Steffele as a Susanna who was the archetype of all nice German and Austrian waitresses and clerks, and Olivera Miljakovic (I think that's her last name) as surely the most charming Cherubino ever, ever, since Mozart wrote it. I saw [Sena] Jurinac twice as Cherubino in 1948, and good as she was she didn't begin to compare for pure charm. I wouldn't mind seeing this Cherubino once a week for the rest of my life. We heard a really good Italian tenor named Carlo Bergonzi in *La Forza del Destino;* he stopped the show for six or eight minutes with his best aria. Simoniata was very good in her first aria, and I don't suppose anybody was ever good in that damnable Rataplan thing. We saw an extremely good *Wiener Blut* done by the Volksoper, delicate, live, and fast, all the principals charming; their *Fledermaus* was loud and crude and looked as though it were given by the League of Middle-Aged Men.

I forget whether Mary told you in her card how wonderfully good Erika Kött was as Zerbinetta in Munich; it was a good, very natural (especially in the first act) *Ariadne.*

I believe the best music we've heard all summer was the first act of *Valkyrie;* at his best he's just a composer on a larger scale than anybody else we heard. I realize this would make a lot more fashionable sentence in 1893 than 1963, but that's a risk you have to take in life. Well, why not go on with such remarks? — we heard a chamber music concert at Salzburg with a Beethoven trio (early) and Mozart and Brahms piano quartets, and the Brahms was incomparably superior to the others. And seeing four Mozart operas in a row made me agree with a shocking remark I once read — that Mozart's melodic gifts, in his operas, seem just a bit too predictable, and when you compare the too-homogeneous melodies with Verdi's best (or, in another sphere, Schubert's) it's hard not to agree; though I never feel this way when I'm listening to Mozart piano concertos or some of his chamber music. How I do hope we get to hear a lot of Verdi in Italy!

We're coming home about three weeks earlier than we planned — we get to New York on the *Christoforo Colombo* on the 18th of November.

It certainly was fun seeing you in Munich; I'm sorry we couldn't have been in Vienna together, too. Our last week or so in Germany was wonderful; the Bamberg Rider's even better than the photographs, walking around Dinkelsbühl in the late afternoons was like walking around a Middle Ages town, and we got fonder of South Germans than ever. "To want to do well and be liked" is a good formula for making foreigners love you — to think that the same people did what they've done!

At Augsburg we stayed at a hotel, the Drei Mohren, where Mozart, Goethe, and the Duke of Wellington stayed; they had the Duke of Wellington's written-out appreciation. At Rothenburg, from a Kunstschmidt (oh, surely, that's spelled wrong), we got a big golden sun with a face and many irregular rays, like an inn sign.

I hope everything's going nicely at your work; Mary sends her love. With all best wishes,

Randall

Jarrell had wide tastes and enthusiasms in music, from pre-Baroque to modern, but a perennial favorite was Mozart, especially the operas. W. D. Snodgrass said Jarrell told him, "When the angels play for God they play Bach; but when they play for themselves they play Mozart."

TO ADRIENNE RICH

Albergo Berchielli,
Florence, Italy
[October 1963]

Dear Adrienne:

I liked both the new poems — "In the Woods" particularly appealed to me. I certainly do like the phrase "Difficult and ordinary happiness,/ No one nowadays believes in you." If you believe in happiness and have ordinary good luck you really can be happy a lot of the time — but most people of our reading-and-writing sort have conscientious objections to any happiness, they'd far rather be right than happy. It *is* terrible in our time to have the death of the world hanging over you, but, personally, it's something you disregard just as you disregard the regular misery of so much of the world, or your own regular personal aging and death. I get a real consolation out of looking at astronomical pictures like the horsehead nebula in Orion: all the different suns the material galaxies will form out of, the little bright spots that are galaxies of hundreds of thousands or millions of suns — most of them with planets — all this in one little patch of space. If something ends, still, how infinitely much there is that isn't ending! The end of the earth isn't the end of the world but more like the death of a person, or the fall of one leaf. I suppose this is a queer rather pathetic-sounding consolation but I mean it, really feel it strongly — the eternal silence of those infinite spaces (or whatever it is) comforts me. There's something so inhuman and incommensurable about the likely end of most beings on earth that anything that can cancel it out needs to be inhuman and incommensurable too.

I'm really delighted that you liked what I wrote about your poems and that it was some good to you. Do send me the changed "Living in Sin." What you said about *Poetry and the Age* made me feel good. I'd send you the terza rima poem ["The Lost World"] except that Macmillan will have copies of the whole book that it is part of, before long, and as soon as they do I'll ask them to send you one.

We were crazy about your friends in Amsterdam [Dr. and Mrs. W. F. van Leuwens]; nothing's so fortifying and reassuring as meeting intellectuals who're just as nice and as much of a joy as any non-intellectuals. I promised to send them a couple of my books and there're a couple of others we think they might enjoy that we're going to send them as soon as we get home. I'm *so* glad you told us about them.

We really have had a wonderful time in Europe — we tried to see all the big galleries except the Prado, we saw ever so much opera, we went to the cathedral in Durham, and saw the Bamberg Rider and the Carpaccio show in Venice, and almost all the Donatellos, and so forth. All in all, we liked Germany best, counting landscapes, buildings, and people (you know how it is, *people* means waiters and waitresses, clerks in stores, hotel people, and passers-by who tell you the way to Nordlingen). I got longing for home and work here in Florence but got to work day and night for two weeks going over my *Three Sisters* translation for the last time, so I'm just thinking dancily of home, home! on the 21st of November.

Mary sends her love. We often see little girls with round, dark heads who remind us of "Thirty-three" and we always say, "Oh, look, there's a little Adrienne one!" We hope you're well and happy and writing lots of poems.

Yours,
Randall

TO ELIZABETH HARDWICK AND ROBERT LOWELL

Albergo Berchielli
Florence
[October 1963]

Dear Elizabeth and Cal:

Don't worry a bit about the typographical errors [two lines omitted from "The X-Ray Waiting Room in the Hospital," which had been published in the *New York Review of Books*]. I didn't mind, and am sure everyone recognized them as such. The new issue [of the *New York Review of Books*] was a very good one, and Mary and I particularly enjoyed Elizabeth's piece about Frost: it was a *very* complicated thing to write about, and you really did do justice to every side. I never have seen anyone say what you did about Frost's (regardless of what he *said* about independence) never going too far and really breaking off with people and the world — there's always Hudson Bay and the fur trader and a small skiff with a paddle blade, but he can wait, they can wait, in a subjunctive clause that stays subjunctive forever.

I always treated him, when we talked, as Gorki did Tolstoy — as a unique natural phenomenon beyond good and evil. I asked and listened, we never had an argumentative sentence. (I *loved* to listen to him, really was fond of him, and knew I was, so to speak, getting to see a waterspout inside a rainbow.) He never saw me without expressing his gratitude to me, oddly enough; he didn't hold any of the unfavorable things I'd said against me, said that I'd made people see the black half of his poetry which had hardly existed for them; loved to repeat that my [*New York*] *Times* review of "Directive" had made it famous, so that from then on every college he went to asked him to read it. (Audiences never followed it after the first six lines.) He was very flattering — in public, too — to audiences I was in. He'd stay with us in Greensboro and talk all day — for one interesting, awful, and touching day about nothing but his family: he was seeing his grand-daughter that night and just seeing her transformed him into a younger, bitterer, uneasier man full of memories of unavenged slights.

Really, though, I existed for him just as the person who'd written those pieces about his poetry — I'm sure he couldn't make heads or tails out of anything else I wrote, and I'm sure he felt faintly, comfortably mocking about everything in me that hadn't written those articles: after all, nothing I did was the way *he'd* have done it. He felt I was an Indian who'd sold him, *given* him, Manhattan Island, and he was willing to keep me on a special little reservation in return. I felt that he talked more like poetry than anybody else I'd ever hear, that his voice made other voices sound a little high in comparison, so what did I care whether he was right or wrong? (He actually *said* that his writing had had all the success he wanted it to, so what did he care what happened with nuclear weapons?) The only cultural try I ever made with him was to read him four or five haiku that I thought close enough to his couplets for him to like; and he really did like them.

I've found this to be a rule in going around the country: every second college you visit will have a man, the equivalent of the [John] Birch Society, who is a good friend of Robert Frost's.

We're going to get home a little before Thanksgiving — I just worked day and night for two weeks here going over my *Three Sisters* translation for a last time. They're going to have Shirley Knight, Anne Bancroft and Geraldine Page for Irina, Masha and Olga; if only they get a really ugly and nice Tuzenbach!

I'll send you some more poems when I get home, and some *Faust* lyric pieces. Mary sends her love — I hope Harvard's nice and the *Review* getting along well.

Yours,
Randall

Lowell was teaching two classes a week at Harvard and commuting to New York. Hardwick, with the aid of Barbara Epstein and others (and a bank loan guaranteed by Lowell), had founded the New York Review of Books *in 1963 during the* New York Times *strike.*

TO MICHAEL DI CAPUA

Albergo Nord Nuova
Roma
[November 1, 1963]

Dear Michael:

We certainly did enjoy your letter — Mary and I were both saying what entertaining letters you write. I was enchanted with the news about the *Bat-Poet* pictures — since it's going ahead so well and the *Rabbit* is stuck in the wilds of Mexico, why don't we just bring out the *Bat-Poet* first? Probably it's best to start with the best of the children's books anyway. Tell Maurice I can't wait to see them.

As you've probably learned already from Mary's postcard, our younger daughter Bea and her husband are going to meet us there in New York, so why don't we all have dinner and go to the opera together, if you can get tickets? And this time, of course, let us take you to everything and we can postpone till later this winter your taking us to anything.

That's funny about "Ball Turret Gunner" and the Air Force Academy objecting to it — but as Tuzenbach says about work, "They've hardly succeeded in sheltering me from it for good — hardly." Actually, flyers always like it and tell me they've read it.

I'd love to write another prose fiction book — please God I'll someday write it or a play! Thanks a lot for what you say about *Pictures.*

[Sviatoslav] Richter was wonderful. We started to send him flowers and then Mary had the inspiration of sending him a present; we picked the prettiest handbag at Gucci's, the sort Mary has, and sent it with a letter saying we hoped he'd allow us to send it to him to bring home to his wife as a souvenir of Florence. We figured having it something for her kept it from being too personal.

It all turned out ideally about the Schmidt translation, it was the Venice one that reached us first, in Florence.

Rome's a very beautiful big city, isn't it? All the trees, hills, and parks are lovely, not to mention the ruins and big buildings. We're afflicted with museums — and shops — closing for All Saints and Victory-over-Austria celebrations; the Vatican Museum's closed for four days straight.

The poetry anthology news is good. Ah, how wonderful America and living in a house are going to be! I certainly feel sorry for expatriates.

Mary sends her love — we'll see you on the 18th.

Yours,
Randall

The good news about the poetry anthology was that di Capua had interested Dell in sharing with Macmillan the costs and profits of bringing the book out in hardback, in an expensive paperback, and then in a mass-market paperback, with the first edition to come out late in 1965 or early in 1966. "So this won't add to our little traffic jam in the spring [1964] but to some future one," Jarrell wrote.

*   *   *

While the museums were closed for the holidays, Jarrell started his poem "Bamberg," continued working on "The Augsburg Adoration," and completed "In Galleries."

The Jarrells in Rome, 1963

TO MICHAEL DI CAPUA

[November 26, 1963]

Dear Michael:

Here are two [publicity] photographs. Mary and I thought the full-face one would be good for the children's books, since it looks kindly. I'll send you the good [Philippe] Halsman photograph later.

We had a *wonderful* time with you in New York; Maurice Sendak's drawings and the opera couldn't have been more fun for us. Home and driving home seemed magic; but President Kennedy's death was, to us, the saddest public thing that's happened in our lifetime, and we can't really think about anything else.

I'll write you soon. Mary sends her love.

Yours,
Randall

Throughout the weekend after the Kennedy assassination Jarrell sat before the television, crying openly at the portrayals of John Kennedy's life, death, and funeral. The Taylors and Hookes were not so deeply affected, and Jarrell understood that, but he never forgave a neighbor he could hear noisily mowing his grass during the funeral procession. To Jarrell, apolitical since the 1940s, Kennedy had brought wit, imagination, and art to Washington and had brought hope to politics. The shooting in Dallas not only extinguished the life of Jarrell's favorite public person but ended Jarrell's brief phase of happy expectancy about America. When the New York Times *asked him to write a Kennedy poem, the only line he could manage was "The shining brown head," and he gave up. Neither Lyndon Johnson nor Robert Kennedy appealed to Jarrell, and so the subscription to the* Washington Post *was not renewed and politics for him became as "feeble-minded" as usual. Added to this major blow was the vexation of the Jaguar's engine trouble that no local mechanic knew how to fix. Being home again after the trip to Europe was something of a letdown. Jarrell lacked energy and consulted his doctor, who prescribed more exercise and continued his bland diet.*

TO MICHAEL DI CAPUA

[January 1964]

Dear Michael:

Here's the dustjacket and, oh joy! here's "The Well-to-Do Invalid" all finished. Let's put it just before "In Galleries." Tell me how you like it.

The weather's a bit warmer, one of my tennis partners is back from his

Christmas vacation and I'm getting lots more exercise. Mary gave me some pink and blue dumbbells for Christmas (they're called *Glamor Belles* and look just like a baby's rattles, a big baby) so I'm getting indoor exercise too. Instead of saying like Vershinin [in *The Three Sisters*], "If only industry could be added to education, and education to industry," I'm going to make my slogan "If only diet could be added to exercise, and exercise to diet."

It was lots of fun talking — Mary sends her love.

Yours,
Randall

"A Well-to-Do Invalid" was included in The Lost World *and is a satiric poem about a marriage Jarrell thought somewhat comparable to Lowell's.*

*   *   *

At this time Lowell made a short visit, bringing with him the poems for his new book For the Union Dead. *Jarrell went over them closely and praised them with all his former enthusiasm. Lowell wrote in a letter afterward, "You stay young, and it's good to think of you, still so honest and hopeful and full of brilliant talk and knowledge, able to judge and make. Your great parade of women [poems] have a delicate splendor, more like bits of Tolstoy than other poets . . . I gather your [Three Sisters] opening will be sometime in June. We'll celebrate when you and Mary come. Our love to you both." (Berg Collection, New York Public Library)*

TO MICHAEL DI CAPUA

[February 1964]

Dear Michael:

The book [*The Gingerbread Rabbit*] looks wonderful — Mary and I were crazy about it. It was particularly clever of you to fix the *To my little Mary* page as you did — the squirrel and nest are even prettier than they are larger-sized later on. We've looked at and looked at it, and I've even read it a couple of times. May all the little children and their mothers love it!

I'm feeling a bit better and it is getting to seem *so* close to spring — surely with spring I'll get all well. The last two weeks have been so warm and sunny; the forsythia's blooming already.

We had a rusty — rustic, that is, chestnut rail fence put around most of our yard and forest, and a row of white pines planted between our forest and the neighbor's house; it makes it all look more like a little ranch in the forest or such.

Thanks so much for the book; it's wonderful. When you send me my ten I'd like to buy fifteen more.

The advertisements in the catalogue looked charming. Mary sends her love.

Yours,
Randall

Not long after this, a letter came from di Capua reporting an intolerable disagreement at Macmillan, and his precipitous departure. This was another shock, like Kennedy's death, that Jarrell was not prepared for.

TO MICHAEL DI CAPUA

[May 1964]

Dear Michael:

I hope everything's going well with you, and I hope you hear from some publisher you really like before long. I've been a little sick but am better now. I believe that the first night of *The Three Sisters* is going to come on June 20; we'll probably come up several days before that so as to do some of the publicity things Barbara Heckethorn wants me to do. I had an awfully nice letter from her about *The Bat-Poet*. I'm sure she's told you the different things she's planning.

I certainly do miss your letters from Macmillan. It feels as if I didn't *have* a publisher any more, compared to what I was used to.

Thanks so much for the bat [from F. A. O. Schwartz]. I didn't even know that toy bats existed.

I was really enchanted with the review of *The Bat-Poet* in the *Library Journal*. It couldn't have been nicer.

How is Maurice? Tell me what you've been doing and seeing. I read [Ernest] Newman's four-volume life of Wagner and enjoyed it a lot; I listened to *Tristan and Isolde*, with the libretto, a couple of times, and I was tremendously impressed with the second and third acts, particularly, of the libretto; they seem to *fit* the music better than any libretto I can think of.

I'm finishing up the last two weeks of school — lots of term papers and exams. A friend of ours [Richardson Preyer] is running for governor and Mary has been helping out in his campaign. She's very well and happy and sends her love. We hope everything is going well with you; write us.

Yours,
Randall

Barbara Heckethorn was di Capua's replacement at Macmillan, and Jar-
rell was dismayed at suddenly being turned over to this stranger. Unlike
Haydn, di Capua had never let his personal problems interfere with his busi-
ness relationship with Jarrell, and it had not occurred to Jarrell that he had
any. He could not blame di Capua, but it was a severe jolt for him to be
obligated to Macmillan for his next three books and the forthcoming Bat-
Poet, *and to have lost the expertise and judgment of this trusted friend who*
had helped him break his writer's block and who was the only reason he had
gone to Macmillan. As usual, Jarrell tried to cheer himself up — and cheer
up di Capua — but his statement "It feels as if I didn't have *a publisher*
any more, compared to what I was used to" was a mild indication of how
shaken he was.

*   *   *

The season of the Pulitzer awards was approaching, and with it Jarrell's
fiftieth birthday. This set him reckoning to Mary that all the poets he was
ranked with — Shapiro, Lowell, Wilbur, Bishop, and Roethke — had won
the Pulitzer Prize before they were fifty. Continuing to count his losses, Jar-
rell remembered the times he had judged for the Bollingen Prize, and that
he had never won that either. In his poem "Thinking of the Lost World,"
Jarrell had written feelingly about his age:

> ... When my hand drops to the wheel,
> It is brown and spotted, and its nails are ridged
> Like Mama's. Where's my own hand? My smooth
> White bitten-fingernailed one?

Along with the loss of his own youth, there was the loss of Mary's.
Where was the young Ingrid Bergman? The mermaid? The Electra? The
Marschallin he had married? Mary was a grandmother and talking poli-
tics all day.

On his birthday, Jarrell was not amused when Malcolm Hooke quoted
Victor Hugo's line, "Forty is the old age of youth and fifty is the youth of
old age." And when Lucy scoffed, "Fifty is nothing, Randall. You're mak-
ing mountains out of molehills," Jarrell answered gloomily, "When you're
depressed there are *no molehills."*

When Jarrell's doctor insinuated that his low spirits were psychoso-
matic, Jarrell left him for an internist the Hookes recommended. After a
careful examination and finding no previous treatment for depression and
no medical history of manic-depressive psychosis, this doctor diagnosed
Jarrell's malaise as a type fairly common among men of middle age and

*ventured that it was probably temporary. Jarrell preferred having a "de-
pression" to having a "midlife crisis," but he acknowledged — half-
amused — Gerhard Hofer's German equivalent* Torschlusspanik, *which
he copied on a card he kept in his billfold and translated as "closing-
door-panic."*

*The internist prescribed a moderate dosage of a newly marketed mood-
elevating drug and check-up office visits every other week. After a month,
Jarrell seemed to feel as listless and drowsy as ever, and he decided to drive to
Cincinnati after the opening of* The Three Sisters *and consult the psychiatrist there who had impressed him in 1958.*

*On June 22, the Jarrells, di Capua, and the Hofers attended a cham-
pagne party in Shubert Alley, followed by the opening performance of* The
Three Sisters *by the Actors' Studio. Under the direction of Lee Strasberg,
Kevin McCarthy played Colonel Vershinin, Geraldine Page was Olga,
Shirley Knight was Irina, and Kim Stanley was Masha. Had Jarrell enjoyed the production, they would have stayed longer in New York and seen it
several times, but he did not. The play simply added to the cycle of disap-
pointments he had experienced during the past six months — "except for
Masha," he granted. "But she was much too fat, poor thing." To Lowell,
he said, "It was a disaster. As crude and exaggerated as Chekhov always is
in this country."*

TO BEATRICE HOFER

Vernon Manor Hotel
[Cincinnati, Ohio]
[June 1964]

Dear Bea:

Here's a little belated birthday present. Mary just read me your lovely
long letter to her. It was ever so much fun seeing you in New York. I'm
getting along well, eating lots of magical home-made ice cream and working on a piece about Frost's letters — I imagine we'll be coming home before too long. Happy Birthday!

Love,
Randall

*The Hofers were keeping Elfie, and part of Beatrice's letter had been about
him.*

*The psychiatrist sharply increased the dosage of the medication Jarrell
had been taking and referred him to a gastroenterologist who lifted most of
the diet restrictions. By lucky coincidence, a foreign-car specialist cured the*

Jaguar's ills; and before leaving Cincinnati, Jarrell finished his review of Selected Letters of Robert Frost, *edited by Lawrance Thompson, enjoyed two operas at the zoo, and proposed a vacation at Blowing Rock, North Carolina. A monthly phone call to the psychiatrist was suggested, but no counseling or therapy, and, with so much going so well, this was not questioned.*

*   *   *

After their return from Cincinnati, the Jarrells spent the rest of the summer in Blowing Rock. They found a rustic cottage with a view of Grandfather Mountain from one porch and the many ranges of the Smokies from another. Jarrell wrote in the mornings, and they took lunch at a pancake house that was in a house, got the mail at the post office, and often took drives among the apple farms between Banner Elk, North Carolina, and the Peaks of Otter, in Virginia. The Taylors had been called to Memphis, where Peter's father and brother-in-law were seriously ill, but the Hofers, the Boyettes, and Irene MacAdams came for visits. Elfie was showing his age, eating poorly, and losing weight, but Jarrell was feeling better every day.

TO HARRY FORD

[Blowing Rock, North Carolina]
[August 1964]

Dear Harry:

It's a real delight to me that you and the people you mentioned liked *The Bat-Poet* that much. This spring I wrote another half-for-children, half-for-grown-ups book named *The Animal Family;* it's much longer, less allegorical, and is all done except for a longish next-to-the-last chapter that I hope to finish this fall.

I'm feeling much better. I had an awfully good doctor in Cincinnati, the best gastroenterologist in that region, and his diet lets me eat dozens of things I hadn't tasted for two years. I derive from what I eat now a hopeful pleasure instead of a settled gloom.

We're living high up in the mountains, so high that we had pieces of cloud in the kitchen, as plain as steam from a kettle; and the probability of meeting with a hot day is about that of meeting Madame de Sévigné at the postoffice.

I was sorry we got to see each other so rushedly in New York; I was all swallowed up in radio and television things, and was still feeling pretty bad. We're going to be in New York for the last week of October (I'm being a Phi Beta Kappa Visiting Lecturer at two colleges there) and we'll see you then.

Have you ever read Christina Stead's *The Man Who Loved Children?* It's the best unknown book I know. I'm part way through writing a long introduction to it — it's being republished [by Holt, Rinehart and Winston] as a new hardcover book twenty-five years after it first came out.

With all best wishes.

Yours,
Randall

*   *   *

Di Capua telephoned saying he had taken a position with Pantheon in the children's book department and would contract The Animal Family *with them. Jarrell, relieved, congratulated him warmly. Di Capua then sent him the four-volume translation of* Eugene Onegin *that Nabokov had done for Pantheon.*

In a letter thanking di Capua, Jarrell wrote, "Oddly enough, the translation is pathetic: flat, tame, literal with some phrases that aren't idiomatic English outside a dictionary. The silly perverse scholarly side of him took over entirely." Jarrell also enclosed the last fully realized poem he would write, "The Player Piano," instructing di Capua to include it with "Gleaning" and "A Man Meets a Woman in the Street" in his new book, Women.

THE PLAYER PIANO

I ate pancakes one night in a Pancake House
Run by a lady my age. She was gay.
When I told her that I came from Pasadena
She laughed and said, "I lived in Pasadena
When Fatty Arbuckle drove the El Molino bus."

I felt that I had met someone from home.
No, not Pasadena, Fatty Arbuckle.
Who's that? Oh, something that we had in common
Like — like — the false armistice. Piano rolls.
She told me her house was the first Pancake House

East of the Mississippi, and I showed her
A picture of my grandson. Going home —
Home to the hotel — I began to hum,
"Smile a while, I bid you sad adieu,
When the clouds roll back I'll come to you."

Let's brush our hair before we go to bed,
I say to the old friend who lives in my mirror.
I remember how I'd brush my mother's hair
Before she bobbed it. How long has it been
Since I hit my funnybone? had a scab on my knee?

Here are Mother and Father in a photograph,
Father's holding me. . . . They both look so *young.*
I'm so much older than they are. Look at them,
Two babies with their baby. I don't blame you,
You weren't old enough to know any better;

If I could I'd go back, sit down by you both,
And sign our true armistice: you weren't to blame.
I shut my eyes and there's our living room.
The piano's playing something by Chopin,
And Mother and Father and their little girl

Listen. Look, the keys go down by themselves!
I go over, hold my hands out, play I play —
If only, somehow, I had learned to live!
The three of us sit watching, as my waltz
Plays itself out a half-inch from my fingers.

In September, Elfie gradually weakened and died in Greensboro. Jarrell dug his grave under a beech tree, carved his name in the bark, and dedicated The Animal Family *to him, but reading, writing, teaching, and tennis distracted him from grieving. He told the Hookes, "It's always awful to lose a pet . . . but it wasn't like losing Kitten." His energy level was soaring, and when asked about his health, he would say, "Richard is himself again. Oh, yes. Oh, yes. God bless his magic pills!" Had the psychiatrist been seeing Jarrell in office visits, he probably would have concluded that the mood-elevating drug had done its work and — as cautioned in the physician's instructions that accompanied it — cut back the dosage to a "maintenance level." However, his contact with the patient was only by phone.*

[October 8, 1964]

Dear Michael:

I've had (it seems to Mary and me) great luck in re-doing *Fly by Night,* now that that great big black thing in the sky, *The Bat-Poet,* isn't overshadowing it. I believe I've got it all smooth now, and what you learn in the beginning about David awake makes David's dream what it is. I'm pretty sure that *Fly by Night* ought to be my next children's book: *The Animal Family* is so long and different that *Fly by Night,* coming after it, would suffer terribly. Coming after *Bat-Poet, Fly by Night* suffers a little from not being an allegory or parable, but it's similar in length, has poems in it, too (poems which are a continuation of the prose more than those in *The Bat-Poet*), has the same talking-animal world, etc., etc. *Animal Family* is realistic, the lynx and the bear never say a word. I think readers of *Bat-Poet* who like the poems will be quite fond of having a *big* poem like "The Owl's Bedtime Story" the climax of the book. Also, Maurice ought to be able to do wonderful illustrations for it. I doubt very much that *Animal Family* can take illustrations.

I've just sent one copy of *Fly by Night* to the *Saturday Evening Post;* I'll tell you what they say about it. This copy of *Fly by Night* ought to get to you on Thursday; if you've time Friday morning call me and tell me how you like it and we can talk about other things, too.

I've cut my Stead piece in two (literally — from 46 pages to 24) to go in the *New York Review of Books,* possibly. I've been feeling so good I've worked hard on a lot of things and made plans for more.

We had a *wonderful* time in New England; a retired professional pianist played us the whole last book of Liszt's piano pieces — only one was ever recorded — that I didn't know whether I'd ever get to hear. They were all that even I wanted them to be — you should hear the third *Mephisto Waltz!*

I've discovered that at Thanksgiving vacation we can come to New York on Monday afternoon, Nov. 23, and stay through Sunday, Nov. 29. Could you get us tickets to *Meistersinger,* Nov. 24 (oh boy!), *Don Pasquale* Nov. 25, *Forza* Nov. 26, *Rigoletto* Nov. 27, *Otello* Nov. 28? We hope you'll want to see some and will come with us. And all of these things are for us to pay for, not Pantheon, of course. Maybe you can get Jean Stafford to go with us, or Maurice.

I'm sure there're other things I meant to say, but won't so I can get this off. Mary sends her love.

Yours,
Randall

We're going to Cal's play [*The Old Glory*] Oct. 31; would you like to go with us?

Jarrell's Stead piece was not sent to the New York Review of Books *but to the* Atlantic, *which asked that it be cut down from twenty-four pages. Rather than do that, Jarrell took it back, and it was published, as intended, as the introduction for Holt, Rinehart and Winston's edition of* The Man Who Loved Children.

Jarrell had been in New England making the first of his Phi Beta Kappa series of readings and lectures. He appeared at Brown University, Clark University, and Wheaton College. On a free weekend, the Jarrells went to Cambridge for a visit with Adrienne Rich and Jarrell's longtime friends Herschel and Barbara Baker.

TO MICHAEL DI CAPUA

[October 1964]

Dear Michael:

I have a lecture at N.Y.U. on Thursday night, so we can't go to the [Dietrich] Fischer-Dieskau; we'll be free Friday and Saturday nights.

We'd rather see *Forza del Destino* (next month) than the Fischer-Dieskau program — how I hope it's Bergonzi. I'll send this note air mail special delivery so you'll get it Saturday morning — sorry I couldn't get it there sooner.

We'll call you Sunday afternoon from the Plaza or you call us — we're going to see Cal that evening. If you haven't the ticket for the play on the 31st tell me then and I'll get one from Cal.

I seem to be giving the same old "Fifty Years of Am. Poetry" at N.Y.U. Wednesday night — all the colleges are picking it for one of their evenings. We'll be completely free all Friday and Saturday — that is, except for the *Falstaff* matinee on Saturday and Saturday evening play.

This letter is a perfect banyan tree of weekday-names and dates.

See you very soon.

Yours,
Randall

Lowell's play, The Old Glory, *was a trilogy based on two of Hawthorne's stories and a Melville novella. Strongly historical, American, and New England,* The Old Glory *was, Jarrell said, "right up Cal's alley." During the performance Jarrell crossed and uncrossed his legs in excitement, ex-*

*claiming in loud whispers, "Oh, that's so clever! That's so like Cal ... Cal
can do this kind of thing in his sleep!"*

*The following day Jarrell joined Lowell and Jonathan Miller in the
two-story library in Lowell's apartment at the Dakota. Script in hand, he
led the others in a line-by-line critique until late in the afternoon, when he
had to leave for the airport. Always an interrupter when excited, Jarrell
went beyond this with excessive talking and swift contradictions. At La
Guardia he spent the hour before flight time in a telephone booth pouring
a torrent of praise and suggestions into Lowell's ear. At home he continued talking about* The Old Glory *until after midnight. Midnight was
now the earliest hour Jarrell would think of going to bed, but he was
waking earlier and earlier, getting by on five or six hours' sleep and no
naps.*

TO MICHAEL DI CAPUA

[December 10, 1964]

Dear Michael:

I've changed my plans a little and will stay in New York all of Tuesday,
Dec. 22. How about my coming to Pantheon at 4 that afternoon, talking
about the anthology and everything else, and seeing Maurice at dinner; we
could all talk about designing *The Animal Family* then. (I've got it pretty
smooth, almost finished and have typed some pages.)

Thanks a lot for the clippings you've sent; they're a lot of fun to see.

"Seventy Years Later" is in Stevens' *Collected Poems* in the section called
"The Rock." "A Flat One" isn't in a book; we should ask permission from
Snodgrass himself, at Wayne State University, Detroit.

I was delighted with your letter to Gerald Gross. Barbara Heckethorn is
going to have a long conversation with him, reminding him of our old
verbal agreement about advertising; she says that the advertisement in the
Times Book Review already seems certain, but we're going to try for the *Saturday Review* one also. She's going to say that she and I (not to mention you)
consider sending the brochure to the Newbery judges a bad idea. In a
month or two — two — I'm going to ask him for a written agreement
about *Faust* advertisements; if he won't I'll consider — to put it mildly —
paying them back the advance and having Pantheon publish it.

I hope they had, at Goody's, one of the on-sale KLH amplifiers [sic:
speakers] for you.

I've been doing *Fathers and Sons* with my class and am taping the classes
in order to get notes for an essay. Gee, a tape recorder's fun and magic-
seeming.

I wrote Paul Schmidt a very long, very cordial letter about [Gogol's] *The Inspector General*. I said I'd be delighted to give him $500 [for a literal translation] and, if Cheryl Crawford produced it, would give him $500 extra.

See you very soon. Probably there are two or three other things I should have written about, but I'm feeling calm but harried and can't remember them. Mary sends her love.

Yours,
Randall

Just got a copy of your letter to Schmidt — it was perfect.

The Stevens and Snodgrass poems were recent additions to Jarrell's poetry anthology in progress.

The Animal Family was a Newbery honor book, and Faust was posthumously released by Macmillan and published by Farrar, Straus and Giroux.

* * *

Jarrell had changed his plans for New York in order to avoid the Taylors' Christmas party; he was put out by Taylor's objections to his astonishing proposal to fire the head of the English department and several faculty members. Still, it was not like the ever-loyal Jarrell to quarrel with Taylor, any more than it was like the never-clumsy Jarrell to bump into, tip over, or drop inanimate objects, as he was now doing. He even scraped the Jaguar sharply against the side of the garage. Nor was it Jarrell's usual way to jump from the anthology to The Animal Family *to a Turgenev essay to translating* The Inspector General, *with* Faust *not finished and the* Three Sisters *introduction not yet begun. While Jarrell liked the security of having several projects in progress, his normal way was to concentrate on one at a time, working tenaciously until that caught hold of him and he could not stop until he had finished it. His new way was to surround himself with half-finished cathedrals and plan even more. What was left of his old self sometimes felt guilty at neglecting* Faust *and* The Three Sisters, *but his new self felt richly inventive, as if anything intellectual was at his command.*

A further distraction that contributed to his being "calm but harried" was his sudden absorption in upgrading his stereo components at Goody's in New York, and in the research required for doing this. Jarrell's intellectual pace was merciless, and his lack of sleep, increased fatigue, and a tormenting ache in his back strained his nerves and drove him to lash out at anyone who crossed him, including Mary. Astounded by the personality changes in the husband she had known so well during the twelve years of their marriage, Mary blamed Jarrell's medication, and at odd moments, when Jarrell himself realized something was not right, Mary pleaded with him to tell his doctor more fully the state he was in; but Jarrell refused. Touchingly afraid of cutting down on his "magic pills," he reported in his long-distance calls only that he felt wonderful, and the depression dosage of the drug continued unmodified into the sixth month.

Voluble but in extreme discomfort, Jarrell went to New York and spent $3000 at Goody's. He wrote di Capua later, "I wasn't irrational, or anything of that sort — but I was elated."

On January 1, 1965, the Jarrells watched Michigan defeat Oregon at the Hookes' amid an atmosphere of strain. Jarrell was in pain from his back and was agitated. For most of the afternoon he stood or paced, since he could not sit in comfort. Talking constantly, he ranged from competing with the sportscaster to chiding Hooke for not finishing Remembrance of Things Past. *Lucy, soon to face cobalt therapy, was subdued and forbearing.*

TO ROBERT LOWELL

[January 1965]

Dear Cal:

I enjoyed your letter and love the thought of you in Egypt — I'm sure the Lowells (the older Lowells, that is) have all sorts of Egyptian connections, were in the old days Egyptians.

I wrote to the Rockefeller Foundation nominating Peter, Elizabeth Bishop, and Bob Watson. Yes, I'd love to have a fellowship myself with which to finish *Faust.*

When you say that [William] Meredith has "a kind of tired, unostentatious devotion to poetry that makes one envious" you're speaking for yourself, not me; I prefer yours or Elizabeth Bishop's or Marianne Moore's, et cetera, et cetera, et cetera.

Thanks for what you say about *The Lost World.*

I'm going to be in New York late this spring and will write you beforehand about things to see and do together.

Have you seen *The Silence* [Ingmar Bergman]? I love it.

Yours,
Randall

Lowell was going to Egypt at the invitation of the American University in Cairo, where he was to give two lectures.

Jarrell's current falling-out with Taylor had no effect on his conviction that Taylor was the Chekhov of our time, and he wholeheartedly recommended him for the Rockefeller grant.

Bob Watson, thirty-eight, wrote wry, realistic, city-based poetry with humor and a twist of the macabre that Jarrell enjoyed. Jarrell valued Watson for being his own person and not belonging to any school or group, and he played the Ransom/benefactor role more than the Tate/mentor role with him. Jarrell had influenced Atheneum to publish Watson's first book of poetry, A Paper Horse, *and he wanted Watson to get the Rockefeller grant. As for Watson, he admired Jarrell's poetry, genuinely liked his older friend, and made every allowance for him, just as Jarrell had done for Frost. Puzzled by Jarrell's estrangement from the Taylors and the Hookes, and at times uneasy with Jarrell's behavior, the Watsons took him in between classes and after class, feeding him, letting him talk or fall asleep on their sofa, and providing him with an island of refuge in the turbulent sea rising around him.*

TO MICHAEL DI CAPUA

[February 8, 1965]

Dear Michael:

Unfortunately, the cortisone injection made my back so painful that I haven't been able to get any of the finished *Animal Family* typed (especially not with examinations). I'll get some typed before we come to New York and I'll get one of these Kelly Girls (or typists to that effect) to finish it Thursday in New York.

We'll surely be able to have dinner with you Saturday night — Otis [Singletary] and Gloria aren't going to be able to come. If you haven't a special restaurant how about La Tocque Blanche, 359 E. 50th? It's moderately priced (well, high-moderately) and terribly good and *pleasant*. The best of our found-through-Joseph Wechsberg restaurants. Provincial specialties, etc., and plenty of dishes with lots of *cooking* involved.

My Russian examinations certainly were fun to read. I had besides all the necessary questions some little factual questions to be answered in a few words; one was, When, where, and in what *costume did Gogol teach Turgenev?* (Answer: At the Univ. of St. Petersburg; when Gogol was temporarily a history professor there; in a black handkerchief tied around his jaw as if he had a toothache — the ends stuck above his head like rabbit-ears.) Almost everybody remembered, but one girl didn't, thought; and put down: — In overcoat.

See you Wednesday,

Randall

Like a shrill record played at the wrong speed, Jarrell could — as if by the flick of a dial — sound almost normal, as the above letter does. At Mary's tiresome insistence, he completed The Animal Family, *but his mind was disturbed all the while by lines of dialogue for a play; and, as Mary wrote in "The Group of Two," "Poems flew at him, short ones, quatrains, haiku, aphorisms, parts of poems . . . beat at his head like many wings." (RJ) In his wakeful midnight hours Jarrell spoke these words into the tape recorder, at the same time playing Liszt's* Etudes d'Exécution Transcendante *on the stereo.*

When Jarrell was lecturing, his notes trembled in his hand, and his piercing voice carried down the hall as he wittily digressed and his spell-bound classes ran overtime. Also, he became a loud and querulous presence in the English department office, and Mary received concerned telephone calls from department members, one of whom said outright, "The man is a holy terror!"

As his personality changed, Jarrell became uncannily fond of two non sequiturs: a sentence reputed to General Sherman about Grant — "I stuck by him when he was drunk, and he stuck by me when I was crazy" — and Marianne Moore's line, "In much madness there is some sense." Feeling disloyal but desperate, Mary consulted the psychiatrist in Cincinnati. While assuring her Jarrell was "the sick one," not she, he advised no action beyond keeping him informed.

The following week, in an absurdly funny introduction of guest lecturer Hannah Arendt that regaled the general audience and dumfounded the faculty, Jarrell, with an ashen face, glittering eyes, and a look of haggard vivacity, talked for twenty minutes about meeting Johnny Unitas, the Colts quarterback. Days later he was urging a mild lady he had just met at a reading to let him show her the cathedral in Durham, England. When, during his third trip to Nashville in two weeks to see his mother, he tipped a waitress with a $1500 check, the Cincinnati psychiatrist, in cooperation with a Greensboro colleague, arranged to have Jarrell admitted to Memorial Hospital in Chapel Hill for rest and observation. Mary wrote in "The Group of Two," "Before it was through with us, this ordeal called forth a desperate valor we'd never have known we had; and Donne's lines '. . . for affliction is a treasure, and scarce any man hath enough of it . . . that is not

... ripened by it and made fit for God ...' came to have more meaning for us than I'd have wished." (RJ)

TO MICHAEL DI CAPUA

[March 1965]

Dear Michael:

Your first letter *was* delayed a week, but I've got them, and have just delayed answering: I've been resting almost entirely, except for writing some new poems and copying the rest. I know it's hard to believe, it sounds like a wish fantasy, but (counting the two-line ones) I've got about a hundred.

I think it might be a good idea to show *Redbook The Animal Family* — show them surreptitiously or informally, so to speak. It was bad luck that *McCall's* had just bought an animal fantasy, wasn't it?

Have you seen Philip Booth's review of *The Lost World* [*Christian Science Monitor,* March 11, 1965]? It's the best review I ever got.

I think I'll be leaving the hospital in a week or ten days. I wasn't illogical or anything of the sort, but I *was* exhausted and I *was* elated — exactly as you saw me when I was last in New York. I was willing to go when people fixed it up for me to go, though I wasn't altogether grateful for the way they fixed it. It's been *very* interesting. I'm all rested and hardly elated at all.

I hope you do come down — I'd love to see you.

Believe it or not, Macmillan's has never sent me an advertising program of any kind: it was supposed to come in eight or ten days; and it's now been, I *believe* — a month and three weeks.

It's all fixed that I'm to go to the Edinburgh Festival, and the Russian trip seems very likely — I'm to get briefed for two days in the last part of April. I'm also going to do some interesting teaching at Clark University in the seven weeks before Edinburgh.

I don't know whether Mary has told you; but she and I are separated and will be divorced after a while.

Do write me about the *Animal Family* publishing things, *et cetera, et cetera, et cetera.* I'd love some extra mail. My current address is South Wing, North Carolina Memorial Hospital, Chapel Hill, N.C.

Affectionately,
Randall

The Russian trip was part of the State Department's cultural exchange program.

Jarrell's doctors had advised him to put off the divorce until he was out of the hospital.

Mary had confided her troubles to her mother, and Irene answered with a letter written at 3:30 A.M.: "I have been re-reading what you say about Randall wanting a separation, and I am very sad for I love you both. If he had been born to me, I could not have loved him more. It is a hard trial and a test of your stamina. But if you accede this would be abandoning him to his own destruction. You and Randall have been faithful, devoted, loving companions for some twelve or more years — you must protect him from himself. That is hard because you are a proud woman and your affection and your pride is humiliated. Your place is at his side 'for better or for worse, in sickness or in health till death do you part.' As soon as Randall's mental film is cleared away he will resume his brilliant career — and he will rise and call you blessed. And I say God bless you both."

TO ROBERT AND BETTY WATSON

> Memorial Hospital,
> Chapel Hill, NC
> [March 1965]

Dear Bob and Betty:

I wanted to thank you for the review Bob wrote — I've never read a better one of any of my books. I imagine I'll be home in a week or so — I'll be seeing you then.

When I went over the Clark University proposition I saw that there's not really a place for Bob in it, but were for Bob ten years ago, I guess I'm in the habit of thinking of us at that age, more or less.

I've been writing a *lot* of poetry.

My mother's pretty ill and unlikely to get better, so I imagine I'll be spending many days in Nashville this spring.

Give my love to the children and yourselves.

> Yours,
> Randall

Watson's long review of The Lost World *first appeared in the* Greensboro Daily News, *and half of it was devoted to an empathetic analysis of the title poem, which he called, in* Randall Jarrell, 1914-1965, *"a poem that speaks to us in mid-twentieth-century America, to our lives, just as Wordsworth spoke to his contemporaries in the early nineteenth century." Watson added that at times Jarrell expressed a "bleakness about life, a kind of cosmic despair reminiscent of Thomas Hardy or even A. E. Housman when the latter says, 'high heaven and earth ail from the prime foundation.' But this bleakness, so justified in view of the history of the twentieth century, is balanced with joy. As the child has his joys, so does the adult. Randall Jarrell insists, for instance, that man and his life can be made exalted through works of art, which are one of the redeeming miracles of life."* (RJ) *As an example of this, Watson cited "In Galleries."*

William Meredith wrote in his review in Book World *that Jarrell had been for twenty years "one of our best poets, in the company of Wilbur, Berryman, Roethke, and Lowell . . . He's written a number of brittle, chilly poems that detach themselves from life with an irresponsible irony — poems like 'The State,' 'Sears Roebuck,' and 'Variations' — . . . [but] at the same time he was consistently producing marvelous, deep-running dramatic poems that from the first were stamped with his voice and his eye for subjective imagery . . . The recognition of his especial vision, which can be counted complete in this fine book, involved abandoning a timid, mechanical skepticism and embracing a wide human involvement." He wrote that the poems "instead of crying, Beauty! horror! [seem] to be saying, life, life . . . with a kind of wondering acceptance."*

In "The Rugged Way of Genius," in Randall Jarrell, 1914–1965, *John Crowe Ransom, writing about the last lines of the last poem in the book, "Thinking of the Lost World," quoted them:*

> I have found that Lost World in the Lost and Found
> Columns whose gray illegible advertisements
> My soul has memorized world after world:
> LOST — NOTHING. STRAYED FROM NOWHERE.
>   NO REWARD.
> I hold in my own hands, in happiness,
> Nothing: the nothing for which there's no reward.

He then commented, "I felt at first that this was a tragic ending. But I have studied it till I give up that notion. The NOTHING *is the fiction, the transformation; to which both boy and man are given. That World is not Lost because it never existed; but it is as precious now as ever. I have come to think that Randall was announcing the beginning of his 'second childhood.' There is nothing wrong about that, to the best of my knowledge. Out of my more extensive acquaintance with this period of life I can say that it begins gently and develops blissfully. And the first stage of it is when the sons and daughters bring grandsons and granddaughters to bless and to play with; they make a wonderfully compatible company . . .*

It should be made known, if I have not already done so, that Randall in all his adult life was a great lover of children and of pets; without that resource, I suppose he could hardly have endured his reporter's job in the Institution."

Robert Lowell wrote in the New York Review of Books *that* The Lost World *was Jarrell's "best book" and in it "he used subjects and methods he had been developing and improving for almost twenty years. Most of the poems are dramatic monologues. Their speakers, mostly women, are . . . unlike Browning's, very close to the author. Their themes . . . are solitude, the solitude of the unmarried, the solitude of the married, the love, strife, dependency, and indifference of man and woman — how mortals age, and brood over their lost and raw childhood . . . Above all, childhood! This subject . . . was for him what it was for his two favorite poets, Rilke and Wordsworth, a governing and transcendent vision. For shallower creatures, recollections of childhood and youth are drenched in a mist of pathos, or even bathos, but for Jarrell this was the divine glimpse, lifelong to be lived with, painfully and tenderly relived, transformed, matured — man with and against woman, child with and against adult."*

Warren made the following statement for the Macmillan advertisements of The Lost World: *"I have read it and reread it with great and growing pleasure, and I am sure it is at his best level — and his best level is something the future will join us in being grateful for, a splendid book."*

Marianne Moore added, in New York Times *ads for the book, "Randall Jarrell is a revelation of how wise is faith in faith — a revelation of how pleasing, how ingenious as words, poetry can be." In* Randall Jarrell, 1914–1965, *about "The X-Ray Waiting Room in the Hospital," "In Galleries," and* The Bat-Poet, *she wrote, "These story-dramas are not labored; they ignite imagination and just stop; they have no end. But the magic never ends."*

TO MICHAEL DI CAPUA

[March 1965]

Dear Michael:

I have been worse — I've actually become a little depressed rather than elated — so I'd better send a hasty note rather than wait. The *Redbook* amount of money is ridiculous — I wouldn't let them have it [*The Animal Family*] unless they offer $3,000 at least. A thousand dollars is pathetic. Go ahead and see whether *Good Housekeeping* will be better. I hate to think of it being shortened [excerpted], but for a lot of money it *might* be better. If they have an interesting offer telephone me here at the hospital and I'll tell you what seems best — though anything you decide is all right with me.

I'll probably be here a good deal longer — I got better for awhile but have retrogressed, lately. Write me or call me whenever you please — it will be fun for me. You yourself may have to make most of the arrangements for *The Animal Family.* If I'm not free to look in libraries for beach pictures, no pictures at all will be best, I guess. I'm so glad it's all finished, since I'm really not capable of finishing it now.

Anytime you can come down I'd love to see you; and if you could bring along cloth samples for the cover of the book (especially beautifully intense blue buckram ones, like the sky or sea) I could pick one. Page samples of the type and paper would be good, too. I can decide things like that, but I *am* depressed enough (and likely, I'm afraid, to be more so) not to want to plan any extended work from myself on it. I'm afraid I won't be able to write the dustjacket. As I said before, thank goodness it's all finished.

Probably it ought to be brought out primarily as a children's book; I'd have the best quotations from *The Bat-Poet* on the back jacket. The front jacket ought to read, I think

THE

ANIMAL FAMILY

RANDALL JARRELL

A STORY FOR CHILDREN

AND GROWN UPS

I think it would be good to give it to read to a lot of the people who liked *The Bat-Poet* best and get quotations for the dustjacket and advertisements. But you know how to do all this — *you* plan. I know you'll make a perfect job of it.

I don't want to sound as if it were all your job and I couldn't help, and I may be exaggerating the extent of my illness, since the last couple of days have been pretty bad, and I may soon be better. Anyway, we'll see.

Thanks for the *Bat-Poet* review; it really is nice.

I'll send this airmail special delivery and it ought to get to you on Monday. Good luck with everything.

Affectionately,
Randall

Although di Capua wanted to come to Chapel Hill, it was not possible for him to drop his work at Pantheon at that time. Through letters and telephone calls he tried to involve Jarrell in every step of the book's production, as

*he had when Jarrell was well. In his frequent calls to Mary, they shared
their anxieties and tried to comfort each other.*

TO MARY JARRELL

Friday noon
[March 1965]

Dear Mary —

Thank you so much for your *nice* letter. I'd already written apologizing
for the telephone call that turned so angry and replying to your angry letter.
Anyway, I want to thank you *extremely* for the last letter — you've never
written a nicer one.

Don't worry, I'm going to stay right here until they want me to go.
Starting tomorrow, I'll have grounds privileges and can walk around the
yard and hospital as I please. I imagine I'll be staying ten days or two weeks
more. I'm a lot more rested and a lot less harried and elated. I'm still writing
plenty of poems, though — I've written four about *South Wing, Third Floor,*
as it's poetically called.

I want to say all over again how sorry I am that things have turned out
this way for us — considering our earlier life and families, it just couldn't
have turned out differently, I think, short of our both being analyzed and
thoroughly changed.

What you say about the poems is a great joy to me. I'll send lots more as
I get more copies of them.

I'll soon make a list of things you might send me — tennis racket, *Inspector General,* etc.

I want to send this right off so as to get it to you as soon as possible. I'll
put poems in the next letter. Here's one of six about the barber at the Hotel
Carlyle:

> The old barber trembled before and after
> But not during my shave.

Affectionately,
Randall

TO MICHAEL DI CAPUA

[March 1965]

Dear Michael:

I want you to disregard almost everything I said in my last letter — I
was not only depressed but very much under the influence of Thorazine, a

drug which makes thought and action so difficult for you that you can't be your real self. Now that I haven't been taking Thorazine for two days I feel refreshingly like my normal self — or rather, I *am* refreshingly my normal self, as you'll see. So the first thing I want to do is make plans about *The Animal Family.* I wish very much that you'd come down to see me weekend after next or whenever is convenient for you — I can see you as much as we please. If you can bring along some pictures of the Oregon, Washington, or California coastline that would be splendid. (Incidentally, do telephone me about anything connected with *The Animal Family* — or for that matter, just telephone me. It will be a great pleasure for me, and a foretaste of the normal world that I'll be returning to before too long.) As you remember, I want three sorts of photographs: (1) The coast seen from out at sea (2) The normal view of the beach, with the surf, the meadow, and the mountains (3) The view from above that the mermaid and hunter see in the last scene, just before they go into the cabin. Tomorrow I'm going over to the University of North Carolina library and start looking for views myself — but if you or other people at Pantheon can find any good ones for me to choose among it will help enormously.

Disregard what I said about anything you decided about magazine publication being all right with me: I'm in good enough shape to make decisions about it. Tell *Redbook* that Mr. Jarrell says that their offer is ridiculous — only if I got three or four thousand dollars would I be willing to consent to the publication of *The Animal Family* in abridged form. I hate to think of its being printed with anything left out — but if *Good Housekeeping* should offer several thousand dollars, I suppose we ought to consider it. I'll be willing to consider less money for its publication unabridged.

I don't want to make this letter too long so I'll end it now. Do call me, Michael, and do plan to come down and see me. I've often told you how grateful I am to you for the series of events that led up to my writing *The Lost World,* but let me repeat it. You're one of the three or four people that help me most and mean most to me, and I hope you'll always remember it. Do what you can about *The Animal World* but don't worry about its magazine publication — that's of very little importance, really.

Yours,
Randall

P.S. Will you please, for *certain,* send me a Verifaxed copy of *The Animal World* special delivery? I've been without a copy too long.
P.S.S. Do anything you can to encourage Sylvia Wilkinson. She will be a good writer for you, as good as Heather.

Sylvia Wilkinson, Jarrell's best fiction student, had finished her first
novel, Moss on the North Side, *and Jarrell hoped Pantheon would*
publish it. In the letter above, he had inadvertently confused Pantheon
with Atheneum, which had published a book by Heather Ross Miller, just
as he confused the titles The Animal Family *and* The Lost World.

TO MARY JARRELL

[March 1965]

Dear Mary:

I was in such a hurry to answer your sweet letter that I forgot to put in
several things. I certainly do realize how hard it was for you simply to obey
the doctor's instructions which put you in a very unsympathetic role. It's
turned out *very* much for the best, though. I needed treatment.

I thought I'd tell you some of the things I'd love to have, if you could
bring them over — and it would be nice to see you, too. I'd like to have the
tape recorder and several of the rolls of tape, if you can find the microphone — I think it's either with the recorder or in a coat pocket; both tennis rackets; two or three solid color ties; four or five shirts (one, that red and
green wool plaid) and two tennis shirts; one of those light Italian sweaters
or the dark blue alpacā one; my English sports coat with the big pockets,
and that beige cotton suit-coat I got last summer; any nice pair of trousers;
two tennis shorts; my raincoat and English cap, so I can walk in the rain if
it rains in this particular movie; the *Inspector General* first act in the pretty
little tool-kit box that the tone-arm came in; the *Faust* manuscript; and
anything else you figure I might want. And thanks so much for sending
me the State Department stuff and all the poems people have sent me
to read.

Affectionately,

Randall

At Jarrell's request, Mary wrote the Cultural Affairs director at the State
Department and the director of the Edinburgh Festival, asking for a one-
year postponement in each case. Clark University was also notified.

The Jarrells tried to follow the analyst's orders to avoid discussing a di-
vorce, and they were able to write, telephone, and see each other about ordi-
nary matters. Both felt resentful and ill-used, however, and there were
outbursts of anger disrupting the artificial calm. In everyone's best interest,
the analyst eventually forbade any communication between them for an in-

definite period. Di Capua continued to telephone and write, Taylor and Watson visited Jarrell once during this period, and Beatrice saw him every other day. The Elavil prescription had been discontinued on Jarrell's admission to the hospital, and his elation subsided but was replaced by a "reactive depression" and progressive melancholia.

*   *   *

On April 18, Jarrell, deeply despondent, read on a back page of the New York Times Book Review *section a short review of* The Lost World, *written by Joseph Bennett, editor of his old nemesis, the* Hudson Review, *and lumped with more favorable ones of Samuel French Morse, Hollis Summers, and Hayden Carruth. Bennett wrote:*

> *Randall Jarrell's "The Lost World" contains four poems of considerable interest where the craftsmanship is clear, the intention honest and skillfully realized in the work: "Bats" with their "needlepoints of sound"; "Woman" serenely and confidently written; "In Nature There Is Neither Right nor Wrong" and the uncannily atmospheric "A Hunt in the Black Forest," the only first-rate poem in the volume.*
>
> *With the exception of the poems mentioned above, the rest of the book is taken up with Jarrell's familiar, clanging vulgarity, corny clichés, cutenesses, and the intolerable self-indulgence of his tear-jerking, bourgeois sentimentality. Folksy, pathetic, affected — there is no depth to which he will not sink, if shown the hole. Cultural name-dropping, hand-cranked puns and gags — a farrago of confused nonsense, a worn-out imagination. There is even a stage Italian out of Hollywood, placed incongruously in the Museo delle Terme; it is all Very Cultured. Jarrell's stance is the fashionable anti-intellectual one of fifteen, twenty years ago. His work is trashy and thoroughly dated; prodigiousness encouraged by an indulgent and sentimental Mama-ism; its overriding feature is doddering infantilism.*

Within days of this, and in such unrelieved depression that shock treatments were being considered, Jarrell cut his left wrist in a suicide attempt. Ironically, this act seemed to release him from his depression, and he sent word to Mary, who wrote back, "Dearest One, I think of you constantly and miss you so much. How I wish we could be back with each other. I hope your poor wound doesn't hurt so much now. I don't know what else to say except I long to have you well and your wonderful self

*again. I'll telephone as soon as they permit it. God bless you and keep you
for me. You're all I want."*

*   *   *

*On April 29, Lowell, back from Egypt, wrote that while he hesitated to in-
trude on Jarrell's privacy, he was heartbroken to hear that he was sick.
Considerately avoiding mention of the* Times *review and any details Taylor
may have given him of Jarrell's condition, Lowell said, "Your courage,
brilliance and generosity should have saved you from this, but of course all
good qualities are unavailing." He went on to say, speaking from experience,
that "what looks as though it were simply you, and therefore would never
pass, does turn out to be not you and will pass. Please let me tell you how
much I admire you and your work and thank you for the many times when
you have given me the strength to continue. Let me know if there's anything
I can do. Courage, old friend."*

*At Jarrell's request, the doctors allowed Mary to visit, and, parking the
Jaguar in front of the building, she saw Jarrell waiting on the steps. When
she ran across the grass calling his name, he smilingly ran toward her, his
good arm outstretched and his injured one in a sling.*

TO MARY JARRELL

[May 1965]

Dearest:

It's Sunday morning, and I've just looked at the roses you brought me
from our own front yard, and put on the nice shoes you brought me — and
now I'm writing this on the clipboard you brought me, and thinking (just
as I did lying in bed) of all the other things you brought me that for so
long made me better and happier and kept something like this from happening to me earlier. You are the one big good real thing in my life, and
I'm *so* glad I met you — we've had hard times together, but so much more
happy and good time, time different from any other in our lives.

I've been remembering our first days in Boulder, and Denver, and Grand
Lake, and how you looked in that yellowish sweater of mine, and all the
time at Princeton — writing so much and talking to you long distance, and
saying goodbye at the airport. And how wonderful it was visiting you at
Christmas. And Yosemite after we were married, and the way it looked
driving to Sequoia on the way back.

I love you,
Randall

TO MARY JARRELL

[May 1965]

My own darling Mary:

Since you've left I've thought about you so much — seeing you made me feel so, *so* much better. I live so queerly in this queer partial little world the patients live in, and it's only when I see you or talk to you that I'm connected to the real one.

I've just looked at all the pictures of you and thought of Washington and Santa Barbara and having our passport pictures taken, and that made me think of all the other places we've lived in or visited since then. I'm very glad we both went to Boulder.

Be mine always the way I'm yours always.

Your own,
Randall

In a note to di Capua about using Sendak's illustrations instead of photographs for The Animal Family, *Jarrell wrote, "I know I'll be as delighted with* The Animal Family *as I was with* The Bat-Poet. *With this book I'll just leave everything to you — next book I'll be well and can help out myself."*

TO BEATRICE HOFER

[May 1965]

Dear Bea —

Thanks so much for my birthday present. I often think about our lunches and how good and sweet you were — nobody's daughter could have done more for him.

I really have been improving — my psychiatrist is *very* good and the medicine's good, too. I think it will take a long time probably but I hope we'll really get down to what has to be changed in me.

I talk to Mary everyday and see her lots, and that's wonderful.

I have unlimited visiting privileges now — do come see me when you've come over to school. I'd love it.

I'm depending on television and conversation to fill my time mostly: since it's impossible to get enough books to fill much time, I try to look at reading as just an incidental extra. I wrote some poems today for the first time.

I hope Gerhard's job and experimental work are going well; give him my affectionate greetings. It'll be wonderful to see you.

Love,
Randall

Jarrell's fifty-first birthday was May 6, and Mary spent most of the day with him.

TO MARIE AND CHUCK BOYETTE

[June 1965]

Dear Marie and Chuck:

When Ramble got your card it made him so happy that he went out in the yard and rolled over and over in the grass and said "Hurray! Hurray!" He said it so loud that it scared a bluebird sitting in its nest in a pecan tree. The bluebird flapped its wings so hard, as it flew away, that it knocked a big green leaf down from the tree — no, two big green leaves, and Ramble reached out and caught them before they hit the ground and guess what? — they weren't pecan leaves, they were dollar bills! One said *Chuck* and the other said *Marie*. Then the bluebird flew back over Ramble's head and sang him a song and the words of the song were:

ONE IS FOR CHUCK AND ONE'S FOR MARIE

AND THEY BOTH CAME OUT OF THE NEST IN THE TREE.

And it was *so* — when Ramble climbed up in the tree and looked at the nest, it was a nest of dollar bills, just the way the bluebird said. So if you ever need another dollar bill just tell Ramble and he will climb up in the tree and get you one. But these two in the envelope are for you to take to the store and buy something extra nice with, to go with a big hug and a big kiss from

Ramble

Marie and Chuck were Mary's grandchildren, aged four and two.

TO BEATRICE HOFER

[June 1965]

Dear Bea:

Thanks so much for my lovely Father's Day card. I'm so sorry for the bad luck that's had me either away with Mary or seeing the doctor every time you've come. The Bismarck biography you left me starts badly but then it became much the best book I've read here at the hospital — I felt intimately acquainted with Bismarck who was a far stranger and more neurotic person than I'd realized.

I had a wonderful Saturday and Sunday at home with Mary — I can't wait to be at home for good. I'm very grateful to the hospital, but it seems an odd irrelevant place for me to be, now. I'm hopeful that, after spending next weekend at home, I'll be able to leave here for good early next week.

You should have heard the canary sing accompanying Brahms and *Traviata* — I didn't know a bird *could* sing so beautifully and it was so strange and marvellous to be hearing classical records, ours or the good music station's — here at the hospital one hears about an hour a month of such music, and that by accident.

I've been reading a pleasant book by a French girl about her year in Russia. You'll have to write your impressions on London. Mary and I were just talking about spending some summer there — it certainly is a lovely city.

I'll see you Thursday night and be able to wish you a happy birthday right at your birthday dinner. All the people here think you're eighteen, so I'd better tell them it's your nineteenth birthday.

With much love,
Randall

Beatrice was actually twenty-three on the twenty-fourth of June, but Jarrell liked to think of her as younger. His comment about writing her impressions of London referred to the Hofers' plans to live there in 1966 and 1967 while Hofer taught at the Imperial College at the University of London.

Jarrell returned home the first of July. He slept normally, ate whatever he wished, and saw a Greensboro psychiatrist once a week. He exercised his wrist daily, according to the orthopedist's instructions, and though he was not playing tennis, he took walks along the country roads. He and Mary had matching sets of binoculars and often sat in the woods silently studying birds in the trees above. Mary wrote in "The Group of Two," "... we got a Hoyle from the library and taught ourselves a beginner's pinochle, then an advanced pinochle. Then Randall scrambled those two together with some added attractions of his own that made a superior pinochle we kept a daily score on. Many afternoons we took our Bicycle playing cards out to the university's lake and played pinochle in the grass in between swims."

In August the Jarrells visited the Boyettes in Belhaven, on the North Carolina coast; and on the flat stretches between the tobacco fields east of

Wilson, Jarrell road-tested the Jaguar at 95 miles per hour and decided that the new English mechanic in Raleigh was "a great find."

TO MAURICE SENDAK

[September 11, 1965]

Dear Maurice:

We loved everything you said in your letter and were *so* touched and pleased by the gift — of all the small drawings of the bat at the side of the page, *that* was the one I liked best. Thank you!

I'm so glad that things have got better for you and that you're, as you say, feeling yourself again. It's been so wonderful to be feeling myself again and to be living at home with Mary instead of nowhere in a hospital. I know how you feel about the bunch of gray hairs — I seem to have collected some myself. But God must be on the side of gray hairs, he makes so many of them.

I feel so lucky and grateful to have had your pictures for both *The Animal Family* and *The Bat-Poet*. *The Animal Family* was harder for you, since you couldn't make the pictures direct illustrations and since the drawing came right in the middle of such a hard time in your own life — and I'm *so* grateful to you for working so hard on them and making them so beautiful. It's hard for me to pick the ones I like best — the one of the moonlight on the sea and the dust-jacket itself are my favorites, almost. It will make so much difference to readers having your decorations rather than a book without drawings — the book will feel rich and full to them in a way it couldn't possibly without what you've done. They really are some of your most original and profound drawings — not only will the readers of *The Animal Family* love them, but there are all the people who get any book you make the drawings for, just because they're your drawings.

What you say about *The Animal Family* makes me feel awfully good. I'd like to have it a good book, and when people like you like it as you do — people with so much understanding and remembrance of childhood, so much magic and imagination of their own — it makes me hope that the book really is what it ought to be.

We'll be coming up to New York later in the fall, and we'd love to have dinner with you and Michael and go to the opera with you, just the way we have in the past. Seeing you as we have has meant a lot to us.

I hope the days with your father will be better now. Our misery about such things is so hard to explain or bear — I guess all one can say is that we can't escape them, and that afterwards we know what matters most to us, what life really seems to us, and are better off in that way; we know that the surface that seemed to matter to us is just the surface, and that it doesn't matter compared to our real life and real self.

I hope you'll have some more work soon that is a pleasure to you. It's nice to think of you reading *Huckleberry Finn* — I hope you'll illustrate some more of the classics, the ones that are particularly close to you, since you do have an absolutely unique gift for embodying a story in your own imaginative creations. I'm hoping so to write a new children's story now that I'm well, and to have the marvellous thrill of seeing your illustrations for it.

> Affectionately,
> Randall

Sendak's father was near death, and Jarrell's mother was in a slow and serious decline.

> * * *

Shortly after Jarrell wrote Sendak, he and Mary went to a party at Frank Laine's log cabin in the woods. Other guests included colleagues from the humanities departments and selected Greek students. The occasion was Laine's purchase of an antique, square, rosewood piano, where occasionally during the evening George Kiorpes of the music faculty played Laine's favorite Chopin. In a dim corner, apart from the others, Laine wanted to discuss with Jarrell Lowell's For the Union Dead *and Jarrell's* The Lost World. *Before long, Laine said, with the kind of cheek born of bourbon over ice, "Well, Cal is a Beethoven of sorts, Randall. And you . . . You are a . . . a Robert Schumann." Jarrell, unperturbed and looking lofty, replied, "That's a clever remark," as if his recent misery had taught him at last that who ranked with whom was truly on the surface of art and that, as he had written Sendak, the surface "doesn't matter compared to our real life and real self."*

TO ROBERT PENN WARREN

[September 1965]

Dear Red:

Thank you so much for your letter. It meant a lot to me. I'm glad you sent me the poem — as I read it every thing in it was extraordinarily real to me.

I've been home from the hospital almost two months, and am my usual self again and very glad to be — I've always wanted to change, but not to change into what you become when you're mentally ill. I was badly depressed last summer and, in getting out of that, got elated and unreasonable, and stayed in the hospital, recovering, from about March 1 to July 1. It feels awfully good to be home with Mary again — school starts soon, and I'll be glad to be teaching.

Really living in the deep woods as you do sounds wonderful, like something out of the past — when you give Rosanna and Gabriel that you're giving them something marvellous, something that very few Americans have any longer.

The last book I wrote, just before I got so depressed, was one about a hunter and his family living all alone in the forest at the edge of the sea. As soon as I get some copies I'll send you one and the children one too — it's another of these books half for children and half for grown-ups.

I know we'll be coming up to New York a couple of times this winter — we'll write you weeks beforehand and make arrangements to come up and stay with you. We'd like it ever so much.

Peter and Eleanor have been having a good summer, partly at Monteagle — they've found another old house (in Sewanee this time) that they're about to buy.

I've been reading a lot of 19th century history, and Mary and I have learned to play cribbage; we spent a week with Alleyne and the children at the beach, but otherwise it's been a Greensboro summer — we're in gentle edge-of-the-country-woods, not in deep woods like yours. I haven't written any poems, but I've been thinking so much about the passage of time, and what it's like to live a certain number of years in the world, that I think it's sure to turn into some poems in the long run.

It was wonderful getting your letter.

As ever,
Randall

Reflecting on his mental illness to Mary, Jarrell said, "It was so queer . . . as if the fairies had stolen me away and left a log in my place."

*   *   *

Between Taylor's trips to Tennessee for family illnesses and funerals, the Jarrells spent an evening or two at their house, with the men talking in the lamplight again, as formerly, and the women quiet. Mainly the topic was Gogol and the Russians, but Jarrell also spoke of Emily Dickinson. There was a hint of wariness in the talk, but a mutually desired rapprochement was in progress, eased in Jarrell's case by his recollections of William James's statement "Wisdom is learning what to overlook" and in Taylor's case by good Memphis manners.

At a party the Taylors gave to mingle writing students with the writing faculty, Jarrell gave most of his attention to Gibbons Ruark, a young poet who had come especially to study with him. (Ruark later wrote A Program for Survival *and* Reeds.*) Jarrell said in the car later, "Parties like that are a good thing. I'm glad we went."*

Not only was Jarrell glad to get back to teaching but he had accepted an invitation to be writer-in-residence at Smith College in 1966–67, and he spoke of finding "a dovey Colonial house like Cleanth's" to rent.

TO BEATRICE HOFER

[September 1965]

Dear Beatrice:

This is a start-of-school letter from a beginning professor to a beginning student. I had my first two classes yesterday — one about Turgenev and one about Hopkins — and it all felt *so* familiar and nice; as Mary and I drove home it was as if I'd never been away.

We had a nice party the night before for the [Joseph] Bryants, the Watsons, and the head of the Art Department [Gilbert Carpenter]. The William Morris scarf was framed and hung on the wall, the new living room was all in its glory, and it was the prettiest party we've ever had. I'm certainly glad you suggested putting the Renoir lithograph over the fireplace; it looks so beautiful and becoming there.

What with seeing you when you came over I haven't been writing you — but I did want to send you those little to-be-used-for-frivolous-things checks that I mentioned when I was talking to you a couple of months ago.

I hope your new classes are as nice as mine and that everything's as nice in Raleigh as it is in Greensboro. See you soon, darling.

Love,
Randall

Beatrice was in her junior year at North Carolina State University.

TO MARY JARRELL

[October 1965]
[Note attached to a wooden birdhouse Jarrell gave to Mary]

To my Mary:

Each of us is the other's bluebird of happiness, but it's nice for us to have, for any wandering bluebird in the world, a little brown house in a tree. Remember the day when the whole flock of bluebirds spent the afternoon in our front yard? I hope they do again this fall . . . I've just been re-reading some of the letters you've sent me and I felt very happy and lucky to have someone love me so and write me so. I love you.

* * *

Although Mary regularly massaged Jarrell's wrist and he had not missed a day flexing it, soaking it in hot water, and squeezing a rubber ball in his fist, it was not responding as it should but seemed to be stiffening and pulling his hand down. A hand specialist in orthopedics at the University of North Carolina medical school recognized the problem at once, saying, "Oh yes, wrist drop or Pollock's Wrist," and he explained how a Dr. Lewis Pollock had studied thousands of such peripheral nerve injuries and treated them successfully with intensive physical therapy and stimulation. The orthopedist prescribed this for Jarrell as part of a daily regimen at the Hand House of the university medical school when space was available and assured him the prognosis was good. A skin graft was not considered.

TO ADRIENNE RICH

October 4, 1965

Dear Adrienne:

I've just been re-reading the last letter you wrote to Mary and me, and I wanted to tell you how good it made me feel, just like your other letters and the things you've said about my books. You've been a real friend to us in my illness and our troubles. I've been home from the hospital over two months and have been my normal self, again, and so glad to be; "so grateful," as Irina says in *The Three Sisters.* I've spent some time going over it once more, to have it ready to print. I haven't written anything. I've love to read the poems you said you'd written this summer. I'm glad you liked *The Man Who Loved Children* that well. When I wrote Christina Stead I quoted several of the things you said. I knew they'd be a great pleasure to her, especially as coming from Monocacy [Baltimore].

The exact things you said about *The Animal Family* certainly were a joy to me. It's so interesting to me to hear how it felt to you . . .

I've been reading a lot of poetry to Mary in the afternoons; I never know whether a poet will seem quite so good as we remembered, or not quite as good. The best Wallace Stevens was awfully good, but oh, it was hard to find it. I longed to have him less verbose and pretty-good, and more concentratedly good. Reading the Hardy and Hopkins I like best was better; there isn't much good Hopkins, but *it's* so good you don't care. How hard it is to write a good poem! How few good poems there are! What strange things you and I are, if we are. When we are! To have written one good poem — *good* used seriously — is an unlikely and marvelous thing that only a couple of hundred writers of English, at the most, have done — it's like sitting out in the yard in the evening and having a meteorite fall in one's lap; and yet, one can't believe that, and tries so hard, by willing and working and wanting, to have the mail man deliver them — and feels so disappointed, even, when he doesn't.

Isn't it interesting when you find your opinion of some poem, over the years, has thoroughly changed? I'd never have believed that I'd like [Robert Browning's] "My Last Duchess" better than "The Bishop Orders His Tomb at St. Praxed's" but Mary and I felt, this time, that "My Last Duchess" is thoroughly better — there is something operatic and general, not personal and exact about "The Bishop" in comparison: the man in "The Bishop" is primarily a representative Renaissance figure, and only secondarily a particular human being — it's the opposite in "My Last Duchess." And there's nothing overdone or lush in it — everything's so thoroughly necessary and exact.

We're going to be coming up to Simmons College the weekend of October 17th. Will you be there? We'd like so much to see you.

Yours,
Randall

Soon after this Jarrell was notified that space was available for him at the Hand House on October 11, and the Simmons College engagement was put off until spring. Bob Watson volunteered to take Jarrell's classes while he was gone and to drive him to Chapel Hill so they might talk over "The Wreck of the Deutschland" and other assignments. Jarrell took a change of clothes, a review copy of Elizabeth Bishop's Questions of Travel, *and the three-volume variorum edition of Emily Dickinson's poetry, in which he was making notes for a critical essay. When Watson arrived, the Jarrells kissed goodbye unabashedly and Randall left Mary outside the house, watching, while he put his things in the car. Before he left, he smiled at Mary, waved, and then impulsively ran back and took her in his arms.*

On Monday, October 11, after an evening walk, Jarrell chatted with Mary on the telephone, saying it was chilly when the sun went down and he wanted a heavy wool sports jacket, winter cap, and leather gloves for his walks. On Wednesday, October 13, he telephoned and told of his visit to the pen where the UNC Tarheel mascot goat was kept, saying, "He was really quite charming and he let me pet him just like a dog . . . To think, I've never met a goat before!" He also described a birthday party the previous evening for another patient, a boy, for whom Jarrell said he had written a silly poem full of puns about ranch hands and old hands at the Hand House.

On Thursday, October 14, about 7:30 in the evening, Jarrell, wearing his dark wools and dark gloves, was walking along the edge of the highway on his way back to campus. He was not visible to the car's driver until too late to be avoided, and in a split second he was sideswiped — "hit from the side," as the coroner said, "not the front, or the front wheels of the car." The Chapel Hill newspaper reported that "the impact spun Jarrell around and knocked him not more than three or four feet" to the side.

Questioned when the patrolman arrived, the occupants of the car first said, "He seemed to whirl," adding after that that "he appeared to lunge in the path of the car." Had Jarrell actually "lunged in the path of the car," he would have been run over, but that was not the case. The coroner found he was hit by the side of the car, not the front or the front wheels. This agrees with the reporter's statement that the impact spun Jarrell around and knocked him to the side, as would have happened since he was vertical. Further evidence of this is shown by the injuries described in the autopsy. All Jarrell's injuries were sustained on his left side, from the abrasions on his left cheek and the fatal blow at the left base of his skull (where, being vertical, he hit and damaged the doorpost and windshield of the car), to the contused left side, to the broken bones in the left foot, which was the only part of his body that came in contact with a wheel.

Although the newspaper reported that "a two-day-old, unfilled painkiller prescription" was found in Jarrell's wallet (which was to be used in case of extreme aching from the physical therapy on his wrist), the prescription had not been filled and the autopsy disclosed "no evidence of intoxication or any other disease process which might have contributed to his demise." These medical findings, plus a thorough three-week investigation of the circumstances, brought the doctor in charge of the autopsy to the conclusion he stated for the media, that there was "reasonable doubt about its being a suicide." In his judgment and that of the coroner and the medical examiners — all of whom had seen the body — Jarrell's death was accidental, and that is what is given on the death certificate.

*   *   *

Jarrell's funeral was held on October 17 in Greensboro at Holy Trinity Episcopal Church, where Mary was a communicant. The casket with its purple pall rested before the altar, and while the organist played Bach prel-

udes on hymns of Luther, friends, students, and townspeople silently filled the church. Jarrell's mother was too weak to attend, and there were no aunts, uncles, or cousins of Jarrell's, only his brother Charles. Charles joined the other honorary pallbearers: di Capua, Jarrell's devoted editor; his closest writer friends, Taylor, Lowell, and Watson; his closest colleagues, Hooke of romance languages and Laine of classics; his longtime tennis partner, Bill Corrigan; and Chancellor Otis Singletary. The men walked up the center aisle in solemn pairs to the music of "And Sheep May Safely Graze" and took their places in the pew across from Jarrell's family of women — Mary, Irene, Alleyne, and Beatrice — and the Order for the Burial of the Dead proceeded.

*   *   *

Jarrell was buried near his home in the pre-Revolutionary Quaker grave-yard of the New Garden Friends. A pin oak stands above him where mock-ingbirds sing, and his flat Moravian-style ledger is engraved

RANDALL JARRELL
Poet
Teacher
Beloved Husband

1914   1965

In the days that followed, Lowell's book The Old Glory arrived, ded-icated to Jarrell and Jonathan Miller and inscribed: "I am heart-broken Randall cannot have this book he loved — and helped." And a note came from Taylor grieving over the loss of his brother-in-law and father as well as Jarrell and saying that his brother-in-law introduced him to Chekhov and Tolstoy; Jarrell taught him how to read them; and his father showed him what they meant. Taylor ended, "I loved all three."

BOOKS BY RANDALL JARRELL

POETRY

ESSAYS

FICTION

CHILDREN'S BOOKS

The Gingerbread Rabbit	1964
The Bat-Poet	1964
The Animal Family	1965
Fly by Night	1976

TRANSLATIONS

The Golden Bird and Other Fairy Tales of the Brothers Grimm	1962
The Rabbit Catcher and Other Fairy Tales of Ludwig Bechstein	1962
The Three Sisters	1969
Faust, Part I	1976

ANTHOLOGIES

The Anchor Book of Stories	1958
The Best Short Stories of Rudyard Kipling	1961
The English in England (*Kipling stories*)	1963
In the Vernacular: The English in India (*Kipling stories*)	1963
Six Russian Short Novels	1963

INDEX